D0016101

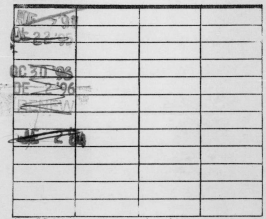

Deobold B. Van Dalen
University of California at Berkeley

Bruce L. Bennett
Ohio State University

A
WORLD HISTORY
OF
PHYSICAL
EDUCATION

Cultural, Philosophical, Comparative

second edition

Prentice Hall, Inc., Englewood Cliffs, N.J.

This revised edition is dedicated to

ELMER DAYTON MITCHELL

Our teacher, friend, advisor, co-author

and a distinguished leader of our profession

A WORLD HISTORY OF PHYSICAL EDUCATION: Cultural, Philosophical, Comparative (second edition) by Deobold B. Van Dalen and Bruce L. Bennett

© 1971, 1953 by Prentice-Hall, Inc., Englewood Cliffs, New Jersey

13-967919-7

Library of Congress Catalog Number: 71-128341

Current printing (first digit)
19   18   17   16   15   14   13   12   11

PRINTED IN THE UNITED STATES OF AMERICA

Prentice-Hall International, Inc., London
Prentice-Hall of Australia, Pty. Ltd., Sydney
Prentice-Hall of Canada, Ltd., Toronto
Prentice-Hall of India Private Limited, New Delhi
Prentice-Hall of Japan, Inc., Tokyo

Figure of runner after a sculpture by R. Tait McKenzie

CONTENTS

part one
PHYSICAL EDUCATION IN ANCIENT SOCIETIES

part two
PHYSICAL EDUCATION IN THE MIDDLE AGES AND EARLY MODERN TIMES

part three

PHYSICAL EDUCATION IN MODERN EUROPE

part four

PHYSICAL EDUCATION IN THE UNITED STATES

part five

PHYSICAL EDUCATION IN OTHER MODERN COUNTRIES

PREFACE

Each recurrent crisis in society gives fresh impetus to the study of educational history and philosophy. The swift sequence of great events quickens an interest in the past. Schools can function effectively as agencies of social progress only if they adjust to a changing civilization. The problems facing education today are the result of a long historical evolution. The degree of success with which they are solved will depend upon an intelligent awareness of the historical and philosophical concepts involved. A vision of the future depends upon an understanding and intelligent interpretation of the past.

Studying the history of educational thought offers unlimited possibilities for comprehending modern trends in our schools and for charting new horizons. No one can hope to appreciate contemporary physical education without a concept of the social forces, conditions, movements, and the philosophies that have come out of the past to shape the institutions of the present day. A study of history brings distant times and conditions into focus to help us understand our modern heritage. Similarly, it helps illuminate and identify approaching guideposts.

The degree of incompatibility often existing between general education and physical education has been of concern to many leaders. If educators believe in teaching the "whole child," they must view education as a *total* process. Physical education must then become more adequately articulated with the general program, and its teachers must more clearly recognize their work as a part of the total process of a child's training and development. At the same time, all other teachers must also have a clear understanding of these inseparable physical and cultural education goals. How to fuse these twin objectives, rather than departmentalize them, is one of the sharpest challenges for modern educational thought.

The general structural organization of the text is based on a historical-philosophical approach. Each chapter title reveals the philosophical characteristics of a historical phase of education through which physical education has passed. Within each chapter, the material is arranged in terms of selective topics: a preview of historical background, aims of education, aims of physical education, promotion of physical education, program of physical education, and methods of physical education. This arrangement also provides the opportunity for a comparative study between periods within the history of a particular country and for comparisons between countries.

In the first edition of this book we acknowledged our indebtedness to a host of fellow workers in the profession. We expressed appreciation to the numerous professional leaders, teachers, and ministries of education abroad that helped us secure authoritative information concerning the development of physical education in their countries. We extended our special acknowledgements to Mr. Yoshio Imamura, Dean of Physical Education, Tokyo University of Education, for assistance in the preparation of the material on physical education in Japan; to Mr. H. Wein, of the Ministry of Education, Israel, for an account of recent developments in the new republic of Israel; to Dr. Ernst Jokl, Union Education Department, Pretoria, South Africa, for suggestions on South Africa and the Near East; to Dr. Arthur Howard, Lucknow Christian College of Physical Education, Lucknow, India, for careful reading of the sections on India; to Mr. Chih-Kang Wu, graduate student in physical education at the University of Michigan, for help with the material on physical education in China; and to Mr. Richard Donnelly, Instructor of Physical Education, University of Michigan, for careful reading of the entire book and making many valuable suggestions throughout its planning and preparation.

We also thanked the following people for valuable assistance in helping us to secure printed materials on the program of physical education in their respective countries: Mr. E. Major, Inspector of Physical Education, Ministry of Education, London, England; Dr. Robert Sutherland, Central Council for Health Education, London, England; Mr. D. G. Ross, Central Council of Physical Education, London, England; Mr. Rolf H. Junker, Newland Park Training College, England; Professor George Belbenoit, School for Boys, Douai, Nord, France; Professor Olle Halden, Royal Central Institute of Gymnastics, Sweden; Major J. Thulin, Sydsvenska Gymnastik-institut, Lund, Sweden; Mr. Agne Holmstrom, Managing Director, Swedish Gymnastic Association, Sweden; Mr. K. Bjerregaard, Director of Real Estate Department of Copenhagen Municipality, Copenhagen, Denmark; Mr. J. Ahl-Nielsen, Kobenhavns Idraetspark, Copenhagen, Denmark; Mr. Peder Trap, Ministry of Education,

Copenhagen, Denmark; Dr. Emanuel Hansen, Danmarks Højshole for Legemsoövelser, Copenhagen, Denmark; Dr. Doris W. Plewes, Department of National Health and Welfare, Ottawa, Canada; Professor Winona Wood, McGill University, Montreal, Canada; Dr. J. B. Kirkpatrick, McGill University, Montreal, Canada. We were also indebted to Dr. Eugene Miller, University of Pittsburgh, and Sister Maria Walburg Fanning, Chestnut Hill College, Philadelphia, for their translations of certain Latin documentary materials.

In the preparation of the second edition, these individuals have contributed significantly and generously in providing information and assistance for the countries indicated:

Argentina: Herme Perez Madrid; *Australia*: H. J. C. Mutton and David Parsons; *Austria*: Werner Haas; *Belgium*: Marcel Hebbelinck and F. Matthys; *Bolivia*: Carlos Pozo Trigo; *Canada*: Roger Dion, Maxwell L. Howell, Robert Osborne, Doris Plewes, and Graham Snow; *England*: F. Michael Holliday and R. E. Pearton; *Finland*: Seymour Kleinman and Keijo K. Kulha; *France*: Raymond Gratereau and Claudel Larcher; *Germany*: Herbert Haag; *Holland*: Jan Bovend'eerdt; *Hungary*: Zoltan Nemeth; *India*: A. M. D'Rozario; *Israel*: Uriel Simri; *Japan*: Kohsuke Sasajima; *Mexico*: Juan Figueroa Peralta; *New Zealand*: D. R. Wills; *Norway*: Robert Hoff and A. Morgan Olsen; *Pakistan*: A. S. K. Chowdhury; *Paraguay*: Ignaio Elizeche; *Philippines*: George G. Tan; *Poland*: Charles Morley; *Romania*: Robert Bartels and Leon Isaac; *South Africa*: Danie H. Graven, J. C. Kelder, Isabelle Nel, and J. W. Postma; *Spain*: Rafael Chaves Fernández and Jacquelyn K. Smith; *Sweden*: Paul Högberg; *Switzerland*: Louis Burgener; *Taiwan*: Gunsun Hoh; *USSR*: Louis Nemzer; *United States*: Raymond Ciszek, A. Gwendolyn Drew, Theodore Harder, Leona Holbrook, and Charles Mand; *Uruguay*: C. M. Carámbula; and *Venezuela*: Manuel Gallagos Carrato and Evelino J. Torres.

In addition we are indebted to many physical education and sports leaders, foreign consulate and ministry of education personnel, and librarians, who have provided us with information through personal letters or supplied us with copies of speeches, minutes of meetings, photographs, archives materials, mimeographed items, and local publications.

Our thanks are also due to the many authors and publishers who have kindly extended permission to use quotations and selected excerpts from their works. Specific credits for these are given throughout the pages of the book.

Finally, we must acknowledge with special thanks the material assistance and the moral support given to us by our wives, Marcella Van Dalen and Helen Bennett.

THE AUTHORS

part one

Physical Education
in
ANCIENT SOCIETIES

1

Physical Education
in
Education for Survival

Human education is as old as humanity. The progress of civilization is so inextricably interwoven with the threads of education that it can be assumed that the one never existed without the other. To gain some insight into man's struggle for survival and significance, we can study the societies men developed before they kept written records, and can trace the role of education in the evolution of modern societies.

From the age of the caveman, the way man has viewed and used his body and mind has had an impact on society. Darkness envelops the cradle of civilization, but on the earth's stratigraphical beds, prehistoric man unwittingly left behind him some fragmentary clues concerning his life. From these clues, a partial panorama of his society and his physical education can be reconstructed. This knowledge can be supplemented by observations of tribal communities in more recent times which, anthropologists tell us, provide a convenient means of interpreting the past through the present.

Aims of Education

Coping with their hostile, unharnessed environment consumed the energies of men in early societies. To insure the survival of the group, they trained youths in *security skills* and *conformity conduct*. The instinct for survival motivated them to teach youths how to obtain food, clothing, and shelter; how to protect themselves from their enemies, whether men, beasts, or nature; and how to conform with the prescribed methods of cultivating the good will of the galaxy of gods who controlled their destiny.

Storms, fire, floods, famines, and other mysterious and fearsome forces in the environment frightened men. They decided each force must have a "spiritual double" that caused it to act as it did, and that with proper propitiation, the nature spirit would respond favorably to their requests. Acting cn this assumption, men evolved a body of rituals, laws, and ceremonies designed to please the gods. Once this exacting code of conduct was formed, no youth was permitted to deviate from it. As John Lubbock remarked: "The savage is nowhere free. All over the world his daily life is regulated by a complicated and often most inconvenient set of customs (as forcible as laws), of quaint prohibitions and privileges."[1]

Group consciousness and group solidarity were emphasized more than individual rights or individual consciousness in primitive societies. "Education began with fixed ways—folkways—with plastic children and eager youths—and with elder-teachers who knew what to do. . . . The outcome was absolute certainty and social stagnation."[2] In other words, the twin objectives of education—collective security and individual conformity —enabled men to survive, but prevented them from effecting many progressive social changes.

Aims of Physical Education

To a large extent general education *was* physical education in early societies, for the environment made great demands on the physical condition of man. Youths who lacked in physical courage, stamina, and skill were a danger to the community. To increase the chances of group survival, the tribe encouraged youths to develop the strength, endurance, agility, and skills needed to withstand the rigors of outdoor life, to obtain the necessities of life, and to engage in aggressive and defensive actions. In addition to acquiring the physical prowess necessary to perform the work required for survival, youths were expected to master the communication media of bodily movement through which they could articulate their wants and fears to the invisible forces that controlled their lives. Exciting games and dramatic dances were promoted to heighten religious fervor and to influence the gods, to impart information about the tribal traditions and cultural heroes, to build an emotional frenzy that would intensify courage and the martial spirit, to develop tribal loyalty, and to create a favorable emotional climate for indoctrinating youths in the folkways of the tribe.

Recreation and procreation were also important to the savage. The

[1]Sir John Lubbock, *The Origin of Civilization and the Primitive Condition of Man* (New York: D. Appleton and Co., 1889), p. 450.
[2]Joseph K. Hart, *Creative Moments in Education* (New York: Henry Holt and Co., 1931), p. 1.

display of the body in the performance of physical feats in various ceremonies probably aided in the selection of mates, and some dances were
performed specifically as fertility rites. Most sports and dances were religious or utilitarian in origin, but some were promoted primarily for
recreation. Children especially must have engaged in play activities just
for fun. Furthermore, as time passed, people forgot the serious religious
purpose of some games and dances and engaged in them primarily for
relaxation and recreation. The joy derived from body movement, social
contacts, and from observing skilled performers and well-developed physiques must have been as satisfying to early man as it is to modern man.

Promotion of Physical Education

Parents, medicine men or shamans, and other tribal leaders informally
acquainted youths with the skills and knowledge they would need as
adults. The initiation and puberty rites provided a more formal type of
education. While these rites varied from tribe to tribe, they all served the
same general purpose: to make the neophytes fully conscious of their adult
status and responsibilities, their duty to their gods and their tribe. Both
boys and girls were initiated, but the ceremony for boys was usually more
elaborate. As a boy approached adolescence, he was sent to the tribal
leaders for instruction. Some initiation ceremonies lasted a few days, some
continued for several months, and some extended over a period of years.
The few youths selected for the priesthood pursued a special course of
study that acquainted them with the secret knowledge which was the
monopoly of the religious leaders.

The physical education program was not terminated with the initiation ceremony. Throughout most of his adult life early man continued to
participate in dances, games, hunts, and war activities. The tribe provided a program for all seasons of the year and all stages of the life cycle.
Ceremonial games or dances were held before and after battles; before
seeds were planted and after the harvest; at birth, puberty, marriage, and
death; and at special times set aside for diversion from labor. Some of
these ceremonies were simple events; others required elaborate preparations and were governed by many rules, lasted for many days, and involved large groups of people.

Program of Physical Education

Little is known of the games of prehistoric times, although a few toys
have been unearthed that correspond to present-day playthings. From observations made of the less advanced cultures of modern times, such as

the American Indians, African Bushman, and Australian Aborigine, we can conclude that the children of early man acquired part of their education by imitating the activities of adults in their play activities. The mothers probably gave their daughters some training in maternal and domestic activities; the fathers introduced their sons to the skills required to shoot arrows, hurl clubs, throw spears, track animals, make weapons, build boats, catch fish, and paddle canoes. Play at war games was an important part of the informal curriculum, for youths had to be accustomed early to the use of weapons and the spilling of blood. Everyday labor and swimming, running, wrestling, and climbing contributed to the physical development of youths. In the initiation rites boys engaged in tests of motor skill and physical courage, feats of strength and endurance, sometimes including ordeals by fire, and ceremonial dances.

Early man must have spontaneously engaged in many nonpurposive play activities, but the ceremonial games and dances associated with religious rites were governed by a mesh of rules and taboos that were carried out in a precisely prescribed manner. Many of the ceremonial ball games of early cultures were associated with fertility rites and some may have been dramatizations of war. Games of chance and betting on the outcome of activities, which were extremely popular pastimes, may have been vestigial survivals of the ancient and serious practice of the arts of divination.

Dance, the media for communicating with the gods and influencing the invisible world, played an exalted role in the life of the early people. Primarily a form of prayer, dance was also a means of socialization and recreation. Nearly every ceremonial occasion had an appropriate dance whose time and place were determined by custom and necessity. Although the characteristics of the dance varied from tribe to tribe, within the group the dances tended to follow definite patterns, and were transmitted in detail from one generation to another.

Dancing was a serious pursuit. The performers dressed in colorful costumes and painted their bodies with symobolic designs. With leaps and gestures, with genuflections and prostrations, they imitated the lunge of animals, the motion of the waves, and the fury of a storm, or expressed the strong emotions of love, hate, fear, and triumph. They performed dances to propitiate their totem—the plant, animal, or nature spirit they considered to be their kin. Bear, wolf, buffalo, rain, sun, and corn dances were performed to protect them from harm, hunger, and economic want; other dramatic dances were performed to purge their bodies and souls of evil spirits. Medicine men and priests executed solo dances to expel the pains and aches from the sick body of a tribesman. In war dances, men imitated all the actions performed in battle. In initiation rites, dance was used to impress youths with the importance of the occasion.

Methods of Physical Education

Imitation, indoctrination, and trial and error methods were the basic means of educating children. In many tribes babies were swaddled fast to a board to make it easier for their mothers to work, but small children enjoyed considerable freedom. They learned through trial and error methods and unconscious imitation; many of their amusements and games were miniature replicas of adult life. For the most part children were taught on an individualized basis by their parents or other elders, and learned skills through a rough sequence of experiences geared to their age and sex. Young boys used small bows and arrows and hunted for small game near home. As they progressed, they took a more active part in the hunt and in the war activities of the tribe.

Special clothing and equipment were designed to cope with the environment, strengthen group identity, increase stamina or skill, and provide for safety. Protective devices were worn in some games and colorful costumes and painted body designs were a part of the prescribed ritual in many dances. Some tribes wore devices, such as cords tied around the ankles or arms, that they assumed would give them strength or some other desired physical attribute.

Youths were motivated to excel in physical activities by the recognition they received from their elders for a good performance, the challenges of their environment, the tales of the physical feats of their gods and culture heroes, the boasting of the older youths and warriors, and ceremonial competitions with their peers. The dazzling costumes, the intoxicating yells, music, and movement, the exhilarating physical exertion, and the emotional frenzy of many games and dances stimulated youths to put forth their best efforts.

Discipline was quite lax among young children, but adolescents submitted to rigorous physical tests and severe discipline during the initiation rites. The emotional appeal of the initiation ritual, the satisfaction of achievement, plus the pressure of competition, provided a successful method of indoctrinating youths with group mores and of impressing them with the wisdom of their elders and the importance of their adult responsibilities.

The formal training provided by the medicine man and priests consisted of a systematic process of indoctrination. Youths were told what to do and how to do it, but little attention was given to informing them about why the prescribed procedures were required. Any acts or thoughts of youths that conflicted with the fundamental beliefs of the tribe were quickly repressed. This practice preserved the culture, but curbed the introduction of new ideas required to evolve a higher level of civilization.

2

Physical Education in Education for the Perpetuity of Civilized Culture

Man has spent thousands of years emerging from his primitive state in all parts of the world. The first light of civilization dawned in the rich agricultural plains of river valleys where ready transportation was available and sufficient food could be grown in the same place generation after generation. Under such favorable conditions, population centers grew denser, work became more specialized, and class or caste sytems evolved. As life grew more complex, the necessity of keeping records spurred the invention of writing. Not only was the growth of learning facilitated by this invention, but there was increased leisure, greater exchange of goods and ideas, and an emergence of varied cooperative enterprises.

As some societies evolved into identifiable cultures, the dominant classes attempted to preserve the status quo. They placed more and more emphasis on conforming to traditional social patterns. By stifling expressions of individuality and suggestions for change, they eventually sacrificed social progress for social stability.

PHYSICAL EDUCATION IN EGYPT

Egypt, situated in the Nile valley where the soil is rich, the sun is favorable, and water is available for crops and commerce, was one of the earliest cultures to emerge from barbarism. Because the people lived in a sheltered location, they were peaceful, but they did know one era of expansion. About the year 1500 B.C., Egyptians reached their greatest glory, conquering Ethiopia to the south and reaching to the Euphrates

River to the east. Then followed a period of decline until Egypt was conquered by Assyria about 700 B.C. After the break-up of the Assyrian empire, Egypt regained its independence and for the first time opened up its doors to foreign visitors, and began to trade, especially with the Greeks. Egypt now disseminated ideas to a younger, more vigorous people. Thereafter Egypt was almost continuously a dependent country, being ruled by Persia, Alexander the Great, and the Greek Ptolemies until conquered by Augustus Caesar and made a Roman province in 30 B.C.

The Egyptians made contributions mainly in science, farming, irrigation, building, and practical household equipment (such as furniture and eating utensils). Some of their accomplishments remain a mystery: we know little about the construction of their great pyramids, their art of embalming, or their methods of weaving linen and working with glass and gold. They devised papyrus, from which our word *paper* is derived, and they invented a partly phonetic, pictorial alphabet. They made remarkable advances in astronomy, devising the calendar of twelve months; they made progress in arithmetic, geometry, and surveying; and they made technical advances in architecture, hydraulics, civil engineering, navigation, and medicine. In the arts, they not only established writing and the recording of events, but also wrote songs and hymns and developed a formalized style of painting and sculpture.

The Egyptians were, according to Herodotus, "excessively religious." They worshipped a galaxy of gods, firmly believed in life after death, and built splendid temples and the massive pyramid-tombs for the pharaohs. Women enjoyed a higher status in Egypt than in most ancient civilizations. The law recognized their right to property, they were not secluded, and those trained as priestesses exercised considerable power and influence in state affairs. Social classes were widely separated, but peasants could— although they rarely did—advance to the upper classes. The pharaoh was an absolute ruler who was worshipped as a god. The nobles, priests, government officials, and the scribes were next highest in prestige. Then there was a privileged class of soldiers who were given the inducement of tax-free land. In the cities there was a middle class of merchants and artisans with little influence, and also a lower class of unskilled laborers, poorly and irregularly paid. Finally, at the bottom of this social structure, were the peasants, heavily burdened with taxes.

Aims of Education

Formal education arose with the development of writing. As keeping records became more and more important in society, the main objective of education was to learn to read and write, for such knowledge gave one status and power. All education was directed toward the practical goal of acquiring a vocation or a profession. In the course of learning to be a scribe so that he could serve as a secretary or steward, a boy would also become acquainted with the moral and religious concepts expressed in the literature he was copying. In a similar fashion, he would gain familiarity with the secular writings, the poetry and songs, the written science of the day. But education was pursued more for its practical advantages in elevating one's position in life than for the enjoyment of knowledge in itself and for cultural appreciation.

Aims of Physical Education

Physical education did not play a dominant role in Egyptian education. Except for a brief period of their history, the Egyptians were not a conquering people, so that there was no need for promoting a military-type physical education program for all citizens. Although the Egyptians made some advances in medicine and apparently saw some relationship between health and cleanliness, they did not relate health to exercise.

The peaceful, practical Egyptians were more interested in the vocational, recreational, and religious objectives of physical education than in military or health objectives. The soldier, dancer, wrestler, and acrobat needed to acquire the skills of their professions. Observing other people perform was a popular form of recreation, while ritual games and devotional dances were a means of realizing religious objectives.

Promotion of Physical Education

Apprenticeship was the mode of education in Egypt. The common people were usually trained in the occupations of their parents, while the upper-class youngsters attended schools for scribes. The priestly class conducted schools for advanced learning, and certain government departments had training divisions for high officials. Physicians, architects, and engineers gained their education as apprentices.

Little is known about the promotion of physical education. The children in the schools for scribes learned childhood stunts and games during their free time. Swimming instruction was sometimes given by a slave of dignified status. Soldiers received instruction and drill in the martial arts from older professional warriors, many of whom were mercenaries. Dancing schools or a dance apprenticeship system probably existed for the temple dancers. Although not an athletic people like the Greeks, the Egyptians did hold gymnastic games in the honor of at least one god. They promoted wrestling matches and bull fights and held many religious spectacles, funerals, public festivals, and private parties that featured dances or games.

Program of Physical Education

In Egypt, swimming was one of the popular sports, even among women. A hieroglyphic symbol was devised for it. Ideographs show that an alternating overhand stroke was already in use. War scenes showing the conqueror Ramses II pursuing the Hittites across a river also show the fleeing enemies using the overhand stroke as well as artificial resuscitation to revive their leader. The nobles had swimming pools on their estates at the time of the Theban period when Egypt was at the height of its power.

The warrior class supplemented military exercises with games and sports to develop skills useful in war. The young sons were sent to barrack schools where they underwent rigorous training in handling weapons and exercised to develop speed, strength, suppleness, and agility. They also practiced wrestling and war dances. Hunting was also important for the soldier class, as it afforded training for war and also rid the kingdom of dangerous animals. Following the introduction of the horse from Arabia about 2000 B.C., both fighting and hunting in war chariots became common pursuits of the noble classes.

The kings and nobility joined in the chase and boasted of their accomplishments. The common people also hunted, trapped, and fished, but they were mainly interested in obtaining food. They used the bow and arrow, spear, bola, harpoon, and boomerang to kill small game, fish, and birds. Crude fishing tackle was available to them as early as 2000 B.C.

From paintings, reliefs, vases, mosaics, and writing (some of them by Greek travelers), we learn that the Egyptians enjoyed wrestling, dancing, and gymnastic games. Wrestling was a well-developed art; it was utilized by the warriors for conditioning, but also by professionals for entertainment. Many scientific holds were developed. It is generally assumed that Egyptians wrestled from an upright position and did not permit any boxing blows such as the Greeks later used as part of the pancratium.

Dancing continued to hold the popular interest even after the Egyptian state emerged from its primitive beginnings. The royal class, however, only took part in the slow, sedate religious dances, leaving the folk, acrobatic, and ribald secular dances to the common people and the professional dancers. The highly esteemed art of professional dancing attracted both men and women performers. Dancing was accompanied by the music of the flute and lyre and the clapping of castanets or the beating of drums. To a modern judgment, the dancing, especially the religious forms, might seem posed and stiff, with unnatural gestures, but the movements seem to be characteristic of the formalistic spirit of all Egyptian art.

As for games, all manner of play activity for smaller children has been found, including toys such as we use today—dolls, tops, hoops, jumping jacks, balls (covered with skin or leather and stuffed with bran or husks of corn), marbles, and many others. Older children tumbling, somersaulting, and performing other gymnastic stunts are shown in the inscriptions. Tests of lifting, single stick fighting, and jousting were introduced for older participants. Dice, "odd and even," and other games of chance were popular. Men, women, and children all played ball games. Ball playing seemed mainly to be a tossing or juggling game; sometimes it was a forfeit game, and whoever failed to catch a ball had to be the donkey and carry the other person on his shoulders while the others continued playing.

Methods of Physical Education

Under the apprenticeship system, youngsters learned by imitating the movement of their parents or tutors. Rather severe discipline and considerable drilling were apparently part of the on-the-job training.

PHYSICAL EDUCATION IN CHINA

The accepted history of China predates Christianity by approximately 2500 years. This oriental country was not only one of the earliest centers of civilization, but one of the most lasting. For thousands of years the Chinese were able to maintain a fixed social pattern, largely because of their system of family organization and ancestral worship. The family was a firmly knit social unit that included grandchildren, children, grandparents, and ancestors. One had to be obedient and reverent not only to the head of the household but also to the spirits of one's ancestors. The cult of family led to the propagation of large family groups and placed a social premium on male children.

Aims of Education

The Chinese sought to maintain the stability of the state by training each individual to perform his prescribed duties according to the pattern established by tradition. The "aim of education was to develop the individual into a man of virtue and culture, and to secure social control through raising up leaders with ability and character to influence the lives of others."[1] To perpetuate the ancient ideals, the government instituted a series of examinations to select students who had most thoroughly mastered the ancient rites, rituals, and teachings for the highest governmental jobs.

[1]Ping Wen Kuo, *The Chinese System of Public Education*, Contributions to Education, No. 64 (New York: Teachers College, Columbia University, 1915), p. 14.

During the early flowering of the culture in the Chou dynasty (1122–249 B.C.), Chinese education embraced physical training as well as the intellectual, moral, and aesthetic training. From the ranks of the scholars the most able and virtuous men were selected for national leadership. Internal strife, which began in about the eighth century B.C., led to a breakdown in the central government and the division of the country into warring states. In the period of educational decadence that ensued schools were neglected, and public offices were frequently inherited rather than merited. Confucius (551–478 B.C.) sought to save society by collecting the moral teaching of the ancients and urging leaders to return to these worthy principles of living. The classical writings gave minutely detailed instructions for proper etiquette and relationships with other people in every phase of daily existence and thereby regulated and controlled every act. Confucius emphasized ethical and moral training, but he did not proscribe physical education activities. Later reformers of the Confucius cult transformed education into a narrow bookish training that focused on the past, rather than the present or future, and tended to ignore the physical needs of the people. The memorization of literature, the endless repetition of ceremonies, and the exacting examination system were so demanding that scholars had no time or energy for physical exercise and athletic development.

The Chinese education provided for the preservation of the family and the existing social order. The family was much more important than the individual. The complete loyalty and obedience to family and ancestral authority, the rigid control of thought and conduct, and the philosophy of hierarchic submission to authority were effective in maintaining order and social stability and perpetuating the culture. This kind of education, however, produced a static rather than a progressive society, for new ideas and changes were tolerated only if the innovation could be justified by the teaching of the ancients.

Aims of Physical Education

In the earlier eras, bodily conditioning played a more important role in Chinese society than it did in later times. The development of a bookish, classical type of education and the spread of Taoism, Buddhism, Confucianism, all of which emphasized the contemplative life, reduced interest in the physical development of the child. Some forms of aesthetic bodily expression were cultivated to heighten the emotional experience in religious rituals. Some physical activities were recreation, and some were promoted to mold moral character and correct conduct. Although militarism existed, it did not cause the Chinese to focus their attention on physical education to the extent that it did in some cultures. Military duties were eventually looked upon as a necessary evil rather than a national ideal. The great masses of peasants toiling in the fields received vigorous exercise from the natural demands of their work; but the national ideal was neither the laboring man, the military man, nor the young man, but the aged scholar who was rewarded by an absence of labor and of exercise. Thus the "desire for age" dominated the Chinese as intensively as the "pursuit of youth" dominates American life today. Such a point of view naturally discouraged physical fitness.

Promotion of Physical Education

Although many modern scholars question the authenticity of the source materials, some authorities believe that more than four thousand years ago the Chinese not only originated schools but also had state education officers and a system of national education examinations. Schools were established for both common people and aristocrats, although common boys of merit could attend the noble schools.

Certain authorities contend that the Chou dynasty had a highly organized national school system that provided for some physical education. One of the five schools located in the capital of the king, was devoted to teaching of rituals, dancing, and archery. Boys entered the lower schools at about eight years of age and higher schools at fifteen. In spring and summer the students practiced archery and dancing and studied music; in the fall and winter they studied reading, writing, and rituals. The youths to be sent to college were selected by the officials of the local governments on the basis of their moral conduct and ability in the arts of war. After the Chou dynasty, government control of schools disintegrated, public examinations were discontinued, and education was often left to private initiative.

During the T'ang period (618–907 A.D.), education was again vigorously promoted. Physical tests were retained in the examinations, but the literary studies increased steadily. By the time of the Ming dynasty (1368–1644), the narrow classical pattern of literary training was deeply ingrained. From time to time, there were attempts to found a military college. The founder of the Ming dynasty, for instance, tried to add military training to the classical curriculum, but even this training was turned into a literary study and the examinations were essays on the archery and horsemanship of the ancients rather than physical tests.

The women's position was inferior to that of men in China. They were subject to their fathers, elder brothers, husbands, or as widows, to their sons. Lower class women did not learn to read, and few upper-class women received a literary education. The practice of binding women's feet precluded vigorous physical activities, but the literature does mention that women danced, some court ladies played polo, a few women were excellent swordsmen, and one even played football.

Program of Physical Education

The general curriculum of the Chinese schools was almost entirely composed of literary studies, but the governmental examinations of the early days indicated that all national leaders were expected to possess some military efficiency. "By the time of Chou . . . the fitness of an official consisted in his ability to excel in playing a musical instrument, shooting with the bow, riding horseback, writing, and arithmetic, while at the same time he was expected to understand the rites and ceremonies of public and private life."[2] In later days, when the government instituted special examinations for military men, these candidates were not required to pursue an exhaustive literary training. Laurie stated, "For the military service a very small knowledge of literature is needed. The special examination consists of physical exercises—the lifting of heavy weights, drawing the long bow, and the drill with the sword."[3]

Many of the sports that developed in China, such as charioteering, wrestling, boxing, and football, were originally devised for their military usefulness or as a means of diverting the attention of troops from hardships or the boredom of idleness.[4] Charioteering gave the Chinese the mobility that was the determining factor in many of their victories. Archery was stressed in ancient times, and various forms were studied. The cross bow came into use about the first century B.C. and the horseback style during the T'ang dynasty (618–907 A.D.). Archery examinations and exhibitions were held often, some of them during ceremonies where the performance was synchronized with music. A form of social entertainment eventually evolved in which the participants tossed arrows into a bottle while music played. Battle axes, spears, and javelins were also used in battle. Throwing stones was a part of the military training about 494 B.C. Various types of swords were developed, and many styles of swordsmanship evolved, particularly between 618 and 1127 A.D. Even scholars took special lessons in swordplay.

Wrestling was as important as archery and horsemanship for men in the army. The sport was also taken up by the people, and from 255 to 618 A.D. two exhibition matches were held each year. The period of the "Five Dynasties" (907–960 A.D.) especially produced many famous wrestlers. Boxing was developed extensively after Buddhidharma came to China about 527 A.D. and evolved the "external system" which consisted

[2]Paul Monroe, *Cyclopedia of Education* (New York: The Macmillan Company, 1919), I: 635.

[3]S. S. Laurie, *Historical Survey of Pre-Christian Education* (New York: Longmans, Green and Co., 1900), pp. 130–31.

[4]E. N. Gardiner, *Athletics of the Ancient World* (Oxford: Clarendon Press, 1930), p. 15.

of eighteen "Arahats" or movements, and emphasized offensive tactics. T'ai Tsu 960-976 A.D.) extended the system to 32 forms; and a century later, Chio Yüan Shang Jên amplified them to more than 170 movements and wrote training rules which stressed systematic living, a vegetable diet, sexual control, and self-discipline. During the Mongol dynasty (1208–1368 A.D.), the Buddhist monks were famous exponents of the art of boxing. At the beginning of the Ming dynasty, Chang San Fung promoted the internal systems of boxing which encouraged the idea of defense. The Chinese boxing, from which the Japanese probably developed ju-jitsu, more nearly resembled the rough and tumble of the Greek pancratium than modern boxing. Participants did not wear gloves and often a quarter staff or spear was employed. Rugged as the sport must have been, military aristocrats were often contestants. The ancient pastime "butting" was introduced in China about 200 B.C. The contestants placed ox skins, horns and all, over their heads, and mounted on the backs of their partners. The opposing two–man teams then proceeded to butt one another.

Football, one of the oldest Chinese sports, was first promoted as a military exercise, but later became a popular sport of the people. In ancient times the football was a round hair–filled ball, made of eight pointed strips of leather, but by the fifth century the inflated ball was introduced. Several types of football were played. In one of the earliest types, six holes were placed at intervals along the side of the field. The game had rules of attack and defense and was conducted in the form of a match. In *The Biography of Piao-Chi*, a general in the Han dynasty discloses that "when they were out in Mongolia the want of food robbed the army of its morale, but Piao-Chi dug holes in the ground and played football."[5] *The Pictorial Book of Football* written by Wang Yün Ch'êng during the Sung dynasty described another football game in which the players take positions and kick the ball to one another in intricate patterns according to specific rules. This game, probably performed more for amusement than for training soldiers, remained popular for centuries.

About the time of the T'ang Dynasty (618–907 A.D.), a game evolved in which two goal posts were used and, later, a game played with one goal post was also popular. The goal, resembling a triumphal arch, was formed of bamboo poles, thirty to forty feet tall, and ornamented with strips of five colored cloths. The goal had an opening of over a foot in diameter, and the players apparently took turns kicking the ball through this hole. Over seventy kinds of kicks could be made in one Chinese game, and several types of fouls existed. Giles found records indicating that ". . . the winners were rewarded with flowers, fruit, and wine, and even with silver

[5]D. B. Van Dalen and Kohsuke Sasajima, "Football Games in Antiquity," *Quest* 4 (April 1965): 69–77.

bowls and brocades, while the captain of the losing team was flogged, and suffered other indignities."[6]

Some of the spirit of good sportsmanship was expressed in a poem about football written by the poet Li Yu (50–130 A.D.):

A round ball and a square wall,
The ball flying across like the moon,
While the teams stand opposed.
Captains are appointed and take their places.
No allowances are made for relationship.
According to unchanging regulations
There must be no partiality.
But there must be determination and coolness
Without the slightest irritation at failure.
And if all this is necessary for football,
How much more for the business of life.[7]

Polo, which probably came to China via Persia, Turkistan, and Tibet between 660 and 700 A.D., was played by many noblemen. One emperor had a minister put to death who criticized his devotion to football, cockfighting, and polo. Another emperor, who reigned in 1163 A.D., had the ground covered with oiled cloth and sand if it rained, so the game could still be played, and at night the grounds were sometimes lighted with candles. During the Sung dynasty the Chinese played a game similar to golf in which they used clubs, hardwood balls, tees, and holes marked with colored flags. Special books were published on how to play the game.

The Chinese were very found of gambling. One historian reported that in one town, in the third century B.C., every citizen loved cockfighting, dog races, shooting dice, and football. A board game, *Liu Po*, and chess were popular. Chess was thought to have originated in China until evidence found in a famous Egyptian tomb revealed that the game was played there at an earlier date. The story has often been related that a Chinese general devised the game of chess for the amusement of his troops during the confining months spent in winter quarters. Han Sing, the commander of this army, called the game *Choke-Shoo-Hong-Ki*, meaning the science of war. The resemblance of the game to military tactics is often noted.

Hunting, fishing, swimming, and flying kites were common pursuits in China. One author reported about 1030–1090 A.D. that children in

[6]Herbert A. Giles, *The Civilization of China* (New York: Henry Holt and Co., 1911), p. 155.

[7]Herbert A. Giles, *Adversaria Sinica*, quoted in Gardiner, *Athletes of the Ancient World*, p. 16; also see "Football and Polo in China," *Nineteenth Century* 59 (March 1906): 508–13.

the south learned to tread water at the age of seven, to float at ten, and to dive at fifteen. Kite flying and kite fighting were highly developed skills. Hunting and fishing were sports pursued for recreation as well as for food. Aristocratic sportsmen organized hunts in which they used horses and dogs, and hawking was practiced as early as 100 B.C. Confucius is said to have been fond of hunting and fishing, but he recommended moderation. He would not shoot at sitting birds and refused to use a net when fishing.

The Chinese practiced a series of light exercises called *Cong Fu*, which resembles the Swedish Ling system. Since disease was conceived by the Chinese to derive from bodily inactivity, mild forms of medical gymnastics, which combined stretching and breathing exercises, were designed to maintain organic functioning, and to prolong human life. These medical gymnastics were usually performed in a sitting or kneeling position.

Dancing was a regular part of the instruction of wealthy youths. In the feudal days, ability in dancing was one criterion for judging character. *The Book of Rites*, an important classic, mentions at least four kinds of dances that were to be performed at great ceremonies. They were named after the objects that the dancers held in their hands—the dance of the shield, the lance, the plume, and the flute. A description of the ancient education of a boy and a girl in the *Book of Rites* reveals, "At thirteen years of age they study music; they read aloud songs in verse. They dance the dance 'Cho.' When they have completed fifteen years, they dance the dance 'Siang.' They learn archery and charioteering."[8] At twenty years, when the young man became of age, "He commences to study the rituals. He can wear clothing made of fur and pure silk; he executes the dance of Ta-hiac (instituted by Yu)."[9] Religious, aggressive, defensive, pantomimic motives constituted the dance patterns. Very early the Chinese began to write a philosophy of the dance, giving expression to the noblest forms of the art. Besides the official ceremonial dances, of course, cruder forms were also practiced on informal occasions.

Methods of Physical Education

Although much has been written about the Chinese methods of literary training, little is known about how they taught motor skills. Students probably learned by doing and by following the example of their elders. Some books provided detailed regulations for various sports, games, dances, exercises, and training programs. The discipline was undoubtedly

---

[8]Ping Wen Kuo, *The Chinese System of Education*, p. 19.
[9]Ibid.

severe with great emphasis on examinations. In the early days the music teachers taught the use of some weapons. Archery was synchronized with music in some ceremonies to cultivate the interior character of man and to effect a perfect union of the body and the mind. In fact, some activities were transformed into ceremonies in which the correct behavior, thoughts, and etiquette were almost more important than the skill of the performance.

PHYSICAL EDUCATION IN INDIA

Evidence that a highly developed civilization flourished in India along the Indus River and the tributary Ravi (ca. 2500–1500 B.C.) was found when the remains of the two ancient cities, Mohenjo-daro and Harappa, were excavated in 1921. There is some doubt about the causes of the decay of these cities and the origins of the Aryans, but it is generally believed that the Aryans came to India from the northwest in about 1500 B.C. and, because of their superior fighting ability, overcame the original dark-skinned inhabitants. The culture of southern India is older than the Aryan civilization, but because of its isolated geographical position little is known about its early existence.

Hinduism, the religious and social system of India, was based on the practice of religious virtue (*Dharma* or piety) and the caste system. Originally the Aryans were a virile and vigorous people who enjoyed life and whose warriors were equal or superior to the intellectual caste. However, as the caste system grew more and more rigid, the strenuous life that was preached by the Bhagavat Gita gave way to contemplative, ceremonial, and mystical religious practices through which men sought absorption into the "Eternal Spirit." By renouncing the enjoyments of this life, personal ambition, and activity, men hoped to annihilate their individuality and achieve fusion with Brahma. Hindu asceticism ranged from the practice of moderation and self-discipline to fanaticism and self-torture. The emphasis on asceticism varied at different times during Indian history, and extreme ascetical practices were probably observed by relatively few.

Buddhism, which exercised the greatest influence between 250 B.C. and 500 A.D., was not a new religion, but rather a reform movement against the excesses of the caste system. While Buddhists eschewed certain sacrificial rites and denounced the extreme self-mortification through which some Hindus sought to acquire spiritual insight, they were critical of self-indulgence and sensual pleasure and proscribed certain sports and pastimes. Moreover, they placed so much emphasis on *Ahimsa*, or non-violence, and passive pietism that they lacked the drive to participate energetically in physical activities and in worldly affairs.

Aims of Education

The Hindus were interested in educating children to seek their place in the divine order and to preserve the caste system. Although Hinduism preached that righteousness, material advantages, and pleasure were worthy of pursuit, all aims were subservient to ultimate salvation. The emphasis was on the next life rather than the present. The youngsters were not strongly inspired to "get on in the world," "to help their fellow men," or to identify themselves with national goals, but rather to devote themselves to caste practices and to seek absorption into the infinite.

The caste system dominated Indian culture just as the family system dominated Chinese civilization. The castes, which were fairly well established by 500 B.C., evolved out of old tribal customs as well as from race, class, and occupational prejudices. The four major castes (*Brahmans, Kshatriyas, Vaisyas,* and *Sudras*) were divided into hundreds of subgroups; a fifth group was known as the *Outcastes.* This social classification confined every being to the status he inherited at birth. The caste an individual was born into determined his occupational, social, and educational opportunities. Caste rules regulated what work he did, what food he ate, whom he married, and with whom he associated.

Although subordinated to the religious objective, the aim of Hindu education was vocational. The system made no allowance for a child's potential abilities, but forced him into the occupation reserved for his caste. The *Brahmans,* who enjoyed the highest position in the social order, were educators and priests. In this capacity they dominated and perpetuated the whole social system. The next two privileged castes were the *Kshatriyas,* who performed the military and governmental duties, and the *Vaisyas,* who worked at business and farming. Of the lower castes, the *Sudras* performed the servant duties. The *Outcastes* were given no occupation other than the handling of leather and waste products, and were forced to live in isolation and degradation.

The educational system of the Hindus was designed to produce the type of citizens their caste system and religious philosophy demanded. The caste system, which kept individuality imprisoned, and the Hindu religion which placed particular emphasis on the next life, brought social stability to India, as ancestral worship did to China. Both cultures, however, lacked the motivating forces for progress that exist when individual ability is allowed freedom to grow.

Aims of Physical Education

Physical education was not important to the aims of general education— because of the religious philosophy that emphasized the abnegation of life, the caste system that elevated the status of the intellectual and degraded many forms of labor, and the enervating climate in much of India. Moreover, during long eras of peace or foreign domination, the need to maintain a high level of physical fitness for protection from external aggression was diminished.

On the other hand, physical education was not completely ignored in India. The stress placed on asceticism and passivity was stronger in some eras than others, and some groups of people considered physical and emotional well-being a prerequisite for spiritual well-being. The development of physical fitness and motor skills was incorporated in the vocational aims of certain groups of people, especially that of the *Kshatriyas* or military caste. Dancing girls, as well, were trained to give expression to religious concepts and to provide recreation for spectators.

Promotion of Physical Education

The ideal pattern of life for a Hindu in the three higher castes was as follows. After a ceremony of initiation at puberty, he became a celibate student living a rather austere life. He then married and was a family man until later middle age when he would retire to devote himself to spiritual matters. In old age, he would give up all earthly ties and become a religious beggar. Only a small proportion of the population lived according to this pattern, but Hindu ideals strongly dominated the life and education of everyone. Some physical education activities, however, were part of the daily religious practices and the periodic festivals and ceremonies. The temple dancers, for instance, received a prolonged and systematic physical training.

In some eras, when the emperors were anointed, special ceremonies were held for them to display their valor and strength and to demonstrate their skill in an exhibition of archery. Special training was provided for military men, and archery was taught in some centers. When the Buddhists were dominant, such as during the long reign of Asoka, the doctrine of nonviolence prevailed and monastic education flourished. Yoga was taught in the monasteries, which attracted students from all over India and from foreign countries.

Program of Physical Education

Because personal cleanliness, hygienic practices, and physical exercises were means by which the Indians sought spiritual well-being, public sanitation and health were given consideration from the earliest times in India. In the cities that existed five thousand years ago, there were excellent closed drainage systems and homes had bathrooms. The literature reveals many instances in which people were punished for defiling public roads or streams, selling spoiled food or adulterated medicine, or polluting public places with dead animals or human corpses.

Interwoven in the religious teaching of the Hindus were many rules for health. All members of the "twice-born" castes (the high three) were to be pure of body and pure of soul. The *Ordinance of Manu*, a sacred book, records such regulations. The use of spirits and intoxicating liquors was discouraged, and the use of certain foods prohibited. Fasting was recommended to cure disease, to stimulate rapt mental meditation, and to restrain the animal nature of man. Bathing, which also symbolized the washing away of sins, was required daily. Even in the earliest society ritualistic cleansing may have been practiced, for a great Bath, measuring thirty-nine by twenty-three feet, and eight smaller baths were found in the ruins of Mohenjo-daro. Chinese pilgrims reported that every morning Buddhist priests left the monastery to bathe in nearby pools and that the Hindus washed before every meal and scoured their teeth with toothsticks. The medical works of the Hindus contained many rules of hygiene that were in advance of European practices until after the time of the Crusades. In fact, Alexander the Great, about 330 B.C., employed Hindu doctors for his army.

The military nobility exercised greater influence in early days than in later times when the *Brahmans* were in power. The men of the military caste were trained for the infantry, cavalry, chariot, or elephant divisions. Archery was especially stressed, but soldiers also learned the use of spears, javelins, battle-axes, swords, and slings. During peacetime, when the army was idle, the men pursued hunting and other sports as pastimes.

The hunting of lions, boars, buffaloes, deer, and birds was a popular pastime in India, and references to fishing are found frequently in the literature. The hunters used bows and arrows, pits, lassos, nets, and dogs. In ancient times monarchs were expected to spend half the year hunting. The sport was pursued for pleasure as well as for practical purposes—as keeping the army active during periods of peace, keeping down the ravages of wild beasts, protecting crops, and catching elephants for the army and for farm work. The Hindus loved to hunt, but the indiscriminate slaughter of animals by the Moguls was repugnant to them.

To the Indians, religious exercises such as the *Pranayam* and *Suryanamaskar* were part of the daily worship. Yoga, a system of religious meditation, incorporated some physical movement. Patanjali, the Sanskrit scholar, compiled the Yoga-Sutra about 200 B.C., but the exercises were known long before his time. Yoga required an intense development of the will to control the body. It consisted of many different meditative postures (*Asanas*) and the regulated control of breathing. Through these exercises, the performer achieved a state of mental relaxation and mental poise that would enable him to maintain ecstatic communion with God.

The yoga exercises of today are different from those practiced in ancient times.

Medical authorities of ancient India, such as Charaka and Susruta, recommended physical exercise (*Vyayam*), oil baths, and massage for maintaining and restoring health. Susruta defined *Vyayam* as movements of the body that produced sufficiently vigorous circulation of the blood and quick respiration to fatigue the individual. Charaka recommended exercise to ward off disease, reduce stoutness, aid digestion, present a pleasing appearance, and delay the encroachment of old age.

Massage and oil baths, which were used extensively in India, were highly recommended by medical men. Ancient medical books gave detailed directions for the massage techniques. Charaka, for example, specified three types of massage—athletic, medical, and hygienic—and mentioned lubrication, friction, kneading, joint movement, vibration, percussion, thumping, stroking, and sweating as some massage techniques.

As for games, dicing and gambling were popular pastimes although the Buddhists attempted to discourage gambling. The game of dice was played separately and as a part of board-games, some of which were quite complex. Betting on animal fights was also popular. Mention is made of bull, cock, elephant, ram, and rhinoceros fights. Polo was probably introduced about the time of the Mohammedan conquest and was particularly popular at the Mogul court in the sixteenth century. Wrestling played an important role in the sports world of the Indians. The Indian club, Dands, the Baithaks exercises, and the Indian massage system have been credited with contributing to the development of outstanding wrestlers.[10]

Children had amusements, such as whistles, rattles, dice, balls, marbles, and models of birds, animals and humans, for large quantities of toys have been unearthed at the sites of early settlements. Some of the figures had nodding heads or were mounted on wheels. Children also played with clay.

Dancing has a long and systematic history in India and was intimately associated with religion. The bronze figure of a dancing girl found in the ancient city of Mohenjo-daro proves the antiquity of the art, and the early literature reveals the people's love of dancing and the important role it played in their religion. In fact, Shiva, one of the trinity of Hindu gods, was known as the Lord of Dance. Both religious and profane dances were performed. The temple girls who danced for their own sins and for the sins of others, began to study religious dances when they were still children; music, reading, and writing were also included in their curriculum. Another class of dancers performed at marriages and banquets. Although the dance remained popular and the art was highly esteemed,

10K. Rajagopalan, *A Brief History of Physical Education in India* (Delhi: Army Publishers, c. 1962), p. 46.

with the growing stratification of society, the performers and their instructors eventually fell into disrepute and suffered social stigma.

Methods of Physical Education

Physical education was to a large extent integrated with religious or vocational education in India. Medical authorities recommended graduated physical exercises for restoring health. Susruta advised that physical exercises vary according to the patient's age and constitution, his diet, the part of the body to be developed, the season, and the environment in which he lives.

3

Physical Education
in Education for Hebrew
Religious and Civic Ideals

The children of Israel were, by tradition, descendants of Abraham who migrated from "Ur of the Chaldees" about twenty-three hundred years before Christ. The story of the migration to Egypt in time of famine, and the escape from bondage under the leadership of Moses; their wanderings in the desert; the settlement of the tribes into secular polity under the rule of David and Solomon; the division of the kingdom into Judea and Israel; and the battles with Assyria and Babylonia which forced the Jews to live in exile, are familiar to all. These great migrations, exiles, and sufferings helped to produce the tough fibers of character found in Hebrew social and religious thought.

Most early people worshipped a galaxy of anthropomorphic gods, but the Hebrews came to envision an omnipotent divine being, a universal God of moral attributes, who lived in close relationship with man and required righteous conduct from his people. As the Hebrew religion developed, a large body of ceremonies, customs, and traditions amassed rapidly; these were transmitted orally until written down to form the *Torah*, probably just before the Babylonian exile. This code helped keep the Jews culturally distinct from their conquerors during the years of exile. After the return from exile, the economic and religious conditions of the Jewish people were so altered that the laws had to be interpreted and expanded in the light of new conditions. These interpretations and commentaries formed the *Talmud*.

Aims of Education

The Hebrews viewed education as a process of training the child in the civil and religious traditions and in the laws found in the *Torah* and the

25

Talmud. Youths were advised to "Fear God, and keep his commandments: for this is the whole duty of man."[1] As early as Deuteronomy, the command appears, "Now these are the commandments, the statutes, and the judgments, which the Lord your God commanded to teach you, that ye might do them in the land whither ye go to possess it . . . ."[2] Authority was no longer based on caste, ancestors, or a military class, but rather was founded on the laws of God.

In Hebrew theocratic history, education developed along with religious ideals. In the early eras, moral training consisted of teaching children to fear the supreme tribal deity Yahweh, to obey his commandments, and to observe the proper sacrifices, feasts, and ceremonies.

After many years, the conception of a tribal deity was transformed into the conception of one God, Jehovah, an omnipotent, omniscient, spiritual and ethical being who could be worshipped by anyone. He was not merely a god of the Hebrews, but a divine ruler of the human race. Furthermore, he was a god of ethical attributes who, rather than merely demanding sacrifices and ritual observances, sought to instill men with a zeal for upright living.

In contrast to early practices, the education of the child emphasized a moral rather than ritualistic approach. The teaching was directed toward ideals of universal peace, social justice, and the brotherhood of man. Unfortunately, after the Jews returned from Babylonian captivity, these high ideals were heavily shrouded in legal abstractions and elaborate ecclesiastical ceremonies that drained them of much of their spiritual vitality.

The Hebrews also sought to develop a strong national spirit through education. After a loosely organized tribal life during the years of Egyptian bondage, the Jews developed, through the leadership of Moses, a national identity and brought the idea of Jehovah into clearer focus by following the laws of Jehovah and their accompanying obligations. The religious ideals of individual righteousness and justice provided a worthy framework for the development of civic harmony and cooperation. These ideals probably originated from a desire to perpetuate a people, but they evolved into a growing consciousness of a universal destiny, that of being God's chosen people. These religious and social ideals were the cornerstones of the Hebrew educational system.

Aims of Physical Education

For the expression of religious ideals and the preservation of national entity, the Jewish people formulated some physical education objectives. Some of these were primarily military; others, like dance and hygiene practices, were directed toward worshipping the Lord. Physical education

[1]Eccles. 12:13.   [2]Deut. 6:1–2.

in Hebrew culture was deeply imbedded in religious and civic ideals, but some physical activities were recreational.

Military training was necessary for these early people who were situated at the geographic crossroads of the ancient world and were subjected frequently to military assaults. For a nation to survive, its future warriors had to develop strength, endurance, and martial skills. In struggling to develop a national spirit and maintain identity, however, the Hebrews did not confine education solely to military ends, as was the case in so many cultures.

The Jewish people valued personal and community hygiene. They sought to be pure in body before God, and observed hygienic laws as part of religious rituals. Physical cleanliness was considered as valuable as moral purity for, the Jews believed, the heart and mind could not be pure unless the body was clean.

Dance was a means of communicating spiritual feeling and strengthening civic loyalty, as well as a rhythmic pattern of holy celebration. Its purpose was not so much to obtain aesthetic pleasure as to give a vigorous expression to religious emotions and to create an *espirit de corps* that gave cohesion to their national spirit.

As the Graeco-Roman influence pervaded Judaism, some new ideals of physical education were introduced. Although inordinate devotion to sports was discouraged, the benefits of moderate exercises were recognized. The Hebrews, however, accepted only those aims of physical education that accorded with the laws of Jehovah.

Promotion of Physical Education

Throughout the entire history of the Jews, the family has been regarded as the fundamental educational institution. The ancient Hebrew family was a patriarchy: the father was not only the supreme ruler, but priest and teacher as well. The mother assisted her husband in child training. The Scriptures impose the duty of instruction upon the parents as their most solemn function: "And these words, which I command thee this day, shall be in thine heart: And thou shalt teach them diligently unto thy children . . . ."[3] Thus the responsibility of educating one's children was a sacred obligation.

During the Babylonian exile, the synagogue evolved as a center for religious instruction, and became an enduring educational institution of the Jewish people. As a result of Babylonian influence, a new class of professional teachers, called scribes, arose after the exile, and a formal system of education was established. Elementary education, eventually made compulsory, was organized on two levels, one for boys between the ages of six

[3]Deut. 6:5–7.

and ten, another for those between ten and fifteen. Beyond the age of fifteen, education was voluntary, but higher schools existed primarily for training of the priests, scribes, and aristocracy.

Physical education, with the possible exception of instruction in the laws of hygiene, was not incorporated in the formal school program. The school day was long and there is some evidence that games were used to break the monotony of the recitation periods, but these were probably nonathletic. At least before the Hellenic influence, physical education rested upon family practices, individual initiative, and military necessity rather than on any formal school organization or athletic festivals.

The early Hebrews had no Olympic Games as the Greeks had, and professional exhibitions and festivals similar to those of the Romans, but they did gather for religious feasts and other social occasions to pit their strength and skill against one another and to participate in dances. The temple served as a unifying force for the Jews as did the athletic games for the Athenians. The great religious feasts were a most impressive educational agency. Dancing was a part of the ceremonies with the temple balconies often serving as stages for the performances. In harvest festivals special places were reserved in the vineyards for dances of thanksgiving. During the Graeco-Roman period, there were more formal agencies of physical education. Places of exercise were built according to Greek models, and Jewish youths were trained to compete in the Olympic Games.

Program of Physical Education

The Hebrew curriculum was fundamentally a religious instruction in Jewish history, laws, literature, and ceremonies. Reading, writing, music, and dancing were part of this instruction, with the addition of simple arithmetic. On the whole, physical education during the ancient times provided for the needs of a hardy agricultural and martial people and did not develop into a systematic curricular training. As the religious laws and literature became more complicated, the students devoted increasing amounts of time to intellectual pursuits and correspondingly less time to sports, dancing, and music.

Without doubt, the early Hebrews admired attributes of physical strength, for some men are indicated in passages of the Scriptures as being very strong. One instance of an exceptional performance of strength is when Jacob saw Rachel approaching and single-handedly rolled away from the mouth of a well the stone that ordinarily required the combined efforts of the shepherds to move.[4] The familiar story of Samson provides another example of a hero's great physical power. Other feats of strength are attributed to David, Jonathan, Abishai, Eleazer, Joab, and Asahel.

[4]Gen. 29:8–10.

Saul, the great war chief, is even asserted to have gathered around him any strong men he saw. The Scriptures emphasize, however, that spiritual strength rather than brute force was often the source of the power of these strong men.[5]

Military preparation was chiefly training in the use of the bow and arrow, sword, shield, spear, and sling. Many passages in the Scriptures chronicle a display of skill that could not have been gained execept through training and practice: "And I will shoot three arrows on the side thereof, as though I shot at a mark."[6] "He hath bent his bow, and set me as a mark for the arrow."[7] The efficiency of Hebrew archery is substantiated by the valiant men of war who could use both hands in "hurling stone and shooting arrows out of a bow."[8] The sling was not merely a school-boy's toy in Biblical days, but a weapon of war. The dexterity of Hebrew slingers was renowned in Biblical literature. Mention is made of ". . . seven hundred chosen men left-handed; everyone could sling stones at an hairbreadth, and not miss."[9] Slings and stones were mentioned in several instances,[10] although David's skill in the use of the sling[11] to slay Goliath is probably the most familiar example.

According to Rabbi Akiba, swimming was one of the three essential things that a father was duty bound to teach his children.[12] Jonathan the Maccabee valued this training when he fled from his pursuers by swimming the Jordan River.[13] That the Hebrews used the breast stroke is inferred from the following passage, "And he shall spread forth his hands in the midst of them as he that swimmeth spreadeth forth his hands to swim. . . ."[14]

A few sports and games enjoyed by some Hebrews were not always looked upon with approval by the general populace. Hunting was never highly regarded by the Hebrews. Nimrod, "the mighty hunter before Jehovah," and Esau, "a skillful hunter, a man of the field," are derogatorily presented in the Bible. In later times, when the Greeks and Romans introduced their games and festivals, the pagan practices, the nakedness of the athletes, and the cruel gladiatorial contests were condemned by the rabbis as offensive. Jewish youth were playing ball games at a very early date and allusions to the sport occur in the later epochs.[15] References appear in the Old Testament such as ". . . and toss thee like a ball,"[16] and later mention is made of handball,[17] punchball,[18] pitch and toss

[5]Judg. 14:6.
[6]1 Sam. 20:20.
[7]Lam. 3:12.
[8]1 Chron. 12:2.
[9]Judg. 20:16.
[10]1 Sam. 17:40; Zech. 9:15.
[11]1 Sam. 17:50.

[12]Mechilts (ed. Horowitz), p. 124; Kiddushin, 29a.
[13]1 Macc. 9:48.
[14]Isa. 25:11.
[15]Kil'aym 23.1, 28.1.
[16]Isa. 22:18.
[17]Sanhedrin 77b.
[18]Tosefta Sabbeth 10 (11):10.

(which appears to have been a primitive volleyball),[19] and some form of polo.[20] Young women in later epochs participated in some of these games, but the rabbis disapproved of such activity.

Religious dances were solemn and ecstatic spiritual expressions for Jewish people of all ages. They held that if it were proper to praise the Lord in song, it was equally proper to praise Him in the dance. Even men participated in dances of joy in praise of the Lord. David danced before the Ark and in the *Psalms* he exhorts his people to "praise His name in the dance,"[21] "praise Him with the timbrel and dance,"[22] Religious dances were performed in connection with the golden calf and at the crossing of the Red Sea.[23] Women danced in honor of Saul and David, "with timbrels of joy and with instruments of music."[24] The great festivals, the Feast of May, the Feast of the Harvest, and the Feast of Tabernacles, included dances in the ceremonies. The "torchlight procession" that took place at the Festival of the Water Drawing included the most distinguished notables.[25] Like all people, the Hebrews celebrated successful harvests and victorious battles with dances. The Bible frequently alludes to such occasions;[26] in one instance, Judith led the women of Jerusalem in a victory dance. The *First Book of Samuel* describes dancing and singing to the tune of tabrets, flutes, and cytheras to celebrate when David had slain Goliath the Philistine. With the Greek influence on Hebrew culture, however, dancing declined as a religious expression, and became an increasingly secular activity.

Jewish dance forms were essentially simple and spontaneous demonstrations of joy. Processionals and round dances predominated. In early periods, Hebrew dancing consisted of violent motion of the feet, energetic leaps and bounds, and hopping in a small area. Dancing was vigorous, strong, and animated.

The Hebrews attained a high degree of personal and community hygiene. They prohibited their people from resorting to charms and magic for the cure of disease as had been the practice in Egypt. The Mosaic laws were directed toward the maintenance of health and the prolongation of life: the Jews were admonished to keep the commandments that they may be strong and prolong their days. Ill health and epidemics were considered an expression of the wrath of Jehovah that could only be appeased through prayer. Nonetheless, the Hebrews anticipated many of the principles of modern sanitation and made real progress in the prevention of disease. Mention is made of the inspection of food, methods of excreta disposal, importance of vital statistics, and diagnosis and notification to

[19]Midrash Eccl. 12:10; Yer Sanhedrin 10:1, 28a.
[20]Hai Gaon to Kil'aym 23.1.
[21]Psalms 149:3.
[22]Ibid. 150:4.
[23]Exod. 15:19–20; 32:19.
[24]1 Sam. 18:6; 21:11.
[25]Sukkah 5:1–4.
[26]Exod. 15:20–21; Judg. 11:34.

the authorities of infectious diseases. The Jews used modern techniques of isolating and quarantining individuals to combat the spread of diseases. Provisions were also made for fumigation and disinfection after contagion as a means of controlling epidemics.

Numerous passages are to be found in the *Talmud* stressing the importance of cleanliness. The most scrupulous observances of all regulations were in regard to baths and ablutions.[27] Washing the hands before meals was a religious duty. The cleanliness applied not merely to the person, but also to utensils: "Rinse the cup before drinking and after drinking."[28] Unclean persons were not expected to seek admission into the temple.

Methods of Physical Education

Except possibly for their military training, and to a small degree in their ceremonials, the Hebrews provided no systematic instruction in motor skills. The fathers, as teachers, were warned against playing with their children and were advised to preserve an austere countenance. If he had a son, the father was told, "Laugh not with him, lest thou have sorrow with him, and lest thou gnash thy teeth in the end."[29]

The child was considered to be willful, perverse, and foolish, and a stern attitude was considered necessary to curb his will. "Foolishness is bound in the heart of a child, but the rod of correction shall drive it far from him."[30] While corporal punishment was advised in the Proverbs,[31] intelligent reproof was thought wiser than a hundred stripes.[32] In Talmudic times, discipline was less severe.

[27]Sabbath 41a, 108b.
[28]Tamid 27b.
[29]Eccles. 30:10.

[30]Prov. 22:15.
[31]Ibid. 13:24; 19:18; 22:15, 23:13–14; 29:15–17.
[32]Ibid. 17:10.

4

Physical Education
in Education for
Greek Individualism

Three great peninsulas—the Spanish, the Italian, and the Balkan—extend from the European continent into the Mediterranean Sea. The Balkans, the home of the ancient Greeks, served as the cultural bridge between the East and the West. Greece was the first European land to become civilized, for the tiny peninsula jutted southeastwardly toward Asia Minor, which extended prominently westward at this point. This proximity provided Greece a contact with Oriental civilization.

The birthplace of Western culture was not only ideally located to receive the older cultures, but also was endowed with an environment particularly capable of nurturing continual progress. Geographically, Greece was a conglomeration of tiny valleys patched with fields of grain and with clumps of olive, fig, orange, and lemon trees. Standing in his fields the Greek could gaze past the grazing flocks and scan the mountain ridges that separated him from his enemies in the next valley. If near enough, he could see the bright sunshine flashing upon the waves that curled and dipped around the broken and irregular seacoast and lapped against the ships in the harbors. The sea provided him with the protection from enemies and paved a pathway to the cultures of other peoples, to commerce, and to colonization. His climate was also a favorable one. The short mild winters were sufficiently stimulating to be energizing, and the long dry summers flooded with sunshine, permitted him to enjoy a vigorous outdoor life.

Politically, Greece was not a united nation, but an assortment of small governmental units. Most of the numerous valleys eventually developed into political centers. In this process the various tribal or clan governments later united under the leadership of one of the larger landowners, who became king. The community and surrounding lands of the valley that he ruled were the origin of the city-state. Numerous independent city-states existed at first, but in time they consolidated into twenty leagues under the most important city-state in each league. Of all these, Athens and Sparta are usually studied as the two distinct and contrasting city-states of the Hellenic culture. Through the progress of the ages, the various governments changed from monarchies to aristocracies, and in some cases political privileges and control were extended to the broader base of democracy. Athens had a government that advanced the farthest toward democracy and individual freedom, while Sparta was representative of a totalitarian government.

Greek society was based on class stratification. In some city-states fifty percent of the people were slaves. Unfortunate captives of conquered cities or individuals who had lost their more favorable social-economic position performed all the manual labor and menial-skilled jobs. Citizenship came with birth and proper education. Only the citizens were free to participate in government, own land, and become educated. Consequently, the discussion of the Greek and his education refers only to the citizens of the city-states.

The Greek citizen devoted himself to serving the state. The political unit was small enough to permit very intimate contact with its operation, and such political activity absorbed much of the citizen's time. He kept himself in readiness to serve the government in war and peace. In those city-states that encouraged intellectual pursuits, the Greek was remarkable for his curiosity and creative imagination. He loved to learn, to travel, to observe, and to philosophize; he was sensitive to color, sound, and rhythm and delighted in expressing beauty in an orderly and practical fashion. As a result, the Greeks bequeathed to the world a rich cultural inheritance that includes sculpture, poetry, architecture, music, oratory, history, science, mathematics, drama, philosophy, and gymnastics. The names of Phidias, Praxiteles, Myron, Homer, Sappho, Pindar, Aeschylus, Sophocles, Aristophanes, Pericles, Democritus, Socrates, Plato, Aristotle, Herodotus, Thucydides, and Archimedes present an honor roll of great thinkers and artists. Their ideas played an active role in the lives of succeeding generations and still permeate our culture. "To Greece, we owe *the love of Science, the love of Art, the love of Freedom*; not Science alone, Art alone, or Freedom alone, but these vitally correlated with one another and brought into organic union. And in this union we recognize the distinctive features of the West. The Greek genius is the European genius in its first and brightest bloom. From a vivifying contact with the Greek spirit Europe derived that new and mighty impulse which we call progress."[1]

[1]Samuel H. Butcher, *Some Aspects of the Greek Genius* (London: The Macmillan Co., 1916), p. 40.

Educational philosophy is inevitable in a society recognizing the principle of progress and growth. In contrast to earlier cultures, Greek education was conceived as a progressive adjustment, with a recognition of the complete individual personality. "The significance of Greek education lies in the fact that here is found a developing conception and standard of life, consequently a conception of education which enlarges through successive periods and in which change is tolerated and development of the individual provided for."[2]

Inasmuch as Greek society was dynamic and progressive, its character changed with each generation. To understand the educational development under this culture, it is necessary to divide the Greek history into four eras: (1) Homeric education, prevailing from the prehistoric period down to the first Olympiad in 776 B.C.; (2) Spartan education, prevailing throughout the entire history of Sparta; (3) early Athenian education, prevailing from the first Olympiad in 776 B.C. to the end of the Persian Wars in 480 B.C.; and (4) later Athenian education, or the "Golden Age" of Greece, lasting from the end of the Persian Wars to the Macedonian conquest in 338 B.C., and the "Hellenistic Period," lasting until the foundation of the Roman Empire.

THE HOMERIC GREEKS

The earliest record of Grecian life is preserved in the literary masterpieces, the *Iliad* and the *Odyssey*. These delightful, lively epics were probably woven from ancient myths and legends by the blind bard, Homer.

The early Greek society was primitive. The people lived a rustic, pastoral life. They had no written laws, no system of coinage, and little specialization of occupation. For the most part, men lived in villages, cultivated nearby fields, and pastured their flocks on the adjacent mountain slopes. Tribal government provided a simple form of political administration. The Homeric period, however, extended over many decades and, embracing a progressive society as it did, cultural and social changes were constantly operating.

Religion was ever present in Greek life. There were household shrines in the village dwellings, special deities became the protectors of each tiny community, and frequent festivals or gymnastic events were held in honor of the gods. Religion nurtured the education, poetry, gymnastics, sculpture, art, music, and architecture of the Greeks. Twelve major gods formed the Olympic council that guided the destinies of the Hellenic people, with Zeus the supreme god of all things.

In addition to the twelve Olympic deities, the Greeks worshipped

---

[2]Paul Monroe, *A Textbook in the History of Education* (New York: The Macmillan Co., 1905), p. 52.

innumerable other gods. The deities were immortal beings, superior to man in ability and subject to none of the restrictions of time, space, and power that limited humans. Yet, the deities resembled humans, for they possessed good and evil qualities, the same moods and whims, the same likes and dislikes.

Although these gods played such an important part in Greek life, the effect of their presence differed considerably from the influence of religion on peoples of other cultures. Greek religion did not inspire its worshippers with awe. The Greeks did not submit humbly to a divine personality who motivated them to be obedient to moral laws such as the Commandments. Their religion lacked a formal code of principles of right, just, and virtuous behavior. Although the Greek religion had little direct influence on the morals of the people, it did enrich other aspects of their life.[3] The Greeks worshipped the beautiful in man and nature. Their gods were idealized humanity, man with a superior intellect and physical capacity. With their natural love of rivalry, the Greeks strove to emulate the gods, the superhumans.

Aims of Education

Individual excellence was the goal of all Greek education. Although probably not perceived as completely as in the philosophical age of Aristotle, this budding educational aim was present in embryonic form in Homeric times. The *Iliad* and the *Odyssey* each personified in its hero one of the two attributes prized in this early concept of excellence. Achilles represented "the man of action," Odysseus, "the man of wisdom." "The aim, then, of education was to develop in every nobleman a combination of these two ideals, each to be tempered to avoid one-sidedness—action, by reverence for the gods; wisdom, by whole-mindedness or control of the appetites by reason."[4] With mind and muscle regarded as the perfect components of education, all efforts were directed toward developing broad individual excellence and public usefulness in the civic councils and on the battlefield.

Aims of Physical Education

The overall aim of physical education was to develop the "man of action." Intermittent warfare was the pattern of Homeric life. Every citizen was a soldier, and physical fitness was a necessity. The early Greek exercises

---

[3]Frederick Eby and C. F. Arrowood, *The History and Philosophy of Education Ancient and Medieval* (New York: Prentice-Hall, Inc., 1940), p. 189.

[4]E. H. Wilds, *The Foundations of Modern Education* (New York: Rinehart and Co., 1942), p. 82.

were calculated to produce the qualities needed for the conduct of war, namely strength, endurance, agility, and bravery. The participation was often spontaneous and a natural recreational expression. The Greeks engaged in activity for the simple love of physical effort and struggle.

The Greeks sought an all-around physical development. Despite their extraordinary love of activity, they were not physical giants as one might expect. Mere strength and bulk appealed to them no more in the human body than in art. "They had not the height of the barbarian or the muscular development of the Assyrians and Romans. It was rather in symmetrical activity than in massiveness or gigantic proportions that they surpassed the other races of their times. In beauty of body they were peerless. . . . No other people, indeed, were ever gifted with so great personal beauty . . . and no others ever so much adored that gift."[5]

Promotion of Physical Education

During the Homeric age there were no formal educational institutions. The agencies of education were the family or clan. The mother or nurse, the father, and the elders educated the children.

The formal athletic meeting as it existed in later years was unknown to the Homeric age. Early Greek gymnastic events were simple and informal. Frequently they were associated with a religious festival or a friendly gathering of men honoring a deceased comrade. As yet no gymnasiums, race courses, nor play areas were available. Any natural environment suitable to the sport was selected for the purpose. Evidence seems to indicate that the athletic events were primarily the activity of mature men of noble birth. In the *Iliad* and the *Odyssey*, the kings and the soldiers of high rank are the contestants in the festivals.

Program of Physical Education

The *Iliad* and the *Odyssey* give us a picture of the role athletic sports played during the Homeric age. In the *Iliad*, Book XXIII, Homer describes the funeral games held in honor of Patroclus, a friend of Achilles. After much lamentation, feasting, and sacrificing of humans and animals in commemoration of his beloved friend, the funeral games commenced. The chariot race, a sport reserved for noblemen, was the first event. Five contestants sprang forward and each yoked a span of swift horses to his war chariot. "Then they all at one moment lifted the lash above his yoke of horses, and smote them with the reins, and called to them with words, full eagerly; and forthwith they sped swiftly over the plain away

⁵J. C. Ridpath, *History of the World* (Cincinnati: Ridpath Historical Society, Inc., 1936), 1:459.

from the ships; and beneath their breasts the dust arose and stood, as it were a cloud or a whirlwind, and their manes streamed on the blasts of the wind."[6] The many accidents that occurred in the course of this race were blamed on partisan gods who interfered on behalf of their favorites.

After the chariot race came the boxing match. Euryalus accepted the challenge of the well-known Epeius. "A girdle first he cast about him, and thereafter gave him well-cut thongs of the hide of an ox of the field. So the twain, when they had girded themselves, stepped into the midst of the place of gathering, and lifting their mighty hands on high one against the other, fell to, and their hands clashed together in heavy blows."[7]

The wrestling match was the next event. Only Odysseus, with a type of artfulness and trickery, and Telamonian Aias, the representative of bodily size and brute force, participated. "Then the twain, when they had girded themselves, stepped into the midst of the place of gathering, and laid hold each of the other in close grip with their mighty hands . . . backs creaked beneath the violent tugging of bold hands. . . ."[8] In this match the Homeric athletes practiced upright wrestling, as distinguished from wrestling on the ground.

After the wrestling match, the foot race was held. There were three prizes and three competitors; among them, in spite of his participation in the preceding wrestling match, was Odysseus. "Then took they their places in a row, and Achilles showed them the goal. . . . Odysseus made prayer in his heart to flashing-eyed Athene (Athena) . . . Athene heard him, and made his limbs light, . . . But when they were now about to dart forth to win the prize, then Aias slipped as he ran—for Athene hampered him. . . ."[9]

The final contest was javelin throwing. The prize was awarded to Agamemnon without a contest because of his well-known excellence in this feat. This event closed the funeral games.

In the *Odyssey*, Homer described another dramatic display of athletic skills. Odysseus, during his adventurous wanderings, came to the blissful island of the Phaeacians and the king of the isle gave a great banquet in his honor. Afterwards, King Alcinous bade the young men to exhibit their skill in sports to the stranger. The Phaeacian athletes thereupon competed in footraces, wrestling, leaping, boxing, and throwing the discus. When they were finished, they invited Odysseus to show his skill in contests.[10] At first he declined, but being nettled by taunts, Odysseus, "leaping up with his cloak about him as it was, seized a discus larger than

---

[6]Homer *Iliad* 23. 358–69, trans. A. T. Murray, Loeb Classical Library (New York: G. P. Putnam's Sons, 1935), 2:521.
[7]Ibid., 682–88.
[8]Ibid., 709–16.
[9]Ibid., 757–74.
[10]Homer *Odyssey* 8. 178–83, trans. A. T. Murray, Loeb Classical Library (New York: G. P. Putnam's Sons, 1924), vol. 1.

the rest and thick, no little heavier than those with which the Phaeacians were wont to contend. . . . This with a whirl he sent from his stout hand, and the stone hummed as it flew; . . . past the marks of all it flew . . . (it) is far the first . . . no one of the Phaeacians will reach this, or cast beyond it."[11] Then Odysseus challenged the Phaeacians to match his throw.

Dancing was another activity the Greek noblemen participated in from the earliest times. While Odysseus was being entertained, King Alcinous ordered the "Phaeacian dancers the best among you to make sport . . . and round stood boys in the first bloom of youth, well skilled in the dance, and they smote the goodly dancing floor with their feet. And Odysseus gazed at the twinklings of their feet and marvelled in spirit."[12] In Book I of the *Odyssey*, Homer, in speaking of the suitors of Penelope, mentions in two instances the dancing of the men. "Now after the wooers had put from them the desire of food and drink, their hearts turned to other things, to song and to dance; for these things are the crown of a feast."[13]

Some sports activities were reserved for the aristocrats, particularly chariot racing, boxing, wrestling, and running. Although the men of high birth also excelled in throwing the javelin, shooting the bow, and heaving the weight, these were primarily the sports of the common soldiers. Homeric men did not have a life of ease, for they participated frequently in sports of the most strenuous type.

Methods of Physical Education

Children acquired their education by imitating the adults, sitting with rapt attention at the feast or funeral games, listening to the exciting tales of the gods as sung by minstrels, memorizing the great epics, and absorbing the wisdom of the council meetings. The older and more experienced men who took over the instruction of the youth gave helpful suggestions to their proteges on how to improve their hunting, gymnastics, and military tactics. Much of the instruction was incidental to the occasion as when Nestor gave sage advice to his son Antilochus on how to win the impending chariot race.[14]

Greek boys were strongly competitive. Rivalry was not limited to athletics, but extended to their art, speech, poetry, and drama. Nor was rivalry confined to individuals, for clans and even cities competed in games. Prizes were usually awarded at each contest. The *Iliad* and *Odyssey* frequently mention awards such as a horse, a tripod, a woman skilled

[11]Ibid., 8. 185–99.
[12]Ibid., 8. 250–65.

[13]Ibid., 1. 150–53.
[14]*Iliad*, 23. 306.

in handiwork. But the prizes were more to honor the man in whose memory the funeral games were held than to attract contestants.

THE SPARTAN GREEKS

In Sparta, the social institutions became progressively more conservative as the nation rose in military power. In the early days society was brighter, more hospitable and refined, with a greater atmosphere of freedom and more cultural activity. As the government became increasingly militaristic, progress in other areas almost stopped. As a result, the Spartans bequeathed very little art, literature, science, or philosophy to the world.

By the eighth century B.C. the city-state of Sparta had begun the aggressive policy of pushing into the surrounding areas until the lower half of the Grecian peninsula was overcome. As the Spartans extended their boundaries, the number of hostile conquered peoples swelled. During the eighth century B.C., the population was composed of approximately 250,000 of the subject peoples and about 9,000 Spartans. To cope with this situation, the Spartans imposed an iron discipline on their own people and molded a military caste devoted exclusively to maintaining their social and political supremacy. The state provided the citizens with land and assigned them serfs to perform the labor on their farms. Other subject peoples carried on the trade and commerce essential for serving their needs. All citizens had only one profession—serving the state as a soldier.

Aims of Education

Because the Spartans were concerned with molding youths for military and collective life, they curbed rather than cultivated all-around individual development. The Spartan constitution, reputedly formulated by Lycurgus about 800 B.C., designed an educational system that would insure a constant supply of manpower to maintain and protect the state. The aim of education was to develop strong, healthy, aggressive youths who could endure stoically the discipline of miltary life and the pain and discomfort of battle. Youths were to be inculcated with one all-consuming desire: to be obedient soldiers, capable commanders, and conscientious citizens.

While boys were being drilled as soldiers, girls were being physically conditioned to bear healthy, sturdy children. Their offspring were prenatally dedicated to the state. Young women were not allowed to develop any tender, protective, maternal affection that might make them fear the loss of a son in war. Indeed, women were expected to experience an exhilarated feeling of self-esteem if a son or husband sacrificed his life in the glory of battle.

As the Spartans became more and more militaristic and conservative, the little encouragement they had given to intellectual and aesthetic development ceased. Every precaution was taken to prevent the growth of forces that might encourage change of the status quo or weaken devotion to the state. Travel was limited, foreign education was prohibited, and the citizens were more or less intellectually isolated from any contacts that could invite comparison or awaken a desire for change. The youths were trained to despise wealth and trade; the acquisition of gold and money was punished; and family life was almost completely destroyed because of its tendency to engender a love of luxury and personal ambition. Not even changes in the rules for ball games were tolerated! Nothing was allowed to survive that was capable of undermining the citizens' complete submission to the government. With this system of education, the Spartans were successful in preserving an orderly, unified state untouched by civil strife for three centuries or more. But their fear of change produced a static society that eventually crumbled because the people knew well the arts of war but nothing of the arts of peace.

Aims of Physical Education

Spartan physical education was designed to develop a "man of action" who possessed brute strength, physical endurance, unflinching courage, and military skill. Even aesthetic bodily expressions were directed primarily toward military ends rather than the creation of beauty and grace. Dance was valued because the rhythm caught the military spirit. Plutarch says, "the military dance was an indefinable stimulus, which inflamed courage and gave strength to persevere in the paths of honour and valour."[15]

In brief, the Spartan Greeks held a very restricted concept of the purpose of physical education. They looked with contempt on athletic training for its own sake. "The attitude of the Spartans toward athletics is expressed in a poem of Tyrtaeus (Bergk, No. 12), in which he declares that he would set no store by speed of foot or skill in wrestling, apart from warlike might."[16] Spartan physical education—indeed all education—was training for war.

Promotion of Physical Education

In Sparta the education of the child was the responsibility of the state. The government controlled his education and welfare from the cradle un-

[15]Gaston Vuillier, *A History of Dancing From the Earliest Ages to Our Own Times* (New York: D. Appleton and Co., 1898), p. 17.

[16]E. N. Gardiner, *Greek Athletic Sports and Festivals* (London: The Macmillan Co., 1910), p. 81.

til retirement. At birth, each youngster was examined by a council of elders to determine whether he was worthy of being reared. Only the healthy and strong children were preserved, for only they could be of service to the warlike Spartans. The weak and sickly were ruthlessly exposed on Mount Taygetus to die.

The mother was responsible for the training and rearing of the child from its birth to the age of seven. In reality she was a state nurse, for the child's education was controlled by the government. The child was not wrapped in swaddling clothes, for the Spartans held that the limbs should be perfectly free to grow unimpeded. From his earliest infancy, the mother trained the infant in the rigorous Spartan regime and refrained from any practice that would develop fear or weakness.

The more formal educational system, called the *agoge*, was supervised by the *paidonomus*, or superintendent. This man, an outstanding and respected citizen, performed his duties without remuneration. He had supreme power to supervise the school system and discipline the youths. In the latter duty, he was assisted by a few officials called "whip bearers." There were also some lower class *agoge* to supervise the children who were not citizens.

Upon the first day of school, the Spartan lad was conscripted by the state and would remain in military service until he was at least fifty years old. Crude barracks housed him, and open fields were his gymnasiums until, in later years, a few athletic buildings were erected. As a student he shared with his fellows the same type of shelter, food, clothing, discipline, and training. "The boys were taken away from home and brought up in great boarding-schools, so that the individualising tendencies of the family life and hereditary instincts might be stamped out, and a general type of character, the Spartan type, alone be left in all the boys."[17] The youths were grouped into companies of sixty-four boys, with one youngster selected as a leader. Four of these companies were combined into a troop which was trained, disciplined, and directed by an *eiren*, a boy of about twenty years, who was responsible only to the paidonomus. The youthful leaders gave orders and inflicted punishment, which the boys accepted with patience and respect. In this manner boys learned how to obey, and how to command.

Youths went through several years of education with a specific name being given to each stage of training. When they were eighteen years old, the boys concentrated on military maneuvers, exercises in arms, and drills in scouting outlying districts of the state. They also spent much time training younger boys and were frequently subjected to tests in military skill.

[17]Kenneth J. Freeman, *Schools of Hellas* (London: The Macmillan Co., 1922), p. 12.

At the age of twenty, the youths took the oath of allegiance to the state, and then they began to engage in intensive military maneuvers and in actual warfare. Until the age of thirty, they were compelled to perform prescribed bodily exercises in addition to their military training. Even during war, the Spartans were not released from their daily physical exercises, but the intensity and duration of the drills were mitigated. On other occasions, physical exercises were done before breakfast and before the evening meal. At the age of thirty, a man gained full citizenship and was expected to marry and to take a seat in the council. However, he still continued to live in public barracks, to eat at a common table, to remain in military service, and to devote attention to training younger boys until he was about fifty years old. But even at this age the state was able to request his continued service.

Every male adult citizen was a teacher in Sparta. The state did not entrust the instruction of youth to professional gymnastic trainers or paid employees. Not being fettered with the duty of earning a living, older men were free to pick young boys to tutor, to inspire, and to discipline. A lad who did not have such a tutor was in disgrace because of his lack of worthiness; a citizen who failed to adopt young proteges to instruct was censured for extreme neglect of duty.

The education of Spartan women was similar to that of men. Girls were divided into different classes and participated in the same exercises as boys, but they had separate training grounds and never lived in public barracks. The home was the residence of female youth. The girls continued their gymnastics until about the age of twenty but gave up exercising in public after their marriage.

The Olympian Games provided an occasion for the Spartan youth to exhibit their prowess. The first recorded Spartan victory was in 720 B.C. when Acanthus won the long distance race. Of the eighty-one victories recorded in the Olympics over the next century and a half, no less than forty-six were won by the Spartans. The results of Sparta's physical education program were well displayed in the national athletic festivals.

After the fiftieth Olympic, Spartan success ceased abruptly. Gardiner argues that Sparta's early success (beginning in 720 B.C. and extending to 576 B.C.) and her later decline, were directly related to her progression toward an increasingly more conservative, narrow, and static society. "Moreover, in the seventh century Sparta was a progressive, enlightened state, fond of poetry and music, taking an energetic part in all the manifold activities of Greek life; only the good effects of her system were yet apparent; its iron rule had not yet produced that narrow spirit of exclusiveness which was fatal to progress. Hence Spartan participation in the Olympic Games not only raised the prestige of the festival, but gave a new importance and seriousness to athletics. Hitherto they had been a diversion of nobles, henceforth they were to be part of the education of the people. The physical education of Greece was largely due to Spartan example."[18]

Besides the Olympics, other festivals enjoyed by the Spartans included exhibitions of gymnastics. In an annual event on the island of Platanistas, the older youths fought a battle often likened to a football game; in August, a festival in honor of Apollo afforded an opportunity to display gymnastic skills; and choral dances were performed on many special occasions.

Program of Physical Education

The Spartan curriculum consisted almost entirely of a military training. Gymnastic exercises were the chief means of education for beginning youths. They engaged in running, fighting, leaping, swimming, hunting, wrestling, hiking, boxing, playing ball, riding bareback, throwing the discus and the javelin, and competing in the pancratium.

The gymnastics were graded to avoid injurious strain. The initial training of the youngsters was primarily composed of running and jumping which conditioned the body and strengthened the leg muscles. To develop their arms the boys began to practice ball playing. All ages enjoyed playing ball, but the youngsters of about seventeen or eighteen years were particularly devoted to such activities, and they were called "ball players."[19] The games were undoubtedly quite different from those played today, but neither the rules nor the number of players are known.

Exercises were gradually increased in dosage and complexity, until older boys were constantly drilling in military evolutions, hurling spears, practicing boxing, and developing wrestling skills. The Spartans recognized wrestling as a sport that gave a man all-around physical development and trained him to take quick advantage of an opponent, thus developing two qualities that would serve him well in time of war.

In addition to the general gymnastic program, training to endure hardships was part of the Spartan system. When youths entered the *agoge*, they enjoyed no life of ease and comfort. The boys slept in public barracks on beds of reeds they had gathered without knives. No blankets warmed them, either in summer or winter. Their hair was close cropped and they usually played quite naked. Only one upper garment a year was permitted each youth after he was twelve. Food was scanty and of the plainest nature. Lads who suffered from hunger could steal extra supplies, a practice that was looked upon as developing a skill useful in war. If the youngster was detected in the act, he was severely punished for

[18]Gardiner, *Greek Athletic Sports and Festivals*, p. 57.
[19]Pausanias 3:14–16 from *Pausanias Description of Greece*, trans. J. F. Frazer (New York: The Macmillan Co., 1913), vol. 1.

lacking the adroitness to forage successfully. Hunting, too, was highly regarded as a means of military training, because it was associated with lurking danger and demanded the alertness, bravery, and shrewd judgment needed on the battlefield.

Fighting, boxing, and the pancratium were also a part of the curriculum, although the latter two were forbidden to the younger Spartans. The older men encouraged boys to fight as a test of their skill. Sham battles were frequently arranged. The pancratium, a rough and tumble fight with no holds barred, allowed kicking, scratching, and gouging. Boxing, an art practiced by the earlier Cretans, was conducted with bare fists and no regulations. The Spartans did not permit their citizens to participate in either boxing or the pancratium in the Olympics, because one of the contestants had to admit defeat, something no honorable Spartan could do. Another rugged type of fighting took place in the games at *Platanistas.* The boys celebrated the eve of the battle with sacrifices. The teams entered the playing area on the island by two bridges, the choice of which had previously been determined by lot. "Thus they fight man against man. But they also charge in serried masses, and push each other into the water."[20] Despite the absence of the ball, the game resembles a football scrimmage.

Spartan women had a state-prescribed gymnastic course comparable to that pursued by men. Plutarch says that Lycurgus ordered ". . . the virgins to exercise themselves in running, wrestling, and throwing quoits and darts; that their bodies being strong and vigorous, the children afterwards produced from them might be the same . . .".[21] Spartan girls regularly participated in wrestling; swimming and horseback riding were also popular sports with them. On state occasions the girls also enjoyed dancing and marching in the public processions.

Dancing had an important place in the education of the youth, and was probably a more serious undertaking for the Spartans than for citizens of other cultures. Lycurgus is credited with instituting the *hormos*, a dance in honor of Diana. In this dance young men pantomimed the gestures of the warriors while the girls danced a symbolic pattern representing woman's work. The religious dance, *caryatis*, was performed before the altar of Diana, and was originally associated with marriage. Another dance in which both sexes participated was the *bibasis*, in which the dancers attempted to spring into the air and kick themselves from behind. One Spartan girl is said to have jumped and kicked herself with her heels one thousand times, which apparently was a feat even in that era, for the fact was recorded on her tombstone.

According to one authority, any performance to measured move-

[20]Ibid., p. 20.
[21]Henry Morley, *Ideal Commonwealths* (London: George Routledge and Sons, 1885), p. 26.

ments was considered a dance in Sparta. Many of the Spartan rhythmical activities incorporated gymnastic performances, marches, or military maneuvers. As a means of welding troops into a complete military unit in respect to all the movements of attack and defense, Greek law prescribed dancing for the warrior. Inasmuch as the Spartan soldiers performed the patterned movements in full armor, the latter also provided strenuous muscular exercise. The most widespread military dance was the *pyrrhic*. Boys began to learn the steps when they were only five. In the *pyrrhic*, naked youths armed with swords and shields rhythmically moved in unison, imitating the maneuvers of individuals in combat. Plato tells us the dance represented the cautious movements for avoiding attack by the enemy such as leaping back, springing to the side, and stooping, as well as such pantomimic offensive movements as hurling spears, shooting arrows, and manipulating weapons. These steps and gestures were performed to flute music.

Methods of Physical Education

The severe and exacting Spartan physical education program conditioned the body to withstand the hardships that war would impose. These militant Hellenes believed that the discipline of youth could not begin too early. Nurses trained children to eat whatever they were given, to have no fear of the dark, and to shun crying as unworthy of a Spartan. As the youngsters grew up, they had little opportunity to escape into privacy and hide from the public's criticism of their every act. They had no home life, but dwelt under the constant supervision of older boy-teachers. Every adult citizen was a self-appointed critic who had the solemn duty of disciplining any erring child. Flogging was the universal penalty for all offenses. The iron scepter of discipline ruled over Spartan boys and continued to rule them after they were full-grown.

Hero-worship played a part in educating the youth. The mothers, in whom state-love had been bred more strongly than mother-love, encouraged the youngsters to aspire to be good soldiers. The tales of the Homeric athletic heroes, the military poetry and songs, were utilized as an emotional stimulus in educating boys. Doubtlessly, the close association with adult men who had no interests in life other than serving in the Army and educating the boys, gave children more teachers per pupil than most cultures have ever known. Naturally, the desire to be singled out and popular among the "foster-father" teachers encouraged boys to put forth their best efforts.

Periodic testing by state officials, *ephors*, was administered to evaluate the boys' physical capacity and citizenship. Youths of eighteen to twenty were given rigid examinations. "And besides, it was written in the law that every ten days the youth stripped naked should pass in public review before the *ephors*. Now if they were solid and vigorous, resembling the work of a sculptor and the engraver, as a result of the gymnastic exercises, praise was accorded them; but if their physique displayed any flabbiness or flaccidity, with fat beginning to appear in rolls because of laziness, then were they beaten and punished."[22] The testing program of the Spartans tried to determine to what degree their youths possessed unflinching valor, uncomplaining endurance of pain and hardship, unsurpassed military skill, and unqualified devotedness to the state.

THE EARLY ATHENIANS

Until the sixth century B.C. the Spartan and Athenian cultures were similar, but thereafter Sparta grew more austere, conservative, and isolated, and Athens developed a more liberal, progressive, and democratic society. Prior to the first Olympic Games in 776 B.C., the Athenians were primarily herdsmen ruled by a monarch. During the next three hundred years many important changes took place. Great landowners acquired sufficient strength to wrest the governing powers from the king and establish an oligarchy. As the Spartans advanced, Athens found it had to maintain, not only chariots, but a cavalry and, eventually, heavily armed troops; as a result noblemen had to admit more men into political power.

Economic developments and political reforms operated to broaden political privileges. As the rich landowners tended to grow richer, they acquired the mortgaged lands of the poorer men, forcing many into slavery. To free the lower-class citizens from these excesses, Solon prohibited the mortgaging of persons, limited the amount of land an individual might acquire, divided citizens into four classes according to their income, broadened the political franchise, encouraged the education of youth, and formulated many of the basic policies upon which the Athenian educational system was developed. Sometime after the death of Solon, some impoverished nobles began to improve their economic position by selling luxury goods to the wealthy. Eventually this new merchant class rivaled the old landed nobles in wealth and demanded political power. The whole early Athenian era was thus a struggle toward more democratic government. The poorer citizens became more powerful during this era of economic expansion and at the same time, slavery increased rapidly. The life of the noncitizen was somewhat more favorable in Athens than in other Greek states, but there remained a gulf between the wealthy citizens, who had the leisure to engage in physical exercises and contests, and the poorer citizens, foreigners, and slaves who had to work for a living.

[22]*Variae Historiae Aeliani* 14:7, quoted in Clarence Forbes, *Greek Physical Education* (New York: The Century Co., 1929), p. 33.

In the early days many free citizens of Athens engaged in manual work and various skilled occupations, but after the fifth and fourth centuries B.C., they constituted only a small part of the producing class.

Aims of Education

Both the Spartans and the Athenians were primarily concerned with training the child to assume his civic responsibilities, but the Athenians were more liberal. Emphasis was not placed on enhancing the youth's personal life, however, but rather on the quality of the service he could render to the state. The Athenians wanted youths to develop not only military skills and courage, but also the virtues and capacities needed for the peaceful progress of the nation. Reverence for the Greek gods, respect for one's elders, and loyalty to the state were civic as well as personal responsibilities.

The Athenian ideal was to unite the "man of action" and "the man of wisdom." To produce this citizen required an educational system that would develop all aspects of a youth's physical and mental potentials into a single, well-integrated personality. No exaggeration, no one-sidedness was to be permitted. Every phase of life was to be in complete harmony.[23]

Aims of Physical Education

Physical education, which was at its zenith in Athens where it flourished as an integral part of national life, was rooted not only in the utilitarian need to prepare citizens for war, but also in the Greek ideals of beauty and harmony. The objective of education, was not the cultivation of the physical alone, but rather the development of the individual qualities *through* the physical. The Greeks gave physical education a respectability that it has never since achieved. They accorded the body equal dignity with the mind. They associated sport with philosophy, music, literature, painting, and particularly with sculpture. They gave to all future civilizations important aesthetic ideals: the ideals of harmonized balance of mind and body, of body symmetry, and of bodily beauty in repose and in action. To these contributions may be added educational gymnastics, the competitive sports of track and field, the classic dance, and the Olympic Games. Although the ancient Games were essentially religious, they represented the first attempt at international cooperation in peaceful endeavors.

Athenian statesmen were apt to stress the military goals of physical education, but philosophers and artists gave the world a new concept of

---

[23]Lucian, *The Dance* 73, in A.M. Harmon, *Lucian with an English Translation* (Cambridge: Harvard University Press, 1936), 5:277.

the aesthetic ideals to be attained by physical exercise. "The Greek, with his keen eye for physical beauty, regarded flabbiness, want of condition, imperfect development as a disgrace, a sign of neglected education. . . ."[24] As the Greeks had high artistic standards in art, literature, and music, they also developed definite patterns of movement and behavior for the achievement of bodily beauty and perfection. Much greater emphasis was placed on the form of the performance, the grace and skill with which it was executed, than on the establishment of records of strength, speed, or endurance. Physical education had to be a perfectly balanced program that completely harmonized with the other phases of education.

Moral training was an important part of the program. Through physical education the youngsters developed self-discipline, courage, humility, determination, and sportsmanship. There was much more emphasis on the formation of character than on the development of strength and athletic prowess.

The Athenians did play field hockey, but for the most part team play and team spirit, so prominent a feature of modern sports, were missing in the Greek competitions. Of this omission, modern writers have commented, "The character of their gymnastic contests led to an exaggeration of the individual ego. . . . Each man contested with his own skill and intelligence against all others. Teamwork in which the individual is subordinated to the group was entirely unknown to Greek gymnastics."[25]

All in all, the youths and men exercising in the gymnasiums of Athens were not indulging merely in a light-hearted, leisure-time amusement, nor were they concerned primarily with developing skills to exhibit for public acclaim. The Athenians participated in arduous exercises because of their zealous desire to become all-around citizens with physical, mental, and spiritual well-being and vigor (*euexia*).

Promotion of Physical Education

In Athens education was much less regulated than in Sparta. Other than maintaining the gymnasium, the state gave no financial support to formal education. Government regulations for schools were more concerned with safeguarding the morals of the youths than with prescribing definite courses of study, methods, or supervision. The government did determine at what age a child should enter school and specified that class size be controlled so that teachers could give proper attention to students. Solon is said to have required that boys be taught to swim. In addition, it was the common practice for the state to pay for the education of boys whose

24Gardiner, *Greek Athletic Sports and Festivals*, p. 88.
25Eby and Arrowood, *The History and Philosophy of Education*, p. 197.

fathers were killed fighting for Athens. Except for these few state regulations, the parents were free to educate their children as they saw fit.

The physical fitness of the infant was determined by the father who decided whether the newborn was to be accepted or rejected. During the first few years of his life the child was in the care of his mother, nurse, or slaves. Spartan nurses were preferred, for their milk was supposed to give the baby strength, and they had a reputation for training children to discipline their emotions. The mothers were uneducated and led such a secluded life that they contributed little to the development of the children.

The Athenian girls, who remained at home until they married, were trained in household arts. Although a few of them learned to read and write, most received virtually no physical or intellectual education. Athenian women did not participate in social and political life with men. Girls entertained men at banquets, but they were usually slaves, foreigners, or *hetairai* who were specially trained in dance and acrobatics.

When the Athenian boy was about seven years old, the home no longer dominated his existence. Meals at home were the only semblance of family life. The boy passed the rest of his time in the company of servants, teachers, and friends. The loose ties of home life encouraged the child to identify himself with his fellow citizens and strengthened his feeling of citizenship.

The early education of Athenian youth took place in two kinds of private elementary schools. The *palaestra* (wrestling school) provided boys with their physical education, and the *didascaleum* (music school) offered courses in literature, music, and some arithmetic. A difference of opinion exists, but the boys probably began to study in both schools about the same time. How they divided their time between them is not known. The *palaestra* was sometimes simply a room attached to a private dwelling with an adjacent playground. The more elaborate of these schools comprised separate buildings surrounded by pillars with extensive play fields and swimming opportunities near by. An open court in the middle of the *palaestra* provided a place for wrestling, boxing, jumping, and gymnastic exercises. Rooms for dressing, oiling, bathing, and sanding the body were at the disposal of the youths. Although most of the activity took place in the court or adjacent play fields, an exercise room with punching bags and balls was also available.

The *paidotribe* was the teacher of physical education. He owned his *palaestra* and charged a stipulated fee. The *paidotribe* hired assistant teachers and professional flute players to serve on the staff. Some Athenians evaluated the qualifications of the various *paidotribes* before enrolling their children in a school, but many parents selected a school on the basis of the cost rather than the quality and quantity of the instruction. Young boys were chaperoned by an old slave known as a *pedagogue* (*paidagogus*), who served them as servant, counselor, tutor, disciplinarian, and guardian. Sometimes the slave served until the boys were eighteen, but more frequently his duties terminated earlier.

In Athens, education was limited to citizens, who still comprised only a small proportion of the total population. The length and quality of the education a boy received in the *palaestra* and *didascaleum* were determined largely by the economic status of his family. The age at which students terminated their education varied from fourteen to eighteen, for the state did not regulate the age limit. At eighteen, youths were examined for the assumption of ctitizenship. If qualified, they participated in a public ceremony that included taking the famed Athenian oath. Between eighteen and twenty years, youths were subject to military service whenever the state needed them,[26] although there was no system of compulsory military training during the early Athenian period.

Throughout most of their adult life, male citizens with sufficient leisure practiced physical exercises in the gymnasiums that were located in a brookside grove of trees just outside of the city. A covered track to be used in rainy weather extended around the court. The great gymnasiums of Athens were the Academy, the Lyceum, and the Cynosarges. The Cynosarges was for some time reserved for the sons of parents who were not both Athenians. In purpose and design the publicly administered gymnasiums were similar to the private *palaestras*, but the facilities were usually larger and more expensive, the patrons paid no fees and no instructors were employed in the early days. The gymnasiums served as clubhouses rather than as formal schools. Some free citizens who had to work for a living probably had little time for the gymnasiums, but many men of all ages spent most of their time at the gymnasium which provided not only exercise facilities but also the intellectual stimulation and the social life that was lacking in the home.

There were no state educational officials of any particular power or authority during early Athenian times. However, the *Areopagus*, the aristocratic governing council, had the power of supervising all civic affairs, including, of course, education. In addition, some public officials, the *gymnasiarchs*, *choragi*, and *trierarchs*, personally financed and supervised the training of boys who participated in special recreational events. As his public service, the *gymnasiarch* selected boys for the torch race, paid the coach, and exercised some authority while the boys were training. The *choragus* selected fifty youths and fifty men to constitute the two choruses for the public festivals in which dancing had a prominent place. During the two months of rehearsals, boys were drilled to perform according to the highest artistic standards. To have had choral training was a mark of distinction for the well-educated Greek. By the end of the

---

[26]Arthur A. Bryant, *Boyhood and Youth in the Days of Aristophanes* (Cambridge: Harvard Studies in Classical Philology, 1907) 18:79–80.

early Athenian period, the *trierarch* was responsible for providing a sailing ship for the nation and he may also have arranged boat races and other aquatic events.

The athletic meetings that had grown out of ancient funeral customs, and the assemblies, marketplaces, juries, and theaters contributed to the education of Athenian youths. The Hellenic holidays held in honor of the gods were dynamic agencies of physical education. "Athens was not the most athletic of the states of Greece; but nowhere was the love of festivals more developed, and nowhere were competitions more various and numerous. The Athenian must have spent a large portion of his life in attending festivals and witnessing competitions."[27] Besides the numerous athletic celebrations that were confined to a single locality, all of the city-states participated in four great "national" athletic contests. These events, known as the Panhellenic games, included the Olympic, Isthmian, Pythian, and Nemean festivals.

The Olympic Games, the most celebrated of the national festivals, were conducted every four years at Olympia, commencing in 776 B.C. The games lasted five days in August and were always accompanied by ceremonies in honor of Zeus. All warring tribes were expected to observe a truce while the games were in progress.[28] Athletes, peasants, noblemen, politicians, and splendid state embassies from all parts of Greece made their way to the games. A city of tents mushroomed on the fields near Olympia. The Panhellenic festivals provided the major force of cultural exchange among the city-states.

In the early days, the Olympics took place in a simple setting. The races were held in the fields which extended from the altar of Zeus to the tomb of Pelops. The spectators observed the contests from the slopes. During the early Athenian period, aside from the priestess of Demeter and perhaps virgins, women were not permitted to attend the games, but the contests were quite democratic in other respects. "In athletic events noble and peasant met on equal terms. The aristocratic prejudice against these popular contests did not yet exist; and though the honor of the Olympic crown was open to the poorest citizen of Greek birth, such was the prestige of the festival that it was coveted even by the highest."[29] The wealthier citizens were actually in a better position to undergo the required ten months of training than the poorer citizens who had to work for a living.

Epictetus has provided a realistic contemporary description of the trials of the spectators who watched the Olympic Games: "True, there are hardships and difficulties in life. Are they not to be found even at Olym-

[27]Gardiner, *Greek Athletic Sports and Festivals*, p. 227.
[28]Some authorities believe that only a guarantee of safe passage for travelers to the Games was made.
[29]Gardiner, *Greek Athletic Sports and Festivals*, pp. 60–61.

pia? Don't you get baked by the sun there? Don't you get crushed by the crowds? Don't you find it impossible to get a bath? Don't you get soaked whenever it rains? Don't you have an overdose of noise, of shouting and exasperation? Yet you steel your heart and put up with it all, because you think that the spectacle makes it worthwhile."[30]

The Pythian festival was probably the second in importance. Originally it was a musical event to honor Apollo, and music continued to be dominant even after Olympic events were added to the celebration. The Pythian festival was held on a plain below Delphi every four years, the third year of each Olympiad. Chariot racing and horse racing were its prominent events.

The Panhellenic games of Isthmia, which also were popular with the Athenians, were celebrated at Corinth during the second and fourth year of each Olympiad. In this festival, athletic, equestrian, and musical events were held, along with boating events in honor of Poseidon, god of the sea. Citizens also engaged in the Nemean games which were conducted every two years in Argolis in honor of Zeus. Compared with the Olympics, the Pythian and Nemean games were local events.

The prizes awarded the winners of the national festivals were not of great material value. Rather, an appropriate wreath was placed on the victor's head in an impressive ceremony. At Olympia the crown was of olive leaves; at Pythia, bay leaves; at Isthmia, dry parsley leaves or pine; and at Nemea, fresh parsley was the award. When the victors returned home, triumphal processions and banquets were held in their honor. The champions were given special privileges and were always highly respected. Solon granted sums of money to winners of great events.

Nearly every month of the year marked the date of some local Athenian festival. The greatest of these was held in honor of the goddess Athena. Although open to outsiders, the Panathenaea was primarily a local celebration lasting for several days. The competitions included horse racing, athletics, torch races, pyrrhic dances, musical contests, recitations, boating, and in later days, even a beauty contest.

Program of Physical Education

The youngsters of the Hellenic world had many sports and games for their childhood amusements. The infant's rattle was a Greek toy said to have been invented by the philosopher, Archytas. The game of rolling the hoop was common. The top, as old as the days of Homer, was a universal amusement. Kite flying seems to have been known, and the swing

---

[30]Quoted in H. A. Harris, *Greek Athletes and Athletics* (Bloomington: Indiana University Press, 1966), p. 141.

existed. Stilts were used by children and also by adults in their dances. Painted clay dolls with movable parts amused the youngsters. Clappers, toy carts, toy soldiers, and hobby horses were found in many homes. Greek children participated in a variety of games similar to the activities of the present day, such as ducks and drakes, blind-man's buff, peg-top, jacks, odd and even, hide and seek, ride a cock horse, and delta. Ball games were favorite pastimes with all the Athenians. More than fifty distinct types of games, with many variations of each game, have been recorded. The Athenians also kept pets.

Informal childhood activities ended when the youth entered school at age seven. In the *palaestra* the youngster did not immediately embark upon a strenuous program. From about the age of seven until twelve, his activities consisted of light exercises and sports, and the teacher encouraged good posture. In these early years younger boys were given training in gesture, a type of exercise for the upper extremities that was used in preparation for dances and for boxing. Other activities for youths of this age were runnning, jumping, rope climbing, leapfrog, and ball games. They were also trained in javelin and discus-throwing but used a smaller discus than adults used.

Strenuous exercises were not introduced into the curriculum until the youngsters had had a few years of general physical conditioning. Older boys participated in a more vigorous program of racing, discus and javelin throwing, jumping, boxing, wrestling, the pancratium, and chariot racing. They continued these activities as they grew into adulthood, for full-grown men were expected to maintain the ability to perform these exercises and to participate in athletic contests.

The great festivals were serious religious observances as well as magnificent sporting displays. The events of the Olympics, reflect the content of the educational curriculum: the foot race, the pentathlon, pancratium, wrestling, boxing, and chariot racing.

Foot races were always important in the Athenian physical education program. In the Olympian contests, foot races were independent events as well as part of the pentathlon. The length of the stadium was equal to a *stade*, a distance of about two hundred yards. There were three types of foot races: the *stade* or short race, the *diaulos* or two-stade race, and the long race, *dolichos*, of seven to twenty-four stades. There were different races for different ages, and some of the festivals classified contestants according to size and strength. The runners assumed a more upright position than the modern crouching stance, but otherwise their form was similar to that of the present day. In the short races, the contestants ran in heats, and the winner of each heat competed in the finals.

In the sixth century B.C. racing in armor was introduced, but it was not taught to the boys. The popularity of this race increased after the Persian Wars in the fifth century. Torch races, which were included in the Panathenaea festival, took place at night and were contests between individuals or between teams. Penalties were exacted for unfair practices in any race.

The pentathlon first appeared at the eighteenth Olympic. It was a selection of events that could produce the best all-around athlete. The pentathlete was a representative of the Greek ideals of harmony and balance as opposed to specialization and one-sided development. The pentathlon consisted of five parts: running, jumping, throwing the discus, throwing the javelin, and wrestling. Considerable controversy exists about the order of events and the method of determining the victor, but he probably had to win at least three of the events.

The jump was part of the pentathlon, but was not an independent event in the Olympics. The athletes competed against each other and the rules were similar to modern contests except that the Athenians used hand weights of stone or metal, called *halteres*, to assist their momentum. The *halteres* differed in size, weight, and shape; some have been found weighing over ten pounds. The broad jump or long jump was the only type of jumping that had any place in the festivals. Unlike today's running broad jumper who takes a long run before takeoff, the Greeks ran a few short, springy steps, like the modern high jumper, to prepare for the takeoff. During the approach, *halteres* were scarcely swung. Immediately before takeoff, the jumper momentarily checked his run, and used the upward and downward swing of the arms with the *halteres* to coincide with the spring of the legs. The use of the weights added to the distance of the jump.

The discus, like the jump, existed only as an event in the pentathlon. Made of polished stone or metal, the standard pentathlon discus was circular, measured about a foot in diameter, and weighed about four or five pounds. Unlike the modern method of hurling after making two or three complete turns, the Greeks employed a relatively fixed position. Artists found the perfectly proportioned body of the discus thrower a favorite subject. Myron's *Discobolus* is a statue which reveals not only the skill of the sculptor but the physical symmetry, vigor, and grace of the early Athenian.

By including javelin throwing in the pentathlon, the Athenians honored the characteristic exercise of their ancestors. Two styles of throwing were practiced, one for war and hunting, the other for athletics. Athletes were interested in distance and form, while warriors were interested in force and accuracy. The athletic javelin was from eight to ten feet long, light, and with a blunt point. It was thrown by means of a fixed thong, attached near the center of gravity, which gave the missile a rotary motion in flight. Javelin throwing was a test of skill rather than of strength.

Wrestling, the last event in the pentathlon, was perhaps the most popular and universal of all Greek sports. The Greeks believed wrestling displayed strength, agility, and gracefulness of body better than any other activity. It was part of the pentathlon as well as a separate event in the Olympics. There were two modes of wrestling, standing and ground wrestling, the former being more common and popular. The contestants stood upright, face to face, and each tried to throw his opponent to the ground without falling himself. Three falls constituted a victory. In ground wrestling, the object was to throw the opponent to the ground where the struggle continued until the opponent admitted defeat. Competitions were conducted in the same manner as modern tournaments. Wrestling gave its name to the *palaestra* and was considered one of the most important subjects in the curriculum.

Boxing, an independent event, was introduced in the twenty-third Olympic. Boxing predates the Homeric age, for in Greek mythology we learn that Apollo defeated Ares. Unlike Homeric athletes, the Olympian contestants used no protective girdle around the loins. Instead of using gloves, the Greeks wound thin ten-foot-long thongs of hardened leather about their palms. Their blows and parries were similar to those used today, but Greek boxers confined their blows almost entirely to the head. Body blows were not practiced and might possibly have been prohibited. In Greek boxing there were no rings, ropes, officials, or rounds, and there were no regulations to prevent hitting a man who was down. Kicking, hugging, and clinching were forbidden. The combatants continued until one was knocked unconscious or was compelled by his wounds or fatigue to accept defeat. In some instances, however, they paused for a rest by mutual consent. Being a slow and defensive sport, Greek fighting lacked the aggressiveness of modern boxing. Because no weight classifications were established, boxing became a sport of the heavyweights.

Several Greek training practices were similar to procedures used today. Sometimes headgears were worn to protect the ears from injury. Boys in the *palaestra* utilized this protective device, but such protection was not used in public competition. In training, men shadow-boxed to perfect the necessary coordinations. In shadow-boxing, the participants sparred with open hands. Evidences indicate that light punching bags were used in workouts.

The *pancratium*, which was introduced as an event in the thirty-third Olympic, was a primitive rough-and-tumble activity combining many elements of boxing and wrestling. When performed at the great festivals, it was regulated to eliminate brutality; biting and gouging were prohibited. Victory was achieved when the opponent admitted defeat. For a long time this sport was limited to adults in the festivals, but youths practiced the sport in the *palaestra* under careful supervision.

Chariot racing was popular as far back as the funeral games of the Homeric Age. The festival races were similar to those in the *Iliad*. Horse racing was as popular as chariot racing, as is evidenced by scenes impressed on coins beginning with the fifth century B.C. Generally, the racing program comprised events for full-grown horses, colts, four-horse chariots, and two-horse chariots. The two-horse chariot race was probably the oldest event. Racing was introduced in the twenty-fifth Olympic; four-horse chariot racing with jockeys dates from the thirty-third Olympic. These sports were limited to men wealthy enough to maintain stables.

Aquatic sports and dancing, not always part of the various festivals, were part of the Athenian physical education program. Swimming was popular among boys who lived near the water, and it was a useful skill for citizens serving in the navy. There are fragmentary allusions in the literature which suggest that swimming was a common accomplishment, and the pictorial vases give us clues concerning the techniques employed. The overhand stroke was used, as well as the side and breast strokes, although these were used less frequently. Plato also mentions a man swimming on his back. The Greeks also knew how to float and tread water. The only known competition in aquatic events was held at Hermione.

Athenian youths were also taught to row, as evidenced by the need for two-hundred-man crews on each trireme. Competitive ship races were sponsored at the Isthmian and more local festivals.

Dancing permeated the lives of the Athenians. "They danced in the temples, the woods, the fields. Every event of interest to the family, every birth, every marriage, every death, was the occasion of a dance."[31] Great festivals in honor of the nine Muses and of Apollo, Artemis, Aphrodite, Athena, and other Greek gods emphasized dancing in the religious ceremonials. Terpsichore, the Muse of dance and choral song, was especially honored. The Dionysian rites were entirely of dancing. The Athenians also performed war dances, but these were more popular in Sparta. Dramatic productions usually required some dancing. As the Athenians celebrated more than forty state occasions annually, the dance played an intrinsic role in their lives.

Greek dancing was an act of religious worship, and it was a total body expression. In describing a boy's performance, Xenophon declared, ". . . I could not help observing; how while he danced no portion of his body remained idle; neck and legs and hands together, one and all were exercised."[32] Athenian dancing was highly dramatic. Originally the rhapsodists had sung or told their tales while dramatizing them with appropriate action. As the Athenians developed their dance forms, they emphasized mimicry, gesticulation, and pantomime—telling a story by the movements of the body. Dancing eventually became an important part of the Greek drama.

[31]Vuillier, *A History of Dancing*, p. 7.
[32]H. G. Dakyns, *The Works of Xenophon, Symposium or the Banquet* (London: The Macmillan Co., 1897), 3:302.

The dance played a synaptic role in the Athenian educational system; it was the point of contact between physical and intellectual education. Dancing was a creative act of expressing the emotional, spiritual, intellectual experience through physical activity. The exercises of the *palaestra* and the interpretation of the poetry and music in the *didascaleum* prepared the boys for participation.

Methods of Physical Education

Athenian youth were trained by imitation and participation. The Greek boys learned by imitating their teachers in the *palaestra* and the more skilled participants in the gymnasium. In dancing, boxing, wrestling, and other sports the teachers developed certain drills or "figures" that children were taught. When the boys had acquired sufficient practice in these skills, the *paidotribe* commanded the desired exercise and critically watched each performance.

The union of sports with religion in athletics motivated youths to attain the manly beauty and superiority in competition that their gods exhibited. They performed not only for their fellow citizens but also for their gods. The boys were inspired to emulate their gods, the great heroes of literature, and the victors in the festivals. Undoubtedly, the prizes, praise, prestige, and privileges granted the winners of the athletic games also intensified their desire to achieve athletic prowess.

From youth to maturity the lads were constantly supervised by parents, *pedagogues*, and *paidotribes*. "Under no circumstances were Athenian boys allowed to fight without supervision. An instructor must be present to see that the contest was fought in accordance with the strict rules of the sport, and to prevent any evil or malicious passion from expression."[33] Discipline in the schools was firm. The *pedagogue* could flog a child, and the *paidotribe* was pictured on vases as a man holding a stick.

Exercises were graded to fit capacities. The boys were grouped according to general ability rather than age. "Care was taken in pairing the boys to bring together only those who were well matched. The weaker and more diffident were matched with those whom they could overcome with good effort. Confidence was developed through self-exertion and the encouragement of the trainers. The overconfident and conceited were paired with boys who were able to defeat them readily. In this way proper self-esteem was fostered."[34] In these ways Athenian education encouraged the individual development of the whole child.

[33]Eby and Arrowood, *The History and Philosophy of Education*, p. 244.
[34]Ibid., pp. 246–47.

THE LATER ATHENIANS

A new epoch in Greek education began after the victorious Persian Wars. Having played a major role in defeating an almost invincible empire, the Athenians were filled with a sense of excitement, well-being, and self-confidence. As individuals and as a nation they were eager to expand and enjoy their new freedom and prestige.

Commerce and industry existed in early Athens, but the period following the Persian Wars was one of extended and accelerated economic expansion. Athens, once a simple, conservative, agricultural community, now became the commercial, cosmopolitan capital of an empire. As citizens acquired more and more slaves and amassed immense fortunes, they had more leisure time to devote to intellectual pursuits. The sparks generated by contact with strange cultures through war and trade intensified their desire to become acquainted with the accumulating masses of knowledge. Because of the intellectual curiosity of the citizens and the economic and social advantages of the city, artists, architects, scientists, mathematicians, and philosophers from many parts of the Mediterranean world gravitated toward Athens. This artistic and intellectual talent catapulted the city into one of the greatest cultural revolutions of history.

Political leadership was revolutionized as a result of the war. The members of the old aristocratic, agricultural ruling class found their authority reduced by the devastation of their estates, the rise of commerce and industry, and the extension of the political franchise. When the right to debate and vote on government problems was extended to a new mass of citizens in return for the part they had played in winning the war, democracy reached its fullest expression. To prepare for their new role, young men demanded a new type of education—an education that would enable them to sway their fellow-legislators, defend themselves in court, and attain political and economic power. The wandering Sophists, who gave lectures on intellectual subjects and taught the arts of reasoning and rhetoric, supplied the new higher education that the youths wanted. Some Sophists were brilliant men, others were glib charlatans, but all of them emphasized intellectual activity, and hence contributed to the decline in interest in physical education.

The Golden Age of Athens provided the soil for the growth and flowering of democracy, unity, and true genius. At the same time, it nurtured the weeds of destruction: unlicensed freedom, rugged individualism, and political particularism. Athens was successful in unifying her neighboring states and transforming this union into a limited empire, but when Pericles attempted to bring about the union of all Greek states after the Persian Wars, he failed. The Greek city-states had the same language, the same religion, and the same games, but local pride, economic rivalry, and fear of Athen's expansionist policies fanned ancient fires of fraternal hatred.

The southern Greeks, led by Sparta, formed the Peloponnesian League; the Northern Confederacy was led by Athens. The prolonged Peloponnesian War marked the beginning of the end of Greek glory. The Greeks never recovered from the effects of the war. During the next century the Athenians came under the domination of the Macedonians and still later they were absorbed by the Roman Empire.

Aims of Education

The scientific and intellectual revolution that took place in the later Athenian period broadened and deepened knowledge, and the critical forms of inquiry that developed caused men to question the traditional ways of viewing the world. Morality based on religion, tradition, and service to the state was met with increasing skepticism and rejection. Educational goals shifted from the old ideal of devotion to the state and fidelity to the gods to the ideal of the pursuit of personal success and happiness. Every man was encouraged to select his own aims, determine his own conduct, and decide the extent of his service to the state. "Man is the measure of all things. Satisfy man!" was the slogan. This philosophy of rampant individualism permeated later Athenian education.

After observing the results of extreme individualism in their society, such conservatives as Aristophanes and Xenophon attempted to arouse the public to the evils of this philosophy. They urged a return to the older order, even recommending the Spartan ideals of complete subservience of the individual to the state. Socrates, Plato, Aristotle, and other philosophers recognized the impossibility of returning to the old social processes. They developed new concepts of education based upon combining the individual will with the interests of society.

Socrates held that seeking truth rather than traditional knowledge was the chief aim of education. Through sound thinking, men were to arrive at the universal truths of piety, temperance, and justice that exist in every man's consciousness. By applying these concepts to life, men would become virtuous and a better world would result. Thus, virtue became the ultimate goal of education. Plato, who held justice to be the ultimate good, denounced training directed toward the acquisition of wealth, physical strength, or mere cleverness. In his opinion, each youth, should be permitted to develop his greatest possibilities for the purpose of serving the state in the way he was best fitted. To Aristotle, the highest goal of education was happiness which was to be realized through good action based on sound reasoning. Happiness included such things as health, fame, honor, friends, children, economic efficiency, and good moral character.

The philosophical systems of these great thinkers had more influence in later times than when they were proposed. The politicians of that day were not anxious to reconstruct education in order to eradicate social ills. Individualism had taken firm root in Athens and flourished until it had completely demoralized the once great empire.

Aims of Physical Education

During the later Athenian period, the schools became concerned with developing a "man of wisdom" almost to the exclusion of the "man of action." The new intellectual education deemphasized the traditional physical and civic aspects of education. Immediately after the Persian Wars, the citizens were still aware of the importance of physical fitness for military efficiency and continued to embrace the high ideals of the early Athenian educators. With the rise of the new intellectualism, the decline of Athenian military power, the replacement of citizen-soldiers by mercenaries, and the rapid rise of professional athletes, youths' interest in physical development was diminished and the *palaestras* became deserted and empty.

Wealthy citizens were contemptuous of the old goals of physical education, but as the lack of exercise and luxurious living took their toll, the possibility of maintaining health and prolonging life through the regulation of diet, exercise, and hygienic practices appealed to them.

Professionalism, with its emphasis on specialization by paid athletes, replaced the earlier Athenian ideal: all-around physical excellence for the sake of serving the state effectively in peace and war. "Hero worship of the successful athlete . . . the centering of the athlete's attention upon himself rather than on any useful social end and the competition of cities for successful athletes all combined to produce a contempt for earlier standards of sportsmanship and morality."[35] Physical education, once a means of building a hardy, vigorous, morally sound nation, was now an agency for undermining and prostituting its power.

Critics who recognized these evils tried to warn the citizens. Aristophanes, in his *Clouds*, an attack on the educational theories of the Sophists, encouraged youths to spend less time in the intellectual atmosphere and return to the gymnasium.[36] Other men were also alarmed at the changes taking place. Xenophon complained that the Athenians "not only neglect to make themselves fit, but mock at those who take the trouble to do so."[37] He emphasized Socrates' conviction that, "No citizen has a

[35]Thomas Woody, "Professionalism and the Decay of Greek Athletics," *School and Society* 67 (23 April 1938): 524.

[36]B. B. Rogers, *The Clouds of Aristophanes*, 1010–1019 (London: G. Bell and Sons, Ltd., 1930), pp. 131–33.

[37]Xenophon *Memorabilia* 3.5.15. trans. E. C. Marchant, The Loeb Classical Library (New York: G. P. Putnam's Sons, 1928).

right to be amateur in the matter of physical training: it is part of his profession as a citizen to keep himself in good condition, ready to serve his state at a moment's notice. The instinct of self-preservation demands it likewise: for how helpless is the state of the ill-trained youth in war or danger! Finally what a disgrace it is for a man to grow old without ever seeing the beauty and strength of which his body is capable."[38] Socrates had appealed for the maintenance of physical education: "For in everything that men do the body is useful, and in all uses of the body it is of great importance to be in as high a state of physical efficiency as possible. Why, even in the process of thinking, in which the use of the body seems to be reduced to a minimum, it is a matter of common knowledge that grave mistakes may often be traced to bad health. . . . But a sound and healthy body is a strong protection to a man. . . ."[39]

Plato, a pupil of Socrates, held that gymnastics should not be promoted as ends in themselves but rather as a means of developing military fitness and healthy bodies to house healthy minds. In the *Protagoras*, he advocated, "Then they send them to the master of gymnastics, in order that their bodies may better minister to the virtuous mind, and that they may not be compelled through bodily weakness to play the coward in War or on any other occasion."[40] Although peace was the state's ultimate objective, it was necessary to be ready to fight if the state was threatened by a foreign aggressor. For Plato, "the moral value of exercises and sports far outweighed the physical value. Vice [he declared] was due to bad education and an unhealthy physical condition; gymnastics served both as a preventative and remedy of the latter, and so contributed to the extirpation of vice."[41]

Plato's concept of man and the human body changed during his lifetime. In *Phaedo* he incorporated the Orpheo-Pythagorean concept of the duality of man and broke with the Periclean "whole man" philosophy which had made physical education an integral part of education. In distinguishing sharply between the mortal body and immortal soul in *Phaedo* and stressing the necessity of freeing oneself from the corrupting influence of bodily appetites, Plato sowed the seeds for the renunciation of the senses and the body and the exaltation of the intellect that prevailed in the centuries that followed. Although essentially a rationalist, Plato eventually recognized the irrationality of man and concluded that moral evil sprang from the irrational or diseased part of man's soul rather than from polluting forces of the body. This shift in Plato's thinking was ignored

---

[38]Cited in Gardiner, *Greek Athletic Sports and Festivals*, p. 130.

[39]Xenophon *Memorabilia* 3. 12. 5–7.

[40]Plato *Protagoras* 326, quoted in Cubberley, *Readings in the History of Education* (New York Houghton-Mifflin Co., 1920), p. 5.

[41]Clarence A. Forbes, *Greek Physical Education* (New York: The Century Co., 1929), p. 103.

by many of his successors who clung to the earlier Platonic concept of dualism which required that man renounce his corrupt bodily needs and cultivate his intellect so that his soul could return to its divine birthplace.

Aristotle considered the education of the rational soul to be important. Since the health of the mind depended on the health of the body, physical education should be promoted prior to intellectual education. He pointed out that physical activity taught the youths courage and good habits, was a means of controlling their passions, and enabled them to vent their animal spirits in a harmless way. Aristotle stressed the military value of gymnastics, but would not permit conquest and war to become the sole aim of the state. He favored athletics as a way of developing strong, healthy, well-proportioned youths who would be able to do all the things virtuous men must do in peace and war.

Promotion of Physical Education

During the later Athenian period the child was usually educated in the home until he was seven years old. From the age of seven to thirteen, he attended the private *palaestra* and music school; from thirteen to sixteen, lectures on intellectual subjects; from sixteen years and upward, classes in rhetoric and philosophy; and from eighteen to twenty (after 335 B.C.) he studied military training.

The activities and facilities provided by the *palaestra* and gymnasium reflected the changes taking place in society. The *palaestras* that were erected to meet the increasing numbers of new students provided more luxurious accommodations. The gymnasiums, once a place where citizens took exercise in a self-imposed and vigorous program, now became pleasure resorts. Here a man could indulge in some light, aesthetic exercises, observe the training of the professional athletes, use the modern hot baths, or join the discussion meetings of the Sophists.

With the rise of professional athletics, the *gymnastes*, or coach, emerged from among the *paidotribes* or retired champions. The *gymnastes* determined what sport a particular physique would most likely succeed in, developed systems for training pupils in particular sports, and employed some knowledge of anatomy, physiology, and dietetics to keep the athletes in good physical condition. The well-known coaches, who were in great demand by aspirant athletes, taught wherever they found the best market for their skills. Wealthy patrons and rich cities were willing to pay them handsomely.

Eventually some teachers began to concentrate on medical gymnastics. The medical *gymnastai* were not so concerned with training a man in a particular skill as they were with analyzing the physical fitness of the individual and preparing him for the condition required for success in athletics. They were expected to know the effect of diet, rest, and exercise on the development of the body. Many critics were contemptuous of the new teachers, regarding them as ignorant charlatans who were trying to invade the medical domain. Other men believed that the new trainers should be honored as the founders of health practices and exercises for the preservation of life.

At the close of the later Athenian period, about 335 B.C., the Ephebic College came into being. Both Plato and Xenophon had previously recommended compulsory military education, but it was the defeat of the Athenians by Philip of Macedon at Chaeronea that aroused the citizens to act. Previously military service had been voluntary, but from lack of volunteers, mercenary soldiers had been employed in increasing numbers. The Ephebic College instituted two years of compulsory military training for youths of nineteen and twenty years of age. Eventually the length of training was reduced, it was no longer compulsory, and intellectual training was introduced.

Although athletic participation was not so popular among the later Athenians as it was in the earlier times, the festivals did not decline in number or importance. Better communications and more leisure promoted a multiplicity of holidays. The embassies arriving at the festivals tried to outdo one another in a display of the wealth, power, and culture of their cities. No longer devoted exclusively to religious and athletic events, the ceremonies furnished opportunities for politicians to announce treaties, truces, and pleas of unity. The mass of spectators also provided an audience for artists, writers, poets, and inventors. The holiday crowds were good customers for merchants, peddlers, acrobats, and quacks. The competitors in the games were no longer gentlemen-athletes who were also able citizen-soldiers, but rather paid athletes who enjoyed a short, glorified, lucrative career. The early Athenians had taken great pride in representing their own city-states, but professional athletes sold their services to any community that wanted to acquire fame by having Olympic victors. The games lost much of their religious significance and became ostentatious commercial displays. Costly prizes replaced the simple symbolic wreaths as awards, and corruption was not unknown. Victories were sometimes purchased, and some athletes were fined for accepting bribes.

Many philosophers, fearing the current trends in education would lead to disastrous results, attempted to blueprint new plans for training youth. Xenophon, one of the severest critics, so admired the Spartan educational policies that he enrolled his own sons in their schools and recommended the adoption of a similar system for Athens. His proposed four-level educational program (boys, *ephebi*, mature men, and elders) was to be a state-supported, state-controlled, compulsory education limited to the upper classes. The youths were to receive a disciplined, military education from the most competent men in the community.

Plato believed that the happiness of the individual and the state was so dependent upon education that the task could not be left to the parent. Furthermore, he made the revolutionary suggestion of extending educational opportunities to girls. In his ideal society, the child was to be cared for by the family and a nurse until he was three years of age. From three until six the youngster was to play in a nursery supervised by a responsible woman playground director. From six to sixteen, he was required to attend a state school. The first five years here were to be spent in military and gymnastic training and in mastering javelin throwing, archery, and riding. The next five years were to be devoted to a study of letters and instrumental music. From sixteen to twenty, a youth would have two or three years of gymnastic and military training. The strictly military gymnastic program Plato advocated was similar to the Ephebic College curriculum later adopted. The officials in charge of education, the most capable men available, were to be appointed by the state. At the conclusion of their military training, boys were to be placed in the classes of society in which they could best serve the state. Those who had exhibited neither courage nor intellectual capacity were to become the industrial workers; those who had not excelled in literary studies but exhibited bravery, strength, and endurance in military maneuvers were to be drafted into the army; the few remaining youths of exceptional intellectual ability were to pursue a rigorous advanced education and were to become the ruling class. Plato had little faith in the human goodness of ordinary men and the capacity of the masses to rule themselves.

Aristotle recommended eugenic mating, the destruction of deformed infants, and population control through abortion. He insisted that the education of boys "be one and the same for all," but did not favor the education of women. In his opinion a boy should be trained at home during infancy. From five until seven, a lad was to visit the schools and become acquainted with their activities. From seven to fourteen the schools were to be concerned primarily with developing moral character through instruction in light gymnastic exercises and later a little literary instruction. Aristotle believed the body should be trained before the mind. At fourteen the pupil was to concentrate on intellectual education for three years. The youth's life from about seventeen to twenty years was to be devoted to severe exercises and a strict diet. A few students were to pursue a higher intellectual education beyond the age of twenty-one; and all men were expected to continue exercising throughout their lives.

Program of Physical Education

In the later period the gymnastics and athletic activities pursued in the *palaestra* of early Athens were still offered, but waning interest did little to encourage a dynamic functioning of the program. "Professionalism was now at its height, and men took more pleasure in sitting at their ease, watching the performances of the athletes, than in themselves toiling at the exercises."[42] Also, the baths now had become popular recreational centers. The more conservative Athenians considered attending the baths an effeminate practice and observed with scorn that young men were more interested in gossiping, gambling, feasting, and watching the ballet and flute girls than in the javelin and discus. Aristophanes declared, "This, this is what they say: This is the stuff our precious youths are chattering all day! This is what makes them haunt the baths, and shun the manlier Games!"[43] The admonition of the elders, however, failed to lessen the popularity of the baths.

A short spurt of military enthusiasm stimulated physical education for a few years after the Persian Wars. The armored race, with runners attired in their helmets and shields, provided a colorful and popular athletic event in fifth-century Athens. Javelin, archery, and equestrian activities also attracted greater attention. Boys who could afford to pay the fees took riding lessons. Colorful parades and military maneuvers of horsemen were frequently held at the gymnasiums and at the festivals. Although the type of participants in the festivals had changed considerably, the list of events was only slightly altered. Many of the old sports, like boxing and wrestling, became largely exhibitions of brute strength. The wealthy aristocrats were no longer interested in participating in most athletic events, but the expensive sports that required maintaining horses and chariots were popular with them.

Dancing remained important in Greek life. The greatest Athenian thinkers and statesmen participated in the dance. Sophocles danced after the victory at Salamis, Aeschylus and Aristophanes performed in their own plays, and even Socrates danced at a banquet. Physicians recommended such exercise for many ills. There were changes taking place in the dance, however, that did not meet with the approval of everyone. At the height of Greek culture, the dance had definite artistic standards of balance, harmony, and order; every gesture had to be perfectly synchronized with the spoken word to heighten effect and meaning. By the end of the fifth century the performers were beginning to cater to the taste of the onlookers, and the dance directors were criticized for presenting profane and vulgar performances.

The Ephebic College provided a program of military physical activities which probably included cross-country runs; patrols; practice in heavy arms, bow, and javelin; mock battles; and equestrian events. The first year was spent in garrison and police duty about Athens. At its conclusion, youths presented drills during the Dionysian festival, took the Ephebic Oath

---

[42]Forbes, *Greek Physical Education*, p. 91.
[43]Rogers, *The Clouds of Aristophanes*, 1052–1054, p. 135.

of Citizenship in an impressive ceremony, and were then presented with spears and shields as a gift of the state. During the second year of training, the young men saw service in different parts of the country and patrolled the borders of the city-state.

The content of Xenophon's ideal school reflects the military character of the Spartan model he admired. In the elementary class of boys, little stress was to be put on physical education, except for some practice with the bow and javelin. In the *ephebic* age group, youths were to divide their time between guard duty, bow and javelin practice, military exercises, and hunting. Xenophon advocated hunting as excellent training for war because it taught courage, endurance, alertness, and adaptability.

Plato did not favor health gymnastics and the professional athletic training, but preferred a modified Spartan system of military training. He proposed a plan in which children would play childhood games until they were six, when they would begin a more systematic study of dancing, riding, archery, and javelin throwing. The strict military-gymnastics training of older youths would include running in heavy armor, hand-to-hand conflicts, hurling of weapons, military pancratium, archery, horsemanship, military evolutions, and military encampment.[44] Plato recommended that every citizen should practice war games at least once a month, and that women as well as men should be trained in military sports and gymnastics.

Aristotle recommended that a child should have a diet that would make him strong and healthy and should get plenty of exercise through play and amusements. But Aristotle was critical of the brutalizing effect that Spartan gymnastics had upon the character of youth and warned against excessively rigorous early training. He advised that "until puberty we should apply lighter exercises, forbidding hard diet and severe exertions, in order that nothing may hinder the growth."[45]

Methods of Physical Education

In the *palaestra* the methods of teaching remained almost the same as in the earlier period, but discipline was less severe. Many individuals complained that both parents and teachers were catering to the whims of children rather than firmly shaping their characters. They affirmed ". . . the master fears and flatters his scholars, and the scholars despise their masters and tutors. . . ."[46] Philosophers warned that such lax methods were producing spoiled, insolent children who not only showed disrespect

[44]Plato *Laws* 830–836.
[45]Aristotle *Politics* 8. 4. 1, trans. H. Rackham, The Loeb Classical Library (Cambridge: Harvard University Press, 1944).
[46]Plato *Republic* 563, from *The Dialogues of Plato* by B. Jowett (London: Oxford University Press, 1924), vol. 3.

for parents and teachers but for the law as well. They lamented the in-effectiveness of motivating youths to aspire toward physical fitness by encouraging them to emulate the gods and great athletic heroes.

The rise of professionalism betrayed the ancient principle of modera-tion and all-around physical development. Athletes who aspired to com-pete in the Olympics trained constantly all year round. The medical *gym-nastai* gave increased impetus to the use of baths and massage in athletic training. The specialized techniques for training youths in different sports and the dietary and exercise regime that some *gymnastai* developed were based more on quackery than on science. Other men endeavored to gain a better understanding of the effect of exercise and diet on health. Hip-pocrates, the father of medicine, devoted considerable attention to diet and attempted to make scientific inquiry into the proper place, time, dosage, and type of activity in which one should indulge.

The new training for professional athletes developed neither intel-lect, health, activity, nor beauty of form. The athletes produced some spectacular records, but their careers were short-lived. The program con-sumed the athlete's entire energy; he had no time to devote to other ac-tivities. Hippocrates criticized the intensive and extensive period of train-ing. Socrates observed that runners over-develop their legs, and boxers, the upper part of their bodies. Euripides in his play, *Autolycus*, scorned the professionals who were "slaves of their jaw and worshippers of their belly." Plato commented that, "The athlete's nature is sleepy, and the least varation from his routine is liable to cause him serious illness."[47] Aristotle pointed out that, "boy victors rarely repeat their success as men." The new specialized methods produced a one-sided development of the human body, disregarding the old Greek ideals of the perfectly propor-tioned physique.

[47]Plato *Republic* 3. 404A.

5

Physical Education
in Education for
Roman Utilitarianism

By the time the crumbling Greek civilization had relinquished its political power to the Macedonians and subsequently to the Romans, the creative genius and spirited patriotism of the Hellenes had been destroyed. The Roman conquerors were a practical, industrious people who possessed a natural executive ability, but lacked the sparkling, aesthetic genius and capacity for intellectual contemplation of the Greeks. The Romans did not develop new philosophical thought or evolve new scientific concepts. Nonetheless, the Western world is indebted to them for many practical contributions to mankind, and for grasping the dying torch of enlightenment from the Greeks and carrying its light into the darkened corners of the universe.

The Latins adapted the culture of the countries they conquered, and applied the theoretical knowledge thus acquired. Applying the scientific principles developed by others, they constructed great bridges, roads, aqueducts, and buildings. As a result of their administrative skill, they laid the foundations for secure institutions; they developed an efficient pattern of governing a huge empire; they promulgated a code of laws that became the model for succeeding civilizations; they formulated the curriculum of an educational system that was to be followed by generations of school children; and they laid the foundation of the Church that later effected Christian moral ideals.

THE EARLY ROMANS

The Italian peninsula was the home of many tribal communities in ancient times. The smallest of these, Latium, was located near the Tiber River and the seven hills of Rome. This tiny political unit developed the energizing force to extend its rule over the neighboring tribes, the organizing ability to unite the Italian peninsula, and the dynamic power to rule the entire Mediterranean world. An initial step in this expansion occurred when the Romans overthrew their northern Etruscan neighbors in 509 B.C. By 275 B.C. Rome had defeated all the important cities of Italy and had given the peninsula a unity the Greek city-states never knew. Sicily, Corsica, Sardinia, and Spain were conquered during the Punic Wars and the Hellenic East fell to Rome in 146 B.C.

When the early Latins revolted against the Etruscans, they founded the Roman Republic which, in reality, was an aristocratic oligarchy. There was no king and the administration of public affairs remained in the control of the noblemen senators and the two consuls elected from their number. A gradual democratization of the Republic took place as the common people demanded and received greater rights and privileges in return for the military service they had rendered in the wars. These plebeians were granted tracks of land, secured representation in the government, and benefited from the new code of laws, the Twelve Tables. By the fourth and third centuries B.C. the common people were enjoying the highest degree of their political and economic freedom. During this era of Roman development, most men enjoyed the independent possession of their own small farms, were cognizant of their individual prerogatives, and were seriously concerned about their governmental responsibilities.

Aims of Education

Early Roman education was geared to train youths to be citizen-soldiers who would effectively serve the state, industriously conduct their individual business and farms, and conscientiously revere their gods and their parents. To attain these objectives, the Romans sought to instill in youths readiness for war, obedience to commands, modesty in behavior, reverence to the gods, respect for the law, and correctness of speech.

The religion of the Romans, which greatly influenced the education of youths, was a businesslike, contractual relationship between men and their gods. The Romans performed the prescribed rituals and gave generously to the gods to gain their support. "Their religion, both family and state, lacked the beauty and stately ceremonial of the Greeks, lacked that lofty faith and aspiration after virtue that characterized the Hebrew and the later Christian faith, was singularly wanting in awe and mystery, and was formal and mechanical and practical in character, but it exercised great influence on these early peoples and on their conceptions of their duty to the State."[1]

[1]Ellwood P. Cubberley, *The History of Education* (Boston: Houghton-Mifflin Co., 1920), p. 58.

Early Roman education stressed moral and military training more than intellectual attainment. While Greeks encouraged the harmonious unfolding of the total personality, the Romans demanded a more definite and practical goal. "More characteristic of his [the Roman's] genius was the striving for . . . some form of excellence or achievement of concrete, even of material, value. . . ."[2] Early Roman education was narrow in scope, but the rigorous training program produced the moral fiber, physical vigor, and military prowess necessary to carve out a great empire.

Aims of Physical Education

For a nation that believed it was divinely elected to rule the world, physical education had one purpose: to make youths serviceable for war. Virgil depicts what was expected:

> "Our infants soon as born to the rivers we first convey, and in the frigid icy stream we harden. In the chase our boys are keen, and harass the woods: their pastime is to manage steeds, and dart the arrow from the bow. Our youth again of labour patient, and to frugality inured, either by the harrow subdue the ground, or batter towns in war."[3]

The Roman curriculum was designed to develop strength of body, courage in battle, agility in arms, and obedience to commands. In contrast with Greek physical education, "the Roman games and exercises were intended only to make men strong and skillful warriors; and it was not for beauty of form or grace of movement, but only for vigour and prowess in battle, that they were honoured by their fellow-citizens."[4] To the Latins, the Greek preoccupation with beautiful proportions, graceful performance, and joyous participation was unbusinesslike dallying in intangibles.

Promotion of Physical Education

The home, Forum, and army were the educational institutions of the early Romans. The state neither directed nor supported education. The Spartan child was educated in military barracks, and the Athenian youngster grew up in the *palaestra* and gymnasium; but the Roman youngster was trained in a well-organized home by his parents. The father determined whether the newborn child should survive, and he continued to

[2]Paul Monroe, *A Textbook in the History of Education* (New York: The Macmillan Co., 1916), p. 176.

[3]*Aeneid*, trans. Davidson, rev. T. A. Buckley, in *Works of Virgil, Aeneid* 9: 603–608 (London: Bell and Daldy, 1866).

[4]A. S. Wilkins, *Roman Antiquities* (New York: D. Appleton and Co., 1878), p. 58.

exert his influence even after the youth was married. The Roman mother, a highly respected and socially active woman, assisted her husband in raising their children. The education of a child was seldom entrusted to slaves. As youths, the lads accompanied their fathers on all of the daily routines: religious exercises, visits to the Forum, business negotiations, and exercises at the *Campus Martius*. In this manner, boys became thoroughly acquainted with the duties they would have to assume in adult life.

Until Greek models were adopted, the Romans probably had no schools, and when primary schools were established by a few private teachers about 300 B.C., they only offered subject matter instruction. The *Campus Martius* and military camps were the physical education schools of the Romans. The *Campus Martius* was a large open area outside the Servian wall adjacent to the Tiber River. Even during the Republic the only building on the field was a temple dedicated to the war god, Mars. In this simple setting every well-bred Roman boy practiced military exercises and games under his soldier-father's guidance.

War was a Roman citizen's chief occupation, and a young man was usually conscripted into the military shortly after donning the *toga virilis*. This ceremony of exchanging his *toga praetexta* for the garment of manhood, which took place between the youth's fourteenth and seventeenth year, symbolized the acceptance of the responsibilities of citizenship. During early times, men between seventeen and forty-seven years were drafted when needed for active service. Older men were employed primarily in guard duty.

From the most ancient times, festivals and games, probably of Etruscan origin, were an integral part of Roman life. At first the games were connected with simple agricultural holidays, but later they assumed an important function in religious rites. Eventually the state established official games, voted sums for their support, and appointed magistrates to conduct them. In addition to these regular events, there were festivals to celebrate triumphs, funerals, and days of thanksgiving. All business was suspended for the celebrations which were free to the public. The early priestly games were performed at the altars, but the state holidays were celebrated at the race courses, for in later years, the festivals lost their original simplicity and religious significance. Except in the earlier era, Roman citizens did not participate in their games. They preferred to observe the performance of slaves and professionals. Thus, unlike the Greek athletic contests, the games did not become functional agencies of physical education for the populace.

Program of Physical Education

Roman youngsters played with hoops, carts, tops, ivory letter blocks, dolls, hobby horses, stilts, toy houses, and pet dogs, birds, and cats. They enjoyed games of blindman's buff, hide and seek, ducks and drakes, odd and even, and many activities using nuts and pebbles. Both children and adults played dice games. Some games used pellets on a board; one of these, *ludus latrunculorum,* resembled chess. Another favorite game was *micare digitis,* which was played to determine the number of fingers an opponent had concealed.

Older boys did not participate in competitive games or gymnastics, but they had plenty of healthy physical exercise while plowing the fields and performing other farm labor. In addition, the Roman fathers trained their sons on the *Campus Martius* in those exercises that would prepare them for military life. Plutarch revealed that Cato taught his son "not only how to throw a dart, to fight hand to hand, and to ride, but to box, to endure heat and cold, and to swim the most rapid rivers."[5]

Ball games were popular with the Romans throughout their history. Different types and sizes of balls were used, some being filled with hair, others with feathers or air. Throwing or catching formed the basis of most games. Classical literature does not record the use of the bat or racquet. Juggling, handball, *trigon, sphaeromachiae,* and *harpastum* were popular. In handball, the players open-handedly hit a ball against a wall, permitted it to bounce on the ground, and then repeated the process as many times as possible. Descriptions of *trigon* are confusing, but apparently three men stood at the corners of a triangle and played with two or more balls. Frequently, they had to catch and toss simultaneously, as the balls were thrown at the caprice of the server. In *sphaeromachiae,* the ground was marked off somewhat as in lawn tennis, and the players formed two teams. *Harpastum* (originally *phaininda*) played with a small hair-filled ball, ". . . was a game in which two or more players threw the ball to one another in such a way as to avoid a player between them."[6] In this vigorous game, which included scrimmaging, the players tackled and used wrestling holds.

The early Roman holidays were devoted almost entirely to horse and chariot races or gladiatorial contests. Athletics, which made up so much of the Greek festivals, were not popular. The brutal gladiatorial combats, which came from Etruria and first appeared at funeral games about 264 B.C., held great appeal for the warlike Romans. In addition, Roman festivals that once were devoted to races and dramatics later became almost entirely theatrical presentations.

Dancing was practiced to a limited degree in ancient times by youths of the most noble Roman families. Ritual dances were performed to supplement the sacrificial ceremonies and dances of a warlike character

---

[5]Plutarch, "Cato the Censor," *Lives,* trans. John and William Langhorne (London: A. J. Valph, M.A., 1832), 3:67.

[6]Norma D. Young, "Did the Greeks and the Romans Play Football?" *Research Quarterly* 15 (December 1944): 312.

but the symbolism and beauty of the dance as a creative expression did not particularly interest the Romans.

War was the prestige profession of the Romans, and the army training program was rigorous. The trainee was drilled in running, jumping, swimming, javelin throwing, and fencing with stationary posts. Cavalry and light troops practiced archery and riding. Field reviews and maneuvers were held frequently. Twenty-mile marches were made about three times a month, being covered at four miles per hour on a forced march. The soldier had to carry his armor, weapons, food, cooking utensils, and several long stakes with him whenever the army was on the move. The total pack probably weighed thirty to eighty-five pounds.

Methods of Physical Education

Tales of the glories of war and the deeds of heroes, and the knowledge that distinction on the battlefield provided a key to fame and personal wealth made youths eager to acquire military skills. They learned by precept and example from their parents and by participating in a strenuous physical training program that was maintained constantly, even during lulls in military maneuvers. Discipline was rigorous: corporal punishment, even death, could be inflicted by fathers or military superiors. However obedience, which was of paramount importance to the warlike nation, was probably instilled in youth more by the example and constant supervision of their parents and public praise of heroic acts than by severe punishment.

In the early Roman methods "is seen the characteristic of the practical education—the doing of the actual thing to be done—with no appreciation whatever of the training and instruction in certain selected activities that possess cultural value because they plant in the very nature of the child germs of a much fuller development in manhood, activities such as characterized the liberal education of the Greeks."[7] The methods of the Romans successfully produced the rugged warriors they wanted.

THE LATER ROMANS

In becoming ruler of the ancient world, Rome acquired a far-flung empire, enormous wealth, and prestige. The stimulating contacts with the Greek and Oriental civilizations expanded Rome's intellectual horizon. The looted libraries, art treasures, erudite slaves, profound philosophers, and medical men acquainted Rome with Greek philosophy, architecture, science, literature, and religion. The conquerors assimilated those aspects

[7]Monroe, *A Textbook in the History of Education*, pp. 190–91.

of Greek culture they considered useful. During the early days of the Empire, Rome had a brief spurt of creative activity, but during the last three centuries, its intellectual efforts were confined mostly to organizing textbooks from the knowledge of the past.

After the Hellenistic wars, several sinister forces converged that weakened and eventually destroyed the Empire. The economic and political rights of the hardy peasant-soldiers who had been the backbone of the Republic were diminished after the fall of Corinth in 146 B.C. The long ravages of war, the floods of grain from abroad, and the burden of debts and mortgages forced many small farmers off the land. The large landowners seized this opportunity to increase the size of their estate and acquire slaves for labor. As the senatorial upper class grew richer and more powerful, the other citizens grew poorer and their political position was slowly undermined. Despite the democratic constitution, the government was controlled by an oligarchy of senators.

Military leaders who won the support of the populace soon threatened the oligarchy of the senate. A series of power struggles between military leaders finally led to the establishment of the Empire in 27 B.C. Under the first emperor, Augustus Caeser, the Romans enjoyed a period of peace and prosperity. This was also an era of considerable cultural activity. Although the power and grandeur of Rome was now at its peak, the seeds of decay were already planted in a treacherous economic pyramid and in a parasitical imperialism. In the later days of the Empire, the rotting seams of the once sound state structure gave way. Emperors were chosen by the army, and in a ninety-year period, Rome had more than eighty emperors. As time passed, the incursions of the barbarians intensified, until Odoacer, a Teutonic leader, deposed the last Roman emperor in the west in 476.

Foreign wars brought riches to Rome, but they also drained her manpower and her treasury, and created internal tension and social disintegration. Both the decadence of the rich and the economic and political deprivation of the small landowners destroyed the moral fabric of a mighty civilization. In the upper classes, the old sense of self-sacrificing patriotism was destroyed by self-seeking individualism; officialdom was corrupt; governors and tax-gatherers plundered the provinces; the judiciary was susceptible to bribery; the army used its power politically; later emperors became absolute despots; and civil freedom and self-government disappeared.

The rich lived in sumptuous town houses and country villas, the masses were crammed into overcrowded tenements. Middle-class citizens, stripped of their lands and democratic rights, displaced by slave labor, and burdened with oppressive taxes, lost their sense of personal dignity. Some sank into serfdom, others abandoned their fields and lived on the public dole in the city, passing their time amid the frenzied excitement of free games. The slave population rapidly increased as the whole economy of Rome came to depend on their labor. Some slaves revolted against the inhuman treatment, but many gained their freedom by manumission, by purchase, or by service in the army, and some freedmen acquired considerable wealth. Family ties among all classes were weakened, morals were lax, divorce increased, birth rates declined, and crime was rampant. Belief in the Roman gods deteriorated because of the influence of the Greek philosophers, foreign cults, and poverty which made men doubt the power of the gods.

Aims of Education

Because the army was professional and the new means of acquiring personal wealth and prestige did not depend on physical labor, the Romans' interest in physical and moral education diminished. Although accepting the Greek ideal of cultivating the intellect, they rejected the objective of promoting harmonious physical development and aesthetic expression, "Thus Roman educational attitudes and school practices, in which mental training alone was stressed, checked the continuance of the Greek tradition of physical education in Europe, the Christian thought almost completely destroyed the tradition for centuries."[8]

The later Romans were interested in training their offspring to become orators rather than athletes. Oratory served a practical purpose in Roman life: The politician seeking votes, the statesman explaining public policy, the lawyer pleading court cases, and the soldier inciting troops to action all required verbal facility. The aims of the orator's education were not confined to mere skill in speech. Cicero insisted that if the orator were to be wise and use good judgment, he must have an encyclopedic, liberal education and a strong moral character. "We are to form, then, the perfect orator, who cannot exist unless as a good man; and we require in him, therefore, not only consummate ability in speaking, but every excellence of mind."[9] The orator was to the Roman what the philosopher was to the Greek, but the Roman considered the orator superior because he possessed not only knowledge but also the ability to put knowledge into action through his power of speech.

As self-government declined during the Empire and the orator could no longer operate in the political arena, liberal education came to be an end in itself. Scholars became involved in tiresome pendantry. Education was increasingly divorced from life and lacked in real social value.

---

[8]James Mulhern, *A History of Education* (New York: The Ronald Press, 1946), p. 176.

[9]Quintilian, *Ad Marcellum Victorium* 1. Preface. 9, quoted in *Institutes of Oratory*, trans. John Watson (London: George Bell and Sons, 1892), p. 4.

Aims of Physical Education

In the later Roman period, men recognized the importance of physical education for the military man and the professional athlete, but the military, aesthetic, moral, and religious motives of physical education held little appeal for most citizens. They engaged in the minimum amount of exercise essential for health and recreation. They exercised either "just for the fun of it" or to prevent systematic weaknesses, to recover from illness, or to avoid the unpleasantness of overindulgence. "It is only natural that, both in Greece and in Rome, when there was no longer need of physical excellence for state service, play became more of an end in itself. Health gymnastics were encouraged both in Greece and in Rome when individual happiness and welfare began to transcend the importance of service to the commonweal."[10] The maintenance of health was a practical aim to the Romans and they employed many Greek physicians.

Although the Romans did not share the attitudes of the Greeks toward gymnastics, they valued some physical education for the schoolboy. Quintilian, a Roman philosopher, argued, "Yet some relaxation is to be allowed to all . . . there is nothing that can bear perpetual labor. . . . Boys, accordingly, when reinvigorated and refreshed, bring more sprightliness to their learning. . . . Nor will play in boys displease me; it is a sign of vivacity. . . ."[11] In other discussion, Quintilian recognized the value of exercising and dancing for youths to achieve natural and graceful gestures as public speakers. Cicero, although critical of Greek gymnastics, approved of a limited pursuit of manly sports, for all men needed some activity.

The festivals revealed the basic difference between the Roman and Greek physical education aims. To the Hellenes, the games were great events in which every man aspired to compete; they were contests between citizens to demonstrate their physical fitness. The Roman regarded the games as spectator entertainments. "To devote to sport the time and energy necessary to secure success at Olympia, to submit for months to the tyranny of a trainer, often a man of no birth or position, and above all to exhibit oneself naked before the eyes of one's fellow-citizens—these were things quite inconsistent with the Roman's idea of his dignity as a citizen."[12]

The Romans promoted games and festivals for political purposes rather than athletic ideals. To win support, politicians vied with one another in producing spectacular games for thrill-hungry mobs. In later times, noblemen maintained schools of gladiators (who could also protect

[10]Thomas Woody, *Life and Education in Early Societies* (New York: The Macmillan Co., 1949), p. 660.
[11]Quintilian, 1. 3, pp. 26–27.
[12]E. N. Gardiner, *Greek Athletic Sports and Festivals* (London: The Macmillan Co., 1910), pp. 163–64.

them from criminals or act as private armies). During the Republic, new games were celebrated to keep up the spirits of a war-weary people. Under the Empire, exhibitions were used as a sounding board of public opinion and to lull a poverty-stricken, overtaxed populace into complacency. The purpose of these games was far removed from the early Roman objectives of inspiring and unifying citizens for state action, and the high objectives of the Greeks in their great athletic festivals.

Despite the decline of interest in physical exercise, some of the first scientific treatises on the subject were written in this later era. Galen, the great philosopher and physician, devoted considerable attention to the influnce of exercise and diet upon health. Although he was a Greek, born in Pergamum in 130 A.D., he lived in the Roman Empire and spent some years in the capital city where he served as physician to the athletes and later to Marcus Aurelius. Galen was critical of the excessive and brutish training program for professional athletes and gladiators. He believed that physical education should enable men to enjoy the glowing health of harmoniously proportioned bodies and should make them alert and physically fit for civil and martial duties. "That form of exercise is best which not only exercises the body but also is a source of joy to the participant. . . . Therefore that form of exercise is recommended which contributes to the health of the body and to the harmonious functioning of the parts and to the strength of the soul. . . ."[13]

Promotion of Physical Education

The Romans were at first critical of Greek education, but they gradually accepted the new literary education and molded it into an organized ladder system that included the school of the *litterator* on the primary level, the school of the *grammaticus* on the secondary level, and the school of the *rhetor* on the higher level. To complete their studies, some boys attended foreign schools or the University of Rome. Women had more education and status in Rome than in Athens, but their training was primarily domestic, except in some wealthy families where scholars were hired to tutor the girls.

The literary schools were academic in nature and did not offer physical education, but several professional and recreational institutions, such as the circuses, festivals, gladiatorial exhibitions, and baths, existed apart from the schools. The army remained an educational institution, but because of the decline of small farmers, soldiers were now recruited from all classes rather than solely from the propertied class. Many citizens escaped from service, and the ranks were filled with poor men and foreigners who followed the most generous leaders.

[13]Galen, "Exercises with the Small Ball," quoted in Young, "Did the Greeks and Romans Play Football?" pp. 313–14.

The free Roman games increased in frequency, variety, length, and magnificence during the later Republic and the Empire. In addition, many new games reflecting a Hellenic influence were added to the old festivals (*ludi*) of the circus and theater. By the close of the Republic there were 76 days devoted to *ludi*; in the era of Marcus Aurelius, 135 were celebrated; and at about 354 A.D., the "Philocalian Calendar"[14] marked 175 such holidays. At one time, 17 of the 29 days in April were spent at the circus, amphitheater, or theater.

The state kept voting greater and greater sums for games. To capture public favor, ambitious politicians supplemented government appropriations with funds from their own pockets and privately sponsored additional games. Although incurring huge debts in this manner, they hoped to recoup their losses by securing profitable provincial appointments as a result of their public popularity. The extravagent expenditures for games were ruinous both for individuals and the public treasury. Although many leaders recognized the evils of this policy they were unwilling to jeopardize their political futures by discontinuing the practice.

With the increased interest in such lavish entertainments, new facilities were provided for the comfort of the pampered patrons. Besides the well-known *Circus Maximus* and *Circus Flaminius*, an additional race track was built in Rome as well as three others outside the city. Usually these structures consisted of tiers of seats built around three sides of a long level track. At first they were built of wood, but later of stone. The immense *Circus Maximus* was about 2000 feet long and 600 feet wide and, according to Pliny, could accommodate 260,000 spectators. The charioteers raced around a fence or *spina* in the center of the arena. Some of the structures were magnificent sights with the sun gleaming upon the white marble highlighting the golden decorations, reflecting from the colored, glass-studded mosaics, and spotlighting the richly carved thrones of the officials.

The circus races were financed by the state or by private individuals, but racing syndicates provided the entertainment. They stabled horses from every part of the Empire and employed a huge staff of trainers, coaches, doctors, and attendants. Each syndicate was identified by the colors its drivers wore and the partisan fans cheered their favorites. In the early days of the Republic, anyone could race, but in later times, respectable citizens did not participate. Nero, however, built a circus and invited a select audience to applaud his imperial skill as a charioteer. The race drivers were usually slaves, although a few won their freedom through exhibitions of skill. The more successful charioteers were the pets of society and received extravagant gifts from wealthy gambling fans.

In early days, gladiatorial combats were held at graves, forums, or

---

[14]This calendar was a table of secular and pagan celebrations contained in a book of chronological information compiled by Furius Dionysius Philocalus in 354 A.D.

circuses, but by about 50 B.C. men began to build wooden and later, stone amphitheaters. The well-known Colosseum, which covered 6 acres, and had walls that were 160 feet high, could accommodate 90,000 spectators. The subterranean area contained chambers for gladiators, dens for animals, and labyrinths of pipes to flood and drain the area for water battles. In the Flavian amphitheater (Colosseum), the marble seats were covered with cushions, awnings protected the citizens from the sun and rain, and the air was refreshed by perfumed fountains; and sixty-four exits minimized congestion as the crowd left at the conclusion of the combats.

The gladiators were mostly slaves, criminals, or captives, but some were freeman who worked for food and wages. They all received their professional education in private institutions, some of which were partially state-supported during the Empire. At least four gladiatorial schools were located in Rome, and some were maintained in other cities. The emperor Caligula had 20,000 gladiators in his school. The dormitories were constructed around a square exercise field where the gladiators received their training under the master and special teachers.

Both Roman and Greek festivals were influenced by the contact of the two cultures. The Greek Olympics declined after the fall of Corinth and became almost entirely local affairs. Sulla violated the sanctity of the Olympics in 80 B.C. by transferring the entire festival to Rome, but this act proved unsuccessful and the games were returned to Greece. Many later Roman emperors revived Greek athletics, partly to maintain the loyalty and unity of the conquered peoples and partly to take advantage of the strategic importance of Olympia as a meeting place of East and West. Augustus, who was genuinely interested in athletics, supported Greek contests, restored the dignity and magnificence of the religious sanctuaries of the Greek festival, and established new Roman games on the Hellenic model. Nero perverted the festivals to flatter his ego. He himself took part in music contests and chariot races, and after being proclaimed victor by obsequious officials, returned to Italy to enjoy a lavish triumph. Nero also constructed a gymnasium for the citizens and instituted the Neronian games which were partly athletic. Although Hadrian instituted a more genuine athletic renaissance and restored the Greek buildings, he could not revive the ideals of the early Greek contests: The evils of professionalism were, by then, too deeply rooted.

At the *thermae*, or baths, which usually incorporated facilities similar to those of the *palaestra* and gymnasium, the Romans were participants rather than spectators. In the early times a rather primitive bath was located near the kitchen, but during the later Republic and the Empire men began to construct public baths in the Greek manner. The first of these buildings, called *balneae*, included two or three rooms that offered ordinary bathing facilities, but later they became elaborate and costly recreational centers, called *thermae*. These were majestic structures with pillars and walls of granite, porphyry, and marble, floors of mosaic and tile, and intricately-designed ceilings supported by lofty arches. In fact, in the sixteenth century, Michelangelo designed a magnificent nave of a church by reconstructing two rooms of a Roman bath.

The larger *thermae* included a small *palaestra*, an adjacent pool open to the sky, and a *sphaeristerium* (a room for playing with balls). The patrons undressed in the spacious *apodyterium*, assisted by slaves. The *unctorium*, or oiling room, was furnished with benches and couches. In the *tepidarium*, one of the most ornamented chambers, warm air or vapor conditioned the bodies of the men for the more intense heat that was to follow in the *caldarium* which provided a hot tub or vapor bath. In the *frigidarium* the patron could take a cold plunge in the pool or have cool water poured over him. Many establishments also contained a *laconicum*, a heat bath, which some authorities believe was used by invalids. This series of rooms was heated by furnaces that circulated hot air beneath the floors and in the spaces between the walls. Some of the larger thermae became immense cultural centers that included libraries, lounges, art galleries, and dining rooms.

The baths were privately-owned, erected by wealthy men as gifts to the city, or constructed from public funds. They were managed by people who leased them and charged fees. In the public baths, the fee was nominal. If no separate *thermae* facilities were available for women, the management usually reserved definite hours for them to frequent the building.

The size and number of baths indicate the popularity of this recreational activity. The elaborate thermae of Diocletian accommodated about 1600 bathers at once and those of Caracalla, 3200. The size of the latter is claimed to have been 220 meters long and 114 meters wide. The popularity of these institutions was not limited to the capital, for most Roman villages possessed at least a simple building. Private homes and country villas had their own baths and some of them had an exercise room.

Program of Physical Education

The Romans could see some value in the Greek system of military training for the *ephebi*, but they scorned the unsoldier-like exercises of the *palaestra*, gymnasia, and athletic festivals. For a time, some Romans retained the old ideal of rigorous military exercises and engaged in boxing, horsemanship, wrestling, and the more vigorous sports. Gradually, however, the gymnasia and warm baths became popular resorts. Roman youths abandoned the *Campus Martius* and lingered for long hours in the hot baths and massage room of the *thermae*, played ball games, participated at the gambling tables, were entertained by dancers at sumptuous banquets, and became devotees of the circuses and the gladiatorial combats.[15]

15John E. Sandys, *A Companion to Latin Studies* (Cambridge: University Press, 1910), p. 230.

In the early times it was scandalous for men of rank to participate in chariot races, gladitorial combats, or Greek athletics, but as time went by some men of prominence, including Nero and Caligula, and even some women participated.

The more sumptuous spectacles in Rome attracted people from all parts of the Empire. One event given by Julius Caesar included dramatic and musical performances, gladiatorial combats, chariot races, athletic displays, and sea fights. Five days were devoted to the wild beast combats. An impressive sham battle provided a miniature war of soldiers, cavalry, and elephants. Three days of athletic competitions were performed at the field of Mars, and a large artificial lake was the scene of a mock naval battle in which biremes, triremes, and quadriremes participated.

On days of the chariot races, men and women of all classes, even some Christians, were attracted to the Circus hours before the games. People placed bets, while the poor eagerly waited to see if the sponsor of the games would have presents thrown among the audience. Everyone gradually found a seat, the emperor, senators, magistrates, and Vestal Virgins occupying special places. With much ceremony, the sponsor of the game and a procession of men proceeded to an altar to make sacrifice, paid their respects before the imperial box, and then the games commenced.

In vaulted stalls with barred doors, the charioteers awaited the starting signal. There were usually four chariots in each race, and, in the later days, as many as twelve. The chariots were low, light vehicles with small wheels to lessen the risk of overturning. Each driver controlled as many as seven horses although a team of four was the most common. From the start, the charioteers struggled for the lead in the seven-lap race around the *spina*, a distance of about three miles. Speed alone was not the decisive factor in these races, for a driver had to negotiate sharp turns around a sandy track and avoid the other drivers as well. Charioteers employed every device to keep the lead and to upset the carts of their competitors. The intense rivalry often resulted in arguments, riots, and bloodshed.

Besides the chariot races, some games included equestrian events in which noble youths might participate. The *desultores* were riding feats in which men jumped from the back of one galloping horse to another. Trained horses performed tricks on wheeled platforms; there was an exhibition of cavalry evolutions by citizens of good standing; and young aristocrats took part in the *ludus troiae*, the semimilitary maneuvers that Virgil described in the *Aeneid*, Book V.

According to Livy, the first exhibition of Greek athletics in Rome took place in 186 B.C., but the citizens were more excited about the panthers and lions brought from Africa as an added attraction at the circus that year. "Even as spectacles the Greek sports did not appeal to his [the Roman's] taste. Brutalized by incessant war, he preferred more exciting contests, and took more pleasure in the gladiatorial shows of his Etruscan

and Campanian neighbors than in musical or gymnastic competitions."[16]
For the Romans the most boring part of the Greek program was the foot
racing, jumping, and throwing, but he did exhibit some interest in the
wrestling, pancratium, and boxing events. Boxing became a murderous
sport under the Romans. The glove, or *caestus*, was strengthened with
pieces of lead and iron, and two or three spikes, probably of metal, extended over the knuckles, making it a lethal weapon.

Originally, the gladiatorial combats were small privately-sponsored
affairs, but later these barbaric events became official spectacles for the
general public. In an early contest, only three pairs of gladiators fought,
but during the third century A.D. a mass of five hundred pairs of men contested in a huge spectacle. The combatants attired in armor and employing
various weapons, fought customarily man against man, but now and
then more thrilling mass battles were conducted. Usually the fighting continued until death decided the victor, unless the mob gave the "thumbs
up" sign that indicated a popular desire to spare the wounded man's life.
In addition to man-to-man combats, there were exhibitions of men against
beasts and beasts against beasts. Even mock naval battles were instituted,
for which the amphitheater area was flooded. In one event 19,000 men
were forced to participate in a miniature war in which hundreds lost their
lives. Small wonder that the Christians, themselves often thrown to the
lions, developed a fanatical antipathy to the cruelty of the games and carried a general aversion to sport into the Middle Ages.

The early Romans washed daily and swam in the Tiber. After the
second Punic War, they began to take hot vapor baths, although such
bathing had once been considered a sign of physical weakness. The rich
indulged in a series of tepid, hot, and cold baths, and then had their bodies
scraped, anointed, and massaged by slaves. In addition to the baths, some
men engaged in pleasant exercises and light competition to stimulate a
hearty appetite and as a general hygienic practice.

During the Empire, gambling games were favorite activities of the
Romans. At private dinners and gambling resorts the wealthy citizens
won and lost huge sums playing odd or even, heads or tails, and dice
games. Some board games, similar to chess and backgammon, were popular amusements for the upper classes.

Although many Romans frowned upon dancing, some boys and
girls attended dancing schools. The *Pyrrhic* and other military dances
were frequently exhibited. Citizens displayed considerable enthusiasm for
the sensational dancing spectacles of the theater and the sensuous performances of the Spanish, Syrian, and Greek slaves at elaborate dinner
parties. The dance was debased rather than ennobled by the Romans, but
pantomime was developed into a precise art, particularly under Pylades

[16]Gardiner, *Greek Athletic Sports and Festivals*, p. 164.

and Bathyllus, two celebrated rival actors, who presented great ballets, dances, and choruses in the theaters.

The indolent life, the gluttonous feasts, and the prolonged drinking bouts often boded ill-health for both the later Athenians and the later Romans. As a result, men turned to health gymnastics, which usually consisted of light exercises and baths. For pleasure as well as for physical well-being, the Romans indulged in sunbathing, swimming, boating, fishing, hunting, riding, and playing a variety of ball games, including one similar to bowling. Life in the country, agricultural pursuits, and moderation in diet were also recommended as a means of maintaining good health.

Since the days of Hippocrates (460–377 B.C.), the Greeks have speculated on the effect of exercises and diet on the health of the body. Although some criticism of Greek physicians was voiced in Rome, medical men soon began to establish lucrative practices. Philostratos, Aretaeus, Galen, Celsus, and many other writers wrote treatises on health gymnastics. Galen (131 B.C.), suggested specific exercises for various parts of the body and further classified these into three groups: exercises for muscle tone, quick exercises, and violent exercises. In the first group he included digging, driving, carrying heavy weights, rope climbing, and resistance exercises. In the second classification he listed running, sparring, punch ball, ball play, and rolling on the ground with an opponent. The violent exercises consisted of a repetition of the first group and an uninterrupted and rapid drill of the second group with weights or in heavy armor. In another esssay, "Exercises with the Small Ball," Galen recommended ball-playing as best of all because it exercised every part of the body, could either be a light or strenuous activity, could be played by all ages, did not require a lot of time or equipment, and had little risk of accident. Galen is credited with being the first man to use the pulse as a means of detecting physical condition.

Methods of Physical Education

The earlier practice of educating children by permitting them to participate in the daily activities of their parents gradually declined.[17] The mild physical exercise most boys received was at the *thermae*, but little is known of the methods employed in physical education. At the same time, the training of soldiers and professional athletes become more elaborate and prolonged. The soldiers underwent intensive periods of instruction and drill. The professional athlete indulged in a prescribed program of diet, exercise, and training in the use of different types of weapons.

[17]Quintilian, 1. 2, pp. 20–21.

part two

Physical Education
in the
MIDDLE AGES
and
EARLY MODERN TIMES

6

Physical Education
in Education for
Medieval Disciplines

The dawn of the Middle Ages found Roman society demoralized. The once magnificent structure of the great Empire was crumbling. The barbarian conquerors hastened the process of disintegration because they had no skill in administering such extensive territories. Men caught in the swirling chaos of fear and terror that followed submitted to defeat. The weak fled to the sanctuaries of the strong, often surrendering their freedom in return for protection. Europe became dotted with hundreds of isolated castle communities where men lived behind barricaded walls. War became an elite profession while the impoverished masses labored in servitude, attempting to make the tiny feudal villages self-sufficient. Trade, commerce, and education almost disappeared; men had practically retrogressed to a tribal life.

The Church, which had stood intact as the barbarians advanced and Rome fell, was the one remaining cultural institution that offered some leadership and provided a bond of unity in the disordered world. The influence of the Christian Church reached into every corner of society, nurturing souls, seeking moral regeneration, and aspiring to soften the warlike nature of the northern tribes. The Teutons settled down eventually; new waves of invaders no longer washed over Europe; the spirits of men began to revive; and a more hopeful attitude toward life developed. As a result of the Crusades, men came in contact with Eastern and Saracenic learning. Curiosity was awakened. As trade and commerce were revived and towns grew in importance, new social classes emerged and larger political units more capable of maintaining order came into being. Universities were born and many new forms of educational institutions were created in an attempt to meet the needs of the age. But this long, slow awakening process covered centuries.

In this chapter the five great forces that moulded the lives of men in the medieval era will be traced: the early Christian Church, monasticism, feudalism, guilds and towns, and scholasticism. Although each of these institutions is discussed separately, it must not be supposed that they were operating in isolation. No attempt has been made to mark the extent of the medieval period by precise dates. The first section goes back to the era of the Roman Empire in order to make clear the role the Church played after the Fall of Rome. Some activities have been pursued into the years sometimes designated as the Renaissance, although in most instances such exceptions are identified by dates or explanations.

PHYSICAL EDUCATION FOR THE EARLY CHRISTIAN DISCIPLINES

At the birth of Christ the Roman Empire was at the zenith of its power, but internal signs of discord were appearing. The early Roman virtues of patriotism, bravery, and service to the state had become old-fashioned and meaningless concepts. No spiritual or moral power seemed to exist that could give hope, comfort, and purpose to the lower classes or could restrain the rich and riotous life of the aristocrats and to direct their energies toward worthy objectives.

Many factors contributed to the successful growth of Christianity. Unlike some philosophies, Christianity was explained in concrete and definite terms based upon emotional appeals that were understood by every one: love for an ideal divine being, sympathy for fellowmen, and fear of eternal retribution. Christianity infused new hopes in the hearts and minds of human beings who had long been neglected by society. The revolutionary idea that all mortals were equal before God imbued the lower classes with a glowing sense of personal excellence and dignity. All men, lord and slave alike, came to be united under the bond of a common religion that taught the brotherhood of man. Under this influence, the slave slowly progressed to the status of the half-free serf and thence to the higher level of the free peasant, the artisan, and the craftsman of the later Middle Ages.[1] Christianity also grew because the early Christians built a well-disciplined, enthusiastic organization that was ready to exercise leadership at a time when it was desperately needed.

The Church came to dominate society in the western Roman Empire. Unlike the state, the Church survived the barbarian invasions and was able to offer leadership to the northern tribes as well as the Romans. In an era in which a multiplicity of small, weak governments kept struggling to remain intact, the Church grew to be an international power wielding considerable civil as well as spiritual authority.

[1]Robert Ulich, *History of Educational Thought* (New York: American Book Co., 1945), p. 72.

Aims of Education

The educational aims of Christianity were more lofty, comprehensive, and universal than pagan ideals. The child was to be trained to live in conformity with the will of an ethical divine being, who commanded his children to love one another even as He loved them. The Christian religion aimed at the moral regeneration of the individual by directing him to lead a Godlike life in order to secure eternal salvation. The Christian philosophy of education also held a promise of social regeneration by placing human relationships on the basis of the universal brotherhood of man and by recognizing the significance of every child of God.

The early medieval world was in need of a moral revolution, and the Church devoted its energy to this spiritual reawakening. "This disciplining and reforming of the European character, after the moral chaos which Roman imperialism had brought into the world, was the necessary condition of all the advances in the fine arts, scholarship, statecraft, and the practical arts which were to be made in the later Middle Ages and in the modern world."[2] Imbuing the demoralized Roman and the warlike Teutons with the Christian virtues was an overwhelming task.

Aims of Physical Education

Jesus, in His own person, represented the finest example of manhood. In Him, body, mind, and soul are found in perfect proportion.[3] Jesus had healthy out-of-door interests and certainly was no ascetic. Although He was familiar with grief and pain and often sought solitude and meditation, He also loved companionship and enjoyed social gatherings. "Hence Jesus did not treat any particular material pleasure or species of social life as inherently wrong. . . . Nothing was definitely required or forbidden; all depended upon the use made of it. . . . He did not condemn the joys and relaxations of this world, nor advocate self-abnegation *per se*. He held that we overcome the world, not by isolating ourselves from it, but by subordinating it to our higher uses."[4]

An exegetical examination of the concepts of body, soul, spirit, and flesh in the *Old Testament* and the *New Testament* revealed that man was viewed as a whole being rather than as a dualistic being.[5] The dualistic

[2]Frederick Eby and Charles Arrowood, *The History and Philosophy of Education Ancient and Medieval* (New York: Prentice-Hall, Inc., 1940), p. 648.

[3]B. D. Brink and Paul Smith, *Athletes of the Bible* (New York: Associated Press, 1914), p. 89.

[4]Frank Graves, *What Did Jesus Teach?* (New York: The Macmillan Company, 1925), pp. 166–67.

[5]D. R. G. Owen, *Body and Soul* (Philadelphia: The Westminster Press, 1956); Wheeler H. Robinson, *The Religious Ideas of the Old Testament* (London: Duckworth, 1913); Daryl Siedentop, "An Historical Note on the Concept of Organismic Unity" (typewritten manuscript, Hope College, 1969).

mind–body or body–soul concept of man was a product of Eastern and later Grecian philosophy. In the *Old Testament*, no Hebrew word can be translated as "body." The Hebrew word that is translated as "soul" in English refers to the psycho-physical totality of man—the whole man. In the *Old Testament*, man does not *have* a soul, he is a soul. In the *New Testament*, the word *soma* is translated "body," but in Paul's usage it meant personality—the whole man. The word *psyche* in later Greek philosophy meant the higher, immaterial, immortal part of man which was in opposition to the lower, material, body (*soma*). But the word *psyche* in the *New Testament* had the same meaning as the Hebrew word for soul—the living being, the whole man. In the *New Testament*, the words translated "flesh" and "spirit" stand not for two opposing parts of the nature of man but rather for two different kinds of man. In the Biblical view man was not a dualistic, but a unified, whole being who might choose to live "unto the spirit" or "unto the flesh."

Some early churchmen, such as Clement of Alexandria, who were attempting to blend Hellenic philosophy with Christian doctrines, did see some health value in exercises, games, and sports, but from the second century A.D. down through the Middle Ages, the early Judaeo-Christian unified concept of man gave way to the Greek and Eastern dualistic concept of man—a being whose debased body obstructed the cultivation of the soul. Consequently, most churchmen opposed physical education, and the Church suppressed many sports and games and failed to include physical education in the school curriculum. This opposition to physical education activities arose not only because of the influence of the Greek dualistic concept of man, but also because of the close association of Roman games with the pagan religion, the debased character of Roman sports and games, and the unfortunate experiences of the Christians in the arena.

Churchmen were particularly disturbed by the religious implications of the games. Attendance at games implied a token demonstration of Emperor worship. Many of the athletic festivals were held in honor of pagan deities, and the demonstrations often included some religious rituals. Tertullian denounced the public games for their pagan origins, and the circus, arena, and gymnasium for their madness, savagery, and vanity. The Church Fathers concluded that such influences were detrimental to Christianity and so endeavored to suppress them.

The Christians eventually came to regard the body as an instrument of sin. The body was mortal and of little consequence to a man seeking eternal salvation. "Save your soul!" was the all-impelling drive of the Christian. Many men came to accept the premise that life in the world to come could best be secured by rising above all thoughts of the body, even to the extent of ignoring and neglecting essential physical needs. In such an atmosphere even the most worthy ideals of physical education could not exist.

Promotion of Physical Education

Early Christian education was very informal, but when the Church became established, catechumenal schools were founded to provide instruction for converts who desired to become members. Parents who wanted their children to receive some general education had to send them to the pagan schools which remained in existence until Emperor Justinian closed them in 529 A.D. Christian agencies of higher learning, the catechetical schools, emerged in the East as the Church began to make more converts among the intellectuals. Both laymen and ecclesiastics attended these institutions. When the Church had perfected its organization, new Christian schools were established and became practically the sole centers of learning in Western Europe. The monastery schools predominated from the sixth to the twelfth century when the cathedral or episcopal schools emerged as the most important agencies of education. Occasionally an enlightened monarch, such as Charlemagne, encouraged and sponsored education, but he used monks and churchmen to carry out his plans. The Church schools were not agencies of physical education, but the Church fostered religious dancing.

Program of Physical Education

The informal education of early Christian youth was moral, religious, emotional, and "other-worldly." In the formative period of the Church, the catechetical schools of the East offered theological and secular studies taught from the Christian viewpoint. The learned Christian fathers who studied and lectured in these institutions integrated the Roman and Greek culture with Christianity and developed much of the early Christian literature and theology. The Western Church powers soon became critical of Greek learning because it was contaminated with pagan immorality and tended to inspire heretical views. When the Western Church established the monastery and cathedral schools, education became confined largely to Church doctrine, theological studies, and rituals; pagan literature, art, science, philosophy, and physical education were neglected.

Some early Church Fathers, particularly those who had received a classical education in the Eastern part of the Empire, did advocate physical education in the schools. Clement of Alexandria recommended wrestling, ball-playing, and walking as worthy pursuits and even believed that suitable exercises for women were desirable. These suggestions were not adopted by the Western Church, but even in the West the changes in social behavior were not effected rapidly. Bishop Sidonius, a fifth century churchman who lived in Gaul, reported that as a boy he enjoyed running, swimming, and hunting. The ball and book were his constant companions. Between masses he played ball or turned to dice and board games. Fishing and boating were pursued on his estate.

Ecclesiastics fought against the Roman practice of indulging in luxurious baths. The church authorities were not necessarily opposed to health and cleanliness, but they felt that nude and mixed bathing were partly responsible for the immoral practices that were undermining Roman society. The defenders of the Christian faith also sought to curb the public games. Christians who attended the activities at the circus or amphitheater could not take communion and no gladiator was baptized until he promised to give up his profession. The persistent campaign of the churchmen was successful. In 394 A.D., Theodosius, an early Christian emperor, abolished the Olympics; and the last gladiatorial exhibition was held in Rome in 404 A.D. Even so, chariot races and beast fights persisted well into the sixth century.

Dancing was a means of religious expression for the early Christians. They celebrated the Church services in hymns and dances. They danced in cemeteries in honor of the dead; they danced during solemn festivals; and they danced on feast days as an expression of thanksgiving. In his writings, Father Claude Ménestrier, a Jesuit priest, has revealed that religious dances were viewed favorably by the early Church Fathers and were actually attached to the rituals. He stated, "Divine service was composed of psalms, hymns, and canticles, because men sang and danced the praises of God, as they read His oracles in those extracts from the Old and New Testaments which we still know under the name of Lessons. The place in which these acts of worship were offered to God was called the Choir, just as those portions of comedies and tragedies in which dancing and singing combined to make up the interludes were called choruses."[6] The choir was apparently a place for dancing as well as for singing the praises of the Lord.

In the course of time the religious dances degenerated. The sacred character of the earlier choreographic art became impregnated with worldly influences and many performances became impious. As a result, dancing was finally discredited in the Christian Church. In 554 A.D., Childebert ruled against dances in his realm and, in 744, Pope Zacharias proscribed ribald performances. It has been said that St. Augustine once remarked, *"Mellius est fondere quam saltare"* ("It is better to dig than to dance").

Methods of Physical Education

Jesus preached the word of God and His actions exemplified His teachings. He adjusted and correlated His lessons to the experiences of the

[6]Quoted in Gaston Vuillier, *A History of Dancing* (New York: D. Appleton & Co., 1898), p. 48.

audiences. He taught by parables, proverbs, and informal conversations. His method was personal and direct, persuasive but not dictatorial, fearless but not coercive. The teaching standards of the early Middle Ages fell short of those established by Jesus. As educational content became systematized, the question and memorized answer method of education was adopted.

PHYSICAL EDUCATION FOR MORAL DISCIPLINE

Monasticism is strongly identified with the early Church, but it did not originate there. Mystic Hindus, as well as Persians, Egyptians, and followers of certain Grecian philosophical sects lived ascetically, frequently seeking their ideals through bodily mortification, silence, and worldly renunciation. The early Christian monks were influenced by these ascetics.

The chaotic conditions in the fourth century stimulated Christian monasticism. Many men sought the sanctuary of cloistered walls. Although the prime objective of the monks was to seek salvation for their souls, some of their rules resulted in significant contributions to society. St. Benedict was primarily responsible for writing the code of behavior observed by the monks. His rule of labor required men to work seven hours and to read two hours a day. This rule led to educational and social benefits for mankind. If monks were to devote time to reading, some type of school had to be provided for novices, and thus remnants of education survived throughout the Dark Ages. Although the men copying books in the scriptoriums were disciplining their souls, at the same time they were preserving the learning of the past as well as maintaining the only libraries of the age. When the monks fulfilled their obligations to perform manual work, they imbued labor with a dignity that it never possessed in cultures where it was reserved for serfs or slaves. The monks practiced the best farming methods, drained swamps, cultivated wastelands, built roads and bridges, established hospitals, developed new methods for craftsmen in leather, wood, and metal, and made contributions to commerce and finance. Furthermore, monastic ideals of obedience and charity had a softening influence upon the Teutons.

Aims of Education

The monk was the "spiritual athlete." He observed the strictest rules and endured the severest training to prepare himself for eternal salvation. The character of the soul was fashioned through bodily mortification, worldly renunciation, and continual prayer. By taking the vows of poverty, chastity, and obedience, he freed himself from any temporal ties to family and to the political state in order to dedicate himself exclusively to preparation for life in the hereafter.

Because the monks had some vocational and intellectual instruction, it is sometimes claimed that their educational aims were temporal as well as spiritual. Their manual labor and literary endeavors, however, were merely a part of their religious discipline. "To labor is to pray" expressed their attitude.

Aims of Physical Education

Monasticism was an educational ideal designed to nourish the spiritual rather than the physical being. Men were to develop the beauty of their souls, not their bodies. Monastic education sought to subjugate all desires and demands of the body in order to exalt the essence of spiritual life. St. Bernard argued, "Always in a robust and active body the mind lies more soft and more lukewarm; and, on the other hand, the spirit flourishes more strongly and more actively in an infirm and weakly body."[7]

In early monasticism, particularly in the East, monks vied with one another by inventing fantastic means of mortifying the flesh. The monasteries of the West, under the leadership of such men as St. Benedict, assumed a more practical attitude. Moderation and restraint rather than physical abuses were recommended. "Nothing harsh and nothing burdensome,"[8] expressed this Western spirit. This new attitude was not adopted out of interest in physical fitness, but because the monks believed the extreme austerities of the Eastern monks impeded the development of spiritual excellence.

The Dark Ages were a sterile period in physical education. The monks censured all physical and aesthetic activities pursued for worldly pleasures. They were reacting against a decadent age in which men pampered their bodies and indulged in sensuous and cruel pastimes. The monks may have carried reform beyond the point of moderation, but they had to instill ideals of self-restraint in men before a sane concept of the interrelationships of body and mind could be restored.

Although physical fitness was never part of the aims of monastic education, the doctrine of labor helped to keep the monks robust. St. Benedict proclaimed, "Idleness is the enemy of the soul, therefore the monks should always be occupied, either in manual labor or in holy reading."[9] This rule of work accomplished some of the same ends as physical education did in other societies. In later days, when the lay brothers

---

[7]Quoted in G. G. Coulton, *Five Centuries of Religion* (Cambridge: University Press, 1923), 5: 532.
[8]Prologue, *The Rule of St. Benedict.*
[9]Coulton, *Five Centuries of Religion*, p. 39.

and serfs performed most of the hard work in the monasteries, the intellectual brothers, who no longer did manual labor, complained of headaches, indigestion, and melancholy.

Promotion of Physical Education

The monasteries and convents were practically the only schools in existence from the sixth to the eleventh centuries, with the exception of the less important cathedral schools, a few secular guild schools in Italy, and the "palace schools" of Charlemagne and Alfred the Great. Girls seeking the ascetic life went into the nunnery, and boys were sent to the monastery. The monastic schools were primarily instituted to educate youths destined to take religious vows of the order (*oblati*), but a few institutions also accepted lay students (*externi*) from noble families. Children entered the schools about the age of seven or eight, although some of them were dedicated to the monastic life by their parents when they were infants. Instruction was given by monks. Toward the end of the Middle Ages, the cathedral schools, which trained the secular clergy of each bishopric as well as a few lay students, surpassed the monastic institutions as educational agencies.

Some mention should be made of the educational revival in the eighth century of Charlemagne's empire, which was carried out under the leadership of the English monk, Alcuin. Charlemagne's empire was still being Christianized when Alcuin established a "palace school" for the education of noble children. This effort was one of the few attempts of the state to sponsor education, but here too the monks were the men who carried out the work.

Program of Physical Education

The monks were drilled in the manners and customs of their order and memorized prayers, sang psalms, studied theology, and worked in the forests and fields. The intellectual program of the monastic schools consisted of the Seven Liberal Arts: the *trivium*, which included grammar, rhetoric, and logic; and the *quadrivium*, which was composed of arithmetic, geometry, astronomy, and music. Many of the lesser institutions offered only rudimentary instruction in one or two of these studies. The curriculum was not really liberal, for practically all subject matter was directed toward theology. Physical education activities were not part of this monastic curriculum.

Western monasteries did not indulge in extreme forms of physical torture, but even so, their standards of health and cleanliness were not at all like those observed today. Food and sleep were reduced to a healthy minimum, with exceptions made for the sick. Hot baths were frowned upon, probably as a reaction to the evils of the Roman public *thermae*. The rules of St. Benedict were interpreted to prohibit even swimming. Men were exhorted to give more attention to cleaning their souls than their bodies.

With such unsanitary conditions, plagues and diseases were common, but the monks looked upon these afflictions as acts of God in punishment for sin. Although prayer was the proper method of seeking cures, the monks, nevertheless, provided the only hospitals of the age and established leper houses. Some monastic orders were established for these specific purposes.

The early monasteries failed not only to provide any formal physical education content in their school program, but also attempted to suppress the spontaneous play of youth. The few lay students who studied in the monasteries were allowed occasional intervals for recreation, but these periods were no more than brief intervals of free play. The boys training to become monks did not enjoy even that much relaxation from spiritual duties. In general, all recreation pursued for worldly pleasure was condemned by all churchmen.

Methods of Physical Education

The main methods of teaching were memorization, imitation, and question-and-answer. In a system which stressed authority and curbed individual expression discipline was administered by the rod as well as by compulsory fasting and confinement. Monastic and nunnery education were not universal; the training was reserved primarily for those who sought an ascetic life.

PHYSICAL EDUCATION FOR SOCIAL DISCIPLINE

As the warlike Germanic tribes gradually penetrated southern Europe, the corrupt, demoralized Roman government was unable to resist their advances or to continue providing essential law-enforcing services. Life and property in the Roman Empire were endangered by raids, banditry, revolts, oppressive landlords, and repeated barbaric invasions. With the impotent government unable to protect and help them, frightened and frustrated people were forced to seek some manner of security. Three institutions besides the Church gradually evolved to answer this need: feudalism, manorialism, and chivalry. Feudalism rendered the services of protection and government; manorialism was quite commonly adopted to meet economic needs; and chivalry was a social and moral code which helped lift medieval life to a higher level of civilization.

Feudalism was the fabric in which the social, economic, and political life of the Middle Ages was clothed. Because medieval society was based on Roman, Teutonic, and Celtic cultures, this new political system became a strange mixture of civilized and barbarian elements. At first, each group developed a feudal pattern according to its own cultural antecedents. Contributions from several cultures were eventually combined to formulate feudal systems, but the pattern varied from region to region and era to era. The feudal system of the Middle Ages was most developed in France, but it also existed in England, Germany, Spain, and Italy, as well as other parts of the world.

In the feudal system all land was held theoretically by the king, except for the property of a small number of free landowners. Unable to rule extensive domains by themselves in these turbulent times, sovereigns delegated some of their territorial and political power to the nobles; in return, the nobles pledged their loyalty to the king and promised to perform military service for him. The nobles, in a similar manner, delegated their lands and political prerogatives to lesser nobles. In this way, the pyramidical structure of the feudal system evolved. Every nobleman was the vassal of another lord, and the king held his rights as a vassal of God. Each vassal had complete political authority over his own domain, which localized government and diminished the power of kings.

Manorialism was the predominantly agricultural economic system that emerged to sustain feudalism, with each village, or manor, attempting to be self-sufficient. The little domestic manufactures and many agricultural services necessary for the operation of the rural economy were all performed by the peasants in return for the protection of the nobles. Manorialism was a natural product of such times.

The serfs, slaves, and freemen who comprised the bulk of the medieval population endured a bitter struggle in their search for subsistence. They had endless obligations to the lord of the manor. They were helpless if he chose to exploit them, for he was their sole judge and ruler. The impoverished peasant remained an ignorant, superstitious, and humble creature, without access to education and with little hope for improving his standard of living.

Modern books and pictures romanticize the rather crude and rugged life of the noble lords and ladies dwelling in the manor. Their castles were actually primitive blockhouses that did not develop into immense masonry structures of towers, keeps, and moats until the later days of feudalism. About the castle or manor was the small manorial village, with the wine press, mill, ovens, carpentry shop, smiths, stables, chapel, fields, orchard, pasturage, and woodlands. A few luxuries—fine armor, iron, and spices—were secured at fairs or from traveling peddlers, but almost all of the necessities were provided by the people of the village. The castle, in which the lord, his knights, and a multitude of servants dwelt, was dark, dank, and drafty. Although the food served was plentiful, it was a monotonous diet that remained unseasoned until after the Crusades introduced spices. Nobles usually ate with their fingers, slept in their clothes, and enjoyed few of the conveniences accepted as commonplace today. When a nobleman was not busy fighting or serving at his overlord's court, he devoted himself to the management of his own estates and to his recreations. He administered justice, checked up on estate affairs, and promoted elaborate entertainments and rugged sports. The noble ladies took an active part in the social life and directed the domestic duties in the castle. Religious observances were, of course, a natural and daily part of the life of everyone.

Although no educational system existed for medieval peasants, noble youths were taught the moral and social code, chivalry. Chivalric ideals dominated their class from the eleventh to the sixteenth century.

Aims of Education

In chivalric education, youths were trained to observe the social and moral customs of war, religion, and gallantry that had bgeen formulated by feudal society. Acceptance of the code of behavior was one of the requirements of knighthood. In a solemn ceremony, the youthful aspirant vowed to serve and obey his lord, his God, and his lady. He was to fight for his lord and to remain loyal to him, exhibiting the virtues of valor, pride, and honor. Secondly, the religious vows of knighthood pledged the youth to defend the Church, protect the poor and oppressed, redress wrong, avoid sin, and perform religious ceremonies—in short, demanding of him the virtues of obedience, chastity, faith, and piety. Thirdly, the knight's code of gallantry pledged him to protect women, to defend widows and orphans, and to fight for his lady. Prerequisite virtues for such services were courtesy, modesty, kindliness, and beneficence. The chivalric code also included training in certain social graces, laws of etiquette, and religious ceremonies.

The chivalric educational goals of war, religion, and gallantry did not originate simultaneously, nor did they receive equal emphasis in all places. The earliest educational objectives of the Teutons were related to the military profession. Later, the Church introduced the religious theme into chivalric standards.[10] The holy wars brought the knights into contact with the East and the lands of the Saracens where some of the ideals of gallantry were acquired. Between 1250 and 1350 the ideals of chivalry came to be most nearly realized, ". . . because the Christian world at that time was

---

[10]F. Warre Cornish, *Chivalry* (New York: The Macmillan Co., 1901), p. 24.

animated with a higher and fuller life.[11] In the later fourteenth, fifteenth, and sixteenth centuries, the educational ideals of knighthood began to decline until chivalric education became an elite training in ornamental ceremonies and artificial manners of court life.

In practice, discrepancies existed between the ideals of chivalry and their realization. The ideals of the knight, who was educated in a narrow, exclusive caste system, were practiced within his own social class; he commonly oppressed the poor and showed absolute contempt for his inferiors.[12] Chivalric education failed to fully realize its ideal, but it served as an ideal of civilized Christianity in a world of savage barbarism. Chivalry did not transform the rude, ravaging Teuton miraculously into a shining knight, but at least it provided him with a pattern of ideals that was better than his previous code of conduct.

> To sum up; Chivalry taught the world the duty of noble service willingly rendered. It upheld courage and enterprise in obedience to rule, it consecrated military prowess to the service of the Church, glorified the virtues of liberality, good faith, unselfishness and courtesy, and above all, courtesy to women. . . . Chivalry was an imperfect discipline, but it was a discipline, and one fit for the times . . . and with all its shortcomings it exercised a great and wholesome influence in raising the medieval world from barbarism to civilization.[13]

Aims of Physical Education

Physical education was the core of the chivalric curriculum, in which youths were to acquire military prowess, social graces, and sports skills. However, unlike the Greek, the medieval noble was not concerned with developing a beautifully proportioned, graceful body, nor was he driven by the patriotism that inspired the early Roman. Physical education was pursued by the feudal noble so that he could fulfill his military obligations and fight for the cause of the Church.

Narrow as the aims of physical education were, a boy was prepared for military life at a time when nobility had no other profession than that of war. The knight was always fighting his own quarrels over a point of honor, following his overlord into battle, going on a crusade, or spending his leisure in strenuous military sports. War rather than peace was accepted as the normal way of life and chivalric education merely reflected this spirit.

11Ibid., p. 17.   13Ibid., pp. 27–28.
12Ibid., pp. 349–50.

Promotion of Physical Education

Education was provided by the home, the castle, and the Church. Some young men interested in church work could attend the monastery or cathedral schools, and in later times, those who desired an intellectual training could attend the universities. The majority of noble youths, however, aspired to become knights, and they received their education in the castle or palace school. Girls were also sent to the castle for their training, which emphasized the courtly graces.

Under the tutelage of his mother, the child began his earliest lessons in the home. Thereafter, the boy was sent to the castle of some secular lord or prominent churchman to continue his education. In youth, he was a page, and the noblewomen, priest, squires, and Masters of Henchmen were his teachers. He might receive training in the liberal arts, but illiteracy was common among the nobles. Upon becoming a squire, he spent considerable time in the company of knights who watched him practice the arts of war. Informal agents of education such as the traveling troubadours, jugglers, tumblers, and minstrels also influenced the youngster in these formative years. These wandering entertainers related the news of other peoples and provided amusement for the court.

The classrooms of the page and squire were the hills and valleys where they hunted; the stableyards, armory, kennels, and hawkpens where they became familiar with the tools of war and sports; the lists where the tournaments took place; the castle halls where dancing and light games were enjoyed; and the battlefields and Crusades where squires attended their knight and observed the practices of his profession.

The formal education of the youth was in two stages. He was trained as a page, or henchman, from the age of seven to fourteen, and as a squire from the age of fourteen to twenty-one. A solemn little religious ceremony marked the page's graduation to the rank of squire. Relinquishing the short dagger of his childhood, he was presented with the sword of adulthood by the priest, who blessed it and offered the boy many sage cautions and instructions concerning its use. The lad then served as a squire for about seven years before he was eligible for knighthood.

If a squire conducted himself well during his period of service, the lord admitted him into the brotherhood. If a boy distinguished himself by a gallant feat, he was dubbed a knight before he reached the usual age. Youths took particular pride in being knighted on the field of battle. If any lord unjustly refused to bestow knighthood, the youth had the right to claim the honor from another lord. Some young noblemen did not seek to be knighted; they remained squires because they were financially unable to assume knighthood.

Conferring knighthood was a religious ceremony that took place on some great military occasion or Church holiday, such as Easter, Pentecost, or even Christmas. Sometimes the lad took a bath of purification the night before the ceremony and spent the hours until morning in a vigil of prayer. The next day, surrounded by the noblemen in their armor and the churchmen in their vestments, he heard high mass. Then the novice knelt before his lord who instructed him in his duties as a knight. The boy then vowed to be true to the ideals of chivalry, and his lord tapped him on the shoulder, dubbing him a knight. After the bishop had blessed the youth's sword and consecrated it to the service of religion and virtue, the proud young man donned his armor and left the church. The rest of the day was usually celebrated at a tournnament, banquet, and other festivities in which the youth participated for the first time as a knight.

Numerous fairs and feast days, as well as tournaments, were means of physical education. Although peasants received most of their physical exercise toiling in their widely scattered fields, they also participated in village holidays. Medieval celebrations were sometimes simple affairs, limited to a day of games, dancing, and religious observances; but there were also elaborate court functions with hundreds of guests, sumptuous feasts, great tournaments, and jugglers, tumblers, troubadours, and other entertainers.

Program of Physical Education

Although a noble youth devoted most of his time to physical education, he also received religious training, drill in etiquette, and some intellectual education. In childhood, the boy was taught all sorts of gymnastic exercises to strengthen his body, including such activities as shooting with a bow, playing with cudgels and backswords, and casting heavy weights. As a youthful page who mingled with adults, observing and absorbing their life, he acquired the particular grace of manner that characterized the true knight.

For squires, the exercises became more rugged. Strength and endurance were developed by bearing heavy weights, running tremendous distances, springing on horseback fully armed without putting a foot in the stirrup, turning somersaults in heavy armor, leaping upon the shoulders of a horseman from behind with no other hold than a hand laid upon the shoulder, scaling walls with and without ladders, swimming with and without light armor, casting lances great distances, and striking heavy balls of wood with large racquets or malls. Besides these exercises, youths practiced riding and managing arms, and attempted to develop the stamina to withstand hunger, heat, cold, and loss of sleep.

The squire also had duties that symbolized his obligation to serve his lord. He attended his lord as valet and bodyguard, assisting him in battle, attempting to rescue him if captured, and guarding the prisoners he took. Upon returning from battle, the squire cleaned his knight's armor, cared for his horse, and served him at dinner. He continued to assist the noble ladies of the castle also, playing chess and backgammon with them, accompanying them on hunts, and singing and dancing for their pleasure. Sometimes, under their tutelage or that of a troubadour, he learned to read or write or learned Latin.

Considerable time was devoted to the development of skills essential for performance in battle. Activities such as quintain and behourd drilled the boys in military techniques and provided experiences of simulated warfare.

In quintain the squires practiced marksmanship with a target that often represented a Saracen. This armor-clad dummy, impaled upon a strong post, revolved at the slightest touch. A lance or sword extended from one hand of the figure and sometimes a shield was held with the other. The object of the drill was to charge the dummy, on foot or horseback, and to pierce it through the middle. In chivalric sport, it was considered unfair to strike an opponent anywhere but on the chest or helmet. A blow too much to the right or left would pivot the dummy so that it would smack the young squire with the shield or lance in rebuke for his clumsiness. There was many variations of quintain. In the pel-quintain, or post-quintain, the young squire, lance and shield in hand, would charge toward a post about six feet high that was fixed firmly in the ground. In human quintain the target was a fully armed opponent who was usually seated on a three-legged stool. His adversary attempted to knock him off the stool with a lance, and he in turn sought to parry these blows and cause the attacker to fall. Tilting at a ring was a variation of quintain. A man riding at full speed attempted to thrust his lance through the ring. If he made a direct hit, the ring would be released and would land on the tip of the lance. Water tub quintain was probably practiced more as an amusement, and possibly even the common people played a variation of this game. A bucket of water was placed upon the top of a post and the objective was to knock it off without getting drenched.

Behourd was another military sport to improve techniques in handling arms. Descriptions of the game vary, but it appears to have been a mock battle in which one group attempted to defend a small fortress while the others attacked. This game provided some experience of the perils of battle. Experienced and mature knights as well as aspiring squires, played behourd and quintain.

From antiquity, military nations have played various athletic games that imitated warfare. During the Middle Ages the heavy cavalry was the most important fighting unit of the army. Therefore the tournament, a contest of armed horsemen, was naturally the favorite peacetime amusement of the people. Tournaments relieved the boredom of peacetime existence and served as a military school for the training of novices and the practice of knights. In later days, with the increasing importance of infantry, archery, and gunnery, the tournaments lost their military significance and became occasions for the lavish display of feudal pageantry.

Authentic records of European tournaments date from the middle of the eleventh century, but they probably existed before that time. In England the tournaments were introduced in the twelfth century by Richard I, who attributed the courage and skill of the French in battle to their practical experience in the tournaments. In the twelfth and thirteenth centuries, this sport was a common pastime of noblemen everywhere. Its popularity survived until the sixteenth century. Both the Church and monarchs often attempted to interfere with the calling of tournaments. They were probably concerned about the loss of life and the worldly atmosphere of gambling, gaiety, and drunkenness in which some of the games were held. In 1179, Pope Alexander III not only forbade the holding of tournaments but refused Christian burial to those who died in them. All repressive attempts were in vain, however, for the sport continued to flourish.

Any important political or miltary meeting was likely to be an occasion for holding a tournament. Knights also found excuses for these games at christenings, weddings, and knightings. The tournaments were so popular that they were even staged during war! Sometimes the king himself sent his heralds through the land to announce that on a certain date he would hold a tournament. On other occasions the events were arranged by a group of independent knights, and messengers were often sent into distant countries to invite all gallant gentlemen to honor the passage of arms. The tournaments were governed by many laws and regulations. Certain formalities had to be observed and an effort was made to have knights meet on equal terms.

The grand tourney or mêlée was the most important event in the tournament and gave its name to the sport. Jousts were customarily included as extra attractions on the program. A joust was a combat between two armed horsemen, and although such events occurred informally in daily life, they had strict regulations in the tournaments. The tournament proper was the mêlée in which many knights fought under conditions similar to war. Regulations attempted to limit all the activities in the program to blunted weapons (arms of courtesy), but sharp lances and swords did come into use and were particularly common in the mêlée. Sometimes crabtree clubs were wielded, and in Germany, the battle-ax was occasionally employed. Men were dressed for battle except that their special tilting helmets covered the whole head and neck.

A flurry of excitement and anticipation existed around the castle in the days preceding the tournament. On the day of the tournament, the galleries for spectators were decked in cloths of silk and gold and trimmed with varicolored banners. The magnificently decorated tents and pavilions that had been erected in the area around the lists, the place of combat, added a further note of color and gaiety to the scene. Strains of warlike music heightened the ever-growing excitement. At either end of the oval arena were the pavilions of the competing knights with their coats of arms prominently displayed. The women in the galleries were dressed fashionably in rich garments and jewels. Against this colorful background, the squires attended their knights, the herald read the rules of the contest, and the starting signal was given. At the blast of a trumpet, the free-for-all tournament was under way. This major event of the fete was by far the most thrilling and perilous. Watching the thirty or forty knights charging from either end of the arena, and hearing the thundering of their horses' hoofs, the spectators braced themselves for the initial resounding clash of lances against armor. Soon a violent battle was raging. Weapons and armor flashed in the sunlight and men and horses were thrown violently to the ground. Successful contestants continued to charge and fight with fury. The captured opponents lost their horses and armour and sometimes had to pay a ransom. Although the rules of the tournament tried to minimize injuries, blood was shed and fatalities occurred frequently.

The jousts, the next event, were less exciting, for the knights fought with blunt weapons. At the blast of the trumpet the two horsemen charged from either end of the oval field. Dashing at full speed, each horseman aimed his lance at the helmet or breastplate of his adversary. The shock of a lance-blow against the armor was terrific. If both men managed to remain seated, they wheeled their horses about and charged a second time. The knight that unhorsed his opponent was usually declared the winner, but sometimes the rules called for him to leap off his own horse and continue the combat on foot. Being encased in armor and using blunt weapons, a knight was in little danger of losing his life. After all the events were over and the chosen queen of the field had bestowed a garland of flowers and a spirited steed on the champion, everyone was ready for the gay round of revelries at the castle.

Knights participated in other games such as *barriers, pas d'armes,* and *à outrance,* which were variations of the tournament activities. In *barriers,* two troops tried to force a barrier placed across the lists using axes, swords, and maces as weapons. In *pas d'armes,* a certain number of knights fixed their shields and tents in a particular pass or spot on the ground, and defended it against all comers. The combat *à outrance* was, in fact, a duel and differed from trial by battle only in being voluntary. It was fought with sharp weapons, and often between two knights of different nationalities or fiefs. This contest was frequently, but not always, the outcome of a private quarrel. Sometimes the combat *à outrance* was undertaken by a number of knights together. Certain jousts held separately from the tournaments were called Round Tables. This name was derived from a brotherhood of knights who jousted frequently together and who, in order to abolish any feeling of inequality or rank, dined afterward at a round table where everyone held an equally honored position.

Hawking and hunting were pursued with the same enthusiasm that the knights held for tournaments and war. Indeed, the hard riding in a wild boar or stag hunt was excellent training for the battlefield. The peasant was forbidded to hunt for his own pleasure or even for food unless granted this rare privilege by his manorial lord. The poor rustic had no recourse or right to complain when wild beasts devoured his crops or when hunters and their dogs trampled his fields of grain. Such injustices gave rise to poaching on the part of the more adventurous peasants.

Hawking consumed much of the time of knights in the intervals between wars. The hawk was the symbol and ornament of nobility. Hounds and hawks were even included in the equipage of the Crusades. The sport was held in such high esteem that a lord rarely appeared in public without a pet hawk on his wrist as a mark of dignity. In the castles, the falconer who caught young birds and trained them was a person of considerable importance. The clergy also participated in this amusement, even though the Church attempted to restrict and even to forbid participation in the sport.

A hawking party of knights and ladies, mounted on beautiful steeds, with pet falcons perched on their wrists, was a common sight. The hawks were hooded and wore little silver bells so that they could be identified if lost. Racing over the fields in search of game birds, the hunters would whip off the tiny hoods at the proper moment and the hawks would swoop after their prey.

Although knights usually preferred rugged, outdoor activities, during inclement weather and on certain holidays they played at less strenuous games. Chess and backgammon were popular; so, too, was dice although frowned on by the Church because of the profanity and gambling that accompanied it. Jugglers also provided amusement. "They threw wonderful somersaults—they leaped through hoops placed at certain distances from one another, they played with knives, slings, baskets, brass bells, and earthenware plates, and they walked on their hands with their feet in the air or with their heads turned downwards so as to look through their legs backwards."[14] As early as 1327, a feat of "rope dancing" amazed the guests at banquets of the French kings, and one mention is made of tight-rope walking 150 feet above the ground.

Dancing became increasingly popular as the Middle Ages progressed, particularly during the Renaissance and later eras when aristocracy reveled in elaborate fetes and balls. In the earlier times, the knights rejected dancing as effeminate, but they looked on as the feminine voices mingled

[14]Paul LaCroix, *Manners, Customs, and Dress During the Middle Ages* (London: Bickers and Son, n.d.), p. 224.

in song and the women danced in the firelight. As feudal society became more and more refined, the men joined their ladies in the dances. Frequently the leaders sang a solo and the other participants joined in the refrain, with clapping and instrumental music providing accompaniment.

Methods of Physical Education

When the young noble began his chivalric training, he was thrust into the active life of the castle and acquired the skills either through observation or participation. He received some formal instruction, but by far the most of his education was gained through an activity program. Through participation in sports of a warlike nature the youths were conditioned for their life on the battlefield. It was held that "a youth must have seen his blood flow and felt his teeth crack under the blow of his adversary and have been thrown to the ground twenty times . . . thus will he be able to face real war with hope of victory."[15]

Constant supervision must have stimulated the boys to put forth their best efforts. The noble knights and ladies who closely observed the performances of the pages and squires and noted their progress exerted considerable social pressure, and the competition among squires must have been keen. Boys sitting in the firelight listening to the troubadours sing in praise of brave and courageous knights, must have been inspired with desire to succeed. The religious ideals connected with chivalry motivated young men to achieve the physical power and skill to fight for the cause of the Church. Discipline for military education is usually strict, and this was especially true in the medieval times.

PHYSICAL EDUCATION FOR VOCATIONAL DISCIPLINE

The rural, feudal society had performed the services essential for survival after the fall of the Roman Empire, but the decentralized governments and the armies of mail-clad horsemen became inadequate during the later Middle Ages. Important developments in warfare had occurred by that time, particularly the invention of gunpowder, which greatly reduced the prestige of the knights. A growing national consciousness and the development of stronger monarchies further diminished the power of the nobles. Eventually, royal law replaced feudal law. The feudal system was further undermined by the revival of trade and commerce, the growth of the towns, and the rise of the middle class. The urban movement gained its first impetus from the Crusades of the eleventh, twelfth, and thirteenth centuries.

---

[15]As quoted by F. W. Cripps-Day, *The History of the Tournament in England and France* (London: Bernard Quarich Limited, 1918), p. 3.

The Crusades set into motion many progressive trends that would affect the whole framework of society. The contacts with other peoples stimulated a desire for foreign foods, clothing, and ornamentation. The men who satisfied the demand for new products soon developed a need for money, credit, banking, and a more adequate administrative system than was offered by the decentralized feudal governments. The activities of the merchants hastened the development of towns near strategic rivers and harbors, trade centers, or important castles and monasteries. Within these urban centers the merchants became a cohesive social unit that was destined to play an important role in history. With the acceleration of trade and commerce, successful merchants acquired a new type of wealth in personal property and capital. This economic power enabled the townsmen to play the nobles, bishops, and kings against one another, and to secure charters granting them rights and privileges of self-government.

The new class of burghers desired to provide their children with an education. Trade and commerce encouraged the pursuit of learning, and towns were natural places in which to establish schools. As a consequence, the townsmen developed a practical type of training through their guild organizations. These were associations of men to secure common objectives, and, by medieval days, there were three well-defined types which contributed to education. These were the religious-social guilds, the merchant guilds, and the craft guilds.

The activities of the religious and social guilds extended Christian charity by contributing aid to poor scholars, comforting the ill, maintaining schools, planning pageants, repairing the church, presenting religious plays, and helping the indigent. The societies were social and recreational as well as charitable.

The merchant guilds were organized by wealthy merchants, usually landed proprietors engaged in wholesale trade who sought to regulate and protect their trade interests. As the merchant guilds grew in importance, they came to be closely associated with the municipal government, so much so that sometimes the two became synonymous.

The artisans and craftsmen organized craft guilds to protect their interests. The weavers, goldsmiths, dyers, tailors, silversmiths, drapers, each banded together to advance the common interests of their individual crafts. The craft guilds fixed hours of work, regulated wages, and established uniform standards of excellence for materials and workmanship. The craftsmen standardized the educational prepartion necessary for practicing their crafts, thus developing a vocational training system. They also sponsored many social and religious projects.

The more democratic spirit emerging in the later Middle Ages, which was manifested in the growth of guilds, was not purely urban in character. Peasants also experienced greater freedom. Many former bondsmen became tenants on their lords' estates through pressure of mass action, peasant revolts, and the purchase of freedom. Some serfs escaped to the cities and secured their freedom if they were not apprehended within a year and a day. Sometimes Christian influence led to the manumission of some serfs when some nobles, on their deathbeds, freed bondsmen to secure salvation for their own souls. Sometimes knights who had depleted their funds in the Crusades were willing to grant privileges to peasants in return for money. Moreover, the Black Death and the general economic revolution made labor so scarce that the bondsmen found themselves in a more advantageous bargaining position.

Aims of Education

Guild training was a vocational discipline that prepared youths for industrial and commercial life, but it was not a narrow training in craft skills. Besides learning a trade, the youths received some intellectual education, and were trained to aspire to high standards of craftsmanship, to perform prescribed religious and social duties, and to develop loyalty and respect for the organization.

Education through vocational training had existed since remote antiquity, but during medieval times it was lifted to a higher plane. As mentioned earlier, monks had considered work part of their spiritual training; similarly the guilds invested work with a sense of social dignity.[16] The guilds were secular, but religion gave direction and cohesion to their social and educational patterns.

Like all social groups, craftsmen also sought to inspire youth with loyalty to the guild and a sense of responsibility for maintaining and strengthening the organization. In later days, this seeking of group solidarity degenerated into maintaining exclusive privileges for the members. Many abuses crept into the guilds and the high standards of craftsmanship also declined.

Aims of Physical Education

The townsmen of the later Middle Ages were never as devoted to physical education objectives as were the knights, although they did perform military service. The peasants and guildsmen, however, did pursue some social, military, religious, and recreational goals through physical education.

Primarily informal, physical education was a means to a social end. Although the Church and guild laws provided a sense of community cohesion, sports and games were employed to heighten this spirit of unity. Some noblemen used physical education activities as a means of social control. Occasional holidays undoubtedly helped to maintain the morale

[16]Toulmin Smith, *English Gilds* (London: N. Trübner and Co., 1870), p. xv.

of the peasant population. Moreover, when emotions were released in sports and dance, they were less apt to explode into peasant revolts.

Militaristic activities existed in medieval towns, for the guildsmen secured certain privileges in return for the military services they could render to kings. Also, in those cities possessing considerable independence, men had to be trained as soldiers for community defense. With military service no longer exclusively aristocratic, military activities did play a significant role in the lives of the townsmen. Occasionally, however, as in England, laws had to be promulgated to encourage the achievement of these militaristic aims.

The association of religion and physical education was naturally strong in a Church-dominated era, but sports and games were not sponsored solely for their spiritual value. For the most part, they were gay and pleasant accessories to religious celebrations. The many religious holidays in the Middle Ages offered a ready excuse for merrymaking!

The medieval townsmen and peasants were not concerned about the intangible values in recreation. For the peasants, physical activities were a relief from a monotonous life of drudgery and squalor. The peasants and guildsmen were zealous sportsmen: ribald humor, drinking, and violence were often a part of their games. They did not govern their sports by many rules and regulations.

Promotion of Physical Education

Education, except for chivalric training, was under Church control up to the twelfth century. With the rise of towns, new demands were made upon education, and much of the initiative to meet these needs was taken over by secular authority. The guilds, of course, employed the master craftsman as the vocational teacher, but they also provided some general education for children. They supported priests who ministered to the religious needs of the members and frequently taught in an elementary school. In England, chantry schools were established by lesser aristocrats or guilds for the chanting of masses and the education of children. Private schools were beginning to be established as were town or burgher schools, some of which taught the traditional Latin grammar curriculum while others were limited to teaching reading and writing in the vernacular.

The sports and games of the later Middle Ages were part of the community life rather than part of the formal educational curriculum. The demands of military service entailed some physical education that in peacetime was pursued largely in rugged sports. Peasants participated in games and dancing on holidays granted them by landlords at harvest time, May time, Christmas, or on such occasions as the knighting of the lord's son or the marriage of his daughter. Church holidays, village fairs and horse sales, school holidays and free time, guild celebrations, state displays and processions usually included sports and games as part of their activities. These events took place in the natural environment of village greens, town squares, narrow streets, nearby fields, and even the church yards.

In the later Middle Ages, the new town schools offered a limited education for the children of the more prosperous townspeople. Boys received vocational education under the well-organized guild training. For a number of years they served as apprentices and later as journeymen, then as master craftsmen when they could go into business for themselves. Children of peasants were rarely educated although records reveal that a few families had to pay their lord extra fees or services because their sons had attended school.

Formal physical education did not exist in these schools. Medieval sports and games were usually spontaneous, although some formal events were planned by guild or municipal officials. On the occasions held in honor of some saint or other religious observance, Church services usually preceded the processionals and games that were held later in the day. The guilds planned days of games that sometimes became quite elaborate. Members of a guild usually lived in the same part of town, prayed together at the same church, participated in the same sports, and served in the same units in the army, so an ever ready organization for any activity was always present. Towns competed in some sports, and held fairs and May Day festivals that also included games.

In an age when sports were often dangerous, it is not surprising that ecclesiastical and political powers attempted to curb some activities. The Church was especially unsympathetic toward games that involved gambling, quarreling, and injury. Ecclesiastics attempted to curb dances, games, and sports when they interfered with religious observances on Sunday or holy days and when they were held in sacred places such as the churchyards and graveyards. On at least one occasion, merchants petitioned the government to forbid sports that led to riots and destruction of property. Accordingly in 1314, Edward II of England proclaimed that men playing football would be imprisoned for disturbing the peace. Edward III and other kings issued edicts declaring all sports illegal, with the exception of archery, which had a military usefulness. A number of laws restricted the playing of games in areas where they would be a nuisance or hazard, such as avenues of the Palace of Westminster while Parliament was in session. These governmental regulations were not always effectively enforced and did not diminish the people's love of sporting activities.

Program of Physical Education

This section gives a general picture of the physical education activities from about the eleventh through the fourteenth centuries. Most of the background material is from England, some from France and Italy, and a little from Germany.

The games played by children in England included base or prisoner's bars, hunt the fox, hunt the hare, cat and mouse, puss in the corner, leap frog, hop-scotch, marbles, tops, odd-even, duck and drake, bait the bear, kites, windmills, diving for apples, bob-cherry, hoodman blind, and hot cockles. Some children's pastimes were also popular with adults, particularly running games, such as base or bars, and blindfold games. Many a village holiday was made merrier by a combat between two blindfolded men. Holding a stick in one hand and a rope that was attached to a stake in the other, both men went round and round trying to hit a pig or goose that had been let loose with them. The spectators laughed heartily as the men thrashed about blindly striking the air or one another more often than the animal.

William Fitzstephen, who died about 1190, wrote an interesting account of the pastimes of schoolboys in twelfth century London. Many of the activities he described reflect the influence of chivalric education.

Every year also at Shrove Tuesday, that we may begin with the children's sports, seeing we all have been children, the schoolboys do bring cocks of the game to their master, and all the forenoon they delight themselves in cockfighting: after dinner, all the youths go into the fields to play at the ball. The scholars of every school have their ball, or baton, in their hands; the ancient and wealthy men of the city come forth on horseback to see the sport of the young men, and to take part of the pleasure in beholding their agility. Every Friday in Lent a fresh company of young men comes into the field on horseback, and the best horsemen conducteth the rest. Then march forth the citizens' sons, and other young men, with disarmed lances and shields, and there they practise feats of war. . . .

In Easter holidays they fight battles on the water [boat quintain]; a shield is hung upon a pole, fixed in the midst of the stream, a boat is prepared without oars, to be carried by violence of the water, and in fore part thereof standeth a young man, ready to give charge upon the shield, with his lance; if so be he breaketh his lance against the shield, and doth not fall, he is thought to have performed a worthy deed; if so be, without breaking his lance, he runneth strongly against the shield, down he falleth into the water, for the boat is violently forced with the tide; but on each side of the shield ride two boats, furnished with young men, which recover him that falleth as soon as they may. Upon the bridge, wharfs and houses, by the river's side, stand great numbers to see and laugh thereat.

In the holidays all the summer the youths are exercised on leaping, dancing, shooting, wrestling, casting the stone, and practising their shields; the maidens trip in their timbrels, and dance as long as they can well see.

When the great fen, or moor, which watereth the walls of the city on the north side, is frozen, many young men play upon the ice; some, striding as wide as they may, do slide swiftly; others make themselves seats of ice, as great as millstones; one sits down, many hand in hand to draw him, and one slipping on a sudden, all fall together; some tie bones to their feet and under their heels; and shoving themselves by a little picked staff, do slide as swiftly as a bird flieth in the air, or an arrow out of a cross-bow. Sometime two run together with poles, and hitting one the other, either one or both do fall, not without hurt; some break their arms, some their legs, but youth desirous of glory in this sort exerciseth itself against the time of war. Many of the citizens do delight themselves in hawks and hounds; for they have liberty of hunting in Middlesex, Hertfordshire, all Chiltern, and in Kent to the water of Cray.[17]

During the era when towns were growing rapidly, the sports of chivalric education were beginning to decline. Tournaments and knightly sports did not disappear quickly as the common people began to imitate the old aristocratic sports. Townsmen and peasants held many games fashioned after tournaments; sometimes they contended seriously in the events, but later it became a fad to burlesque the old sports of knightly splendor. In the days of Edward III (1312–1377), an amusing tournament was held in which country people mounted on any beast they could find fought with flails. In France, the burgesses held tourneys, jousts, and *pas d'armes*, called by a variety of names. These rowdy events became immensely popular.

In Italy, in the thirteenth century and thereafter, certain games developed that performed the same function for the mechanics and artisans as the tournaments did for the knights. When the armed cavalry of the nobility declined in importance in warfare, the bulk of the communal armies was composed of guildsmen's sons who served as foot soldiers. In times of peace these boys participated in the rugged sports of a militant nature, such as *giuoco del mazzascudo*, *giuoco del ponte*, *palio*, and *giuoco del calcio*.

In most of the cities of Tuscany and Umbria during the thirteenth and fourteenth centuries, *giuoco del mazzascudo* was played. This game, resembling a tournament, was fought on foot with the club (*mazza*) and shield (*scudo*) as weapons. Customarily, the battle of clubs and shields took place in the village square.

The Companies entered the piazza, to the sound of music and with waving banners; each side taking up its position at its own *bocca*. Then

---

[17]William Fitzstephen, *Description of London*, as quoted in John Stow, *The Survey of London* (Manchester: George Routledge and Sons, 1893), pp. 118–19.

began a series of single combats, among lovers, upon whose shields were painted the faces of their ladies . . . by dint of blows and strength of arm, after the old knightly way. . . . Then, a blast of trumpets recalled the combatants to the ranks; a second blast, and both armies entered the lists, and took up their positions in ordered files. . . . At the third blast, the battle joined. . . . The struggle continued until one side or the other was beaten out of the field. . . .[18]

Giuoco del ponte, the mimic battle fought on the principal bridge of the city of Pisa from the close of the fifteenth century to 1804, appears to have been a variation of the old game of *mazzascudo*. The most celebrated of these events was held on January 17, the Feast of St. Anthony. Citizens living on the northern bank of the Arno were usually represented by six squadrons composed of thirty to sixty men each, who fought a like number of selected citizens of the southern bank.

In *ponte*, they no longer used the club and shield employed in *mazzascudo*, but substituted a *targone*. This narrow shield-shaped instrument of stout wood was about five times as long as it was wide at the top, with the bottom half the same width as the top. A contestant manipulated the weapon by means of two handles fastened in the same position as the arm straps of a shield would be. This shield was used apparently both to thrust and parry. Despite the fact that the game of *ponte* was rough, few mortal accidents occurred because the participants were well protected by iron helmets, leather doublets as well as breast and back pieces of iron, and thick, padded gauntlets.

The colorful and imposing ceremonies and pageantry associated with the *ponte* were characteristic of the Renaissance. On the day of the game all attention was focused on the bridge. When the air was rent by the blast of trumpet notes, the armies on either side of the river marched across the bridge toward one another until they met at the dividing line. At first the men were able to do no more than push and shove, but as more room was available with the breaking of ranks, contestants began to jab with the *targone* or to wield them as clubs. Some men tumbled off the bridge and continued to struggle in the water. The object, of course, was to rout the enemy and capture his territory.

The *palio*, a race, was the favorite sport of many medieval Italian communes. The word *palio* itself means flag or banner, as the practice in medieval times was to offer yards of silk or woolen cloth known as *palii* as prizes for winning horse races. Eventually, *palio* came to signify not only the prize for the contest, but the race itself. Although the *palio* was generally a horse race, it could be a foot race, chariot race, donkey race,

---

[18]William Heywood, *Palio and Ponte, An Account of the Sports of Central Italy from the Age of Dante to the XXth Century* (London: Methuen and Co., 1904), pp. 102–3.

or even a boat race. These races, or *palii*, seem to have originated during the thirteenth century.

Although almost all Italian holidays were religious in nature, they also were graced with colorful dramatic processions and enlivened with exciting *palii*. A brief listing indicates the multiplicity of the races: *palii* given in honor of guild saints, *palii* given to commemorate a battle, to celebrate the deliverance from the rule of a tyrant, to placate the divine vengeance, to celebrate a city's release from excommunication, and to celebrate the arrival of sacred relics. The most famous Florentine *palio* was held for St. John the Baptist. In honor of the Virgin, the Pisans conducted both land and water *palii*. On the first Sunday in Lent Verona held two *palii*; the first was a horse race and the second a foot race. Later, a third *palio*, a foot race for women, was added. Sienna, in mid-August, celebrated the famous religious festival and great fair in homage to the Assumption of the Virgin. As early as 1200, this occasion included processions and dancing in the piazza, revelry and amusements by buffoons and jugglers, and about 1310 the *palio* was added to the activities. This event with all its medieval trappings still survives.

A colorful parade took place on the day of the *palio*. Trumpeteers and fifers in bright green and blue liveries raised their silver instruments to produce a spirited tune. Behind them came the horsemen riding two by two, and then the parade of people carrying candles. Finally, the *palio*, the prize, was borne on an oxcart. It could be a beautiful piece of gold brocade or yards of luxurious, scarlet velvet, fashioned by a master craftsman through months of exacting labor. Similar to races today, the horses were ridden by jockeys dressed in the colors of their employers. In later times, the *palii* were less closely associated with religion. The prizes increased in value, and racing became a rich man's sport.

Giuoco del calcio, in the early days, was a free-for-all fist fight with the ball playing an insignificant part in the game. By the sixteenth century, the game had evolved into a sport that resembled rugby. A rectangular area fenced in by posts and rails served as the playing field. One side of the field was called "the wall" and the other "the ditch." Players, hitting the ball with their fists or feet, attempted to force it over the opponents' "goal line," which extended across the entire end of the field. A touchdown was called a *caccia*, and the team making the greater number of *caccie* won the game. A player was allowed to kick, strike, throw the ball, or to run with it. There were certain fouls in the game, such as kicking the ball into the "ditch" side, and two fouls were equal to a *caccia*. Teams changed sides after a *caccia* or two fouls had been scored.

Twenty-seven men played on a team in *calcio*: fifteen forwards, who followed the ball and usually dribbled it, five halfbacks who tried to break the rush of the opposing forwards, four threequarters who gave direct blows to the ball, and three fullbacks. This game, developed much later than the others.

Sports were taking hold in other parts of Europe during the later Middle Ages. Archery had been employed in the old feudal armies, but it became increasingly important at the beginning of the fourteenth century, especially in England. When the country no longer depended upon the armed lancers for protection, but upon the archers, kings made the practice of archery compulsory. In view of the war with France, King Edward III issued the following proclamation of 1365:

> We . . . command you . . . that everyone of the said City, strong in Body, at leisure Times on Holidays, use in their Recreation Bows and Arrows . . . and learn and exercise the Art of Shooting; forbidding all and singular on our Behalf, that they do not after any Manner apply themselves to the throwing of Stones, Wood, Iron, Hand-Ball, Football, Bandy-ball, Cambuck, or Cockfighting, nor such other vain Plays, which have no Profit in them, or concern themselves therein, under Pain of Imprisonment. Witness the King at Westminster, the twelfth Day of June.[19]

Richard II passed a similar law some forty years later, and the law was reenacted by Henry IV in 1401. In 1447, the Commons petitioned the king that ". . . no person should use any unlawful plays [such] as dice, quoits, football and such like plays, but that every person mighty and able in body should use his bow, because that the defence of this land standeth much by archers."[20] The years English youth spent in perfecting their marksmanship were rewarded by important victories against the French at Crécy, Poitiers, and Agincourt.

The crossbow and the longbow were both used during the Middle Ages. The crossbow was introduced by Genoese archers and was used during the Crusades. This weapon, which was shorter than the longbow, was fastened on a stock and discharged by means of a catch or trigger. It had to be "cocked" before each shot, and in this interval a longbowman could shoot several arrows. The Englishmen preferred the longbow, because it had greater velocity and range than the crossbow. The longbows were about the height of a man and the arrows used at Agincourt were a yard in length.

Despite the fact that Edward III and later monarchs attempted to force every man to practice archery to the exclusion of every other pastime in England, many other sports were pursued, particularly wrestling, quoits, bowling, handball, bat-and-ball games, football, and tennis.

[19]Sir Walter Besant, *Mediaevel London, Historical and Social* (London: Adam and Charles Black, 1906), 1: 74.
[20]G. G. Coulton, *Medieval Panorama* (New York: The Macmillan Co., 1938), p. 596.

Wrestling bouts were frequently held between English towns, and almost any village festival provided this sport as part of the entertainment. "The citizens of London, in times past, are said to have been expert in the art of wrestling, and annually upon St. James day they were accustomed to make a public trial of their skill."[21] The wrestling bouts of ancient London were more like a battle than a friendly competitive sport. The sport became such a nuisance that, in the time of Henry IV, 1411, a proclamation was made forbidding wrestling within the city of London under threat of forty days' imprisonment.

Quoits was a popular pastime in the Middle Ages. Probably the sport originated from the ancient practice of soldiers amusing themselves by bending an old horseshoe into a circle and casting it like a discus. Throwing for distance was replaced by a game relying on skill more than strength, in which players attempted to toss at stakes.

In many respects, tennis, *jeu de paume*, and fives, which are mentioned so frequently in the literature, were similar games. Fives, referring to the fingers of the hand, was a type of handball originating in Ireland, and it was also played in England. The French game of *jeu de paume* (palm), later known as court tennis, is not to be confused with modern lawn tennis. It evolved as a definite game in the thirteenth century and became increasingly popular. The French enjoyed an outdoor as well as an indoor version of the sport. Some authorities are of the opinion the game originated in the monasteries and Church schools, for the sport was particularly enjoyed in ecclesiastical circles. The tennis court may have received its shape from the cloisters in which early games were played. Outdoors, the French played over an embankment rather than a net. Originally, the ball was hit with the palm of the hand rather than a racquet. At first the wool-stuffed leather ball was quite large, but later it was reduced in size. The earliest indoor court was probably built in France in 1230. Tennis became popular in England under Edward III, who built a court in his palace and encouraged the sport.

The Romans were familiar with bowling and possibly some Roman soldiers brought the game into northern Europe. A bowling game played with pins was practiced in Germany, perhaps first in the churches and later among the upper class laymen. Early pins, alleys, and balls were rather crude. The outdoor alleys of the fourteenth century were of clay or cinders. Rules for the game differed in various cities, for in 1300 A.D. only three pins were used in some parts of Germany, while as many as seventeen were employed in other places. Bowling at pins spread throughout the low countries and became very popular, but it was not fashionable in France, England, Italy, Scotland, or Ireland.

The English, instead, were enthusiastic about lawn bowling, or bowls,

---

[21] Joseph Strutt, *The Sports and Pastimes of the People of England* (London: Wm. Tegg and Co., 1850), pp. 80–81.

which was played at least as early as the thirteenth century. Strutt has given this description of the game: "Here are two small cones placed upright at a distance from each other; and the business of the players is evidently to bowl at them alternately; the successful candidate being he who could lay his bowl the nearest to the mark."[22] Lawn bowling was sufficiently popular in England in 1299 to warrant the organizing of the Southhampton Town Bowling Club in that year.

Billiards may have evolved when men attempted to adapt lawn bowls to indoor conditions. These experimenters varied the game to suit the confined indoor areas by using sticks of wood to hit the ball and ruling that the ball had to pass through certain arches before approaching the goal. Eventually, however, sportsmen transferred the game to the table, the sticks becames cues, and the arches were discarded in favor of pockets. Thus, lawn bowls evolved into a game resembling modern pocket billiards. When this development took place, the old game formerly played with sticks on the floor was revived as croquet.

Games played with a bat and ball, possible forerunners of cricket, were in evidence in the reign of Edward III. According to Strutt,[23] goff or bandy-ball, at this time called by its old Roman name of "cambuca," was played with a leather ball stuffed with feathers and a bat called a bandy. Club ball was similar to goff except that one was played with a curved bat and the other a straight one. Strutt classifies trapball as "anterior to cricket," placing it back as far as the fourteenth century. The trap used to elevate the ball, which was struck by the batsman, gave the game its name.

A primitive type of football was probably played in England as early as the twelfth century. Football was always strictly a kicking game; carrying the ball in the hands as in rugby did not originate until the nineteenth century. When rugby developed, the old kicking game of football became referred to as soccer. (American football, which is largely a blend of soccer and rugby, is comparatively recent.)

Football was a rough sport that gave vent to the animal spirits of townsmen and peasants alike. Scores of men of nearby villages would meet at a midpoint, and each team would try to kick the ball through the city gates of their rivals, or some other prearranged goal. The goal posts of modern football symbolize these simple origins. Attempts were made from time to time to abolish the sport, partly because men were neglecting archery and partly because of the roughness of the game. A monastic chronicler of the fifteenth century stated:

> "The game at which they had met for common recreation is called by some the foot-ball-game. It is one in which young men, in country

[22]Ibid., p. 266.
[23]Ibid., pp. 102–08.

sport, propel a huge ball not by throwing it into the air but by striking and rolling it along the ground and that not with their hands but with their feet. A game, I say, abominable enough, and, in my judgement at least, more common, undignified, and worthless than any other kind of game, rarely ending but with some loss, accident, or disadvantage to the players themselves."[24]

The British love of racing may have developed from their early horse shows. In the twelfth century, at Smithfield, just outside of London, horse sales were conducted every Friday. Citizens of the town and nobles attended these events to watch the boys ride the spirited steeds. Fitzstephen related, "The boys who mount the wing-footed by threes or twos according to the match . . . contended for the love of praise and hope of victory, plunge spurs into the loose-reined horses, and urge them none the less with whips and shouts."[25] The men at the horse sales who took great interest in these races began to include them in other affairs.

Although the ecclesiastics sought to curb dancing throughout the Middle Ages, considerable evidence indicates that the people did not heed their admonitions. In France, and more particularly in Spain, the dance remained a vital part of the life of the people. Sacred dances continued to be performed in the Spanish churches. In the Cathedral of Seville, for instance, choreographic celebrations of the Nativity and dances of choirboys were presented. In the southern countries the religious pageantry was heightened by the dance. Strolling ballet groups would dance in religious parades—usually a dramatic presentation of allegorical scenes—while the litter bearing the costly statues of patron saints of the guild proceeded through the streets.

Despite the frequent synods and councils condemning dancing, the common people loved to participate in this form of recreation. They celebrated their patron saints' days, weddings, May days, and harvest festivals with dancing. The folk dances were usually tumultuous and vigorous, with much jumping, hopping, and whirling.

Methods of Physical Education

At this time youths received little formal instruction in physical education. Presumably they acquired their skills in sports and games through the imitation of others, helpful suggestions from older players, and actual participation. On some holidays, games for children preceded or followed those of adults, thus stimulating the youngsters to imitate the skill of their elders.

[24]Cited in Coulton, *Five Centuries of Religion*, pp. 83–4.
[25]As quoted in Stow, *The Survey of London*, p. 27.

PHYSICAL EDUCATION FOR INTELLECTUAL DISCIPLINE

From the eleventh to the fifteenth centuries a gradual intellectual awakening occurred in the Christian world. Cities continued to grow as commerce and trade developed. The emerging national governments, as well as the Church, needed educated men to carry out administrative duties. The enthusiasm for scholarship also increased, especially in the fields of law, theology, and medicine. This era also saw progress in art, architecture, and the development of a vernacular literature.

From the sixth to the eleventh centuries, the teachings and beliefs of the Church went largely unchallenged. As a result of their contact with Moslem culture, Crusaders brought back to Europe new religious views, and concepts of Aristotelian science and dialectics. These ideas stimulated a new skepticism which asserted itself in the Christian world and stimulated intellectual activity.

The Church had previously been hostile toward any rationalistic attempts to defend the revealed truths; by the eleventh century, its attitude had changed. The theologians attempted to vanquish heresy by rendering the doctrine of the Church intelligible to reason. This philosophical process was known as scholasticism. The theological scholars sought to define, systematize, and restate Church doctrine, supporting the revealed truths by logic and reasoning to answer any challenge of dogma. Some outstanding scholastics were Scotus Erigena, Anselm, Abélard, Peter Lombard, Albertus Magnus, and Thomas Aquinas.

The founding of universities was a natural outgrowth of the quickening intellectual interests. Students flocked to the cities where great teachers lectured. Many of the northern institutions, such as the University of Paris, sprang from the old cathedral schools in which the clergy had pursued dialectics and scholastic theology, but some institutions had a somewhat different origin. In the south, students gathered at Salerno, which had developed into an intellectual center of medical learning because of contacts with Jewish and Arabic scholars as well as with some ancient Greek writings. Northern Italian cities, such as Bologna, attracted men to study law as a result of the rediscovery of *Justinians Digest* and the current needs for defining law. By the time of the Renaissance there were seventy-nine universities in Europe.

Aims of Education

The scholastics labored diligently to support the beliefs of the Church. Using dialectic arguments, they sought to strengthen Church authority and its theological foundations. Scholasticism was a narrow and exacting, essentially theological, intellectual discipline, but it also influenced the study of law and medicine. Later ages severely criticized scholasticism;

nevertheless, this movement legitimatized intellectual interests after centuries of scholastic inactivity in the Christian world, and produced scholars in a society that had few learned men.

The universities that originated during the later Middle Ages aimed to train men for leadership in three fields: the Church, government, and teaching. Within these new educational institutions, men explored the knowledge acquired from the Moors and ancient Latin and Greek sources and endeavored to make this learning harmonious with the beliefs of the Church.

Aims of Physical Education

Scholasticism was devoted to definite and limited intellectual objectives. Because of the preoccupation with theological scholasticism, and because many ascetic attitudes toward the body still persisted, the need for physical education went unheeded. External uncleanliness and health negligences were thought to be no hindrance to the elevation of the mind. St. Thomas Aquinas did give some limited praise to the value of bodily exercise in the development of man, but for the most part scholastics ignored such an idea.

Promotion of Physical Education

About the eleventh century, the monasteries began to decline in educational importance. Cathedral and parish schools operated by the secular clergy gradually became the dominant educational institutions. In each parish, children were supposed to receive some elementary education from the priest, at least in the elements of religion. The cathedral schools, established to train the clergy of each bishopric became agencies of higher learning. Largely from the cathedral schools, but also from monastic and secular origins, the universities were established. None of these gave formal attention to physical education, but they did bring young men of many nations together and these men participated in some unorganized sports and games.

Universities did not possess campuses. They were merely guild associations of students and masters, with representatives from the two groups performing the executive duties. Outside of the classrooms, students organized themselves according to the nation of their origin. The professors, also organized into guilds, came to be divided into four faculties: arts, law, medicine, and theology. Students first studied liberal arts and then theology, although some devoted themselves to law or medicine. As corporations, the universities secured many rights, privileges, and immunities from civil and Church authorities.

Program of Physical Education

Physical education was not part of the university curriculum, nor did the university authorities encourage participation in sports and games outside of school. No doubt the lack of physical education resulted in leisure-time activities of a degraded nature. Students participated in street brawls, boisterous practical jokes, carousals, drinking, gambling, vice, serious fights between "town and gown" (citizens against students), and mortal combats between "nations." The famous St. Scolastica's Day riot of 1354 between town and gown started as a quarrel in a tavern and ended in an armed battle in which many students were wounded and some killed.

When university authorities did take cognizance of recreational activities, they usually acted in a negative or hostile manner. Some of their restrictions are quite understandable, for in that day many games and sports involved gambling and were so rough and undisciplined that they caused damage to life and property. The Statutes of Kings College included some typical prohibitions of the early universities. No student was to keep hunting or fishing nets, or ferrets, falcons, or dogs. Playing dice, hazard, ball, and all sports involving gambling were prohibited. Students could not shoot arrows, cast or hurl stones, javelins, wood, or clods in the precincts of the college where property might be destroyed. Dancing and wrestling were also forbidden in the Chapel, Cloister, or Hall, because of the possible damage to reredos and windows. At Montpelier, students who danced outside of their own houses would be expelled, and some institutions penalized youths who went about the city singing and dancing in masked bands. Although hawking was permitted at St. Andrews, the dangerous game of football was forbidden. In some schools, bathing in the river was against the rules.

There are enough references to university students participating in sports to indicate that such activity was not entirely suppressed by the authorities. During the time of Peter Abélard when "the lecture [was] over, the stream would flow back over the Little Bridge, filling the taverns and hospices, and pouring out over the great playing meadow, that stretched from the island to the present Champ de Mars. All the games of Europe were exhibited on that international playground; running, jumping, wrestling, hurling, fishing and swimming in the Seine, tossing and thumping the inflated ball . . . and especially the great game of war, in its earlier and less civilized form. The nations were not yet systematically grouped, and long and frequent were the dangerous conflicts."[26] A tournament or a dance was sometimes given at the installation of the rector of a university. The founder of Corpus Christi allowed moderate hawking

---

[26]Joseph McCabe, *Peter Abélard* (New York: G. P. Putnam's Sons, 1901), pp. 79–80.

and hunting on holidays as well as games of ball for the sake of healthy exercise.

When scholars began to study medicine more intensely, one might expect that greater interest in the body and health would be exhibited. Significant progress in anatomy and physiology was not made at this time, however, for men were studying rather inadequate translations and not directly from Greek sources. The study of anatomy was considerably handicapped because medical schools were only allowed to dissect a corpse for students every two or more years.

Methods of Physical Education

Scholasticism was an intellectual and religious training. Very precise methods of study in logical analysis, syllogistic reasoning, disputation, and debate, as well as lectures were employed. Physical education was never a part of the curriculum.

7

Physical Education
in
Humanistic Education

The seeds of progress sown in the Middle Ages came to bloom in the Renaissance. There were many complex factors which contributed to Europe's general awakening. Contacts with Moslem learning, the rediscovery of Aristotle's writings, the establishment of universities, all were the stirrings of a new spirit of inquiry. The Crusades, revealing the cultural wonders of the East, foreign peoples, new ideas, and new trade possibilities, stimulated intensive economic and intellectual activity. With all of these stimulating events taking place, medieval man was no longer content to preoccupy himself completely with "otherwordliness."

Just as the growth of trade and commerce undermined the structure of feudalism, the new spirit of intellectual inquiry undermined the structure of scholasticism. The Renaissance man was not merely intrigued with foreign goods and ideas, but also was convinced that the ideas discovered in classical literature held the key to civilization. Acquaintance with the Greek and Roman classics increased his resistance to the suppression of personality that had characterized medieval life. The new era released mental activity from the limited areas of theology and encouraged the free development of the individual's aptitudes. The new humanistic environment nourished the genius of a distinctive group of men who collected, corrected, restored, interpreted, and imitated classical literature and art and modified the moral and educational assumption of the medieval world.

This unfolding of the free intellect and creative spirit took place in a turbulent world. The era was characterized not only by commercial and intellectual activity, but also by the destructive influences of chronic war, the struggles between the Church and secular authorities, the oppressive rule of tyrannical despots, the rumbling of peasant revolts, and the horror of devastating plagues. The Renaissance was constantly in the shadow of the Black Death which struck terror in men's minds comparable to the threat of the atomic bomb today. Authorities estimate that one-third of the Italian population perished from the plague. Nevertheless, this vibrant and challenging era was studded with men of genius, including Leonardo da Vinci, Michelangelo, Cellini, Columbus, Magellan, Galileo, Luther, Gutenberg, and Rabelais.

Three great movements swept Europe between the fourteenth and seventeenth centuries: *Humanism*, the first to appear, was followed by *Moralism* and *Realism*. These three movements did not start everywhere at the same time nor did they progress at a uniform rate, or in the same way. In this and the next two chapters, the purpose is to trace the origin and development of each movement rather than to study distinct historical periods.

Humanism originated in Italy and was later carried to the countries over the Alps. Because Humanism manifested itself somewhat differently in Southern and Northern Europe, the two phases will be discussed separately in this chapter. The educational movement in Italy represents *individual humanism*; and the later movement of Northern Europe, *social humanism*.

PHYSICAL EDUCATION IN INDIVIDUAL HUMANISM

Italy was the nursery of the humanistic movement, for feudalism had never crushed Italian individualism into complete submission. The Italian peninsula provided the natural environment for a revival of learning: it had many towns, including some Roman ruins, the vernacular was similar to Latin, and some Roman literature had remained as a part of the culture. Moreover, many Greek scholars sought refuge in Italy after Constantinople fell to the Turks in 1453. Sufficient wealth and leisure also existed in Italian cities of the Renaissance to promote a revival of Greek, a restoration of Latin, and a reevaluation of what the classics had to say.

Petrarch, the first modern scholar, exemplified the spirit of Humanism. By replacing logic and scholastic philosophy with the classical studies, he did much to initiate the critical spirit that inaugurated the Renaissance and hastened the destruction of medieval dogmatism.

The work that Petrarch initiated was carried on by a distinguished group of scholars and schoolmasters. Petrus Paulus Vergerius (1349–1420) wrote the first and most widely read humanistic tract on education entitled *On Good Morals and Liberal Studies* (*De Ingenius Moribus et Liberalibus*), which became the "textbook" of later schools and scholars.

Vittorino da Feltre (1378–1446) and Guarino da Verone (1370–1461) established the pioneer schools of humanism at Mantua and Ferrara, respectively. Leone Batista Alberti (1404–1472), a poet, artist, philosopher, musician, and architect, wrote a treatise, *On the Care of the Family,* which presented an interested layman's attitude toward education. Aeneas Sylvius Piccolomini, later Pope Pius II (1405–1464), discussed the proper training for youth in a letter, *De Liberorum Educatione.* Mapheus Vegius (1405–1458), a scholar of classical education who was associated closely with the Church, wrote a book entitled *On the Education of Children (De Educatione Liberorum).* Castiglione (1478–1529) portrayed the ideal, distinguished gentleman and cultured lady of knightly society in his famous book, *The Courtier (Il Cortegiano).*

Italian physicians were among those in the humanistic movement who emphasized the importance of physical education. Girolamo Cardano (1501–1576) and Hieronymus Mercurialis (1530–1606) were both familiar with classical scholarship and wrote books discussing the values of exercises in maintaining health.

Aims of Education

A changed point of view was reflected in the philosophies of the men who formulated the objectives of humanistic education. Leone Alberti, Vittorino da Feltre, and Aeneas Sylvius Piccolomini all reaffirmed the Athenian ideal of seeking the harmonious development of the whole personality. The humanists wanted to fashion a physically sound youth with an alert and fertile intellect; a citizen who was prepared to participate in the practical affairs of adult life; a cultured gentleman who was socially adept, skilled in arms, learned in letters, sensitive to beauty, and impeccable in manner. The humanists sought to reconcile the active civic and the contemplative scholarly life. How different were these ideals from the restrictive goals of Medieval education! This change has been expressed by an educational writer as follows:

> The education of the Middle Ages, over-rigid and repressive, which condemned the body to a regime too severe, and the mind to a discipline too narrow, is to be succeeded, at least in theory, by an education broader and more liberal; which will give due attention to hygiene and physical exercises . . . which will give the preference to things over words; which, finally, instead of developing but a single faculty, the reason, and instead of reducing man to a sort of dialectic automaton, will seek to develop the *whole* man, mind and body, taste and knowledge, heart and will.[1]

[1]Gabriel Compayré, *The History of Pedagogy* (Boston: D. C. Heath and Co., 1890), pp. 83–84.

Italian humanism provoked progress in all fields and reconstructed values of life. It synthesized Christian morality with Hellenic individualism, but failed to incite social action. Men were so preoccupied with their individual attainments and desires that existing traditions and conventions were never outwardly questioned. The extension of freedom and of self-expression became more and more unrestrained. Humanism suffered not only from this overindulgence in personal license, but also from Ciceronianism, so called because of a devotion to a narrow, formal training in the classical languages and literatures. Ciceronianism was hardly more liberal than scholasticism. The aesthetic, social, and physical goals of humanism were gradually removed from the program. Early humanism perished before it flourished, but later, its spirit united with other forces to contribute to the culture of the modern world.

Aims of Physical Education

Physical education was an integral part of early humanist education which sought the harmonious development of all aspects of man. Practically every great humanistic philosopher emphasized the need for devoting attention to physical development and proficiency. Many of them engaged in the mind-versus-body and arms-versus-letters debates and sought to effect a perfect marriage of these forces.

Vergerius, who believed that arms as well as letters were important in the training of a prince, argued, "We cannot forestall the reality of war . . . but by training and practice we can at least provide such preparation as the case admits."[2] Vegius recommended physical exercise "for training the youth in the arts of war which seem to be necessary both privately and publicly for preserving safety."[3] Pope Pius II, declared that "Every youth destined to exalted position should further be trained in military exercises. It will be your destiny to defend Christendom against the Turk."[4] Ecclesiastics and laymen both gave sanction to the military objective of physical education.

The humanists embraced the classical ideal of the "sound mind in the sound body" as the highest objective of physical education. An excellent physical organism was correlative to an active intellect. Alberti propounded that the body nourished the mind and that any defect in the body would damage the corresponding mental power. Vittorino once ob-

[2]W. H. Woodward, *Vittorino da Feltre and other Humanist Educators* (Cambridge: University Press, 1905), p. 115.

[3]Mapheus Vegius (Maphei Vegii Laudensis), *De Educatione Liberorum et Eorum Claris Moribus,* Libri Sex; A Critical Text of Book I–III by Sister Maria Walburg Fanning (Washington, D. C.: Catholic University of America Press, 1933), p. 106.

[4]Woodward, *Vittorino da Feltre,* p. 138.

served two youths discussing their lessons while other boys were out playing. Declaring that "it was not a good thing in a boy," he sent them off
to join the others in games. Vegius recommended exercises because they
make students ". . . more attentive and more eager, and there will be
avoided in them the thing which is wont to ruin any good disposition:
dejection and despondency."[5] Vittorino da Feltre along with other humanists believed that to maintain brisk intellectual activity, studies should
alternate with games and exercises to relax and refresh the mind from labor. Pope Pius II argued that an exercise developing muscular activity
and personal carriage ". . . not only cultivates grace of attitude but secures the healthy play of our bodily organs and establishes the constitution."[6] Alberti pointed out the necessity of gymnastics and sound health
as essential to the development of a harmoniously proportioned body.

The works of the great artists of the Renaissance gave proof that the
world once again viewed the human form as a revelation of beauty. The
humanists recommended physical education as a means of imbuing youth
with the self-discipline that could curb self-indulgence, effeminacy, and
habits that enervate the body and the mind. Physical skills were to be
performed with ease and grace, without ostentatious display, and one-
sided development of the body was to be rejected just as emphatically as
overneglect.

Promotion of Physical Education

Humanism found its first home in the privately established institutions for
the sons of wealthy merchants, bankers, and aristocrats. The ruling dukes
and the merchant princes of Italy, anxious to increase the fame of their
cities and their own personal prestige, lavished huge sums of money to
create fashionable, cultural centers of humanism. With such financial
backing Vittorino da Feltre, Guarino da Verona, and numerous other
schoolmasters put humanistic education into institutionalized form.

La Giocosa,[7] the court school established by Vittorino da Feltre, at
Mantua, exemplified one of the finest institutions of humanistic learning.
The school was a palace on a ridge that commanded a magnificent view
of the river valley. On three sides, it was surrounded by large grassy
meadows that provided an ample exercising and playing area. Vittorino
had the interior of the building stripped of all sumptuous furnishings and
had the walls redecorated with frescoes of children; the rooms were large,
sunny, and well-ventilated. The playgrounds and woods were considered
just as important parts of the school as the classrooms, and in summer

---

[5]Vegius, *De Educatione Liberorum*, p. 107.
[6]Woodward, *Vittorino da Feltre*, p. 138.
[7]Translated literally, "La Giocosa" means "The Pleasure House."

months, the excursions into the surrounding mountains and countryside further extended the facilities for learning. A cheerful, healthy, happy atmosphere pervaded La Giocosa; for Vittorino believed that a pleasant environment was conducive to good work as well as sound character.

Vittorino da Feltre also gave careful attention to the selection of the masters and attendants in his school so that his pupils would associate only with the most worthy characters. Vergerius directed that "tutors and comrades alike should be chosen from amongst those likely to bring out the best qualities, to attract by good example, and to repress first signs of evil."[8] Dancing masters were employed in court schools, and some of them gained great prominence by teaching classical dancing and preparing children to take part in the theatricals and processions that were so characteristic of Renaissance life.

Humanistic schools were organized rather informally. The activities and degree of participation in them were determined according to the individual needs and capacities of the child. Boys and girls were sometimes taught together and, for the most part, by the same methods. However the curriculum for girls was designed with consideration for their special aptitudes, personal vocations, and future social positions.

At La Giocosa, Vittorino and his staff instructed the Gonzaga children plus a group of selected youths from wealthy families, some of them from as far away as Germany. A few sons of outstanding scholars and some promising poor boys were also admitted. To all of them, Vittorino acted as father, looking out for their food and clothing, sharing in their games and pleasures, and supervising their manners and morals.

Program of Physical Education.

The medieval curriculum, so largely devoted to theology and dialectics, gave way in the Renaissance to the new humanistic learning. Students studied Greek and Latin—language, literature, and oratory—mathematics, moral philosophy, natural history, music, drawing, painting, and dancing, all augmented by physical training. However, the curriculum and the ideals the early leaders propounded and translated into action soon became narrowly intellectualized.

Vergerius, the early pioneer of humanistic studies, advocated that a youth should engage regularly in games and exercises that would prepare him for military duties, "So, too, our youth must learn the art of the sword, the cut, the thrust, and the parry; the use of the shield; of the spear; of the club; training either hand to wield the weapon. Further, swimming, . . . running, jumping, wrestling, boxing, javelin-throwing,

[8]Woodward, *Vittorino da Feltre*, p. 100.

archery, thorough horsemanship, in sport or in war—these are all need-ful to the full training of the soldier."[9]

Vergerius did not limit his recommended exercises and sports to a disciplined military program, but included a variety of activities for relaxation, although rejecting emphatically either coarse or effeminate pastimes. He advised the pursuit of activities requiring energy and vigor. He argued that it would be wiser if a boy ". . . found in the sharp exertion of ball-play the best refreshment alike for jaded spirits and for bodily fatigue. So, too, others seek recreation in hunting, hawking, or fishing and so keen is their enjoyment, that the severe efforts which these pursuits demand are cheerfully borne."[10]

In the school of Vittorino da Feltre, a continual outdoor program of exercise in all weather was compulsory. The boy participated in ball games, leaping, fencing, riding, running, and hiking. For those who would have to perform military duties as adults, exercises in arms were provided. Vittorino also devised a program of gymnastics to meet the needs of civilians. The health and diet of the boys were watched carefully.

The recommendation of Aeneas Sylvius Piccolomini (Pope Pius II) gave a greater support to physical education than was ever expressed by medieval churchmen. He favored racing, dancing, and swimming for women as well as men, and even discussed the need for sex education for children. In writing to the King of Bohemia about the proper education of a youth, he remarked,

> As regards a boy's physical training, we bear in mind that we aim at implanting habits which will prove beneficial through life. . . . A boy should be taught to hold his head erect, to look straight and fearlessly before him and to bear himself with dignity whether walking, standing, or sitting. . . . Games and exercises which develope the muscular activities and the general carriage of the person should be encouraged by every Teacher.[11]

The ideal personality, according to Alberti, was the product of some physical training. Censuring idleness, he advocated vigorous exercise as an excellent means of hardening the body and warding off sickness and infirmity. In his opinion, youths should engage in active sports involving dexterity, endurance, strength, skill, and coordination. Alberti recommended ball games, fencing, leaping, swimming, and riding, but he rejected tourneys as too rough.

Castiglione sketched the physical training of the ideal courtier as follows:

[9]Ibid., pp. 113–15.
[10]Ibid., p. 116.

[11]Ibid., pp. 137–38.

I would have him well built and shapely of limb, and would have him show strength and lightness and suppleness, and know all bodily exercises that befit a man of war: Whereof I think the first should be to handle every sort of weapon well on foot and on horse. . . . Moreover I deem it very important to know how to wrestle . . . and to play at tilting and jousting. . . . It is fitting also to know how to swim, to leap, to run, to throw stones. . . . Another admirable exercise, and one very befitting a man at court, is the game of tennis, in which are well shown the disposition of the boys, the quickness and suppleness of every member, and all those qualities that are seen in nearly every other exercise. Nor less highly do I esteem vaulting on horse, which although it be fatiguing and difficult, makes a man very light and dexterous more than any other thing; and besides its utility, if this lightness is accompanied by grace, it is to my thinking a finer show than any of the others.[12]

Although some humanists saw advantages in dancing, others condemned it as having a softening influence on the child. Vergerius feared the enticements of dancing might lead to immorality.[13] Vegius agreed. He argued, "Although Socrates and Scipio are recorded to have indulged in dancing occasionally, although these same sports were included by the Lacedaemonians among their exercises on the ground that they were useful for war, and although they were also prominent in the religious rites of the ancient Romans, in no way can we give our approval to them because they are the source and origin of many evils and cause young men to become wanton and corrupt."[14] Guarino da Verona, on the other hand, saw some virtue in dancing as an aid to graceful carriage. Castiglione also favored dancing of a dignified character. Some philosophers did not favor dancing, but aristocrats considered it a highly desirable social asset.

During the Renaissance, artists such as Leonardo da Vinci studied anatomy in order to portray the human form correctly. Renaissance painting reveals great technical perfection in depicting the muscular structure of men. Italian physicians also began to take new interest in the structure and function of the human body. Mercurialis in his tract, *De Arte Gymnastica*, described the ancient gymnasia and gymnastics and urged the employment of physical exercises for their hygienic value. Although the works of these medical scholars were largely compilations of the knowledge of the Greeks and the Romans, they served to encourage contemporaries to consider the greater use of exercise as a means of preserving health.

Disease and its relationship to the body were explored during the

---

[12]Count Baldesar Castiglione, *The Book of the Courtier*, trans. L. E. Opdycke (New York: Charles Scribner's Sons, 1903), pp. 29–31.
[13]Woodward, *Vittorino da Feltre*, p. 117.
[14]Vegius, *De Educatione Liberorum*, p. 109.

Renaissance. The hundreds of tracts from all parts of Europe that were written to explain the causes, symptoms, and treatment of the Black Plague were among the first large-scale attempts at instruction in public health. Most writers stressed the contagious nature of the disease and the necessity for isolation, quarantine, and fumigation; some mentioned the importance of cleanliness, sanitation, and moderation; others speculated about the corrupt, poisonous vapors in the air and the planetary influences. The age of scientific study had not arrived, but the new inquiries were creating an environment that would later encourage such development.

Methods of Physical Education

The humanistic educators considered how to teach as much as what to teach. Several writers stressed the importance of self-activity, self-expression, individual differences, progressive training, and positive discipline.

Basically, the humanists stressed emulation, having "the examples of living men, known and respected for their worth, . . . held up for a boy's imitation."[15]

One of the most refreshing ideas emphasized by the humanists was that the teacher should seek to understand and respect the personality of each individual. Vittorino maintained an ample staff and insisted upon small classes so that the instructors could become familiar with each student and fashion a program suitable for his abilities, temperament, and tastes. For a child in delicate health, Vittorino devised special exercises; for young aristocrats who would follow military careers, he emphasized drill in arms; for others, he provided a more general program of gymnastics. Vergerius was another scholar who recognized differences in personality. He urged, "In choice of bodily exercises . . . it will be necessary to consider to some extent the case of each individual boy."[16]

In the court schools, systematic methods of physical instruction required that care be taken to gradually increase the dosage and intensity of exercise observing constantly the specific condition of each child. Vergerius cautioned, "In childhood much care must be taken lest growth be hindered, or the nerves of the body be strained, by severe exertion. . . ."[17] Vegius urged that in the physical education of boys ". . . moderation ought to be employed, so that, until they have reached the age of puberty, they should be ordered to refrain from unnatural and violent exercises, lest their growth, which is a continuous process, he hindered."[18]

[15]Woodward, *Vittorino da Feltre*, p. 98.
[16]Ibid., p. 114.
[17]Ibid., p. 114.
[18]Vegius, *De Educatione Liberorum*, p. 106.

The personality of the teachers and the high level of interest they were able to stimulate in pupils rendered severe discipline unnecessary in schools such as Vittorino operated. The masters and boys lived more or less a communal life sharing pleasures, interests, and games. Alberti believed that subject matter should be made attractive and interesting, combining instruction with amusement to make it more enjoyable. Children were to be made conscious of their abilities and powers to do things, encouraged to participate in games and recreation, and urged to help one another. Constructive criticism, praise, and healthy rivalry between boys or sections of a class were methods employed to encourage youths to high endeavor. Pope Pius II expressed his idea of the proper type of discipline as follows:

> A boy must be won to learning by persuasive earnestness, and not be driven to it like a slave. . . . In fine, the master, as Juvenal says, does in reality exercise a parental function toward his pupil and should not be satisfied unless he attracts a corresponding filial affection.[19]

PHYSICAL EDUCATION IN SOCIAL HUMANISM

Humanistic studies did not reach northern Europe until a century after it had vitalized Italian cities. Intercourse with Italy, whether through the travels of students or military missions, eventually brought the countries of the north into close touch with the humanistic centers of the south. By the time the new learning had begun to decline in Italy, Italian students had wandered into France and Germany, spreading the spirit of humanism as they went. Northern students began to throng to Italy seeking the new learning. Humanism soon aroused the northern nations into a vigorous intellectual life. The movement was accelerated by the invention of the printing press (with movable type) by Johann Gutenberg, which made possible a rapid and extensive dissemination of the classics as well as the education treatises and research works of the Renaissance.

The struggle to introduce humanism in the north called for courageous and able men who were willing to battle against the conservative forces resisting reform. This challenge was met by Erasmus, Agricola, Melanchthon, Thomas à Kempis, Reuchlin, Wimpfeling, Sturm, Ascham, Elyot, Budaeus, Corderius, and Thomas More. These pioneering scholars expanded the curriculums in existing schools, organized new humanistic universities and secondary schools, and labored to secure royal support for the new educational movement.

Towering above all of his contemporaries was the Dutch scholar, Desiderius Erasmus (c. 1466–1536), a bitter foe of credulity and ignor-

---

[19]Woodward, *Vittorino da Feltre*, p. 137.

ance and a dynamic reformer. Convinced that education was the most effective means of reforming current abuses, he published the classics that he thought best suited to improve society, prepared Latin and Greek grammars and textbooks, and produced a number of educational treatises. The influence of Erasmus extended throughout Europe and stimulated many others to participate in the humanistic movement. Among them, the men who made the greatest contribution to physical education, were two Englishmen, Sir Thomas Elyot and Roger Ascham.

Aims of Education

The north European educators modified the spirit of humanism, but the fundamental principles remained intact. Elements of the new Italian learning were selected and adapted to meet the needs of the various national groups. "The peoples of the North, especially those of Germanic stock, were naturally more religious than the brilliant and mercurial Italians. With them the Renaissance led less to a desire for personal development, self-realization, and individual achievement, and took on more of a social and moral color."[20] The aim of education for these humanists was not so much the glory of the individual as the advancement of mankind.

In discussing the broad aims of the new learning, Erasmus suggested, "The first and most important part is that the youthful mind may absorb the seeds of piety; next, that it may love and thoroughly learn the liberal arts; third, that it may be prepared for the duties of life; and fourth, that it may from the earliest years be straight-way accustomed to the rudiments of good manners."[21] The northern humanists hoped through education to achieve reform by eradicating the ignorance and superstition upon which abuses bred.

Although northern education was somewhat restricted to social and religious ideals, it nevertheless possessed a critical, investigating, and intellectual spirit. After 1600, however, these characteristics began to disappear and the classics were no longer read to capture their spirit and meaning. Learning degenerated into a formal study of language, style, and form. This Ciceronian humanism unfortunately remained the dominant educational pattern for several generations.

Aims of Physical Education

Some northern European educators were cognizant of the organic unity of body and mind and recognized a constant interplay between them, but

[20]F. P. Graves, *History of Education during the Middle Ages and the Transition to Modern Times* (New York: The Macmillan Company, 1910), p. 141.
[21]Ibid., p. 151.

as a group they never grasped the concept of physical education held by the early Italian humanists. Erasmus, who clung somewhat to asceticism and stressed the difference between the ignoble body and the divine soul, designated the position that physical education held in social humanism when he declared, "We are not concerned with developing athletes, but scholars and men competent to affairs, for whom we desire adequate constitution indeed, but not the physique of a Milo."[22] Although Erasmus attached some significance to the importance of physical exercise in childhood to prepare the body for future intellectual labors, he never attained the Greek feeling for physical beauty and fitness.

Unlike their contemporaries in the Church, schools, and colleges, Sir Thomas Elyot and Roger Ascham who were associated with the Tudor court, seem to have been profoundly inspired by the earlier humanistic attitude toward physical education. Being interested in the education of the young courtier, who was to serve as a statesman and a soldier, they directed their physical education programs toward preparation for military life, promotion of mental alacrity, and maintenance of health. Elyot advised, ". . . it were moche better to be occupied in honest recreation than to do nothynge."[23] He cautioned that continual study without some exercise would exhaust the spirit, hinder the digestion, and make man's body subject to sickness. Roger Ascham, living a little later than Elyot, expressed a similar interest in physical fitness for youth.

It is difficult to determine the causes for the general indifference toward physical education in the north, but a number of complex conditions may have been responsible. When north European educators became interested in adopting the new learning in their countries, they did not come in contact with the schools of Vittorino da Feltre, but instead with those later institutions that had drifted toward Ciceronianism. Early Italian humanists had emphasized the all-around development of the individual and thus had readily recognized the value of physical education. German humanism, which focused more upon social and religious reform than upon the individual, never became fully aware of this value. Furthermore, the northern humanists were so quickly plunged into the Reformation that they did not have full opportunity to extend their educational ideals to include the physical development of youth. When the new learning was introduced into Church schools and universities in the north these institutions, unlike the knightly court schools in Italy, had no tradition of physical education in their program upon which to draw.

[22]Desiderius Erasmus, *De Pueris Instituendis*, trans. W. H. Woodward, *D. Erasmus Concerning the Aim and Method in Education* (Cambridge: University Press, 1904), p. 202.

[23]Sir Thomas Elyot, *The Boke Named The Governour* (London: Kegan Paul, Trench, and Co., 1883), 1:269.

Promotion of Physical Education

Humanism was first introduced into the existing schools of Europe and other institutions were gradually organized to carry out the aims of the new learning. The Brethren of the Common Life, a nonmonastic humanitarian group dedicated to teaching, were pioneers in bringing the classical studies to northern Europe. The German Prince Schools, or *Fürstenschülen*, were like the court schools of Italy. The *Gymnasium*, formed from the existing burgher and cathedral schools, represented the best humanistic secondary schools in Germany. The term "gymnasium" did not imply physical education; the name was derived from the ancient gymnasia of Greece and the curriculum was classical and religious. When Colet founded St. Paul's school in London, he introduced the new learning and, shortly thereafter, all the grammar schools associated with guilds, cathedrals, monasteries, and parish churches were fashioning themselves after this model. The universities, which had long harbored scholasticism and sometimes offered opposition to the new learning, gradually began to accept the classical studies.

Physical education was recommended in a few educational treatises, but a definite program was never adopted. Students did participate in some games and sports, but usually as extracurricular events enjoyed during free time or on holidays, rather than as organized class activities. Many youths, whether studying with private tutors or at school, received instruction in sports, games, and dances from special masters.

Sports, games, and exercises were not closely associated with Renaissance schools, but a variety of activities were sponsored by the courts and guilds. Henry VIII constructed tennis courts at Hampton Court in 1529, a royal cockpit in St. James Field, and bowling alleys at Whitehall. Many Italian masters were imported to provide instruction in fencing, falconry, riding and hunting.

Fencing schools sprang up throughout Europe, and some social fencing guilds were formed. One of the most famous fencing associations in Germany was the Bürgerschaft von St. Marcus von Löwenberge, founded in 1480. The members, called Marxbrüders, held fencing examinations once a year and gave letters of privilege to candidates who were to be allowed to teach. In England in the first half of the sixteenth century, a guild called Masters of the Noble Science of Defense was formed which held examinations for fencers. In France, the *Academie d'Armes*, an association of fencing masters, was organized about 1570 and was recognized by Henry III.

Fencing schools, bowling greens, tennis courts, cockpits, and bearbaiting pits were favorite centers of amusement. During the pleasure-loving Renaissance, life was enlivened by the rich pageantry of sumptuous religious feasts, dramatic carnival masques, gay public festivals, and magnificent jousts and tournaments. In Venice citizens enjoyed two hundred fete days which included religious parades, regattas, sham fights, bull and bear baiting contests and acrobatic contests. It was indeed a merry England where the citizens "take pleasure to see some pageant or sight go by, as at a coronation, wedding and such like solemn niceties; to see an ambassador or a prince received and entertained with masks, shows and fireworks. The country hath also his creations, as may-games, feasts, fairs and wakes. . . ."[24]

Program of Physical Education

Although a few northern European educators advocated physical education, the broad program of the Italian court schools was not adopted by the secondary institutions of northern Europe. Physical education was not a part of formal education until the eighteenth century.

Few humanists were as concerned with the physical development of the child as Thomas Elyot, a contemporary of Henry VIII. In *The Boke Named the Governour*, he devoted attention to the physical education activities for youth. Running, hunting, and hawking were acceptable, and wrestling won Elyot's approval if proper precautions were taken to prevent injury. Lifting and throwing heavy stones or bars, exercising with dumbbells, and play at tennis were recommended. He thought swimming an honorable exercise that would prove profitable in war in addition to such military activities as riding spirited horses and managing the sword, battle-axe, and longbow. Although the English educator preferred vigorous exercises, he would tolerate playing at cards, "tables" (backgammon), and chess because some wit was employed. Idleness and play at dice were condemned by Elyot, but dancing received his approval. Elyot devoted seven chapters of his book to dancing and declared, "I am nat of that opinion that all daunsinge generallye is repugnant unto vertue."[25] He described football as unfit for a gentleman, ". . . wherein is nothinge but beastly furie and exstreme violence; wherof precedeth hurte, and consequently rancour and malice do remaine with them that be wounded."[26] A considerable portion of his book was devoted to physical education and each activity recommended was thoroughly documented from classical sources.

Roger Ascham, who became tutor to Princess Elizabeth, later Queen of England, discussed his concept of the proper physical education in *The Scholemaster*. He urged that ". . . young gentlemen should use, and

[24]Joseph Strutt, *The Sports and Pastimes of the People of England* (London: Wm. Tegg and Co., 1850), pp. 19–20.

[25]Elyot, *The Boke Named the Governour*, 1:203.

[26]Ibid., 1: 295–96.

delight in all courtly exercises, and gentlemanlike pastimes."[27] Ascham summarized briefly the activities of which he approved. "Therefore to ride comely, to run fair at the tilt or ring; to play at all weapons, to shoot fair in bow, or surely in gun; to vault lustily, to run, to leap, to wrestle, to swim; to dance comely, to sing, and play on instruments cunningly; to hawk, to hunt; to play at tennis, and all pastimes generally . . . be not only comely and decent, but also very necessary for a courtly gentleman to use."[28] Ascham's activities were a blend of the old chivalric training and the recommendations of the Italian humanists.

Bright pictures of school life in a German university of the fifteenth and sixteenth centuries are preserved for us in the refreshing dialogues, *The Paedologia*, written by Petrus Mosellanus in 1518. These dialogues between students reveal that, although boys may not have had physical education in their formal curriculum, they did enjoy games and dancing. In these dialogues the youths discuss the activities they plan to attend in the town. A circus excites their interest and they are intrigued with the announcement of rope walkers, dancing Russian bears, and a sham battle of mail-clad horsemen. In one dialogue Petrus discusses his habits of bathing, admitting that he doesn't indulge in the extravagance more than six times a year.[29]

Archery, which had risen in importance as a means of warfare, continued to hold that position during most of the fifteenth and sixteenth centuries. Henry VIII passed three acts obliging ". . . every king's subject to practice shooting with the low bow."[30] Roger Ascham's *Toxophilus*, was a treatise on the art of shooting with the bow. Ascham pleaded, "I have laboured only in this book, showing how fit shooting is for all kinds of men; how honest a pastime for the mind; how wholesome as exercise for the body; not vile for great men to use, not costly for poor men to sustain. . . ."[31] In the book he discussed in detail every phase of shooting: selection and care of equipment, many warnings of faults to avoid, various styles of archery, and advice on proper methods and techniques of shooting. Despite Ascham's loyalty to bows and arrows, the English army relegated them to a secondary position after 1588 when their experiment with firearms against the archers in the Spanish Armada proved highly successful. That battle sounded the death note of archery as a military weapon.

Cockfighting was an ancient sport in England. During the twelfth century royalty was amused by this pastime, and the schoolboys of Lon-

---

[27]Roger Ascham, "The Scholemaster," *The Whole Works of Roger Ascham*, ed. Rev. Dr. Giles (London: John Russell Smith, 1864), 3:139.

[28]Ibid., pp. 139–40.

[29]Petrus Mosellanus, *The Paedologia; Renaissance Student Life*, trans. R. F. Seybolt (Champaign: University of Illinois Press, 1927), p. 48.

[30]Strutt, *Sports and Pastimes*, pp. 56–57.

[31]Roger Ascham, "Toxophilus," *The Whole Works of Roger Ascham*, 2:6.

don were allowed to bring their cocks to school on Shrove Tuesday to delight themselves in a match. The sport became so popular in the reign of Charles I (1625–1649) that Van Dyke painted a picture of the court watching a match. In the later days this cruel pastime was promoted by syndicates for paying spectators.

The brutish sports of bull and bear baiting by dogs were popular in England under the Tudors, and, indeed, did not become illegal until 1835. During later times these sports became the pleasures of the lower classes and were patronized furtively by the aristocrats.

During the fifteenth and sixteenth centuries tennis continually gained in popularity. The racket, or bat, came to be substituted for the palm of the hand, and the ball was commonly stuffed with human hair. Men bragged about the number of sweat shirts they used at tennis, and were attracted to the gambling associated with the game. Some effort was made to reserve this fashionable sport for the courtier and the gentleman, but one writer in 1558 mentions artisans, joiners, and hatters playing at tennis. Nearly every city had a tennis court in France. Noblemen in England enjoyed the conveniences of a tennis court, but the lower classes frequently used the fields and streets. Henry VIII himself was exceedingly fond of tennis; nevertheless, in 1535 he forbade anyone to keep a tennis court, and in 1541 tennis was enumerated among the "unlawful games" in order to enforce longbow practice.

Although all authorities do not agree, golf probably originated in Holland. When the Scotch and English were introduced to the game, they adopted it as a national sport. During early times many edicts attempted to abolish the game in order to promote the practice of archery, and Sabbath prohibitions continued to appear throughout the years. Finally, James IV (1488–1513) was invited to play with a group of nobles, and became intrigued with the game. His granddaughter Mary, Queen of Scots, was devoted to golf. During her reign, in about 1552, the famous club, St. Andrews, was established.

Playing cards were used in the thirteenth and fourteenth centuries in Europe, but their popularity increased in the fifteenth and sixteenth centuries. The cards were hand-painted, thus making a deck a rather expensive possession. During the reign of Queen Elizabeth I, the deck of cards was reduced to fifty-two. Ruff and honors was the game played at her court. During the seventeenth and eighteenth centuries, the coffee houses and private clubs of England took up cards. The game Elizabeth once played was changed to swabbers, which later was altered and called whist. This game developed into bridge whist, auction bridge, and the contract bridge of today.

After the introduction of firearms, soldiers abandoned their heavy armor and long swords and adopted the rapier blade. With the rapier becoming a part of man's attire, dueling increased; this contributed to the rapid rise of fencing schools. Roger Ascham in *Toxophilus* remarked that a number of manuals on fencing were published at this time.[32]

During the Renaissance a number of books concerning health and medicine were published in northern Europe. Charles Estienne, a French humanist, produced *Anatomy* in 1546; John Banister, a well-known surgeon, was the author of several medical works. Dr. Linacre, a contemporary of Elyot, who obtained his medical degree at Padua in 1496, translated Galen's *De Sanitate Tuendâ*. A medical treatise, *The Castle of Health,* written by Sir Thomas Elyot, imparted what he knew about medicine to the laity. A number of minor writings of the sixteenth century also discussed methods of maintaining health.[33]

The courts of Europe were passionately fond of dancing. Lavish fêtes, balls, ballets, and masquerades were highlights of the social life of the courtiers and their ladies. Usually the dances originated among the peasantry and were modified to suit the dignity of the court. In the process of adaptation, many of the vigorous, earthy, country characteristics were refined into low bows, graceful curtseys, stately poses, toe pointing, and simple walking and gliding steps.

At the time of the Black Death, when life was considered a macabre dance that led to the grave, the Dance of Death was popular. In this dance, which was sometimes performed as a masque, men dressed as skeletons and danced with performers who represented the different stations of society. The dance revealed how deeply men were preoccupied with death in this age of wars, famine, and plague.

Dances varied from one part of Europe to another, but there was also a general tendency to adopt dances of foreign lands. The *basse danse, branle, haute, pavane, volte, courante, saraband, allemande, gaillarde,* and *brawls* were favorite dances of this era. The slow, grave, stately *basse danse* was originally performed only by the aristocracy. The *haute danse* or *danse baladine* included rounds, *bourrées* (clog steps), *farandoles*, and much pantomiming. These free and easy dances were also popular with the common people. *Les branles*, a family of figure dances accompanied by singing, remained in vogue until the seventeenth century. The *pavane*, sometimes called the peacock dance, was one of strutting, posing, curtseying, retreating, and advancing, pacing in cadence. The *volte* was composed of gliding steps and is considered the forerunner of the waltz. In England, the carole, the round, and the morris dances that appeared in feudal days were still performed in later centuries. "In the sixteenth and seventeenth centuries, when villagers assembled every holiday, and on Sunday evenings, after the prayers, to dance upon the green, every parish of moderate population had its piper. The numerous hornpipes, jogs,

[32]Ibid., p. 88.
[33]Frederick Furnivall, *The Babees Book, Early English Meals and Manners* (London: N. Trübner and Co., 1868), 32:247, 252.

rounds, and bagpipe tunes of that time may thus be accounted for."[34] May Day was a great festival of dancing for everyone.

The ballet, which became fashionable during the Renaissance, provided one of the most elegant aspects of court social life. The lavish fête given in honor of the Duke of Milan in 1489 is generally credited with the restoration of dancing and the stimulation of the ballet. Dancing came to absorb royalty in France after Henry II was killed in a tournament in 1559, a happening that caused the abandonment of the old knightly sport. The king, queen, and courtiers took part in these early presentations. The professional theatrical ballet did not appear until the later seventeenth century. The richly-jeweled, royal performers, costumed elegantly in costly gowns, presented historical and mythological scenes, sometimes combining music, dancing, speeches, and pageantry. Illustrious births, marriages, and important public events were celebrated with a ballet. Churchmen were sometimes patrons of these performances and were even known to have taken part in them.

Methods of Physical Education

The social humanists were noted for their interest in improving the methods of teaching languages and literature. Erasmus and Ascham expressed some modern pedagogical ideas. Most humanists pleaded for less brutal discipline in the schools; however, under Sturm, education again became systematized and formalized, resulting in a return to harsher discipline. The invention of the printing press, which had an impact on society comparable to that of the development of the computer today, gave increased emphasis to textbook methods of education.

During the fifteenth and sixteenth centuries, a few books appeared discussing particular sports and games. Curiously enough the very first of these books, *Gentlemen's Academie* or *Boke of S. Albans*, was written by a woman, Dame Juliana Bernes. She published two volumes, one concerning hawking, hunting, and heraldry, and the second pertaining to fishing. Roger Ascham believed that archery and the cockpit were important enough to justify writing about them. Several volumes on the art of fencing also appeared at this time. In 1587, Everard Digby published *De Arte Natandi* because he believed the number of deaths of Cambridge undergraduates by drowning warranted the scientific teaching of swimming. *The Booke of Hunting* by Turberville discussed the sport that had remained one of the popular pastimes of the nobles. *Orchésographie*, 1588, by Jehan Tabourot (*nom de plume*, Thoinot Arbeau) is still referred to as an authority on dancing. The authors concerned with games, sports, and dancing usually included methods of learning.

[34]William Chappell, *Popular Music of Olden Times* (London: Chappell and Co., 1859), 2:792, as quoted in Helen H. Paul, "The Metamorphosis of the Circle Singing Game in England" (Master's thesis, University of Pittsburgh, 1935), p. 33.

8

Physical Education
in
Educational Moralism

The Reformation represents one of the most extensive and complex cultural transformations of modern times. Europe had experienced a substantial increase in trade and commerce, an amazing extension of exploration and discovery, and the steady rise of capitalism. Medieval man had been exposed to natural science, the gradual emergence of national consciousness, and the growing sense of individual worth. If the feudal and Church organizations were to survive in the sixteenth century, they had to adjust to the needs of the emerging culture. Feudalism failed to meet this challenge and, in many parts of Europe, soon disintegrated. Although the Catholic church survived, the Protestant revolts diminished its supremacy.

Humanism rather unintentionally supplied the intellectual fuse for the Protestant Reformation. The early humanists, dissatisfied with scholasticism and the allegorical mode of interpreting the Bible, saw Platonic philosophy and the new critical techniques used in studying the classical and Church literature as tools that would illuminate rather than undermine Christian doctrine. Long before Luther, the men who were engaged in an intensive study of the classics and the early Christian community began to criticize the moral, political, and financial corruption of the present-day Church and to plead for a return to the original simplicity and purity of the early Christians. Their intention was to eliminate flagrant abuses, not to tear the Church asunder.

Some ecclesiastics had recognized the need for a purification of their practices and were turning toward a reformation movement before the sixteenth century. But before this internal renewal of the Church could be achieved, Luther ignited a revolt that, when fanned by strong political and economic forces, burst into a conflagration that destroyed the unity of Christendom.

During the Middle Ages, secular and spiritual interests had become intermingled. The civil power assumed by the clergy in organizing the chaotic post-Roman world had repeatedly been the source of much irritation. Churchmen held many powers that rising monarchs of the sixteenth century believed should be the prerogative of the state. In Germany, one third of the land was owned by the Church. Irritated with the power the Church was exercising in their domains and with the wealth that was being drained to Rome, a number of German princes reponded to Luther's appeal to free themselves from the tyranny of Rome. They were willing to support the religious revolt in order to break the civil power of the Church.[1] Rather indirectly the spirit of capitalism also encouraged the reformers, for the merchants found it to their advantage to support the kings who were able to grant them privileges, rights, and protection. Thus the Protestant Reformation was born of intense religious feeling, but it was also nurtured by the budding spirit of capitalism and nationalism.

The Protestant religious upheavals were succeeded by the Catholic Counter-Reformation, and a moral reformation generally known as Puritanism. The stress on morals, emphasized both in Catholic and Protestant churches, was cultivated most intensively by the Calvinists. With a strict internal discipline, the Calvinists sought to destroy what, to them, was the false, worldly Church and replace it with the true Church.

Religious tolerance did not result from the Protestant Reformation or from the Puritanical moral reforms. Popes and kings, Catholics and Protestants, were equally unwilling to allow the individual freedom of conscience. Many European monarchs refused to countenance individual determination of religious belief; they held that religious unity was essential to political unity. Their citizens were required to adhere to the official Christianity of the state church or suffer harassment, banishment, imprisonment, or death.

The religious intolerance that came in the wake of the Reformation stimulated the colonization of the New World. The waves of migrants coming to America corresponded roughly to the fluctuations of the political-religious conditions in their homelands. Many Puritans in England who opposed the Catholic rituals of the Anglican church fled to New England; many Anglicans sought refuge in Virginia when the Puritans gained power under Cromwell. The subsequent overthrow of the Puritan Commonwealth marked another exodus of Quakers, Catholics, and Puritans from England. Religious and economic reasons also motivated migrations from other nations. French Huguenots established settlements along the coastal Carolinas, and the Dutch founded a colony in New York. Anxious to propagate the Catholic faith in the New World,

---

[1]Encyclopaedia Britannica, 11th ed., s.v. "reformation" (James H. Robinson), 32.5.

the teaching order of Jesuits explored the St. Lawrence, the Great Lakes, and the Mississippi Valley Basin, carrying on their missionary work wherever they went.

PHYSICAL EDUCATION IN PROTESTANT MORALISM

Early Protestants emphasized the right of the individual to discover the truth contained in the Bible for himself without turning to the collective judgment of the churchmen in seeking the rule of faith. The reformers, however, did not long allow such freedom. As soon as the doctrines and disciplines of the various religious sects assumed definite forms, the Protestants became less liberal and more conservative. Each sect was certain that it upheld the true interpretation of the Scriptures. Thus, unlike Catholicism, Protestantism never established a unified church. It was initially divided into three major sects and developed into numerous subdivisions.

The main forms of Protestantism appearing in the sixteenth century were Lutheranism, Calvinism, and Anglicanism. Lutheranism triumphed in northern Germany and in the Scandinavian countries. Calvinism arose in Switzerland and spread throughout Europe. In France, the Calvinists were known as Huguenots, in Scotland and England as Presbyterians, in the Netherlands as the Dutch Reformed, and in other parts of the Continent as the Reformed Faith. After Henry VIII severed relations with Rome, religion in England was delegated to the National Anglican Church.

Leaders of the Protestant Reformation found that the renovation of the church required many efforts in behalf of education. Martin Luther (1483–1546) translated the Bible into the vernacular so that everyone could read it and wrote catechisms for both children and adults. Vigorous pronouncements demanding better education were made in his *Letter to the Mayors and Aldermen of all the Cities of Germany in Behalf of Christian Schools* and in his *Sermon on the Duty of Sending Children to School*. The active reorganization of education was done by Luther's colleague, Bugenhagen, and the humanists Melanchthon and Sturm.

Ulrich Zwingli (1484–1531), the theological predecessor of Calvin in Switzerland, also made education an integral part of religious reform. His *Brief Treatise on the Christian Education of Youth* gave marked attention to physical education. John Calvin (1509–1564), a French Protestant who fled to Switzerland seeking religious asylum, became deeply involved in the formulation of religious instruction and the establishment of schools. John Knox (1505–1572), the Calvinist who led the Protestant revolt in Scotland, in the *Book of Discipline for the Scottish Church*, proposed an educational system of a very democratic nature.

The Reformation and the humanistic movements paralleled each other. They never coalesced, but a close relationship existed between them as well as between the personalities involved in their leadership. Humanism was an aesthetic and literary movement of aristocratic leanings; the Reformation was an ethical and religious movement of national and popular character. Nearly all reformers were humanists, but not all humanists were reformers. Whether allied or conflicting forces, humanism and moralism shaped education during the ensuing centuries.

Aims of Education

The aims of Protestant education reveal that they were constructed in an era of religious reform which was deeply influenced by the rise of nationalism and economic development. Education was designed not only for personal salvation but also for competency in performing home, occupational, and state duties.

Developing the highest type of Christian manhood was the ideal of Protestant education. At first, the reformers held that the individual should read the Bible, which, through the invention of the printing press, was now available to all men, and in the light of his own reasoning, determine the most worthy pattern of Christian living. But this liberal concept of education was soon abandoned. Distrusting individual judgment and self-discipline as the principal means of achieving Christian ideals, the Puritan moralists became convinced that they had to supervise the conduct of men in order to enforce compliance with the rigid codes of behavior devised by them. Religious education, after having enjoyed a brief glimpse of freedom, was slipped into a new yoke that was as confining as the straitjacket of medievalism.

The cultivation of good citizens as well as deeply religious personalities was the objective of the Protestant sects everywhere. The Protestants held that the individual was to be capable of discharging his civic duties as well as of meeting his religious obligations. Luther declared, ". . . that society, for the maintenance of civil order and the proper regulation of the household, needs accomplished and well-trained men and women."[2] Calvin as well as Luther believed that the welfare of the government depended upon the intelligence and virtue of its citizens. The early American colonies emphasized religious training ". . . and other employments which may be profitable to the commonwealth."[3]

The leaders of the Puritanical movement wove the moralistic aims of education into a pattern that harmonized with the growing capitalistic spirit. The Protestants did not demand that men renounce their worldly pursuits in order to seek salvation. Work was an expression of service to

[2]Martin Luther, *Letter to the Mayors and Aldermen of the Cities of Germany in Behalf of Christian Schools,* as quoted in F. V. N. Painter, *Luther on Education,* (St. Louis: Concordia Publishing House, 1928), pp. 180–81.
[3]A. B. Hinsdale, "Documents Illustrative of American Educational History" in *Report of the United States Commissioner of Education* (1892–93), 2:123.

God and a means of effecting a higher morality. The educator had to instill not only the traits of piety, virtue, and honesty in the hearts and minds of children but also the Protestant work ethic: respect for industry and thrift and abhorrence of idleness and frivolity. "Time and talents were not to be wasted. . . . No one should be unemployed; even the man of leisure should find some occupation which would be of service to the common weal."[4] Under Protestantism, economics were an inextricable part of the overall religious and moral pattern of educational aims. The virtues of labor were exalted.

Aims of Physical Education

During the Reformation, the Protestant sects relegated physical education to an inferior position and intensively endeavored to curb worldly pleasures. The development of physical education was thus held back for generations.

The early reformers did not stress physical education, but they saw greater value in it than the puritanical sects. Luther advocated that children be allowed to associate with one another. He recognized that pleasure and enjoyment were as important to good health as food and drink. He highly approved of gymnastics as a means of maintaining personal fitness and of discouraging participation in degrading pursuits. Luther declared,

> It was admirably provided and ordered by the ancients that the people should have honorable and useful modes of exercise. . . . Accordingly, I pronounce in favor of . . . music, and the knightly sports of fencing, wrestling, etc., of which, the one drives care and gloom from the heart, and the other gives a full development to the limbs. . . .[5]

Luther advocated the cultivation of buoyant health to enable an individual to devote energy to labor and to Christian service, hence, achieving both religious and economic aims. He stated,

> It is the part of a Christian to take care of his own body for the very purpose that, by its soundness and well-being, he may be enabled to labour, and to acquire and preserve property, for the aid of those who are in want that thus the stronger member may serve the weaker member, and we may be children of God . . . fulfilling the law of Christ.[6]

---

[4]H. G. Wood, "Puritanism," *Hastings Encyclopedia of Religion and Ethics* (New York: Charles Scribner's Sons, 1919), 10:514.

[5]Henry Barnard, *German Teachers and Educators*, trans. from Karl von Raumer's *Geschichte der Pädagogik*, 1:142–43 (Hartford: Brown and Gross Co., 1878), p. 158.

[6]Martin Luther, "Concerning Christian Liberty," *Luther's Primary Works*, trans. Henry Wace and C. A. Buchheim (London: Hodder and Stoughton, 1896), pp. 279–80.

Zwingli, the Swiss religious leader, appreciated the values of physical education far more than many succeeding Protestant reformers. In his opinion, all sports and games had to be directed toward worthy purposes. "Games played with one's companions, at proper times, I allow," declared Zwingli, "provided they are games that require skill and serve to train the body."[7] He also sanctioned activities for the pleasure they afforded youth, as along as they were morally unobjectionable. He advocated military training "so far as it was necessary for defense of the fatherland." This early Swiss reformer presented the people with a broader goal of physical education than was allowed to flourish under John Calvin.

Calvin was so animated with a burning desire to perfect the moral discipline of men that he banned most amusements. Recognizing that he could not completely suppress the natural desire for play, Calvin conceded that men should participate in "honest games," but he devoted more attention to applying external restraints to physical education than to developing its goals. For example, the *By Laws of the Academy of Geneva* recommended a period of recreation on Wednesday "but in such a way that all silly sports be avoided."

Some cultures have been able to advance moral goals through physical education, but the Puritans prohibited such a possibility. First, their exaltation of labor and detestation of idleness placed play outside the pale of approved social behavior. Thus, physical education could not survive unless it was devoted to economic goals. Secondly, the Puritans desired to eliminate any activity tainted with Catholicism; consequently, they abrogated many medieval holidays and prohibited Sunday amusements through which social-recreational objectives of sports and games had once been attained. Thirdly, the Puritans' determination to improve morals through spiritual vigilance and external discipline because a fanatic proscription of nearly every natural desire of man. To create a perfect system for policing morals, the Puritans developed a strait-laced code of laws that practically reduced legitimate recreation to "seasonable meditation and prayer."

Some limitations on the scope of physical education were not dominated by religious motives but rather by a class consciousness. The Puritans, who believed in working hard, were nettled by the rich, leisure-loving aristocrats who were such sports enthusiasts. Externally, they directed their attacks against the moral laxity of the upper classes. Subconsciously, they were employing their economic and social discontent as a religious justification for outlawing the enjoyments of the wealthy. "These two influences, spiritual reform and economic envy, can never be disentangled. They were both present in the sixteenth and seventeenth centuries, and

[7]Ulrich Zwingli, *The Christian Education of Youth*, trans. Alcide Reichenback, (1899), p. 90. (Reprint of the original Swiss edition, 1526.)

they have been present in every later day manifestation of the Puritan spirit."[8]

The harsh demands of the wilderness in America thrust the detestation of idleness upon the colonists. In this primitive environment every moment was precious and had to. be devoted to essential labor. Play was expendable and had to be condemned. The Puritans, however, tried to enforce this point of view upon the people long after economic conditions had improved. The dogmatic laws prohibiting idleness were reluctantly relaxed only after years of struggle.

Unconsciously, the colonists gave indirect approval to some forms of physical education even in the early days. They recognized the economic value of a sound physique in meeting the challenges of the New World; but, at the same time, surfeited with their daily back-bending toil, they saw no need to provide additional exercises for health's sake. The Puritans, however, indirectly satisfied their needs of social-recreational experiences through group participation concerned with obtaining food, clothing, shelter, and military protection. In short, the early Puritan recreational pattern was cut expertly to fit their economic needs.

As frontier conditions were gradually conquered and business and political interests increased in the colonies, the complete dominance of Puritanism was somewhat relaxed. By the eighteenth century, the Virginians and the Dutch, who had always been more free and pleasure-loving peoples, were paying little attention to the restrictions on recreation that had existed in earlier days. The southerners, primarily Anglicans, experienced less religious restraint than the Puritans. The warmer climate and richer soil was less demanding of their energies, and the employment of slave labor gave them greater leisure. These conditions were all favorable to the development of sports, games, and dances.

As the stern battle for security and stability was won along the New England seacoast, even the Puritans expressed a growing interest in amusements. Alarmed churchmen struggled to curb this incipient movement, but they could not stem the tide. Later immigrants who had come to New England for political and economic reasons rather than religious ones, were not so puritanical as their predecessors. As wealth and leisure increased the Puritan's sense of security and opportunity to enjoy amusements, the group activities that had once been tolerated because of their economic worth came more and more to be recognized and enjoyed for their social-recreational values.

Promotion of Physical Education

When the Roman Catholic church no longer functioned as the official agency of education in many parts of Europe, the Protestant reformers

[8]Foster R. Dulles, *America Learns to Play* (New York: D. Appleton Century Co., 1940), p. 9.

had to establish their own school systems. Having enjoyed the support of governmental authorities in the revolt, the Protestant churchmen sought their cooperation in developing education, and thus laid the foundations for state control and support of education. Eventually, the civil authorities began to displace the churchmen in exerting jurisdiction over education.

The Protestant schools were of three types. Latin grammar schools gave youths of wealth or intellectual promise a theoretical and cultural education, and many of the graduates went on to universities. The elementary schools, known as dame or parish schools, offered the masses a limited education that was often supplemented by some type of apprenticeship. Elementary students did not go on to Latin grammar schools. Preparation for Latin grammar studies was secured from tutors or in private classes. Little or no relationship existed between the elementary and secondary institutions. A dual rather than a ladder system of education developed in Europe with different schools for different classes of people. Protestant schools both in Europe and America either failed to function as agencies of physical education or assumed such duties in a limited capacity. The New England colonists expected the elementary school to offer disciplined training only in the catechism and the three R's. The students in the Latin grammar schools and universities for the most part were studying for the ministry, and it was deemed unbecoming for them to participate in rugged, noisy amusement. The rules of various European institutions indicated that a few hours a week were frequently devoted to recreation, and brief holidays were granted as a relief from study. At the Academy of Geneva, students were allowed recreation from noon until three o'clock on Wednesday. In Scotland, "In 1649, the scholars of the grammar school of Elgin had play from two to four on Tuesdays and Thursdays and on Saturdays from two P.M. till five."[9] The town council of Dunbar required ". . . that there should be a fair proportion between work and play . . . to impart to the school a healthy tone, and to the scholars an *esprit de corps*. . . ."[10] Whenever recreational periods were allowed, they were generally supervised by older students or masters, whose duties were primarily to prevent unseemly conduct and to limit participation to approved activities.

The Church, which had acted indirectly as an agency of physical education during the Middle Ages, did not continue to function in that capacity under Protestant leadership. Sundays and holy days in medieval times were celebrated by attending mass and afterwards participating in games, sports, dancing, and merrymaking. The Protestants proscribed the observance of these special Catholic holidays in their churches. Christmas and other holidays were abolished altogether by the Puritan Parliament

---

[9]James Grant, *The History of Burgh Schools of Scotland* (London: Wm. Collins Sons and Co., 1876), p. 170.
    [10]Ibid., p. 170.

in 1647. That many people were not happy about the restrictions placed upon these customary days of merrymaking is indicated in the following extract from *Father Hubburd's Tales* in 1604: "Do but imagine now what a sad Christmas we all kept in the country, without either carols, wassail bowls, dancing of Sellingers Round in the moonshine nights about Maypoles, shoeing the mare, hoodman blind, hot cockles, or any of our Christmas gambols—no, not so much as choosing king and queen on Twelfth Night."[11] The puritanical New Englanders, like their European brethren, discouraged all such holidays, and "any person who observed it [Christmas] as a holiday by forbearing of labor, feasting, or any other way was to pay five shillings fine. . . ."[12] The Dutch in New Amsterdam seemingly had more forbearance, because they continued to celebrate St. Nicholas Day as well as May Day and Shrove Tuesday.

Sunday amusements, which had been socially acceptable during the Middle Ages, were frowned upon by the Protestants. This was not initiated by the earlier reformers, for Luther would have allowed people to engage in whatever work or pleasure they deemed proper after church service. Even though Calvin forbade all work on the Lord's Day, he was observed by his follower, John Knox, to be playing at bowls on a Sunday. The later Puritanical reformers, however, sought vigorously to apply Old Testament strictness for the observance of the Sabbath.

The conflict over Sunday amusements became so sharp that some fun-loving citizens of Lancashire petitioned the king for permission to enjoy their customary, merry pastimes. As a result, James I wrote the *Basilicon Doron* to pronounce that the people of the realm were free to enjoy Maypole festivities, dancing, archery, leaping, vaulting, and other lawful amusements after observing Sunday worship. He argued that this day was the only occasion that working men were free from labor and could participate in sports. The Puritans, deeply incensed over this act, had the book burned publicly when they came into power.

In America, rather severe penalities were exacted for participation in pleasurable pursuits on the Sabbath. In New London, a man was fined twenty shillings for sailing a boat, a hunter in Plymouth was whipped for shooting, and many a New Englander was punished for unseemly walking or riding on Sunday. The blue laws of Vermont demanded that, "Whoever was guilty of any rude, profane, or unlawful conduct on the Lord's Day, in words or action, by . . . running, riding, dancing, jumping, was to be fined forty shillings and whipped upon the naked back not to exceed ten stripes."[13] The Virginians also banned all dancing, card playing, hunting,

---

[11]William Chappell, *A Collection of English Airs* (London: Chappell and Co., 1893), as quoted in Helen H. Paul, "The Metamorphosis of the Game," p. 69.

[12]Alice M. Earle, *Customs and Fashions in Old New England* (New York: Scribner's Sons, 1896), p. 215.

[13]Alice Morse Earle, *The Sabbath in Puritan New England* (New York: Charles Scribner's Sons, 1891), p. 248.

or fishing on the Sabbath, but they did not rigidly enforce these laws in later years. The Dutch were quite tolerant about Sunday pastimes except during the sermon hours.

Apart from their concern for the Sabbath, the Puritans, both in Europe and America, imposed restraints on participation in many popular amusements. In Geneva, Calvin and his Puritanical followers passed regulations on almost two hundred pastimes. In England during the reign of Edward VI, the reformers crusaded against dancing and resolved to cut all Maypoles down; "Merry Scotland became for the time a grim, earnest place, when the tide of Reformation burst as a torrent, and swept away even innocent amusement. . . ."[14]

A multiplicity of statutes prohibiting sports, games, and dancing also appeared in New England, and in the early days Virginia had many laws just as strict as those of the Puritans. Dancing was forbidden in taverns or at weddings in Massachusetts, and the magistrates attempted to stop boys from kicking a football about Boston streets. How unhappy the boys of Albany, New York, must have been in 1713 when the constable confiscated their sleds and broke them into pieces, declaring that they were disorderly and a shame and scandal to their parents because they enjoyed coasting down the snow-covered hills. On hot summer days, mischievous New England boys must certainly have tried to escape the spying of the town tithingman who kept watch to prevent "boys and all persons from swimming in the water."

The New Englanders did not suppress a number of informal physical education agencies that were dedicated to practical purposes. Organized hunts were acceptable recreational activities as well as a practical means of securing food; house and barn raisings provided considerable physical exercise, as well as pleasant social experiences. Official holidays operated as slightly more formal agencies of physical education. The first Thanksgiving in Plymouth was not a day devoted solely to religious observance; indeed, it was not a day, but a week of feasting and recreation. Military training days were especially important events. The Pilgrims had six training days a year. In 1645, the court of Massachusetts ordered that all boys between ten and sixteen years should receive practice with the bow and arrow, small guns, and half pieces. The village commons were drill fields and playgrounds of the community. In 1639, about 1,000 men exercised on the Boston Commons on training day.

In the South, where the planters did not live as close to one another as did the New England farmers, group activities could not be organized as easily. The house parties of Virginia became a popular means of bringing the scattered planters together for a few days of merrymaking, dancing, sports, and games. Training days and county fairs attracted the Tidewater people on special occasions as did the race tracks in a later day.

[14]Gaston Vuillier, *A History of Dancing* (New York: D. Appleton and Co., 1898), p. 421.

Although schools and the community rarely acted as agents of physical education, commercial interests recognized that recreation could be profitable. All along the Atlantic seaboard, the inns and taverns became centers of amusement that promoted various games and diversions. A few race tracks appeared in Virginia and New York, while bowling greens, so popular with the Dutch, were scattered throughout the colonies.

Program of Physical Education

The study of religion was the core of all school curriculums of the Reformation. The elementary school program included reading, writing, and sometimes crude arithmetic, but emphasis was placed upon learning the catechism, creed, Lord's Prayer, and the Ten Commandments. In the Latin school and the university, the course of study stressed the religious aspects of the classical humanistic training. Latin and often Greek and Hebrew were taught. It was desired that students should be able to read the Bible and the writings of the Church Fathers in the original. Logic, eloquence, and rhetoric were frequently added to the curriculum, and a few educators advocated the study of history, natural science, and music. Luther and Zwingli both recommended gymnastic training, but such activities were not included. Free play was allowed in the brief recreational periods, but only approved activities were permitted. The existing records reveal more information concerning games banned than those enjoyed.

Realizing it was the nature of children to run and play, Martin Luther advocated the inclusion of sports, particularly fencing and wrestling, in the school program. In contrast to many reformers, he approved of dances if they were properly chaperoned. Luther, himself an enthusiastic bowler, did not condemn physical education activities that were morally sound, but denounced vigorously all others.

Ulrich Zwingli, the Swiss reformer, proposed a variety of physical education activities for the curriculum. His program of running, jumping, some throwing (or putting the shot), and wrestling, was similar to the old Greek *palaestra* course. A plea for moderation permeates his discussion.[15]

In the strict theocracy of Calvin, moral conduct was supervised carefully. Calvin declared, "As I see that we cannot forbid men all diversions, I confine myself to those that are really bad."[16] The pleasure-loving people of Geneva, who once had enjoyed the festivals, masquerades, and dances, found their lives regulated strictly. Those who played at cards or dice could be punished by public exhibitions in the pillory, and to dance at a wedding or a feast was also a crime. Calvin was more moderate in his restrictions than some of his followers; even in old age he enjoyed a

[15]Ulrich Zwingli, *The Christian Education of Youth*, pp. 91–92.
[16]Preserved Smith, *The Age of the Reformation* (New York: Henry Holt and Co., 1920), p. 171.

pleasant walk or a simple game of quoits or "clef."[17] The later Puritanical Scotch and English followers of Calvin were noted for their campaign to suppress amusements.

Despite the many similar prohibitions on amusements in New England, life was not so austere as some accounts infer. In spite of the gloomy contemplation of sin and the fear of eternal damnation, the stern New England fathers were never completely successful in crushing the play spirit of youth. The vast number of laws directed toward the suppression of recreational activities[18] suggests that many "wicked backsliders" in the community did not limit themselves to those approved forms of recreation.

Children had few and very crude toys, but by 1695 a Mr. Higginson advised his brother in England that a market for toys existed in the colonies if they were imported in small quantities. By the time of the Revolution, the following games were popular: "chuck-farthing; kite-flying; dancing round May-pole; marbles; hoop and hide; thread the needle; fishing; blindman's buff; shuttlebock; king am I; peg-farthing; knock out and span; hop, skip, and jump; boys and girls come out to play; I sent a letter to my love; cricket; stool-ball; base-ball; trap-ball; swimming; tip-cat; train-banding; fives; leap-frog; bird-nesting; hop-hat; shooting; hop-scotch; squares; riding; rosemary tree."[19] Boys were prohibited from playing football by law in Boston, but they engaged in the game frequently enough to teach it to the Indians, for a traveler in America in the seventeenth century writes of it as an Indian game.[20]

Although many New Englanders may have sought their recreation by attending funerals, long Lecture-Day sermons, or public punishments, some gayer events relieved the monotony of their daily labor. On the occasion of the first Thanksgiving at Plymouth, the governor sent four men fowling for enough game to serve the assembled colonists and Indians for a week. Chief Massasoit and some ninety Indians presented their hosts with a few deer for the feast. While the women prepared the food, the colorfully-clad Indians watched their white brothers "exercise their arms" and probably competed with them in shooting with bow and arrows as well as in running, jumping, leaping, and wrestling contests.

An air of joviality also pervaded the military "training days." Religious services opened the ceremonies, but a more gala atmosphere prevailed on the village commons where the drills were held. The military exercises were climaxed by the granting of the awards for the best marks-

[17]In the game of clef, the keys were pushed on a table, the aim being to bring each contestant's nearest to the farther edge without falling off.

[18]William Bradford, *Bradford's History of Plymouth Plantation*, ed. Wm. T. Davis (New York: Charles Scribner's Sons, 1908), p. 126.

[19]Alice M. Earle, *Child Life in Colonial Days* (New York: The Macmillan Company, 1927), pp. 346–47.

[20]Ibid., p. 358.

manship. After the drills, the men took pleasure in exhibiting their strength and skill in impromptu wrestling matches, jumping contests, and rough-and-tumble fights.

The solemn Harvard commencements were supplemented by a gay, unofficial program of horse races, nine-pins, card games, and contests of strength. To curb such frivolity, in 1730, the authorities set commencement day thereafter for Friday. There would be ". . . less remaining time in the week to be spent in frolicking."[21] The date for the graduation exercises was also shifted from fall to spring with the hope that farmers would be too busy with their plowing to descend on the town for a holiday.

Group work offered the early settlers some limited opportunities for recreation. Barn and house raisings, corn huskings, log-rollings, and plowing bees were in themselves a test of physical competence. The feasting and merrymaking after the work was completed was often spontaneous indulgence in dancing or sports.

Dancing was the subject of many a sermon, but even the eloquent preaching of Increase Mather fell upon many deaf ears. A century of increasing prosperity in the New World found colonists anxious to imitate the social life of England, and as early as 1719, both sons and daughters of Boston blue bloods received dancing lessons. The ball given by the governor of Boston in 1713, which lasted until 3 A.M., would certainly have shocked the earlier New England settlers.

The amusements of the inns and taverns were frequently banned, but popular demand encouraged cockfights, animal baitings, shooting matches, "shovel-board," billiard games, dicing, card playing, ninepins, quoits, bowls, and dancing. To increase business, the tavern keepers would offer prizes for "shooting at the mark." Playing at cards—"the devil's picture books"—which was also popular at the village inn, had to be carried on surreptitiously, but as time went on the events were even announced in the newspapers.

The woods and waters of the New World offered abundant supplies of game and fish for the profit and pleasure of all colonists. Even New Englanders approved of such sports. All along the Atlantic seaboard, the pioneers bagged pigeons, quail, turkey, opossum, raccoon, squirrel, wolves, deer, bear, and fox. When hunting was no longer a part of daily labor, men continued to pursue the pastime as a sport. Group hunts of a social-recreational as well as economic nature were held on certain festive occasions even in the early days. Usually the colonists depended upon their skill with a gun to secure game, but bows and arrows, pits, log pens, and nets were also utilized. Colonial anglers, employing improvised rods or the Indian techniques of fishing with the net and spear, explored the

[21]Alice M. Earle, *Customs and Fashions in Old New England*, p. 223.

inland lakes and streams and also tried deep sea fishing. In the early eighteenth century, angling truly became a sport. Two fishing clubs, which became exclusive sporting and social centers, were organized along the Schuylkill River in 1732.

The Virginians, who had been enthusiastic sportsmen in England, kept their play spirit even during the harsh days of early settlement. In 1611, when colonists were starving, Sir Thomas Dale was amazed to find them playing at bowls quite merrily. He had to threaten them to insure their application to stern working duties. Because the Anglican Virginians did not view sports and games as sinful, they could engage in diverse forms of amusements without feeling guilty. They held fairs and engaged in horse racing and cockfighting; fox hunting remained dear to their hearts.[22] They also enjoyed ninepins, card playing, dicing, fishing, and boating.

The Dutch in New Netherlands were tolerant toward diversions, and this attitude remained when New York became a British colony. The bowling green was well patronized by the burghers who enjoyed their traditional sport of ninepins. (Rip Van Winkle is still a legendary figure of Dutch bowling!) In later days, the taverns built stone or wooden platforms for a game of *kaetzen* or *kolf*. In *kaetzen*, which resembled handball, a sphere filled with horsehair was palmed against a tree, post, or wall. Women employed racquets when they played the game. In *kolf*, a primitive kind of golf, heavy wooden clubs were utilized. Sometimes the game was played on ice, so it may have resembled hockey more than the modern game of golf. Naturally, in a colony so rich in game and fish, the men were devoted to hunting and fishing. A Dutch law of 1656, attempting to enforce church attendance, reveals that the citizens were also fond of ". . . dancing, playing ball, cards, tricktack (a complicated kind of backgammon), tennis, cricket, or ninepins, going on pleasure parties in a boat, car, or wagon. . . ."[23]

The winter months were a joyous season of coasting, ice skating, and sleigh-ride parties in New Netherlands. When ice carnivals were held, booths and tents were set up on the icy ponds for the purpose of selling drinks and candies. Young people strapped their skates on their boots and sailed out to cut figures and fancy capers on the ice. Some boys pushed girls in swan-shaped sleighs across the pond, and others raced with their friends or organized hockey games. Sleigh-ride parties were exceedingly popular in New York under British as well as Dutch rule.

When the English ruled New Netherlands, the royal governors and wealthy citizens were anxious to imitate the recreations fashionable in

[22]Hugh Jones, *The Present State of Virginia* (New York: Joseph Sabin, 1865), p. 49.

[23]Edward Channing, *A History of the United States* (New York: The Macmillan Company, 1925), 1:536.

England. Fox hunting was imported, but it never won the approval of the Dutch. The English had always loved horse racing, and the sport proved to be particularly popular in New York.[24] The race track at Salisbury Plain, later known as Newmarket, was the scene of yearly races after 1670. His Majesty's representatives in New York and the wealthy traders were also fond of giving lavish balls and dances.

Methods of Physical Education

Schoolmasters in the dame schools and Latin grammar schools did not give instruction in sports, games, or other recreational activities. Youths learned such activities from their peers, parents, or elder members of the community. In colonial America, the Indians served the white men as teachers of woodland lore and instructed them in new methods of trapping, fishing, and hunting. Just before the Revolution, an era of increased wealth and leisure, a few dancing masters were beginning to give instruction to wealthier children.

PHYSICAL EDUCATION IN CATHOLIC MORALISM

Protestantism did not become entrenched in all countries of Europe. A number of nations, particularly those of southern Europe, remained Catholic. In Italy, where the secular leaders were closely allied with the Church, Protestantism made scant progress. The Spanish religious crusades against the Moors, which ended in political unification for the people of the Spanish peninsula, had further intensified their Catholicism. Political motives prompted some monarchs to seek the friendship of the Church. When French kings found the Protestants attempting to check their royal power, they turned to the papacy for support.

The religious reforms made within the Catholic church were instrumental in maintaining the supremacy of the authority of Rome throughout southern Europe. Even before Luther, leading ecclesiastics exerted efforts to improve the character of the clergy and the practices of the Church. The Protestant revolts greatly stimulated this movement. The Council of Trent (1545–1563) swept away many of the abuses that needed correction, reaffirmed emphatically and defined more clearly the doctrines of the Church, and enacted provisions encouraging education. This vigorous and militant campaign to revitalize the Church and to check the spread of Protestantism, was known as the Counter-Reformation.

---

[24]Alice M. Earle, *Colonial Days in Old New York* (New York: Charles Scribner's Sons, 1912), pp. 220–21.

The Catholics recognized the value of education as a means of winning the dissenters back to the Church and of deepening the spiritual life of the people. Many prominent clergymen devoted their energies to reorganizing the parish schools and to providing more and better teachers. One famous religious teaching order was established by a former Spanish knight, Ignatius de Loyola (1491–1556). While recovering from battle wounds, he decided to dedicate his life to the service of God. Loyola's efforts culminated in the establishment of the Society of Jesus, commonly known as the Jesuits. To strengthen the Church, this religious order built a strong, well-organized, thoroughly trained teaching force and operated noted educational institutions throughout the world.

All Catholic orders were animated by a religious motive, and many were dedicated to a social ideal as well. Some of the orders devoted themselves to education, some to missionary work, some to attending the sick, and some to social rehabilitation. Cardinal Sadoleto and Cardinal Silvio Antoniano were two churchmen who are of particular interest to students of physical education. Cardinal Sadoleto (1477–1547) in his treatise, *On the Correct Upbringing of Children (De Liberis Recte Instituendis)*, adhered to many of the early humanistic ideals of physical education. In 1584, Carinal Antoniano also gave consideration to the physical development of the child in his discussion on *The Christian Education of Children (Dell' Educatione Christiana dei Figliuoli)*. This treatise was a careful compilation from ancient authorities, Renaissance sources, and Church Fathers.

Aims of Education

Religious moralism was the basic objective of the Counter-Reformation educators. Much of the success of Catholic schools rested upon the religious aim of education to which all teachers were dedicated.

With indefatigable energy the Jesuits labored to fulfill the motto of their society, "All for the greater glory of God." Their ideal of Christianity was not a religious withdrawal from this world, but rather a lifetime of practical activity dedicated to training Christian leaders of the Church and state.

Training in religion was the basis for the extension of elementary schools during the Counter-Reformation. The rule of the Christian Brethren expressed this by declaring, ". . . the Brothers of the Society shall labor continually by prayer, by teaching, by vigilance, and by their own good example in the school, to promote the salvation of the children entrusted to them by bringing them up in a truly Christian spirit. . . ."[25]

[25]As quoted in F. P. Graves, *A History of Education During the Middle Ages and the Transition to Modern Times* (New York: The Macmillan Company, 1910), pp. 229–30.

Although spiritual and moral training dominated the education of poorer boys and girls, some attempts were made to prepare them to earn a living.

The Catholics did not accept the individualism of the Renaissance. As is observed in the *Ratio Studiorum* of the Jesuits, churchmen were advised that, "Also in things which contain danger for creed and faith, nobody shall introduce new questions on any important topic, nor an opinion, without sufficient authority or without permission of his superiors. . . ."[26] The educators required the submission of the individual to the authority of the Church.

Aims of Physical Education

The severe asceticism of the Middle Ages was not accepted by the Counter-Reformation educators. The body was once again envisaged as a medium for serving higher purposes. Health and recreational goals of physical education were recognized not as ends in themselves, but as means of attaining moral and spiritual objectives. As a result of periods of recreation, man was to be refreshed for renewed activity in God's vineyards.

Physical fitness was emphasized repeatedly by the Jesuits as the necessary prerequisite for serving and glorifying the Creator. Loyola contravened the medieval ideal of rejecting the body. "Let your mind be filled with the thought that both soul and body have been created by the Hand of God; we must account to Him for those two parts of our being; and we are not required to weaken one of them out of love for the Creator."[27] Disciplining the will rather than castigating the flesh was to be the means of achieving an enriched spiritual life. The body was considered the tool of the spirit, the receptacle of the soul; since it was divinely created, the Christian was to keep it in perfect condition for the service of the Lord.

Cardinal Antoniano expressed the sentiments of the Catholic clergy and laymen who recognized the value of physical education. Antoniano believed the child had to develop a robust, vigorous physique in order to meet the hardships of life. He emphasized that ". . . recreation revives strength of mind and body, and equips the individual to return to his labors with body refreshed and mind active."[28] Antoniano advocated recreation for everyone, but especially for children. "If therefore, recreation is necessary to mature men, how much more should we concede to

[26]Ibid., pp. 219–20.

[27]As quoted in R. H. Quick, *Essays on Educational Reformers* (New York: D. Appleton and Co., 1897), p. 62.

[28]As quoted in Sister Mary Laurentana Zanfagna, *Educational Theories and Principles of Cardinal Silvio Antoniano* (Washington, D. C.: Catholic University of America Press, 1940), p. 38, (translated from the Italian).

children, who by nature are . . . very fond of motion . . . it gives growth and perfection to the limbs. . . ."[29] Antoniano saw games as a means of developing the mind and training a graceful and healthy body. He also recognized that through play educators could instil some qualities of character in the hearts and minds of youth. "In playing games children not only exercise their bodies and their wits; they learn to act with fairness and come to feel something of the joy that arises from companionship and friendly rivalry in common occupation."[30]

Not all Catholic educators were interested in the physical development of the child. The Port Royalists, who established secondary schools, paid little heed to physical education, although they were progressive in other respects.

Promotion of Physical Education

In the countries that remained loyal to Rome, education continued to be under the firm control of the Church. Parish schools multiplied and many new teaching orders were established. The Jesuits, Oratorians, and Port Royalists founded secondary level educational institutions. The Brethren of the Christian Schools, the Piarists, the Order of the Ursulines, and the Sisters of Notre Dame all attempted to establish elementary schools. Jean Baptiste de la Salle (1651–1719), who founded the Institute of the Brethren of the Christian Schools, was as important to the development of elementary education as the Jesuits were to secondary and higher schools.

Catholic nuns, notably the Ursuline Sisters, were devoted primarily to teaching girls. Catholic interest in feminine education was stimulated by Fénelon (1651–1715), Archbishop of Cambrai, who wrote the famous treatise, *The Education of Girls*. Madame de Maintenon (1635–1719), considerably influenced by Fénelon, established a progressive school for girls at Saint Cyr.

The new teaching orders organized education into a standardized, efficient system. The uniformity of the organization, the continuity of the administration, the minute attention to details, and the well-disciplined body of teachers may have caused some educational rigidity; but they also provided the schools with considerable stability and the machinery for accomplishing their religious aims. The extensive *Ratio Studiorum* of the Jesuits served as an administrative manual.

The careful selection and training of teachers by the Catholic teaching orders contributed to the improvement of education. The Brethren of the Christian Schools established the first normal schools, and the Jesuits, Oratorians, and Port Royalists also developed teacher-training programs. The Jesuits required that each prospective member possess

[29]Ibid., p. 39.   [30]Ibid., p. 53.

good health, a fine physique, an unblemished character, gracious manners, and a promising intellect. Members were prepared for their work as teachers through long years of study.

The Jesuit schools were usually well-equipped with dormitories, classrooms, and playgrounds. Attention was given to the physical welfare of the students. The Jesuits believed that lessons should be brief—about two hours in the morning and again in the afternoon—so that neither the health of the teacher nor of the students would be impaired by overwork. The *Ratio Studiorum* insisted, "Just as earnestness is necessary in literary exercises, so is some vacation important. . . ."[31] At least one day each week was to be allowed for rest, and several short vacations and holidays were also prescribed. Boys were sometimes taken on trips to farms.

Many girls grew up with little formal education. Mothers were often content to leave the tutoring of their daughter in the hands of dancing masters and governesses. The new teaching orders of nuns did provide convent education for many upper-class girls, but the rule of silence and the devotion to religious duties discouraged any lively exercise. The progressive school of Madame de Maintenon at Saint Cyr, although dedicated to religious instruction, was less ascetic. A playground and recreation rooms were provided for a variety of activities. Children were given two recreational periods daily, one extending from dinner until two P.M. and another in the evening. Special one-day holidays were periodically granted. A medical examination was required of every girl entering Saint Cyr, and students developing serious diseases were removed from the school.

Program of Physical Education

The content of the Catholic curriculum on the elementry level was limited largely to the three R's and religion; some vocational training was sometimes offered. The vernacular was always used in these schools except for Latin which was taught in the higher grades. The Jesuit secondary schools offered a religious and humanistic training, and all classes were taught in Latin. The upper Jesuit schools were similar to Protestant universities, offering philosophy, theology, Church history, and canon law.

Physical education received greater recognition in the Catholic schools of the sixteenth and seventeenth centuries than in other educational institutions. Specific recommendations for games, sports, and dances are found in a number of treatises. Cardinal Sadoleto warned parents not to repress the child's desire to play. He recommended the ancient exercises of ball playing, javelin throwing, running, and riding. Spontaneous outdoor exercises of a spirited and energetic nature were to his liking.

[31]Edward A. Fitzpatrick, *St. Ignatius and the Ratio Studiorum* (New York: McGraw-Hill Book Company, 1933), p. 135.

Book III of Cardinal Silvio Antoniano's treatise was devoted largely to a consideration of the diet, sleep, dress, and recreation of youth. Beginning with the prenatal life of the child, he observed that the sound body of the mother was essential, and he advised certain physical exercises for her.[32] Physical exercises and games were an integral part of education. Ball games were considered beneficial because they make boys ". . . more erect and more eager and enable them to meet sadness and depression with unruffled brow."[33] Small children were not to take part in activity requiring too much physical exertion or skill. When sufficiently developed, young men could engage in horseback riding, hunting, boxing, jumping, and fencing. Dancing was condemned by Antoniano.

The Jesuits did not limit their teaching to the classroom. In order to advance Catholicism, the Order utilized the theater as a means of religious propaganda. Dancing was considered very important by aristocratic society in the seventeenth century, and so the Jesuit ballets were very popular. Their productions were supervised by the most famous dancing masters of Europe.

Fénelon proclaimed educational principles that revealed his admiration for Hellenic culture. He advised, "The most useful thing during the first years of infancy is to take care of the health of the child. . . . Let a child play and mix instruction with play."[34] As tutor to. the Duke of Burgundy, he prescribed plenty of outdoor exercise, including running and jumping; only the simplest of food was served his royal charge.

The "Prospectus" of Saint Cyr announced that girls attending the schools would enjoy frequent amusements and that all means, even games, would be employed to help develop their reason. Madame de Maintenon described the ideal student as one who enjoyed the periods of recreation and participated actively in games, dances, and running. All roughness was forbidden during recreation; boisterous games were not permitted indoors, but quieter activities, such as skittles, chess, and draughts, were sanctioned.

Health and physical education were given consideration in the elementary schools of Jean Baptiste de la Salle. The teachers inspected the child twice a day in regard to cleanliness, and classrooms were to be kept thoroughly ventilated. During recreation, children were to perform exercises to develop and strengthen their bodies.

Methods of Physical Education

The general policy of all Catholic educators was close supervision of children at study or at play. In some schools this may have imbued classes

[32]Sister Mary Laurentana Zanfagna, *Educational Theories*, p. 32.
[33]Ibid., p. 38.
[34]As quoted in Kevork Sarafian, *French Educational Theorists* (Los Angeles: C. C. Crawford, 1933), p. 76.

with a repressive spirit, but in other institutions this supervision afforded a worthy opportunity for offering children real leadership. The friendly and interested teachers on duty in the recreation rooms or playgrounds encouraged a true spirit of gaiety and relaxation.

To promote interest in intellectual subjects in Jesuit schools, the boys were awarded the leadership of a squad for superior work, honor societies were organized, pupils were paired as rivals, and classes were divided into competing groups. At Saint Cyr the girls who were most successful in games were awarded small money prizes which they in turn usually donated to charity. The Port Royalists, who displayed little interest in physical education, opposed such rivalry between students. They believed that youths should only try to exceed their own past efforts.

In general, discipline in Catholic schools was firm but not harsh. The rod, employed so generously in other institutions, was seldom seen, for rigid regulations governed the utilization of it. The zeal of the teachers, methods of motivation, close supervision, and efficient organization of the schools eliminated many disciplinary problems.

9

Physical Education
in
Educational Realism

The Italian humanists of the fifteenth century and the northern reformers of the sixteenth century both showed great promise of encouraging intellectual freedom and extending knowledge. But the later humanists rejected the broad, rich curriculum of the early Renaissance. They narrowed the humanistic studies to a few classics, principally the writings of Cicero which came to be considered the sole instrument for developing an educated man. This formalistic trend was also evident in the work of the northern Protestant reformers. As the different sects became established, each tended to suppress individual judgment and to require unquestioning obedience to the authority of the church.

Realism arose as a movement of protest to these conditions. While most men were preoccupied with classical learning, a few, such as Copernicus, were seeking the solution to problems by new methods of scientific inquiry. Soon these scientists and explorers were making discoveries that discredited certain laws of the ancient scholars and demonstrated that the classics did not hold the final and total sum of all knowledge. The originators of realism moved away from the medieval obsession with salvation and projected themselves beyond the authority of the past. They demanded a broader curriculum for youth and a training that would directly relate to the realities of life on this globe.

Although the realistic thinkers pleaded for educational reform, the religious wars that followed the Reformation placed obstacles in the path of the movement. Yet, at a time when men's energies were being drained by the Thirty Years' War in Germany, the Puritan Civil War in England, and the Huguenot wars in France, the new educational spirit managed to manifest itself in three distinct stages known as verbal realism, social realism, and sense realism. Verbal and social realism relied largely upon the knowledges of the past, but efforts were made to redirect these facts, applying them in utilitarian ways. Sense realism marked the emergence of the modern scientific method.

PHYSICAL EDUCATION IN VERBAL REALISM

The verbal realists, like the humanists, believed the classical languages and literature were the highest product of human thought and therefore most worthy of man's pursuance. Fundamentally, the two groups accepted the same sources for their educational content, but they held different concepts of the scope and aims of education. The verbal realists condemned the shallowness of humanistic studies and sought to direct learning toward more meaningful goals. Among the distinguished scholars who were early exponents of verbal realism, three were most noteworthy: the Spanish Juan Luis Vives, the French François Rabelais, and the English John Milton.

Juan Luis Vives (1492–1540) received a scholastic training as a young man, was introduced to humanism at the University of Paris, and later became a friend of Erasmus and Thomas More. His educational works include *On a Plan of Studies for Youth* (*De Ratione Studii Puerili*), *On the Instruction of a Christian Woman* (*De Institutione Feminae Christianae*), *Concerning the Teaching of the Arts* (*De Tradendis Disciplinis*), and *Concerning the Mind* (*De Anima*).

François Rabelais (c. 1483–1553), originally dedicated himself to the Church but later left monastic life to study medicine and to write vitriolic criticism of ecclesiastical abuses and educational inefficiencies. In his satirical works, *The Life of Gargantua* and the *Heroic Deeds of Pantagruel*, he depicted the education of his day. The mythical Gargantua first attended an ordinary school of the Middle Ages, spending years laboring over grammatical drills and exercises and did ". . . profit nothing. . . ."[1] After being given a potion to make him forget all he had learned, the huge schoolboy renewed his education according to a more realistic pattern. Although the new type of education Rabelais suggested had little effect on the schools of that era, his ideas influenced such men as Locke, Montaigne, and Rousseau.

John Milton (1608–1674), who devoted himself to public service during the time of Cromwell, was one of the most erudite men of his day. In 1644, he published a brief *Tractate on Education*, in which he attacked the current educational methods and suggested ways of improving them. Although a confirmed classicist, Milton did think of education as a discipline for the actualities of life.

---

[1]François Rabelais, *The Works of François Rabelais*, trans. Sir Thomas Urquhart and Motteux (London: H. G. Bohn, 1849), 1:148.

Aims of Education

The verbal realists believed that comprehending the ethical precepts and meaning of the classics was more important than analyzing their grammatical and literary forms, or their logic and dialectics.

Juan Vives insisted upon relating education to useful objectives. "This must be the first rule of any study . . . ," he declared, "to order all our inquiry with reference to the practical needs of life, to some definite advantage of mind or body, or to the end of personal piety."[2] Again, more concisely, "Having acquired our knowledge, we must turn it to usefulness, and employ it for the common good."[3] Vives' aims of education were all subordinated to his dominant goal of happiness which was religious piety. Knowledge was the way to know God; the end of all wisdom was the uplifting and improvement of human life.

Rabelais demanded an education that would lead to ". . . freedom of thought and of action instead of the complacent dependence on authority, whether of Schoolmen, classicists, or Church."[4] He argued for the development of the whole man. "Together with the intellect, the senses are to be trained; the body, as well as the mind, is to be nurtured; character and a religious spirit are to be developed; and the pupil made competent to take his place in a world of men, and to perform with ease and dignity all that manhood demands."[5] Although the education Rabelais proposed was somewhat literary, it was encyclopedic in scope, and had a practical bearing on man's duties in society.

Milton was primarily a classicist, but he would not limit education to intellectual achievements. A moral goal pervaded the Puritan's educational ideas with emphasis given to physical and aesthetic objectives. Studies were to be in terms of preparation for life. Milton proclaimed, "I call, therefore, a complete and generous education, that which fits a man to perform justly, skillfully, and magnanimously all the offices, both private and public, of peace and war."[6]

Aims of Physical Education

The physical development of students were given little consideration in the scholastic and later humanistic schools. The realists once again re-

[2]W. H. Woodward, *Studies in Education during the Age of the Renaissance* (Cambridge: Cambridge University Press, 1924), p. 203.

[3]J. L. Vives, *On Education*, trans. Foster Watson (Cambridge: Cambridge University Press, 1913), p. 283.

[4]Paul Monroe, *History of Education* (New York: The Macmillan Company, 1910), p. 447.

[5]F. P. Graves, *A History of Education during the Middle Ages and the Transition to Modern Times* (New York: The Macmillan Company, 1919), p. 244.

[6]John Milton, *Of Education; Areopagitica; the Commonwealth* (Boston: Houghton-Mifflin Company, 1911), p. 9.

minded the pedagogy that man had a body that needed to be developed as well as a mind.

The aims of physical education emphasized by Vives reinforced his major objective of education—religious piety. Physical exercises were to provide a regenerative force upon which the mind could draw when exhausted and to develop a vitalized body that would support greater mental powers. Any overemphasis of physical education, Vives censured, and any promotion of physical education for increasing military efficiency, he denounced as incompatible with the Christian doctrine of love. In this last belief, Vives differed with the opinions of Rabelais and Milton.

The medical training of Rabelais no doubt shaped his ideas on physical education. He recognized the recreational value of exercises and their importance in counterbalancing intellectual effort. He also appreciated that hygiene and nutrition were related directly to man's ability to perform his duties in life. Inasmuch as chivalry still influenced institutional forms, Rabelais' objectives were confined primarily to preparation for the gentlemen's occupation of war.[7]

Milton desired to utilize physical education for the duties of war. Being closely associated with the Cromwell government, he urged, ". . . it were happy for the commonwealth, if our magistrates . . . would take into their care . . . the managing of our public sports and festival pastimes . . . such as may inure and harden our bodies by martial exercises to all warlike skill and performance. . . ."[8] Physical training was to keep youth, ". . . healthy, nimble, strong and well in breath . . . make them grow large and tall, and to inspire them with a gallant and fearless courage, which . . . will turn into a native and heroic valor. . . ."[9] Milton also appreciated that, ". . . the spirit of man cannot demean itself lively in this body, without some recreating intermission of labour and serious things. . . ."[10] Nevertheless, the physical recreation Milton recommended was primarily military and was imbued with the Spartan rather than the Athenian spirit.

Promotion of Physical Education

The ideas of the verbal realists were not incorporated by the schools of the day, but their philosophical writings became a part of the heritage that was to influence pedagogy for generations.

Vives disapproved of sending young boys away to school. He believed tender young bodies could be better nourished to good health and increased strength under the supervision of parents. At eight years, how-

[7] Rabelais, *Works*, p. 348.
[8] J. Milton, "Reason of Church Governments," *Prose Works*, ed. J. A. St. John (London: H. G. Bohn, 1848), 2:480.
[9] Milton, *Of Education; Areopagitica; the Commonwealth*, p. 125.
[10] Milton, *Prose Works*, p. 480.

ever, children should enroll in public day schools rather than private boarding academies. Besides outlining such revolutionary policies as establishing publicly financed schools, the Spanish philosopher recommended paying teachers from government funds, and even wanted to found a school for training teachers.

Rabelais' educational scheme was a tutorial system in which Gargantua's life was systematically regulated as to hours of rising, of work, or eating, and as to the nature and duration of studies and physical exercise. A period of exercises followed both the morning and afternoon studies. Physical exercises and diets were changed to meet inclement weather.

Milton proposed that youth be educated in an academy providing education for boys between twelve and twenty-one years. The day's work was to be divided into three parts: studies, exercises, and diets. Milton advised, ". . . about an hour and a half ere they eat at noon should be allowed them for exercise, and due rest afterwards. . . ."[11] Military drills were to engage the boys for two hours before supper. Thus, a good portion of the day was to be devoted to physical education. In addition, in the spring of the year, older students were to ride forth in companies to all quarters of the land.

Program of Physical Education

Vives, like all the verbal realists, advocated a comprehensive educational program and included many of the physical activities popular in the classical times. He favored javelin throwing, ball playing, running, leaping, wrestling, vigorous walking, tennis, and football. He did not mention military exercises, and he censured dancing, dice, and cards.

Rabelais' description of Gargantua's physical exercises included most of the commonly known exercises and sports of the day. The proposed curriculum was beyond ordinary human potentialities. Gargantua's physical activities for the day were outlined as follows: "Then for three good hours he had a lecture read unto him. This done, they went forth . . . unto the meadows where they played at the ball, the long-tennis, and at the *pile trigone,* most gallantly exercising their bodies, as formerly they had done their minds."[12]

After lunch and a period of studying, Gargantua resumed his exercises. Donning a complete suit of mail, he participated in grueling feats of horsemanship and exercised with his lance, battle-axe, pike, and various types of swords. With great skill he took part in the vigorous activity of the hunt.

[11]Milton, *Of Education; Areopagitica; the Commonwealth,* p. 24.
[12]Rabelais, *Works,* pp. 176–77.

He played at the balloon, and made it bound in the air, both with fist and foot. He wrestled, ran, jumped, not at three steps and a leap . . . but at one leap he would skip over a ditch, spring over a hedge, mount six paces upon a wall. . . . He did swim in deep waters on his belly, on his back, sideways, with all his body, with his feet only, with one hand in the air, wherein he held a book, crossing thus the breadth of the River Seine. . . . Coming out of the water, he ran furiously up against a hill, and with the same alacrity and swiftness ran down again. He climbed up trees like a cat, leaped from the one to the other like a squirrel. . . . He did cast the dart, throw the bar, put the stone, practise the javelin, the boar spear or partisan, and the halbert. He broke the strongest bows in drawing, bended against his breast the greatest cross-bows of steel. . . . The time being thus bestowed, and himself rubbed, cleansed, wiped, and refreshed with other clothes, he returned fair and softly. . . .[13]

Finally supper came, lessons were read, and discussion followed before retiring.

Indoor recreation replaced sports during inclement weather. On rainy days, Gargantua and his fellows "did recreate themselves in bottling up of hay, in cleaving and sawing of wood, and in threshing sheaves of corn at the barn. . . . He went through the halls and places appointed for fencing and there played against the masters themselves at all weapons. . . . He went to see jugglers, tumblers . . . and considered their cunning, their shifts, their summer-saults. . . ."[14]

Gargantua's teacher advocated that one day a month be profitably spent in the country without books or lectures, and ". . . there spend all the day long in making the greatest cheer that could be devised . . . playing, singing, dancing, tumbling in some fair meadow . . . and fishing for frogs and crabs."[15] Although much of Rabelais' program is of a military character, the "country day" was solely an invigorating and recreational nature.

Milton's physical education program was almost exclusively military. He stated, "The exercise which I commend first, is the exact use of their weapons, to guard, and to strike safely with edge or point. . . . They may be also practised in all the locks and gripes of wrestling wherein Englishmen were wont to excel, as need may often be in fight to tug, to grapple, and to close."[16] About two hours before supper Milton wanted youths ". . . to be called out to the military motions . . . that having in sport, but with much exactness and daily muster, served out the rudiments of their soldiership. . . ."[17]

[13]Ibid., pp. 180–81.
[14]Ibid., pp. 183–84.
[15]Ibid., p. 185.

[16]Milton, *Of Education; Areopagitica; the Commonwealth,* pp. 24–25.
[17]Ibid., p. 26.

Methods of Physical Education

Vives was particularly advanced in his concept of education methods. Desiring to study the operation of the mind and to apply his findings to improve instruction, the Spanish scholar became one of the forerunners of empirical psychology. Recognizing individual differences, he desired that teachers should observe children to determine the best training to suit their abilities. He also advised that followup conferences be held during the year to exchange observations concerning the progress of the pupils.

Rabelais denounced formal, authoritarian methods. Through a pleasant, informal program he hoped to capture the interest of children. Excursions, which would permit students to collect first-hand information, were part of his program. Children were to be constantly in the company of learned tutors who would observe the character and natural bent of each pupil and use the most natural methods to develop his potential.

PHYSICAL EDUCATION IN SOCIAL REALISM

Scholastic and humanistic learning remained aloof from contemporary life. The verbal realists had taken a step toward making education more functional by urging students to read the ancient classics for the ideas expressed in them rather than merely studying their form and style. The social realists moved one step further by directing education toward a preparation for the practical life of a gentleman. Although they would not discard bookish instruction, they insisted that it was not enough to understand the wisdom of the classics but that the knowledge must be applied to living. The question to be asked was, "Is he a better man and more accomplished in the art of living as a result of his education?"

Michel de Montaigne (1533–1592), a French essayist, living during an era of religious persecution, was a representative of social humanism. His educational views, expressed in two essays, *On the Education of Children* (*De l'Institution des Enfants*) and *On Pedantry* (*Du Pédantisme*), reveal surprisingly modern ideas.

Aims of Education

Montaigne conceived education as the process of shaping an aristocratic youth to live the life of an accomplished gentleman. To him, learning was not to develop grammarians and logicians but to prepare men to lead active and happy lives. Such an ideal implied educating the whole man— physically, mentally, and morally. "I would have his outward manners, and his social behaviour, *and the carriage of his person* formed at the same time with his mind. It is not a mind, it is not a body that we are training; it is a man, and he ought not to be divided into two parts."[18] To Montaigne, physical awkwardness, social maladroitness, and intellectual unproductiveness indicated educational failure.

To shape a man for a useful life did not mean specialized or professional training. A boy's studies were to make him capable of distinguishing truth from error, good from evil, so that he would select the right and best course of living. Montaigne criticized parents who ". . . look only toward furnishing our heads with knowledge; of judgment and virtue not a word is heard. . . . We labour to stuff the memory, and leave the understanding *and the conscience* empty."[19] Although Montaigne would never have divorced religion from life, the type of education he advanced was more Grecian than Christian. His moral objectives reflected the Realists' concept of man.

Aims of Physical Education

Montaigne aimed to combine the physical with the emotional, spiritual, and intellectual to form an integrated personality capable of sustaining the demands placed upon it. Physical education was conceived essential to the total educative framework. "The body has a great share in our being, it has an eminent place there; and therefore its structure and composition very properly receive consideration."[20] Physical education was formally acknowledged as a prerequisite for the development of man, for through the physical, man's mental and moral powers were to be activated.

With the physical, intellectual, and spiritual life of man all so interdependent, Montaigne complained, "They who go about to disunite our two principal parts, and to separate one from another, are in the wrong. We must, on the contrary, reunite and rejoin them. We must command the soul not to draw aside and entertain herself apart, not to despise and abandon the body. . . ."[21] Those who narrowed educational aims to favor the body were just as severely censured by the French philosopher as those who favored the soul; for both had lost sight of their real objective, which was the education of the whole man.

In some respects, Montaigne preceded Locke in viewing exercises as a "hardening process," but his idea was considerably moderated. He believed, however, that a boy broken to the "pain and harshness of exercise" would be better able to meet the pain and harshness of life. Montaigne held that a youth's emotional equilibrium was as dependent upon the vitality of the body as the intellect. *"It is not enough to toughen his*

---

[18]Michel de Montaigne, *The Essays of Michel de Montaigne*, trans. Jacob Zeitlin (New York: Alfred Knopf, 1934), 1:145.

[19]Ibid., 1:117.

[20]Ibid., 2:303.   [21]Ibid., 2:303.

spirit, his muscles also must be toughened. For the spirit is too greatly strained if it is not supported, and would have too hard a task to discharge two offices alone."[22] The body and mind were envisioned as complementary forces, acting in unison, and focusing toward a healthy, thinking, acting individual.

Promotion of Physical Education

Montaigne desired that the child be educated by a tutor rather than by his parents or the schools. He observed ". . . it is not right for a child to be brought up in the lap of his parents; their natural affection makes them too tender and lax, even the wisest of them."[23] He also censured the school as an agency of education. "Do but observe him when he comes back from school. . . . All you shall find he has got is, that his Latin and Greek have made him more vain and presumptuous than when he went from home. *He should have brought back a full mind, he only brings back a swollen one; and has only inflated instead of enlarging it."*[24] Montaigne advised that the child's tutor be selected with great care, for upon him would depend the whole success of the youth's education.

Program of Physical Education

The curriculum advocated by the French philosopher was broad and comprehensive. Because it forms the judgment and character, philosophy was to be the principal study. The traditional subjects, logic, rhetoric, geometry, and physics, were considered less important. Although Latin and Greek were retained, emphasis was also placed on the contemporary languages, which scholars had previously ignored. The consideration given to health and physical education in the curriculum represented another departure from the educational practices of that day.

The physical education program was designed to make the youth capable of living a vigorous and active life. Montaigne advised, "Harden him to toil and cold, to wind and sun, and to dangers that he ought to despise; wean him from all effeminacy and delicacy in clothes and sleep, eating and drinking; accustom him to everything."[25] Other than suggesting running, wrestling, dancing, hunting, riding, and fencing, Montaigne did not elaborate on the content of a physical education program.

Methods of Physical Education

Of the teaching methods of his day, Montaigne complained, "Our schoolmasters are eternally shouting into our ears as though they were pouring

22Ibid., 1:133.   24Ibid., 1:120.
23Ibid., 1:133.   25Ibid., 1:145.

into a funnel, while our business is only to repeat what the others have said."[26] Denouncing such practices, he pointed out that if a man were to be trained for a life of action, he must be given an opportunity to explore, sample, and practice the art of living. Of the teacher, therefore, he said, "I would not have him do all the thinking and speaking: I would have him hear his pupil speak in turn."[27] Montaigne thought a tutor should be a pleasant, resourceful individual, who could attract students to their studies and make them relish learning without rigor and constraint. This concept of the relationship between teacher and pupil was revolutionary in a day of "memory schools" that were ruled by the rod.

PHYSICAL EDUCATION IN SENSE REALISM

As the Renaissance continued to penetrate medieval thought, more scholars began to regard nature and the universe with a critical and inquisitive spirit. These intellectual rebels made outstanding contributions during the sixteenth and early seventeenth centuries.[28] These included: in the field of mathematics, the decimal fractions by Stevin, the use of the abstract symbols in algebra by Cardan, the analytical geometry of Descartes, and the development of logarithms by Napier; in the field of astronomy, the heliocentric theory of Copernicus, the charting of the courses of the planets by Kepler, and the discoveries of the celestial phenomena by Galileo; in the field of the physical sciences, the utilization of magnetism by Gilbert, and the invention of the barometer by Torricelli; and, in the field of the biological sciences, the discovery of circulation of blood by Harvey, the drawings of dissection of the human body by Vesalius, and the rejection of many medical theories of Hippocrates and Galen by Paracelsus who began to treat disease by pharmaceuticals. Despite the opposition these scientists often had to endure, the world gradually came to accept their work.

Most of the discoveries of the scientific pioneers resulted from new methods of attacking problems. Copernicus, finding himself dissatisfied with the Ptolemaic explanation of the universe, reviewed all previous literature on the subject and finally formulated his own theory. The scientific method, which required using independent judgment and observing nature as a means of seeking truth, stimulated the enthusiasm of the men who are identified as sense realists. Among the philosophers who wrote about the new methods of scientific thought and applied them to education, were Francis Bacon, Richard Mulcaster, and John Amos Comenius.

Francis Bacon (1561–1626) was the author of the *Advancement of Learning, The New Atlantis,* and *Novum Organum.* Although Bacon's

[26]Ibid., 1:130.   [27]Ibid., 1:130.
[28]Henry Morley, *Ideal Commonwealths* (London: G. Routledge and Sons, 1893), p. 263.

ideas were not new, his writing gave them such vivid expression that they stirred deeply the thinking of many educators.

Richard Mulcaster (c. 1531–1611), headmaster of Merchant Taylor's and St. Paul's schools, wrote two volumes on education, the *Elementaire* and *Positions*. *Positions* gave proof of his keen interest in physical education; for the subtitle declared it as necessary to train for "health in their bodie" as for "skill in their booke."

The pedagogical genius, John Amos Comenius (1593–1670), commands the respect of educators of all ages. As a Moravian bishop during the religious strife of the Thirty Years' War, he suffered bitter persecution; yet, wandering in exile, he continued to devote himself to the religious cause of his people and sought to focus attention on the need for educational reform. His influence spread throughout Germany, England, Sweden, Poland, and Holland. Comenius was a prolific writer. He produced over one hundred works in Czech and Latin, including *Great Didactic, The Vestibule of the Gate of Tongues Unlocked, The School of Infancy,* and *The World in Pictures*. His simplified language textbooks were widely adopted, but his educational theories, prophetic statements of modern educational philosophy, were largely neglected until the nineteenth century.

Aims of Education

The sense realists culminated the realistic movement with their scientific thinking. The verbal realists had initiated the reform by insisting that students read the classics to secure knowledge rather than to practice grammatical exercises; the social realists still clung to the classics, but insisted that the wisdom acquired must be applied to everyday living; the sense realists believed that information about life could be discovered in the forces and the laws of nature. The sense realists proclaimed that understanding came through the senses—through hearing, feeling, tasting, touching, and seeing—and they desired to have education directed toward sensory training. They refused to regard the classic philosophers as infallible or as the only source of truth.

Typical of all sense realists, Bacon asserted that intellectual life had to give the individual power to deal with reality. Man through his senses and his powers of observation, was to discover the basic laws of nature and utilize this information for the service of mankind. Bacon delineated the progress that could be realized by inductive reasoning unlocking human thought.

Richard Mulcaster demanded an education that would be more useful. He wrote, "*Education* is the bringing up of one, not to live alone, but amongst others. . . ."[29] In further requiring that men be trained in ac-

---

[29]Richard Mulcaster, *Positions* (London: T. Vautrollier, 1581), p. 185. (When necessary for intelligibility, Mulcaster's spelling has been slightly modernized.)

cordance with the laws of nature, Mulcaster was a sense realist. "The end of education and training is to help Nature to her perfection. . . ."[30] Mulcaster's objectives were focused on the child rather than on content.

Comenius was more influenced by his deep religious convictions than by the spirit of the scientific age. He believed that the ultimate objective of education was to attain eternal happiness with God, but he was convinced that "Nature is God's work, and is an enemy of man only in so far as he does not *know* it. He must, then, be taught to know nature; and to know himself."[31] The Moravian bishop expressed great faith in the power of education to regenerate the individual and society.

Aims of Physical Education

The theory that ideas are acquired through the senses naturally focused attention on the body. Curiosity about the physiological laws governing the body and the mind opened the pedagogical door wider for the establishment of an improved physical education.

Bacon briefly mentioned physical education in his philosophical writings. He noted ". . . there seemeth to be a relation or conformity between the good of the mind and the good of the body;"[32] He ". . . divided the good of the body into health, beauty, strength, and pleasure."[33] In reference to health, Bacon felt ". . . there is scarcely any tendency to disease which may not be prevented by some proper exercise."[34] (Of course, he did not know the germ theory of disease.) He recommended that athletic skill should be practiced sufficiently for use, but excessive exercise could only serve for "mercenary ostentation."[35]

Perhaps more than any other writer of the day, Richard Mulcaster insisted upon the importance of physical education. In educating a youth, he advised to ". . . consider the strength of his bodie, no lesse than we do the quicknesse of his witte."[36] The body and the mind were to assist one another in the proper execution of their duties, so one was not be made ". . . stronge, and well qualified, the other left feeble, and a prey to infirmitie."[37]

Although Mulcaster recognized that exercises could serve recreational as well as military purposes, he was interested in employing them

---

[30]As quoted in Graves, *A History of Education during the Middle Ages and the Transition to Modern Times*, p. 251.

[31]S. S. Laurie, *Studies in the History of Educational Opinion from the Renaissance* (Cambridge: University Press, 1905), p. 151.

[32]W. A. Wright, *Bacon, The Advancement of Learning* (Oxford: Clarendon Press, 1900), p. 216.

[33]Ibid., p. 216.

[34]James L. Spedding, D. D. Heath, and R. L. Ellis, *The Works of Francis Bacon* (London: Longman and Co., 1901), 4:384.

[35]Ibid., 4:394.

[36]Mulcaster, *Positions*, p. 22.   [37]Ibid., p. 40.

to maintain good health. Mulcaster lamented that the absence of health had prevented many men from developing their full potentialities. He urged that health should not be reserved for consideration in old age or when illness had developed, but was to be one of the major objectives of education. Whatever nature bestowed upon the body of youth, Mulcaster believed, should be assisted and bettered by exercises. He asked, "But now what place hath exercise here? to helpe nature by motion in all these her workings, and wayes for health; to encrease and encourage the naturall heat, that it maye digest quickly and expell strongly; to fashion and frame all the partes of the bodie to their naturall and best behaviour. . . . And be not these great benefites? . . . to helpe life to continue long?"[38]

Comenius, although a theologian, exalted the soul by attending the body. In his words, "Above all things it should be the parents' first care to preserve the health of their off-spring, since they cannot train them up successfully unless they be lively and vigorous; for what proficiency can be made with the sickly and morbid?"[39] He devoted a whole chapter in his *School of Infancy* to physical education.

Comenius possessed a unique insight into the play life of the child. He saw play as a natural educational process and cautioned that to restrain it would result in deficiencies in the harmonious development of the mind and body. Children's games and pastimes were to be encouraged, for such participation was nature's wholesome medium for developing their wits, manners, and habits. Parents were advised that "It is better to play than to be idle, for during play the mind is intent on some object which often sharpens the abilities. In this way children may be early exercised to an active life without any difficulty, since Nature herself stirs them to be doing something."[40] He also believed that amusements would contribute to emotional equilibrium, for the happier heart and stronger body resulting from play would together insure sound mental health. Comenius reminded parents of the proverb, ". . . a joyful mind is half health. The joy of the heart is the very life-spring of man. . . ."[41] He would not deny children any little occupation that stirred up their spirits unless it was contrary to piety and morality.

Promotion of Physical Education

To appreciate the contributions of the sense realists, one must have a visual picture of the schools of that day. The schools were organized on

[38]Ibid., pp. 45–46.
[39]J. A. Comenius, *School of Infancy*, ed. W. S. Monroe (Boston: D. C. Heath and Co., 1901), p. 23.
[40]R H. Quick, *Essays on Educational Reformers* (New York: D. Appleton and Co., 1904), p. 143.
[41]Comenius, *School of Infancy*, p. 33.

a two-track system, offering a limited elementary training to poor youth and a classical education for the sons of gentry.

At a time when most schoolmen were interested only in higher education, Richard Mulcaster perceived the importance of early training. From approximately the sixth to the twelfth year, he would have all children attend a vernacular elementary school. From their twelfth to the sixteenth year, selected students would attend grammar school and begin their Latin studies. University life was to follow for the more competent students. Mulcaster made the revolutionary suggestion that one college of the university should train teachers on the same basis as the other schools educated doctors and lawyers. Some three hundred years elapsed, however, before the art of teaching was considered a sufficiently important skill to require specialized training.

Physical education was not to be left to chance in Mulcaster's proposed system. He warned parents, "neither is it enough to saye, that children wille stirring alwaie of themselves, and that therefore they neede not any so great a care, for exercising their bodies. . . . Wherefore as stilnesse hath her direction by order in schooles, so must stirring be directed by well appointed exercise."[42] The physical education classes were to be taught by the same individual in charge of the youth's intellectual training.

Richard Mulcaster looked for three qualities in a physical educator. First, he was to be "ravished with the excellencie and worthynes" of his profession, for ". . . being well resolved in the excellencie of his owne subject he will both himselfe execute the better, and perswade other sooner to embrace that with zeale. . . ."[43] Secondly, the prospective teacher was to have sought knowledge of his subject in the writings of such men as the learned Galen and the Italian Hieronymous Mercurialis, who took ". . . paines to sift out of all writers, whatsoever concerneth the whole *Gymnasticall* and exercising argument."[44] And, thirdly, the physical educator was to use discretion in applying teaching methods.

Mulcaster gave careful attention to a healthful school environment. In selecting school sites, he cautioned teachers to observe whether a plot would provide sufficient fresh air and light and an ample and proper space for a playground. Being a practical schoolman himself, Mulcaster advised teachers not to give up exercises because they lacked perfect playgrounds but to make the best use of existing conditions.

Comenius advocated the same education for everyone regardless of social status. The external school organization was to be divided into four levels of six years each. A School of the Mother's Knee (ages 1–6) would be located in the home. The vernacular school (ages 6–12) would be located in every village and would offer basic knowledge to everyone.

---

[42]Mulcaster, *Positions*, pp. 23–24.   [44]Ibid., p. 128.
[43]Ibid., p. 127.

A Latin School (ages 12–18) established in every province would prepare those desiring to enter the professions. A university (ages 18–24) erected in every kingdom would train leaders and teachers for the future. In a graduate center, a School of Schools, all the great scholars of the universe would gather to pursue research for the good of mankind and the glory of God. Every child was to proceed through these institutions, as far as his natural abilities and interests would permit him to go. The first two steps of training were to be compulsory and ability rather than social station was to determine how much further a youth was to ascend the educational ladder. Two centuries passed before this ideal of universal education was put into limited practice.

Comenius believed that the internal organization of the school should be planned in harmony with the child's development. In early infancy the parents were to encourage their offspring to play and were even to play with them. He added,

> Although the parents and attendants may be of great service to children in all these matters, yet children of their own age are of still greater service . . . consequently, boys should meet daily and play together or run about in open places; and this ought not merely to be permitted, but even provided for, with the precaution, however, they do not mingle with depraved associates. . . .[45]

As pupils proceeded through school, Comenius would consistently allot time for exercise and games. School work was to be limited to four hours for younger students and six hours for older youths. For each study period, one-half hour of relaxation was to ensue and no homework assigned. For more mature students, Comenius allotted eight hours of the day to sleep, eight to work, and the remaining eight to meals, exercise, and recreation, and general health care. In many ways, he anticipated modern attempts to reorganize education in terms of child growth and development.

Textbooks, facilities, and equipment as agencies of education were not underestimated by the sense realists. Illustrated books, maps, pictures, and models were to be utilized as a means of sense training, and a playground was deemed an essential part of the facilities.

Program of Physical Education

The sense realists, for the most part, recommended a broad curriculum. Teaching in the vernacular was exalted. Classical languages were still taught, but only as a means of seeking knowledge rather than as ends in themselves. Many sense realists urged that students be given more time

[45]Comenius, *School of Infancy*, pp. 42–53.

to study natural phenomena, and most of them included physical education in the curriculum.

Many chapters in Mulcaster's *Positions Concerning Training Up of
Children* were devoted to physical education. Some of these were: Of
Dancing, Why it is blamed and now delivered from blame; Of Wrestling;
Of Walking; Of Running; Of Fensing, or the use of weapons; Of Top and
Scourage; Of Leaping; Of Swimming; Of Riding; Of Hunting; Of Shoot-
ing; Of Ball. Mulcaster's discussion on the value of exercise in each
chapter revealed that he was largely reliant on Galen and Mercurialis for
his knowledge of the body.

According to Comenius, when imaginative children sought enjoyment in imitating the activities of their elders, they should be encouraged,
and toy replicas of adult objects should be provided for them. Because
youngsters love to construct things, Comenius believed they should be
allowed to build walls and houses with wood and stones. "In a word,
whatever children delight to play with, provided that it be not hurtful, they
ought to be gratified rather than restrained from it. . . ."[46] Even in the
later school life, when a boy devoted most of his time to his studies,
Comenius would permit and even encourage him to play games.

Methods of Physical Education

The rise of scientific thinking influenced all aspects of teaching, but it
activated more changes in the area of methods than in any other phase
of education. Bacon, in publicizing inductive thinking, exhorted students
to develop critical attitudes, to make observations, to collect facts, and
to engage in original investigations. Emphasis had previously been placed
on deductive reasoning, which begins with a premise, a generalization
which is accepted as a settled statement of truth, and from it conclusions
are drawn. Deductive logic teaches and proves what is already known or
assumed to be true; inductive logic, advocated by Bacon, tried to establish
general principles after making many observations and collecting many
facts concerning particular phenomena. Bacon would have men end with
generalizations and not begin with them. Bacon was not an educator and
did not apply his methods to the schools, but he had electrified a circuit
for seeking knowledge that was to illuminate the techniques of teaching.

Mulcaster, after studying the ancient Greek and Roman methods of
conducting exercises, suggested a similar but less elaborate plan: ". . .
to *apparell* our selves for the purpose, to *begin* our exercise first slowly,
and so grow on quicker, to *rebate* softly, and by gentle degrees, to *change*
our sweatie clothes, to *walke* a little after, last of all our bodies being
setled, to *go* to our meate."[47] In other chapters of his book the English
schoolmaster gave similar consideration to the proper time to exercise and

---

[46]Ibid., p. 45.   [47]Mulcaster, *Positions*, p. 122.

the proper amount of exercise. The duty of the teacher, in his opinion, was to study the natural ability of the child and "to help nature to her perfection." Recognizing the individual differences of youths, he reminded the teachers that ". . . children that come to schoole dwel not in one house . . . they be not of one age, nor fit for one exercise, and yet they must have some."[48]

Comenius denounced the schools of his day as "slaughterhouses of the mind," as, indeed, they were. Tender six-year-old youngsters entering school were glutted with Latin vocabularies and forced to labor for years over rules of grammar. Proceeding through a confused maze of memorization, rarely associating things with words, children could only find learning a very unpleasant experience. Teachers had to rely on fear to motivate learning.

Comenius desired to improve pedagogical procedures and much of what he had to say has since been established on a more scientific basis. He believed that teaching should proceed from the simple to the complex, from the known to the unknown; that examples should come before rules; frequent repetitions help to fix ideas; new knowledge should be tied to old; the scope of materials should be limited to the child's experience; explanations should be clear, simple, and, if possible, humorous; studies should be graded and organized to follow the natural pattern of the child's development. In short, the student should be led in every possible way to love learning.

Comenius insisted on moderation in all things. "To express the matter in a few words, let their health sustain no damage from bruises, from excess of heat or cold, from too much food or drink, or from hunger or thirst."[49] He believed in allowing youngsters to play with one another, for "When they play together, children of about the same age, and of equal progress and manners and habits, sharpen each other more effectually, since the one does not surpass the other in depth of invention; there is among them neither assumption of superiority of the one over the other, nor force, dread, or fear; but love, candor, free questionings, and answers about everything; all these are defective in us, their elders. . . ."[50]

The great Czech scholar was thinking in terms of the intellect when formulating most of his methods, but much of his advice is also applicable to the teaching of health and physical education. Whenever possible the student was to come in contact with the object he was studying or at least a picture or representation of it. For example, Comenius suggested that students would learn far more anatomy from one skeletal model than from reading several volumes on the subject. Such suggestions were eventually to mature into the modern demand for laboratory work, experiments, field trips, and visual aids.

[48]Ibid., p. 131.   [50]Ibid., pp. 42–43.
[49]Comenius, School of Infancy, p. 32.

10

Physical Education
in
Educational Disciplinarianism

The seventeenth century was an age when men were still trapped in religious and civil turmoil and engaged in a dramatic struggle between reason and authority, liberty and despotism. Between the Reformation and the Age of Enlightenment of the eighteenth century, the merchant class acquired greater social prestige and political power. Bold seamen exploring little known continents returned to the homeland laden with riches and glowing stories of their discoveries. A spurt of creative genius in arts and letters presented the world with imperishable masterpieces. Above all, science gradually became the commanding spirit of the times. Men, challenged by the work being done in mathematics, astronomy, and medicine, sought methods of thought that would bring the same accuracy and precision to other endeavors. By the end of the century, the world was blazing with intellectual curiosity and scientific interest.

John Locke (1632–1704) crystallized the ideas that were the keynote for the Age of Enlightenment. Son of a Puritan lawyer, he lived during the reign of Charles I, throughout the Cromwell regime, the Restoration of Charles II, and the expulsion of pro-Catholic James II. When William and Mary of Orange ascended the English throne, Locke returned to his native land after having spent years of exile in Holland. Throughout these troubled times, the philosopher had fought for religious toleration and denounced the divine right of kings.

Locke's opinions concerning religious tolerance and the political rights of man and his concept of the source of knowledge have been firmly woven into the fabric of modern educational life. Rather than conceiving of the mind as impressed prenatally with information and beliefs, he described it as a blank tablet (*tabula rasa*) on which experience would slowly write the story of life. Learning, therefore, was a product of sense perception and mental reflection. Knowledge was obtained by noting relationships among the data supplied by the senses and from them deriving meaningful concepts and generalizations.

Locke's interest in education was not limited to philosophical considerations. Having studied medicine, he thought in terms of both body and mind more naturally than many scholars; also his own inadequacy of health and vigor made him acutely aware of the need for physical fitness; and having established the relationship between the senses and reason, he naturally directed more attention toward the body than men preoccupied with the soul or reason alone. Locke expressed his philosophy of education in a number of treatises. His *Essay Concerning Human Understanding* had educational implications, but two other of his publications, *Some Thoughts Concerning Education* and *Conduct of the Understanding*, were more exclusively devoted to the training of the child.

Locke became a pivotal figure in history, exhibiting characteristics of the old order and opening an approach to a new epoch of thought. Endless arguments have been put forth to classify him, but his position has remained unique. Influenced tremendously by Montaigne, he was a social realist, directing all education toward the development of a gentleman of affairs. He was also a sense realist in that he thought ideas are secured through the senses. His *tabula rasa* theory destroyed the old concepts of the youth as a miniature adult and opened the way for an education based on the natural development of the child. Locke was a disciplinarian in that he stressed the continual practice of desirable behavior habits. His ideas, however, do not coincide with a number of the theories of the later disciplinarians.

Aims of Education

Disciplinarian education aimed to inculcate those habits in a young aristocrat that would result in the attainment of the highest character and refinement. The objective was to teach the individual to thwart those natural desires not in harmony with reason and to discipline himself habitually to practice desirable ways of acting and thinking. In Locke's opinion it was ". . . only practice that improved our minds as well as bodies, and we must expect nothing from our understanding any further than they are perfected by habits."[1]

A well-disciplined character could be achieved only by a youth possessing a sound mind in a sound body.[2] Thus Locke could educate the

[1]John Locke, "Conduct of the Understanding," in J. W. Adamson, *The Educational Writings of John Locke* (New York: Longmans, Green and Co., 1912), pp. 197–98.

[2]John Locke, "Some Thoughts Concerning Education," *Essays by John Locke* (London: Ward Lock and Co., 1883), p. 9.

whole man, disciplining him mentally and physically, and developing his bodily vigor to support his intellectual powers. Having provided for the physical fitness of the youth, the English philosopher specified four other qualities every gentleman desired for his son: virtue, wisdom, breeding, and learning. These behavior components were to be bred and nourished within each individual by a continual process of physical and mental discipline.

Locke did not accept the traditional definition of learning. He explained, ". . . I do not propose it [learning] as a variety and stock of knowledge, but a variety and freedom of thinking, as an increase of the powers and activity of the mind, not as an enlargement of its possessions."[3] Learning was to focus on reason; it was to be an active process of habit formation and not a passive process of fact accumulation.

Aims of Physical Education

Although the development of character was the principal part of the disciplinarian education, health was to be established first. The English philosopher envisioned physical fitness as basic to education, for he realized that the temper and strength of the body regulated the possible attainment and disposition of the personality. Locke's physical education program for the child was to create a strong constitution, to develop healthful habits of living, to provide refreshing recreation, and to develop the skills necessary for a gentleman in society, including the ability to bear arms.[4] Locke declared, "How necessary health is to our business and happiness, and how requisite a strong constitution, able to endure hardships and fatigue, is, to one that will make any figure in the world, is too obvious to need any proof."[5]

In *Some Thoughts Concerning Education,* Locke recommends that the body be developed to withstand hardships but he counterbalances this "hardening process" by encompassing recreation as an essential part of education. Locke recommended ". . . he that will make a good use of any part of his life, must allow a large portion of it to recreation. . . ."[6] He declared that when wearied either by physical or intellectual labor, the individual should turn to other activities to refresh ". . . the part that has been exercised, and is tired. . . ."[7] Although a broad interpretation was given to recreation, physical exercise was to constitute a major portion of it. Exercise was not only to harden the body but also to refresh the intellect and thereby assist in establishing sound mental health.

In that aristocratic period, physical education was also directed toward social objectives. Every noble youth was expected to acquire the

---

[3]Locke, "Conduct of the Understanding," p. 216.
[4]Locke, "Some Thoughts Concerning Education," p. 17.
[5]Ibid., p. 10.   [7]Ibid., p. 154.
[6]Ibid., p. 150.

physical skills necessary for a gentleman of fashion. "Besides what is to be had from study and books, there are other accomplishments necessary for a gentleman, to be got by exercise. . . ."[8] Such accomplishments included self-discipline, self-confidence, perfect carriage, and graceful motions as well as health and strength.

Promotion of Physical Education

After weighing the advantages and disadvantages of public and private instruction. Locke concluded that the child should be placed under the watchful eyes of a tutor who could carefully supervise his moral character. The governor was to be more than a sober and scholarly man, he was also to possess good breeding and a knowledge of the world. Special dancing, fencing, and riding masters were to meet similar qualifications.

Program of Physical Education

Locke initiated his treatise on the education of youth by outlining a simple regimen for the preservation and improvement of health. In general, he advocated "plenty of open air, exercise, and sleep. . . ."[9] Strict measures were to be used in toughening children's bodies and building up their resistance, but natural play was not to be suppressed. "They must not be hindered from being children, or from playing, or doing as children; but from doing ill. All other liberty is to be allowed them."[10]

In advocating exercise, Locke was thinking mainly of those skills necessary for an accomplished gentleman, such as swimming, dancing, riding, and fencing. Swimming was included because it would be a great advantage to a man's health and might save his life. Riding was essential for it would be useful to a youth of breeding both in peace and war. Fencing was endorsed by Locke with reservations. He thought that real skill required more practice than a busy man of affairs could devote to it and also that this sport often encouraged youths to engage in duels and thus endanger their lives. Locke concluded that he would rather have his son be a good wrestler than be an ordinary fencer. In expressing such an opinion, he reflected the changing social attitude toward duelling: " . . . with the rise of the merchant class, preferring commercial to combative competition, duelling began to be condemned and severely repressed."[11] As for dancing, Locke gave it full approval. "Dancing being that which

[8]Ibid., p. 149.   [9]Ibid., p. 24.
[10]Ibid., p. 45.
[11]Preserved Smith, *A History of Modern Culture* (New York: Henry Holt and Co., 1930), 1:525.

gives graceful motions all the life, and, above all things, manliness and becoming confidence to young children, I think it cannot be learned too early, after they are once of an age and strength capable of it."[12]

Recreation was defined in quite modern terms by Locke. As used by the original Latin writers, recreation had meant "recovery from illness," but Locke wrote this definition of recreation: ". . . Recreation is not being idle (as everyone may observe), but easing the wearied part by change of business. . . ."[13] To counterbalance man's predominantly sedentary labors, he recommended physical exercise. He stated, "A gentleman's more serious employment I look on to be study; and when that demands relaxation and refreshment, it should be in some exercise of the body, which unbends the thought and confirms the health and strength."[14]

Locke reminded men that gardening, carpentry, working in iron, and "other manual arts, which are both got and exercised by labour, do many of them, by that exercise, not only increase our dexterity and skill, but contribute to our health too, especially such as employ us in the open air. In these, then, health and improvement may be joined together, and of these should some fit ones be chosen, to be made the recreation of one, whose chief business is with books and study."[15] He defined a good recreation as an activity that men delight in and that will also leave them refreshed and relaxed as well as serving a useful and profitable purpose afterward. For this reason, he opposed cards and dice, which many men of fashion pursued passionately in the coffee houses of the day, as being more apt than not to tire men and give them more vexation than their regular employments in life.

Methods of Physical Education

Speaking for the aristocratic class, Locke advised, "That gentlemen should use their children as the honest farmers and substantial yeoman do theirs."[16] Criticizing parents because ". . . most children's constitutions are either spoiled, or at least harmed, by cockering and tenderness,"[17] he warned them that a hardy constitution could be developed only by consistently practicing sound health habits. Instructing the child about desirable habits was not considered sufficient because "Nobody is made anything by hearing of rules or saying them up in his memory; practice must settle the habit by doing, without reflecting on the rule. . . ."[18] Parents and tutors were charged with the responsibility of directing pupils into desirable health patterns.

[12]Locke, "Some Thoughts Concerning Education," p. 149.
[13]Ibid., p. 154.
[14]Ibid., p. 153.
[15]Ibid., p. 152.
[16]Ibid., p. 10.
[17]Ibid., p. 10.
[18]Locke, "The Conduct of Understanding," p. 191.

Locke desired that education should be a process of moral and physical discipline rather than intellectual instruction. He believed that the child should submit to authority, but he did not favor corporal punishment or constant chiding. Neither did Locke propose the pursuit of particular exercises merely because they were difficult, disagreeable, and dull, in order to give youth practice in the control of inner desires. Discipline for discipline's sake was not a part of Locke's thinking; he favored a purposeful discipline that would cultivate desirable habits.

In some respects Locke's suggestions were rather severe, but he wished to make the process of habituation as pleasant as possible. Establishing a balanced discipline was his objective, for, ". . . he that has found a way, how to keep up a child's spirit, easy, active, and free; and yet, at the same time, to restrain him from many things he has a mind to . . . has . . . got the true secret of education."[19] This objective could best be achieved in the English philosopher's opinion by initiating studies when the youngster's interest was keenest as well as by motivating him to take delight in his work. Public praise and private censure were also emphasized as worthy techniques for making youths ". . . find delight in the practice of laudable things. . . ."[20] Any resemblance to stern, formal, discipline was absent from Locke's discussion on the recreation of children. "Recreation is as necessary as labour or food: but because there can be no recreation without delight which depends not always on reason, but oftener on fancy, it must be permitted children not only to divert themselves, but to do it after their own fashion, provided it be innocently, and without prejudice to their health. . . ."[21] If later formal disciplinarians referred to Locke to justify their dull, coercive, and harsh methods of teaching, they must not have been fully acquainted with his writings.

Children were to have the pleasure of owning playthings, but not to the extent of being surfeited with them. Locke believed that the possession of too many toys would instill a pride in quantity of possessions rather than interest in their use. He suggested that children should be encouraged to devise their own toys. The English philosopher was also convinced that play could make intellectual studies more attractive. Teachers were advised to invent games that would help youngsters learn to read or spell. Teachers were also advised that careful observations made of children in play situations would assist tutors in studying the character of their charges and in evaluating their natural dispositions, aptitudes, and inclinations.

[19]Ibid., p. 32.   [21]Ibid., p. 79.
[20]Ibid., p. 79.

11

Physical Education in Educational Naturalism

The eighteenth century, known as the Age of Enlightenment, marked a philosophical rebellion against the enslavement of the individual. When Copernicus, Brahe, and Kepler explained certain universal truths discovered through a study of nature, they paved the way for the work of Locke, Voltaire, and Rousseau. If natural laws operated in the physical world, some intellectuals concluded that they also operated in the realm of government, education, and economics.

The most scathing attack on French society was made by Jean-Jacques Rousseau (1712–1778) who cried out, "civilized man is born, lives, and dies in a state of slavery." There was a growing resentment against burdening the masses with excessive taxation, subjecting them to arbitrary arrest, regulating their business ventures, and forcing them to serve the whims of the aristocracy. Rousseau charged that the institutions of civilization had created inequality, oppression, and slavery, and his zealous appeals for reform won many adherents. He declared that the laws of nature endowed men with certain inalienable rights that have priority over all inherited powers.

Rousseau's indictment of French education was as unsparing as his attack on society itself. In that age the child was expected to live by the same standards as a mature adult. Little boys had their hair curled, powdered, and pomaded, were attired in embroidered coats, dainty frills, knee breeches, and silk stockings, and carried swords by their sides in the same manner as their fathers. A little lass of six wore a long, hoop-skirted dress and an elaborate coiffure with false curls and, in addition, was bound up in a tight corset. She was an imitation of a fashionable lady and was expected to act like one.

Just as vivacious, active youngsters were forced into adult attire, they were expected to absorb a pedantic, adult-type learning. Any deviation from the accepted pattern was attributed to the natural depravity of children which necessitated the severest discipline. Memorization and recitation were the only activities of students; testing memories and keeping order were the major duties of teachers. Rousseau's "return to nature" was a war cry against these conventional attitudes toward education.

Comenius and Locke, prior to Rousseau, had proclaimed an education according to nature when they urged that children become familiar with their natural environment by using their senses for observation and that teaching should proceed in accordance with natural laws of child development. Rousseau accepted and expanded upon his predecessors' viewpoints. Both Comenius' and Locke's aims of education subjected the child to authority—Comenius to the will of the Bible, Locke to the demands of society. Rousseau, however, desired to free the child from every bondage, permitting a completely natural development of his individual personality.

Educational naturalism, beginning with Rousseau, has exercised a prodigious influence over modern civilization. He laid bare the defects and abuses of society and education, and rendered clear the relationship between education and human welfare. His doctrines also influenced political and social theory. The democratic structure of American government and education owes much to Rousseau's theories, especially his emphasis on individualism and personal rights.

Among Rousseau's contributions to literature were: *Discourse on Political Economy* (1755), *The Social Contract* (1762), *Émile* (1762), and *Considerations on the Government of Poland* (1773). His ideas concerning education were primarily set forth in *Émile*, a volume tracing the training of a child from birth until his marriage to the ideal girl, Sophie. Paradoxical and untenable as some of Rousseau's ideas were, his writing also contained much fundamental truth. Rousseau was a theorist who never attempted to test his ideas in practical school situations, but he keynoted many educational reforms that followed.

The doctrine of naturalism was rejected in France until after the French Revolution, but German educators began to experiment with these ideas before the close of the century. Johann Bernhard Basedow (1723–1790), a German schoolmaster, was influenced tremendously by Rousseau. His school, known as the Philanthropinum, made one of the first attempts to put naturalistic education into practice. Basedow's chief pedagogical works, *A Book of Methods (Das Methodenbuch)* and the *Elementary Book (Das Elementarwerk),* outlined his views on educational reform. Gerhard Vieth (1763–1836), another outstanding teacher in Germany, and a contributor to the movement wrote an *Encyclopedia of Bodily Exercises (Versuch einer Encyklopädie der Leibersübungen)* which contained a history of physical education and his own system of exercises. In the later half of the eighteenth century, a number of new schools were patterned after Basedow's Philanthropinum. Among the most famous of these schools was the Schnepfenthal Educational Institute established by C. G. Salzmann (1744–1811).

Johann Friedrich GutsMuths (1749–1839), who is regarded as the "grandfather" of modern physical education, was one of the teachers in Salzmann's school. The pre-eminence of GutsMuths rests upon nearly fifty years (1786–1835) of teaching and upon the volumes that he wrote on physical education. His two great works were *Gymnastics for the Young* (1793), which formed the basis of modern physical education, and *Games* (1796), which described and arranged 105 games into natural classifications according to the skills they developed. Other of his contributions included *Manual of the Art of Swimming* (1798), *Mechanical Avocations for Youths and Men* (1801), *Book of Gymnastics for the Sons of the Fatherland* (1817), and a *Catechism of Gymnastics: a Manual for Teachers and Pupils* (1818). His *Gymnastics for the Young* underwent several revisions and was translated into many languages. Outside of physical education, GutsMuths wrote numerous geography texts and rendered an important service to education by editing 53 volumes of the *Library of Pedagogical Literature*.

In the Age of Enlightenment, the body became the object of scientific interest. Medical men began to study anatomy and physiology, and a number of treatises appeared concerning exercises and their influence on health. In 1705, Francis Fuller's *Medicina Gymnastica* appeared and went through several editions. Between 1700 and 1720, Friedrich Hoffman (1660–1742) published several essays that were later referred to by GutsMuths, including "On Motion, the Best Medicine for the Body," and "The Incomparable Advantages of Motion and of Bodily Exercise, and How They Are to Be Employed for the Preservation of Health." Clement Joseph Tissot (1750–1826), a famous French physician, contributed "Medical and Surgical Gymnastics: An Essay on the Use of Motion and of Different Exercises of the Body in the Cure of Disease," which also appeared in translations.

Aims of Education

"Everything according to nature" expressed the aims of educational naturalism. A natural education was to free the youngster, to allow him a complete development of his own nature, his own powers, his own natural inclinations. Rousseau's educational plan would protect the child's natural goodness and purity from contamination and enslavement by society. He declared, "Everything is good as it comes from the hands of the Author of Nature; but everything degenerates in the hands of man."[1] Ultimately, Rousseau hoped this process would contribute to the construction of a society based upon the natural laws of equality, temperance, simplicity, fraternity, and liberty.

Natural education recognized good health and rich sense experiences as primary goals. Whereas for centuries the dominating desire had been to drive children toward moral and intellectual objectives as soon as possible, the naturalists claimed that children were not sufficiently mature to assimilate such learning. They believed that youth was the natural time to build a sturdy, skillful, physical organism capable of supporting the mental and moral powers when they did emerge. If, to the contrary, the body were allowed to remain feeble, it would never be able to nourish a vigorous soul and intellect.

Natural education was to train a youth for a good and happy life. "Life is the trade I would teach him. When he leaves me, I grant you, he will be neither a magistrate, a soldier, nor a priest; he will be a man."[2] In Rousseau's opinion, such an education would help man adapt himself to an everchanging environment.

In visualizing an ideal state where men enjoyed the natural rights of liberty and equality, Rousseau thought children should be imbued with love of country and loyalty to its democratic purposes. "It is education that must give the souls of the people a national form, and so shape their opinions and their tastes that they become patriots as much by inclination and passion as by necessity."[3] Again, "If children are educated together on a footing of equality . . . it cannot be doubted that they will learn in this way to cherish each other as brothers. . . ."[4] Being influenced strongly by the doctrine of "liberty, equality, and fraternity," Rousseau and his fellow naturalists supported the idea of a general, democratic, and universal education.

Rousseau's "everything according to nature" doctrine found immediate acceptance, particularly in Germany. Basedow reiterated the theme. At his Philanthropinum, it was believed that ". . . the chief purpose of education should be to prepare the child for a useful, public-spirited and happy life."[5] A self-contented, cheerful, enthusiastic disposition; a virtu-

---

[1]J. J. Rousseau, *Rousseau's Émile or Treatise on Education*, trans. W. H. Payne (New York: D. Appleton and Co., 1926), p. 1.

[2]J. J. Rousseau, *Émile on Education*, trans. B. Foxley (London: J. M. Dent and Sons, 1911), p. 9.

[3]William Boyd, *The Minor Educational Writings of J. J. Rousseau* (taken from the "Considerations on the Government of Poland") (London: Blackie and Son, Ltd., 1911), p. 141.

[4]Ibid., p. 45.

[5]Hugo Göring, *Ausgewählte Schriften, mit Basedow's Biographie* (Beyer: Langenslza, 1880), p. 42, as quoted in T. Misawa, *Modern Educators and Their Ideals* (New York: D. Appleton and Co., 1909), p. 95.

ous character; a "sound mind and sound body"; these attributes were considered more important than the accumulation of knowledge, social accomplishments, or elegant manners.

Aims of Physical Education

Naturalism gave major emphasis to health and physical education. Rousseau declared, "The training of the body, though much neglected, is . . . the most important part of education, not only for making the children healthy and robust, but even more for the moral effect, which is generally neglected altogether, or sought by teaching the child a number of pedantic precepts that are only so many misspent words."[6] The naturalistic concepts of physical education included investing the child with adequate motor skills, providing him with worthy recreation, hardening his body to meet emergencies of every sort, and teaching him how to work and play with his fellows.

Rousseau agreed with Locke that a child had to develop a healthy constitution to withstand the impacts of life. He felt that this theory conformed with nature's laws, for "She keeps children at work, she hardens them by all kinds of difficulties, she soon teaches them the meaning of pain and grief."[7] In many ways, Rousseau was as severe as Locke in his concepts of the hardening process.

The close relationship between the mind and body was realized more perfectly by Rousseau than by many of his predecessors. "It is a lamentable mistake," he announced, "to imagine that bodily activity hinders the working of the mind, as if these two kinds of activity ought not to advance hand in hand, and as if the one were not intended to act as guide to the other."[8] Rousseau argued ". . . to learn to think we must therefore exercise our limbs, our senses, and our bodily organs, which are the tools of the intellect; and to get the best use out of these tools, the body which supplies us with them must be strong and healthy."[9] Although many educators ignored Rousseau, others were stirred deeply by the assertion, "Would you cultivate your pupil's intelligence, cultivate the strength it is meant to control. Give his body constant exercise, make it strong and healthy, in order to make him good and wise . . . make a man of him in strength, and he will soon be a man in reason."[10] Such arguments did much to reinstate physical education as an integral part of education.

The cultivation of the senses was considered an equally important part of physical education. Through playing games, the youngster, accord-

[6]Boyd, *Minor Writings of Rousseau*, p. 145.
[7]Rousseau, *Émile on Education*, p. 14.
[8]Ibid., p. 82.
[9]Ibid., p. 90.
[10]Ibid., p. 82.

ing to the naturalists, would become familiar with the world around him. Sense training would make the child capable of judging heat and cold, hardness and softness, size, number, and shape; would help him to learn to estimate height, width, length, breadth, and distance. Rousseau believed such experience would enlarge the pupil's realm of knowledge much more than secondhand material from books.

Recreation was essential in natural education. Rousseau proposed strenuous physical activity for his imaginary pupil, Émile, ". . . which interests him by its novelty, which keeps him in good humor, gives him pleasure, occupies his attention, and keeps him in training. . . ."[11] Recreation was to be the counterbalance of life. "The great secret of education," according to Rousseau, "is to make the exercises of the body and of the mind always serve as a recreation for each other."[12] He was just as opposed to excessive indulgence in recreation as he was to its absence.

Rousseau thought that physical education should train children for democratic citizenship in the ideal state. If a democratic state were to emerge, games and exercises were to accustom them ". . . from an early age to discipline, to equality, to fraternity, to rivalry, to living under the eyes of their fellow-citizens and seeking public approbation."[13] Educators of the next century elaborated upon these ideals.

The program that GutsMuths instituted at the Salzmann school harmonized with Rousseau's ideals. GutsMuths harbored no doubt concerning the influence of the body on mind and character. Health rather than knowledge was to be the basic objective of education, for "learning and refinement are to health and bodily perfection what luxuries are to necessaries. Is not then our education depraved, when it aims at a luxury, and neglects our greatest and most essential want?"[14] He further pointed out, "Nature would willingly be active till the four and twentieth year in improving the corporeal faculties, as well as the mental: but we counteract her endeavours. . . ."[15] The main objective of gymnastics was to bring about the harmonious development of mind and body, rendering both equally sound and energetic.

GutsMuths resented the education of the day which enforced inactivity on the child. He insisted on a hardening process that would inure the pupil to some pain, fortify him against the elements, render him adroit, agile, firm of nerve, give him presence of mind in event of danger, and ". . . foster in his mind the germs of courage, perseverance, activity, and reflection on the objects of Nature."[16] By thus promoting physical strength

[11] Rousseau, *Rousseau's Émile or Treatise on Education*, p. 237.

[12] Ibid., p. 184.

[13] Boyd, *Minor Writings of Rousseau*, p. 146.

[14] C. G. Salzmann (incorrectly credited to Salzmann), *Gymnastics for Youth* (Philadelphia: Wm. Duane, 1802), p. viii.

[15] Ibid., pp. 7–8.   [16] Ibid., p. 7.

and beauty, GutsMuths was confident that the child would acquire the serenity, self-confidence, and stability of a sound personality.

Promotion of Physical Education

Rousseau held that education was derived from three agencies—nature, man, and things. Because nature's function was based upon permanent elements in the individual's constitution, all other agencies of education had to be synchronized with it. Nature was the all-important agency of education; man and things were merely supplementary agencies to carry out her purposes.

Whether a child should be educated by a tutor or in a public school was to be determined by the kind of culture in which he lived. Rousseau, being opposed to the autocratic society of his day, proposed a private education for Émile. Living in a rural culture, exposed to a minimum of social contacts, and possessing no costly toys, Émile would be forced to depend upon his physical environment and his own inner nature for his learning experiences.

Rousseau was rather pessimistic about the possibility of the immediate development of a democratic society. If a popular government could be established, based on the consent of the people, he believed all children should be required to attend national, public schools. Rousseau was given an opportunity to devise a plan for the national education of Polish children some ten years after his publication of *Émile*. His scheme provided for the employment of gamemasters and the erection of a gymnasium. He advised that youths ". . . should not be allowed to play separately at their own fancy, but made to play all together and in public. . . . "[17] Through group activities, the schools would weld a common spirit and the emotions and responses that would solidify national feeling.

Where the old educational system had forced the child to fit the school, the new educational system tried to organize the school for the child. Rousseau believed that between birth and maturity, children passed through several natural stages of development, each of which unfolded certain distinct desires, interests, and capacities. His school program was to be adapted to harmonize with the emerging functions of each respective stage.

A school program based on the naturalistic philosophy came into existence in 1774 in Basedow's Philanthropinum. Although small, the school became a focal point for all those desiring educational reforms. Students enrolled from several countries. Such distinguished men as Goethe and Kant voiced their support of the bold experiment. The Philanthropinum initiated the first modern physical education program. In the better

---

[17]Boyd, *Minor Writings of Rousseau*, p. 145.

knightly schools of that time, special masters were employed to conduct fencing, dancing, riding, and gymnastic lessons. Basedow entrusted these activities to regular members of the staff. Basedow suggested that one hour in the morning and two hours in the afternoon should be devoted to games, gymnastics, sports, and recreation, and two hours to manual labor. The new school offered a great contrast to other institutions of its day. The children wore simple uniforms that did not restrict freedom of movement. They romped in the court gardens and gymnasiums. The classes were entrusted to Johann Friedrich Simon, who is regarded as the first teacher of modern physical education. Simon was succeeded by Johann Du Toit. This famous school served as a center that trained many teachers who carried its purposes and program to other institutions.

The Schnepfenthal Educational Institute, established by Christian Salzmann, was modeled after Basedow's school and attempted to carry out the naturalistic ideas of education. Lessons in gymnastics were held from eleven to twelve in the morning. From lunch until two o'clock, the children were allowed to engage in games, and, similarly, in the evening these activities alternated with other entertainments. Sunday afternoons were devoted entirely to amusements, excursions, and relaxation. The classes were usually conducted in a pleasant open space under the trees where the initial equipment included a jumping ditch, a balance beam, and a pair of upright poles. During inclement weather the classes were held indoors. Salzmann employed Christian Carl André as a teacher of physical education until this work was turned over to GutsMuths in 1786. Physical education in these institutions received more attention than it had at any other time since the days of ancient Greece.

Program of Physical Education

Traditional subject matter was rejected by Rousseau. The studies in his naturalistic curriculum harmonized with five successive stages of social, physical, and mental development. These stages foreshadowed the recapitulation theory of the next century.

From birth to five years of age, the child was in the *animal* stage, and therefore in need of much physical activity. Rousseau gave Émile, his fictitious pupil, absolute freedom to exercise. The hardening process was also begun during these early years. Gradually, Émile was to be trained to endure baths of varying temperatures.

From five to twelve years of age, Émile was in the *savage* stage, a young "Robinson Crusoe." His activities were to consist largely of a wide variety of games, plays, and sports that would strengthen his body and make for better sense discrimination. The child was to have none of the usual academic and moral studies, for he was not mature enough to indulge in abstract reasoning or to comprehend teachings about virtue and truth. Rousseau advised the tutor to exercise the child's ". . . body, his limbs, his senses, his strength; but keep his mind idle as long as you can."[18] The motto was *Do nothing, allow nothing to be done; let nature take her course!*

In childhood, as in infancy, Émile was to exercise in the open air, to run, shout, and jump to his heart's content. The tutor shouid ". . . let him learn to perform every exercise which encourages agility of body; let him learn to hold himself easily and steadily in any position, let him practise jumping and leaping, climbing trees and walls. Let him always find his balance, and let his every movement and gesture be regulated by the laws of weight, long before he learns to explain them by the science of statics."[19] The hardening process was to be intensified during childhood. Émile was to play barefooted and bareheaded, indoors and outdoors, winter and summer. The boy was to become accustomed to an uncomfortable cot and to receive only the plainest foods.

During childhood, through his games and sports, Émile was to gather sense experiences that would provide him with the raw materials for his future thoughts and reasoning. To Rousseau, a ball game contributed significantly to the development of neuro-muscular and spatial learnings. For a boy ". . . to dash from one end of the room to another, to judge the rebound of a ball before it touches the ground, to return it with strength and accuracy, such games are not so much sports fit for a man, as sports fit to make a man of him."[20]

Early adolescence, between the ages of twelve and fifteen, was a *pastoral* stage. Rousseau believed that the powers of reason and judgment were then beginning to awaken in the youth, hence formal intellectual instruction could begin. Émile, however, was to pursue only those studies that interested him or that were of immediate use. Agricultural activities and the manual arts were to acquaint him with the works of man and to keep his body in exercise.

Later adolescence, between fifteen and twenty years of age, was labeled the *social* stage of a child's development. Emile's reasoning powers would have matured sufficiently to grasp complex concepts so he was ready to study social, religious, and moral problems. In regard to sex education, Rousseau suggested ". . . let them learn at an early hour that which it is impossible always to conceal from them. . . ."[21] Replies to all questions must be given with ". . . the greatest simplicity, without mystery, without embarrassment, and without a smile. There is much less danger in satisfying the curiosity of the child than in exciting it."[22] Proclaiming that ". . . reading, solitude, and idleness, an aimless and sedentary life. . . ."[23]

[18]Rousseau, *Émile on Education*, p. 58.
[19]Ibid., p. 104.
[20]Ibid., p. 111.

[21]Rousseau, *Rousseau's Émile or Treatise on Education*, p. 198.
[22]Ibid., p. 197.
[23]Ibid., p. 236.

may influence his imagination and arouse his passions, Rousseau would divert Émile's senses by "exercising his body" in vigorous physical pursuits.

The fifth or *adult* stage of Émile's training culminated in his marriage to the ideal girl, Sophie. She, strangely enough, was allotted a conventional education that almost completely contradicted all the naturalistic principles upon which Émile's education was based.

In Basedow's naturalistic school, the Philanthropinum, education was viewed as a physical as well as an intellectual development. Basedow first adopted the traditional knightly exercises of fencing, dancing, riding, and vaulting; but Simon, the physical education teacher, supplemented this program by introducing what he called "Greek gymnastics," consisting of running, jumping, throwing, and wrestling. A diamond-shaped jumping ditch was constructed so that children could first practice jumping at the tapered ends and work toward the eight-foot jump at the middle as they became more proficient. Vertical poles were erected for high-jumping exercises and a balance beam was also devised. A swing slung between two trees became a favored apparatus. Younger students enjoyed playing with hoops and the seesaw, while older youngsters participated in games of tennis, shuttlecock, fives, skittles, and ball. Under Simon's successor, Du Toit, swimming, skating, archery, gardening, woodworking, and marching were introduced. Playing soldier, excursions into the country, walking and hanging on oblique ladders, and carrying bags full of sand with the hands outstretched horizontally were also added to the activities. Basedow even anticipated the idea of a summer camp. One of the advertisements of his school promised—if the enrollment were sufficient—to provide a two-month summer camping period to give youngsters an opportunity for bathing, hunting, fishing, jumping, climbing, and boating, as well as the study of geography and the natural sciences.

At Salzmann's Schnepfenthal Institute, Christian André first patterned the physical education program after that in operation at the Philanthropinum. With more experience, he added activities such as throwing at the target, pole-vaulting, running through a jumping rope, and running uphill and downhill. He also taught some movements to improve the students' posture. Games and amusements occupied the students during the afternoon and evening relaxation periods.

When GutsMuths took over André's work, he continued most of the exercises initiated by his predecessor. He also experimented with new activities and apparatus and delved into the classics seeking further information. GutMuths divided activities into three classes: gymnastic exercises, manual labor, and social games. Some of the chapter headings on exercise in his text, *Gymnastics for the Young,* give an insight into the materials he used: (1) Leaping, including hopping, standing jump, running jump, vaulting, leap frog; (2) Running; (3) Jaculation, including slinging, bow, dart, discus; (4) Wrestling; (5) Climbing, including pole, mast, ladder, rope; (6) Balancing; (7) Lifting and Carrying; (8) Dancing, Walking, and Military Exercises; (9) Bathing and Swimming. Among various types of manual labor that he thought suitable for children were cabinetmaking, bookbinding, basketmaking, and particularly gardening. Terraces about the Salzmann school were covered with patches of flowers and vegetables, with each student cultivating his own little garden. Now and then, the whole school went into the woods for a picnic. Occasionally, older children packed their baggage on a wagon and went on a hiking excursion for several days.

In short, the physical educators in the naturalistic schools adapted the learning materials and experiences to the characteristics of the child and to the natural environment.

Methods of Physical Education

In naturalism the child became the focal point of education. "Observe Nature, and follow the route which she traces for you,"[24] was the slogan. From such a guide for educational procedure, the modern principles of growth, pupil-activity, and individualization have emerged. Physical educators, as well as general educators, have adopted these instructional methods.

According to Rousseau, all educational experiences were to be selected in accordance with the abilities of students at their particular stage of growth, for the commonest error of teachers was that "We never know how to put ourselves in the place of children; we do not enter into their ideas, but we ascribe to them our own. . . ."[25] No concepts were to be taught that were beyond the comprehension of children, nor were drill, memorization, threats, compulsions, and prodding to be employed to force learning upon children. The body was to be free to develop as nature intended, not according to any set routine. In Rousseau's words, "Nature provides for the child's growth in her own fashion, and this should never be thwarted. Do not make him sit still when he wants to run about, nor run when he wants to be quiet."[26] Rousseau advised mothers to leave a baby's limbs free and to permit him to crawl about as he desired, stretching and developing his legs day by day. At all stages of growth simple, loose garments were to be selected.

"Without doubt," Rousseau stated, "we derive much clearer and much more accurate notions of things which we learn for ourselves than those which we gain from the instruction of others. . . ."[27] To him self-

[24]Ibid., p. 13.
[25]Ibid., p. 141.

[26]Rousseau, *Émile on Education*, p. 50.
[27]Rousseau, *Rousseau's Émile or Treatise on Education*, p. 152.

directed activity on the part of the child was much more valuable than lessons dominated by the teacher. Children were to learn by observation and experience, by thinking their own thoughts and reaching their own conclusions. The teacher could arouse the child's curiosity, but only through his own activity was the child to satisfy it.

Natural education stressed individual differences, because "Each mind has its own form according to which it must be governed; and for the success of our undertaking, it is necessary that it should be governed by this form and not by another."[28] A student was not encouraged to surpass a rival; rather, he was to be taught to measure his progress in terms of his own growth. The tutor was to help him compare his performance with that of the previous year by saying, "You have grown so many inches; there is the ditch which you jumped and the load which you carried; here is the distance you threw a stone and the course you ran at one breath. Let us see what you can do now."[29] Always, naturalistic methods demanded that learning must proceed in terms of the individual.

[28]Ibid., p. 60.   [29]Ibid., p. 161.

part three

Physical Education
in
MODERN EUROPE

12

General Preview
of Physical Education
in Educational Nationalism

To be declared a man without a country is a terrifying thought in modern society; even so, the political concept of a modern nation and the emotional attachment to a fatherland is of relatively recent origin. Although nationalism had its source deep in antiquity, it did not become a distinctive force until the middle of the eighteenth century. By the twentieth century, it had become a torrent engulfing the entire world.

Nationalism does not readily lend itself to a simple definition. Although it often implies common aspirations, racial origin, homeland, language, religion, and culture, all of these elements are not always present. Yet loyalties based upon a national ideal are prerequisites to nationalism.

Rudimentary elements of nationalism appeared even in antiquity. The aristocratic Greeks were of common descent, held some common aspirations, and enjoyed active cultural and political participation. Nevertheless, the desire for a unified national state never became a potent force with them. Their loyalties remained with their local city states rather than with Greece. Although the Romans acquired extensive territories and developed common laws, their Empire was imposed upon many conquered peoples whose loyalties remained with their own group rather than with Rome. The many subjects of the Empire were never assimilated and integrated into a common culture possessing a vigorous national spirit. In the Middle Ages, the tiny feudal units did not approximate a cultural or national entity. The universal control of the Church over religious life and many of the medieval activities acted against the growth of the emotional and political fervor needed to promote nationalism. Nevertheless, some dominant elements necessary to the formation of states emerged from the vague and shapeless universalism of the Middle Ages.

In the transition between the feudal era and modern times, a new Europe was in the process of creation and dynastic states were gradually emerging. The Crusades helped to develop a sense of solidarity, particularly in France, while the Christian-Moslem wars fostered nationalistic sentiments in Spain. Economic and commercial expansion tended to break down provincialism and necessitated interdependence of larger geographical units. The Commercial Revolution gave rise to the middle class, which allied with strong princes to establish centralized states. Rising monarchs utilized the Protestant movement as a means of seeking political independence from the Holy Roman Empire. The invention of the printing press and the replacement of Latin by vernacular languages made possible the mass dissemination of national literature and the expression of national aspirations. By the end of the eighteenth century most of western Europe, with the exception of Germany and Italy, had ceased to be feudal. These latter countries and those in eastern Europe waited nearly another century for national unification.

The American and French revolutions stimulated nationalistic and liberal movements all over the world. The spirit of individualism and faith in liberty that had been nourished by the Renaissance and the Reformation eventually brought forth the cry of "liberty, equality, and fraternity." When the middle classes revolted against the tyranny of kings, demanding certain rights as citizens, they prepared the way for democracy. Loyalty to a prince was then transferred to a nation—*their* nation. This personal identification with the nation heightened the spirit of patriotism, and intensified national sentiment to a degree unknown in earlier society.

The idea that there can be no patriotism, no loyalty to the state without liberty, as expressed by Rousseau, must be considered with reservation. Dictators have proven that intensive national loyalty can be cultivated in the absence of a strong democratic spirit. In the nineteenth and twentieth centuries, both authoritarian and liberal governments have successfully solidified sentiment behind their particular brand of nationalism and often they have employed the same techniques. Pride in military might; citizen armies; theories of racial superiority; indoctrination in the national political philosophy; cultivation of a super-patriotic national history and literature; emotionalized symbols, such as flags, banners, emblems, anthems, and holidays; the glorification of folk literature, dances, and music—all these measures have been utilized to create an intensive nationalistic spirit.

The Industrial Revolution also fanned the flames of nationalism. The rapid development of the factory system and the urbanization of society soon created a demand for new sources of raw materials and new markets for manufactured goods. After 1870, in most large countries the emphasis was shifted from the unification of the state to the exploitation of foreign territories. Missionaries, adventurers, business interests, and fortune seekers poured into the colonial possessions along with the movements of surplus populations from the homeland. This expansion of national imperialistic policies held a dramatic emotional appeal that intoxicated people with patriotic pride. But the rivalries between states created ominous jealousies, stimulated secret alliances, and increased the demand for larger armies and navies to protect and extend national properties. Eventually, the clash of interests engulfed most of the peoples of the earth in two great world wars.

In the nineteenth century, education came to be accepted as the most effective means of providing for the welfare and progress of the nation. Previously, education had been considered the private privilege of parents and religious groups, but these agencies were not considered adequate to nurture the spirit of nationalism and insure national solidarity. All modern countries—monarchies, democracies, and totalitarian states—came to accept the establishment and maintenance of schools as essential national policy. Popular education was conceived to be the business of the nation and vital to its welfare.

In general, nationalism calls for a universal education to produce citizens loyal to the state and willing to work for its best interests. Nationalistic education implies indoctrination in the particular political ideology of the state, development of the ability and willingness to fight for the fatherland, cultivation of an exalted love of country, and the attainment of a social homogeneity.

Educational nationalism stresses the cultivation of civic virtues in contrast to the religious and humanistic goals which previous societies emphasized. The character and intensity of this civic training is in a large part determined by the particular political concept of the relationship of the individual to the state: whether the individual exists for the state, or the state for the individual. From the one point of view, civic training places emphasis on informing the youth of his obligations to the state; from the other point of view, of his rights and privileges, as well as equipping him to assume the duties of citizenship. Adherents of the concept that the state is universal and omnipotent denounce an education that liberates personal capacities. To them, human life takes on value only when it serves the special interests of the state. Opposed to this point of view, liberal nationalists believe that the state will realize its greatest enrichment if each individual is allowed to refine his skills to their fullest expression.

Although the ultimate end of nationalistic education has often meant death on the battlefield, it has also been responsible for improving the status of mankind. In analyzing nationalistic education, E. H. Reisner recognized some of its contributions to society:

It must be observed that national interest has provided the effective dynamic of social reform and better human husbandry. In the interest of pack strength the individuals had to be made more intelligent, more productive, more loyal, and better contented. On the spiritual side it must be credited with a positive enlargement of human personality. The citizen, conscious of his identity with an historical tradition and a living cause and willingly devoting himself to his country's need, is more of a person than the peasant who knows nothing and cares for nothing beyond his immediate local and personal affairs. To lift the individual to the vistas of national consciousness and loyalty was a great human accomplishment. Perhaps it ought to be regarded as the necessary halfway station on the upward road to a lively consciousness of human kind.[1]

Peaceful relations between countries are not yet achieved in modern society. Perhaps this goal can eventually be attained even within the framework of nationalism. Some educators urge that the schools contribute toward this objective by stressing cultural rather than militant nationalism. They desire not only to transmit the national heritage to their own youth, but also to make them conscious of the contribution each nation can make to humanity. If properly directed, nationalistic education may yet find the basis for the "interplay and cooperation between the best spiritual contributions of each national group in the interests of a sane and sound development of world civilization and culture."[2] Certainly, nationalistic aims of education need not be considered inherently evil nor inherently incompatible with international peace and good will.

National education extols civil ideals; its general purpose is to fashion social and political homogeneity. National sentiment is usually promoted through teaching a common language, history, geography, literature, and folklore. Religious and moral types of education are sometimes used in the inculcation of a sense of cultural solidarity. Physical education is often incorporated in the curriculum to promote the physical fitness and skills necessary for national preservation, and its potential civil and social values are recognized as a means of instilling patriotism and a community spirit. Vocational education has also become a respectable part of the curriculum of the schools since the Industrial Revolution. Although primarily intended to produce efficient workmen, the experience of recent wars has also made it obvious that as a guarantee of national stability and strength, the training of an "economic army" is as essential as the military training of the troops.

[1]E. H. Reisner, *The Evolution of the Common School* (New York: The Macmillan Company, 1930), pp. 230–31.
[2]I. J. Kandel, *Comparative Education* (Boston: Houghton-Mifflin Company, 1933), p. 14.

Nationalism tends to create an educational system that is state-supported and state-controlled. The national system of education is highly centralized in most European countries. In the United States, however, the federal government does not control education, as that function is the exclusive prerogative of the states. In theory, nationalistic education is the function of the state and is usually compulsory and gratuitous.

Until the present century, European schools were of a dual nature. The elementary schools were for the masses and the secondary schools were for the upper classes. The two types of institutions came into being separately and, until recently, were not related. Religious training and the three "R's" composed the greater part of the elementary school curriculum. It was almost impossible for an elementary pupil to transfer to a secondary institution, for he was not instructed in the Latin and Greek prerequisites. Youngsters from wealthy families usually secured their preliminary training from tutors or in special preparatory schools. Between nine and twelve years they entered the secondary schools where they pursued a rigorous program of predominately classical studies. Upon graduation and after passing examinations, toward which all of their training was directed, most of the secondary school scholars proceeded to the universities and eventually to the leading positions in the state and church. During this century, a reform movement has made progress in equalizing educational opportunities. Primary education has been enriched and extended, provisions have been made for the transfer of elementary pupils to secondary schools, more technical and industrial training has been offered, and fees for secondary education have been reduced or abolished in many countries. All governments are not proceeding at the same pace, but the trend seems to be toward providing all children with educational programs as a means of strengthening the national well-being.

13

Physical Education
in
German Educational Nationalism

Germany at the turn of the nineteenth century was a conglomeration of some 300 sovereignties, ecclesiastical states, and free cities. Politically these governments were at variance with anything resembling harmonious thought or action, but culturally they shared many sentiments. Fear of the Napoleonic shadow being cast over Europe finally forced these countries into closer cooperation. When Prussia, one of the leading states of Germany, sent her professional troops against the citizens' army of Napoleon in 1806, they were decisively defeated in the battle of Jena and had to submit to the humiliating Treaty of Tilsit. Men realized that French domination threatened to disperse the remaining fragments of the German states. Many leaders keenly felt the need for uniting all the German states.

German interest in unity was reinforced when the spirit of nationalism became allied with the democratic aspirations of the common people. Having been aroused by the ideals of the French Revolution, they were ready to attack both class and political divisions. Not only a free nation, but a free people, became the popular goal. Feudalism had lingered longer in Germany than in most countries, so naturally the new political concepts aroused the hopes of common men and made them promote the spirit of nationalism and liberty.

German kings and aristocrats welcomed the general desire to unite and overthrow the French, but they feared that the enthusiasm for democratic doctrines among the masses might lead to the destruction of their own rights and privileges. However, the ruling powers became so anxious to resist the French that they decided to risk the acceptance of popular support. The Germans joined with others to defeat Napoleon at the Battle of the Nations at Leipzig in 1813.

After the war, however, the efforts of the people were not rewarded with the founding of a united Germany or with the granting of constitutional liberties. Many patriots were disappointed in the weak German confederation of thirty-eight practically independent states that was created by the Congress of Vienna. Metternich, the Austrian prime minister who played a leading role in negotiating the peace treaties, advocated that monarchs employ the severest methods to defeat all movements that threatened their divine authority. Repressive decrees were issued and the liberals were silenced. For a brief time in 1848 democratic agitators were active again, but the resurgence soon collapsed.

Although the people failed to attain a united German nation in 1815 by democratic methods, this objective was later realized as a result of commercial necessity and military ambition. The Industrial Revolution compelled the numerous sovereignties to cooperate in a tariff union, thus adding strong economic bonds to the common cultural, racial, and language ties that already existed. Political unification was finally achieved in 1871 under the leadership of the Prussian "Iron Chancellor," Otto von Bismarck. With shrewd diplomacy and an efficient military machine, he consolidated the various German states and created the German Empire as an enlarged Prussia dominated by a military regime.

The élite of the Prussian army were not adherents of democratic government. They believed in a benevolent autocracy, the glorification of the armed power, and a citizenry who would faithfully follow those who brought them victories and prosperity. To strengthen Germany's position, they advocated the formation of alliances, industrial development, the acquisition of colonies, and the checking of the growth of socialism among workers. Eventually, dynastic and nationalistic ambitions combined with commercial needs to foster an aggressive spirit in Germany that led to open conflict with the rest of Europe in 1914. With the collapse of her military power in 1918, the democratic forces that had grown since the Industrial Revolution had an opportunity to assert themselves.

The Weimar Republic (1919–1933), established after World War I, was a brief experiment in democracy between the era of autocratic empire (1871–1918) and the totalitarian National Socialism (1933–1945). The Germans who had followed the orders of a military regime for decades, found self-government difficult. Political self-determination had been thrust upon them before they had fully assimilated the responsibility to govern by consent. Pressing problems immediately faced the newly installed officials. Many political parties arose, each so opposed to the others that they could not cooperate in formulating a united policy. Bureaucratic sabotage, as well as the influence of the reactionary upper class and the military clique, contributed to the failure to secure popular support. Inflation, depression, and unemployment built up such discontent that the Germans were willing to surrender their freedom and right of self-government to any strong regime that would promise to eliminate the unpleasant realties they faced. Hitler and the National Socialist Party (Nazis) rode into power in 1933 by claiming they would revitalize the German nation and win the Fatherland its rightful place in the world. The Treaty of Versailles became a convenient scapegoat for all German ills. The Nazis quickly transformed the democratic government into a totalitarian state ruled by the National Socialist Party. The resulting society was quickly geared to a program of aggressive expansion.

Nazi dreams of a "1,000-year Third Reich" vanished with the Allied victory in the war, and a shattered and devastated Germany in 1945 was divided into four political zones under an Allied Control Council composed of France, England, Russia, and the United States. After three years Russia withdrew from the Council and the three western powers in 1949 established the Federal Republic of Germany, or West Germany, which consisted of eleven states or *Länder*, including West Berlin. A few months later the Russians created the smaller German Democratic Republic (GDR).[1] The Federal Republic is based on the autonomy of its eleven states. Over sixty million people live in West Germany which has an area of 96,000 square miles. About fifty percent are Protestants, mainly Lutherans, and forty-five percent are Catholic. The West Germans have made a remarkable economic recovery since the war.

For decades physical education in Germany paralleled the politics of the nation. During the early days, it was most pronounced during liberal movements only to be suppressed during reactionary periods. This was because the first gymnasts were political liberals under the vigorous and colorful leadership of Friedrich Ludwig Jahn (1778–1852). Jahn was first and foremost a German nationalist, a champion of liberalism, a defender of the common man. He campaigned energetically for a united Germany and developed an intense hatred for anything foreign. He is honored both as the father of German gymnastics and of the Turner societies (see below), but actually he was not a physical educator in a professional sense. He did publish in 1816 one book on physical education, *German Gymnastics, (Die Deutsche Turnkunst)*. But to Jahn, "physical education was not the goal; it was a means to a national end."[2] Because of its initial affinity with liberalism, physical education was generally suppressed after the War of Liberation until the 1840s.

At this time Adolph Spiess (1810–1858) organized gymnastics for school use and secured their adoption as an integral part of the educational curriculum. His two volumes, *System of Gymnastics* (*Die Lehre der Turnkunst*) and *Manual of Gymnastics for Schools* (*Turnbuch für Schulen*), formed the basis for the standard of physical education in

---

[1]See section at the end of this chapter for a discussion of physical education in the German Democratic Republic.

[2]Hans Kohn, *Prelude to Nation-States: The French and German Experience, 1789–1815* (Princeton, N. J.: D. Van Nostrand Co., Inc., 1967), pp. 270–71.

German schools. Later, Hugo Rothstein (1810–1865), a contemporary of Spiess, introduced the Swedish Ling gymnastic system and attempted to impose it on the army and the schools. After 1870 and until World War I, the Spiess and Rothstein systems coalesced and formed the German program of school physical education.

By the turn of the twentieth century, the increasing tempo of industrial and urban existence and the budding reaction to the formalism and militarism in the schools resulted in the development of the playground, sports, and youth movements. Konrad Koch (1846–1911), August Hermann (1835–1906), and Emil Theodor Gustav von Schenckendorff (1837–1915) contributed to the establishment of playground programs and aroused an interest in athletics. Karl Fischer lent his magnetic leadership to the youth movement. Richard Schirrmann was the motivating force behind the Youth Hostel program. These informal and liberalizing influences, however, were submerged or militarized when the National Socialists came into power in 1933.

The giant of German physical education and sports in the twentieth century was unquestionably Carl Diem (1882–1962). He assumed leadership of the expanding sports movement when he began his long service on the German Olympic Committee in 1906. He was a key figure in efforts to achieve peace between the Turners and the sports enthusiasts before the first World War. Diem headed a commission which visited the United States in 1913 and returned with many ideas to improve the German program and practice. He inaugurated the German Sport Badge in 1913 based on a Swedish proficiency test, and 2.3 million Germans received this coveted award during his lifetime. The famous teacher education institution, *Deutsche Hochschule für Leibesübungen*, started in Berlin in 1920, was his brainchild, and he served as vice-president until the school was taken over by the National Socialists in 1933. Diem was instrumental in the reopening of the *Sporthochschule* in Cologne in 1947, which provided needed and well-qualified leaders for the difficult reconstruction period. The masterful organization of the 1936 Olympic games in Berlin was his responsibility and, as a part of the games, he conceived the Youth Camp to which thirty physical education students were invited from each participating country. His influence and work were curtailed by the Nazis after 1936, so he began excavations at Olympia in Greece which were finally completed in 1961. Among his numerous writings is the comprehensive work, *World History of Sports and Physical Education (Weltgeschichte des Sports und der Leibeserziehung)*, published in 1960.[3]

The name of Carl Diem must stand at the top echelon of great leaders in sport and physical education from all countries and for all ages.

---

[3]Herbert Haag, "Life and Work of Professor Dr. med. h.c., Lit. D. Carl Diem. The Father of Modern Physical Education in Germany," mimeographed, n.d. This is the main source for the paragraph.

Aims of Education

During the nineteenth century, German elementary schools strove to produce literate, submissive, God-fearing citizens who would be loyal to the autocratic government. The masses were trained to be economically efficient in their modest vocations and well-satisfied with their positions in life. The purely intellectual secondary schools, with their exacting and rigid standards, were largely inaccessible to the common people. During the Weimar Republic an attempt was made to transform the German schools into more democratic and liberal agencies. In the elementary schools, at least, somewhat more recognition was given to freedom and individualism. The Weimar Constitution stated that the objective of the schools was "to provide youth with a moral education, a sense of responsibility to the state, individual and professional efficiency in the spirit of German nationality and of international reconciliation." When the National Socialists came into power, the schools became agencies of political indoctrination that were to transform boys and girls into the pattern desired by the Nazi party. Creating physical fitness for farm, factory, and military life was given precedence over intellectual development.

Education in the Federal Republic of Germany was not radically changed from the pre-Nazi days. It was still rooted in a class-dominated society although it professed to "give every young person with the ability and desire for education access to any kind of educational institution and also to prepare for democratic citizenship."[4] Yet in the mid-1960s less than six percent of university students came from working-class homes. Reform, pressed by government and industry, is under way, but resistance is strong and progress is slow.

Aims of Physical Education

After the defeat of the Germans by Napoleonic forces, the philosopher Fichte awakened ideals of freedom and independence in the minds of the weak and demoralized German people. He urged the leaders to employ education as a means of saving the nation. He emphasized that physical education should be given attention as well as intellectual studies because such training was indispensable to a nation seeking to recover and maintain her independence.

The most determined nationalistic trend in physical education had its inception in Germany under Jahn. In forceful language he pleaded for a high standard of physical proficiency. "Gymnastick Exercises are intended to restore the just proportion of the two principal parts of human education, moral and physical, the latter of which had been neglected for the space of several ages. As long as man has a body, it is his duty to take care of it and to cultivate it, as well as his mind, and consequently gymnastick exercises should form an essential part of education."[5]

To Jahn, gymnastics were not merely the means of augmenting physical powers, but a tool for achieving political goals as well. German freedom and strength devolved upon the youth of the state and therefore the supreme aim of physical education was to develop sturdy citizens possessing a love for their homeland and the aggregate strength necessary to throw off the rule of the oppressor.

Unlike most leaders with militaristic aspirations, Jahn bolstered, rather than crushed, the spirit of individualism. The Turner movement breathed of freedom. The motto which Jahn coined, "Frisch, frei, fröhlich, fromm," connotes "bold, free, joyous, and pious."[6] For the first time the common man was encouraged to participate in a popular movement. Men were keeping physically fit with the idea not only of securing freedom for their nation, but also greater personal freedom, and more rights for the masses. To accomplish such objectives, physical education had to be broader than militaristic in scope. Jahn also recognized that Germany's future greatness rested on increasing the mental and moral vigor of the people. Gymnasts were expected to adhere to high standards of personal conduct.

Spiess is known as the founder of school gymnastics in Germany. Unlike Jahn, he conceived of gymnastics as a pedagogical rather than a political process, as a definite aspect of school life rather than a popular movement. Spiess held that educators should concern themselves with the whole life of the child, not just with his mind. In his words,

> Gymnastic exercise in our schools should be the means of educating the body, in the same measure as the other branches educate the mind, and, like the other branches, be taught from the beginning. The school, in teaching gymnastics, develops mainly the common physical activities, orders and regulates them, endows the pupil with the powers of freer and more graceful motions, and nurses within him a desire for exercise and games of all kinds.[7]

Spiess devised a progressive series of exercises in keeping with his purposes of producing systematic bodily development and habits of obedience. He was successful in introducing physical education into the schools of Ger-

---

[5]F. L. Jahn, *Treatise on Gymnastics*, trans. Charles Beck (Northampton: Simeon Butler, 1828), p. 151.

[6]Karl von Raumer, "Physical Education," *American Journal of Education* 8 (March 1860): 203.

[7]A. B. C. Biewend, Selections from A. Spiess' Works, *Essays Concerning the German System of Gymnastics* (Milwaukee: Freidenker Publishing Co., n. d.), p. 7.

many because his objectives harmonized with the autocratic political and educational philosophies of the era. With considerable pride, he emphasized that gymnastics was the one subject that teaches how to practice and display discipline. Although he endeavored to seek an efficient and thorough development of all parts of the body, such objectives were achieved through submission, training of the memory, and quick and accurate responses to commands.

Between 1840–1860, Rothstein, an officer and teacher in the German army, became an adherent to the Swedish Ling system of gymnastics and imported it into Germany where he was successful in introducing some aspects of it into the schools and army. As a result, the philosophies of both Spiess and Rothstein are reflected in the following official statement made at the end of the century:

> School gymnastics should, by means of appropriately selected and well-ordered exercises, promote the bodily development of the children, strengthen their health, habituate the body to a natural and pleasing carriage, increase the strength, endurance, and dexterity of the body in the use of its members, and secure the adoption of certain useful forms of dexterity, particularly with reference to future service under arms in the army of the Fatherland. Throughout the entire course of instruction . . . it is essential . . . to accustom them [the children] to quick apprehension and accurate execution of commands, and to teach them ready subordination to the purpose of a greater whole.[8]

Before the beginning of the twentieth century, dissatisfaction was being expressed with the prevailing educational philosophy and some leaders were demanding a reevaluation of the goals of physical education. Critics charged that little or no thought was being given to the new educational theories of making the whole child the center of the educational process; that intellectualized subject matter and discipline dominated the thinking of the educators; that the schools remained inflexible to new ideas and were pervaded by a military spirit; and that the crowded, repressive conditions of city and industrial life demanded better health and recreational planning.

The German leaders of the playground, youth, and outing movements strove to secure participation in healthy out-of-door sports whereby young people were to be released from introspection and worry and given the opportunity to realize the rights of freedom in personally and socially

---

[8]*Leitfaden für den Turnunterricht in den Preussischen Volksschulen,* Berlin, 1895, as quoted in Edward M. Hartwell, "On Physical Training," *Report of the Commissioner of Education for 1897–1898* (Washington, D. C.: U. S. Government Printing Office, 1899), 1:547.

constructive ways. The new play and youth movements broadened the concept of physical education.

After World War I, under the Weimar Republic, physical education was not dominated by militaristic and nationalistic aims. In striking contrast, the objectives were directed toward restoring the health of the people, providing them with recreation, and inculcating ideals of democratic living. As a result of the war, bodily regeneration became an important consideration in the rehabilitation of the nation. Postwar conditions also emphasized the need for recreation as a means of relieving the tensions of weary citizens, checking the moral breakdown of discouraged youth, and preventing the unemployed from resorting to anarchy.

When the National Socialists came to power, they quickly established the preeminence of the state over the individual and clearly identified an all-embracing nationalistic military purpose of physical education. In order to build up an efficient war machine, the Nazis insisted that all social classes should respect the work done in the factories and fields and take pride in possessing bodies capable of performing such labor. Hitler emphatically stipulated the nature of the schools he wanted. "The racial state must build up the entire educational work in the first instance not on the pumping in of empty knowledge but on the development of healthy bodies."[9] To the Nazis, a constitutionally weak child was considered a national liability; the robust youth, an asset. The Third Reich demanded assets.

In strong terms the Nazis denounced individual development of the personality as an educational goal that would endanger the welfare of the nation. The National Socialists believed in a "nation-centered" rather than a "child-centered" school.[10] This principle was emphasized in a decree which stated that ". . . physical education and sport are not for the enjoyment of private persons; physical exercise is rather a substantial part of the national life and the fundamental element of the national educational system. Physical education and sport must be deprived of all individualism and must become nationalistically popular. . . ."[11] The Nazis were devoted to a Spartan program of rigid discipline and strenuous physical activity. The product of this program was the Nazi youth. To a degree possibly unparalleled in all history, he possessed fanatical loyalty, blind courage, and martial spirit.

In the postwar era, physical education in West Germany sought to educate the whole person through physical activity within a framework

[9]Adolph Hitler, *Mein Kampf* (Munich: F. Eher, 1927), p. 452.

[10]Von Tschammer und Osten, "Physical Education as a Part of Citizenship Training," *Leibesübungen und Körperliche Erziehung* (December 1933), p. 535.

[11]Quoted by Joseph S. Roucek, "The Subjugation of German Physical Education to German Fascism," *School and Society* 19 (August 26, 1933): 281.

that was Christian, democratic, and humanistic. The term, *Leibeserziehung* (physical education), gained preference over *Leibesübungen* (physical exercise) and reflected this changing philosophy.[12]

Promotion of Physical Education

Before 1806, physical education was not a part of the school curriculum in Germany except in a few isolated, experimental schools under the leadership of such men as Basedow, Salzmann, and GutsMuths. It was not until Jahn dedicated himself to the work that physical education became a potent factor in German national development and a popular institution of the people.

JAHN AND THE TURNERS: Jahn was not committed to a career in gymnastics. He began teaching in German boys' schools, first in Graue Kloster in 1810 and later at Plamann's Pestalozzian School for Boys. As was the practice, Wednesdays and Saturdays were "half-holidays." On these afternoons when no classes were in session, teachers occasionally accompanied students on expeditions into the country. Jahn became an enthusiastic promoter of these events. Beginning on a small scale, he took the boys out into the country and encouraged them to practice vigorous physical activities. Working with them he devised some primitive apparatus, such as horizontal oak limbs to be used as hanging bars, straight sticks to hurl at marks, and jumping standards. From this simple, informal beginning grew the idea of the *Turnplatz* (playground).

In June 1811, Jahn completed and opened his first *Turnplatz* on the outskirts of Berlin. Friedrich Friesen, a teaching colleague, aided Jahn in its management. The *Turnplatz* was similar in purpose to the early Greek palaestra, except that it was patronized on a more democratic basis. The playground was an enclosed rectangular area equipped with a small hut or arbor for dressing and a few roughly-made pieces of apparatus, including ladders, high jumping standards, horizontal bars, climbing masts, inclined ladders, balance beams, pole-vaulting standards, rope climbs, broad-jumping ditches, a figure-eight-shaped track, and a wrestling ring within one end of the track. Activities requiring considerable space were conducted outside of the fenced area. To meet the expenses of maintaining the grounds and keeping the equipment in good condition, the children were assessed a small fee. A common uniform helped to erase barriers of class distinction and promoted a feeling of social equality among the boys, a most revolutionary act in that almost feudal era. During the months of July and August groups met on Tuesdays and Fridays as well as on the customary Wednesday and Saturday half-holidays.

[12]Wolfgang Karbe, "Physical Education and Sports in East and West Germany," *Physical Educator* 19 (October 1962): 108–10.

In the next year, 1812, an enlarged *Turnplatz* was completed with additional and more elaborate facilities including a new running track, jumping ditches, the first model of parallel bars, vaulting bucks or horses without pommels, and hanging and climbing devices. The equipment, although crude in design and construction, was the forerunner of our modern heavy apparatus. New members from all classes of society joined in the program. Jahn yielded to the request of adults who desired to engage in *Turnen*, setting aside Sundays and certain holidays for their use of the facilities. At times, spectators by the hundreds lined the sides of the *Turnplatz* to watch the participants.

When the War of Liberation broke out in 1813, Jahn and Friesen were among the first to join the armed forces seeking to free Germany from the Napoleonic domination. Most of the Turners quickly followed their example. Despite the war the *Turnplatz* remained open and exercises continued under the direction of Jahn's assistant, Ernst Eiselen. During this period gymnastics was publicly financed for the first time.

In the tidal wave of patriotism that swept throughout Germany as the last of the French troops left the soil of the Fatherland, the Turner societies enjoyed an amazingly spontaneous growth. The whole nation became enthusiastic about gymnastics and honored Jahn as a public hero. He completed his book, *German Gymnastics*, and men in other German states turned to it for guidance in the construction and management of the Turner program.

However, under the reactionary rule of Metternich, the Turner establishments came to be regarded as preparatory schools for revolutionary training. These fears seemed justified when a Turner, Karl Sand, murdered an antiliberal dramatist, Kotzebue, in 1819. The Prussian king abolished the Turner organizations; Jahn was arrested and never again served as an active leader. Although the Turners were generally restricted for the next twenty years, their work was permitted to continue in some German states. Even in Berlin Eiselen was allowed to operate several gymnasiums.

A new Prussian king in 1840 removed the restraints on gymnastics and the Turners flourished once more. The Revolution of 1848 caused a temporary setback, and many members emigrated to the United States. In the 1860s Turners decided to remain unconditionally aloof from all political affiliations and thus acquired full state approval. In 1868 the National Union of German Gymnastic Societies (*Deutsche Turnerschaft*) was organized with 128,491 active members. Membership grew steadily and by 1915 there were over a million Turners in 11,769 local societies.[13] The National *Turnfeste*, in which hundreds of participants simultaneously displayed their gymnastic skills, became as important a part of national life in the German Empire as the World Series baseball games are in

---

[13]Fred E. Leonard and George B. Affleck, *A Guide to the History of Physical Education* (Philadelphia: Lea & Febiger, 1947), p. 105.

America. The exhibition held in Leipzig in 1913 lasted five days, and 60,-000 Turners performed before an audience of 250,000 people. Germans emigrating from their homeland carried their gymnastic exercises to every part of the globe, organizing new societies to carry on the activities.

Jahn did not attempt to put gymnastics in the formal course of study in the schools. The *Turnvereine* tended to supplement the intellectual training of youth, but the societies were divorced from school organizations. The clubs were composed of children and adults from all classes of society. Gymnastics were not officially made a part of the school curriculum until after the birth of the Turner movement, and followed quite a different pattern. In order to describe the development of the program, attention will be focused on Prussia, for in Germany there was no centralized Bureau of Education; each state independently organized its own.

SCHOOL GYMNASTICS: There was little agitation for school gymnastics in Prussia until 1836 when medical men began to make strong appeals for such work. An article by Dr. Karl Lorinser entitled "On the Protection of Health in the Schools" charged officials with exclusively training the intellect at the expense of emotional balance and physical fitness of youth, thus endangering the national vigor. A decree of 1842 officially recognized physical education instruction as a state function and a ministerial order two years later prescribed the establishment of school gymnasiums and voluntary physical education classes for male secondary schools and teacher training colleges. A Turner, Hans Massmann, who was put in charge of the program, endeavored to institute the informal gymnastics of Jahn and club activities into the schools. His efforts were not successful, and the Minister of Education ordered the installation of the Spiess system.

The German school gymnastics (*Schulturnen*) owed their distinctive and valuable program to Spiess and his followers. Although most of his work was done in Switzerland and Hesse, his influence extended to all German states. Spiess enjoyed the title of "founder of school gymnastics and gymnastics for girls in particular." As a young man in Switzerland, he had experimented with integrating physical education into the regular curriculum. He was given considerable encouragement by the head of the school, Friedrich Froebel. As a result of his pioneer efforts, Spiess was offered a position in the Grand Duchy of Hesse in 1848. The authorities requested that he organize classes, train the required number of teachers, and supervise the operation of the program. By 1852, Spiess had opened in Hesse a new gymnasium, 100 by 60 feet, surrounded by a double *Turnplatz*. Both indoor and outdoor facilities were constructed so that classes would not be interrupted because of the weather or season. The indoor gymnasium, which was the first of its kind in Germany, could be divided into two rooms by a movable partition. The new gymnasium attracted visitors from many German cities, and within a few years the Spiess system was carried to all parts of the Fatherland.

Spiess hoped to secure the acceptance of bodily exercises in the curriculum on the same basis as the academic subjects. He believed that gymnastic instruction should be extended to girls as well as to boys. In his planning, gymnastics were to be required rather than voluntary, with only physicians' certificates accepted as excuses for absences. Elementary classes were to meet for one hour every day while older students would have slightly shorter sessions. All teaching materials were to be suitably graded for each sex according to the age group. Classes were to be conducted during the school hours by pedagogically trained instructors who understood the art of teaching and the development of children. The principle that the school should be concerned with the whole life of the child, physical as well as mental, gradually gained wider acceptance. Educational authorities of the German Empire began to adopt the Spiess system as the basic program for the schools. Later it was slightly modified to include certain Swedish concepts of gymnastics.

When Hugo Rothstein introduced Ling's Swedish exercises into Germany, he insisted that all work should follow the Ling system. This aroused a storm of protests from the followers of Jahn and Spiess, from leaders of the Turner movement who denounced Rothstein's program as too militaristic, and from medical men who attacked it from the physiological and anatomical side. A manual of physical education for elementary schools was revised in 1868 to compromise the differences of opinion over the two systems. This compromise plan was generally accepted down to World War I with minor changes.

After 1860 Prussia became a leader in school gymnastics. In 1862 physical education was made compulsory for boys in the elementary schools. The requirement for boys in secondary schools was increased from two to three hours weekly in 1892. Two years later authorities decided to require physical education for girls, first in the secondary schools and later in the elementary schools. *A Manual for the Physical Training of Girls in Prussian Schools* was published in 1913.

TEACHER TRAINING: The teacher-training program in Germany probably had its inception in 1815 when Jahn attempted to train a few leaders, but for the most part his students were not school men. Massmann organized a Central Training School for Teachers of Gymnastics in 1848 which offered a three-month course, but it failed within two years. The Royal Central Gymnastic Institute established in 1851 under Rothstein's direction met with greater success. At first, the Institute consisted of two divisions, the military and the civilian, but later they became completely separated. The civilian school moved to new quarters and changed its name, eventually being known as *Landesturnanstalt*. The full course of instruction extended about seven months for men and six months for women. Because there was such a great demand for teachers, the Royal Central Institute could not take care of all the work; therefore, arrangements were made to give some classes outside of the school but under its auspices. Several cities made preparations for state examinations for teachers. Later, five-month training courses were offered in Prussian universities for qualified teachers or students who had completed four semesters of work. To be certified as a gymnastic teacher in Prussia prior to World War I, a student had to pass a state examination, both theoretical and practical. Certified physical education teachers held faculty status and were responsible to school administrators.

SPORTS AND THE PLAYGROUND MOVEMENT: Soon after the Franco-Prussian War, sports were first introduced into Germany from England. August Hermann, a teacher in Brunswick, brought a ball from England and started rugby in 1874.[14] Cricket began two years later and by 1900, thanks to the efforts of English students, businessmen, and officials, some Germans were also enjoying rowing, track and field, tennis, soccer, and other sports. A few schools at the secondary level began to provide time for sports participation similar to the plan of the English public schools.

The sports movement was sharply contested by the Turner societies who also opposed German participation in the Olympic games. The Turners stressed mass participation and nationalism; the sports advocates, high skill levels and international competition. Carl Diem tried to reconcile the two groups and proposed the word *Leibesübungen* to include both areas.[15] After the 1912 Olympic games, Diem headed a commission to visit the United States and observe the nature of American physical education. The commission advocated running games, the use of athletic contests involving strength, the value of individuality, specialization in sports to promote personal preferences, and construction of playgrounds.[16] They also brought back a coach to train German athletes for the 1916 Olympic games which were scheduled for Berlin but cancelled by the war.

Germany assumed world leadership in the playground movement and in advocating outdoor play and games for school children to supplement the indoor gymnastics of the Turnverein. Unexpected support came from a Prussian judge, Emil Hartwick, who wrote an influential pamphlet in 1881. He urged that students give the morning to the mind and the afternoon to the body and spirit. At a national convention in 1889 Emil von Schenckendorff and Gustav Eitner aroused additional enthusiasm for playgrounds, and this led to the formation of the Central Committee for

14Ibid., pp. 134–35.

15Haag, "Life and Work of Carl Diem," p. 2.

16Liselott Diem, "Federal Republic of Germany—Health, Physical Education, and Recreation," in C. Lynn Vendien and John E. Nixon, eds., *The World Today in Health, Physical Education, and Recreation* (Englewood Cliffs, N. J.: Prentice-Hall, Inc., 1968), pp. 128–29.

the Promotion of Games in Germany. This committee for the next two decades helped to secure facilities, published booklets with authoritative descriptions of games, arranged teacher training courses, called national conventions in the interest of play, and publicized the playground movement through the press.[17]

The germ of the German youth movement was cultivated in 1896 in a gymnasium at Steglitz, a suburb of Berlin. A group of boys, with the assistance of a sympathetic teacher, Karl Fischer, sought freedom in hiking and open-air activities. Some eight years later the *Wandervögel* (literally, wandering birds) was formed and enjoyed rapid growth. A decree of 1911 encouraged organizations to place buildings at the disposal of the wanderers. In the same year the Prussian Diet voted three and one-half million marks to further the work. Hostels soon sprang up all over Germany. The seventeen shelters providing for 3,000 people in 1911 had multiplied to eighty-three shelters, providing for 20,000 people, by 1913.

THE WEIMAR REPUBLIC: During the early days of the Weimar Republic, physical education received strong official support and there was wide acceptance of sports, games, and out-of-door activities. The regulations of 1921 revived playground activities and required an increased number of gymnasiums and teachers. Other provisions required all schools heretofore without physical education to incorporate it into their curriculums. The number of hours per week and number of years to receive instruction in physical education were gradually increased. Some institutions obtained a daily hour of instruction, besides setting aside one afternoon a week for play and one day a month for hiking. Physical education was recognized on the same basis as any other school subject. It was a requirement for grade promotion and a prerequisite for graduation. Achievement records appeared on report cards. Even the universities, the strongholds of intellectualism, began to foster some athletics.

Numerous physical education facilities were constructed in the period after 1918. In spite of war damage and a ruinous inflation, many municipalities embarked on a massive public works program to provide jobs for unemployed ex-servicemen. Between the years 1919 and 1928 in Prussia alone, appropriations were authorized for 833 playgrounds, 273 gymnasiums, 322 recreational places, 269 bathing beaches, and 274 youth hostels. So extensive was this effort that the Weimar Republic "came nearer to providing adequate physical education facilities for all its citizens than any other large country has done hitherto."[18]

The education of teachers moved forward with the opening of the *Deutsche Hochschule für Leibesübungen* in 1920. It was located in the

[17]Leonard and Affleck, *A Guide to the History of Physical Education*, pp. 143–45.
[18]J. G. Dixon, et al., *Landmarks in the History of Physical Education* (London: Routledge & Kegan Paul, 1957), p. 140.

Berlin stadium and associated with the University of Berlin. A physician, Dr. August Bier, was appointed president and Carl Diem served as vice-president. It offered a four-year curriculum with a scientific emphasis backed up by facilities for research. This school also gave short-term courses for sports leaders and coaches and acquired an international reputation for the excellence of its work until it fell victim to Nazi manipulation. Another professional institution was the *Landesturnanstalt* in Spandau, under Neuendorff, which devoted minimal attention to sport. Also various universities established institutes of physical education. The first university appointment of professor of physical education was given to Karl Altrock at Leipzig in 1925, and the first doctorate was granted five years later.

During this period, the German people from all classes of society flocked to sports in greater numbers than ever before. Weekends were widely devoted to leisure activities. Women, tanned and physically fit, joined with the men in hiking, swimming, skiing, running, and other strenuous sports. The youth movement was revived and considerably expanded, supported by practically every political, religious, and professional organization.

The various sport and gymnastic societies were thoroughly organized. The many local clubs united their efforts and formed national commissions to represent their interests. Most of the school youth organizations were members of the RDJ (National Commission of German Youth Associations) and the JH (National Commission of German Hostels). The RDJ combined a variety of youth clubs in a loose federation that aimed to promote the health and physical education of youth. The JH was a commission founded to promote the hostel movement. Wilhelm Münker, commission secretary, was recognized for his ability in having over a thousand new hostels built in the 1920s.

Adult recreational clubs of the Republic belonged to one of three commissions: (1) the nonpolitical DRL (German National Commission of Physical Education); (2) the socialistic ZK (The Central Commission for Workers' Sport and Physical Education); and (3) the communists KRS (The Communistic Sport Commission). The DRL, the strongest of the three, was a federation of thirty-eight public and private unions, representing more than 30,000 clubs, totaling more than 6,000,000 members. This commission, directed by Diem, gave professional advice to members, assisted organizations in raising money, conducted research, sponsored conventions, furthered the National Olympic games, helped found the *Deutsche Hochschule für Leibesübungen* in Berlin, increased playground areas, conducted athletic meets, and worked to achieve compulsory physical education in the schools. The DRL pursued Diem's idea of a German Sports Badge as a mark of physical proficiency and over a quarter of a million of them were awarded between 1919 and 1933. The second largest sports commission, the ZK, was a federation of socialistic athletic societies with more than 1,000,000 members. The ZK conducted athletic meets, aided in building a training school, and carried on activities similar to the DRL but always slanted toward socialistic goals.[19] The third recreational commission, the KRS, was organized in 1931 by the communists who broke away from the ZK. Spreading propaganda was its chief objective.

During the Republic, the state did not directly control the athletic and sport clubs nor their commissions, but a federal committee, *Reichsbeirat für Körperliche Erziehung*, was established in 1920 to help distribute funds set aside for physical education and to act in an advisory capacity. The committee was composed of representatives of the five national commissions, the RDJ, JH, DRL, ZK, and KRS. It acted as a liaison board between the private physical education clubs and the government.

THE NATIONAL SOCIALIST REGIME: When the National Socialists came into power, there was already built up a vigorous centralized physical education administrative structure convenient for their purposes. The Nazis soon seized control of all sport, athletic, and youth organizations, as well as the school physical education programs that had existed under the Republic. To make their political system secure, they believed it essential to place physical education on all levels under government control and to coordinate and synchronize it with the totalitarian pattern. In 1933, Hitler appointed Hans von Tschammer und Osten, a military man, as National Sport Commissioner. The latter immediately set about to disband or reorganize the existing amateur sport and youth societies. The new Sport Commissioner ordered, "There must be a lessening of the multitude of sport leagues in order to improve the control over them, and to lighten the financial obligation. . . . The right leaders, who can foster the correct spirit, must be selected to conduct the sports and *Turn* Unions. . . . Only those unions in the *Führerring* will be allowed to conduct athletic meets, festivals and demonstrations."[20] The government now had complete supervision of sport clubs; to survive, they had to conform to Nazi policies. The *Deutsche Turnerschaft* was dissolved in 1935.

Having determined to simplify and unify out-of-school sport agencies, the National Sport Commissioner selected sixteen unions to carry out the work. Every amateur club was required to become a member of one of the following unions: German Turners, Football, Track and Field Athletics, Heavy Athletics, Swimming, Winter Sports, Riflery, Water Sports, Wandering, Cycling, Motor, Tennis, Bowling, Sports Physicians, Teachers, and Youth Groups. To complete his organization, the National Sport Com-

---

[19]Constitution of ZK, (n. d.) p. 2.
[20]Von Tschammer und Osten, "Der Neuaufbau des Deutschen Sports," *Leibesübungen und Körperliche Erzichung*, no. 10 (June 1933), p. 218.

missioner established the national *Führerring*, an association composed of one representative from each of these sixteen unions. Similar provincial, district, and local Führerrings were set up to carry out orders from the national office.

While the Nazis vituperated the Weimar Republic, they made full use of the numerous facilities for sports and physical education constructed during that despised era. The major effort by the Nazis in this direction was to build the stadium and other accommodations in Berlin for the 1936 Olympic games.

Hans von Tschammer und Osten also directed the recreational program for labor. He was head of the Sport Division of the *Kraft durch Freude* (KdF), Strength Through Joy. This organization, established in 1933, was patterned after Mussolini's National "After Work" Institution, and in 1938 was placed under the direction of the German Labor Front, the party-controlled association that replaced all of the 169 workers' and employers' unions dissolved by the Nazis. A gigantic effort was made by the KdF leaders to organize the leisure time of the entire German nation in harmony with National Socialistic Party purposes. To avoid duplicating the efforts of the amateur clubs, the KdF did not undertake any sport competitions.

Of the eleven departments of *Kraft durch Freude*, the Sports section and the Travel, Hiking, and Vacation sections were related to physical education. The Sport section was designed to attract the approximately 25,000,000 adults who were not members of regular athletic clubs associated with the sixteen unions represented in the national Führerring. It employed more than 2,000 trainers and teachers. Any Aryan German citizen was eligible to obtain a membership card, which could be renewed yearly for about ten cents. For a very low fee he could join one or more of a wide variety of classes. Swimming lessons that would have cost forty cents in a private club were available to members for seven and a half cents. Members were also eligible for reduced rail fares and could secure sport equipment at special prices.

The division of Travel, Hiking, and Vacation of the *Kraft durch Freude* organized cruises to other countries, provided accommodations at inns and resorts, and arranged hiking trips. The prices were so low that hundreds of thousands who formerly could not afford to travel were given an opportunity. A sea trip from Hamburg to the Norwegian fjords cost about $1.75 per day; a trip to Lisbon and the Azores about $1.00 per day. The German masses felt the *Kraft durch Freude* was the first step in the realization of greater opportunities for them, and the movement undoubtedly did much to strengthen party loyalty.

Although young people might participate in the *Kraft durch Freude* and Amateur Athletic Unions, the government authorized certain other agencies to concentrate on providing a physical education program for them. These were: (1) the schools, (2) Hitler Youth Clubs, (3) the *Landjahr*, (4) Labor Service, and (5) Military Service.

The Reich Minister of Education, Dr. Bernhard Rust, controlled the work done in the schools. Physical education received greater emphasis than any other subject except German culture. In the lower schools, pupils usually received two to three class hours of training a week. In the upper grades, four or five classes per week were scheduled as well as periodic hikes of one or more days. Some secondary institutions also provided country homes for vacations and week ends.

In order to attend secondary school, students had to pass tests which assessed their physical as well as their intellectual capacity. The physical tests were sufficiently easy so that few youngsters failed. However, students could be dismissed from school if they showed little desire to endure physical hardship. Physical education was a required subject for which marks were given. Students could be withheld from graduating with their class if they failed to pass physical fitness tests. The annual Sports Day at each school was an important occasion. All pupils who could attain the standard set for five athletic events were granted a Reich Sports Medal. Students who exhibited exceptional physical fitness and qualities of leadership were selected to attend a special school preparing them for important party and military positions.

In higher institutions of learning, physical education was given considerable recognition. All university students were obliged to take classes for three semesters, and those training to become teachers took a daily lesson through their entire course. If students desired to qualify as teachers in physical education, they pursued a year of additional study at one of the University Physical Training Institutes which were attached to every university in Germany. The Nazis repeatedly emphasized that "youth must lead youth" and a number of institutions offered short courses, with a strong party indoctrination, for training youth leaders in physical education.

The Reich Youth Leader of the National Socialist Party directed an elaborate program to attract youngsters and to indoctrinate them in the party ideology. The Hitler Youth was divided into three age groups, the *Pimpfs*, 6 to 10; the *Jungvolk*, 10 to 14; and the Hitler *Jugend* (Hitler Youth), 14 to 18. The latter group was composed of four branches: HJ proper, HJ marines, HJ flyers, and HJ motorized division. The girls had similar organizations. They belonged to the *Jungmädel* (Young Girls) until they were fourteen and then were members of the *Bund Deutscher Mädel* (League of German Girls) until they were twenty-one years of age.

When the school day was over at 1:00 P.M., students in their Hitler Youth uniforms were busily engaged in club activities. Usually the afternoons, some evenings, and weekends were devoted to party work, instruction in Nazi ideology, and premilitary drills. Frequent use was made of the Youth Hostels that had sprung up all over Germany. In the Hitler Youth club meetings, military order and discipline were maintained at all times. When boys entered the Hitler movements, they were given a number and an efficiency card. Club leaders, who were usually Storm Troopers, regularly marked the military abilities, club promotional examinations, and ideological growth of each youngster on his efficiency record.

The *Landjahr* and Labor Service also acted as agencies of premilitary training. After 1935, youths beyond the age of compulsory school attendance (fourteen or fifteen years of age) were required to spend approximately one year in the country following a schedule of organized farm work, physical training, and ideological indoctrination. This project was initiated to assist children from crowded industrial areas to increase their physical vigor, to become more conscious of their duty to the state, and to develop an understanding of country life and how to maintain a food supply.

The final step of the premilitary training was six months of Labor Service required sometime between the ages of eighteen and twenty-five. Youths were moved from one part of the country to another in an effort to break down any provincialism.

Culminating all the physical training, of course, was the induction into actual army life. As early as 1935, Germans were drafted into the armed forces for two years. They were certainly not raw recruits. They were physically fit, disciplined youths, accustomed to group life and outdoor hardships, and ready to receive their specialized military training. After serving two years, exceptionally able young men with proven party loyalty became eligible for service in the Storm Troops and the Elite Corps.

Under National Socialism, all teachers were quickly brought under strict regimentation. Eventually, every instructor was expected to become an actively participating member of the party. Civilian clothes almost disappeared from the teachers' meetings, for professional prestige came with the Storm Trooper's uniform. To further control the profession, the Nazis replaced all teacher organizations with the National Socialistic Teacher Association (NSLB). The physical education branch of the NSLB was composed of five offices: school physical education, propaganda, sports, gymnastics outside of the schools (*Geländesport*), and aviation. The state gave a recognition to physical educators that they had never enjoyed in the era of intellectualism, but professional prestige was secured by relinquishing their freedom.

THE FEDERAL REPUBLIC: Following World War II, enormous problems had to be faced as the German people struggled to return to normality. Physical education was temporarily sidetracked, partly because of more pressing needs and partly a natural reaction against the identification of physical education with the Hitler regime. In the Federal Republic each of the eleven *Länder* exercised its own authority over culture and education. In 1956 all the state ministers of education officially declared the need for physical education in the total education of youth. Throughout West Germany, most children in the lower grades have two hours a week for physical education, and secondary school youth receive three hours. Sometimes there are an additional two hours for sports one afternoon a week. The vocational schools, however, generally have little or no physical education. At the universities, physical education is largely voluntary, but sports clubs provide competitive opportunities.

The energetic Carl Diem perceived the urgent needs in teacher education after the war, and he was primarily responsible for the opening of the *Deutsche Sporthochschule* in Cologne in 1947.[21] J. G. Dixon of the English Military Government provided necessary support for this project. The new school flourished under the skilled leadership of Diem and his wife, Liselott Diem, and enrollment grew from 100 in 1947 to 1200 in 1969. This total included a number of students drawn from many other countries. Greatly enlarged facilities were completed for use in 1963. The *Deutsche Sporthochschule Köln* is a state college which provides a three-year curriculum for teachers of physical education and a one-year course for youth and sports association leaders. Three-year courses are also given at the Bavarian Sports Academy and the State College for Physical Education in Mainz.

Other students prepare for physical education by attending a department of physical education at one of nearly thirty universities. They go for four years and must major in one or two other subjects besides physical education. The conservative German university faculties are slowly accepting physical education on an equal basis with other subjects. A doctorate in the department of physical education is possible only at Frankfurt, Tübingen, and Bonn; elsewhere the dissertation has to be written in another department.

The promotion of physical education and sports under the Federal Republic has been severely hindered by the lack of facilities. This problem was aggressively attacked in 1960 by the announcement of the Golden Plan developed by the German Olympic Committee. A careful estimate was made of the exact needs for playgrounds and sports centers in Germany, and then a bold, fifteen-year construction program was proposed at an estimated cost of 6.5 billion Deutschmarks ($1,625,000,000). Support was sought from the local, state, and federal governments. These facilities will be for the use of schools, clubs, and the general public. The *Deutsche Sporthochschule* in Cologne has an Institute for Facilities to assist in the planning and construction of indoor and outdoor areas.

[21]Diem had hoped to rebuild the former *Hochschule* in Berlin but this was made part of the Soviet zone after 1945.

The reestablishment of the whole structure for sports organizations took place soon after the war. The German Sport Association (*Deutscher Sportbund*) was formed in 1950 to provide a national authority. In 1966 it had a membership of over seven million and embraced 35,000 sport clubs and 41 federal sport associations. The soccer union had 2,240,000 members and the gymnastic association had 1,640,000 adherents.[22] The work of the clubs and the sport associations is financed in part by a national soccer lottery to the extent of 50 million marks ($12,500,000) a year. The local communities, who own over 90 percent of all sport facilities, allow the clubs to use them at little or no cost.

A major promotional event in West Germany is the Federal Youth Games which are held each summer and winter for all youth 10 to 20 years of age. Five million participate annually in a variety of events with the emphasis placed on achieving certain levels of performance and fitness based on age and sex in friendly competition. Those who achieve a given point total receive a certificate signed by the President of the Federal Republic.

The German Sport Federation in 1952 carried on the German Sport Badge program originated by Carl Diem in 1913. It provides classification for both sexes from the age of 12 to 40 and over. Participants must perform in one event from each of five groups: swimming, jumping, running, throwing, and an endurance event. For the year 1964 alone, 150,000 people won badges, and the total for the period from 1952 to 1967 exceeded one million.

The *Deutscher Sportbund* initiated another program in 1959 called the Second Way, or *Zweiter Weg*. The purpose was to try to reach the millions of West Germans who did not belong to a sport club and did not take part in sports. Studies showed that most club members were men under 30 years of age, and some communities had no clubs at all. Several steps were taken. Since 55 percent of all clubs centered around one sport, they were encouraged to offer additional activities. Another approach was to give a variety of instructional courses in recreational activities for men and women on weekends, holidays, and for short periods of three months. Stress has been placed on rhythmic gymnastics and games, swimming, tennis, judo, badminton, skiing, and dancing. A third step was to train more leaders through free short courses.[23] The *Zweiter Weg* was particularly directed at women. Only one adult woman in 65 belonged to a club, and it was estimated that only 2.2 percent took part in sports. The languid *Frau* of the 1960s apparently was no match for her athletic counterpart of the 1920s.

[22]Diem, "Federal Republic of Germany—Health, Physical Education, and Recreation," pp. 129–30.
[23]Jürgen Palm, "The 'Second Way' for Sport in Germany," in International Council of Sport and Physical Education, *Sport and Leisure. Report of the First International Seminar* (Stuttgart, Germany: Verlag Karl Hofmann, 1965), pp. 30–31.

Sports leaders were responding to the fact that a booming economy in the 1960s had given the German people more money and leisure time than they had ever known.

Program of Physical Education

Jahn, the early leader of German physical education, made many contributions to the program in that field. Participating in fundamental activities in a national setting was the basic consideration of Jahn's program. When he accompanied students on excursions into the country, he encouraged spontaneous activities demanding big muscle movements, such as running, jumping, walking, vaulting, throwing, climbing, lifting, wrestling, swimming, and stunts on apparatus. To teach the boys to work cooperatively Jahn incorporated interesting, popular games such as "robber and traveler." As the youths tramped along, Jahn led them in patriotic songs, related stories from German history, exhorted them to work for the future of the Fatherland, and assiduously cultivated their desire for liberty. During the winter months, some of the exercises were continued indoors, especially fencing with light broadswords and crossbow shooting at targets. More than half of Jahn's book is devoted to gymnastic exercises. Jahn recognized the value of games but felt they should require sufficient motion to render the body active and strong. He advised:

> A good gymnastick play should not require too great and extensive preparations; it should be easy to be understood, and yet founded on a certain rule and principle; it should not entirely, or to a great extent, depend on chance; it should occupy a sufficiently large number; it should not require too large a space unproportioned to the number of players; it should not require idle lookers on; but on the contrary, each should be occupied; it should afford a fair proportion of labor and rest; it should not be uniform and without variety; it should require active and dexterous players, in order to be played well; it should be of such nature as to be always played with zeal and interest."[24]

As the Turner societies took root and entered upon their precarious existence, they began to retreat from the open-air *Turnplatz* into indoor halls. There was a tendency to relegate free and spontaneous movements to a minor position, and to minimize games, jumping, running, and hiking. In confined quarters, classes in fencing and exercises on horizontal bars, parallel bars, and ladders were most suitable. Apparatus work became more systematized at this time, stunts were perfected, nomenclature was established, and tables of progression were written. A subtle metamorphosis took place during the indoor period that made the Turner program slightly narrower in scope and a little more formal in procedure.

[24]Jahn, *Treatise on Gymnastics*, pp. 141–42.

When physical education was gradually introduced into the school curriculum, the Spiess system of gymnastics was adopted. Although earlier educational leaders had anticipated many of the activities he used, Spiess fashioned them into a system adapted to the harmonious development of the child. He also devised some new exercises and apparatus more suitable for younger children and girls. Hanging teeter-totters, walking stilts, giant swings, rail slides, miniature climbing ladders, and poles were features in his work. Because he did not approve of Jahn's squad leader system, Spiess tended to disregard individual activities and apparatus work that could not be adapted to group instruction. Spiess classified apparatus work into hanging and supporting exercises, to be performed on such equipment as horizontal bars, parallel bars, ladders, ropes, poles, oblique boards, horses, bucks, scaling walls, giant strides, stilts, skates, and sleds. Spiess himself stressed free exercises and marching. Free exercises were those performed without apparatus or with only such as could easily be carried in the hands. These were used because they offered an efficient way of exercising a large group and yet insured sufficient activity for each part of the body that needed development. Marching exercises were extensively used because they provided a quick and orderly method of moving large numbers of pupils at once as well as helping to develop an erect and graceful carriage. Spiess, being musically gifted, arranged many of the free exercises and marching drills to be performed with music accompaniment. The founder of school gymnastics recommended that some time should be given to play at the end of every lesson and also advised that youngsters be taken on excursions into the open country. Although he sanctioned games, sports, hiking, and dances, he never allowed them to dominate his program. Later disciples of the Spiess system tended to omit them altogether.

The Swedish Ling influence brought to Germany by Rothstein, introduced classes in calisthenics, military gymnastics, fencing, bayonet and rifle drills, and corrective and aesthetic gymnastics. The Turnvereine in Berlin and elsewhere protested because Rothstein rejected work on parallel bars as physically harmful and made light of Jahn gymnastics. Although the Ling system lost its dominance over the German program, it nevertheless left a permanent imprint.

In the 1870s, when Koch and Hermann, the pioneer leaders of the playground movement, took boys out-of-doors on their free afternoons and let them engage in such games as prisoner's base and *Kaiserball*, it was quite an innovation. Youngsters, of course, welcomed the opportunity to play native games and the newly-introduced English rugby and cricket. The revised manual of 1895 mentioned sixteen running games and seven ball games in addition to intensive apparatus work, marching, and free exercises. A later manual of 1909 for schools without indoor gymnasiums omitted the Spiess marching exercises, limited the apparatus work, but advocated running, hiking, games, and track and field events.

Most of the organized games which became popular in Germany were imported from England and other countries. One exception was the game of handball which originated in Germany just after 1900. The first rules were published by a sport teacher, Carl Schelenz.[25] German handball is quite unlike the court game. It was first played outdoors with eleven players on a side and resembled soccer except that a goal is scored by throwing the ball into the goal from outside a semicircular area. Small-field handball, with seven on a side, was started in Denmark by Holger Nielsen. Since then the game has moved indoors as well and is widely played in almost every European country under the name of *Hallenhandball*.

Outside the schools, the Olympic committee of 1895 stimulated participation in swimming and track and field events, and several private clubs sponsored particular sports. The general public exhibited an increased interest in mountain climbing, swimming, rowing, hiking, and winter sports. As yet, however, most parents were not tolerant of games and sports, expecting the children to apply themselves earnestly to the strict academic and army training of the times.

After World War I, under the Republic, military training was forbidden and the whole nation suddenly became intensely recreation-minded. The influence spread both within the schools and in the extra-curricular and adult programs. Young people and adults, on foot or bicycle, ranged over the countryside during the day and slept in barns or hay lofts at night. Water enthusiasts dotted the canals and rivers with their canoes and rowing shells. In every town, neighbors gathered at the playgrounds and open fields in the evening for games of soccer, handball, or *Schlagball*. Other sport lovers tried golf, bowling, tennis, and dancing. In the fall, people began to look forward to the winter for skating, skiing, bobsledding, and ice hockey.

The emphasis on gymnastics and the sports movement in the early twentieth century, however, triggered a protest reaction which produced rhythmical gymnastics and modern dance. A leader in this new direction was Rudolf Bode who studied the eurhythmics of Jacques Dalcroze in Switzerland. He developed the movements for his "expressive gymnastics" (*Ausdrucksgymnastik*) out of primitive dance forms, the play of children, sports, and the natural stretching actions of animals and children. Bode used "joyful swinging movements" to achieve general efficiency in movement for dance, sport, and industry and to make the body, mind, and nervous system plastic and relaxed.[26] Bess Mensendieck was a physician who was critical of Swedish gymnastics for women; she formulated exercises, based on the pelvic region, which arose out of the particular functions of women in housework and other daily tasks. Rudolf Laban began

[25]Langhoff and Mundt, *Hallenhandball* (Berlin: Sportverlag, 1958), p. 5.
[26]Hinrich Medau, "Introduction to Dr. Bode's Expressive Gymnastics," *American Physical Education Review*, 34 (January 1929): 8–10.

his analysis of the scientific structure of human movement. Mary Wigman studied under Dalcroze and Laban but then went on to develop the "first thoroughly practical and feasible modern dance technique."[27] She sought to use the body expressively and freed dance from its subordination to music. The themes which she portrayed were highly nationalistic, emphasizing the pessimistic philosophy so intimately a part of Teutonic culture. Naturally, as Wigman's influence was carried to other European countries and to the United States, the resulting dance forms became more varied. Others who contributed to rhythmical gymnastics and modern dance developments were Hilda Senff, Dorothea Günther, Hinrich Medau, and Gretl Palucca.

The schools of the Weimar Republic reflected a more democratic attitude than their Prussian predecessors. Rhythmical gymnastics replaced the mechanical exercises, and athletics and sports became an important part of the program. From April until November, outdoor activities such as dancing, games, wandering, swimming, and track and field were emphasized. Calisthenics were relegated to winter months or inclement weather. Afternoon play periods were devoted to soccer, handball, *Schlagball* (a type of baseball), and *Faustball* which was similar to volleyball but played with one hand. Teachers were also urged to give attention to orthopedic and corrective work for the physically handicapped. Inasmuch as young men no longer had to pursue the two or three years' compulsory army service, they were free to go on wandering hikes or trips to school land-homes in the country.

In the Third Reich, the physical education programs were slanted toward military objectives. Hikes became disciplined marches, woodcraft assumed overtones of army maneuvers, and many games were utilized for pretraining in military tactics.

In lower schools, the Nazi program consisted of gymnastics and play patterned after the child's natural movements. Later, some apparatus exercises were used for greater body control. Great emphasis was placed on massive developmental movements, but little attention was given to correctives. In girls' schools, rhythmics were stressed. Track and field sports, team handball, soccer, football, *Schlagball*, and swimming were important in the program, and hiking was required one half-day a month. Before being admitted to the secondary school, a pupil had to pass a physical test which included running, climbing, and obstacle racing.

The secondary school program was similar but more advanced. Hikes were scheduled for at least one full day a month. Lower secondary students marched twelve to eighteen kilometers and higher classes covered twenty to thirty kilometers. During the course of hikes, as well as on other occasions, instruction was given in *Geländesport*, a semimilitary training

[27]Jan Veen, "Mary Wigman's 80th Birthday," *Journal of Health, Physical Education, and Recreation* 38 (February 1967): 56.

that included endurance marches, country craft, movements over different kinds of terrain, tracking and spying, silent forays on the enemy, obstacle races, throwing hand grenades, wall scaling, jumping, throwing, crawling, creeping, and hurling. Boxing, which had been abolished in Prussia in 1912 as too dangerous for educational purposes, was reintroduced to inculcate an aggressive spirit. Rifle shooting, gliding, and flying instruction were also promoted in the schools.[28]

In the universities, the required physical education program for all students consisted of gymnastics, cross-country running, light pentathlon training, small bore rifle shooting, team games, and life-saving. In addition, men attended boxing classes, and the women, dancing classes. Voluntary participation in a variety of sports was available after the completion of the required work.

The Hitler Youth clubs provided training in organized games, gymnastics, boxing, wrestling, jiu-jitsu, swimming, light athletics, shooting, hiking, scouting, and first aid. The *Geländesport*, which assumed a military character, was a very important club activity. Motoring, sailing, aviation, and gliding were offered to groups when facilities were available. Drills, competitions, and efficiency tests were commonly accepted procedures. The efficiency tests for youths fifteen to seventeen years included 100- and 3,000-meter runs, long jumps, throwing, putting the shot, chinning, swimming, and sometimes cycling. There were also efficiency tests in shooting, marching, and various items of the *Geländesport*.

During the *Landjahr*, youths lived in the country, working on farms for half a day, and participating in a program of sports, play, and political instruction during the remaining hours. During their six months of Labor Service, youths carried out work beneficial to the country, including reclamation and reforestation projects, as well as work on reservoirs and harbors. An hour or more a day was also spent in athletics, competitive sports, and drills. All physical education culminated in compulsory service in the army, where the youths received intensive, technical military training.

Moreover, in the Third Reich, through the medium of the sport clubs and the *Kraft durch Freude* the general public was offered a variety of voluntary recreational classes in general physical training, swimming, light athletics, preparation courses for National Sports Badges, boxing, jiu-jitsu, rowing, sailing, tennis, riding, rifle and pistol shooting, skittles, fencing, cycling, rollerskating, golf, folk dancing, courses for invalids and other physically backward people, skiing, sailing, gliding, and campcraft.

Under the Federal Republic, physical education in the various states dropped the Nazi military emphasis. The Conference of Ministers of Education in 1966 recommended that more stress be placed upon sports,

---

[28]Hans Heintz, "Fostering Airmindedness in the Secondary Schools," *Leibesübungen und Körperliche Erziehung*, no. 16 (September 1933), p. 376.

games, and gymnastics. Boys and girls at the primary level have gymnastics with free movement, tumbling, small and large apparatus activities, basic movement activities, and games. Boys will have some soccer. Children in the intermediate grades have the same program (except for basic movement activities) plus basketball, volleyball, and track and field. The secondary schools offer these and sometimes other sports such as rowing, skiing, hiking, and ice skating if feasible. Physical performance tests are given twice a year.[29] Some of the states are encouraging swimming where pools are available. In 1966 in West Berlin, for example, 80 percent of the children finishing primary school had their swimming certificate; for Bremen the total was 89 percent.[30] Special attention is given to children with disabilities.

A useful piece of apparatus, the *Stegel*, was invented in 1952 by a teacher, Lenchen Kunow, in the town of Lueneburg. It consists of three 13-foot long beams held by two triangular supports at each end. The height is adjustable and various attachments make it handy for climbing, chinning, balancing, jumping, swimming, volleyball, and fistball. The *Stegel* was particularly designed for small schools operating on a limited budget.[31]

Physical education in the German schools at the end of the 1960s is still inadequate. Children attend school six days a week and take ten or twelve subjects. This heavy curriculum often means a sacrifice of physical education classes. An estimated fifty percent of the elementary schools have no indoor gymnasiums. Teachers of physical education are in short supply, the pay is low, and they lack full academic status.[32]

Methods of Physical Education

Jahn, a liberal in thinking and acting, was a foe of systems, stiff formality, and mechanized programs. Freedom of action was the rule on his playground. Boys attended because they enjoyed the exercises and games; no compulsory methods were employed. With his enthusiastic personality and rare gift for leadership, Jahn kept the work varied, lively, and interesting.

Greater formality and organization appeared as more students participated in the activities, but Jahn remained firm in his conviction that

[29]International Council on Health, Physical Education, and Recreation, *Physical Education in the School Curriculum*. ICHPER International Questionnaire Report, pt. 1, 1967–68 rev. (Washington, D.C.: ICHPER, 1969), pp. 31–32.

[30]*International Yearbook of Education, 1967*, (Geneva: International Bureau of Education, 1968), p. 175.

[31]Hermann Gall and Marian Webb, "Little Bridge that Goes Over Fences," *Journal of Health, Physical Education, and Recreation* 33 (December 1962): 27–28.

[32]Peter Richter, "Physical Education in Germany," in William Johnson, ed., *Physical Education Around the World*. Monograph no. 1 (Indianapolis. Ind.· Phi Epsilon Kappa, 1966), pp. 24–25.

procedures should not become mechanical and rigid. When the gymnasts reported to the Turnplatz, they usually started with the exercises each preferred; then, after a brief rest period, they were grouped in squads according to age. In later days, Jahn's coworkers systematized exercises as guides for instructors. Each squad leader (*Vorturner*) demonstrated proper execution of the movements, gave encouragement to the beginners, carefully observed the development of his group, and kept records of attendance and proficiency. Youths learned by imitating the physically proficient Vorturners, but conscientious participation and keen rivalry were also factors in the learning process.

Jahn was always conscious of the individual differences of pupils. He also cautioned that leaders must always be on the alert to prevent injuries and overexertion. He insisted that squad leaders ". . . must be able to make a judicious selection from the single parts of a compound exercise. In inspecting the younger and weaker, they should consider that the object is general preparation for gymnastick exercises, not performing particular exercises or feats."[33] Jahn recommended that children be classified in groups according to age, size, and ability.

Although stern methods were not a part of Jahn's program, he did believe that supervision was necessary to preserve order, avoid injury, and help pupils perfect their skills. Discipline on the playground was firm but friendly; group decisions were made by a council and enforced by the boys themselves.

Jahn's objectives were basically nationalistic, but there was nothing militaristic in his methods. Exercises proceeded according to demonstration, emulation, and cooperation. A number of techniques were employed to motivate youth: the wearing of a common uniform, awarding badges bearing important dates in German history, giving inspirational talks, conducting patriotic group singing, and holding gymnastic exhibitions on historic holidays.

Spiess had a different methodology. He believed that order was imperative to good teaching. He was convinced that Jahn's system of depending upon initiative and interest was too casual to achieve a thorough physical development. Seeking to devise a more systematic type of training, Spiess reviewed the mass of gymnastic materials, tabulated the various attainable positions and movements of the trunk and limbs, and graded and classified the exercises of his selection. He presented the results in a practical manual, *Turnbuch für Schulen*, which listed the desirable activities for each age and sex, from the simple to the complex. By selecting the proper sequence for his class, the teacher could proceed to exercise the class members from head to foot in a thorough and exacting manner. Drills were precisely executed, first according to count, then as

[33]Jahn, *Treatise on Gymnastics*, p. 155.

a whole routine, and finally, they were often performed to music. There was only *one* correct way to perform these movements. To land with feet apart in a jump or vault was unforgivable. Apparatus work was as carefully regulated as calisthenics. Pupils were graded on their performances and took examinations in gymnastics on the same basis as in intellectual subjects.

Group drills appealed to Spiess because of their efficiency. Pupils stood in circles or rows, and were subjected to the commands of a single teacher. This system, although ignoring the nature of the individual and stifling interest and initiative, did effect an automatic willingness to respond to commands and insured that every part of the body was being systematically exercised. Although a formalist, Spiess did consider the individual differences of children to the extent that he urged instructors to seek variety in selecting exercises and to relax discipline when necessary. He was such a gifted teacher that his classes may not have felt the restrictions of his methods. Followers of Spiess, however, tended to rely more and more upon stereotyped procedures, which, of course, are always easier than creative presentations. The later introduction of the Ling gymnastics by Rothstein, if anything, served to accentuate the formality of the program.

After the German Republic was established, physical educators were encouraged to experiment with new methods that would allow the child greater freedom of self-expression. Teachers sought to encourage the creative spirit in children and to permit them considerable choice in selecting their activities. Informality and freedom were keynotes of the program. The stiff exercises performed in a precise manner by count gave place to a more flowing, natural, rhythmical style. Many of the retired army officers disappeared from the schools.

In trying to adopt more democratic educational practices, leaders met considerable confusion and controversy. Creative teaching required skills that many instructors lacked. They yearned for their old, formal, disciplinary procedures that were so easy to administer. The conservatives complained that children were becoming too self-assertive under democratic methods and that excesses of individualism were leading to license and destroying respect for authority.

When the Nazis came into power, they were determined to employ methods that would attract youth to their projects and at the same time would create well-disciplined soldiers. Spartan severity was carried throughout the entire physical education program. Lessons were usually divided into three parts: warming-up exercises, apparatus and agility exercises, and games. Class sizes were kept reasonably small. Careful medical histories, systematic physical measurements, and records of achievements in specific sports were kept. Propagandistic indoctrination and strict discipline replaced the free, creative, informal procedures of the Weimar

Republic. In the classroom, on the playground, and on the wandering tours, every type of emotional appeal was used to fire adolescents with enthusiasm for such a rugged regime. The wealth of recreational opportunities and the government's efforts to provide the best equipment and facilities completely captured the support of youth. Nazi methods were based upon manipulation of the individual through mass psychology. Colorful parades with waving banners, flaring torches, and countless marching men culminated in gigantic athletic exhibitions and stirring speeches. Young people were exposed to propaganda in all their activities. The appeal of uniforms, swastikas, sport badges, service stripes, and the Hitler salute had a tremendous effect on the imagination of adolescents. Boys and girls were made to feel that their nation needed them, and they responded to the call with fanatical earnestness and enthusiasm.

After the war, there was a return to more democratic and informal teaching methods. Some German teachers began to use the methods of movement education whereby the teacher does not give exercises but simply sets the stage for experimentation by the child. Liselott Diem outlined this teaching process as follows:

1. Play. The children get to know themselves through unrestrained activity.
2. The movement task. The child decides how he will achieve his goal through a spontaneous response.
3. The exercise is formed. The child learns the best technique for efficient performance by going through a naive phase, a reflective phase, and a self-learning phase.[34]

PHYSICAL EDUCATION IN THE GERMAN DEMOCRATIC REPUBLIC

The German Democratic Republic (GDR), or East Germany, was created by the Russians in 1949 in the aftermath of World War II. It included East Berlin and five states from prewar Germany. It embraces an area of about 42,000 square miles and has a population of 17 million. Eighty percent are Protestant although the practice of religion is officially discouraged.

The GDR has undergone considerable hardship in trying to recover from the damage and losses of the Second World War. Much of the heavy industrial equipment was claimed by the Russians for war reparations. There was a severe labor shortage in the 1950s when seven percent of the population crossed over into West Germany. This exodus was ended by

---

[34]Liselott Diem, "Basic Movement Education with Simple Elements in Primary Schools," *International Council on Health, Physical Education, and Recreation, 9th International Congress, 1966* (Washington, D.C.: ICHPER, 1967), p. 104.

the erection of the Berlin Wall in 1961. Industrial and agricultural production greatly improved in recent years although it has not matched that of West Germany.

The Russians quickly set up a strong central government in 1949 and completely overhauled the educational system to meet the needs of a Communist state. The old classical *gymnasium* was replaced by the ten-year polytechnical school which stressed vocational preparation and co-operated closely with industry and agriculture.

Physical education is used as a means of producing more effective workers, followers, and defenders of the state. The general approach is reminiscent of the Nazis except that the goals of Marxist socialism are substituted for National Socialism.[35] Two to three periods of physical training are required in all grades through the college and university level. A great many school sport clubs exist for children to attend outside their regular school lessons. It was estimated in 1968 that about one-fourth of all school children belonged to a club.[36] Special schools in a variety of subjects including sports are available for the talented child who transfers in from the regular school either at the seventh or tenth grade level. University students also have sports clubs; at the Technical University in Dresden, for example, there are 20 different sports offered and 1800 students participate.[37]

Most East German schoolchildren belong to one of the youth organizations which follow the Russian plan. Those in the first three years of school belong to the Young Pioneers, and pupils in the fourth through eighth forms join the Ernst Thälmann Pioneer groups. The Pioneers offer a variety of activities, both academic and athletic, and sponsored the First International Children's Camp of the World Federation of Democratic Youth in 1960.[38]

The principal institution for training teachers of physical education is the German College for Physical Training (*Deutsche Hochschule für Körperkultur*) in Leipzig which was started in 1950. The course for teachers is four years long and a doctorate may be earned in three additional years. The college has fine facilities for research and instruction adjacent to the new 100,000 seat Leipzig stadium. Another important school for sport officials and primary school teachers is at Blankenburg.

An essential component of physical education in the GDR is the practice of mass sports because they are believed to develop discipline in addition to mental and physical strength. Five German Sports and Gym-

[35]Wolfgang Karbe, "Physical Education and Sports in East and West Germany," *Physical Educator* 19 (October 1962): 110–11.

[36]*Sports in the GDR*, no. 2 (1969), p. 3 of insert.

[37]*Sports in the GDR*, no. 3 (1969), 24–27.

[38]W. Rosenkranz and others, *Polytechnical Education For All* (Dresden: Verlag Zeit im Bild, 1965), pp. 34–36.

nastics Festivals of the GDR have been held between 1954 and 1969. The last one was in Leipzig over a five-day period. The competitors are supposed to be individuals not qualified or interested in international compation. They met in soccer, team handball, bowling, track and field, swimming, orienteering, volleyball, and also put on demonstrations in calisthenics and gymnastics. The first Spartakiad of Children and Youth occurred in 1966, and the second one two years later had 13,000 participants in twenty-three sports. Another mass participation device used is sports badges.

The national organization for the thirty-six sports associations is the German Gymnastics and Sports Federation which has tripled its membership since 1950 to almost two million in 1969. The five most popular sports associations, in rank order, are soccer, gymnastics, angling, bowling, and team handball. In the 1968 Olympic games East Germany was represented by its own team for the first time, and its athletes collected a total of twenty-five medals to take fifth place among the nations of the world.

14

Physical Education
in
Swedish Educational Nationalism

By the seventeenth century the mighty warriors of the House of Vasa had built up such a significant power in northern European life that Sweden ruled an extensive empire in the Baltic including Finland and important areas along the southern Baltic coast. When Peter the Great of Russia decided to cut a "window" into the Baltic Sea for his landlocked nation, he ignited a conflict with Sweden that soon flared into open warfare. In the early eighteenth century, the youthful Swedish king, Charles XII, flung his troops against his Russian foes and eventually lost most of the southern and eastern Baltic provinces. A century later, Sweden surrendered her remaining possessions south of the Baltic as a result of her participation in the Napoleonic wars. The severest blow came when Russia conquered the whole of Finland in 1808 and thereby stripped Sweden of one-third of her territory. The desperate status of their once mighty empire kindled an intensive patriotism in the hearts of the Swedish people. As in Germany after the Napoleonic defeats, philosophers, poets, intellectuals, and soldiers were fired with a desire to rebuild the prestige and honor of their country.

Per Henrik Ling (1776–1839), who was to become the founder of Swedish gymnastics, was at this time inspired to start upon his life's work. As a student in Sweden and during a five-year stay in Denmark, he was profoundly influenced by the philosophers and poets of both countries who instilled in him a deep respect for his Scandinavian heritage. After acquiring considerable skill in languages, Ling turned to literature and became engrossed in the sagas of the Norsemen of old. While in Copenhagen, he engaged in fencing lessons and is said to have noticed an improvement in an afflicted arm. Intrigued with the effect of exercise on the body, he visited the private gymnasium which Nachtegall has started in

1799, a few years after GutsMuths had published *Gymnastics for the Young*.

Signe Prytz,[1] a Danish scholar, maintains that Ling was strongly influenced by Nachtegall; Albert Wiberg,[2] a Swedish scholar, contends that Ling may have become interested in physical education before he left Sweden. Wiberg points out that several articles on gymnastics had appeared in the press in 1789; during the next decade, Swedish teachers had returned from their travels with enthusiastic reports about the work of GutsMuths; as early as 1779, Johan Murberg included a statement on physical education in proposed regulations for the schools, and in 1794, a few years before Ling left for Denmark, Fisherström delivered a speech before the Swedish Academy of Sciences on the need for physical education. Wiberg suggests that Ling may not have found anything new in Nachtegall's work, for it is possible that prior to his arrival in Denmark he had read GutsMuths' book and the work on medical gymnastics written by the French physician, C. J. Tissot.

When Ling returned to Sweden in 1804 as a fencing master and a lecturer in Norse literature and history at the University of Lund, he soon won permission to introduce gymnastics and swimming and received invitations to give instruction in other cities. When Sweden was forced to surrender Finland to Russia in 1808, the idealistic young teacher was moved by a strong patriotism similar to that which had activated Jahn in Germany. To Ling, gymnastics and literature coalesced into one purpose: to imbue the weakened descendants of the Goths with new strength and courage. To this end he poured forth patriotic poems, epics, and plays and became a recognized literary leader of the Romantic Movement. With the same zeal, he cultivated the friendship of King Charles XIV, acquainted him with the value of physical training for the Swedish soldiers, and gained the necessary support for his gymnastics program. His literary works were mostly poems and plays, but he also wrote some gymnastic treatises. His principal works in this field are *Reglemente för Gymnastik* (Manual for Gymnastics), 1836; *Reglemente för Bajonettfäktning* (Manual for Bayonet-Fencing), 1836; *Soldat Undervisning i Gymnastik och Bajonettfäktning* (Soldiers' Manual of Gymnastics and Bayonet-Fencing), 1838; and a book entitled *General Principles of Gymnastics*, commenced in 1831 and published after his death in 1839 by his associates, C. A. Georgii and Dr. P. J. Liedbeck.

Aims of Education

In the nineteenth-century Swedish elementary schools the masses were imbued with a love and loyalty for their nation and acquired those funda-

[1]Signe Prytz, *P. H. Ling Og Hans Gymnastikpaedagogiske Indsats* (Copenhagen: Ejnar Munksgaard, 1941).

[2]Albert Wiberg, *Gymnastikhistoriska Studier* (Växjo: Nya Vaxyobladet, 1949).

mental skills necessary for reading the Bible and performing their daily tasks. Secondary education, primarily for the children of the well-to-do, was a classical, intellectual training for the preparation of clergymen and public officials. Broader purposes of education have slowly evolved until today the Swedish people seek the complete, individual development of all children. Educational opportunities have been expanded without reference to social class or sex. An effort is made to cultivate the individual capacities of the children and to lay a foundation for their future vocational pursuits. Emphasis is given to providing a civic training that will deepen the youngsters' understanding and appreciation of the national ideals and institutions of their country. The future Swedish citizen will thus be capable of undertaking his responsibilities and enjoying his freedom in a democratic, Christian society.

Aims of Physical Education

Patriotic motives impelled Ling to promote gymnastics that would make his countrymen strong in body and capable of defending the fatherland, but he did not confine his thinking to military objectives. He aimed to develop the body through carefully selected movements. "By theory of gymnastics," he declared, "we mean the doctrine of bodily movements in consonance with the laws discernible in the organism. . . . these laws aim at a complete agreement among the parts of the organism, and . . . health is the expression of this harmony."[3] To achieve these ends, physical education was to extend in four directions: military, medical, pedagogical, and aesthetic.

Imbued with the nationalistic purposes of raising the physical standards in the army, Ling's program was highlighted by emphasis on power, alacrity of action, and the ability to endure strain. As a modern pioneer in the field of medical gymnastics, he was also concerned with the possibility of restoring health to the weak through exercises. Pedagogical gymnastics were to develop the potentialities of the body, creating an erect well-balanced, and perfected organism that was under the control of the will of the individual. Aesthetic gymnastics were to give bodily expression to inner feelings, emotions, and thought.

Although Ling devoted himself primarily to military and medical gymnastics, he did not have a narrow concept of physical education. He believed all military, medical, pedagogical, and aesthetic goals were interdependent. The men who carried on his work, however, tended to restrict, rather than to expand, his philosophical framework. The stereotyped pro-

---

[3]Edward M. Hartwell, "Physical Training," *Report of the Commissioner of Education for 1897–98* (Washington, D.C.: U.S. Government Printing Office, 1898), 1, 543.

gram they established, directed primarily toward military ends, was not popular. Not surprisingly, by the early part of this century, their program was subjected to considerable criticism, which led to a more comprehensive conception of physical education.

In the Swedish schools today, the aim is to develop an understanding of physical activity as a means to health and recreation and to build a healthy population capable of working effectively in modern society. To counterbalance the one-sided effect of intellectual and industrial life, gymnastic exercises are used to promote the harmonious functioning of every part of the body, to maintain the normal mobility of the joints, and to improve the functional efficiency of the muscles and the circulatory, respiratory, and nervous systems. Through exercise, students learn how to relax physically and mentally, to move gracefully and economically, to achieve an aesthetically pleasing posture, to perform common work movements properly, and to maintain their youthful vigor as long as possible. An effort is made to provide a stimulating program that gives the participants a sense of well-being and satisfaction with ample scope for the imagination and initiative of pupils, and cultivates a lasting interest in leisure-time activities and the preservation of the beauties of nature. The subject is used to develop good manners, self-discipline, self-confidence, courage, perseverance, consideration, cooperativeness, teamwork, fair play, and leadership ability.

Promotion of Physical Education

Ling left Copenhagen in 1804 about the same time the Danish government opened the Military Gymnastic Institute. After teaching at Lund for a few years, he took a position at a cadet school outside of Stockholm and sought support for training teachers at the university. After being rebuffed by the university chancellor, he drafted a proposal for a national gymnastics school similar to the one operating in Denmark. Because of the recognition Ling had won as a poet and dramatist, he was able to present his petition to people in power. The patriotic temper of the times, stimulated by the unsuccessful war against Russia, made the King and the Crown Prince receptive to the idea of establishing an institute that might regenerate the army and the nation. In 1813, the government consented to establish and support the school which was later to become known as the Royal Central Institute of Gymnastics (GCI) at Stockholm. The first classes were held in 1814 in an abandoned cannon factory converted into a gymnasium. For the remaining twenty-five years of his life, Ling directed the Institute.

Lars Gabriel Branting, who came to the Institute seeking medical treatments, was such a talented and enthusiastic youth that Ling encouraged him to remain as a student. Branting attended medical school for many years and served as a teacher under Ling. Upon Ling's death, he succeeded him as director of the Institute, a position he held for twenty-three years. During these years, the staff was enlarged and the Institute began to attract international attention. Ling's son, Hjalmar, joined the staff in 1843 and began to develop gymnastics for school children. The first regular woman teacher, Gustafva Lindskog (1790–1851) was appointed in 1848; later when a course for girls was begun, Ling's daughters, Hildur and Wendla, also taught at the Institute. While Branting was director, the Institute became rather well-known, for many foreign visitors came to the school and Carl August Georgii became a foreign missionary for the Swedish system of exercises. Georgii, an army officer and highly respected gymnastic teacher, served at the Institute for ten years before Ling's death. Later, living abroad for many years, he introduced the Ling gymnastics in France and England.

In 1862, Colonel Gustav Nyblaeus succeeded Branting and continued to serve as director of the Central Institute until 1887. During these years he effected a reorganization of the school. The length of the courses was increased to two years of six months each (October to April), and a training course for women teachers was inaugurated. In 1864, the Institute was divided into three sections—military, medical, and pedagogical —each having a head teacher. Nyblaeus, who had been trained as an army officer, directed the military division; Hjalmar Ling, the son of the founder of the school, directed the educational division; and Truls Johan Hartelius, a physician, directed the medical gymnastics.

The Central Institute (GCI) was established to train both civilian and military pupils, but army men made up the bulk of the student body. When Nyblaeus resigned in 1887, the directorship was filled by a succession of army officers who were probably responsible for the military character of the gymnastics as well as for the higher status gymnastics teachers attained in Sweden compared with other countries. But in 1934 the military instructors acquired a training school of their own, and civilian leadership was finally established at GCI in 1946, with Dr. Erik Hohwü Christensen, who had studied at the Lindhard laboratories in Denmark, appointed as director. Christensen was succeeded by Paul Högberg. In 1967 the Royal Central Institute of Gymnastics (GCI) was renamed the Institute of Gymnastics and Sports.

Since 1950, the Swedish people have extended compulsory education from seven to nine years and have reorganized their entire school system. Previously, they had maintained parallel school systems, an elementary school system open to all students, and a secondary school system which accepted academically adept students mostly from the upper and middle classes. A comprehensive school (*enhetsskola* or *grundskola*) is now being established to educate all children together, irrespective of social class, during the nine-year span of compulsory education. Vocational guidance begins in the sixth grade. In grades seven to nine a variety of electives are offered geared to the various educational and prevocational alternatives available above the comprehensive school. In the ninth year, the comprehensive school is divided into gymnasium preparatory, general education, and prevocational sections. After the ninth year, the students who do not follow the academic program may enter various vocational training schools; the students who complete the academic secondary program usually take the *studentexamen* to qualify for admission to a university.

The National Board of Education, which is appointed by the Council of State and operates under the jurisdiction of the Minister of Education and Ecclesiastical Affairs, has a department of physical education with both men and women inspectors. Large cities employ supervisors to assist elementary teachers, mainly by demonstrations. Formerly all elementary teachers had to study physical education; now they have the choice of physical education or music. Regular classroom teachers, who receive no special training beyond that provided in normal schools, teach physical education classes and handle the outdoor day activities in the elementary schools. But programs are worked out for them and demonstrations are held once a month to show them how to conduct their classes.

Beginning in the seventh grade, and in the fifth grade in the larger cities, full-time gymnastics teachers are made responsible for physical education classes. They also plan and supervise the outdoor-days program, but other teachers, students, and personnel from the voluntary clubs assist them. Physical educators also supply much of the leadership for the activities that gymnastics and sports organizations, in cooperation with the schools, provide outside of the school timetable. Most schools have their own sport clubs which are members of the Swedish Association for Athletics and Sports in School, which in turn, belongs to the Swedish Sports Federation that governs all sports.

Secondary school gymnastics teachers do not teach other subjects as they do in Denmark. They receive somewhat lower salaries than other teachers, but they may receive extra pay for the direction of outdoor days, the direction of sports, or as leaders of school traffic wardens. Their national professional organization is the Swedish Society of Teachers of Physical Education (*Svenska Gymnastikläraresällskapet*) which publishes an official journal, *Tidskrift i Gymnastik*. Female graduates of GCI also have a professional organization.

For many years the Royal Central Gymnastic Institute (GCI), which Ling founded, trained teachers for the schools and the army as well as physiotherapists. But military instructors acquired their own school in 1934, and the training of physiotherapists was moved to the Royal Caroline Institute in 1956. The standards at GCI, which is now known as the

Institute of Gymnastics and Sports, are high. The prerequisite for admission is a Leaving Examination from the upper secondary school, but over fifty percent of the applicants have an academic degree in one or more subjects, such as psychology or education. The instructional program, which consists of theoretical subjects, gymnastic and athletic activities, and practice teaching, is a two-year course and is free. The theoretical instruction is tied in with the institution for research at GCI. Research is carried out in physiology and functional anatomy, but not in psychology and education. The main areas of research are physical education, aviation physiology, and industrial or work physiology. The equipment includes a treadmill, pressure chamber, animal experimentation apparatus, whole body counter, and facilities for blood and gas analysis and measuring body density.

Physical education was introduced by law in secondary schools in 1820 and in elementary schools in 1824. The subject is required in all grades and also in folk high schools and teacher-training institutions, but not in universities. Marks are given in physical education every term after the third grade, but, for the most part, they are not taken into account when evaluating promotion from one grade to another. About 135 to 150 minutes a week are devoted to physical education, plus six to twelve "outdoor days" which are usually divided into half-days on the elementary level. Schools are allowed to arrange their own outdoor days whenever suitable, for each class or for the whole school. Since 1925, many Swedish children have enjoyed a one-week, midwinter sports holiday in the mountains, which is provided through the cooperative efforts of the Swedish Tourist Association, the Society for the Promotion of Ski-leaping, and the State Railways. A nominal fee is charged for the entire vacation, including room, board, and transportation.

Sweden's secondary school buildings have spotlessly clean gymnasiums that are usually well-furnished with apparatus, lockers, and showers. Equipment may include one to three Swedish horses, one or two bucks, vaulting boxes, wall bars, floor beams, vertical ropes, oblique ropes, benches, and wall and window ladders. In many primary schools equally good facilities are available and much use is made of miniature apparatus. Government appropriations are available for building facilities. The national school program makes provisions for gymnasiums in every school, except elementary schools with less than seventy-five pupils. Construction plans for playgrounds include pits for high jumping and broad jumping and a track, but many of the sports activities are conducted at community or voluntary club facilities. Because of the increase in the school population and the lack of construction during the war and postwar years, 1940–1950, some schools do not have adequate facilities. A number of modern gymnasiums have been built in recent years, but playing courts and swimming pools are provided only in the better-off communities.

As a pioneer in the field of medical care, Sweden planned medical supervision as early as 1830 and has appointed health officers for secondary students since 1868. Doctors and nurses make regular physical inspections; vaccinations and tuberculin tests are standard procedures; and dental examinations with free or inexpensive care are available. In 1950, a compulsory health insurance law went into effect which extended the already fairly advanced socialization of Swedish medicine to include sick relief pay and three-quarters of the doctor's charges. In 1946, a daily free lunch program for primary pupils was effected. Since 1885, Stockholm and other urban centers have conducted summer colonies for underprivileged children.

The early attempts to initiate voluntary gymnastics and fencing clubs in Sweden resulted in mediocre success. Unlike the Turners in Germany, the Swedish gymnastics organizations featured semimilitary activities and developed such a rigid and formal program that they had less than a thousand members at the turn of the century. When the Swedish gymnastic programs and methods were revised, interest was revived, The addition of sports and games also encouraged amateur participation in clubs.

Sports were accepted in Sweden somewhat more slowly than in other countries, probably because of its long, cold winters, the military influence at GCI, the inbreeding at GCI because only graduates were able to become staff members, and the relative ease and cheapness of providing gymnastic drills in the schools. The oldest sport club in Sweden, still existing, the Uppsala Swimming Club, was founded in 1796, but the sports movement did not get under way until the end of the nineteenth century. The leader of the movement, Viktor Balck, observed English games while on a tour with a gymnastic team in 1880. Upon his return to Sweden, he organized groups to promote sports, founded the *Sporting Times* (*Tidning för Idrott*), introduced sports activities to military conscripts, and between 1907 and 1909 served as the director of GCI. The upper class, the military schools, and the high schools were the first to accept athletics. The farmers, industrial workers, and academicians saw little value in such activities at first, but by the turn of the century, urban development and the rise in the ranks and status of the middle class had created conditions favorable to the development of sports.

Today, most of the gymnastic and sport clubs in Sweden are attached to a governing association or union that obtains facilities, trains instructors, and arouses public interest in the clubs' activities. Some of the larger organizations are the Amateur Athletic Association, the Football Association, The Gymnastic Association, the Swedish Association for Athletics and Sports in Schools, and the Ski Association. Forty of these associations, representing over ten thousand clubs and one million members, have allied with the central governing body, the Swedish Sports Federation (*Sveriges Riksidrottsförbund*), which came into being in 1903.

The Swedish Sports Federation makes financial recommendations to the government, distributes funds, advises groups on setting up and maintaining establishments, serves as the "supreme court" of sports, supports the youth and recreation divisions in the clubs, cooperates with industrial recreation programs and youth movements, and represents Sweden in foreign countries in matters dealing with sports. The Federation administers the Sports Polyclinic at the Stockholm Stadium where staff members provide health examinations for members, give advice on sports, and carry out scientific studies. The national sports institute at Böson for training volunteer instructors, teams, and athletes, which is supplemented by Olandergården at Vålådalen in the mountains, is equipped for every form of sports activity. A gymnastics folk high school at Lillsved also offers thirty-week courses and a number of ten-day courses. Hundreds of the volunteer instructors in sports and gymnastic organizations enroll in full-time, short-term, or weekend courses to improve their leadership skills.

To arouse and maintain interest in physical fitness, the national federation has awarded the National Sports Badge since 1907. The tests passed by the recipients are fairly strenuous and demand all-round development. Most of the associations belonging to the national federation have since introduced badges for the activities they supervise. With the approach of World War II, the Gymnastics Association started a physical fitness drive by offering a special "Lion's Badge" for passing a standard test. The Swedish Walking Association, which had previously offered a "Hiker's Badge," introduced the National Walking Contests in 1939. A "Field Sports Badge" was created for soldiers and civilians alike.

Since World War II, the physical fitness-recreation movement has gained momentum. Over five thousand companies have become involved in developing an industrial recreation program and extensive sport facilities for their employees and their families. Over one million workers have taken part in the various sports events and the soccer and ice hockey leagues that have been formed. "Sport 60," which was started in 1960 to stimulate interest in physical fitness and was repeated in subsequent years, requires a minimum standard of performance in skiing, walking, gymnastics, cycling, swimming, and orienteering (a combination of cross-country running and path finding with a map and compass) to qualify for a badge. A few years ago, invitations were sent out to form family exercise clubs, the idea being to have families compete against one another, block by block and city by city. Badges and diplomas were devised to stimulate interest. When the "4 M" physical fitness campaign was initiated in 1962, all sports and physical education organizations supported the program.

The success of the sporting movement in Sweden has been achieved largely through the fees of sport club members, the efforts of the unpaid sport club instructors, and special sources of financial support. The Central

Association for the Promotion of Sports, founded in 1897, was permitted in 1908 to establish a lottery and to use the profits for the construction of sport facilities. The Association built the Stockholm Stadium, established the Sports Museum, and did other notable work before it handed over the lottery funds in 1931 to the Swedish Sports Federation. In 1914, the central government gave the first annual grant to the Swedish Sports Federation. Two decades later, much more substantial financial assistance was made available when some revenues from gambling were diverted to sports. Since Sweden took this step in 1934, most European countries have followed her example.

The "football pools" in Sweden were originally operated by private companies, most of which were foreign. To curb this drain on Swedish funds, the government established a state-controlled company, A. B. Tipstjänst. Some of this revenue now passes directly to the Swedish Olympic Committee, but most of the money is dispensed by the Swedish Sports Federation. This money enables the sports associations to build facilities to provide technical and advisory services, to train instructors, and to provide medical supervision of sports and sports facilities. Government grants are given not only for the support of urban facilities and activities, but also for the promotion of outdoor pursuits, such as skiing, sailing, hiking, and climbing.

In most communities the athletic facilities are either owned or governed by sporting associations. In addition to the assistance provided by the central government, municipal governments help build and administer sports facilities. Even the smaller towns have well-developed sports complexes which may include soccer fields, a track, and tennis, volleyball, and basketball courts. Some communities have an ice arena, a swimming area or a pool, and a gymnasium. Almost all towns have laid out trails for hiking and skiing and some illuminate them in the evening. A number of marked trails have been laid out in Sweden for cross-country skiing with huts at intervals for one day's skiing or hiking. School children use the local parks and sports association facilities on outdoor days. Conversely, the schools are open to the public until eleven o'clock in the evening. This type of cooperation reduces costs for the schools, the clubs, and the community.

The Scandinavian countries have been pioneers in adopting progressive social legislation. Vacations for all workers was discussed for a number of years, and by collective agreements, all employees were eventually guaranteed vacations with pay. The government also restricted the right of private citizens to monopolize nature. Many public camping sites were developed; the Cooperative Housing Society constructed several cooperatively owned resorts with children's camps nearby for low-cost family vacations, and the Swedish Tourist Association provided seaside and mountain huts on the same basis. Allotment gardens with small weekend summer cabins attached, cheap rental for plots, and loans for cabins also became a part of Swedish life.

Program and Methods of Physical Education

At the University of Lund, Ling taught fencing and vaulting with a horse, introduced swimming, and acquainted his students with the GutsMuths-Nachtegall gymnastics. In addition to teaching, he studied physiology and anatomy and attended dissections with the objective of developing a gymnastic system based on the laws of the human organism. At first Ling used apparatus freely and activities that were full of movement, but he eliminated many exercises later in his career because they did not conform to his scientific theories.

Very early, Ling introduced the posture-correcting element of Swedish gymnastics and devised free movements as preparatory exercises for the lighter apparatus work which he favored. Free exercises strongly appealed to him. In summarizing their advantages he claimed,

> (1) That more can exercise at one time under a teacher. (2) That such movements can be made in a great variety of places, e.g., on the march, in barracks, quarters, a schoolroom, or in a school yard. (3) That the trouble and expense of providing and keeping apparatus in repair are eliminated. (4) That the fact that the entire squad or class must make the exercises at the same moment promotes strength and agility and rapid attainment of bodily control. (5) That the execution of gymnastics at the word of command re-enforces the effect of strictly military drill. (6) That free movements are more easily adaptable to the bodily peculiarities of individuals. (7) That they are better than machine gymnastics for overcoming awkwardness and stiffness.[4]

The military needs of that era no doubt influenced Ling's enthusiasm for free exercises.

Ling subordinated "exercises on apparatus to the needs and nature of the body, while Jahn subordinated the body to the nature of the gymnastic machines."[5] In Ling's opinion, much of the German apparatus work was too complicated and had a questionable effect on the body. Ling and his successors utilized some of the existing equipment but also invented some new equipment more suitable for achieving the simple movements they favored. The Swedish apparatus included stall bars, booms, saddles, window ladders, low combination benches, vaulting boxes, climbing poles, and the horizontal, vertical, and oblique ropes.

[4]Ibid., p. 545.   [5]Ibid., p. 544.

Although Ling classified exercises into four groups—pedagogical, aesthetic, military, and medical—he devoted himself to the last two types. Between 1836–1838 he published his manuals for military gymnastics and bayonet fencing which were officially adopted by the army and later used extensively by foreign troops. During the first years in Stockholm, Ling began to experiment with medical gymnastics for the relief of physical disabilities. These exercises were divided into three types: active, passive, and duplicated movements. In the *active* group, the patient was to practice by himself. The *passive* movements were to be performed upon the patient's body without his having to resist or assist the activity. In *duplicated* movements, the patient either was to resist the effort made by the gymnast or, while the patient performed, the gymnast was to make suitable resistance for the strength of the patient. Ling's medical gymnastics became widely known abroad, but some physicians strongly opposed them.

The teachers who carried on Ling's work after his death made contributions to various parts of his projected program. Lars Branting, who succeeded Ling as Director of the Institute, devoted himself to medical gymnastics and was one of the first to point out that exercise was beneficial to the nerves and blood vessels as well as the muscular system. Gustav Nyblaeus, who succeeded Branting as Director, studied gymnastics systems in other countries and published manuals on fencing and gymnastics and military exercises for elementary schools. Truls Johnan Hartelius, a physician and head teacher of medical gymnastics under Nyblaeus, wrote manuals on anatomy, physiology and histology, and hygiene, as well as a work on medical gymnastics. Hartelius also served as the first editor of *Tidskrift i Gymnastik*, a periodical devoted to gymnastics which is still published today.

Physical education had been introduced in the schools in Linköping prior to the time that Ling established the Institute, and by 1807, the government had drafted a regulation recommending the establishment of similar programs at every place of learning. But gymnastics were not developed specifically and systematically for school children at the Institute until after Hjalmar Ling, the surviving son of Per Ling, joined the staff in 1843. Hjalmar went to France in 1854 where he studied anatomy and attended lectures on experimental physiology; later, he introduced Swedish medical gymnastics in Berlin. In 1866, he published two pamphlets on gymnastics and a work on kinesiology. Per Ling had used some simple tables of movement; Hjalmar systematized his father's work and arranged the exercises in a fixed plan that would exercise the whole body from head to toe in a single lesson. Taking the mass of gymnastic materials, Hjalmar Ling divided them into groups according to the effects produced upon the individual and provided for an orderly progression within each group. From his graded series, appropriate exercises for the different sexes, ages, and abilities could be chosen and combined into the "day's order" or "table." To further adapt gymnastics to school use, he invented apparatus suitable for children, particularly that which would facilitate mass activity.

The Swedish system as developed by the Lings and their successors was characterized by the great care given to the selection and arrangement of exercises. The activities for a single "day's order" were coordinated not only in regard to one another but in respect to the tables that had preceded and those that were to follow. This principle of "progression" and the precision and correct execution of the movements characterized Swedish gymnastics. Unlike the Germans, who performed several exercises on one or two pieces of apparatus in a lesson, the Swedes tended to utilize all the equipment during each session, often performing only one exercise on each piece. Mass drills were favored, with the whole class, or not less than half of it, participating at the same time under the command of a teacher. Squad leaders and memorized drills did not readily lend themselves to the continuous, progressive, comprehensive, Swedish gymnastic system.

Many bitter battles were fought over the Swedish exercises, but they were adopted, sometimes in a modified form, in Great Britain, Denmark, Belgium, Greece, Romania, and many other countries. Ling may not have been an authoritative physiologist and his pioneer efforts were naturally limited by the scientific knowledge of his day, but he insisted that gymnastic teachers must have both theoretical knowledge and practical ability and prophesied that the zeal for the program would die out if "doctors and gymnasts did not continue to nourish it scientifically." But his successors, who were all graduates of the Institute and many of them army men, followed the dictates of military tradition. By the turn of the century, the program consisted of dull, rigid, routines. The artificial patterns of movement were characterized by strained positions, an exaggerated posture, and much continuous muscular tension. The medical gymnastics were particularly criticized.

Throughout the Scandinavian countries critics began to call for a restatement of Ling's original principles in the light of modern scientific developments. As early as 1912, a committee appointed by the king recommended that secondary schools substitute civilian for military teachers. Women were the first to break with the rigid positions of the Ling exercises and to make movements more plastic. Elin Falk published her three-volume work in 1915 and 1916. Major J. G. Thulin, who also pioneered in the reform movement, developed programs for women and children and published works on men's gymnastics. By midcentury, the work of Maja Carlquist and her girls from the Sofia Club were known internationally.

Today in Sweden the gymnastics program consists of freestanding exercises with or without hand apparatus, such as balls and skipping ropes, improvisations of movement, with or without music, and exercises on apparatus. To the traditional Swedish equipment (beam, bench, box, buck, and wall bars), schools have added horizontal and uneven parallel bars, weight lifting apparatus, and rings. Exercises from other countries, such as the Danish mat exercises, have been adopted. In place of the many exercises demanding continual tension of muscles with pauses for restriction, movement gymnastics are employed in which tension and relaxation follow one another in a rhythmical pattern and muscles have time to recover during the movement. Because psychological as well as physiological needs are kept in mind, greater stress is placed upon making the activities pleasurable and applying them to the practical demands of life.

The "present-day gymnastics have become a movement-gymnastics which recognizes all that is necessary in posture-gymnastics for the maintenance of form and control, and makes use of the intrinsic power of rhythm, with its emphasis on delight and ability to aid in relaxation and the concentration of energy. Games and athletics and other free forms of applied exercises contribute further to the liveliness and pleasure of the lessons and fulfill the developmental purpose of gymnastics in relation to the practical demands of life."[6] Although the Ling principles remain the basis of Swedish physical education, the program has been expanded and improved in accordance with advances made in physiological, psychological, and pedagogical research.

Gymnastics still provide the core for Swedish physical education, but during the past thirty years ball games and sports have begun to play a more important role. The premilitary training which constituted a part of the program from 1940 to 1945 was terminated after the war. At present, for about one month in the autumn and in the spring, outdoors instruction in provided in sports, games, track and field events, and swimming, if the weather allows. During the long winter, physical education classes are primarily indoors. Gymnastics are given priority, but they are supplemented by games, ball games, dance, indoor sports, and swimming where a pool is available. When the weather permits, classes are taken outdoors for ice-skating, skiing, ice-hockey, bandy (a type of hockey), and orienteering.

Rhythmic gymnastics, which received their impetus from Ernst Idla, are very popular with the older girls. Circuit training and bicycle-ergometers are popular with the boys. Instruction in how to lie, sit, stand, lift, walk, and carry have been introduced to prevent lumbar ailments and injuries and to help youngsters achieve a pleasing posture. In Stockholm, the advisor in biotechnology visits vocational guidance classes and gives practical and theoretical lessons in work techniques and industrial hygiene. All students receive instruction concerning the effects of exercise on the

---

[6]J. G. Thulin, *Gymnastic Hand-book* (Lund: Sydsvenska Gymnastik-Institutet, 1947), p. 20.

body, the rules of hygiene, the rules of safety in traffic and sports, the conservation of nature, and the services of voluntary sports organizations. Special classes of corrective exercises are provided for students with posture problems, flat feet, or other disabilities.

On field days and open air days, which are spent on the playing fields, in the forests, or on the mountain slopes, students are permitted to choose among a number of games and sports with the expectation that they will find one to pursue in later life. They may take part in various types of ball games, athletics, skating, skiing, orienteering, swimming, rowing, shooting, tennis, or golf. Teachers are concerned, however, for part of sports-day time is being usurped for instruction in traffic safety, fire drills, first aid, child care and other activities, while the number of weekly lessons for physical education have decreased.

Syllabuses for classes and open air days are used on all levels. The National Board of Education works out daily exercises and field day exercises for elementary teachers. Whenever the curriculum is reorganized or a syllabus is drawn up, the scientific department of the Institute of Gymnastics and Sports is requested to provide scientific advice. Teachers on the upper level no longer have to conform to an inflexible system. They are given considerable freedom to develop their programs, but they must be prepared to have their work appraised by specialists.

Special leisure-time activities are organized after school hours in sports, gymnastics, music, drama, and other activities, and gymnastics are particularly popular. The voluntary clubs assist in the development of these programs. No regular varsity competition is provided, but the teachers and pupils who govern the Swedish Association for Athletics and Sports in Schools arrange for school and district contests and draw many students into sports participation through the award of School Sports Badges. Apart from track and field events, contests are held for skiing, orienteering, ball games, swimming, sailing, and marksmanship. The Autumn School Championship, which has taken place each year since 1912 in Stockholm Stadium, is an important national sporting event. Demonstration days in which all members of a class publicly exhibit their accomplishments are a part of school life.

The Anglo-Saxon sports of cricket, rugby, and baseball are uncommon in Sweden, but soccer football is played universally and is followed by crowds of enthusiastic spectators. Skiing and orienteering are practiced everywhere; sometimes the whole family participates. Perhaps the most popular sport stars are the participants in cross-country skiing and track and field events, particularly in long-distance running. Sports in trials of strength are favored, especially wrestling, boxing, weight lifting, and tugs-of-war. Shooting is popular and is encouraged by the government. Swedish horsemen are internationally known and basketball is becoming more popular, particularly in the schools. Tennis and golf are increasingly popular.

Swedish athletes have won many gold medals in the Olympics, for many years dominating the modern pentathlon. They have had strong entries in wrestling, shooting, rowing, kayak, canoeing, equestrian events, fencing, cycling, and boxing. Sweden has also been outstanding in soccer and ice hockey.

During the 1930s, the "sports for all" movement and the competition it provided gave impetus to a "gymnastics for all" movement. When the Swedish Gymnastics Association sponsored the first Lingiad in Stockholm in 1939, commemorating the centenary of Ling's death, the event attracted participants from thirty-seven countries. Since World War II, the voluntary gymnastics programs for youths and adults, ranging from easy forms to competitive forms, have expanded. Special exercise routines have been devised as an aid to athletic training. The fitness programs for "gymnastics in the home," which were first broadcast in 1929, remain popular. The first "gymnastics for the housewife" class attracted seventeen women in 1942; within three years, thirty thousand women were participating. The teachers of these classes pay particular attention to strengthening the back and feet muscles that receive so much use. Special tables of exercises have also been constructed to relieve industrial workers and clerks from the monotonous tasks of the day and to counteract the effect of habitual working positions. Teachers circulate from department to department to conduct five to ten minutes of exercise. Exhibitions of the rhythmical gymnastics performed to music by the "Sophia Girls" and the "Idla Girls" have attracted international attention.

Today, every sixth Swede owns a car and every sixth Swede belongs to some organization that promotes sports, gymnastics, or outdoor activities. The high standard of living, the mobility of the people, the favorable social legislation, the variation in climate, the long seacoast, the many streams and lakes, the vast scenic areas in the mountains and forests provide the prerequisites for recreational life.

During the brief summer, the Swedes become sun worshippers. On Midsummer's Eve, merrymakers dress in folk costumes, dance around Maypoles, and climb to the top of a hill to watch the early sunrise heralding the summer season. From that day on, the Swedes abandon their apartments and farm homes and hike, or cycle, or pile into cars, boats, and trains to get to the mountains, forests, lakes, streams, and seaside beaches. They sleep at hostels, pitch a tent at one of the many camping sites, or visit the family cottage. Throughout the summer, the white sails of their boats dot the waters. At surf-washed beaches, they swim in chilled waters. They fish in the lakes and rivers, hike through the woods and mountains, search for mushrooms and berries, and work on their summer cottages.

As the winter months approach, the Swedish people look forward to a long, vigorous sports season on skis and skates. Skis, which have been in existence for hundreds of years in Sweden, are a necessary means of locomotion in many parts of the country. Long distance skiing, jumping, slalom, and downhill running are vigorously engaged in, particularly in the gay company that gathers at tourist stations located in the forest and mountain districts. Ice games, such as ice hockey, bandy, curling, skate-sailing, and ice-yacht sailing are as popular as the snow sports. The performance of Swedish skiers and skaters in the Winter Olympics regularly attests to their skill.

Swedish folk dances are still loved. On special holidays some of the modern Swedes will don the colorful costumes of their native district and enjoy a merry holiday of singing and dancing. Most of the folk dances are lively and spirited although more sedate types, showing the influence of the French court dances, also appear. Many of the forms are predominantly pantomimic, using occupational or courtship themes.

Physical Education
in
Danish Educational Nationalism

When the raids of the Nordic seamen were at their height, the Danish kings held Britain and southern Norway in sway with a precarious power structure that was later solidified in alliance with the Catholic church. Norway and Sweden were brought under Danish rule in 1397, and this Scandinavian union lasted until 1523 when Sweden broke away. After Lutheranism was accepted by the Scandinavian people in the sixteenth century, the Catholic Latin schools were reestablished as Lutheran institutions, vernacular reading schools were developed, and the ability to read was eventually made a requirement for confirmation, and, hence, for marriage.

In the late sixteenth century, Denmark experienced prosperous years, but the wars that followed brought a period of decline, intensified the burghers' hatred of the nobles, and brought about the establishment of an absolute monarchy in 1660 which lasted until 1848. For some time under absolutism Danish agriculture remained stagnant, taxes were heavy, and the nobles exacted more and more labor from the peasants. But with the approach of the French Revolution, free trade was encouraged, economic conditions improved, the ideas of the Age of Enlightenment were accepted in government circles, and a period of great reforms began. Land reforms were passed, the peasants were emancipated in 1788, the Jews were given full social rights in 1814, and criticism of the narrow classical-religious training in parish schools led to the appointment of the Great School Commission in 1789. The Great School Commission helped bring about the secondary school law of 1809 and the Education Act of 1814 which provided for a system of state-operated elementary schools.

The industrial awakening of England, the French Revolution, and the Napoleonic wars fostered a steadily increasing prosperity for the Danes. But the practice of using naval convoys to protect trading vessels during the Napoleonic wars precipitated a conflict with England which resulted in the loss of Norway to Sweden and of Helgoland to England in 1814. The price for being on the losing side in the Napoleonic wars was high. With her foreign trade almost wiped out, the failure of the banks, and the falling prices of farm products, Denmark suffered bankruptcy and stagnation. After a low point in 1820, conditions improved. The rise in grain prices, increase in the number of free landowners, emergence of a new national sentiment, and adoption in 1849 of a liberal constitution with popular suffrage, corresponded with the political and economic tides of the European liberal movement of 1848.

The new prosperity was soon threatened by Bismarck's ambition to build the German Empire. The Danish people received a crushing blow when the duchies of Schleswig-Holstein and Lauenburg were taken in the War of 1864. The loss of one-third of their territory and two-fifths of their population created economic conditions comparable to those occurring after the Napoleonic wars. In the days of humiliation following the War of 1864, the people sought a new source of courage and strength in nationalism.

One of the pioneers of the new Danish culture who sought to lift the Danes out of their deep gloom was the poet-bishop, Nicolai F. S. Grundtvig (1783–1872). To arouse a sense of national awareness in young adults and to prepare them for the political liberty that was spreading in the mid-nineteenth century, he envisioned a new type of school. The folk high school, which came into being in 1844 to provide a "fatherland education based on the mother language,"[1] inspired the Danish people to build a vigorous society. In voluntary classes, students and teachers informally examined man's achievements in the past and present, discussed how to live a meaningful life, and forged new ideals for their country. The folk schools did not emphasize memorizing facts, military training, or the practical aspects of farm life, but rather gave rural youths something that "has proved to be of vastly greater importance—broad culture, a devotion to home and soil and native land, a confidence and trust in one's fellow man, and a realization that success in life is measured by standards other and higher than mere money-making. The results of an adherence to ideals such as these have been a welding together of the people in Denmark which accounts for their remarkable success of cooperation as it has been worked out in every form."[2] The Danish folk schools were a compelling example of the ability of education to revitalize national life.

The Danes have built up a high level of culture with no great dis-

---

[1] Willis Dixon, *Education in Denmark* (Copenhagen: Centraltrykkeriet, 1959), p. 62.

[2] Peter Sandiford, ed., *Comparative Education* (London: J. M. Dent and Sons, 1918), p. 460.

parities in the distribution of wealth. To cope with World War I, depressions, changing trade conditions, and the years of Nazi occupation, the Danes revolutionized their export products, organized consumer-producer cooperatives, increased their agricultural and industrial production, devised a comprehensive system of social welfare, collaborated with other Scandinavian countries, and solidified their political structures.

When physical education had its renaissance on the continent, Denmark was one of the first countries to participate in the new movement. The pioneer in this field during the first half of the nineteenth century was Franz Nachtegall (1777–1847), who held the position of Director of Gymnastics. The inspectorship was held by four different army officers until 1904, when school gymnastics were divorced from the military with the appointment of a civilian inspector, K. A. Knudsen.

In 1909, the University of Copenhagen added to the faculty, doubtless earlier than any other university, a *Docent* in anatomy, physiology, and theory of gymnastics. Dr. Johannes Lindhard, who was appointed to this position, did much to place the profession on a more scientific basis. He retired from the university in 1935 and from his post as Rector at the Physical Training Teachers College in 1940, and was succeeded by Dr. Emanuel Hansen, and then by Dr. Asmassen. Other outstanding leaders who have contributed to Danish gymnastics are H. G. Junker, Niels Bukh, Agnete Bertram, Else Thomsen, Ann Krogh, and Jørgine Abildgaard.

Aims of Education

The pioneer Danish school legislation of 1814 sought to educate youth to be good Christians and useful citizens. These same goals have been repeated in official pronouncements down to the present day. The Danish people want "to strengthen the children's feeling for ethical and Christian values, inspire them with respect for human life and for nature, teach them to love their homes, their people, and their country, to consider the opinions of other people, to appreciate community between the peoples and the fellowship with the other Scandinavian nations."[3] Although no specific decree or directive outlines the pattern of secondary education, a liberal and humanistic spirit prevails.

Aims of Physical Education

Physical education in Denmark, as in most European countries during the nineteenth century, was dominated by nationalism. The primary objectives were the development of soldierly competence and of patriotism.

[3]Ministry of Education, *Survey of Danish Elementary, Secondary, and Further (Nonvocational) Education* (Kobenhavn: Universitets-Bogtrykkeri, 1947) p. 6.

In the turbulent days of the early nineteenth century, Nachtegall, like Jahn and Ling, was caught in the swirling forces of historical events. His original goal had been to develop a sturdy populace through early and effective school training, but the threat of Napoleon impelled him to direct his plan to meet a more rigid and narrow military requirement. When the Napoleonic wars were over, Nachtegall once again recommended giving attention to all-round bodily fitness as a source of national vitality and solidarity.

After the death of Nachtegall in 1847, gymnastics dwindled in popularity, and the leadership reverted to military men. When the first rifle clubs were organized, as the conflicts with Prussia and Austria approached, emphasis was placed on training for national defense. But after the bitter defeat in the War of 1864, the gymnastic movement played a somewhat different role. The folk high school leaders employed exercises as a means of enlivening the spirits of the disheartened people, improving their health, giving them opportunities to enjoy good fellowship, and acquainting them with the satisfactions and accomplishments that could be realized through cooperative action. In describing the difference between these broad objectives and the previous limited gymnastic goals, an early folk high school principal explained, "These gymnastic exercises are not at all designed as a form of training for a military or any other special purpose; nor are they intended merely to develop strength and agility in the human body, they aim at the improvement of the whole person. They will become a link in human education and training."[4] The folk school idea of developing not only physical fitness but personal dignity and civic responsibility became an expression of national sentiment.

During this century, Niels Bukh (1880–1950), the folk school gymnastic leader of the Ollerup Gymnastic High School, gave particular attention to rural young folk. Believing that occupational habits lead to ill-proportioned physiques and a deterioration of the mechanisms of movement, he strove to counteract these effects. Bukh aimed to maintain lifelong working capacity and vigor. Although he retained the folk high schools' traditional objectives, his greatest stress was placed upon suppleness, strength, and mobility, which he interpreted to be the greatest physical needs of rural youth.

The objective of physical education today in Denmark is *"to promote the physical health of the children* by helping them to develop their bodies harmoniously, training their motor functions (nervous, muscular and articulatory systems), bringing them into good physical condition, and giving them good habits of hygiene; *to promote the mental health of the children* by letting them feel the pleasure of physical activity, and by ex-

---

[4]Quoted in Holger Begtrup, Hans Lund, and Peter Manniche, *The Folk High Schools of Denmark and the Development of a Farming Community* (London: Oxford University Press, 1936), p. 63.

ploiting the special potentialities of the subject for developing such qualities as the ability to cooperate, self-discipline, sense of order, initiative and self-reliance; *to teach the children the importance of keeping the body in good condition and of using it properly*, so that they are stimulated to continue physical training and open-air life after they have left school. The subject shall thus be not merely one in which the children acquire skills and enjoy recreation, but also one in which they gain experience and knowledge by which they can profit both while attending school and later in life."[5]

Promotion of Physical Education

When Nachtegall opened his gymnasium in Copenhagen in 1799, it was the first institution of its kind to be established in modern Europe. His exercises gradually gained recognition in the schools and soon spread throughout the military. As a result of Nachtegall's skillful leadership, Denmark became one of the first European countries to introduce physical education as a school subject, the first to offer teacher-training courses, and the first to provide a manual for instructors.

An ordinance of 1809 stated that instruction in gymnastics in the secondary school would be furnished whenever possible. In 1814, Denmark introduced a pioneer compulsory education law for all children from seven to fourteen years of age and at the same time ordered that grounds, equipment, facilities, and gymnastic classes should be provided for all elementary school boys. Owing to the lack of trained teachers and the impoverished conditions following the Napoleonic wars, communities were very slow in complying with the law. In 1828, follow-up legislation was passed, authorizing physical education for all boys, and more energetic measures were taken to insure that the acts were put into effect. Classes were not initiated for girls until a decade later, and legislative edicts did not require them until 1904.

The preparation of physical education teachers in Denmark was originally provided by military agencies. King Frederick VI founded a Military Gymnastic Institute in 1804 and appointed Nachtegall as the director. This school, the first of its kind, was supplemented in 1808 by the Civil Gymnastic Institute for the instruction of teachers which, because of economic conditions, was closed in 1814. Although gymnastics became a compulsory subject in the teacher-training institutions in 1818, an effective program was not quickly realized. When Nachtegall was appointed as superintendent of civilian and military gymnastics in 1821, he renewed

[5]Danish Ministry of Education, "Physical Education in Danish Schools." Excerpts from Teachers' Manual of 1960, Chapter XI, "Physical Education" (mimeographed, n.d.), p. 3.

his efforts to assist public school teachers. He collaborated on a *Manual of Gymnastics* for elementary schools and secured the king's authorization for its official distribution in 1828. Six years later, a similar volume was published for secondary teachers. In 1828, Nachtegall established a normal school at the Institute, and in 1839, approved a plan to train women. He offered students opportunities to do practice teaching, using public and charity school classes for the purpose. The Institute, however, remained primarily military in character and the new courses were short-lived. After they ceased to exist, no adequate instruction was provided for teachers until the turn of the century.

A quiescent era during the middle of the nineteenth century seriously threatened gymnastics with extinction. Frederick VI, who had been a pupil of Nachtegall and who always supported him loyally, died in 1839. He was succeeded by Christian VIII, who took little interest in gymnastics. Nachtegall resigned his position as director of the Military Gymnastic Institute in 1842, and military leaders replaced him. His successor, Captain Niels Georg la Cour, was unable to maintain the same esprit de corps. The military men tended to remain aloof from general school life, which did not improve the status of physical education. Even in the army, gymnastic exercises came to be looked upon as a matter of discipline and punishment.

After the war with Austria and Prussia in 1864, interest in physical education was revived, for the Danes turned to gymnastics as a means of invigorating the nation and stirring up national pride. As in Germany, the movement originated with young adults. Two nongovernmental institutions were primarily responsible: the rifle clubs (*Skytteforeninger*) and the folk, or people's high schools (*Folkehøjskolerne*).

The threatening situation before the War of 1864 had precipitated the organization of voluntary rifle societies, patterned after those in England. After the war, these organizations assumed more and more the character of gymnastic societies as they expanded their activities, holding general competitive meets, and erecting their own gymnasium and play areas.

The folk high schools, which became increasingly popular after 1864, were unique Danish institutions. Although they welcomed everyone, most of their students were farming youths between eighteen and twenty-five years who had completed elementary school. These schools, which have survived until the present, are either privately owned or are self-perpetuating corporations. Some state support is now given, but only nominal state supervision. Attendance is voluntary. The rural boarding pupils spend a few months in pursuing a general education without specializing or having to pass examinations. The curriculum usually includes courses in language, singing, national literature and history, gymnastics, homemaking, and agriculture. Most of the folk high schools offer a general cultural course, but some of them concentrate upon gymnastics, nursing, athletics, or have a labor or international slant.

In 1884, the Ling Swedish gymnastics were introduced by the Danish engineer, N. H. Rasmussen, at the Vallekilde Folk School in Zealand. From there it spread rapidly to other folk schools and to many rifle clubs. The Ling system eventually made its way into the elementary and secondary schools, as well as the university. There was much controversy before its acceptance. Army officers, many of whom taught in the school, particularly objected to any change from the old Danish-German system. Finally, the government appointed a commission to study the problem, with the result published in 1899 as a *Manual of Gymnastics*, which was subsequently authorized for official school use. The *Manual*, following Ling's general principles, adopted almost all of the Swedish exercises, and added a few of the most valuable Danish ones.

In response to the interest in Ling gymnastics, a special one-year course for elementary instructors was instituted in 1898 at the State Training School for Teachers. To meet the demand for teachers trained according to the *Manual* of 1899, a number of short-term courses were offered during the early part of the century. In 1904, the first civilian, K. A. Knudsen, was appointed as state inspector of gymnastics. A law requiring all teachers to have professional training further emphasized the desire to put physical education under civilian rather than military leadership. The first independent civilian school for physical education teachers was established in 1911. It was known as the State Institute of Gymnastics and later renamed the Physical Training Teachers' College of Denmark. Regular sessions and various short courses were organized to meet the demand for more instructors. In 1909, an academic physical education curriculum was introduced in the university as a preparatory program for students who wished to teach the subject in the secondary schools. Thus the University of Copenhagen was probably the first to introduce gymnastics as a scientific discipline and to establish a laboratory for the study of physical education.

The democratization of the public school has slowly gained momentum during this century. The effort to replace the separate elementary school system for the masses and the gymnasium for the upper classes with a unified school system began with the passage of the Secondary School Act of 1903, although substantial progress was not made until after the Education Acts of 1958. The Danish elementary school now consists of seven grades with a "gentle division" of students on the basis of ability after the fifth grade. One to three additional grades may be offered that include practical studies for students who will leave school at the age of fourteen. After the seventh year, some of the more able students enter a three-year, lower secondary school department (*realafdeling*) and take the *Real* examination which leads to the gymnasium. The three-year gymnasium program, culminated by an examination (*studentereksamen*), gives access to the university.

In Denmark today, there is an effort to hold children in a common stream longer and to provide more content in the curriculum for non-academic students. Free public education was extended to the secondary school in 1954. In recent years, some smaller schools have been replaced by central schools. On the lower secondary school level, where most of the studies are academically oriented, some vocational guidance and family and sex education have been introduced. In the upper secondary schools students choose between two departments, languages and mathematics; beginning in 1968 such departments introduced a joint social-science stream. Among the other innovations in the gymnasium are the provisions for vocational guidance and some joint classes for students in different streams. The school year usually consists of forty weeks of classes which are held six days a week. The present laws make education compulsory between the ages of seven and fourteen, but youths are encouraged to remain in school longer. Many Danes still believe that a child should start to work at fourteen and continue his education in evening schools, Youth Schools, trade and technical courses associated with apprenticeship, or folk high schools.

Physical education is compulsory in all elementary and secondary schools for 100 and 150 minutes per week, respectively. Physical education is not an examination subject, but an annual grade is given which is included with other marks in calculating the examination average. At the universities, the subject is voluntary, but through sports clubs and *Universitetets Studenter-Gymnastik* about a third of the student body participates in activities. Physical education is also important in the folk high schools and a part of the training of military conscripts.

Physical education in the primary and *real* schools is supervised by a state-appointed Inspector of Gymnastics and his assistants. Teachers in grammar schools are supervised by a General Inspector of Education, with assistants in the various subjects. Secondary school teachers are university trained, and physical education instructors also teach academic subjects for which they are certified. University students who minor in physical education take anatomy, physiology, and the physiology of exercise and concurrently take a one-year course at the Physical Training Teachers' College of Denmark, which is closely associated with the University of Copenhagen. Students who major in the field take the same subjects as those who minor in the field, but they also take a special course in physiological laboratory exercise, work in a self-chosen physiological study, and are encouraged to do research. Primary school teachers attend teacher colleges for four years where they are trained in all school subjects including about 560 lessons in physical education. If they want to teach in the larger towns, they may take a one-year course in physical training at the Danish Teachers' High School (*Danmarks Laererhøjskole*) or the Physical Training Teachers' College of Denmark (*Danmark Højskole for Legemsøvelser*). The military teachers of gymnastics and games receive their training at the Military Gymnastic Institute which was established in 1808.

Research in physical education was initiated early in this century. A chair in gymnastic theory was established at the University of Copenhagen in 1909, and a Laboratory for the Theory of Physical Education was established in 1918. Dr. Johannes Lindhard, the first professor and head of the Laboratory, who did much to separate scientific facts from traditional beliefs and quackery, is primarily known for his work in the physiology of circulation and muscles. In the Laboratory for the Theory of Physical Education, which has the Krogh bicycle, ergometric equipment for gas and blood analysis, and for strength-testing apparatus, and both low-pressure and climatic chambers, research work is done in respiration and circulation, physiology of the muscle, measures of strength, and the effect of obesity on the cardiovascular system. Considerable physiological research has been carried out, but the psychological effects of physical education have received little attention.

In Denmark, World War II postponed the construction of facilities according to the Education Act of 1937. This act required local councils to provide a gymnasium with baths and dressing rooms at every school for children over twelve, and to provide grounds for games and for track and field athletics. After the war, a circular in 1946 ordered each country school without a gymnasium to build one and equip it with wall bars (for at least half of the largest class), counter balance beam, fixed iron bar for somersaults, one little buck, one little box, jumping stands, weighted rope, one long skipping rope, two forms with balance rib, one vaulting mat, one small agility mat, and one jumping pit.

By the mid-fifties, almost every city school and about half of the rural schools had gymnasiums, but many of them were smaller and less suitable for team games than gymnasiums in the United States. Rural schools can provide playing fields more easily than schools in large towns, but even rural schools are not adequately supplied. Outside of school hours, gymnasium and athletic fields are made available to youths and to gymnastic and sports organizations. State grants cover fifty to seventy-five percent of the cost of gymnasiums and playing fields. Although many communities have obtained available grants for swimming pools, the number of swimming facilities is still insufficient.

The playground and youth movements in Denmark are more recent than those in England and Germany. In 1891, the Copenhagen Playground Association opened the first public playground. In 1897, a national Committee for Danish School Children's Coordinated Games was instituted and given government funds to promote games for children, train teachers in the work, furnish advice to communities, and equip playgrounds. Local communities were expected to match all government contributions and many quickly accepted this aid. Danish youth organizations took their inspiration from England, where such activities developed earlier because of the more intensive industrialization and urbanization. In 1902, the Boys' Voluntary League (*Frivillegt Drengeforbund*) was patterned after the English Boys' Brigade. The Youths' Sports League was founded in 1905, the Danish Boy Scouts in 1909, and the Danish Girl Guide Corps in 1911. In 1910, special YMCA scout troops were formed, and since 1919, the YWCA has had its own Girl Guide program. The Danish National and Community Life and Folk High School movement as early as 1894 initiated an organization for older youth called the Danish Young People's Association. The main youth organizations today are affiliated with the Youth Associations Advisory Committee.

In Denmark, more voluntary instructors are available for gymnastics than for sports. Town clubs draw most of their teachers from the military and public school gymnastic instructors. Many rural clubs send youths to special folk high schools for training. These graduates then serve their local clubs as voluntary teachers.

The first folk high school for gymnastics was founded at Ollerup by Niels Bukh in 1919. A school for women was founded at Snoghøj in 1925 by Jørgine Abildgaard and Anna Krogh. In 1938, an Athletics High School was established at Gerlev; in 1943, the Jutland Athletics School was started at Vejle; and more recently, schools have been established at Viborg and Sønderborg. Besides enrolling rural youths, the folk high schools also accept foreign students, either in regular sessions or in specially-designed short courses. Because Danish-trained instructors are in demand in foreign institutions, two folk schools have offered classes conducted in English, the H. G. Junker Institute for Women at Silkeborg (now closed) and the Holtze Institute for Men at Fredensborg.

Several gymnastics and sports organizations provide programs for adults and for youths who have left school. The Danish Sports Federation, which was founded in 1896 and draws most of its members from cities, has divisions for gymnastics, swimming, shooting, soccer, handball, riding, bicycling, orienteering, sailing, athletics, boxing, and most other amateur sports. The Federation organizes national championships, represents the respective sports in international competitions, helps develop playing fields, and provides facilities for medical control of all sportsmen. To stimulate interest in sports participation, the Federation helped institute a sports badge (*idraetsmaerke*) in 1921. The badges can be won by three age groups: school children, juveniles, and adults. Tests with successive bronze, silver, and gold grades are arranged for various sports.

The Danish Rifle, Gymnastics, and Sports Association, which stem from the rifle clubs formed before the War of 1864, sponsors shooting matches, gymnastics, and athletic championships. The members of this association and the members who broke away in 1930 to form the Danish Gymnastics Association come mostly from the rural areas. The Danish Workers' Sports Federation, which was formed in 1946 but includes some old sports clubs, also sponsors sports tournaments and has experimented with introducing brief gymnastics breaks during working hours.

The Danish Youth Hostels Association and Danish Rambling Club, which cooperate closely, were formed in 1930. These associations provide young cyclists, hikers, and travelers with cheap means of travel at home and abroad and an opportunity to enjoy life in the open air. The youth hostels in the various towns, each with its dormitory, common room, kitchen, and sanitary facilities, provide accommodations for over fifty thousand Danish members and many foreign visitors.

The Danish Sports Federation received its first annual grant from the government in 1903. The Football Pools Act of 1948 greatly improved the financial status of sports clubs and open-air activities. Profits from the state controlled pools are now allocated for the advancement of sports, voluntary service movements, open-air activities, cultural activities, and scientific research. Sports and gymnastics clubs are also permitted to use school facilities after school hours and on weekends. If these facilities are unsuitable, clubs build their own playing fields, halls, and swimming pools with the help of the local government, voluntary donations, and the contribution of labor by the members.

The Danish Holiday Act of 1938 assured almost every citizen of a minimum twelve-day vacation with pay, in the case of full employment. If an individual works for wages during the vacation period, he loses his holiday allowance. To utilize this vacation, many clubs and folk high schools have organized lectures, gymnastics, and sport activities. Favorable terms on small allotments of land for a tiny cottage and garden have been won by the "garden colony movement." The Society for the Preservation of Denmark's Beauty Spots maintains attractive camping grounds. The Danish People's Holiday Society, representing trade unions, sponsors miniature holiday towns with individual cottages for families, arranges with farmers to open their homes to city folk for small fees, plans with trade unions in foreign countries reciprocal excursions that feature at least a day's visit as a guest in a private home, and secures otherwise-empty berths on tourist boats at low cost.

The Copenhagen Sports Park (*Københavns Idraetspark*) is a unique institution. Prior to 1911, athletics were pursued in incidental areas and in buildings without special accommodations. The Copenhagen Sports Park was built to provide for sports engagements: a swimming pool, thirty-five short-range shooting galleries, six halls for drilling and exercising, one hall with two indoor tennis courts, and an athletic stadium, hockey grounds, and football grounds. The supreme authority was vested in a board of governors representing the municipality, sports organizations, the Copenhagen inspector of physical culture, and others. Financing of the huge project was accomplished by means of the income from a cinema, restaurants, and shops surrounding the park, a small subvention from the municipal government, and the proceeds of sports events and training fees. As the city continued to grow, other sites were developed in the city and in suburban areas.

Program and Methods of Physical Education

The Danes did not originate a system of physical education. They selected and adapted German, Swedish, and English gymnastics and sports, subjected them to scientific inquiry, and refashioned them into a distinctively Danish character. In the early nineteenth century, Nachtegall devised the first Danish program, duplicating GutsMuths' conception of gymnastics with very few alterations. Activities were conducted on hanging ladders, climbing masts, and rope ladders. Students practiced jumping, vaulting, running, balancing, swimming, tug-of-war, and military drills. A wooden horse was employed for vaulting, and mats were used to prevent serious injuries. Although mats may have been employed previously, this is the first mention of their use. Hikes and games do not seem to have been given the same consideration by Nachtegall as they were by GutsMuths.

Although Nachtegall divided his small repertoire of exercises into seven groups, he provided no methodical sequence for each group. He relied upon the teacher's good judgment to mix the exercises properly for all-round development and class interest. The gymnastics of GutsMuths, in the form Nachtegall had given them, were later supplemented with exercises from German *Turnen*, using rings, trapeze, parallel bars, and horizontal bars. Greater formality and organization appeared as physical education became more militarized. Exercises were done to command, individual expression was expunged, and uniform and precise movement exemplified teaching methods for a number of years. This led to a declining interest in physical education.

The substance of the Swedish Ling system has been deeply rooted in the Danish program since shortly before the turn of the twentieth century. The most active champion of the Swedish system was K. A. Knudsen, the state inspector of physical education for thirty years. The Swedish and Danish gymnastic classifications were similar. All exercises were divided into three groups: introductory, principal, and final. The *introductory* category included leg, neck, and arm exercises. The *principal* category consisted of span bendings, heaving, balancing, lateral, abdominal, and dorsal exercises, marching and running, jumping and vaulting, and agility exercises. The *final* classification was composed principally of breathing exercises. In devising the gymnastic lesson, Knudsen advised teachers to select exercises from the different groups that harmonized with one another in strength, form, and coordination and that provided for the development of the whole body. The easier exercises were to be placed at the beginning and end of the lesson with the more strenuous ones in the middle, thus providing for a steady increase in effort with a tapering-off toward the close of the class period. Teachers were to provide a change between free standing and apparatus work, slow and quick movements, and mass and individual exercises. The tables of exercises were also to be adapted to the age and sex of the students.

Under Bukh, Swedish gymnastics in the folk schools underwent a change in the second decade of the twentieth century. In the Swedish exercises, considerable time was used in ordering pupils and in maintaining held positions. Bukh devoted more time to movement and confined the held positions to brief phases between exercises. In his "motional exercises," he emphasized vigorous rhythmical movements that flowed into one another and intensive stretching motions to promote elasticity, flexibility, and freedom. His day's order had eight divisions: leg, arm, neck, lateral, stomach, dorsal, marching, and vaulting exercises. The Swedish divisions of span bending, heaving, balancing, and breathing were omitted. Three main types of exercises were used by Bukh: those needed to develop flexibility, strength, and coordination or agility. Advanced students engaged in "athletic gymnastics," consisting of a number of simple and plastic positions that taxed the limits of a performer's powers and demonstrated that he could master feats that were difficult in character and accomplishment. Bukh's system dispensed with the beams, benches, Danish horse, and the buck; he used only wall bars, vaulting boxes, and Danish agility mattresses. A typical lesson was composed of introductory marching, thirty to thirty-five minutes of continuous free standing movements, and then five to ten minutes of vigorous and passive exercises on the wall bars. The lesson often concluded with ten minutes of hurricane vaulting, agility work, and a march around the gymnasium while singing a spirited song. Modern gymnastics for boys have been influenced by Bukh; his exercises are particularly popular among folk school graduates.

Nachtegall had experimented with gymnastics for girls as early as 1838, and exercises suitable for women were studied from time to time thereafter, influenced especially by the French between 1860 and 1870. Dr. A. G. Drachmann, a Danish medical man who published a handbook of gymnastics in 1869, questioned whether women should do the same exercises as men. His system was further developed by Paul Petersen (1845–1906) who started a school for female teachers. The system influenced instruction in Danish schools, but it was forced into the background as the Ling exercises gained in popularity in the 1880s and 1890s. In 1914, Dr. Lindhard published his book, *The Special Theory of Gym-*

nastics, in which he attacked the Ling gymnastics because they did not give sufficient consideration to the physical and psychical differences between men and women. One of the first changes in women's gymnastics was introduced by Elli Björksten, a Finnish teacher, who replaced the rather static, stiff Swedish exercises with free, rhythmical movements. The folk school at Songhøj helped popularize this form of gymnastics. Another departure from the Ling system was instituted by Agnete Bertram, a pupil of Lindhard, who taught at the University and established a school for training female gymnastics instructors in the 1920s. Opposed to mechanical drills, she sought to make the work more natural, to place greater emphasis on the aesthetic aspects of exercise, and to replace posture gymnastics with movement gymnastics. Her exercises were full of motion; they flowed from one to another without a break and were often performed to the accompaniment of music. Many of the exercises that are used today in Danish schools reflect the influence of Bertram and Björksten.

The present physical education program in Denmark follows the traditional continental system of placing the greatest emphasis on gymnastics. Games and athletics have grown in importance in recent years, but the belief is still held that they do not achieve the all-around development and basic neuromuscular discipline resulting from gymnastics. Hence, from late fall until early spring, classes are devoted primarily to gymnastics. The 1899 *Manual of Gymnastics* has long been out of use; teachers are free to select exercises that are suitable for their students, but they are provided with some general guides by the Board of Inspectors.

In the lower grades, a number of minor games are played, particularly longball (*Langbold*), an ancient continental ball game. Team handball is the most popular game for older girls. Boys prefer team handball and soccer. Track and field events have gained a footing in Denmark more slowly than games, and systematic training for girls has not gained general favor. The athletic activities usually include all the exercises for the School Athletic Badge: running, jumping, throwing, and relay racing.

Some of the older girls are taught folk dances, but modern dance is not a part of the curriculum. Swimming is taught where facilities are available; certificates are given for passing tests which include life-saving. The swimming season is short, however, for most schools use outdoor pools. In the upper secondary grades, hygiene, human anatomy, and physiology, including sex education, are usually a part of the curriculum. In most instances, this instruction is given in periods that are allocated to physical education above the required minimum.

Students are expected to dress for class and to shower afterward. Great stress is placed on cleanliness as well as upon other hygienic practices. Annual tuberculosis examinations, weighings, and measurings, with other medical observations and findings are entered on the child's records. The school doctors do not provide treatment, but the Danish hospital service and national health insurance usually assure excellent treatment at little or no cost to the individual. Similarly, dental examinations are given periodically and some work may be done in the school clinic. Free school meals are provided for children who need them, and they are available to all students in some schools.

Most schools provide extra-curricular gymnastics and sports. No regular varsity athletic program is sponsored, but some competitions are arranged between schools. Some schools have open-air days or half-days for cross-country and orienteering exercises, sports meetings, and winter sports. Sports days, which emphasize group performance rather than individual performance, are organized frequently by groups of schools. Every few years, the grammar schools arrange national sport rallies which consist of gymnastic displays as well as competitions in athletics and games. The Danish people attach considerable importance to the physical education exhibitions given by school children and young adults. Folk high schools give exhibitions in tours of the country; mass demonstrations are held at camps; town and village clubs entertain the populace with gymnastics, athletics, games, and dances. Danish gymnasts on foreign tours draw international attention.

Watching television and visiting with friends are the principal leisure activities in Denmark, and about a quarter of the population attends the cinema regularly. Fifteen percent of the whole population and almost half of the 15–35 age group pursue some form of athletics. Football (soccer), gymnastics, and the Danish game of handball are the most popular sports. Denmark is the only Scandinavian country in which field hockey and cricket are played. Persons over thirty years old enjoy swimming, tennis, Danish handball, shooting, and fishing. The Danes are enthusiastic soccer players and fans. Their amateur teams play against professional British teams, and the international football match with Sweden is the big game of the year.

Soccer was introduced in 1879 by the Copenhagen Ball Club which had been formed in 1876 by people interested in *langbold* and cricket. Tennis was introduced in 1883 and golf in 1898. Danish handball originated at a grammar school in 1898, where the physical training teacher, Holger Nielson, drafted the first rules. This is a modification of field or team handball, with seven, instead of eleven, players on a side. Hockey was introduced by F. Knudsen, an ardent champion of the game. Fencing has a long tradition and has always been an important subject at the Army Gymnastic School, but it is not a sport of the general public.

On the Danish peninsula and the hundreds of adjacent islands, water sports are enjoyed. The mild winters do not encourage ice and snow sports, but as soon as warm weather appears, the Danish people flock to the sand dunes, beaches, wooded hills, and country lanes. Rowing is pursued for pleasure and for sport, and children growing up along the seashore or near inland lakes become expert swimmers and sailors. Clubs for rowing and yachting were founded as early as 1866; swimming became a competitive sport in 1880, but participation was limited until indoor pools were built in 1925–27.

Lovers of the open road and outdoor life have accounted for the tremendous growth of the rambling movement. Denmark claims to have a higher number of hikers in proportion to the population than any other nation. The multitude of bicycles weaving in and out of traffic symbolizes not only a convenient method of transportation but also a popular vehicle for sport. Since the Dansk Bicycle Club was founded in 1881, interest in cycling as a sport has always been great.

The historical competition of *ringridning* (ring-riding) has origins that go back to the knightly tournaments. This colorful sport, in which riders at full gallop use a lance to unhook a ring suspended by a rope between two posts, is chiefly pursued in South Jutland. Many men continue to participate in the annual tournaments until after the age of seventy. The Shrovetide tournament riders on the Island of Amager take turns hitting a suspended barrel with a stick, though the barrel no longer holds a cat as was once the custom.

Dance has long enriched social life in Denmark. Danish youths follow all forms of popular dance. In the village halls, Danish folk dances have long created a lively atmosphere as the villagers perform the schottische, Crested Hen, Little Man in a Fix, masquerade, varsovienne, or the minuet. Much of the country social life centers around such occasions. In the city, the ballets have enriched cultural life for over two centuries, offering classical performances as well as more modern interpretations.

16

Physical Education in French Educational Nationalism

For almost a century before the French Revolution, intellectual leaders believed that their institutions had ceased functioning satisfactorily. The economy was essentially feudal, and the nation was on the verge of bankruptcy as a result of royal extravagance and the unsuccessful struggle with England for world empire. France was composed of differentiated social strata with glaring contrasts between the luxury-loving privileged class and the poverty-stricken masses. Politically, the ideology of divine right was employed to justify the absolute power of the king. The reformers used the theory that all men are endowed with natural rights, conferred by God himself, to provide the necessary leverage for dislodging authority and privilege. The supreme need was liberty—freedom from social and political bondage. To liberty, the French added "equality" and "fraternity."

Nationalism had existed in France before the Revolution, but the necessity of defending the new liberties from attacks by foreign powers made the spirit of patriotism flare brighter, and the military successes under Napoleon continued to fire national pride. The years of international rivalry, especially between France and Germany, constantly renewed the spirit of nationalism even to the present day.

Shortly after the French Revolution, the authorities made a deliberate effort to maintain the nationalistic fervor of the citizens by establishing a strong centralized government. To protect itself from monarchist and clerical interference, the government had to control education. When Napoleon came into power, he established a centralized system of education that has endured until the present day. "National subjects" dominate the course of study. Classes in French language, literature, history, geography, civics, and music are carefully oriented toward nationalism. From his first days in elementary school until his last days in compulsory military service, the youth is thoroughly imbued with patriotic precepts.

A French physician, Clement Joseph Tissot, published a book on medical and surgical gymnastics in 1780 that was translated into German and Swedish. But most of the gymnastic theories and practices that were introduced in France were borrowed from other nations. A Spaniard, Colonel Francisco Amoros (c. 1770–1848), laid the foundation for the French military and school program in the two-volume *Manuel d'Éducation physique, gymnastique et morale*. Another early teacher, Phokion Clias (1782–1854), who had trained soldiers in Switzerland and England before being invited to France, prepared a manual, *Elementary Courses for Gymnastic Exercises*, whose principles were influenced by GutsMuths and Jahn. But a Frenchman, Baron Pierre de Coubertin (1863–1937), was the man who envisioned the modern international physical education ideal and realized it in the renewal of the Olympic Games. De Coubertin's chief literary contributions were *L'Éducation en Angleterre* in 1888, *Souvenirs d'Amérique èt de Grèce* in 1897, and *Une Campagne de vingt-et-un* in 1908. Among other physical education leaders of the early twentieth century are Jules Simon, George Demeny, Philippe Tissié, and Lieutenant George Hébert.

Aims of Education

The French have traditionally instilled in their children a reverence for the cultural contributions that France has made to the world. The elementary school has cultivated loyalty to national ideals, has stressed the use of a common language as a unifying force, and has insisted on the mastery of fundamental skills and knowledges. For generations, the upper and middle class students attending the secondary schools have pursued a predominantly classical education. After much debate modern languages and historical and scientific subjects were accepted. The objective of the secondary schools and universities has been to prepare an intellectual elite, a corps of leaders who would serve as the custodians of French culture and spread it throughout the world.

In 1947, an educational reform commission recommended the adoption of broader and more democratic aims of education. The Langevin Commission urged that *all* children be allowed the maximum development of their abilities, without suffering limitations of social or economic status. The Commission recommended that the school should develop manual, technical, and artistic talents equally with the intellectual. Although traditional education was to be retained, the Commission believed this training should be paralleled by preparation of "elites in the other walks of life." The principles of the Langevin Commission have guided French education down to the present day.

Aims of Physical Education

When the church controlled the schools of France, emphasis was on saving souls and training youthful intellects rather than on developing physical potentials. When Amoros and Clias introduced gymnastic programs, their objective was to enhance the military potentialities of youth. Spontaneous interest in physical exercise was not characteristic of the French, but being alert to any threat of national safety, they saw the value in a physical education program to meet defense needs. Except for this military objective, physical education was not acknowledged as a pedagogically sound or socially desirable method of developing future citizens.

After the Revolution of 1848, physical education dwindled, but enjoyed a renaissance after the disastrous Franco-Prussian War of 1870. Leaders charged that a physical and moral degeneracy had undermined the vitality of the nation. Pierre de Coubertin, in particular, sought to help France rebuild her national strength. Through sports, he hoped to build up a new type of French manhood with the physical vigor, moral discipline, and self-control necessary to maintain the honor and integrity of the country.

Drawing inspiration from the ancient Greek Olympic Games, de Coubertin sought to cut across nationalistic lines with an athletic spirit and sportsmanship creed that would serve three broad purposes: "First, to spread physical education and sports around the world; second, to raise the standard of physical achievement; and third, to bring the young people of all continents together in order that links of friendship might be formed to replace the deadly contacts of international war."[1] Even though his dreams of worldwide peace were shattered by two world wars, the Olympics have focused attention on the health and physical skills of youth and have inspired improvements in physical education and recreation programs in many nations.

After World War I, French gymnastic organizations exhorted youths to remember that "When a citizen is born in France, he is born a soldier." National sports federations clearly defined patriotism as among their major objectives. They pointed with pride to the rifle range beside the playing field as a symbol of the efforts to protect France's uncertain future. A report to the President of the Republic in 1934 urged achieving these mili-

---

[1]"The Lessons of the XIV Olympiad," *Physical Recreation* 1 (January–April 1949) :18.

taristic aims. "If . . . the nation is to live and flourish . . . it is . . . necessary that its children should grow up under the most favorable conditions of development; that they become strong and efficient for war . . ."[2]

After France's humiliating defeat during World War II, greater emphasis was placed on the recreational, social, and moral goals of physical education. The public recognized this phase of education as a way to counteract the deleterious effects of industrial and intellectual life as well as the ravages of war. Today, the French are concerned not only with good health and developing speed, strength, and resistance, but also with giving bodily activity an aesthetic, intellectual, and moral dimension through muscular suppleness, tactical skill, and courageous conduct. Considerable attention is given to individual physical and social development, but the nationalistic purpose of physical education remains dominant. By providing more support for physical education and sport programs, the government hopes to help youths affirm their own personal worth and develop the initiative, judgment, self-discipline, self-confidence, teamwork, and leadership qualities that will win world prestige for France.

Promotion of Physical Education

Between the Battle of Waterloo and the Revolution of 1848, gymnastics were introduced in France, particularly in the army. The Spanish refugee, Colonel Francisco Amoros, established his first gymnasium in Paris at the private school of M. Durdan in 1817. After the French Minister of War observed an exhibition given by Amoros, he detailed a group of men to take the gymnastic course in order to prepare themselves as future army instructors. Encouraged by such support, Amoros planned the *Gymnase Normal Militaire et Civil* with a great open-air gymnasium, and became the director when it opened in 1820. The instruction was primarily for soldiers, but selected private pupils were also admitted. In 1831, Amoros was appointed national director of all French gymnastics, but disagreements between him and the government resulted in the closing of his classes in 1837. Meanwhile, in 1834, he had opened his private institution *Gymnase Civil Orthosomatique* where he continued to teach for fourteen years. For noncommissioned officers, he offered six-month courses to train them as instructors in their own regiments.

Phokion Heinrich Clias, the gymnast who constructed programs for the Swiss and English military forces, was invited to France in 1841. Although he was sixty years old and had already retired, Clias assumed several responsibilities in Besançon and instructed at the city schools, the normal school, and the nearby military garrison. Later, he became Superin-

2Quoted in L. H. Weir, *Europe at Play* (New York: A. S. Barnes and Co., 1937), p. 64.

tendent of Gymnastic Instruction in the elementary schools of Paris, a position which he retained until the Revolution of 1848, when he returned to Switzerland.

A period of stagnation ensued in French physical education between 1850–1870. During these years, two former pupils and associates of Amoros were instrumental in founding the Military Normal School of Gymnastics at Joinville, which eventually supplied schools and the army with teachers. Interest in physical education revived after the Franco-Prussian War. Many new gymnastic societies were formed. In the academic world, laws requiring gymnastics in the curriculum were passed in 1872, 1880, 1887, and 1905. The exercises were made compulsory for boys and then for girls, first in the public schools and later in private and church schools. Although physical education came to occupy an officially recognized place in the curriculum, its practical values were far from appreciated. The work was relegated to special teachers, usually graduates of the military institute at Joinville.

Although the official primary gymnastic course at the turn of the century looked formidable, it was seldom followed. There was no gymnastic apparatus in most lower schools, swimming facilities were negligible, and the drills themselves were sterile and complex. These factors, along with a law which held teachers personally responsible for any accidents, contributed to the general apathy toward physical education.

In the secondary schools, the physical education programs were not supported by the scholastically-minded faculties. In Paris, pupils who desired music, fencing, gymnastics, dancing, boxing, swimming, or riding lessons could take them only during leisure hours. Some schools also programmed physical education classes during the student's leisure time. Although no special costumes were required, the boys divested themselves of their coats and waistcoats. Showers were not a part of the regular gymnasium facilities, but most of the lycées sent pupils to the nearby public baths at least once a month for hot baths and more frequently for footbaths. Although most of the Paris lycées had rugby and association football teams, the schoolboy's schedule was too crowded to allow much participation in athletics.

Most schools had no physical education facilities, but a few secondary schools in Paris had gymnasiums that were in excess of 50 x 30 feet and two stories high, usually well-lighted but not well-ventilated. The floor space was often divided into two areas: the floor proper, and a lower area covered with eight to ten inches of tan bark or sawdust where the fixed apparatus was located. The equipment was simple, consisting of parallel bars, flying rings, climbing ropes, horses, jumping boards, horizontal bars, wands, and dumbbells. Large classes were divided to permit some students to work on the heavy apparatus in the pit while the rest carried out Swedish evolutions on the floor. In the smaller provincial schools, the gymnasium was often open to the air on one side, the floor was a thick layer of loam, and the equipment was meager and crude.

Because of the lack of support by the Ministry of Public Instruction, the physical education movement did not develop as rapidly in France as it did in other countries. For a long time the army and the gymnastic and sports societies provided most of the leadership. Demolins provided some impetus for action in 1895 when he published *A Quoi Tient la Supériorité des Anglo-Saxons?* The Olympics and the YMCA directors with the American Expeditionary Forces during World War I stimulated interest in track and field events and sports. After World War I, an effort was made to effectively organize physical education in the schools. In 1922, a committee was appointed to study methods, time schedules, teacher training, and the promotion of games in schools and universities. In less than a year, physical exercises were included in the elementary curriculum for two hours a week. In 1923, provisions were made for training personnel to effect the program. In most provincial schools, however, the official directives were not enforced. By an edict of 19 January 1925, all secondary school pupils were to have two hours of physical education a week, but lack of funds prevented the strict application of this principle in practice.

The physical education movement failed to gather much momentum, because expenditures for education were low, the academic program was overloaded, and an extremely class-conscious system of school organization existed. Separate national directorates controlled separate systems of elementary, secondary, and technical education. The primary schools educated the children of the lower economic groups from seven to fourteen years of age. The upper elementary schools prepared students for normal schools, for a trade, or for clerical, industrial, or agricultural employment. The state lycées and municipal colleges provided a classical-cultural education for upper-class youths and a few gifted poor students from the ages of seven to seventeen. A rigorous course of formal studies developed the critical thinking ability and communication skills of secondary students and prepared them for the baccalauréat examination. This examination was the only pathway to the universities and the *grandes écoles* and ultimately to most positions of leadership in government, the professions, and industry. Since transfer from the elementary to the secondary school was extremely difficult, the future economic and social status of children was, to a large degree, determined the first day they entered school.

Under these circumstances, French youths felt more bound to their social class than to their generation. Their life was quite different from that of American youths. The number of pupils who did not pass to the next grade each year was high, school attendance laws were not strictly enforced, and children of farmers and workmen usually left school and went to work at an early age. In 1939, only eleven percent of the children beyond the age of fourteen continued in school and only thirty-five percent in 1958. The school day and school year were longer than in the United States. Few provisions were made for student self-government, social activities, and athletics; boys and girls were usually separated for instruction; and many public secondary schools were regimented boarding institutions. Because passing examinations was extremely important, most classwork consisted largely of formal lectures and note-taking which were directed toward questions that might appear on examinations.

Pressure for change built up after the two world wars. After World War I, when men from all strata of society fought side by side, some teachers began to question the dual system of education and pressed for a unified school system, the *école unique*. After the defeat and occupation of France during World War II, blame for the lack of leadership was placed on the inequality of educational opportunities and the policy of educating according to a nostalgic cultural tradition rather than to the mushrooming technological age. The scathing report of the Algiers Commission of 1944 and the comprehensive Langevin Plan recommended reform. The Delbos Act of 1949 and the reform decree of January 1959 effected many of the Langevin recommendations.

Since 1959, a vigorous effort has been made to give equal educational opportunities to all youths. To democratize education, the school leaving age has been raised to sixteen years of age, the examinations have been changed, the development of secondary and higher education has been accelerated, the number of scholarships and grants have been increased, and the administration of education has been reorganized to eliminate the vertical separation of the elementary, secondary, and vocational schools and to coordinate the work of all inspectors.

All students now receive the same elementary education up to the age of eleven, and all programs above the elementary level are considered secondary education. A system of guidance has been established on the lower secondary level to aid students in choosing their upper secondary school programs. The classical studies have been retained, but more attention is being given to technical, scientific, and vocational education. The secondary school is no longer exclusively for the intellectual and moneyed elite.

The whole question of education in France is considered from the national point of view. The Ministry of National Education is responsible for the supervision of all education, both public and private. Under the Minister of Education is the Secretary-General and several administrative divisions or directorates, which extend through the organizational levels in France, the country being divided into academies which, in turn, are divided into departments and communes. For each academy, a rector serves as the head of the university and all other educational establishments in the academy. The Minister of Education and his directors are assisted by a body of general inspectors who are specialized in individual school subjects. Each rector is assisted by specialist inspectors and by an academy inspector in each department. Efforts are being made to decentralize some aspects of the educational system, but the strong state control still leaves little room for local authority or initiative. National education authorities control the courses of study and standards of examinations; the training, certification, and appointment of teachers; and the regular inspection of the work of each teacher.

In the early days, physical education was under the supervision of the Ministry of War and the Ministry of Public Instruction, but gradually more and more authority was shifted to the latter. In 1929, a Physical Education Bureau was established by the Ministry of Education which later acquired departmental status. After World War II, the Undersecretary for Youth and Sports who served directly under the Minister of Education, was in charge of the physical education program which was subdivided into three directorates or departments: Youth Movements and Popular Education, Sports, and Physical Education. No definite relationship existed between the Directorate of Physical Education, which organized the required school program, and the Directorate of Sports, which coordinated the extracurricular sports associations for the schools and general public as well as the national premilitary training.

During recent years, the status of physical education, especially sports, has improved. In 1958, a High Commission for Youth and Sports was responsible for an expanded program of physical education, sports, and youth activities. In 1963, the High Commission was transformed into the Secretariat of State for Youth and Sports, the youth activities were extended, and the budget for 1964 was increased to four times the amount of the 1958 budget. Another advance was made in 1966 when the Secretariat, which had been under the Ministry of National Education, became the Ministry of Youth and Sports.

The Minister of Youth and Sports, who holds cabinet rank, is "responsible for the study of problems relating to youth and action in favour of youth."[3] He is in charge of physical education and sports education, leisure-time sports, recreation and popular education programs, leadership training programs, sport installations and equipment, and medical and sanitation supervision in schools, sports clubs, and camps. "Organizational measures applicable in schools and university establishments and regulations concerning teachers of physical and sport education are adopted in agreement with the Minister of National Education."[4]

The Ministry of Youth and Sports has regional and departmental personnel to carry out its programs and works with the national and regional sports advisory bodies, the Ministry of National Education, the rec-

[3]Ministère De l'Éducation Nationale, *Le Mouvement Éducatif en France Pendant L'Année, 1965* (Paris: Institut Pédagogique National, 1966), p. 51.
[4]Ibid., p. 51.

tors of the academies, and the leaders of the sports, recreational, and cultural programs of civilian societies, sport federations, industrial enterprises, and labor groups. In each academy, a chief inspector for youth and sports and departmental inspectors organize programs and sports examinations, supervise medical programs, and coordinate sports activities. The Inspecteur Principal Pédagogique supervises the teachers of physical education and sports in the academy in accordance with the directions given by the Ministry of National Education.

To make the importance of physical education clearer to students, their parents, and the intellectual community, the subject has been made a part of the school examinations. At the close of elementary school, candidates for the *certificat d'études* must pass the examination for the *Brevet Sportif Populaire*. Since 1959, physical education has been an obligatory part of the baccalauréat and for certificates of technical education. In 1962, the subject was included in the *Concours Général*, a difficult competitive examination given to outstanding students of the public schools in each major discipline.

Elementary school physical education classes, which are usually taught by the classroom teacher, are held for 150 minutes a week. On the secondary school level, where each subject is taught by a specialist, physical education classes are held for 180 minutes a week, with the addition of an open-air afternoon. Students who desire to engage in sports and athletic competitions can join one of the many school sports clubs. Sports competition is conducted on Thursday afternoon in the elementary and secondary schools and on Wednesday afternoon in the universities. In 1953, the universities, which in the past had not considered sports and exercise as a legitimate part of education, were requested to promote exercises and sports. However, there was little progress (because of a lack of interest, funds, facilities, and personnel) until 1963, when a Commission for Physical Education and University Sports was set up for each rector to promote and implement programs.

Private, rather than government associations have traditionally sponsored the school sports programs in France, while instructors have usually served in both the association and the public school physical education programs. In the past, few students have engaged in competition but an effort is now being made to draw more of them into active participation. In private schools, the Sports Union for Free Instruction (UGSEL) supervises the athletic clubs. In the public schools, the Sports Union of Primary Education (USEP) organizes games and encourages participation, but avoids prematurely introduced competition. For many years, the Scholastic and University Sports Union (OSSU) organized sport activities in secondary schools and universities. After a long struggle with the government, certain compromises were made and the OSSU was replaced by a public agency, the Association for School and University Sports (ASSU).

Physical education instructors are the driving force in ASSU which includes more than 4,000 clubs. The Administrative Council of the ASSU is headed by the Minister of Youth and Sports and includes both public officials and representatives of sports associations.

France was behind the other European countries in devising a national sports badge test. The first serious attempt to launch a countrywide physical fitness campaign was made in 1937 when Leo Lagrange developed the *Brevet Sportif Populaire* (BSP), which was divided into several age levels. To reach those groups who were not receiving physical exercise in the school programs or in the compulsory military training program beginning at age twenty, the *Brevet Sportif Populaire* was revived and extended after World War II.

Because France initiated her modern physical education and community recreation programs somewhat later than many countries, she has many obstacles to overcome. Most secondary schools were originally constructed without any sport facilities. Prior to World War II, the supply of gymnasiums and playing fields was inadequate, and many facilities antiquated. The loss of some facilities during the war, the postwar population surge, the extension of compulsory education, and the rapid increase in leisure time has placed a burden on existing installations. As rapidly as the national economy will permit, the Ministry of Youth and Sports is assisting local communities in providing facilities. Since 1956, no school could be built without the necessary installations. A four-year program launched in 1961, which has since been renewed and expanded, resulted in the construction of 1200 stadiums and playing fields, 600 gymnasiums and sports-halls, 600 swimming pools, 600 youth centers, and many holiday camps and other types of installations. Normal facility standards, however, have not yet been met.

Not only the shortage of facilities, but also the shortage of qualified teachers has impeded the development of physical education in France. Some training programs were established to train civilian gymnastic instructors prior to World War I, but for many years the military academy at Joinville supplied the schools, the army, and the sporting associations with most of their physical education teachers and developed most of the outstanding athletes in France. After World War I, many civilian instructors were pushed aside when army men were again appointed to direct physical education in the schools. Some of the army men were not qualifield for the work, however, and civilian teachers gradually began to fill more and more of the positions, particularly after improved training programs were provided for them. In 1927, the universities started to organize Higher Institutes of Physical Education in order to provide qualified leadership for the revised curriculum. In 1933, a decree established the two national Superior Normal Schools of Physical Education, one for men and one for women. The graduates of these schools taught in the preparatory schools for elementary school teachers. To overcome the serious shortage of teachers, training programs were established which increased the number of physical education instructors from 6,818 in 1958 to 12,281 in 1964, but this increase was not sufficient to meet the need.

Several types of schools train physical education personnel. First year physical education students are more and more being trained in preparatory classes attached to certain high schools. The Regional Centers for Physical Education and Sports (CREPS) prepare candidates for teaching certificates. They also train sports and recreation leaders for sports clubs, nationalized enterprises, vacation resorts, and out-of-school youth movements. The Regional Institutes for Physical Education and Sports (IREPS), generally attached to the schools of medicine at each university, also prepare physical education teachers. The two national Superior Normal Schools of Physical Education (ENSEPS) admit the best students on a competitive examination basis and prepare this elite corps of future leaders for the second part of the teaching credential.

The National Institute of Sports (INS), which was established at Joinville after World War II and houses one of the most up-to-date complexes in Europe, provide training programs for the athletes who participate in national and international competitions; prepares coaches for schools, associations, clubs, industry, and the military; trains officials; and conducts a medical sports-research program. Schools for yachting, rowing, and skiing and mountaineering are also administered by the INS. The INS is adjacent to the Superior Normal School for Men and one of the Regional Centers and has cooperative relationships with them and the Inter-Armed Forces Sports Group of Joinville.

Physical education personnel in France fall into several categories. Elementary teachers take some physical education classes and tests as part of their preparatory training. The *maîtres*, as distinguished from the professors or specialists, pursue two years of training after obtaining a lower secondary school certificate or an equivalent diploma. *Maîtres* serve in some of the same schools as professors, but they receive lower pay, work longer hours, and are responsible for teaching activities rather than theoretical, supervisory, or rehabilitation work. Many *maîtres* become directors of community out-of-school programs, work with sports clubs or sports associations, or serve industrial enterprises that sponsor sport programs.

Students who wish to become professors pursue a year of basic studies in Regional Centers, Regional Institutes, or preparatory classes that have been established in some lycées. They take the examination for the first part of the teacher's certificate one year after the baccalauréat, and competitive examinations to gain admittance to the Superior Normal Schools where they prepare for the second part of the teacher's certificate. Their training requires a total of four years after the baccalauréat. ENSEPS students, who are considered civil servants and are paid a salary (full grants), agree to serve as teachers of public education for ten years. Their degree entitles them to teach in all senior high schools, CREPS, IREPS, and ENSEPS. To widen recruitment, IREPS and some CREPS train teachers in the same way as ENSEPS; the students in these programs do not receive a salary, but they may receive maintenance grants. To promote the interests of teachers of ENSEPS, an organization, *Amicale des Anciens Elèves d'ENSEPS*, has been formed which publishes *Education Physique et Sport*.

A number of other publications are also available in France, such as *L'Homme Sain*, published by the French Federation of Educative Gymnastics; *INS*; *L'Education Physique, Revue de Kinestherapie*; *Annales de Cinésithérapie et de Rééducation Physique*; and SIEPEPS (Society of Information and Pedagogical Studies of Physical and Sportive Education) which is published by the syndicate of physical education teachers.

For almost a century, military men provided a home for French sports in the famous Joinville School (1852-c.1945). After the school was dissolved, it was replaced first by the Armed Forces Sports Center (1946), then by the Joinville Battalion (1956), and later by the Inter-Armed Forces Sports Group of Joinville (GSIJ) (1960) which is now in Fontainebleau. The GSIJ, in cooperation with the Ministry of Youth and Sports and the coaches of the National Sports Institute, trains the athletes who represent the armed forces in national and international sports meetings. Draftees who are accepted for this program devote as much as fourteen months of their total army training to their sport specialty. Not surprisingly, Joinville has provided a third or more of the French athletes in recent Olympics.

Some gymnastics and sports societies were organized in France in the nineteenth century, but they experienced their greatest growth after World War I. To get financial support from the government and to provide some physical conditioning for the great masses of youth who left school at an early age, they often included a premilitary training as a part of their activities. In time, the diverse clubs banded together into unions and federations, which, in turn, became members of the National Committee on Sports, a central governing body which coordinated their activities and settled differences between them. Today, the Ministry of Youth and Sports maintains a close liaison with the sport federations and the French Olympic Committee. The sport federations receive grants from the government which amount to more than four million dollars per year with the largest grants being made to the athletics, swimming, skiing, and basketball federations.

Better medical control of sports has been effected in recent years. In 1953, a ministerial decree made it compulsory for all sportsmen under twenty-one years to obtain medical certificates. Research in sports medicine is encouraged by the Secretary of State for Youth and Sports; special courses, certificates, and awards are offered in the field.

The renaissance of an international spirit of sports originated in France when Pierre de Coubertin established the modern Olympic Games. As a young man, Coubertin observed the general apathy of the French populace toward gymnastic societies. While visiting British schools, he was impressed with their many football, cricket, track, and rowing competitions. Believing that these activities might be the source of the physical vigor and the moral discipline that enabled the British to rule a huge empire, he sought to propagate such activities in France. Under his leadership, the *Union des Sociétés des Sports Athlétiques* was organized in 1891–1892, consisting of 200 French athletic clubs. Having unified these groups, de Coubertin began to lay the foundation of international matches between France and England in 1892. Later, he disclosed plans for a revival of the Olympic Games, and in 1896 the first modern Olympic Games took place in Greece.

Program and Methods of Physical Education

In the nineteenth century General Amoros devised the first gymnastic program in France, utilizing many of the Pestalozzi's ideas, but also displaying much originality. All exercises were executed according to a methodical progression. First free exercises were performed to make the body supple, these were frequently accompanied by singing or were timed by a metronome. Next came activities upon apparatus, balancing exercises, dumbbell exercises, marching, leaping, climbing, vaulting, and jumping. According to the published atlas of Amoros, he was one of the first gymnasts to employ rings, inclined boards and ladders, rope ladders, giant strides, a strength-testing machine, and the trapeze. The Amoros system was retained in the army and in the schools for a number of years. Clias, who succeeded Amoros, offered a combination of the exercises of GutsMuths and Jahn in addition to some form of activity called *Kallisthenics*. The apparatus he employed included the horizontal beams, parallel bars, poles, ropes, climbing masts, giant strides, and the horses.

Between 1848 and 1870 little gymnastic interest was exhibited in France, but an important research project was carried out. In 1867, G. B. Duchennes, the founder of the science of kinesiology, published his *Physiology of Motion* which was the first complete record of the kinesiology of the human muscular system based on empirical evidence. In his investigations, he used electrophysiological methods to analyze human movements in both normal and diseased subjects.

After the War of 1870, the Belgian exercises, which were predominately German *Turnen*, were temporarily adopted. Later, the Swedish Ling system was introduced and was considered an improvement. Until about 1890, classes were limited to formal exercises, although for extra fees students could also engage in fencing and target shooting. Thursday school holidays were often devoted to extra study periods, a visit to the museum, or a mild walk in the country. During the noon recreation period, older boys sometimes played tennis or handball and the younger students amused themselves with marbles, toys, and romping about the playground. The little interest in sports that did flare up was spontaneous, sporadic, and unorganized. Athletics were usually confined to "scrub" games during the afternoon recreation periods. A few interscholastic soccer games, track and field meets, and fencing matches were held, but general participation was unknown.

During the twentieth century, the French have been divided on the type of physical education programs to be adopted. R. Tait McKenzie once wrote that "France is a battleground for systems." Since the turn of the century no less than five systems—Ling, Demeny, Joinville, Ministry of Education, and Hébert—have had their sponsors. George Demeny, who was first an advocate of the Ling gymnastics, later withdrew his support because he considered the Swedish system to be more suitable for adults than youngsters. In designing a new classification, Demeny tried to include only those movements known to have a beneficial effect upon the subject. He sought to improve posture and bodily vigor. Free movements were to be used, but these were smooth, relaxed, and graceful in contrast to the stiff and held positions of the Swedish system. Complete, harmonious and continuous movement characterized his program. Irene Popard, a pupil of Demeny, took his basic exercises and designed an outstanding educational and corrective program for women. The Joinville and Ministry of Education systems accepted much of Demeny's work but included other features that they favored. Hébert, who was inspired by the magnificent physiques that primitive peoples developed as a result of their natural movements, evolved a program of "natural exercises" which included walking, running, jumping, climbing, balancing, weight lifting, combat, and swimming. The 1945 instructions for teachers recommended a combination of Ling, Hébert, and Demeny exercises. Initiated by the publication of *Physical and Sports Activities from Birth to Maturity* in 1962, a reform program is under way which promises to lead to the development of a more flexible program.

Traditionally, organized sports have not held the same position in French schools as in English and American schools. From the age of five, French youngsters attend school until four-thirty every afternoon, and most of them never participate in organized play. Intellectualism is the French ideal; the schools have always been serious places of study and have not usually been associated with extracurricular activities. In secondary schools and universities where standards have always been strict, studies difficult, and examinations strenuous, most students have looked down upon lessons in gymnastics and have ignored sports. Generations of French university students have plodded from their tiny rooms to classes, and then to cafés where they have discussed politics, rather than sports.

The French are beginning to believe that physical activity is not sufficiently emphasized in the schools. Since World War II, they have conducted some experiments to demonstrate the value of exercise and sports. Many students have benefited from the therapeutic exercises that are provided in the numerous classes in Centers of Physical *Reeducation*. The "Half-Time Pedagogical and Sports Program" experiments, which began in Vanves in 1951 revealed that reducing the academic work load, increasing the time for physical activities, and providing supervised study and rest periods not only improved the physical development of students but also made them more sociable and independent, and increased their incentive. Moreover, the students attained a scholastic standing equal to that of students in regular classes. The mountain ski classes which were introduced in 1953, and ocean sailing classes which were introduced in 1964, have also aroused keen interest. The participants in the winter program are accompanied by their teachers, physical education teachers, and ski instructors. During the morning, regular classes are held; the afternoon is reserved for physical activities. Part of the expense is borne by the family, part by the state. Dr. Max Fourestier of Vanves has provided the leadership for these experimental programs.

The content of the required elementary and secondary school curriculum is also changing. Traditional gymnastics are retained, but there is now greater emphasis on sports. The schools are moving toward the harmonization of physical education, sports, and nature activities. The elementary program consists of postural gymnastics, functional gymnastics, natural exercises, and exercises leading up to sports, games, and track and field events. The secondary program is similar with the addition of rhythmics for girls and swimming where facilities are available. The physical education program is being enriched and expanded, but leaders feel that the schools should make better use of the half-days devoted to sports, place greater emphasis on training students for leisure activities, and draw more secondary school and university students into active sports participation.

Leisure was once a privilege reserved for the cultured elite in France. For the masses of workers and for children from lower economic groups, recreational opportunities are relatively recent. Despite the many deterrents to progress, the Ministry of Youth and Sports, in cooperation with the many private and public agencies, has done much to improve the leisure life of youth and adults. In addition to the physical activity programs that have been developed in the schools at all levels and in the armed services, programs have been developed by industrial firms and labor groups, religious and community youth organizations, vacation colonies, ski stations, and sports clubs. New recreation-oriented professions have been established. Young people are trained to serve as counsellors of popular education programs and supervisors of leisure time activities. Over 50,000 sport clubs have been formed in France which have issued over three million certificates of proficiency. The largest sport federations are those of soccer, skiing, and basketball, but tennis, swimming, cycling, judo, gymnastics, athletics, equestrian sports, volleyball, and team handball are also popular. Music, art, and other cultural pursuits have extensive organizations to promote them.

Today, young workers may participate in the sports programs that the law requires industrial enterprises to provide for apprentices, join sport clubs, attend boxing or football matches, or race through the countryside on their bicycles. Excitement runs high during the gruelling bicycle race, the *Tour de France*, and when France is playing for the European rugby title. During summer, vacationers pitch tents or live in youth hostels. During the winter, many of them take advantage of the low cost ski vacations which the government sponsors. Some youths participate in vacation tours or in work projects that the Ministry of Youth and Sports sponsors at home and abroad.

17

Physical Education
in
English Educational Nationalism

It seems incredible that the world's most powerful nation was a small country with few natural resources, ranking seventieth in size among world states and possessing two percent of the world's population. This is the story of England who started the Industrial Revolution in the eighteenth century and developed the richest manufacturing industry in the world. During the reign of Queen Victoria when "Britannia ruled the waves," England established an empire that, in 1900, encompassed one-fourth of the earth's land and one-fourth of its people. The twentieth century has been quite different, for England was hard hit by two world wars which cost 1,100,000 lives, while the British Empire has been steadily diminishing in size and influence. The Emipre was officially dissolved by the Statute of Westminster in 1931 and replaced by the British Commonweath of Nations. England suffered during the depression of the 1930s and again during the Battle of Britain in 1940–41 when the entire populace responded to Winston Churchill's eloquent call for "blood, toil, tears, and sweat" and the British stubbornly blocked Hitler's plans for world conquest.

In the quarter century since the Second World War, England has been a leading nation in trade and industry, but it is no longer a major military power. It has faced a series of economic crises brought on by its position at the hub of the sterling area, the role of sterling as a major trading currency, the lack of adequate domestic capital investment, the outmoded and inefficient trade union structure, and the decline of its major traditional industries. Despite England's unsuccessful efforts to join the Eureopean Common Market, it is still a rich nation, and Englishmen enjoy the benefits of increased affluence. Britain's stable political system goes hand in hand with a freedom of individual expression and action that is difficult to match. In recent years serious social problems have arisen which threaten the old order—racial segregation, juvenile delinquency, and the development of an adolescent subculture at variance with the values of society at large.

Historically dedicated to individuality and freedom, the British developed a decentralized type of school administration based largely on local and voluntary initiative. Before 1870, all English schools were private, religious, or charitable in nature. The poor who received any formal education attended the parish, "dame," or charity schools, many of them deplorable in character. The wealthy had tutors or paid fees to attend the preparatory and grammar schools. Some attended the famous public schools, such as Eton, Winchester, Harrow, and Rugby, which were actually exclusive private schools for upper-class children. The state eventually assumed some responsibility for education in 1833, without, however, displacing either private or church schools. The first step taken was token aid to existing institutions. Finally, the Education Act of 1870 decreed that locally elected boards of education should set up and manage elementary schools wherever the voluntary facilities were inadequate. Attendance was neither compulsory nor free until some years later.

The government was even more dilatory in providing support for secondary education. Gradually, however, elementary schools began to add extra years of instruction. About 1900, the state began to aid privately operated (secondary) grammar schools if they would reserve "free places" and scholarships for promising elementary pupils. After 1902, local authorities established their own grammar schools. Except for "free place" students, fees were exacted at almost all of these secondary institutions. As a result, many youths were excluded. Gradually, more "free places" were added, and the legal age for leaving school was raised.

The Education Act of 1944 pointed the way for all children to receive a secondary education, at least until the age of fifteen, through a tripartite system consisting of the secondary school for general, non-academic education, the grammar school for academic education leading to the university, and the technical secondary school for vocational training. However, the strong class lines in English society limited the value of the act, and the academic attainment still depended on one's socio-economic background. A more recent innovation has been to broaden the secondary modern school curriculum so that the academically-strong student can take a course the last two years leading to the external examination and admission to a university.[1] About 75 percent of secondary school pupils attend the modern school. Opportunities and facilities for higher

[1]Robert M. Marsh, "The Secondary Modern School in England," *Bulletin of the National Association of Secondary-School Principals* 41 (March 1965): 79–80.

education have been increased by the creation of twenty new colleges and universities since 1950.

Recreation opportunities, at least in an informal sense, have generally been available for all classes of people in England. The mild climate has encouraged outdoor pastimes and both the nobles and the commoners have traditionally been interested in sports. Between the fourteenth and sixteenth centuries, English kings issued repeated edicts forbidding certain sports so that citizens would devote themselves solely to the practice of archery for the defense of the nation. During Puritan times most sports were prohibited on moral grounds. The days of the Restoration signified a merry revival for pleasurable pastimes, and many towns had teams in sports, such as cricket. The English historian, George Trevelyan, described a team from Kent which had Lord Sackville as a member and a gardener as the captain. Trevelyan went on to observe: "If the French *noblesse* had been capable of playing cricket with their peasants, their chateaux would never have been burnt."[2]

The advent of the Industrial Revolution, however, radically changed the lives of the great mass of people who left their country and village life for the crowded city slums and factories. Laboring for twelve or sixteen hours a day even in childhood, lacking their customary rural recreations, and suffering from poverty and unsanitary conditions, the workers tended to sink into alcoholism and general physical and moral degradation. The demand for reform became so strong that social legislation was finally enacted. The vote was extended to new segments of society. Child labor laws were passed. Longer leisure hours were secured as well as increased recreational facilities. During the twentieth century, consistent efforts were made to provide universal public education, with modern physical education and recreational programs, as well as increased health and medical services. After 1950 the increased affluence was manifested in the growth of leisure opportunities available to everyone. The Englishman, with his traditional love of sport, turned even more to physical activity for his recreation.

The systematic physical exercises originating in Germany and Sweden in the post-Napoleonic period were early brought to England. Karl Völker, a pupil of Jahn, opened a gymnasium in London in 1825. A few years earlier British officers traveling in Switzerland observed the gymnastic training that Phokion Clias was giving to troops. They were so impressed that they invited him to London to institute this work. A few decades later, Archibald Maclaren (c. 1820–1884) received a similar request from the army. He was a Scotsman who had studied medicine, gymnastics, and fencing in Paris before becoming a pioneer in the development of physical education in England. Maclaren's manual, *A Military*

---

[2]George M. Trevelyan, *English Social History* (New York: Longmans, Green & Co. Ltd., 1942), p. 408.

System of Gymnastic Exercises for the Use of Instructors (1862), was adopted by the army, and his book, *System of Physical Education, Theoretical and Practical* (1869) is a classic in its field. Numerous Scandinavian and English pioneers also introduced innovations and reforms into modern British physical education.

A major development in the 1950s and 1960s was movement training. Influenced by Rudolf Laban's modern dance and movement analysis, certain women teachers applied dancelike techniques to gymnastic activities.[3] This eventually became known as modern educational gymnastics whose leading proponent was Ruth Morison. She wrote three books: *Educational Gymnastics* (1956), *Educational Gymnastics for Secondary Schools* (1960), and *A Movement Approach to Educational Gymnastics* (1969). The movement has not only affected British physical education, but it has had a substantial effect in the United States, Germany, and some other countries.

England's great contribution to world physical education has unquestionably been her sports and games. They were carried to all parts of the Empire and the world by military personnel, civil servants, public officials, businessmen, and students attending boarding schools and universities. Many countries sent observers to the English public schools to watch the boys at sports. An American historian of physical education, Fred Leonard, recognized England's preeminence in this field when he wrote: "In variety of sports cultivated, elaborate attention to details, and the perfection of play attained in games like cricket and football she was long without a rival."[4]

Aims of Education

English education generally has been free of the nationalistic philosophy of other countries because its insular position and strong navy have relieved the fear of invasion. Because of the decentralized nature of British education and the variety of schools, the English have formulated no official philosophy to be imposed on the schools. The Ministry of Education from time to time broadly defines the purpose of education, but teachers have considerable autonomy in determining their own goals and programs. During this century, the class consciousness of English education has gradually diminished. Elementary training, which once provided instruction in the three R's for poor children, has been transformed into a more vital

[3]Laban left Germany during the Nazi regime and came to England in 1936. After the war he and Lisa Ullmann founded their Art of Movement Studio in Manchester, which moved to Addlestone in 1953. It is now known as the Laban Art of Movement Centre.

[4]Fred E. Leonard and George B. Affleck, *A Guide to the History of Physical Education* (Philadelphia: Lea & Febiger, 1947), p. 202.

program. One publication in 1937 defined the function of the school "as being (1) to provide the kind of environment which is best suited to individual and social development; (2) to stimulate and guide healthy growth in this environment; (3) to enable children to acquire the habits, skills, knowledge, interests, and attitudes of mind which they will need for living a full and useful life; and (4) to set standards of behavior, effort, and attainment, by which they can measure their own conduct."[5]

The traditional aim of secondary education at the grammar schools and the public schools has been academic attainment and this is still true today. In addition, the public schools are concerned with social development directed toward the preservation of the class values of English society. The development of a more egalitarian secondary education than that created by the tripartite system has shifted emphasis away from academic instruction and towards the development of the individual and his social integration. The trend toward a common form of secondary education in Britain is creating a convergence of aims. The secondary modern school teacher must become "more aware of the intellectual dimensions of his task,"[6] and the grammar school teacher must become aware of the sociological dimensions of teaching.

Aims of Physical Education

The concerted effort to strengthen national unity, intensify patriotism and develop military fitness through physical education, as exhibited in continental countries of the nineteenth century, was less emphatic in England. In contrast, the British emphasized the cultivation of sound character, social qualities, and general physical fitness.

The Napoleonic wars did have their repercussions in England as is evidenced by the militaristic nature of both the Clias and Maclaren physical education programs. Nevertheless, these pioneer teachers both urged that gymnastic instruction should be extended to civilians as well as soldiers. Clias was convinced that gymnastic training, in addition to creating bodily efficiency, could also impart those moral qualities and social graces essential to a well-rounded personality. Maclaren believed that systematic exercise was necessary for civilian as well as army life. By constructing drills for the troops he expected to secure the bodily components most essential for soldiers—strength, mobility, dexterity, and stamina. But he contemplated a more extensive program that would provide gymnastics for all citizens rather than merely giving ". . . added strength to the strong,

[5]*Handbook of Suggestions for the Consideration of Teachers and Others Concerned in the Work of Public Elementary Schools* (London: H. M. Stationery Office, 1937).

[6]Eric Hoyle, *The Role of the Teacher* (London: Routledge & Kegan Paul Ltd., 1969), p. 16.

increased dexterity to the active, speed to the already fleet of foot. . . ."[7] Activities for nonmilitary men were to stress health. Maclaren believed that exercise was a necessary antidote for the ". . . long hours of work, late hours of rest, jaded frames, weary brains, jarring nerves"[8] of daily life.

Team games have long been traditional in British public schools. Though Wellington was supposed to have said that the battle of Waterloo was won on the playing fields of Eton, it is not to be inferred that schools were devoted to perfecting military skills. Rather, the public schools have always emphasized the socializing influence of games and the use of them to promote leadership, loyalty, cooperation, self-discipline, initiative, tenacity, and sportsmanship—all qualities needed in the administration of a great colonial empire. In the process of attaining these traits, nationalism is imbued in the boy. The totality of these traits have come to be accepted as the highest product of English character.

At the turn of the century, the Swedish system of gymnastics adopted by the British had a military bias, but gradually other objectives were added. A statement published in 1945 listed these aims:

> (a) Secure and maintain high standards of bodily health, physique, and vigour; (b) develop qualities of character, high social ideals and the team spirit, *e.g.*, hardihood, courage, perseverance, fair play and friendliness; (c) foster an appreciation of the joy of physical fitness; (d) cultivate quick and accurate co-ordination of thought and action; (e) develop easy, graceful bodily movement and poise; (f) develop general motor skill and specialized recreational and occupational skills; (g) help to correct bodily distortions due either to heredity or environment; (h) provide opportunities for self-expression and self-testing; (i) encourage the pursuit of wholesome leisure-time activities.[9]

Since World War II physical education has reflected the increased concern for personal and social development. As a nonexamination subject, physical education remains outside the mainstream of secondary education in England and has compensated by emphasizing social aims. But there is now a growing realization that physical education offers unique opportunities for individual personality development and new dimensions for social education. As summarized in a 1969 publication, the major objectives for physical education are "to develop normal physical growth,

[7]Archibald Maclaren, *A System of Physical Education, Theoretical and Practical,* 2d ed. (Oxford: Clarendon Press, 1885), p. 22.

[8]Ibid., p. 23.

[9]National Association of Organizers of Physical Education, *Physical Education: Its Aims, Scope and Organization* (Chelmsford, Essex: The Association, 1945), p. 5.

body control and fitness, personal skills, social accomplishments, and character training and social behavior."[10]

Promotion of Physical Education

The military events at the turn of the nineteenth century gave impetus to the establishment of gymnastic training for military men in many countries. Nachtegall in Denmark and Ling in Sweden found support for their programs from army circles. The English followed a similar pattern in 1822 when they invited Clias to establish gymnastic training for the military services. He was given the rank of captain and made superintendent of physical training in the royal military and naval academies. Following an injury, he retired in 1825 and returned to Switzerland. Clias stimulated a brief interest in gymnastics in London which was carried on by several others. Karl Völker operated a *Turnplatz* and was involved in the founding of the London Gymnastic Society.[11] Gustavus Hamilton and Signor Voarino promoted various exercises for girls and women, and both men wrote books.

About the middle of the nineteenth century, interest in gymnastics was revived when Archibald Maclaren, who had been operating a fencing school, opened a private gymnasium in Oxford in 1858. Two years later the army asked him to revise its physical training program. He trained a group of noncommissioned officers sent to him. After finishing their course, these young men returned to a new army gymnasium at Aldershot and created a normal school to train other military teachers of gymnastics. In this manner, Maclaren's system was introduced and carried out in the army. The Scotsman also urged that physical education should become a regular part of the school curriculum. Moreover, he argued, if the soldiers and school boys of England could benefit by regular gymnastic exercises, so too could the men in the factories and shops. Despite Maclaren's efforts on behalf of physical education, the schools and the army eventually turned to the Ling gymnastics.

SWEDISH GYMNASTICS: While Maclaren was carrying out his work, envoys from Sweden were making great claims for the value of their exercises. The Ling system was introduced to Britain by Lientenant Govert Indebetou in 1838, by Lieutenant C. Ehrenhoff in the early 1840s and especially by Carl A. Georgii in 1850. All were graduates of the Central Institute of Gymnastics of Sweden, and all established private schools in

---

[10]International Council on Health, Physical Education, and Recreation, *Physical Education in the School Curriculum*. ICHPER International Questionnaire Report, pt. 1, 1967–68 revision (Washington, D.C.: ICHPER, 1969), p. 27.

[11]"Prospectus of the London Gymnastic Society," *American Journal of Education* 1 (August 1826): 502–506.

London. Georgii's classes were in operation from 1850 to 1877. In 1878, the London School Board invited Concordia Löfving, a graduate of Central Institute of Stockholm, to give gymnastics courses to teachers. She was succeeded after three years by another graduate of the Central Institute, Martina Bergman (later Madame Bergman Österberg), who also served as superintendent of physical education in girls and infant schools of London. Similarly, Captain J. D. Haasum initiated teacher training for men. These pioneers largely provided the leadership for the gymnastic system that gradually pushed military drill out of the curriculum and was later officially adopted by the English authorities.

Although there was an attempt to make physical education compulsory in the elementary schools in 1885, it was not until the twentieth century that real expansion occurred. The Swedish system of exercises was adopted by the navy in 1903, the schools in 1904, and the army in 1906. The Boer War of 1899–1902 drew attention to the serious deterioration of the British physique. As a result, several commissions were appointed to study means of improving the physical condition of the nation. Following the recommendations of these commissions, the Board of Education published the first official *Syllabus of Physical Exercises* in 1904. It was largely based upon the Swedish system. This syllabus was subsequently revised in 1905, 1909, 1919, and 1933, carrying the principle of freedom and enjoyment in gymnastics further and increasing the emphasis on games and athletics.

SCHOOL AND COLLEGE PHYSICAL EDUCATION SINCE 1944:   The dominance of the Swedish system was finally broken by the Education Act of 1944 and postwar conditions. Highly regimented exercises with a therapeutic core became inappropriate to the needs of schoolchildren and were out of keeping with the prevailing educational climate. Physical education was put under the control of the Ministry of Education and removed from the control of the Chief Medical Officer of Health. This change cleared the way for an official move from a health-and-posture-based syllabus to an education-based one. The 1933 *Syllabus of Physical Training for Schools* was replaced by *Physical Education in the Primary School*, a two-part publication prepared by the Department of Education and Science. Part One was entitled *Moving and Growing* (1952) and Part Two was called *Planning the Programme* (1953). The movement approach thereby obtained a foothold, gaining stimulus from the newly-devised forms of apparatus based upon wartime obstacle pieces, the ideas of Laban, and the desire of various women physical educators to explore new principles of movement.

Even today in England there is no compulsory physical education in the schools nor is it an examination subject for a general Certificate of Education or university matriculation. Nevertheless, physical education is universally taught and has a significant role in the modern curriculum. Infant school children (five to seven years) generally have two short lessons a day. In the primary schools physical education is usually taught daily by the classroom teacher. In the state secondary schools regular physical education instructors or at least some classroom teachers with specialist training are employed. For both boys and girls four periods a week are allotted to physical education; two of these are given over for sports and games. Pupils in cities may be transported by bus to the nearest playing fields. One sports area in London covers 132 acres.[12] There is a tendency in the grammar schools to allow academic work for examinations to press physical education activities out of the time table. Secondary schools are organized into houses which serve as units for intramural competition and an overall league championship. On Saturday mornings interschool competition, based on age groups, is held in rugby, soccer, field hockey, track and field, cricket, basketball, and swimming. There may be five or six teams in each sport from one school. Girls compete in net ball, rounders, field hockey, tennis, swimming, cricket, and track and field.[13]

In most of the public schools considerable importance is attached to team games. The first cricket match between Eton and Harrow occurred in 1805. By the mid-nineteenth century competition in cricket, rowing, track and field, and soccer were regular events. Thomas Arnold and Edward Thring of Rugby and Uppingham were headmasters who made organized games compulsory as a means of training character. Today games are conducted two to four afternoons a week on extensive facilities. Eton, for example, has thirty soccer and rugby pitches or fields. Other accommodations are provided for track and field, swimming, fives, squash, and tennis. One of the masters with a sports background, probably an Oxford or Cambridge "Blue," supervises the program. Some schools have recently organized a department of physical education with a qualified teacher in charge, who may help with the sports also. Fencing, boxing, and gymnastics are often handled by retired noncommissioned military officers. The first gymnasium was built at Uppingham in 1859, but gymnastics and systematic physical training have never approached sports in their acceptance or recognition. The public schools and games program indirectly inculcates a national spirit. Boys from all parts of the country and the Commonwealth become acquainted with the athletic prowess and governmental services rendered by famous "old boys" who have helped to make school tradition and British history.

[12]Peter C. McIntosh, "Health, Physical Education, and Recreation in England," in C. Lynn Vendien and John E. Nixon, eds., *The World Today in Health, Physical Education, and Recreation* (Englewood Cliffs, N. J.: Prentice-Hall, Inc., 1968), pp. 163–65.

[13]Michael Ellis, "Physical Education in Great Britain," in William Johnson ed., *Physical Education Around the World*, Monograph no. 1 (Indianapolis, Indiana: Phi Epsilon Kappa, 1966), p. 5.

The county colleges that provide compulsory part-time studies for young workers are expected to promote a strong physical education program. These publicly supported institutions offer classes one day a week, or two half-days, to people under eighteen years of age not receiving full-time education elsewhere.[14] The organizers of the county college movement have suggested that one and a half of the eight periods in the day should be devoted to physical education and that participation in voluntary and weekend activities should also be encouraged.

Only one university, Birmingham, has any required physical education. A one-year requirement was instituted there in 1940 in a wartime environment to develop physical fitness, and it has remained ever since. Originally, the gymnasiums of many universities were supervised by an Organizer. The modern practice is to have a department of physical education, although the program is mainly recreational. Each of the thirty-two colleges at Oxford and the twenty-three at Cambridge has its own facilities. For intramural and extramural competition the organizing, scheduling, financing, and coaching is done mainly by the students. A university will be represented by four or five teams in each sport who play other university teams, sometimes before only a handful of spectators. Practice sessions, once casual and informal affairs, have become more formalized and are conducted by specialist coaches. The traditional concept of the amateur sportsman is still very strong in England, and there is little of the attitudes and practices which characterize big-time college athletics in the United States.

EXPANSION OF FACILITIES: Since 1900 there has been a continuous increase in provisions for physical education. The National Playing Fields Association, started in 1925, has raised about five million dollars by donations for the construction of play fields and playgrounds. Independent schools, many of which were built when land was readily available, often have better sports grounds than state schools. The Education Act of 1944 required local authorities to provide facilities for physical education and recreation. Progress in facilities suffered a serious setback during the war due to the destruction of schools by bombing and the military take-over of buildings and playing fields. Under the Camps Act of 1939 a number of permanent, hutted camps were built in the country to accommodate children evacuated from the cities to escape German bombing attacks. After the war, urban local authorities sent children to these shelters for a brief outing each year. Although the regular academic work was carried on during the camping period, much greater attention was given to outdoor activities. In spite of these efforts a recent study showed that only thirteen

[14]Ministry of Education, *Youth's Opportunity* (London: His Majesty's Stationery Office, 1946), p. 30.

percent of the schools in problem areas of England had good outdoor space and seventy-seven percent had less than half the prescribed acreage.[15]

In response to the need for swimming facilities, the London County Council has experimented with construction of an inexpensive indoor pool made of wood and covered with plastic which can be put up in the classroom. A gymnastics aid is the Cave-Southampton apparatus which can be swung out away from the wall to permit hanging, climbing, vaulting, heaving, balancing, jumping, and other fundamental movements.[16]

TEACHER TRAINING: Teacher training was first offered in Britain by Maclaren about 1862. This work was primarily for military men. About a decade later, courses in Swedish gymnastics for civilians were initiated for both women and men. Mme. Österberg started a Training College for Teachers of Physical Education at Hampstead in 1885 which ten years later became Dartford College. She served as director for thirty years and trained hundreds of women in Swedish gymnastics. Many Scandinavian leaders such as K. A. Knudsen, H. G. Junker, and Braae-Hansen were also brought to England to conduct classes for teachers. For a long time the most common qualifications held by physical educators were either a diploma from a Scandinavian school, experience in instruction in the army, or knowledge gained in short courses in England.

The linking of an academic background to the professional training of physical educators occurred with the opening of the Carnegie College of Physical Education in 1933 and Loughborough College two years later. Carnegie gave a one-year specialist course in physical education for those students who were graduates of either a university or a training college. Loughborough offered a three-year specialist program similar to that of the women's colleges.

The McNair report in 1944 urged that the training of physical education teachers should take place within the general context of teacher training. One-year specialist courses for men were started at three general colleges and the women's colleges were brought into the new university Institutes of Education. In 1960 the normal two-year period of general teacher preparation was increased to three years and, in order to cater to the subsequent supplementary courses, a number of general colleges were designated as "Wing" colleges and organized specialist courses in physical education. University graduates can gain a training in physical education by completing a one-year postgraduate course at Loughborough and Carnegie (for men), or Chelsea (for women). The Robbins report in 1963 recommended four-year courses at training colleges (hence to be called

[15]Sir Alec Clegg, "Physical Education: Who is Against?" *Education* 126 (30 July 1965): 252.
[16]M. L. Howell and M. L. Van Vliet, *Physical Education and Recreation in Europe* (Ottawa: The Fitness and Amateur Sports Directorate, 1965), pp. 64–65.

Colleges of Education) leading to a Bachelor of Education degree. Most of these colleges offer physical education as an area of study. The first of these students graduated in 1968.

British universities are still reluctant to give degrees in physical education, but Birmingham University took the initiative in 1946 and provided a general arts degree with physical education as one of the subjects. In 1969 the University of Leeds launched a one-year postgraduate Master of Arts course in physical education and the University of Loughborough a one-year Master's course in response to increasing demands for training managers for sport centers. As yet there is little high level research in physical education in England. Degrees awarded for original work at the doctoral level have to be conducted in related areas of study.

The leading professional organization for physical education teachers in England is The Physical Education Association of Great Britain and Northern Ireland. It started in 1899 and was originally restricted to teachers of Swedish gymnastics and women. For many years it was known as the Ling Physical Education Association, and it has played an active role in the growth of the profession. Two of its official publications were the periodicals, *The Leaflet* and *Physical Education*, which merged in 1970 to become the *British Journal of Physical Education.*

ORGANIZATION OF SPORTS: Since the earliest time in England, a great many informal agencies have provided recreation for the general public. Sport associations began to appear in the nineteenth century as follows: riflery (1860), association football (soccer) (1863), field hockey (1866), yachting (1875), cycling (1878), and athletics (track and field) (1880). Many new governing bodies have since been formed. The amateur championship competitions sponsored by most of these governing bodies have a colorful history. Ancient fairs often had races, wrestling matches, and boxing bouts on their programs. Formal athletic meets (track and field events) sprang up in many parts of the country by the mid-nineteenth century. In 1864, the first two large-scale meetings were held: the Civil Service Sports Meeting and the Oxford and Cambridge Sports Meeting. Amateur championships were held in London in 1866 and thereafter for fourteen years. It is interesting to note that many early associations often disqualified men as amateurs if they had been employed for wages as a mechanic, artisan, laborer, or had engaged in any menial duty. By 1900, a number of clubs had opened their ranks to all men irrespective of class or occupation. Today, representatives of sports associations participate in a multitude of local games, as well as national and international events. They have participated in the Olympics since their reestablishment in 1896 and in the British Empire Games since they were first held in 1930.

The various sports-governing bodies keep close contact with educational and recreational agencies and constantly try to capture the interest of schoolchildren. They schedule national and international championship competitions, formulate uniform rules, try to improve standards of performance, hold demonstrations and lectures, issue books, pamphlets, and films on their specialties, arrange training courses for coaches and youth leaders, award badges and certificates to qualified coaches, and select participants for the Olympic Games.

The orginal organization of sports along social class lines is evidenced by the numerous single-activity sports clubs which owe little intersport or community allegiance. It is most obvious at the national level where the 41 national governing bodies work autonomously to meet their own needs and show no spirit of cooperation.[17] Many sport associations adhere to the middle-class tradition that "those who play should pay."

The status of coaches outside of schools is generally low. Traditionally sports were largely run by honorary officials and coaching was usually done by amateurs. In 1947 a policy change occurred by the decision to appoint national coaches with 80 percent of their salaries coming from the Ministry of Education. Geoffrey Dyson received the first post in track and field. However, most coaching help still comes from people who have received a certificate by completing a course offered by a governing body at a sports center.

RECREATION: Early developments in recreation for youths were initiated by voluntary bodies after 1900. Sir Robert Baden-Powell, an Army officer, outlined his idea for a scouting program in 1902. A few years later, he and his sister helped to organize the Girl Guides. The YMCA and YWCA, both of which began in England in the mid-nineteenth century, also began to devote greater attention to recreation for young people. The Juvenile Delinquency Report of 1920 suggested that boys and girls leaving school became better citizens if they were members of some club or youth organization. Eventually the Youth Service was created as an educational agency concerned with leisure activities and the citizenship training of youths.

The British system of organization of recreation is quite haphazard and lacking in uniformity in contrast to some of the highly centralized European plans. The leaders of British physical education have stated:

> It may fail to show the spectacular results of the government-controlled schemes operating in other countries, but our peculiar British patchwork quilt of sports organizations, although perhaps the despair of the grand planner, provides the surest guarantee that our love of sport will never be made a political weapon capable of being misused if its control fell into the wrong hands.[18]

[17]The Wolfenden Committee on Sport, *Sport and the Community* (London: The Central Council of Physical Recreation, 1960), p. 12.

[18]G. A. McPartlin, "Developing Sport in Great Britain," *Physical Recreation* 1 (April–June 1949): 5.

Some order has been maintained by the work of one major coordinating body, the Central Council of Physical Recreation (CCPR). This group was founded in 1935 as the Central Council of Recreative Physical Training by two organizations interested in physical culture—the Ling Physical Education Association and the National Association of Organizers and Lecturers in Physical Education. It is a voluntary organization whose purpose is "to encourage the development of all forms of games, sports, outdoor activities, and dancing as part of post-school recreation."[19] The CCPR is not directly concerned with the provision of facilities. It has received partial financial help from the national government since 1937. In the year 1965–66, for example, the government gave one million dollars to the Council which raised a similar amount on its own through voluntary contributions and fees for services rendered. The scope of the CCPR is revealed in the fact that in 1966 it consisted of 212 organizations and 80 individual members and promoted nearly 50 activities.

The Central Council of Physical Recreation is a servicing, advisory, and stimulating body. It employs 50 full-time representatives (not coaches) who are distributed in nine regional offices. Their general functions are as follows:

1. Introduce beginners to sport and outdoor activities.
2. Stimulate interest in improving performance.
3. Advise on training and recreative matters.
4. Arrange conferences and develop cooperative efforts between various agencies, particularly in providing facilities and bettering technical skill.
5. Assist in the training of leaders, coaches, and referees.[20]

The CCPR operates three National Sport Centers. The first was established at the historic Bisham Abbey on the Thames river in 1946, and it emphasizes river sports such as rowing, sailing, and canoeing. Subsequent centers were developed at Lilleshall (1951) and Crystal Palace. The latter opened in 1964 and is by far the most elaborate as it provides new facilities for track and field, soccer, and cricket, plus a sports hall, three swimming pools, and a dormitory. The cost of seven million dollars was paid by the London County Council. The Central Council also conducts a National Mountain Center at Plas y Brenin in North Wales and a National Sailing Center at Cowes.

The CCPR is cooperation with other recreational agencies does outstanding work in training part-time recreational instructors. Hundreds of local, regional, and national courses are offered during the evenings, week-

[19]Geoffrey H. G. Dyson, "The Development of Sport in England through the Central Council of Physical Recreation," *Journal of the Canadian Association for Health, Physical Education, and Recreation* 33 (October–November, 1966): 6.
[20]Ibid., pp. 6, 32.

ends, and holidays. Often athletes of national repute are recruited to teach. To establish some standard of qualification for nonprofessional physical education personnel, the CCPR developed the National Test for Leaders of Physical Recreation in 1940. This proved to be an effective incentive for raising teaching standards. Among other activities the Council arranges displays, lectures, demonstration classes, films, competitions, sports days, youth rallies, sports-training holidays, physical education festivals, Fitness Weeks, and Sports Weeks. Many handbooks and pamphlets are published by the CCPR as well as an official magazine, the quarterly *Physical Recreation.* To encourage physical recreation in industry, the CCPR sends representatives to give advice on programs, to promote work-time classes, to assist with organization of the leisure-time activities of employees, and to give guidance on construction of facilities. The welfare departments of many industrial concerns have sponsored amateur rugby teams, cricket elevens, and track teams for many years.

The Central Council appointed a committee headed by Sir John Wolfenden which reported the need for a sports development council in 1960. Five years later the newly elected Labor Government established the United Kingdom Sports Council "to advise the Government on matters relating to the development of amateur sport and physical recreation services and to foster cooperation amongst the statutory authorities and the voluntary organizations concerned."[21] The establishment of the Sports Council marks a change in principle: if sport is to play its full role in the life of the nation, then a planning and coordinating structure is necessary. The work of the national Sports Council is carried out by eleven regional sports councils who coordinate facilities planning on a regional basis. There has also been a steady growth of sports advisory councils at the county and borough level.

England is the home of the Outward Bound program featuring vigorous, tough outdoor activities for young men and women. Important in this development was Kurt Hahn, a German school teacher, who came to Britain in 1933 and founded the Gordonstoun School in Scotland. He instigated a badge system for successful achievement. In 1941 he started the Aberdovey Outward Bound Sea School and nine years later the Eskdale Outward Bound Mountain School. Four additional schools have since been opened and they run a total of sixty courses per year.[22]

One of Hahn's students at Gordonstoun, the Duke of Edinburgh, was influenced by this experience and initiated the Duke of Edinburgh's Award Scheme in 1956. A similar plan for girls began 2 years later, and by 1966 participation exceeded 100,000 boys and girls from 14 to 20. Gold, silver,

[21]Central Office of Information, *The Sports Council* (London: Her Majesty's Stationery Office, 1966), p. 8.
[22]Peter C. McIntosh, *Physical Education in England Since 1800* (London: G. Bell and Sons, Ltd., 1968), pp. 264–65.

and bronze medals are given to boys for performance in service, expedition, pursuits, and fitness; to girls for design for living, interests, adventure, and service.

Another notable achievement in England has been the Stoke Mandeville games for the severely handicapped. These games were first organized in 1948 by a neurosurgeon, Dr. Ludwig Guttmann, at the Spinal Injuries Center in Stoke Mandeville. Twenty-two handicapped veterans competed in archery at the same time that the Olympic games were going on in London. More sports were added each year with other countries invited to send their players. In 1957 there were 360 contestants from 24 countries, and it has continued to grow.

Program and Methods of Physical Education

The traditional love of vigorous outdoor games and sports, deeply ingrained in English character, strongly influences the physical education curriculum. Previous chapters traced the early development of some pastimes that have since evolved into popular modern games. Cricket stems from crude ancient games in which curved sticks and balls were used. With the passage of time, the rough game of Elizabethan football has been refined into association football and rugby. The origin of rugby is engraved on a tablet at Rugby School which reads as follows: "This stone commemorates the exploit of William Webb Ellis who, with a fine disregard for the rules of football as played in his time, first took the ball in his arms and ran with it, thus originating the distinctive feature of the Rugby game A.D. 1823." Soccer has become identified with the working classes, and rugby is associated with the upper classes. Legalized gambling on soccer matches amounted to an estimated $469 million for the 1967–68 season. A popular game for girls, netball, is a modification of basketball which was brought to England by Mme. Österberg. The Dartford students and an instructor, Mary Hankinson, developed the netball rules which prohibit dribbling and allow uncontested shots at the basket which has no backboard.

Although games and sports were generally native, gymnastics originated on the Continent. The exercises of GutsMuths and Jahn were both taught by Clias and Völker. Clias invented an apparatus called the triangle which was essentially a movable horizontal bar suspended by ropes from a swivel support in the ceiling. Voarino highly recommended it for his students.[23] Maclaren, who had studied various systems in Europe, developed his eclectic system. He was a research pioneer who photographed and measured height, weight, chest, forearm, bicep, calf, and thigh to de-

[23]Signor Voarino, *A Second Course of Calisthenic Exercises* (London: James Ridgway, 1828), p. 93.

termine the appropriate exercise for the individual. He arranged a gradual progression of exercises for the standard pieces of apparatus. He felt that games and sports alone could not provide the uniform and harmonious development of the entire body. Maclaren's work had a considerable influence on Dudley Sargent in the United States.[24]

During the later nineteenth century, physical education, when it did exist in the lower schools, consisted principally of singing games and action songs, or "drills" with tambourines, hoops, wands, dumbbells, and clubs. After the Education Act of 1870, it was suggested that "physical drill" for schools should be comprised of those parts of the *Field Exercise Book* under the heads of Squad or Recruit Company Drill. In 1890, the term "physical exercises" was substituted for that of "drill," but the army handbook still provided teachers with their basic activities.

The Swedish system of Ling dominated English physical education for several decades after 1900, although gradually, a more informal and recreative approach was used. Teachers sought to make the exercises more dynamic, adventurous, and exhilarating. Organized games were permitted during the regular school schedules as early as 1906, and many teachers used their own time and money to treat their students to the pleasures of soccer, track and field, and cricket. Today, games are an integral part of the program. An effort is made to develop leadership by giving older pupils a chance to organize, coach, and umpire games.

Modern educational gymnastics evolved out of Laban's prewar experimentation with modern dance in which he identified the four movement principles of time, weight, space, and flow. After the war, many teachers began to apply Laban's movement principles to gymnastics. A division developed between modern dance and educational gymnastics because proponents of the latter brought in apparatus work which the dance movement purists rejected. Ruth Morison regards educational dance and educational gymnastics as separate areas, but feels that they complement each other and that both should be in the school curriculum.[25]

Modern educational gymnastics is an integral part of the primary school physical education program and is conducted by both men and women teachers. The material for the program may be described in three categories:

1. Compensatory movements: leg, trunk, and arm and shoulder girdle.
2. General activities: walking, running, skipping, jumping, leap-frog, through-vault, crouch jumps, catsprings, rolls, handstands, cart-

[24]Bruce L. Bennett, "The Life of Dudley Allen Sargent, M.D., and His Contributions to Physical Education" (Doctoral dissertation, University of Michigan, 1947), pp. 34–35.

[25]Ruth Morison, *A Movement Approach to Educational Gymnastics* (London: J. M. Dent and Sons Ltd., 1969), p. 3.

wheels, balancing, pulling, climbing, swinging, contests, throwing, bouncing, hitting, kicking, heading, and aiming.
3. Games: chasing and dodging, races, and group.[26]

In her 1969 book, Morison outlines the program for educational gymnastics in this manner:

A. General management of the body in:
  1. Actions emphasizing locomotion:
    a. transference of weight
    b. travelling
    c. flight
  2. Actions emphasizing balance:
    a. weight bearing
    b. balancing skills
    c. actions of "arriving"
    d. on and off balance
B. Specific control of movement in:
  1. Bodily aspects of action
  2. Dynamic aspects of action
  3. Spatial aspects of action
C. Handling (of the apparatus)
D. Relationships (partner and group work)[27]

Essential to the full implementation of these activities are all kinds of equipment and apparatus. Bats, hoops, bean bags, ropes, poles, skittles, canes, and a variety of balls are necessary pieces of small equipment. The more fixed or heavy apparatus includes nets, poles, planks, ladders, ropes, and anything else that will support the weight of children. The teacher tries to see that *all* children are engaged in movement. Children are encouraged to learn through exploration, repetition, and creation in an informal structured setting. They are expected to learn from other children as well as from the teacher who makes sure that "progress is neither forced or checked."[28]

In addition to educational gymnastics, primary school children also have games, dancing, and, if possible, swimming. Boys may be introduced to soccer and cricket and the girls to netball. Teachers often organize competitive games, swimming galas, and expeditions for their pupils on weekends and during school holidays.[29]

[26]Department of Education and Science, *Planning the Programme* (London: Her Majesty's Stationery Office, 1953), p. 33.
[27]Morison, *A Movement Approach to Educational Gymnastics*, p. 20.
[28]Department of Education and Science, *Planning the Programme*, p. 11.
[29]International Council on Health, Physical Education, and Recreation, *Physical Education in the School Curriculum*, p. 28.

At the secondary school level, girls continue to have modern educational dance and gymnastics, with the addition of national and ballroom dancing, track and field, tennis, rounders, and field hockey. Boys have gymnastic activities for muscular development, weight training, and circuit training. The variety of sports participation in the weekly double period will depend on the availability of staff and facilities for soccer, rugby, track and field, Olympic gymnastics, tennis, field hockey, fencing, badminton, rowing, sailing, and trampoline work.

A unique English contribution to programs of physical education is circuit training. This idea was first put into practice at Leeds University in 1953 by Graham T. Adamson. Circuit training is directed at improving muscular strength, power, and circulo-respiratory endurance by progressive loading based on the individual's work rate. The student does a specific activity at each of nine or ten stations within a designated time limit. Performance demands are increased as fitness develops.[30] Circuit training is popular for the older secondary school boys, college men, and in some of the sports associations. It has also been carried abroad to several other countries, including Canada and the United States.

Although the public schools educate only a small percentage of English youth, their strong team-games program has had a decided influence on British life. When the state-supported schools were established, they also adopted organized games. Today, in the fall term, these traditional schools play rugby, association football, hockey, and tennis; in the spring, they take part in cricket, rowing, swimming, and tennis. Sports such as fives, rackets, fencing, wrestling, squash racquets, many events of track and field, and cross-country running are performed throughout the year. Some gymnastics and military training may be given.

An obvious development since 1945 has been the growth of participation in outdoor educational activities in schools and the community. Derbyshire was the first Education Authority to open an Outdoor Pursuits Centre in 1951, and twenty-two other authorities have followed suit. Many schools now take their children to outdoor education or mountain centers for weeks at a time, often during the holidays where they can enjoy camping, canoeing, sailing, rock climbing, hiking, swimming, and expedition work. These activities have recently found great favor among the populace at large and have added a new dimension to British recreational life.

[30]Graham T. Adamson, "Circuit Training," *Physical Educator* 13 (May 1956): 68–69.

18

Physical Education
in
Soviet Educational Nationalism

Sprawling across Asia and extending well into Europe, the Union of Soviet Socialist Republics covers one-sixth of the world's territory. Between the frozen tundra of the Arctic and the cotton belt of the south, more than 244,000,000 people speaking over 150 languages and representing 169 ethnic groups claim citizenship in the fifteen Soviet Republics. Within a few decades these peoples have experienced a dramatic transformation of their ways of living and thinking. Their nation in the Tsarist days was a backward monarchy on the fringes of European politics. They have seen it rise to the position of a military, political, and industrial power in world affairs.

In the chaotic and turbulent days following the October Revolution in 1917, the Communists began to attack the problems of building a new society. They charged that the existing social and economic injustices resulted from weaknesses in the capitalistic system. Therefore, capitalism, individualism, and nationalism were to be destroyed and a collectivistic, classless, and international society was to be established. The individual citizen of old Russia had to be adjusted to the new society. He had to be completely merged into a collectivistic culture and molded to think and act in communal, rather than individualistic, patterns.

The Communists desired to create a union of workers of all countries in the Socialist World Soviet Republic. Communist principles would establish a society in which all men would become so cooperative and brotherly that state rule would "wither way." The utopian goal was envisioned as an era of unrestricted abundance when true Communism will be achieved, and the slogan of Marx, "from each according to his ability, to each according to his need," will be realized. Until then, the state was to be directed by a dictatorship of the proletariat under the control of the Communist Party.

At present, the USSR is a socialist state which, according to the constitution, is dominated by the axiom, "from each according to his ability, to each according to his work." This, however, is considered as a temporary step.

The USSR, constitutionally, is a federation of Soviet Socialist Republics, the largest of which is the Russian Socialist Federated Soviet Republic. Politically, the people are organized into a series of local councils, or soviets, which elect higher district and regional representatives, culminating in the Supreme Soviet. However, the real governing power on all levels is in the hands of the Communist Party, which has an elaborate organization of its own.

In the power struggle which followed Lenin's death in 1924, Josef Stalin emerged victorious and ruled the Soviet Union with an iron hand until his death in 1953. On the domestic front he concentrated his efforts on industrializing the country and collectivizing agriculture. In foreign affairs he sought to guarantee the security of the Soviet Union. He made a number of agreements with capitalist nations and pursued vigorous anti-Fascist policy. The USSR even joined the League of Nations in 1934. Stalin's success in mobilizing the Soviet people to smash the German invasion during World War II was a major contribution to the Allied victory, and the USSR emerged from the war as a leading world power. Stalin solidified his country's position by establishing the satellite nations behind the Iron Curtain which consisted of Poland, Hungary, Romania, Bulgaria, Czechoslovakia, East Germany, Albania, and Yugoslavia. The last two countries were able to break away from Soviet rule, but revolutions in Hungary and Czechoslovakia were crushed by Soviet troops. The early Communist hope of an international uprising of workers against their capitalistic oppressors was abandoned in the 1950s, and the policy of peaceful coexistence was inaugurated by Nikita Khrushchev. This policy was also undoubtedly influenced by the nuclear stalemate which existed. Under Khrushchev and his successors, Leonid Brezhnev and Aleksei Kosygin, life for the Soviet people improved with increased production of consumer goods and some easing of censorship and oppression by the government. A strong spirit of nationalism came out of the Second World War which was heightened by Soviet scientific successes in developing nuclear weapons and in orbiting the first man around the earth.

The Soviet Union was slower than most European nations in developing a modern national system of education. Although the foundations were laid in the eighteenth century, educational progress in a feudal society was slow. The schools of Tsarist Russia were based upon class distinction, the instruction offered was very academic and formal, and the nation had a very high degree of illiteracy although much improvement occurred in the twenty years before 1914.

After the Revolution, the Communists worked to establish a universal, free elementary school system to wipe out the illiteracy of the workers and peasants. Education was to become a means of securing Communism against elements of the pre-Revolutionary society. Polytechnical or vocational education was especially encouraged in the 1920s as a necessary phase of industrializing the country. In the 1930s, under Stalin, schools began to emphasize mathematics and science in order to meet the need for scientists.[1] Soviet scientific successes in the space race in the 1950s caused considerable consternation among other countries, especially in the United States. By the mid-1960s eight years of schooling were required, and the general level of education in the USSR was comparable to most western countries. Soviet education has produced a citizenry dedicated to serving and preserving the state.

Physical education before 1917 existed only in a very limited form and sports participation was largely the prerogative of the wealthy class. Morton estimated that not more than fifty thousand people out of a hundred million were involved.[2] But this situation was completely changed after 1917. The function of physical education in a Communist society was stated in 1925 by a Party decree as follows:

> Physical culture must be considered not only from the standpoint of physical education and health and as an aspect of the cultural, economic and military training of youth (the sport of rifle markmanship and others), but also as one of the methods of educating the masses (in as much as physical culture develops will power and builds up endurance, teamwork, resourcefulness and other valuable qualities), and in addition, as a means of rallying the broad masses of workers and peasants around the various Party, soviet, and trade union organizations, through which the masses of workers and peasants are to be drawn into social and political activity.[3]

The Party made the resolution in 1948 for all organizations to take steps "to insure a rise in Soviet athletic records so that within the next few years Soviet athletes may beat world records in all major sports."[4]

Two principles which underlie the whole Soviet system of physical education are *massovost* (mass participation) and *masterstvo* (profi-

[1]Robert Ulich, *The Education of Nations* (Cambridge, Mass.: Harvard University Press, 1967), pp. 264–71.
[2]Henry W. Morton, *Soviet Sport* (New York: Collier Books, 1963), p. 156.
[3]John N. Washburn, "Sport as a Soviet Tool," *Foreign Affairs* 34 (April 1956): 490. Copyrighted by the Council on Foreign Relations, Inc., New York.
[4]*Kultura i Zhizn*, 11 January 1949, quoted in Morton, *Soviet Sport*, p. 80.

ciency), and their application has produced phenomenal results. The direction and development of physical education in the Soviet Union have been an integral part of the total indoctrination planned by Party leaders. As a result, sports permeates the whole of Soviet culture and society.

The theory of Soviet physical education is based in large part on the teachings of P. F. Lesgaft (1837–1909) and Ivan Pavlov (1849–1936). Lesgaft stated that all life phenomena can be explained in environmental terms and that heredity was unimportant. He believed that physical exercise improved the intellectual processes and felt that people should be able to isolate and consciously control specific body movements and then apply them to any practical activity. Lesgaft was critical of foreign systems of gymnastics. The physiologist, Pavlov, declared that exercise was important for improving the functioning of the central nervous system and produced physiological functioning in general. Exercise was also conducive to a cheerful mind.[5]

Aims of Education

Under the Tsar, education existed for the elite and its aim was to produce "orthodoxy, autocracy, and nationalism."[6] From 1895 to 1917 an effort was made to provide some technical education to supply workers for new industries, but national illiteracy was still widespread.

Communist education has been guided by Marxist-Leninist philosophy combined with a desire for national expansion and scientific development. Ulich identified five basic principles of Soviet education:

1. The individual is always part of the social organism which is the state. Man is interpreted as a materialistic and collectivistic being.
2. Children are to be trained as fighters, pioneers, or warriors. This is done by encouraging physical culture, self-discipline, courage, and the capacity for resisting adversity and overcoming obstacles.
3. Education is centralized and controlled by the Party even though the individual republics may be granted administrative power.
4. Labor is central to education. Schools should be closely connected with industry and agriculture.
5. The teaching of science and a materialist atheism is stressed which denies the practice of religion and the institution of the church.[7]

A statement of purpose was given by the All-Union Komsomol Central Committee in 1959: "The main task of the school is to prepare the

[5]Morton, *Soviet Sport*, pp. 113–16.
[6]Gusta Singer, "Health, Physical Education, and Recreation in Communist States," in C. Lynn Vendien and John E. Nixon, eds., *The World Today in Health, Physical Education, and Recreation* (Englewood Cliffs, N.J.: Prentice-Hall, Inc., 1968), p. 352.
[7]Ulich, *The Education of Nations*, pp. 280–84.

upcoming generation for life, for useful labor, to inspire in youth a deep respect for the principles of socialist society."[8]

Soviet youths are trained to work unceasingly for the fulfillment of state goals. The willing subordination of self and the supreme readiness to serve the socialist cause is the basic quality of Soviet patriotism. These goals are also attained through an extensive program of adult education and the organization of leisure time by the government for useful and socially-approved purposes.

Aims of Physical Education

In Tsarist days physical education and sports participation existed mainly as a leisure-time activity for the wealthy. In the years following the 1917 Revolution, leaders of the new government were first concerned with military training as they sought to preserve their regime's very existence and to defend a country which has the longest frontier in the world. During the 1920s physical education became part of the movement toward mass education and collectivism. Emphasis was placed on mass activity, team competition, and group life. There was official disapproval of individual excellence and record-breaking performances. As the Soviet Union worked hard to develop its industrial potential, the health and fitness of the workers was considered by Party leaders to be a significant factor in raising labor productivity. Workers were told that it was their patriotic duty to be strong and to turn out more goods and products for the benefit of the state. Sports and physical education were also the educational means for building a new society and for attracting citizens into Party-sponsored activities.

Thus, up to the time of World War II, the purposes of physical education, an essential part of Soviet life, were to prepare for the defense of the country, to increase economic productivity, and to develop loyal citizens eager to subjugate their individual interests and desires to the social and political ideals of Communism.

After the Second World War, another purpose was added—the use of sports as a way of acquiring international prestige and for proving the superiority of socialism over decadent capitalism. This change actually began in the mid-1930s when young Russians were exhorted to "surpass bourgeois sports records and . . . raise the banner of Soviet physical culture to new unprecedented heights."[9] This new emphasis on athletic proficiency (*masterstvo*) did not mean an abandonment of the principle of mass ac-

---

[8]Mildred Y. Foster, "A Comparison of the Programs in Physical Education in the United States of America and the Union of Soviet Socialistic Republics" (Master's thesis, Springfield College, 1967), p. 28.

[9]*Krasnyi Sport*, 6 January 1935, quoted in Morton, *Soviet Sport*, p. 35.

tivity (*massovost*). The relationship of these two principles was clearly expressed by a top Soviet official, Mikhail Kalinin, when he declared: "In our country physical culture is sport for the people, in our country millions participate in the physical culture movement. And it is obvious that talented athletes will sooner be found among these millions than among thousands, and it is easier to find talented athletes among thousands than among hundreds."[10]

Since 1950 the Soviet Union has fully exploited the propaganda value from the success of their athletes in international competition. Their athletes abroad serve as cultural diplomats, and sports are truly an instrument of Russian foreign policy.

In the late 1960s the USSR seemed to give more recognition to health as an aim, and a recent booklet asserted that Soviet physical education is geared "to improve man's health, to provide for his all-round, harmonious development and to prolong his life."[11] This statement resembles the purposes of physical education as cited in the recent literature of western countries.

Promotion of Physical Education

Although eight or nine million pupils were in primary and secondary schools by 1914, little is known about their physical education program and probably little was done. The new government showed its regard for physical education by appointing a Supreme Council of Physical Culture in 1923 which consisted of authorities from the Commissariats of War, Public Health, Public Instruction, Interior, and Labor, as well as representatives of the Central Committee of the Communist Party, the Union of Communist Youth, Labor Unions, and the Moscow Soviet. By the same decree a council of physical culture was established in every district, county, and local soviet. The local body was composed of members of the physical education staffs in the schools, physicians in charge of medical control, labor organizations, representatives of the local soviet, and the community unit of the Red Army. This group was responsible to the local soviet as well as to the Supreme Council of Physical Culture which provided a centralized administration to carry out governmental policies. Subsequently, school programs in physical education were separated from sports and were placed under the Union-Republic Ministries of Education. The USSR was probably the first country in the world to establish physical education as a regular department of government.

[10]Washburn, "Sport as a Soviet Tool," p. 494.
[11]*U.S.S.R. Ball Games.* Published for the 1968 Olympic Games in Mexico. No place of publication, publisher, or date given and pages are not numbered.

Physical education held a prominent place in the general system of instruction and was compulsory for all grade levels. The requirement consisted of daily morning calisthenics for about fifteen minutes before school in addition to the scheduled physical education periods. The morning exercises were held outdoors if the weather permitted and were based on skills learned in the regular gymnasium period. In the lower grades, they were conducted by the classroom teacher or by an older pupil of outstanding ability. Beginning with the fifth year these classes were taught by specialized gymnastics instructors.

Before and after the Second World War, physical education was required of all students two or three times a week, 45 minutes each time. During the war a decree temporarily raised the secondary school requirements for military and physical training from 6.2 percent of the school time to 11 percent.

Since 1945 many observers of Soviet education have reported that physical education is regularly practiced at all levels from the kindergarten through the university. In addition pupils participate in free exercises before school, play games during the 20-minute recess, and engage in the physical education program during their practice periods away from school in agriculture or industry.[12] After school more than half of the students, especially from grades five through ten, are active in sport clubs which meet several times a week guided by the physical education teachers. These clubs provide competition in four age-level groups in fifteen sports —basketball, volleyball, water polo, cycling, gymnastics, track, swimming, diving, table tennis, tennis, soccer, shooting, canoeing, chess, and team handball. Competition begins at the intra-class level and goes up all the way to an all-union championship.[13]

Students from 12 to 18 years of age who show special talent in physical education may attend one of two thousand sport schools where they receive specialized instruction by highly qualified teachers in a particular sport or activity They go after their school for two to four hours a week and during vacations for five hours a day, five days a week. There are also some sports boarding schools where athletically gifted students complete the last two years of secondary school and receive training in their sport specialty.[14]

University students must take sports during the first two years and also learn how to swim. They may elect their activities from gymnastics, swimming, basketball, track, tennis, skiing, motor cycling, soccer, volley-

[12]Singer, "Health, Physical Education, and Recreation in Communist States," pp. 357–58.

[13]M. L. Howell and M. L. Van Vliet, *Physical Education and Recreation in Europe* (Ottawa: The Fitness and Amateur Sports Directorate, 1965), pp. 10–12.

[14]Frank S. Minnerly, "Physical Education and Recreation in Soviet Russia," *Journal of Physical Education* 58 (November–December 1960): 28.

ball, or mountain climbing. Each institution also has a number of sports clubs for competition.[15]

TEACHER TRAINING: After the Revolution, Party officials found very few experienced physical education teachers, and some of these were unacceptable because of their bourgeois associations. The Tsarist army had established an Officers' General Gymnastic School in St. Petersburg in 1909 which had become a center for research in physical culture and gave a ten-month course in anatomy, physiology, hygiene, history, and methods of teaching indoor and outdoor sports.[16] The P. F. Lesgaft Physical Education Institute was started in Leningrad in 1919, and the next year the State Institute for Physical Culture and Sports was founded in Moscow. Because of the shortage of teachers it was necessary to devise short-term courses as emergency measures. The All-Russian Conference on Physical Culture in 1924 deemed it essential to train school doctors, organizers, teachers for schools, and leaders for clubs, circles, and labor unions. By 1929 qualifications were raised so that teachers in pedagogical, medical, and higher institutions were required to have four years of training in state institutes; secondary and vocational school teachers were to be graduates of three-year technicums of physical culture; and all primary school teachers were to receive specialized courses in physical culture as a part of their regular curriculum.

In the post-World War II Soviet Union, three levels of teacher training were described by Singer as follows:

1. The first or lowest level is the physical education technicum. This takes five years and follows eight years of schooling. The graduates serve as assistant instructors, and most of them continue their education by taking night school or correspondence work.
2. The second level is the departments of physical education in the pedagogical institutes. This is a four- or five-year curriculum taken by graduates of the ten-year school. These graduates can teach physical education in primary schools or in secondary schools if they have an academic background.
3. The third or highest level is the physical education institutes. This is a four-year course for students who have completed eleven years of previous schooling. Institute graduates become secondary school teachers, coaches, sport directors, and administrators of sports and physical education.[17]

[15]Glyn Roberts, "Physical Education in Russia," in William Johnson, ed., *Physical Education Around the World*, Monograph no. 1 (Indianapolis, Ind.: Phi Epsilon Kappa, 1966), p. 54.

[16]Morton, *Soviet Sport*, p. 159.

[17]Singer, "Health, Physical Education, and Recreation in Communist States," pp. 361–62.

The first and second level schools are under the Union-Republic Ministries of Education, but the third level institutes are under a special authority for physical education and sport. There is a movement to raise the standards of the technicums and thus bring levels one and two closer together.

The USSR has eighteen institutes of physical education whose students are carefully selected for admission by a comprehensive testing program. There are four departments—Pedagogical, Sports Coaches, Night School, and Correspondence—and also a Coaches School which gives refresher courses for those in the field.[18] The curriculum is rigorous with almost the same amount of time devoted to activities and methods as is given to academic content. Supervised teaching begins in the first year with one day a week at a nearby school and continues throughout the remaining years. The senior student teaches for two months at the school where he will be placed after graduation.[19] All students must attend two winter camps and three summer camps.

Ever since the physical culture movement began in the USSR, it was held that the program should be based upon scientific research. Research in sports and physical education is a vital part of teacher education and is highly regarded. Institute faculty members have reduced teaching loads and are expected to do research and writing. Areas of particular concentration are exercise physiology, sports medicine, sports psychology, and kinesiology, especially studies in cinematography and electromyography. Research is closely coordinated with the teaching of children and the coaching of athletes. There are three scientific research institutes for physical education located in Moscow, Leningrad, and Tbilisi in Georgia. Superior institute students can go on for postgraduate work toward the degree of *Kandidat Nauk* which requires at least three years of research and is comparable to the doctorate.

To sum up, teachers and coaches enjoy a status and social acceptance seldom found in other countries outside the Soviet sphere of influence. Teachers and coaches receive comprehensive training at the same educational institutions; this minimizes the rift between the two professions, often observed in some other countries. Coaches seem to occupy a favored position; Minnerly reported that they received $375 a month while the teachers earned about $250 and many of them had a second job.[20]

NONSCHOOL AGENCIES: For pupils in the fifth through seventh years of school, there are physical culture circles that meet after school two or three times a week and also take Sunday excursions and winter skiing trips. In the higher grades, these collectives are largely devoted to sports. During the summer an estimated 80 percent of city children go to one of

[18]Minnerly, "Physical Education and Recreation in Soviet Russia," pp. 28–29.
[19]Ibid., p. 29.   [20]Ibid., p. 29.

8,000 pioneer camps for at least three weeks. The camps offer a good deal of theoretical work, but each camp has a physical educator who supervises the morning exercises and sports.

The Pioneer youth organization is one of three youth groups created by the Communist Party to work with the younger generation in Soviet ideology. These are the *Octobrists* for children from seven to ten, the *Pioneers* for ages ten to sixteen, and the *Komsomols*, or members of the Young Communist League, for ages sixteen to twenty-five. Some Komsomols serve as counselors for the Pioneers, while members of the Pioneers perform similar services for Octobrists. Admission to the younger group is available to all, but the process becomes a little more selective on higher levels.

The Soviet Union has attempted to build a chain of recreational and health facilities such as camps, Parks of Culture and Rest, sanatoriums, rest homes, gardens, travel stations, swimming pools, ski stations, libraries, theaters, and laboratories. Communist youth societies usually have a club room in the school, and in larger cities there are the Pioneer and Komsomol Palaces. Many of these are former palaces of the Tsars, and the newer buildings are very attractive and fully equipped for a wide variety of activities ranging from art and astronomy to games and sports. A trained staff is on hand for instruction and supervision. Moscow alone has twenty such palaces.[21] Trade unions and voluntary sport societies either provide separate facilities for youths or include children's sections in their own buildings. The types of accommodations, of course, vary widely, but all of these organizations make some effort to sponsor junior athletics and dancing circles. The sports centers and Pioneer camps available for youth are either free or charge a low fee, thus encouraging everyone to participate. Touring clubs, sports circles, and Houses of Pioneers make the arrangements for juvenile hiking excursions, routing them to the tourist stations that offer sleeping accommodations. The Parks of Culture and Rest, some of which are built specifically for children while others have special sections reserved for youth, have an organized program like playground programs in the United States. People of all ages are offered a variety of activities, such as open-air concerts, talent shows, amusement rides, games, athletic competition of a more recreational nature, and others. In the winter, park areas are flooded for ice-skating.

Workers in various factories, offices, and industries generally have two 15-minute periods each day for group calisthenics given by volunteer leaders who have been certified as a Social Coach following a three-month training course.[22] These exercise breaks are considered necessary to provide relaxation for the workers and to increase production for the company

[21]"Physical Education and Sports Training in the U.S.S.R.," *Journal of Health, Physical Education, and Recreation* 36 (October 1965): 8.
[22]Minnerly, "Physical Education and Recreation in Soviet Russia," p. 29.

and the state. All citizens are strongly encouraged to follow radio programs every morning which give ten minutes of music and exercise.

SPORTS ORGANIZATIONS: The primary unit in the vast network of sports participation in the Soviet Union is the local sports *kollektiv*, or physical culture club. The first clubs were formed in the 1860s by wealthy citizens and nobles in St. Petersburg and Moscow for yachting, ice-skating, cricket, and gymnastics. The St. Petersburg Circle of Sports Amateurs was organized in 1887 for tennis, cycling, and swimming, and ten years later soccer matches began. There was obviously a foreign influence at work here. The Sokol groups started around the end of the nineteenth century, and members engaged in gymnastics, track and field, outdoor sports, and military excursions. They gained enough momentum to organize the Union of Russian Sokols in 1910. Morton estimated that there were approximately one hundred sport or gymnastic societies by 1905. Interest in sports quickened following Russia's defeat at the hands of Japan in 1905. Russian cyclists appeared in international competition, and N. Panshin won a gold medal for figure skating in the 1908 Olympic Games. Russian athletes did poorly at Stockholm in 1912, and this led officials to hold the first Russian Olympiad at Kiev in 1913 in an effort to improve athletic performance. A second one was held the next year at Riga before the war intervened.[23]

Following the Revolution, the sport clubs were regarded as counterrevolutionary, and they either were taken over or dissolved by the Party. But there were a number of activities such as a mass physical culture parade in 1919 and a national swimming meet in 1921 while military clubs practiced skiing, swimming, boxing, wrestling, and weight lifting.

The most famous sport society, *Dynamo*, began in 1923 and was sponsored by the secret police and security guards. About the same time several of the republics organized the Supreme Council of Physical Culture as a permanent coordinating agency. Control of the sport societies was tightened considerably under Stalin when the All-Union Council of Physical Culture was created in 1930. This was succeeded by the All-Union Committee for Physical Culture and Sport Affairs under the new constitution in 1936. The present body, the Union of Sport Societies and Organizations of the USSR (USSO) was announced by Khrushchev in 1959 as a democratic group, but it remained under the control of the Communist Party. The USSO has broad responsibility for general participation in physical education and sports, improvement in international competition, proper functioning of physical education institutes, rules and policies for all sports societies, and standards of all institutions concerned with training physical education teachers, coaches, and others.[24] There is also a Physical

---

[23]This paragraph is based on Morton, *Soviet Sport*, pp. 156–60.
[24]Singer, "Health, Physical Education, and Recreation in Communist States," p. 356.

Culture and Sports Committee under the Council of Ministers of the USSR which apparently has primary responsibility for school physical education.

The bulk of sports participation for the people is provided by the 25 trade union sport societies for their 24 million members. They own vast numbers of stadiums, gymnasiums, fields, and other facilities, and supply huge amounts of sporting equipment to their members. They employ 20,000 coaches and conduct the massive Trade Union Games. The first of these games was held in Leningrad in 1932 and the ninth games, embracing finals in 26 sports, occurred in 1969 in Moscow.[25] Some of the most powerful sport societies are *Dynamo*, the *Central House of the Soviet Army*, *Lokomotiv* for transportation workers, *Torpedo* for auto workers, *Burevestnik* for university students, and *Spartak* for producers' cooperatives. Each society has a minimum of twenty-four sections, one for each sport which is offered.

The task of providing sport opportunities in the villages and rural areas has been very difficult. The formation of sport societies has proceeded slowly, and there is a definite shortage of facilities and coaches. In 1952 All-Union competition was begun in soccer and several other sports for collective farmers only since their level of play is somewhat inferior to that of their urban brothers.

FACILITIES: Soviet figures on the extent of facilities for sport and physical education are impressive, even allowing for some exaggeration. According to recent sources, the USSR had 3,000 large and medium stadiums, 40,000 gymnasiums, 85,000 soccer fields, 250,000 volleyball courts, and 1,361 swimming pools.[26] However one accepts these statistics, there can be no denying the reality of the imposing Lenin Stadium complex in Moscow which covers 464 acres. The stadium itself was completed in 1956 and seats 105,000 spectators. Under the stadium are 14 gymnasiums, several restaurants, 2 theaters, and housing accommodations for 500 athletes. The complex includes a 20,000 capacity stadium for tennis, volleyball, basketball, and field handball, a 15,000 seat stadium for swimming, a 10,000 seat stadium for ice hockey, basketball, and boxing, and numerous other courts, fields, and playing areas. A full-time staff of over a thousand physical education teachers, coaches, and doctors is maintained to direct the use of these enormous facilities for many different kinds of programs and events.[27]

All physical education and sport facilities are owned by the government, municipalities, industries, educational institutions, trade unions, or the army. There are no private or commercial sport facilities of any kind.

---

[25]"Millions of Competitors," *Sport in the USSR*, no. 8 (1969): 3, 7; also *The Moscow News*, 14 August 1965, p. 15, quoted in Foster, "A Comparison of the Programs in Physical Education," pp. 57–58.

[26]Sergei Pavlov, "A New Stage," *Sport in the USSR*, no. 4 (1969): 3; see also *USSR Ball Games* previously cited.

[27]Minnerly, "Physical Education and Recreation in Soviet Russia," p. 30.

Sport society members pay annual dues of thirty-three cents. The cost of this mass program is borne by the government, industry, trade unions, and collective farms. The government allotted 7.6 billion rubles (about $8.3 billion) in 1968 under the heading of sports and public health, but no further breakdown of expenditures was made available.

A comparative study of figures for various sports facilities since 1945 indicates that the Soviet Union has engaged in a massive building program. Nevertheless, USSR leaders recognize that some serious problems do exist. There were, for example, less than 75 indoor swimming pools in 1962. More large indoor sports arenas are needed. In some communities sports facilities are built by local organizations without due regard for the needs of the population at large.[28] Officials are also concerned that all sport facilities receive maximum utilization by the people, but at the same time there are complaints that the superior athletes receive privileged treatment.

MASS FESTIVALS: Mass competition in the Soviet Union is promoted in a variety of ways. One Sunday each summer is set aside as Physical Culture Day and is an occasion for parades of athletes, mass gymnastic exhibitions, and exciting games and meets. As a climax to the pageantry and exhilaration of the day, prominent political and physical culture leaders give speeches exhorting the people to make greater progress, to bring more people into the physical culture movement, and to capture new honors in sports and gymnastics.

Another great sport festival is the *Spartakiada* which was first held at the opening of the new Lenin Stadium in 1956. Since then it has been held every four years in the year preceding the Olympic Games. The fourth *Spartakiada* in 1967 was also the occasion of the fiftieth annniversary of the October Revolution. This festival involves millions of athletes in twenty or more events who begin competition at the local level and gradually progress upwards to the finals. It encourages mass sport participation but also serves to select the best athletes for further national and international competition.

SOVIET ATHLETES: When the USSR was first established, its teams were not permitted to compete with opponents representing bourgeois governments and would only meet other workers' sports organizations. The Olympic Games were described as a bourgeois-inspired device "to deflect the workers from the class struggle while training them for new imperialist wars."[29]

In the mid-1930s talented athletes began to receive special privileges such as better living quarters, good jobs, extra food supplies, and lavish vacations at Black Sea resorts. In 1945 Pravda announced that athletes would get cash awards for superior achievement. However, when the USSR applied for permission to engage in the 1952 Olympic Games, they de-

[28]Pavlov, "A New Stage," p. 10.   [29]Morton, *Soviet Sport*, p. 70.

clared that this kind of incentive had been discontinued. Soviet athletes were under heavy pressure to win when they first entered the international scene, and the army team which lost a match to Yugoslavia in 1952 was disbanded. In their intense desire for success, the Soviet Union has approached sports with total dedication, maximum effort, and extensive use of modern scientific procedures. A good example of the efficacy of Soviet methods can be seen in ice hockey. The first official hockey game to be played in Russia was in 1946. Their first international match was two years later and in 1954 they won the world title. In 1956 the Russian hockey team captured first place in the Olympic Games.

Soviet athletes are commonly accused of professionalism although within the country all athletes are considered as amateur. They consider it no violation of amateur status for an athlete to teach physical education or coach sports. When athletes from an industry enter a meet, all expenses for food, travel, and lodging are paid for by the trade unions and physical culture committees. The factory employing the athlete releases him for the final training period and the contest itself, paying him full wages. The Soviets consider this no more objectionable than for a college in the United States to pay tuition, room, board, books, and an allowance for a skilled athlete. The entire situation emphasizes the inadequacy of present regulations concerning amateur sport, especially in view of the trend toward year-round training for athletes.

Soviet women are given equal opportunities with the men to engage in sports and physical education, and many of them have received international acclaim. The USSR provides high level competitive opportunities for the skilled female athlete—a fact which has surely contributed to a recent movement in that direction in the United States.

SPORTS AND MEDICINE: An important part of sports and physical education is a close relationship with the medical profession. The duties of the school doctor include teaching sanitation, hygiene, and first aid, giving medical examinations, maintaining adequate records, directing the pupil assignments based on physical condition and ability, establishing contacts with parents, and supervising children's hot lunches, summer camps, and all competitive events. Medical care and inspection are also given to members of trade union sports societies, physical culture circles, and the other sports clubs. All members of athletic organizations must submit to physical examinations twice a year. Sports doctors have supervision over all contests or mass meets. They check sanitary standards, inspect the conditions of the grounds, render first aid to athletes and spectators, and exercise absolute authority in protecting the health of participants before, after, and during competitions.

The USSR has led the world in the operation of reconditioning centers for its workers. Many of the centers are palatial buildings located in resort areas such as the Black Sea and the Caucasus. About half the people who come are considered to be prophylactic cases exhibiting symptoms of fatigue and potential cardiovascular and circulatory disturbances which reduce their working capacity. They stay for about a month under medical supervision and engage in a daily routine of physical exercise, special diets, and health lectures and discussion. The physical activities include gymnastics, calisthenics, hiking, tennis, volleyball, *gorodki*, rowing, and swimming.[30]

Programs and Methods of Physical Education

In pre-Revolutionary Russia, educational content was based upon the aristocratic, intellectual models of the feudal centuries. Gymnastics and sports were not held in high esteem. The method of physical education in the schools during this era, if any, was the system devised by P. F. Lesgaft. His program of exercises was similar to the Ling system, in spite of his opposition to foreign influences.

PHYSICAL EDUCATION IN THE SCHOOLS: The physical culture content is theoretically based in the work of Lesgaft and Pavlov but is also the result of selecting and adapting a variety of activities from other countries. The Soviet program, both in and out of school, is modeled after the calisthenics of Germany and the Scandinavian countries and the sports and games from England and America. Naturally, many native activities have been retained and the whole curriculum has been modified to conform with Soviet ideology and conditions.

Provisions have been made for the physical culture of the citizenry from infancy to old age. Physical education for preschool children is based on the children's natural liking for active games. Children in the first two years of school receive gymnastics and games with some rhythmical activities. In the third and fourth years they are instructed in elementary track and field skills plus skiing and basketball.[31] During these years children learn how to walk correctly, they develop their strength, suppleness, and resistance, and they often learn to love sports, "the highest form of physical culture."[32]

In the secondary schools the program consists of free exercises, track and field, skiing, basketball, volleyball, and team handball. Cross-country skiing or swimming is taught if facilities permit. Boys and girls meet separately at this age for their classes. Girls also have dancing and boys have

[30]Wilhelm Raab, *Organized Prevention of Degenerative Heart Disease* (Burlington, Vermont: n.p., n.d.), pp. 12–15, 19–21.

[31]Howell and Van Vliet, *Physical Education and Recreation in Europe*, pp. 9–10.

[32]Georgi Techetikov, "Exercise for Young and Old," *World Health* (October 1967): 32.

military exercises. Schools follow the curriculum prescribed by the ministries of education for their republic, but there is some variation for local differences. A typical class begins with a short warm-up period before going into the learning phase of the lesson for a half hour or so. A tapering-off activity will conclude the lesson. Classes in physical education are ordinarily about the same size as for other subjects—usually 25 to 30 pupils. Teaching tends to be rather formal with good discipline and class control. The instructional emphasis is upon achieving skill and perfection rather than having fun, which does come as a by-product of purposeful accomplishment. Yessis believed that the general level of the physical education curriculum in Soviet schools is somewhat more advanced than in the United States.[33]

All school children are given a medical examination at the start of each school year, and those with a medical excuse must attend class and help the teacher. Students are examined and given grades for physical education on an equal basis with other subjects.

DANCE: An important element in the life of the Soviet people is dance. Russian ballet has long enjoyed an international reputation. The classics remain a part of the Soviet repertoire, but ballet masters have presented many modern productions reflecting themes of socialist realism. Soviet choreography comprises not only the ballet but many other dance forms. Groups of skilled artists travel throughout the country presenting programs of folk, character, and gymnastic dances. Many programs are designed especially for children. Dancing is not limited to the talented artists but is a popular and spontaneous expression of the masses. The wealth of folklore from the many different cultures enriches the dance idiom. The treasured dances of the multi-national peoples of the USSR are displayed in All-Union Dance Festivals. Here, Ukrainian, Georgian, Turkmenian, Byelorussian ensembles, each in national dress, move in graceful and intricate patterns, translating their respective traditions into dance expressions.

AWARD PROGRAMS: In 1931 the Soviet government launched an awards system to encourage the masses to develop their physical fitness under the title "Ready for Labor and Defense" (*gotov k trudu i oborone*), or GTO. Three grades for boys and girls were set up:

1. BGTO badge (Will be Ready for Labor and Defense) for youth up to 16 years of age. Tests cover morning calisthenics, rope and pole

[33]Michael Yessis, "What We Can Learn from the Europeans, East and West," *National College Physical Education Association for Men Proceedings of the 70th Annual Meeting,* 1966, p. 127. The rest of this paragraph is based on Minnerly, "Physical Education and Recreation in Soviet Russia," p. 30; Singer, "Health, Physical Education, and Recreation in Communist States," p. 357; and Arthur A. Esslinger, "Health, Physical Education, and Recreation Programs in the USSR, *"Journal of Health, Physical Education, and Recreation* 29 (September, 1958): 35.

climbing, 60-meter dash, high jump, broad jump, 50-meter swim, skiing, grenade throwing, and hiking.

2. 1st level GTO for 16 to 18 years. The same events as the BGTO except standards are higher. Boys have rifle shooting.

3. 2nd level GTO for 19 years and over. Requirements for the same events are still more demanding, and men must demonstrate a familiarity with motors, or have a license to drive a motorcycle, an automobile, a tractor, or a motorboat. They must be able to handle a sailboat, or pass a mountain climbing or parachute jumping test.[34]

These tests are widely used throughout the country and the GTO awards are administered by the Komsomol organization. In 1959 a point system was initiated to provide better motivation and higher levels of achievement.

Men and women who have received the GTO badge are then eligible for special awards given to athletes. This system was started in the mid-1930s when the Party decided to stimulate high-level athletic performance. Successive steps lead up to the coveted title of Master of Sports which is granted to national champions and Olympic winners. From this select group, a few may go on to be designated as Merited Master of Sports. Highly successful coaches are recognized as Honored Coach, and even sports officials may be similarly rewarded.

SPORTS PARTICIPATION: The Soviet people are enthusiastic sportsmen. Soccer is undoubtedly the favorite team sport. The peak of sporting enthusiasm is aroused over the championship soccer title and the Cup tournament. Qualifying rounds are conducted throughout the republics and on the days of the big final games in Moscow, the Lenin Stadium is crammed with partisan fans.

The games of basketball and volleyball, which are familiar sports in many other countries, are well known in the Soviet Union. Golf, baseball and American-style football are not usually played; nor are cricket, lacrosse, and rounders. Tennis is growing in popularity but is not as widely played as in the West. *Gorodki* is a typical native game resembling American bowling or English skittles more than anything else. On a cement base a yard square, pins about six inches long are arranged in a flat design. Participants stand some thirty feet away with clubs and attempt to hit the pins. Another game is *lepta* which is somewhat like cricket.

Gymnastics has its appeal to the citizens who belong to physical culture circles. The gymnastic demonstrations at junior and senior national championships and sports parades are spectacular events. "Light athletics," which includes our track activities but excludes the throwing events, are also extremely popular. The shot put, discus, and javelin, along with box-

---

[34]Morton, *Soviet Sport*, p. 41.

ing, wrestling (Graeco-Roman and Georgian—not catch-as-catch-can), weight lifting, and heavy apparatus work are known as "heavy athletics." Hiking and excursions into the country on rest days and during vacations have become common, often including whole families. Added features of hiking include night marches, finding the way by map and compass, outdoor cooking, setting up camp, and studying nature. Bicycling is another attraction, particularly in rural areas. The Caucasus and Pamirs offer peaks higher than the Alps for those aspiring to achieve the medal of the Soviet Alpinist. The Soviet people proudly proclaim their skill as sharpshooters, and many pursue the militant sports of parachute jumping and gliding. Horse races can be seen in some of the larger cities on Sundays. Chess is highly regarded as a sport with national tournaments receiving as much attention as athletic activities.

Water and winter sports claim the attention of sportsmen in season. When the swirling snowstorms make their appearance and freezing weather arrives, the people enjoy skating, skiing, and ice hockey. All schoolchildren living in the winter areas are required to learn to ski. Sometimes their only means of transportation depends upon this skill, and during the war such training proved of great value. Mass cross-country ski races attract thousands of participants. When the warm weather returns, the people again flock to the beaches, rivers, lakes, and ponds for swimming, sailing, rowing, and even water polo.

The omnipresence of sports in Soviet life made a forceful impression on one reporter from the United States who described the numerous statues of sport figures in the parks, the continuous use of the innumerable sport stadia and fields, the calisthenic exercises given over the radio, and the number of sports programs on television. He attributed this situation to six reasons: (1) government support; (2) eight-hour working day with time for leisure; (3) the passion for mass activity; (4) excellent facilities at no cost; (5) the propaganda barrage on the values of fitness; and (6) the withdrawal of citizens through sports from economic and political problems.[35] To these factors Morton would add the poor and overcrowded urban housing accommodations which cause the people to look for leisure and recreational activities outside their homes.[36]

The inseparable relation between physical culture and political reality is ever present. Huge pictures of national heroes are hung in the clubrooms and carried in the parades. The words, "Ready for Labor and Defense," appearing on the GTO badges, stand as constant reminders of Communist objectives. The youth organizations with their salutes, red neckties, and red stars are imbued with a strong patriotic spirit; their banners carry such mottos as "We are building a new world." Collectivist

---

[35]Jerry Cooke, "Sports in the USSR" *Sports Illustrated* 7 (2 December 1957): 39–40.
[36]Morton, *Soviet Sport*, p. 27.

habits are carefully cultivated through games and sports where group work rather than individual skill is emphasized. The continual provision for mass activities accustoms students to operate obediently and efficiently as a member of a group.

According to Soviet estimates, one-fourth of the population takes part in some kind of active sports or physical exercise. It must be realized that many problems exist, in spite of exultant accounts and optimistic figures. Soviet physical educators themselves complain that physical education in the primary grades is poorly taught by the classroom teacher with no systematic program. They report that children are not allowed to go outside for recess, and there is too much emphasis on the academic work. There is a lack of gymnasiums and equipment. Charges are made that the institutes of physical education stress individual athletic perfection rather than the teaching of physical education to children. Some lament the excessive use of sport grounds by organized teams and athletes preparing for competition, and others criticize the sport festivals and exhibitions because they feature the sports taught at the sport schools and not the activities learned in the school curriculum.[37] Sergei Pavlov, chairman of the Physical Culture and Sports Committee, admits that much needs to be done to improve the distribution of sporting goods and equipment to meet the growing demands of the people.[38]

These are complaints which are echoed by many other physical educators in their own countries. The Soviet method differs sharply from that used in England, for example, and yet both approaches are highly effective. Possibly the highest tribute to the Soviet system came from former citizens interviewed by the Harvard University Russian Research Center. Most of these people agreed that the system of sport and physical culture under government sponsorship was the one aspect of Soviet life which they would not want to change.[39]

[37]Ibid., pp. 49–50.   [38]Pavlov, "A New Stage," p. 10.
[39]Morton, *Soviet Sport*, pp. 211–12.

19

Physical Education
in Educational Nationalism
in Other European Countries

Caught in nationalistic intrigues, alliances, and wars of the nineteenth century, the other nations of Europe have clung tenaciously to their own distinctive patterns. Even with independence lost and regained according to the fortunes of war, they have managed to preserve many of their old folkways. This was particularly true in the case of those recreational activities close to the people such as play, games, and the dance. In some cases —as with *boccie* in Italy, *pelota* in Spain, skiing in Norway, orienteering in Sweden, and all native folk dances—activities once local in nature have been introduced to other countries and become part of their culture as well.

Most of these countries lived under the threat of aggression so that the need to keep the citizenry strong, patriotic, and alert was ever present. The German and Swedish systems of gymnastics not only proved to be a ready-made answer to the call for universal physical fitness but also they instilled a unifying patriotic fervor as well. These systems were conceived for nationalistic goals and were readily adopted by other nations living under similar conditions.

The interest in both competitive and recreational sports was primarily a twentieth-century development. The English team games, when first transplanted to the Continent, were slow in taking root. The interest spread, however, when the sports of track and field were demonstrated in the modern restoration of the Olympic Games. In addition to these influences, the YMCA began to reach out in foreign lands, and the American, British, and Dominion soldiers brought their recreational sports to Europe with them in World Wars I and II. Most team sports originated outside the Continent, excepting team handball which came from Germany and Denmark. Besides sports, Europeans began to take advantage of the natural recreational opportunities of their countries. They developed a greater interest in the out-of-doors, forsaking gymnasium activities to some extent, for swimming, boating, hiking, mountain climbing, skating, skiing, orienteering, tourism, and others.

The growing sports interest brought a more democratic spirit into the nationalistic developments. The democratic approach recognizes the participant's desire to share in the planning and progress of the activities in which he engages, his desire to depart from rote and the expected, and to cope with the problem-solving of the unexpected. In the case of both individual and team sports unexpected situations keep arising that call for perception, understanding, judgment, decision, and response. The traditional gymnastic systems were affected by democratic sentiments, and the new Austrian School of Natural Gymnastics discarded the formal approach in favor of an individual, problem-solving technique.

Russia's decision to engage seriously in international athletic competition after the Second World War was of monumental importance for the cause of sport. Other nations in the Communist bloc followed Russia in this regard, and thus sports became a primary part of national physical education programs throughout Europe. The countries least affected by the swing to sports were probably Spain and Portugal. Gymnastics and calisthenic exercises still appeal to many people, but by 1970 their role has become subordinate to sports. National leaders too realize that sports can produce military fitness just as effectively as vigorous gymnastic exercises. Sports have the added advantage of building initiative and self-reliance and of providing recreation.

In the discussions that follow in this chapter, each country will be studied from the standpoint of its unique contributions, as well as to give credit to the influences that have come to it from the outside.

PHYSICAL EDUCATION IN AUSTRIA

Austria has 7,400,000 people who live in an area of 32,400 square miles, a small remnant of the once-powerful Austro-Hungarian Empire. Ninety-nine percent of the citizens speak German and ninety percent are Roman Catholics. Austria emerged from World War I as an independent republic for a brief, troubled existence which was abruptly terminated by the Nazis in 1938. After the Second World War, Austria did not regain freedom from foreign occupation until 1955.

As might be expected, Germany has strongly influenced Austrian physical education. The ideas of GutsMuths and Jahn were introduced early in the nineteenth century by Eduard Milde. The Stephani brothers, Albert and Rudolf, taught the gymnastics of Eiselen and Spiess in the 1840s, and the first Turnverein was organized in 1861. These efforts contributed to the passage of a law in 1869 requiring two hours per week of physical education for primary school children although it was not enforced. The same requirement was enacted in 1909 for secondary school boys and four years later for secondary school girls. Shortly before 1900, Swedish gymnastics and English sports made their appearance.[1]

Early in the twentieth century Austrian physical educators began to experiment with content and methods and to break away from the formal program. One of these men was Adalbert Slama who initiated an organized natural system of gymnastics in 1909. His initial efforts were considerably expanded and given a scientific basis by Karl Gaulhofer and Margarete Streicher after the First World War. Both individuals were teaching at the University of Vienna when Gaulhofer was appointed federal consultant for physical education in 1919. He shortly called upon his colleague for assistance and for the next ten years they collaborated to produce *Natürliches Turnen* or Natural Physical Education.[2] It became known throughout Europe as the Austrian School and, as a contribution of major importance which paralleled the work of Wood and Hetherington in the United States, it merits some elaboration here.

Gaulhofer and Streicher viewed physical education as an integral part of total education. They declared: "One can omit neither the mental development nor the physical. Where one must not do anything in the mental development that might hurt the physique so one must not do anything in the physical development that might hurt the mind. Only then it is possible to speak of harmonious education."[3] They believed that physical education must strive for the development of the whole man and therefore should help the individual to *become* something, rather than to *do* something. They emphasized the development of movements for daily life and vocational activity.[4] Physical education should be based on movements which are natural to the human body. They described a natural movement as one leading "from one status of balance to another by applying not only muscular power, but by also utilizing proper distribution of the bodily masses."[5] Natural movements were both beautiful and efficient. Physical

[1]Hans Groll, "L'Éducation physique en Autriche," in Pierre Suerin, ed., *L'Éducation physique dans le monde* (Bordeaux: Editions Bière, 1961), pp. 31–32.

[2]Nicolaas J. Moolenijzer, "Physical Education in Austria," in William Johnson, ed., *Physical Education Around the World*, Monograph no. 3 (Indianapolis, Ind.: Phi Epsilon Kappa, 1969), p. 3.

[3]Karl Gaulhofer and Margarete Streicher, *Natürliches Turnen* II (Vienna: Verlag für Jugend und Volk, 1949), p. 174, quoted in Nicolaas J. Moolenijzer, "The Concept of 'Natural' in Physical Education: Johann Guts Muths—Margarete Streicher" (Doctoral dissertation, University of Southern California, 1966), p. 110–11.

[4]Karl Gaulhofer and Margarete Streicher, *Natürliches Turnen* I (Vienna: Verlag für Jugend und Volk, 1949), pp. 76–81, quoted in Moolenijzer, "Physical Education in Austria," pp. 110–111.

[5]Gaulhofer and Streicher, ibid., p. 152, quoted in Nicolaas J. Moolenijzer, "Implications of the Philosophy of Gaulhofer and Streicher for Physical Education" (Master's thesis, University of California at Los Angeles, 1956), p. 40.

activities were selected so as to produce the natural joy and pleasure which are inherent in movement by children.

The Austrian School listed four categories of exercises: normalizing, forming, achievement, and stunts. The first group included exercises for flexibility, relaxing, and muscle-strengthening to correct slight defects and return the body to its natural condition. Forming exercises sought to establish effective patterns for functional postural alignment and movement for work and daily life. Exercises of speed, endurance, and power predominated in the achievement group that were directed toward overcoming a goal or defeating an opponent in order to bring out the individual's optimal personal performance. There was no effort to compete with standard norms or records of time or distance. Sample activities would be hiking, self-defense, competitive games, swimming, and winter sports. The fourth group, stunts, were those activities which gave the individual personal satisfaction. They embraced a wide range of movements with or without apparatus, exercises using wands, balls, ropes, Indian clubs, and dancelike movements.[6]

The general method used in teaching Natural Physical Education has been aptly described by Moolenijzer:

> Natural exercises are a purposeful means of teaching. These consist of movement assignments. The children receive an assignment that involves movement, that lies within the limits of their physical powers and abilities. The assignment is presented in a language that is akin to the child's and therefore within the limits of his mental capacities. No descriptions are given as to which movements should be used. Further, no requirements concerned with the execution of the movements are given. It is the child's responsibility now to solve this problem as well as he can. This demonstrates quite clearly that the child must utilize his physical and mental facilities to achieve his goal.[7]

It is apparent from this brief description that movement education in England and the United States resembles that of the Austrian School.

In the trying years following 1945, *Natürliches Turnen* continued to serve as the basis for Austrian physical education. Some modifications came from the work of Hans Groll which emphasized the social aspects of physical education. The requirement for physical education was raised from two to three hours in the 1960s. However, facilities in the primary schools are generally inadequate. Sports competition among the schools increased in the 1950s and 1960s. A new development in the mid-1960s

[6]Moolenijzer, "The Concept of 'Natural' in Physical Education: Johann Guts Muths—Margarete Streicher," pp. 171–192.

[7]Moolenijzer, "Implications of the Philosophy of Gaulhofer and Streicher for Physical Education," pp. 42–43.

was the offering of voluntary sport lessons (*Neigungsgruppen*) to small groups of students in addition to the required physical education classes. A distinctive feature is the tremendous national school ski instruction program. All secondary school students must attend a one-week ski camp as part of the curriculum. Excellent instruction is given in downhill and cross-country skiing and elementary jumping. The international reputation of Austrian skiers reflects the quality and scope of this program. A determined effort is being made to teach swimming but the lack of indoor pools is a major obstacle.

Teachers of physical education are educated at four Institutes of Physical Education associated with the Universities of Vienna, Graz, Innsbruck, and, most recently, Salzburg. They take a four-year course, but the physical education student must also major in another subject. The profession of physical education in Austria has gained considerable academic status and prestige in recent years, and in 1968 Dr. Friedrich Fetz was appointed to the first chair of physical education (*Ordinariat*) at the University of Innsbruck. Coaches and sports instructors are qualified by taking a two-year course at one of the Federal Sport Schools which were started in 1946. These graduates cannot be employed in the school systems although there is now some pressure to allow them to teach school physical education because of a shortage of fully qualified teachers.

Austria has many associations for specific sports such as cycling, team handball, swimming, boxing, soccer, track and field, gymnastics, tennis, and others. Hiking, which is extremely popular, is promoted by Alpine clubs. An unusual accomplishment was the conversion of the flood plain of the Danube River at Vienna for recreational purposes in 1966. This area provided ten soccer fields, two basketball courts, and space for volleyball, *korbball*, and free play.[8] The usual team sports do not have the widespread appeal found in so many countries; certainly intense specialization is less common. Austria, probably more than most other countries, has managed to keep physical education and sports in an educational perspective.

PHYSICAL EDUCATION IN BELGIUM

Belgium is a country of 9,700,000 people who live in an area of only 11,800 square miles. It has been an independent nation since 1830 and consistently has pursued a policy of neutrality, but unfortunately it became a battleground during the two world wars of the twentieth century. The people are mainly Roman Catholic, but there are two ethnic groups of about the same size and two official languages. Flemish is spoken by the

---

[8]Nicolaas J. Moolenijzer, "Playground of the Open Door," *International Relations Council Newsletter* (Winter 1968): 10.

Flemish population in the north, and French by the Walloons who live in the south.

During the nineteenth century, several physical education systems competed for attention. The first was imported by a Frenchman who in 1840 opened a gymnasium in Brussels and taught the exercises of Francisco Amoros. The Swedish Ling gymnastics were initially introduced in 1861 and eventually taught in the schools in the 1890s. Carl Euler came to Brussels in 1863 to teach the Jahn-Eiselen gymnastics in a normal school. In the meantime, Jacob Happel opened his own school for teachers in 1860 and offered a Belgian system of gymnastics. Considerable controversy developed among the advocates of the different systems. The Swedish supporters achieved recognition in 1899 when a commission recommended that the Brussels schools should adopt the Ling gymnastics. The commission also favored swimming instruction and outdoor games.[9] The first law which required physical education in the upper elementary grades was passed in 1842, but the lack of trained teachers and a general apathy among educators made enforcement difficult.[10]

Following World War I, American and British influences stimulated an interest in sports and games, rather than in the formal Swedish gymnastics. This informal trend disturbed educational and medical authorities in the early 1930s, particularly the abuse of sports by children at too early an age. Many youth organizations with outdoor programs were encouraged, such as the Scouts and Guides and the Junior Red Cross. Between the two wars, school physical education was under the Ministry of Arts and Sciences in cooperation with the Ministries of the Interior and of Health. These agencies were especially interested in corrective and rehabilitation programs for children with physical or mental abnormalities. They also stressed medical inspection before athletic competitions.

Since World War II, school physical education programs have stressed gymnastics and games for the younger children. In the 1960s there was a distinct trend away from the formal, drill-type lesson toward a more natural approach and a broader understanding of bodily movement. In the secondary schools, soccer, swimming, basketball, volleyball, team handball, and track and field as well as gymnastics, were taught to boys and girls who generally attended separate schools. Some schools have organized teams in these sports for outside competition. Belgian physical educators are trying to integrate sports into the traditional curriculum and achieve maximum educational and recreational values. The Ministry of National Education in 1968 published a provisional program for secondary schools which listed six principles for lesson planning. Under one principle, motivation, psychological derivations through game-play forms of exercise were

[9]Maurice Van Der Stock, "L'Education physique en Belgique," in Suerin, *L'Education physique dans le monde*, p. 43.
[10]Ibid., p. 42.

recognized.[11] Physical education is generally required at all grade levels for two or three 45-minute periods a week although in the late 1960s there was a tendency to reduce the time. Some school gymnasiums, which suffered heavy bomb damage during World War II, have not been rebuilt and other facilities are old and out of date. Outdoor play space for children seems to be limited.[12]

The preparation of physical education teachers is provided by Higher Institutes of Physical Education associated with four universities which are all under the Ministry of Education. The first of these institutes was established at the University of Ghent in 1908. The others are at Liège, two at the University of Brussels, and two at the University of Louvain. The curriculum is four years, leading to the licence degree. At least one year after receiving his licence degree and upon presenting an original dissertation, a student can also earn the Doctor in Physical Education. The Institutes are attached to the School of Medicine. A noteworthy professional event was the authorization of a chair of physiology and biometrics applied to physical education at the University of Ghent in 1966. Teachers of physical education in elementary schools take a two-year course offered at a number of other institutions. In addition, provincial schools offer an evening program of about 240 hours to prepare leaders and trainers for various youth groups.[18]

Belgium has a National Institute of Physical Education and Sport (INEPS) which supervises sports grounds and associations, prepares Olympic teams, offers short courses for trainers and teachers, conducts research in sports medicine, and maintains a documentation center.

The sports interests of the people of Belgium center around soccer in the winter and cycling in the summer. There are over 2,000 soccer clubs with 300,000 active and amateur members and as yet no professional players. Cycling is participated in by thousands of amateur riders in their clubs. In addition there are a hundred professional cyclists who rank among the best in the world in international racing. Basketball captured Belgian youth after World War II and over a thousand outdoor courts were in use by 1969.

The name of Henri De Genst ranks high among the leaders in Belgian physical education and sport. He was a government school inspector of gymnastics for many years and served as an officer in several professional organizations. He wrote a three-volume history of physical education, and in 1914 he went to Bolivia for several years where he established

[11]Robert Decker, "Plan of a Physical Education Lesson," *Gymnasion* 6 (Autumn 1969): 19

[12]Jack Hewitt, "The Education of Physical Education Teachers in Belgium," *Physical Educator* 25 (October 1968): 137.

[13]Council for Cultural Cooperation of the Council of Europe, *Physical Education and Sport* (Strasbourg: Council of Europe, 1964), pp. 76–81.

Swedish gymnastics and soccer. Another internationally-known Belgian was Count Henri de Balliet Latour who succeeded Baron de Coubertin as president of the International Olympic Committee in 1925. Antwerp was the scene of the 1920 Olympic Games, and Belgium has been the meeting place for many international conferences of physical educators, beginning with the founding of a European gymnastics federation in 1881 which later became the International Gymnastics Federation.

PHYSICAL EDUCATION IN BULGARIA

The People's Republic of Bulgaria is a mountainous country located on the shore of the Black Sea. It is home for about 8,500,000 people and covers an area of 42,800 square miles. Eighty-five percent of the inhabitants are of the Eastern Orthodox faith although religious worship has been discouraged under Communism. Bulgaria broke way from almost five hundred years of Turkish rule with Russian military assistance in 1877–78 and adopted a constitution in 1879. It allied with Germany in both world wars and then was occupied by the Russian army in 1944. Since that time it has been a Russian satellite nation.

A spirit of nationalism was instrumental in the founding of the first gymnastics association in 1878 which stressed the development of physical vigor and patriotism through marching, riflery, and fencing. Other gymnastic clubs followed, many of them like the Czechoslovak Sokol. In 1880 gymnastics became a school requirement, but there were few teachers and less money for a program. Twelve gymnastic teachers from Switzerland came to Bulgaria by invitation in 1893 and worked in the normal schools. Several Russians also contributed to the development of physical education before 1900. Bulgaria was officially represented at the first modern Olympic Games in 1896 and had one athlete in competition.

Sports were relatively late to arrive on the scene and the first soccer club was not established until 1913. In the 1920s clubs were formed for basketball, tennis, swimming, rowing, and skiing. In a military situation in 1931 physical education was made compulsory for all boys and girls up to twenty-one years of age, whether in or out of school.

Under the Communist government, physical education is required for two hours a week to develop "strength, speed, stamina and desirable personal social habits" and to prepare students for socially useful labor. In the elementary schools children have gymnastics, calisthenics, running, walking, jumping, throwing, games of low organization, sports, national folk dances, and occasionally marching to get ready for special parades.[14] In 1965 a weekly halfday for sports participation was introduced. At the

[14]Peter J. Georgeoff, *The Social Education of Bulgarian Youth* (Minneapolis: University of Minnesota Press, 1968), pp. 101–02.

same time numerous school sport clubs were created for gymnastics, track and field, volleyball, basketball, team handball, soccer, skiing, and swimming.[15] University students have a two-hour weekly requirement for their first two years and then may take four hours a week from the third year on.

One important school for physical education teachers is the Higher Institute of Physical Culture, Georges-Dimitrov, founded in 1944. It offers a four-year course for physical education teachers and a two-year course for sports trainers and club leaders. The curriculum provides time for the practice of swimming and rowing on the Black Sea and for winter sports on Mt. Pirine. The Vassil-Levski Technicum was started in 1949 to prepare physical education teachers for the lower grades. Physical education teachers also work for the various sports groups outside of the schools.

The general organization of sports adheres closely to the Russian model. General control rests with the Bulgarian Union for Physical Culture and Sports which claimed over a million members in 1961. A huge Spartakiade was held in 1958 and 1959. The construction of new facilities has centered on soccer fields, swimming pools, cycling tracks, and courts for volleyball and basketball. Bulgaria exhibited extraordinary talent in wrestling at the 1964 and 1968 Olympic Games when it won five events and collected nine silver and bronze medals.[16] However, the Politburo was not satisfied with this performance and accused the local party organizations, the trade unions, and the Ministry of Education of indifference to the development of sports. A thorough shake-up was ordered to insure a wider scope of participation for the 1972 Olympics.[17]

PHYSICAL EDUCATION IN CZECHOSLOVAKIA

Czechoslovakia occupies a strategic location at the crossroads of Europe and has been a site of conflict for centuries. As Bohemia, it fell under Hapsburg domination in 1620, and remained part of the Austrian Empire until 1918 when the new Republic of Czechoslovakia was proclaimed. The fledgling country was occupied by Nazi troops in 1939. In the three years after the war, Czechoslovakia was drawn into the Soviet sphere of influence and officially became the Czechoslovak Socialist Republic.

Czechoslovakia in 1969 had a population of 14,300,000, and it occupied a land area of almost 50,000 square miles. The official languages are Czech and Slovak. About three-fourths of the people are normally Roman Catholic although the Communist regime subjugated the Church in 1949.

---

[15]International Yearbook of Education, 1966 (Geneva: International Bureau of Education, 1967), p. 47.

[16]The major part of this section is based on A. Vassev, "L'éducation physique en Republique populaire de Bulgarie," in Seurin, L'Education physique dans le monde, pp. 67–70.

[17]Atlas (December 1969) :B.

The tradition of physical education in this country may be traced all the way back to the work of the great teacher, John Amos Comenius, in the seventeenth century (see Chapter 9). The next notable physical education leader was Miroslav Tyrs, who, with the assistance of Jindrich Fügner, founded the Sokol (Falcon) organization in Prague in 1862. Tyrs was an admirer of the ancient Greeks, and he sought to develop the physical and mental efficiency of the Czech people through voluntary and democratic discipline.[18] The Sokol pledge required all members to be faithful to the ideals of "freedom, equality, brotherliness, and a love of country."

The Sokol idea took root not only in Czechoslovakia, but in other countries as well. A women's and girls' division was added in 1869 and the first national festival, or *slet*, was held in 1882. These gala gymnastic celebrations were dramatic displays of group proficiency of movement, timing, and grace. Ten *slets* were held prior to 1941 when the Germans dissolved the Sokols because of their strong nationalistic nature. The eleventh *slet* in 1948 shattered all precedents. Ninety-eight thousand school children and 273,000 men and women participated in a mass display which lasted for two weeks. The Sokols used the occasion to express their displeasure with the new Communist premier of their country, and this turned out to be the last *slet*.

Prior to World War II, there were other gymnastic organizations drawn from political or religious groups such as the Social-Democrat Party, the Communist Party, and the Catholics. Several of them emulated the Sokols by holding occasional festivals. As in France, premilitary training for youth was conducted by the private gymnastic societies with the government furnishing funds and some teachers. With the rise of athletic sports, a policy of mutual assistance was developed between sports and gymnastics societies.

After 1948 physical education in the school was put under the Ministry of Education and Culture. Two or three hours are required each week. The general purpose of physical education is to "secure physical work and moral preparation of youth for socially beneficial work, for the defense of the country and for a cultural life in a socialist society."[19] The younger children have basic gymnastics for good posture and health, climbing, balancing, games, and folk dancing. They are also taught elementary principles of sport training for track and field, swimming, skating, and sledding. Another activity is tourism, which is a general term used for hiking, climbing, knowledge of nature and the results of human work, and skills necessary for living out of doors. The program for older children continues these activities plus sports such as skiing, basketball, team hand-

---

[18]Jarka Jelinek and Jaroslav Zmrhal, *Sokol: Educational and Physical Culture Association* (Chicago: American Sokol Union, 1944), pp. 15–19.

[19]L. Reitmayer, "Physical Education in the Czechoslovak Schools," *Physical Educator* 23 (May 1966): 84.

ball, volleyball, soccer, and ice hockey.[20] However, school facilities for many activities are extremely poor, and sports-minded students find their main outlet in the 7,000 sports clubs which exist outside the schools. The above program is supplemented for some grades by recreative trips to the mountains and one- to three-day camping excursions. School children with various disabilities must take specialized physical training until they are able to rejoin their regular class. A new development has been the creation of specialized schools for gifted children. By 1967 nine of these schools had been established in physical education.[21]

Unlike most European countries, university students in Czechoslovakia must take physical education for four years, but it is not necessary for the fifth year. In the first two years, students attend special training courses lasting from ten to fourteen days in the summer and winter. Students can participate voluntarily in the Slavia physical training sports clubs started in 1963. Every two years university sports championships are held under the title of Czechoslovak Universiads.[28]

The professional education of physical education teachers requires five years of study at the Institute of Physical Training and Sport either at Charles University or Comenius University. The Institutes have eight chairs as follows: Theory of Physical Training, Anatomy and Physiology, Hygiene and Medical Control, Sports Gymnastics, Sport-Games, Light Athletics, Swimming, and Tourism. These students have to take other studies besides physical education. Teachers for the primary grades attend Pedagogic Institutes and take two other subjects in addition to physical education. There is also a Scientific Research Institute for Physical Training and Sport.[23]

Sports are guided by the Czechoslovak Physical Training Union with its two million members in various units which are found in factories, businesses, and communities. The YMCA in the 1920s played a major part in organizing associations for volleyball and basketball. The "Y" also conducted the first organized summer camps.[24] The Sokol *slet* was replaced by the first All-National Spartakiade in 1955. This is held every five years, and most events take place in the mammoth Strahov Stadium in Prague which has a field area of 300 by 200 meters and seats 250,000 spectators. Participants are selected after nationwide local and district competition. A good idea of the sports activities of the Czech people may be obtained

---

[20]Ibid., p. 84.

[21]*International Yearbook of Education, 1967* (Geneva: International Bureau of Education, 1968), p. 137.

[22]Reitmayer, "Physical Education in the Czechoslovak Schools," p. 88.

[23]International Council on Health, Physical Education, and Recreation, *Teacher Training for Physical Education.* Questionnaire Report, pt. 2, 1967–68 Revision (Washington, D.C.: ICHPER, n.d.), pp. 25–26.

[24]Lewis W. Riess, "Physical Education in Czechoslovakia," *Journal of Health and Physical Education* 3 (October 1932): 13.

from a listing of the events of the Third Spartakiade in 1965: ice hockey, skiing, cycling, track and field, swimming, sports gymnastics, Czech handball, team handball, soccer, basketball, tourism, chess, and military events. Up to 16,000 individuals performed at one time, and separate groups consisted of children, adolescent boys and girls, and men and women.[25] A native game is *házená*, which began around 1905. It is very similar to small field handball and is played largely by women. Men began to play field and indoor handball after the Second World War when some Prague students brought back the rules from France.[26]

The government is working toward a goal of one hour of physical training daily for all young people. A great deal of money is spent each year to build new accommodations for sports and physical education and to encourage broader participation through the Pioneers and the Union of Youth. More qualified teachers and leaders are needed, but in the meantime much has been accomplished with volunteer assistance.

PHYSICAL EDUCATION IN FINLAND

Finland lived under Swedish and Russian rule for eight centuries until 1917 when it declared its independence after the Bolshevik Revolution in Russia. It engaged in two wars with Russia in 1939 and 1944 without losing political integrity, and the Finnish people are universally admired for their courage, honesty, and loyalty. The country embraces 130,000 square miles, most of which is lake, forest, or swamp. There are 4,700,000 million people, of whom 92 percent belong to the Evangelical Lutheran church. The official languages are Finnish and Swedish; the latter is the first language of 7 percent of the people.

The origins of modern physical education in Finland go back to the 1830s when a Swedish citizen opened a private gymnastics institute and swimming pool in Helsinki. In 1834 Giacchino Otta, an Italian and a graduate of the Royal Central Gymnastics Institute in Stockholm, founded the Institute of Physical Education at the University of Helsinki. The proclivity for Swedish gymnastics began to yield to the German gymnastics in the 1860s. The first teacher of physical culture at the Jyväskylä pedagogical institute brought in the German system, and Mathilda Asp, who had studied in Germany, opened a private school for women gymnastics teachers in 1869. Viktor Heikel, the "Father of Finnish Gymnastics," was an advocate of German gymnastics when he initiated a one-year course for training men teachers at the Helsinki Institute in 1882. The Asp school was moved to the Institute in 1894 and the training of women teachers continued

[25]*III Spartakiade*, Prague, 1965 (Prague: Sport and Tourism Publishing House, n.d.).

[26]Langhoff and Mundt, *Hallenhandball* (Berlin: Sportverlag, 1958), pp. 12–13.

there. While the men were emphasizing German gymnastics, however, the women decided to adopt the Ling system.[27] In the meantime, physical education had been accepted as a voluntary subject in the school curriculum in 1843 so that there was a genuine need for teachers.

In the twentieth century, Finnish physical educators, Elli Björksten and Hilma Jalkanen, began their own modifications of these foreign systems. Both women taught at the Institute of Physical Education in Helsinki. In the 1910s Björksten, dissatisfied with the Swedish exercises, developed rhythmical movements with emphasis on form and beauty of execution. She sought to harmonize the mind and the body. Björksten believed that gymnastics for women should proceed along its own lines.[28] Her work had some effect in Denmark, England, Poland, and Norway.

In the 1930s Hilma Jalkanen, influenced by the ancient Greeks as well as by Delsarte, Mensendieck, Bode, Laban, Medau, and others, developed exercises which were based on total body movement. She believed that movement should begin in the hip region and flow up the spinal column through the arms and fingertips and out into space. She sought a sequential flow of action with no rigidity anywhere. Posture was considered in relation to the body in action or at rest, and not just in a static position. Like Björksten, Jalkanen looked for beauty of movement and harmony of mind and body.[29]

These ideas have contributed to the development of the "New Rhythmic Gymnastics" as practiced by Finnish women today. It integrates the natural movements of play, the rhythmic qualities of the dance, and physical qualities of strength and coordination with an aesthetic grace to eliminate bodily inhibitions and ultimately to develop poise.[30] The women extensively use balls, clubs, hoops, sticks, and cymbals to produce rhythmic, dynamic total motion, and to find self-expression and a sense of relaxation, joy, and pleasure. Women leaders object to the heavy apparatus which they consider to be more suitable for men. The Finnish Women's Physical Education Association, founded by Elin Kallio in 1896, has always been against highly organized athletic competition for women. Kallio is fondly regarded as the "founder of women's gymnastics."

In the required school program of physical education, boys and girls are together the first four years for gymnastics, track and field, ball games, skiing, and folk dances. After that classes are held separately with more

[27]Finnish Society for Research in Sports and Physical Education, ed., *Physical Education and Sports in Finland* (Helsinki: Werner Söderström Osakeyhtiö, 1969), p. 91.
[28]Bertelsens, "A Danish Physical Educator Speaks," *The Progressive Physical Educator* 30 (May 1948): 30. Miss Bertelsens' first name was not given.
[29]Margaret P. Duggar, "Gymnastic Festival in Finland," *Physical Educator* 17 (October 1960) :111–13.
[30]*Finland's National Gymnastic Teams.* Official program of touring teams to the United States in 1959.

time devoted to sports. Swimming, skiing, and orienteering are considered essential to the national welfare and receive special emphasis. Other sports taught are basketball, volleyball, soccer, team handball, *pesäpallo* (Finnish baseball), skating, and ice hockey.[31] Older boys also have weight lifting but do not use weights exceeding a hundred pounds. Finland was one of the first countries to use mimetic instruction for teaching sport skills. Teachers try to teach basic techniques as early as possible and then give supplementary instruction thereafter. Most of the larger schools have a gymnasium, and smaller schools will equip a regular classroom with apparatus. Primary schools must have a playground area for ball games and track and field. Schools in the larger cities, however, lack open area, and they will use the public sports grounds.

Most schools have their own clubs for voluntary exercises in gymnastics and sports competition. National tournaments are conducted each year for all secondary schools in basketball, soccer, and *pesäpallo*. Considerable competition is conducted on a mass basis for athletic badges or to obtain performance records which can be compared with those of other schools. All students in a school will engage in a cross-country ski race on one of the seven days set aside as workdays for sports. In addition to these opportunities, about half of the boys and one-fourth of the girls from 14 to 18 years of age also belong to an outside sport club.

Teachers of physical education were prepared solely at the Institute of Physical Education at the University of Helsinki for many years. In recent times students attend for three years and then teach a year at a normal school for certification. However, in 1963 a Department of Physical Education was established at the University of Jyväskylä which will lead the way to offering the higher academic degrees—the M.A., Licentiate, and Ph.D.—in physical education. In 1968 the department became a Faculty of Physical and Health Education. Primary school teachers receive some physical education at the seminaries or teachers' colleges and do student teaching in physical education. The sports institutes at Vierumäki and Nastola were designated as sport leadership colleges and gave a one-year course for sport directors which was extended to two years in 1968. There are a dozen other sport institutes for coaches and sports instructors.

Research in sport and physical education is conducted at the Institute in Helsinki, the University of Turku, and the University of Jyväskylä. The Finnish Society for Research in Sport and Physical Education has been functioning since 1929. The Finnish Research Council for Physical Education and Sports was created in 1967 under the Ministry of Education.

Sports in Finland are under the control of the Finnish Central Sports Federation (SVUL) which began in 1900. In 1969 all federations had

[31]Finnish Sociey for Research in Sports and Physical Education, *Physical Education and Sports in Finland*, pp. 12–14.

1,400,000 members—an amazing number when compared against the total population. Sports clubs with the greatest membership are track and field, skiing, soccer, orientation, and *pesäpallo*. A soccer pool provides most of the state monetary support. Over the years Finnish athletes have distinguished themselves in long distance running, skiing, wrestling, and the javelin throw. Paavo Nurmi won four events in the 1924 Olympics.

The national game of *pesäpallo* was devised by Lauri Pihkala after observing baseball in the United States. Following some years of experimentation, the first rules of *pesäpallo* were published in 1922. A major difference from baseball is that the pitcher, who is also the catcher, stands next to the batter and tosses the ball in the air so that it will descend on a round platter. The batter hits the ball on the way down. *Pesäpallo* makes two major adaptations to Finnish conditions—the field is narrower in a country where open space is limited, and the game is more active where the climate is colder.[32]

The Finnish people display a refreshing enthusiasm for their physical education work. The gymnastic exercises, the sports, and the dances are all characteristically vigorous. Even though the exercises may be somewhat formal in themselves, there seems to be a group feeling of informality in executing them, rather than one of dictated leader dominance. Although the Finnish people seek for perfection in their group exercises, their athletics, and their dance expressions, they still retain a spontaneous play attitude toward the activities in which they are engaging.

PHYSICAL EDUCATION IN GREECE

The historic land of Greece, or Kingdom of Hellas, combines the beauty of rugged mountains with scenic islands set against the blue of the sea. Although the glory of ancient Greece is still very real to Greek citizens today, the modern country dates its independence only from 1830 when four centuries of Turkish rule were terminated with the assistance of Great Britain, Russia, and France. In the Second World War Greece was occupied by German, Italian, and Bulgarian troops for four years before regaining its freedom. Then followed several years of internal struggle before stability was achieved in 1949. The 1969 population was estimated at 8,800,000 and its area is 51,000 square miles. Almost all people belong to the Greek Orthodox Church.

Following independence, Greece in various ways showed reverence for its classical tradition. Efforts were made to revive the Olympic Games in 1859 and 1872. When the modern games did begin in 1896, they were properly held in Athens at a new stadium built to ancient specifications.

[32]Jussi Biork, Pauli Vuori, and Roy Pangle, "Pesäpallo," *Physical Educator* 21 (May 1964): 60.

It was located on the site of an ancient stadium within view of the Acropolis. A physical education requirement of two periods a week was set by law in 1834, but it was not implemented at the time. When the Greeks believed that the modern Olympic Games had lost the ancient spirit, they started the Delphic festivals in 1927. After two festivals, the idea was abandoned because of a lack of financial resources. This is the irony of the modern Greek situation: an economically poor and politically unsettled country which lacks the means to recapture the best of its ancient traditions.

Apart from these dedications to the past, Greece has shaped its modern physical education after the patterns of Germany, France, and Sweden. In the 1830s it came into close touch with the German program through Hans Massmann; later, with the Swedish system when it came into vogue in Germany and France. When the Ling gymnastics were officially adopted by German military authorities in the middle of the last century, this influence was felt in Greece. In fact, Greece still retained the Swedish system almost without change until World War II. Jean Chryssafis, one of the great physical education scholars of modern times, provided able leadership as Director of Physical Education in the Ministry of Education during the late 1920s and 1930s.

Since 1950, Greek school children generally have had two to three periods a week for physical education but the dominant activity remains Swedish gymnastics. Folk dancing offers an opportunity for both rhythmical and vocal expression. Track and field and swimming are given to older children, but other sports have been very slow to be accepted. During the 1960s, however, school teams began to compete in basketball, team handball, soccer, and volleyball in addition to track, cross country, and swimming. School facilities, both indoor and outdoor, for most sports are still sparse.[33]

The National Academy of Physical Education was founded in 1939 and is the only college for teachers of physical education. Graduates of the three-year curriculum receive a diploma and can teach at the secondary school level. There is no certification for physical education teachers for the lower grades. Since teachers of other subjects are graduates of a four-year curriculum at a university, physical education teachers obviously have inferior status.

About 2,000 sports clubs provide out-of-school activities in Greece. The most popular are soccer, track and field, basketball, swimming, and volleyball. They are supervised by the Secretary-General for Sports whose budget comes from the soccer lottery. The YMCA also has played a recognized role in providing facilities and leadership for fifty years.

[33]International Council on Health, Physical Education, and Recreation, *Physical Education in the School Curriculum.* ICHPER International Questionnaire Report, pt. 1, 1967–68 Revision (Washington, D.C.: ICHPER, 1969), p. 35.

Greece deserves great credit for inaugurating the International Olympic Academy in 1961, sponsored by its National Olympic Committee. The Academy meets every summer at Olympia for seminars, lectures, and recreation, drawing students and teachers from all over the world. The Academy is a distinguished effort to unite the best of the ancient and modern worlds, and it is most appropriate that it be done by Greece.[34]

PHYSICAL EDUCATION IN HUNGARY

The landlocked country of Hungary was once a powerful kingdom and a partner of Austria in a great empire. All this was lost in the first World War when it had to give up two-thirds of its land and half of its inhabitants. In World War II, Hungary sided with Hitler and was occupied by the Russians in 1944. Several years later the Communist Party gained complete control, and Hungary fell into the Soviet orbit. A short-lived revolution in 1956 was put down by Russian troops, and Communist authority was restored.

Hungary today has 10,200,000 people and an area of 36,000 square miles. About two-thirds of the population are Roman Catholics and 20 percent are Calvinists, but all religions have been relentlessly oppressed by the state government. The official language is Magyar.

Because of their location astride the Danube River, it is not surprising that the cities of Buda and Pest had swimming pools as early as 1830. Rowing was also a common activity on the Danube. A gymnastics club was started by a French army captain in 1833, but more important was the opening of the Pest Gymnastics Club in 1867 by Elek Matolay and Tivadar Bakody. Bakody was a physician who had studied the Swedish system while living in Poland. In 1875 the Hungarian Athletic Club, the first of its kind in Europe, was organized and held a meet which included three track events and boxing.[35] German gymnastics were also practiced.

The first ball games came late in the nineteenth century. A soccer game was initiated by a Hungarian youth who had moved to England and returned for a visit in 1896. The next year an Englishman formed a tennis club. Three Hungarian athletes were in the first modern Olympic Games and all three won medals.

Just before the First World War, a group of Hungarian physical educators and sports leaders visited Sweden, Denmark, and Germany. They decided that they preferred the Swedish system because it was more scien-

[34]A valuable source for this section was Vassilis Klissouras, "Greece: Health, Physical Education and Recreation," in C. Lynn Vendien and John E. Nixon, eds., *The World Today in Health, Physical Education, and Recreation* (Englewood Cliffs, N.J.: Prentice-Hall, Inc., 1968), pp. 173–189.

[35]József Vetö, ed., *Sports in Hungary* (Budapest: Corvina Press, 1965), pp. 13–14.

tific, but they considered sports to be an essential part of the program too.[36]

After World War I severed its ties with Austria, Hungary began life as a smaller but independent and nationalistic country. Physical education was required for two one-hour periods a week plus a two-hour afternoon period. In the upper grades an additional hour was added for boys. All colleges and universities instituted a two-hour requirement for the first year. The Horthy regime also organized the Levente (Young Hero) movement, comparable to the Turner and Sokol societies. Membership was compulsory for boys from 12 to 21 years of age. Attendance was required two hours a week, usually on weekends. The program was made up of physical activities, which included agricultural work as well as sports and outing events.

The school program of physical education before 1940 was devised from many sources. A typical demonstration was an admixture of modern Swedish exercises, Danish flexibility exercises, Swiss rhythmic calisthenics, Finnish mimetic gymnastics, relaxation exercises, German apparatus activities, individual and dual tumbling, mass relays, and English and American sports.

Since 1945 the government has given even greater support to physical education for youth although the content of the school program appears to be more limited. Games, calisthenics, gymnastics, track and field, and dancing for girls are the principal activities. However, this is supplemented by the school sports clubs for upper grades which meet twice a week under the physical education teacher and provide interscholastic competition in track and field, gymnastics, basketball, swimming, and team handball. One stated purpose of the program is to "make physical education an everyday habit."[37] There are, in addition, sport schools for children from 12 to 18 years of age which teach all subjects and give specialized instruction in specific sports. College students find their outlet for sports through the major sport clubs, and many of them play on national teams.

In the field of teacher education, Hungary attained international recognition through its Royal Hungarian College of Physical Education (*Magyar Királyi Testnevelési Föiskola*), founded in 1925 in Budapest. The first director was Imre Szukováthy. Students studied for four years with access to the most complete library on physical education in the world. Included in its collection were rare volumes of ancient and medieval authors. In the post-World War II era, it became the Hungarian College

[36]Sándor Molnár, "Physical Education in Hungary," in William Johnson, ed., *Physical Education Around the World*. Monograph no. 2 (Indianapolis, Indiana: Phi Epsilon Kappa, 1968), p. 20.

[37]International Council on Health, Physical Education, and Recreation, *Physical Education in the School Curriculum*, p. 38.

of Physical Education and continued to train teachers for schools, pedagogical institutions, and universities. A three-year course leads to the certification of coaches. An Institute for Scientific Research in Physical Education is also part of the college. Physical education teachers for the lower grades complete a three-year course at one of the pedagogical colleges.[38]

The organization of sports is designed to reach all citizens of all ages and to bring people into activities frequently instead of once or twice a year. The central authority is the National Federation of Sports and Physical Culture. The largest club is for soccer, with table tennis, track and field, team handball, volleyball, and chess following in that order. Hungarian athletes are well known on the international scene, especially in soccer, fencing, and water polo. László Papp, a boxer, became a national hero for winning a gold medal in three successive Olympics.

A massive program for youth and adult fitness was launched in 1961 as the Kilián Physical Exercise Movement. Contestants win points to obtain badges representing different levels of accomplishment. Every one has to be able to swim. Other events consist of running, field events, gymnastics, and throwing. An earlier badge test competition for youth began in 1949. This was the MHK, "Ready for Work and Combat." The Young Pioneer movement culminates in Pioneer Olympic championship competition for the 10- to 14-year age group in team handball, gymnastics, tourism, table tennis, and track and field. One-fourth of the school children belong to these clubs. Village Spartakiades are held every year for the rural residents. A recent step is to give five-minute breaks several times a day in the workshops and factories for gymnastic exercises. After some initial resistance by workers, this program has become better accepted.[39]

A final word must be said about the *Népstadion* or People's Stadium opened in 1953 in Budapest. It seats 100,000 spectators for soccer or track and field and is encompassed by other sporting facilities. One of these is the *Kisstadion* or Minor Stadium which can accommodate 20,000 people for basketball, team handball, and ice sports. A marvelous natural resource is Lake Balaton which is almost fifty miles long and three miles wide, but it has an average depth of only ten to fourteen feet. It is a paradise for all water sports in the summer; winter weather converts it into a huge ice rink for everything from skating to ice yachting.

PHYSICAL EDUCATION IN ITALY

The history of Italy can be traced for 2500 years, although the modern state was not created until 1861 under the leadership of Count Camillo Benso di Cavour and Giuseppe Garibaldi. Italy was enlarged according to

---

[38]Molnár, "Physical Education in Hungary," p. 24.
[39]Vetö, *Sports in Hungary*, pp. 164–67.

the First World War peace treaty and became prominent in European politics, but Fascism and Benito Mussolini led to Italy's ruin in 1945. Italy today has 53 million people living in a territory of 116,300 square miles. The population is culturally quite homogeneous since 95 percent are Roman Catholic and the universal language is Italian.

During the first half of the nineteenth century, the limited attention given to physical education was concentrated on military gymnastics. After Italy became independent, gymnastics, divorced from its military function, became a required subject in the schools by a law passed in 1878. Another law, passed in 1909, required every secondary school to have a gymnasium and an open play area, but this law was not enforced.

The Fascist Party lost no time in taking over physical education by adding a Department of Physical Education, known as the *Opera Nazionale Balilla* (ONB), to the Ministry of Education. School programs were outlined in state manuals and featured marching, calisthenics, apparatus gymnastics, mass games, and track and field activities; generally, four hours a week were allotted to these subjects. Education for the young children was based largely on the methods of the renowned Maria Montessori, a government school inspector from 1922 to 1934 who achieved extraordinary success through the use of play activity and sensory training. She criticized the formal gymnastics and developed various kinds of apparatus for natural, large muscle activities appropriate for the age and developmental level of children.

Following World War II, the physical education requirement was continued on the basis of four thirty-minute periods each week. Lower-grade children have rhythmic activities and lead-up games with emphasis on doing a variety of movements in a creative way. Children are allowed to progress at their own rate of speed.[40] In the 1960s a trend toward some aspects of movement education was noticeable. However, many elementary schools still have no physical education at all. Upper-grade pupils have exercises with or without apparatus, track and field, volleyball, and basketball. Girls have rhythmics, games, gymnastic exercises, and sport games.[41] A new addition to the program is remedial gymnastics for pupils with minor defects.

A strong effort began in 1952 to promote secondary school competitive athletics through school sport clubs. By 1967 there were 2600 such clubs with a membership of 1,200,000 pupils. Teams compete at the school, province, regional, and national levels in track and field, basketball, volleyball, swimming, skiing, fencing, tennis, and gymnastics. Teams are supervised by the school physical education teachers, but competition is

[40]Arthur Weston, "Physical Education in Italy," *Journal of Health, Physical Education, and Recreation* 29 (March 1958): 68.

[41]International Council on Health, Physical Education, and Recreation, *Physical Education in the School Curriculum*, p. 43.

not highly organized. The best school athletes play for the private associations. The national sport of soccer is prohibited under school administration, but it is played by boys everywhere else.[42] At the university level there is practically no physical education.

A training school for teachers of physical education, the Academy of Physical Education (*Academia Fascista di Educazione Fisica*), was instituted by the government in 1928. Its offerings ranged from a two-year teaching certificate to a doctorate degree after six years of work. The candidates were carefully screened through rigid medical, motor proficiency, and emotional examinations. In the postwar period teachers of physical education obtain a diploma from one of the higher institutes of physical education, *Instituti Superiori di Educazione Fisica*. These are all associated with universities such as Rome, Naples, Turin, Bologna, and others. The institutes are usually under the administration of the medical school. The theory courses in physical education are formally taught in the universities as academic subjects, but the methods and skills courses are handled by sports instructors at sport facilities completely separate from the university. A graduate of this three-year curriculum is authorized to teach physical education or coach a school team, but he cannot teach any academic subject.[43] Primary school teachers are prepared by completing a four-year, high-school-type course which they enter at the age of fourteen. A National Association of Physical Education for teachers was formed in 1955.

Italy's first sports organization was the Genoa Cricket and Football Club founded in 1893. The cricket was soon dropped, but the football was destined to excite the passions of millions of Italians in the years to come. The Fascist Party organized an elaborate out-of-school sports program through the ONB and many recreation centers and play areas were constructed all over the country. Four types of youth organizations for boys and girls from eight to eighteen years of age were sponsored: the *Balilla, Avanguardisti, Picole Italiane*, and *Giovanni Italiene*. The military spirit was fostered by the wearing of black-shirted uniforms of the national Fascist Party. The Party aims of patriotism, health, fun, and military fitness were carried out by gymnastics, sports, athletics, camping and outing, winter sports, shooting projects, and manual labor assignments. Fascist goals were also fulfilled by various premilitary and compulsory military programs for young men and by government-directed adult recreation programs.

The Italian National Olympic Committee (CONI) was formed in 1942 and has become the most powerful sports authority in Italy. It is financed by the soccer lottery and promotes sports in a variety of ways. It

[42]Ibid., p. 44.
[43]Jack E. Hewitt, "Physical Education Teacher Training in Europe," *Journal of Health, Physical Education, and Recreation* 35 (September 1964): 64–65.

started Youth Centers in 1954 to train professional athletes, and today there are sixty of these which hold classes from November to June. The CONI completed construction of the grandiose National Forum in Rome which Mussolini had started. This facility was the site of the 1960 Olympic Games and features a 100,000-seat stadium for soccer and track. It has other accommodations for tennis, swimming, fencing, gymnastics, and basketball. There are sixty marble statues in the Stadium of Statues. The CONI also has been very active in developing the school sports clubs.

Italians are naturally attracted to sports of dexterity and speed, and they have shown their expertise in soccer, fencing, cycling, skiing, bobsledding, and car and boat racing. A popular native sport is *boccie*, an outdoor lawn bowling game. The appetite of Italian sport fans is whetted by four daily newspapers devoted entirely to sports.

Italy's contributions to modern physical education are in the realm of scientific exploration rather than in the development of a distinctive system. The experimental work of Angelo Mosso in physiology of exercise, especially with fatigue, is a classic in its field, and the original approach of Maria Montessori to work with preschool children has been an inspiration for the growth of nursery schools over the world. In connection with physical anthropology, certain Italian schoolmasters have made notable advances in work with physically handicapped children. Much of this work is carried on in open-air schools and in camps, with some methodical gymnastics but with much more emphasis on natural, spontaneous exercises individualized for each child.

PHYSICAL EDUCATION IN THE NETHERLANDS

The Netherlands is the most densely populated country in Europe with 12 million people in an area of 13,000 square miles, two-fifths of which is below sea level. Historians generally agree that the modern state of Holland was created by the Union of Utrecht in 1579. Two years later, Holland declared its independence of Spain and has avoided foreign domination ever since except for a brief period under French rule from 1795 to 1813 and the German occupation of World War II.

Eighty percent of the Dutch people are about equally divided between membership in the Roman Catholic and the Protestant churches. There is complete religious freedom, and the government subsidizes all schools. A wide diversity of theory and practice in education exists, even under a national Minister of Education.

In physical education, the Netherlands has mostly received rather than initiated new ideas. The main influence came from Germany in the nineteenth century, first with GutsMuths' system and then with the Jahn-Eiselen system which Carl Euler introduced in 1850. This was followed by the German school gymnastics developed by Adolph Spiess. There was a flurry of interest in Swedish gymnastics after 1900 and these were adopted by the Dutch army in 1917.

After the First World War, several new influences were felt. Two professors from the Academy of Physical Education at The Hague, P. Dekker and J. Penders, sought to develop a system of Dutch gymnastics by combining the German exercises with the Swedish calisthenics and adding games and track and field. Sports were introduced, as well as the rhythmical gymnastics taught by Stebbins, Mensendieck, Dalcroze, Laban, Bode, and Wigman.[44] The program of the Austrian physical educators, Gaulhofer and Streicher, was the most significant. Gaulhofer, in fact, became the director of the Academy of Physical Education at Amsterdam in 1932 and served until his death in 1941.

The Austrian program retained its popularity after the Second World War, but Dutch physical educators and the Royal Dutch Association of Teachers in Physical Education formulated a program known as the "Basic Teaching Plan." Exercises were classified in the progressive development of functional movements such as walking, running, jumping, climbing, throwing, rolling, etc. These activities were the core of the school program, but time also was devoted to swimming, track and field, hiking, skating, and games. The goals and purposes of physical education were to be consistent with those of general education.[45]

Physical education was required in the elementary schools by laws passed in 1890 and 1920, but poor facilities and few teachers discouraged progress. Similar legislation for the secondary schools was enacted in 1863 and 1920 with similar results. Since 1945 a fifty-minute period two or three times a week has generally been respected by the high schools and reluctantly by the classical schools.

Teachers of physical education are prepared in five four-year academies located at Amsterdam, The Hague, Groningen, Tilburg, and Arnhem. Admission is highly selective. Academy graduates are qualified to teach in both elementary and secondary schools. Many elementary school pupils are taught by their classroom teachers who receive some physical education instruction in the teachers' colleges. No professional physical education courses were offered in the Dutch universities until 1969 when Klaas Rijsdorp and C. C. F. Gordijn were appointed to the first professional chairs at the universities in Utrecht and Amsterdam, respectively. Physical educators have two professional organizations, the Royal Dutch Associa-

[44]M. Kupers, "L'Education physique en Hollande," in Pierre Seurin, ed., *L'Education physique dans le monde*, p. 190.

[45]Jan Broekhoff, "Physical Education in the Netherlands," in William Johnson, ed., *Physical Education Around the World*, Monograph no. 2, pp. 47–48.

tion of Teachers in Physical Education, founded in 1862, and the Roman Catholic Association, St. Thomas Aquinas, founded in 1950.

Sports activities for the people of the Netherlands center in the various sport clubs or associations. The largest is the Royal Dutch Soccer Association started in 1889 by a sportswriter, Pim Mulier, who also introduced track. In 1966 the Soccer Association had 3,035 member clubs and over half a million individual members. Professional soccer arrived in 1954 because many of the outstanding Dutch players were being lured away by other countries. After soccer, the most popular clubs for men are skating, gymnastics, swimming, sailing, and tennis. Women enjoy gymnastics, skating, swimming, tennis, team handball, and korfball. Bicycling is a universal sport common to both sexes. Another large organization is the Netherlands Walking Federation which sponsors the famous Four Days' Walk in Nijmegen during the last week in July. This colorful event, first held in 1909, drew over 14,000 men, women, and children from eighteen nations in 1967 and sorely taxed the housing facilities of the community. Competition is graded from men who walk 55 kilometers each of the four days to small children who do 10 kilometers a day.

A favorite indigenous game is *korfball* which has been played since the early years of this century. Similar to basketball, it is played outdoors on a large field with a soccer ball. There is a basket at each end of the field placed on a pole 11½ feet high without a backboard. A team consists of six boys and six girls who try to score baskets by passing the ball down the field. Basketball and volleyball became popular after World War II.

In 1928 Amsterdam was host to the Olympic Games. Interest in swimming and track and field events has been enhanced by the excellent Dutch showing in them. One of the greatest Olympic performances of all time was achieved by Fanny Blankers-Koen in the 1948 Olympics at London. A thirty-year-old mother of two children, she won four gold medals.

In the Netherlands there is a definite separation between sports and physical education. The various sport organizations are supervised by the Physical Training and Sports Division of the Ministry of Cultural Affairs, Recreation, and Social Work. The Ministry operates three institutes which provide a two-year program for training sports leaders. One for men is at Overveen, another for women is at Arnhem, and a third at Sittard is co-educational. The graduates of these sport institutes have not been able to teach in the schools and could only work with the sports clubs. However, in 1969 for the first time, institute graduates were allowed to teach physical education in the elementary schools because of a serious shortage of professionally qualified teachers. Many physical educators use their spare time to serve as leaders and coaches in the sport associations. The Ministry is also encouraging villages to build community centers with a gymnasium, and it is urging schools to open their physical education facilities to the sport associations.[46] In the late 1960s there was a tendency for the municipal councils to give more money to the sport organizations to provide more activities for teenagers.

Most sport associations belong to the powerful Dutch Sport Federation which is substantially supported by a lottery based on the results of the professional soccer games. For 1966 this amounted to 10 million dollars. The Federation recently began a National Sport Center at Arnhem, and it supports research in sports medicine and workshops for coaches.[47]

The status of physical education in Holland has improved considerably in the last twenty years. Outdoor space is at a premium and there is still a real shortage of gymnasiums and swimming pools. Physical education classes at the universities are voluntary but show increased growth, and university administrators evince more interest in better sport facilities for their students. The profession is well organized with competent leadership. A visiting teacher from the United States recorded her impressions in these words: "Bicycling, the gymnastic background including vigorous work on apparatus, the emphasis on swimming, all indicate . . . . that Dutch children are active and healthy, and enthusiastic teaching in the schools is intended to keep them so."[48] It can also be added that the comprehensive sports clubs provide vigorous activities for Dutch men and women long after their school days are over.

PHYSICAL EDUCATION IN NORWAY

Norway, once the home of the intrepid Vikings, is a land of mountains and magnificent fjords, and its way of life has always been affected by the sea and its northern neighbors. It has been an independent nation since 1905 when its 91-year-old union with Sweden was peacefully dissolved. Prior to this, Norway had been united with Denmark from 1397 to 1814. Today it has about 3,800,000 people living in an area of 125,000 square miles; 96 percent of the population belong to the Evangelical Lutheran state church.

During the nineteenth century physical education in Norway reflected ideas from Denmark, Sweden, and Germany. While Norway was still united with Denmark, some Norwegian officers attended Nachtegall's institute in Copenhagen, but after 1814 Norwegian military personnel went to the Royal Central Gymnastics Institute in Stockholm for further training. In 1870 Norway opened its own Norwegian Gymnastic Central School for

---

[46]Physical Training and Sports Division of the Ministry of Cultural Affairs, Recreation, and Social Work, "Government Participation in Physical Education and Sport" (mimeographed, n.d.), pp. 1–4.

[47]Broekhoff, "Physical Education in the Netherlands," p. 52.

[48]Julia R. Grout, "Physical Education in Holland: Observations and Impressions," *Physical Educator* 16 (December 1959): 151.

Physical Exercises and Use of Arms in Oslo. The practices of Basedow, GutsMuths, and Jahn had some effect during this time also.

Two early laws in 1848 and 1860 recommended the teaching of gymnastics for boys in the elementary schools. In the secondary school curriculum physical education became an accepted subject in 1869. Local sports clubs were started during the 1850s in rifle shooting, gymnastics, and skiing. These clubs were brought together by the first national association in 1861.

The Swedish influence generally dominated the Norwegian school program until the 1920s when women's gymnastics were supplemented by the rhythmical movements taught by Elli Björksten in Finland. In recent years educational gymnastics from England have been introduced under the leadership of Helfrid Ruud. The general purpose of the modern school program in physical education is to help pupils become familiar with their bodies and to learn how to develop them effectively and to use them best.[49] Children in the lower grades take as many as three periods per week of physical education and have a wide variety of exercises such as swinging, hanging, balancing, climbing, throwing, running, jumping, and tumbling activities on the mat, floor, or grass. Freestanding or calisthenic exercises are given frequently with stress on posture training. Other activities are low organized games and an introduction to volleyball, basketball, and team handball. Skating, skiing, and swimming are also taught.[50] The number of schools with a swimming pool has jumped from 11 in 1950 to over 300 in 1969. Otherwise swimming takes place in the rivers, lakes, or ocean bays. Recent emphasis has been placed on teaching in the playlike and individual way.[51]

In the upper grades additional time is devoted to various ball games such as soccer, team handball, volleyball, and basketball, as well as to gymnastics, track and field, swimming, and life saving. The curriculum also includes rhythmic activities and folk dancing. Orienteering from Sweden has become very popular, and circuit training from England has been introduced as well. Finally, all of the winter sports may be offered to older students: hockey, bandy, figure skating, speed skating, and cross-country skiing.

School competition in sports is supervised by the National Council for School Sports established in 1922. Because of the difficulty in traveling, however, due to distance, weather, and the terrain, most competition is of an intramural nature. Badge tests are given in track, orienteering, ski-

---

[49]*Programme for Physical Education* (Oslo: The Royal Norwegian Ministry of Church and Education, 1963), p. 2.

[50]Robert D. Hoff and Randi Norman, "Physical Education in Norway," in William Johnson, ed., *Physical Education Around the World*, Monograph no. 2, p. 59.

[51]International Council on Health, Physical Education, and Recreation, *Physical Education in the School Curriculum*, p. 57.

ing, swimming, and other activities by the schools. At the University of Oslo there are student sport clubs for track and field, skiing, orienteering, team handball, rowing, fencing, and soccer.

From 1870, physical education teachers were trained at the Central Gymnastics Institute whose name was changed in 1915 to the State College of Physical Education (*Statens Gymnastikkskole*). This college never gave courses lasting more than a year and a half. It was succeeded in 1968 by the completely new Norwegian College of Physical Education and Sport (*Norges Idrettshögskole*) which offers a two-year course for all teachers of physical education. Programs for graduate and postgraduate studies in physical education are in the planning stage. There are seventeen teachers' colleges which provide required courses in physical education for all classroom teachers. Some of these colleges give an additional one-year course in physical education.

The central sports organization in modern times is the Norway Sports Association (*Norges Idrettsforbund*) which embraces thirty-three sport federations and receives financial aid from soccer betting pools and the government. It confers the Norwegian Proficiency Badges on youth and adults and sponsors ski field days and family sport days. In 1967 the Sports Association officially launched a project known as TRIM. This is a national effort to promote participation in sports and physical activity by the entire populace for its own well-being. TRIM was the subject of an international conference at Oslo in 1969 attended by representatives from a dozen countries and the Council of Europe.

Professional sport does not exist in Norway. The world's most famous ski jump is the Holmenkollen Hill located near Oslo. Skiing is almost a way of life in Norway and is a common mode of transportation in the winter. There is little interest in slalom or downhill racing.

Physical education and sports in Norway have been greatly accentuated since 1945. There are still schools in rural areas which have no gymnasiums and do not meet the weekly physical education requirement. This problem has been alleviated by government financial assistance to almost 400 villages since 1950 for the construction of social community houses (*samfunnshus*). They are usually located close to schools and are surrounded by parks with sport facilities. They have multiple use by the schools, the sport clubs, and the community.[52]

PHYSICAL EDUCATION IN POLAND

The history of Poland since it first became an independent kingdom in 1025 has been a tale of invasion, revolution, and partition. In 1918 Poland

[52]A. M. Olsen, "Norwegian Community Centres," *Gymnasion* 2 (Summer 1965): 10–12.

became an independent republic, until Nazi occupation in September 1939. With the Russian army invading in 1944, Poland became a Communist state and a Soviet satellite. The Polish People's Republic now covers an area of 120,700 square miles with almost 33 million people. Ninety-four percent of the population are Roman Catholic.

Turbulent political conditions and low economic standards did not permit much concern for physical education in the nineteenth century, but the first of the Sokol societies was formed in 1867. During its short life as an independent nation, from 1918 to 1939, Poland formulated one of the best programs of physical education and sports among the European countries.

Physical education became part of the school curriculum right from the start by the Teachers' Diet in 1919. A 1922 law made a playground essential for all elementary schools and a gymnasium compulsory for all secondary schools. Early priority was given to the Swedish system but women's gymnastics were considerably modified by the ideas of Agnete Bertram of Denmark and Elli Björksten of Finland. Most secondary schools had special teachers for gymnastics, usually both a man and a woman. Extensive use was made of the native folklore and dance. Gradually sports came into the curriculum to claim equal attention. Basketball and volleyball, for example, were introduced by graduates of Springfield College in Massachusetts.

Following World War II Poland faced an enormous task of reconstructing both its material and human resources. By an act of 1961 physical education was required for two hours a week in all classes from the lowest grade through the second year of the university. Children with physical defects are given four hours of rehabilitation or corrective gymnastics and sports activity. Primary school children have gymnastics, play and games, rhythmics, dance, skating, skiing, swimming, hiking, and cross-country. The older children have these subjects plus team handball, volleyball, track and field, soccer, and ice hockey. After school, boys and girls each have two hours a week to work on winning their sport badges. Those interested in other sports join the school sports clubs which arrange competition and are supervised by a physical education teacher.[53] The highly skilled students can join the Interschool Sport Clubs. University students may elect physical education after completion of the two-year requirement. Thirty-five thousand of them belonged to the Sport Union of Students in 1967 and enjoyed national and international competition.

The new republic's serious concern for physical education was shown by its immediate efforts to provide teachers. The Faculty of Physical Education at the University of Poznan was recognized in 1919, the State Insti-

---

[53]International Council on Health, Physical Education, and Recreation, *Physical Education in the School Curriculum*, p. 72.

tute of Physical Education at Warsaw started in 1925, and the Faculty of Physical Education at the University of Cracow resumed in 1927 after a brief existence in 1913–14.[54] The first director of the Poznan institute was an able scholar and writer, Dr. Eugeniusz Piasecki, who founded a quarterly magazine, *Wychowanie Fizyczne* in 1920, and wrote a history of physical education, *Dzieje Wychowania Fizycznego*, published in 1929. He was influential in forming a Council for Scientific Physical Education in 1927. The Institute at Warsaw eventually became the Academy of Physical Education in 1938. These institutes all offered a three-year course which had a strong scientific basis. Because of the hiking and camping emphasis, much attention was given to first aid, massage, fatigue, and medical gymnastics.

In the post-World War II period, the curriculum was lengthened to four years and the institutes were changed to Colleges of Physical Education with university standing. A new College of Physical Education was established in Wroclaw. The colleges also prepare coaches for various sports, train instructors for medical rehabilitation work, and do research. In 1959 the Academy of Physical Education in Warsaw and the Scientific Institute for Physical Culture were authorized to confer the doctor's degree. The latter was founded in 1953 with three basic departments for research: physiology, medical control, and theory and methods of physical education. In the first seven years of the new doctoral program at both institutions, 85 students received degrees, of whom 20 percent were women.[55] Teachers of physical education for the lower grades go to one of three two-year schools. All programs of school physical education and teacher education are under the supervision of Aleksander Gutowski who is Director of the Department of Physical Education of the State Committee for Physical Culture and Tourism.

All sports in Poland are part of a comprehensive organizational structure designed to encourage maximal participation by the populace. The core of the whole structure is the individual sports clubs for thirty different activities. Favorite Polish sports are soccer, basketball, boxing, cycling, fencing, track and field, skiing, and swimming. In Olympic competition in 1964 and 1968 Polish women did especially well in track and the men were strong in boxing and weight lifting. The Rural Sports Group Association (LZS) encourages sports in rural areas by providing facilities, training leaders, and organizing Spartakiades. The Polish Tourist Society maintains extensive tourist and hostelling accommodations, rents out equip-

---

[54]Janina Kutzner, "L'Education physique en Pologne," in Seurin, *L'Education physique dans le monde*, p. 306.

[55]Aleksander Gutowski, "Dissertations for the Degree of Physical Education Doctor in Poland," *International Council on Health, Physical Education, and Recreation, 10th International Congress, 1967* (Washington, D.C.: ICHPER, 1968), pp. 169–70.

ment, and organizes excursions. The Society for the Promotion of Physical Culture encourages large scale participation not only in recreational sports but also in dancing, music, and singing for the entire family. A unique institution is the Physical Culture Museum in Warsaw which was started in 1955. It has collections of ancient and modern sports equipment, medals and prizes won by Polish sportsmen, old prints, documents, photographs, and various kinds of sporting art. Considerable money for sports facilities is raised through state-organized lotteries on Polish and international contests.[56]

The efforts of Poland to develop a comprehensive program of physical education and sports with competent leadership merit commendation. There is still a shortage of qualified teachers in the rural areas and for the primary schools, and more gymnasiums and swimming pools are needed. But these self-admitted shortcomings may be a reflection of high standards and expectations. In 1967 alone, 380 new gymnasiums and 180 temporary gymnasiums were constructed.[57] The number of graduates in physical education was six times higher in 1965 than in 1961. Programs for in-service training and summer courses have been greatly enlarged.[58] In a five-year period ending in 1964, a million people learned to swim and 35 swimming pools (12 indoor) were built.[59] These accomplishments in the midst of most difficult circumstances testify to the long-standing regard for the value of sports and physical education which exists in the minds and hearts of the Polish people.

PHYSICAL EDUCATION IN PORTUGAL

The corporative Republic of Portugal has been independent since 1143 with only two interruptions. It was under Spanish rule from 1580 to 1640 and again yielded its sovereignty to France during the Napoleonic Wars. Portugal became a republic in 1910 but was politically unstable until António de Oliveira Salazar became dictator in 1932 and established some stability within the country through totalitarian procedures. Portugal has a land area of almost 35,000 square miles for 9,400,000 people, most of whom are Roman Catholic.

The first influence on physical education in Portugal was probably that of Francisco Amoros in the early nineteenth century. The Swedish

[56]This paragraph is taken from *The Organization of Physical Education and Tourism in Poland* (Warsaw: State Committee for Physical Culture and Tourism, 1961), pp. 24–31.
[57]*International Yearbook of Education*, 1967, p. 344.
[58]Ibid., 1966, p. 292.
[59]Fritz Balz, "Preliminary Report on the ICHPER Swimming Questionnaire," *International Council on Health, Physical Education, and Recreation, 8th International Congress, 1965* (Washington, D.C.: ICHPER, 1966), p. 107.

system came into the country before 1900 and continues to play a significant role. The first sport club was started in 1855 for rowing and sailing, and in 1875 the Portuguese Gymnastics Club was created and helped to develop physical education for the youth.[60]

School physical education was required by a decree issued in 1901. After the republic was established in 1910, the responsibility for physical education was assigned to school physicians who were told to "evolve a method based on scientific principles which will strengthen the race, not spectacular gymnastics but something which will give us robust and resistant men."[61] The new constitution of 1933 required two weekly periods of physical education in the secondary schools in order to improve the health and vigor of the individual and the nation. The program of physical education for secondary schools places a heavy emphasis on the Swedish exercises through calisthenics and apparatus. Schools and universities have some sports competition in track and field, soccer, basketball, volleyball, fencing, team handball, and sailing, which is administered by a national authority outside the school. Primary school physical education consists of Swedish gymnastics and games to correct various defects in children.

Prior to 1940 gymnastics teachers were prepared at several institutions, including a High School of Physical Education. In that year the government placed the teacher-training curriculum in physical education under a new National Institute of Physical Education. The Institute has impressive facilities adjacent to a large stadium in Lisbon.[62] Graduates must complete a three-year course and then teach a fourth year in order to become a professor of physical education. Again, the course work reflects a strong Swedish influence, and Portuguese students are often sent to study at the Royal Central Gymnastics Institute in Stockholm.

Many sport clubs exist for the public, and these tend to be less formal than the school program. Soccer is tremendously popular. In 1936 the Portuguese Youth (*Mocidade Portuguesa*) was founded by the government. Membership was required for all youth from 7 to 14 years of age and was voluntary after 14. Activities stressed physical fitness and military preparation, and older youth were taught by retired military personnel. The girls had a separate program featuring exercises, games, drama, sewing, and singing.[63]

Physical education in Portugal has been slow to change its traditional content and formal methods. However, a government manual provides detailed information for making equipment and laying out fields for the fol-

[60]José Salazar Carreira, "L'Education physique au Portugal," in Seurin, *L'Education physique dans le monde*, pp. 318–19.

[61]*Directrizes e Organização duma Initiativa do Estado Novo*, 7, quoted in Leora J. Sheridan, *Secondary Education in Portugal: Its Origin and Development. An Essential Portion of a Dissertation* (Philadelphia: By the author, 1941), p. 20.

[62]Salazar Carreira, "L'Education physique au Portugal," p. 323.

[63]Sheridan, *Secondary Education in Portugal*, pp. 35–36.

lowing activities: gymnastics (largely Swedish apparatus), team handball for seven and eleven players, track and field, basketball, fencing, soccer, field hockey, roller hockey, tennis, table tennis, and volleyball.[64] Perhaps in time schoolchildren will benefit by the inclusion of these sports in the school physical education curriculum.

PHYSICAL EDUCATION IN ROMANIA

The modern Socialist Republic of Romania is the outcome or a succession of wars and treaties which have altered the boundaries of the country for hundreds of years. Michael the Brave achieved a unity from 1593 to 1601 which did not occur again until 1918. During World War II Romania suffered heavy damage and finally, in 1948, became a Communist state under its northern neighbor, Russia. As of 1969 Romania occupied 91,660 square miles of land with a population of 18 million. The main religion is the Orthodox Eastern Church which is under state control.

The Romanian people have enjoyed sports and folk dances for centuries, but the initial organization of physical education as a school subject was in 1864. The first sports club for fencing, gymnastics, and target shooting began in Bucharest three years later. A gymnastics club got under way in 1879 and the Romanians tended to prefer the Swedish system to the German. Soon after 1900, clubs in soccer and boxing were founded. Rugby was imported from France. In the 1930s Romanian athletes began to merit international recognition.

Since World War II, physical education in the schools has increasingly emphasized sports instruction and competition. The usual requirement of two hours weekly was supplemented in 1965 by an additional hour every two weeks for sports. Physical performance tests are administered quarterly. Pupils in the intermediate and secondary grades take part in national competition in track and field, gymnastics, volleyball, basketball, team handball, skiing, swimming, and soccer. In 1967 a specific effort was made to form student sport clubs where children met to train for a sport under qualified teachers. Students attend sports training camps in the summer and ski camps in the winter. One innovation of the early 1960s was the establishment of special secondary schools which provided extra time for physical education. One such school in Bucharest has ten specialists in physical education.[65] University students also compete for national championships. This increased attention to sports was reflected at the ad-

[64]António M. Carmona e Costa, *Educação Física, Suas Instalações*, vol. 1, (Lisbon: Gabinete de Divulgação da Fundação Nacional para a Alegria no Trabalho, 1954).

[65]Don Anthony, "Physical Education and Sport in England and Rumania: Observations and Remarks," *International Review of Education* 14, no. 1 (1968): p. 83.

ministrative level when the two services of Physical Education and Sports in Schools and Physical Education and Sports in Higher Education became directorates in the Ministry of Education.[66]

The Institute for Physical Education in Bucharest dates back to 1922 and is one of the oldest of its kind in eastern Europe. A four-year course of study, of university status, prepares graduates to teach physical education at all grade levels, to become coaches, and to serve in leadership positions with sport organizations and councils.[67] Teachers of physical education for lower grades take a three-year course at a pedagogical institution. A good deal of effort is devoted to scientific study at specialized research institutes. Specialists in sports medicine undergo rigorous and thorough preparation in both theory and practice.

The ruling body for all sports clubs and sport federations is the Union of Physical Culture and Sport which controls all aspects of sports. It embraced 34 sports and 2.5 million members in 1961. Boys and girls with above-average ability in sports attend special after-school sports schools at the town stadiums for expert instruction. Another device for mass competition is the Agriculture Cup contest held in the villages. Young men and women engage in track and field, gymnastics, swimming, soccer, and volleyball. The closest thing to a national sport is the native game of *oïna* which resembles baseball. Another old Romanian game is *trînta*, a form of Turkish wrestling.

The impressive growth and development of physical education and sport for the last twenty-five years in Romania seems similar to Russia in many respects—mass participation in a variety of activities, special training for skilled athletes, sports medicine, and the scientific study of sports. Certainly physical education and physical educators are fully accepted and respected in Romanian life.

PHYSICAL EDUCATION IN SPAIN

The history of Spain has been marked by violence and insurrection for centuries until it finally became a republic in 1931. Five years later a bloody civil war broke out which ended with General Francisco Franco creating a Fascist dictatorship. The current population of 32,600,000 is ninety-five percent Roman Catholic. The area of Spain is 195,000 square miles.

Spain's first physical educator was Francisco Amoros, who was appointed director of the Royal Pestalozzian Institute in Madrid in 1807. His

---

[66]*International Yearbook of Education*, 1967, p. 351.

[67]Mihai Epuran, "General Training of Physical Education Teachers in Romania," *International Council on Health, Physical Education, and Recreation, 11th International Congress, 1968* (Washington, D.C.: ICHPER, 1969), pp. 61–62.

work in Spain ended when he was forced to leave the country with the retreating Napoleon for political reasons. In the last twenty years of the nineteenth century a few German turnvereins were formed, and Swedish gymnastics were introduced. The army eventually decided to adopt Swedish gymnastics and created the Central School of Gymnastics in Toledo in 1919 based on the Stockholm model. Sport societies started around 1900, and by 1925 there were 200 sport or gymnastic associations.[68]

The educational system in Spain is highly centralized, and a program of physical education is outlined for all grade levels. However, it is apparent that the school curriculum, which is strongly influenced by the Catholic Church, concentrates on classical and religious subjects. School physical education suffers from lack of time, facilities, and trained teachers. If physical education exists in an elementary school, it will consist of gymnastic exercises, games, rhythmical activities, folk dance, and picnics. Secondary school students may have track and field, basketball, team handball for seven players, volleyball, soccer, gymnastics, *pelota española*, and first aid if facilities are at hand. An innovation of the 1960s was joint classes for mothers and young children held in clubs. Games, exercises, and music constituted the major part of this program.[69]

All aspects of sports and physical education are under the control of the National Delegation of Physical Education and Sports (DNEFD). A National Institute (*Instituto Nacional de Educación Física*) was authorized in 1961, and it recently moved into fine new facilities at the University of Madrid. The Institute prepares male teachers of physical education through a four-year course and promotes scientific and cultural research in sports and sports medicine.[70] Women teachers are trained at the Julio Ruiz de Alda Superior School. Other physical education teachers have been trained at the José Antonio School in Madrid, while the military school at Toledo has prepared teachers and sports instructors.

Soccer, bull fighting, and *pelota* are the most popular sports. Spanish soccer teams such as Real Madrid have won international acclaim for their excellence. Bull fights are a major attraction for every tourist to the country, and the Basque game of *pelota* has been imported to Latin America and the southern United States as *jai alai*. It is played in a special building or *frónton* by players who throw and catch a hard ball played off the walls of a three-sided court with the aid of a basket contrivance (*cesta*) strapped to the hand. Enthusiastic crowds bet on their favorite players.

[68]Ricardo Villalba Rubio, "L'Education physique en Espagne," in Seurin, *L'Education physique dans le monde*, p. 126.

[69]Consuelo Perez, "Matrogimnasia," *International Council on Health, Physical Education, and Recreation, 11th International Congress, 1968* (Washington, D.C.: ICHPER, 1969), pp. 115–16.

[70]*Instituto nacional de educación física y deportes* (Madrid: n.d.).

PHYSICAL EDUCATION IN SWITZERLAND

A little over six million people live in the beautiful country of Switzerland with its glaciers, lakes, rivers, and picturesque hamlets perched high in the mountains. Protected by the Jura mountains to the northwest and the rugged Alps to the south, Switzerland has been able to maintain its independence and has had no foreign invasion since 1798. It is a democratic confederation of twenty-five cantons and half-cantons. There are three official languages: German, spoken by 75 percent of the people; French, spoken by 20 percent; and Italian, spoken by 4 percent. Approximately 57 percent of the population are Protestant and about 40 percent are Catholic. Each of the cantons is autonomous so that educational organization, curriculum, and methods vary considerably. Yet the Swiss have achieved a remarkable political and educational stability in spite of the diversities in racial stock, language, and religion.

Historically, no other country of comparable size has exerted a more profound influence on education than has Switzerland. The ideas of Rousseau and the philosophy of naturalism were accepted and put into practice by Johann Heinrich Pestalozzi (1745–1827), Philippe Emmanuel de Fellenberg (1771–1844), and Johann Jakob Wehrli (1790–1855).[71] All three men taught schools in which the children regularly participated in games, gymnastics, and outdoor activities. These schools were observed by visitors from many countries and the writings of Pestalozzi, especially *Leonard and Gertrude* and *How Gertrude Teaches Her Children*, have inspired countless educators and revolutionized educational systems throughout the world.

Two well-known physical educators spent some time in Switzerland in the first half of the nineteenth century—Phokion Clias and Adolph Spiess. The ubiquitous Clias, as an officer in the army, taught vaulting, swimming and wrestling to his troops in 1814 and introduced some of the gymnastics of GutsMuths at an orphan school in Berne the following year. He published a small manual on gymnastics in 1816. Adolph Spiess, usually associated with Germany, actually spent half of his professional life in Switzerland. He came to Burgdorf in 1833 to teach at an elementary school headed by Friedrich Froebel, equipped a *Turnplatz* on the Jahn plan, and set up an indoor hall. He also taught at a normal school and was active in the Swiss Turners who had held their first Turnfest in 1832. While in Switzerland, Spiess developed his own adaptation of Jahn's exercises for school use and tried them out in Basel before returning to Germany in 1848.[72]

[71]Hugh M. Pollard, *Pioneers of Popular Education, 1760–1850* (Cambridge, Mass.: Harvard University Press, 1957), pp. 23–63.

[72]Fred E. Leonard, *Pioneers of Modern Physical Training* (n.p.: Young Men's Christian Association, n.d.), pp. 19–25.

At the end of the nineteenth century Jacques Dalcroze conceived his famous eurhythmics system while teaching music at the Geneva conservatory. Dalcroze sought to develop the music education of his pupils by using body movement to interpret the music with close attention to rhythmical accuracy.[73] Two of his pupils, Rudolf Bode and Mary Wigman, made important contributions to rhythmical gymnastics and modern dance in Germany.

The history of physical education in Switzerland has been influenced by the country's need for self-defense from its larger and more powerful neighbors. Pestalozzi offered military drill and riflery for the boys at his Yverdun institute. But the accepted need for military service has not had a stifling effect on physical education, in or out of the schools. The ability to hike, climb mountains, ski, and shoot has not been attained at the expense of other physical education activities.

Compulsory gymnastics were first begun in 1874. A new law in 1947 required all schoolboys to have three hours a week of gymnastic training although an afternoon of sports and games could be substituted for the third hour.[74] Of late, the Swiss have strongly emphasized the rhythmic element in their group gymnastics. The vigor of the movements is accentuated by a periodic emphasis or beat; there is a wavelike ebb and flow to them as they are performed. The use of rhythm lends zest to the gymnastic performances and provides a total workout. The school program for primary and intermediate grades consists of swimming, skating, and skiing, in addition to gymnastics, calisthenics, climbing, running, throwing, jumping, and games. Secondary school students also have track and field, cross country, and orienteering along with gymnastics and calisthenics. Apparatus gymnastics are particularly popular in German Switzerland. Most schools in Switzerland have modern gymnasiums with play areas outside. The schools do not generally sponsor teams or competition in sports.[75]

Prospective teachers of physical education receive their bachelor's degree, after which they take a two or three-year course at the Universities of Basel, Lausanne, or Geneva, or at the Federal Polytechnical School at Zurich. Other courses are also given at the Federal School for Gymnastics and Sport established in 1944 at Magglingen (or Macolin). This well-equipped school performs many functions such as giving short courses for physical education students from the university, conducting courses for military personnel, and training sports leaders and coaches.[76] Research in

[73]Florence E. Goold, "The Eurhythmics of Jacques-Dalcroze," *American Physical Education Review* 20 (January 1915): 36.

[74]Ernest Hirt, "L'Education physique en Suisse," in Seurin, *L'Education physique dans le monde*, p. 372.

[75]International Council on Health, Physical Education, and Recreation, *Physical Education in the School Curriculum*, p. 69.

[76]Richard H. Pohndorf, "Swiss Federal School for Gymnastics and Sport," *Physical Educator* 17 (May 1960): 71–73.

the science of sport is carried on by the universities and at Magglingen. The University of Basel has an interesting sports museum.

Although gymnastics occupy a dominant place in the school curriculum and military preparation, the Swiss have not neglected sports. In fact, over one-tenth of the population belong to one of the fifty-two sports associations. Soccer, brought to Switzerland by some English schoolboys, is first in popularity. Cycling is also widespread and the annual *Tour de Suisse* is a highlight for the Swiss citizenry. Hiking is almost universal and all forest lands are open to the public, regardless of ownership. The Swiss Ski Association was founded in 1904 and has had undiminished growth. In recent years orienteering has acquired many new participants. The abundant water resources encourage all kinds of aquatic sports. Rowing began in 1862 with an impromptu boat race on Lake Zurich between two Englishmen and four Swiss youth. The government has set up a voluntary, premilitary instruction program for young men out of school. Over half of those eligible take part in a program of athletics, gymnastics, orienteering, camping, hiking, swimming, skiing, and mountain instruction.[77]

In reviewing the history of this remarkable nation, it seems plausible to suggest that gymnastics and sports have made no small contribution to the cohesive spirit displayed by the diverse ethnic groups of the Swiss population.

PHYSICAL EDUCATION IN YUGOSLAVIA

The country of Yugoslavia is a multinational state of almost 100,000 square miles on which live twenty million people. The name itself was proclaimed by King Alexander I in 1929 in an effort to foster unity among his heterogeneous people. There are six republics—Serbia, Croatia, Slovenia, Montenegro, Macedonia, and Bosnia-Hercegovina—and three separate languages—Serbo-Croatian, Slovenian, and Macedonian. The national diversity applies to religion also; forty-seven percent of the people are Eastern Orthodox, thirty-six percent are Roman Catholic, and 11 percent are Moslem. The borders of Yugoslavia are contiguous with seven countries, a factor which has contributed to a long history of war and conflict. The Yugoslavs were overrun by German troops in 1941, but after the war the Communist party took control. In the past two decades, however, the country has been able to pursue a policy of political nonalignment under Marshal Tito.

The first institution to have physical education was the military academy of Serbia in 1884. A gymnastic society had been started almost thirty years earlier, and it was only gradually that sports were introduced from

[77]E. Hirt, "Physical Education in Switzerland," *Physical Educator* 22 (December 1965): 180.

Germany, Czechoslovakia, and Austria. By 1900, swimming, cycling, and soccer had been started. A school for instructors which taught the Swedish system opened in 1894.[78]

As the result of extensive educational reform in 1954, physical education and health were given special subject status in the elementary school. At all levels in the educational system, physical education is required two or three hours a week. Physical fitness testing and awards are also part of the program. The primary schools suffer from a lack of indoor facilities and trained teachers. The schools arrange considerable intramural and interschool competition in a variety of sports—basketball, soccer, team handball (most popular), tennis, table tennis, swimming, rowing, skiing, cross-country, and gymnastics. University students have no required physical education but do have their sports federations.[79] Equipment is provided by the university but accommodations are very limited.

Physical education teachers for secondary schools take a four-year course at one of four High Schools of Physical Culture in Belgrade, Zagreb, Sarajevo, or Ljubljana. There are a number of pedagogic schools which offer two-year preparation for teachers in primary or industrial schools. The Yugoslav Institute for Physical Fitness is a national center in Belgrade which coordinates all government programs in five areas: school physical education, sport, sport medicine, facilities, and recreation.[80] There are also eight scientific institutes for physical culture which provide sports teaching and do research on a variety of topics.

The people of Yugoslavia have a keen interest in sports which has been fully encouraged by the state and federal governments. Eight-five percent of all athletic facilities have been built since 1945; these are financed by government subsidies, contributions from industry, collections, and lotteries. The six largest sports clubs in order of membership for 1964 were riflery, rowing, mountain climbing, soccer, team handball, and volleyball.[81] Yugoslavians have a particular aptitude for ball games as shown by a record of international success in soccer, water polo, basketball, and team handball. The highest organization for sports is the Council for Physical Culture of FRRY which supervises associations in 34 sports. The Partizan Federation particularly promotes mass participation in gymnastics, track and field, cross country, swimming, and camping, and periodically sponsors mass festivals called *slets* for all ages, beginning at seven years.

[78]Miro Mihovilovic, "L'Education physique en Yougoslavie," in Seurin, *L'Education physique dans le monde*, pp. 413–14.

[79]Miro Mihovilovic, "Physical Education in Yugoslavia," *Physical Educator* 15 (October 1958): 111–13.

[80]M. L. Howell and M. L. Van Vliet, *Physical Education and Recreation in Europe* (Ottawa: The Fitness and Amateur Sports Directorate, 1965), p. 4.

[81]"Sports and Physical Culture in Yugoslavia," mimeographed reprint from *Review* (March 1964), n.p.

Reference should be made finally to the rich folklore of the country. Much material on Yugoslavian native dances has been compiled by Ljubitza Yankovitch, a scholarly woman versed in folk culture. The national dance, *Kolo*, is performed as enthusiastically by the men as by the women. In fact, many of the vigorous dances are done by groups of men only.

part four

Physical Education
in
THE UNITED STATES

20

General Preview
of Physical Education
in
Education for Democracy

The arrival of a courageous little band of settlers in Virginia in 1607 marked the beginning of the American colonies of England. Yet after nearly a century, the total population of all the colonies was only 200,000, about the size of Grand Rapids, Michigan today. These people inhabited a narrow fringe of land extending along the Atlantic coast. Schenectady, New York, was only a frontier outpost, and the population of New England did not extend beyond the northern boundary of Massachusetts except along the sea. The number of English colonists was supplemented by German, Dutch, French, and Scotch-Irish settlers. Residents of Boston, New York, Philadelphia, and Charleston enjoyed a culture drawn largely from the Old World and seemed to have little in common with their fellow colonists who lived in windowless log cabins on the frontier less than one hundred miles away.

The years prior to independence saw the population of America increase to about two million people. Venturesome settlers pushed the frontier into present-day New Hampshire and Vermont, into Central New York along the Mohawk Valley, and into the Allegheny and Blue Ridge Mountains of Pennsylvania and Virginia. The largest city was Boston with 30,000 inhabitants, but other important cities were Philadelphia, New York, Charleston, Baltimore, Salem, Newport, and Norfolk. The culture, interests, and attitudes of the city and coastal dwellers contrasted sharply with the farmers and hunters on the frontier, and political rivalries developed as the older districts sought to prevent political control from passing to the new western settlements.

Provincial America in the eighteenth century also began to show a liberalism and other characteristics that varied from European practice and customs. The limitless expanses of land and its ease of acquisition made the development of a landed aristocracy difficult. Wages were high because men were scarce, and the penal code in America was far less severe than in England.

Education generally clung to institutions and practices patterned after Old World antecedents and actually showed little change or adaptation to New World conditions and needs. However, by the middle of the eighteenth century, the old Latin grammar school had clearly revealed its inadequacy, and the first academies were being founded to provide a non-classical education for students going into business and trade rather than to college.

The aims of general education and the philosophy and practice of physical education during the early colonial period have already been discussed in Chapter 8, "Physical Education in Educational Moralism." The growth and development of physical education from the colonial period to the present will be described in the next five chapters. During this time, four movements or themes were particularly significant for education and physical education in the United States. These themes, in chronological order were: the military emphasis, the scientific movement, educational developmentalism or child-study, and social education. Each needs to be well understood in the study of the history of American physical education.

The *military emphasis* is usually related to a strong nationalistic spirit, in general, and to wartime conditions in particular. It is characterized by total subservience and allegiance to the purposes of preparing for war, carrying on war, or trying to prevent war by maintaining a strong military force. In democratic countries such as England and the United States, this theme has been mostly limited to periods of actual warfare. One major exception, however, occurred in the United States when a strong national movement for physical fitness began in the middle 1950s.

The *scientific movement* in education refers to the use or application of scientific procedures to the problems of education. Scientific procedures are objective, impartial, mathematically precise, and subject to verification by any competent observer.[1] The sense realists of the sixteenth and early seventeenth centuries who looked upon nature and the universe with a critical and inquisitive spirit were the pioneer scientists. Further improvements in scientific methods occurred in the natural sciences during the nineteenth century through the contributions of Charles Darwin in biology, John Dalton in chemistry, Michael Faraday in physics, and Charles Lyell in geology. Recognizing the significance of the methods and findings of these men, Herbert Spencer urged that science courses and scientific methods should receive more attention in educational institutions, and such courses began to appear in the school curriculums in the last quarter of the

[1]Elmer H. Wilds, *The Foundations of Modern Education* (New York: Rinehart and Co., 1942), p. 507.

century. About the same time, Wilhelm Wundt in Germany established the first psychological laboratory; and in England Francis Galton and Karl Pearson developed statistical methods for biology, eugenics, heredity, sociology, and psychology that became the foundation for statistics in education.

These were some of the men and ideas that lay behind the scientific movement in education. The work of Galton and Pearson led to the sciences of biometry and anthropometry which were carried on in this country by James McKeen Cattell. The real application of statistics and quantitative research to education was made at Columbia, by Edward L. Thorndike who published *Mental and Social Measurements* in 1904. Another great leader in the scientific study of education was Charles H. Judd at the University of Chicago.

Scientific education has made little effort to determine what the aims of general education should be. It has questioned the usefulness or utility of educational content, but has mostly developed efficient methods and effective measurements. Once objectives or aims have been set up in an educational system, scientific education will determine whether those objectives are being achieved and whether they are being achieved in the best way. In recent years, some thoughtful scientists have become concerned about purpose and direction. This may indicate a return to philosophical thinking which was brushed aside in the rush for scientific education.[2]

Some of the more notable effects of scientific education include the following:

1. Development of the I.Q. test by Binet, Simon, and Terman.
2. Educational achievement tests in handwriting, arithmetic, spelling, reading, physical education, etc.
3. The use of educational surveys for schools and school systems.
4. Measurement by the objective-type test that can be constructed by the individual teacher and the results interpreted on the normal curve.
5. Curriculum reconstruction based on some kind of scientific study. Bobbitt, Bonser, and Charters were pioneers in the early efforts.
6. Provisions for individual instruction such as the Dalton plan, the Winnetka plan, and nongraded elementary schools.
7. Technological devices for better instruction such as educational television, language laboratories, and teaching machines.
8. The professionalization of teacher-preparation. Careful preparation and training is a prerequisite to the intelligent and effectual use of scientific techniques in education. The normal schools for training elementary school teachers developed first. Then, with the

[2]Frederick L. Whitney, *The Elements of Research* (Englewood Cliffs, N.J.: Prentice-Hall, Inc., 1950), pp. 12–16.

establishment of public secondary education, the universities began to be interested in establishing classes in pedagogy, which in turn led to departments of education, and later to schools of education. Departments of education were established at Clark University in 1889 when G. Stanley Hall became its first president, at Teachers College in 1888 (affiliated with Columbia University in 1893), at New York University in 1890, and at the University of Chicago in 1891. Following 1900, the universities of the Middle West exerted leadership in the new movement for the scientific study of education and the establishment of separate schools of education.[3]

The last seventy years have produced a trend toward intensive scientific education with its insatiable spirit of inquiry, its experimentation, and its quantitative measurement.

The term *developmentalism* describes that movement in education where the focus shifted from the curriculum and subject matter to the child himself. This trend is also called the child-study movement in education. Serious study was concentrated on how the child develops, how he learns, and what needs and interests he has. The findings, in turn, were related to the use of tests and measurements to determine abilities, capacities, and needs.

Pestalozzi, Herbart, Froebel, and Fellenberg were early contributors to developmentalism; but new findings in psychology since the last quarter of the nineteenth century have been an important factor in this movement. The impetus to educational developmentalism came from Germany where Preyer published a remarkable study, *The Mind of the Child*. The prime figure in this movement in the United States was G. Stanley Hall, who studied at Harvard under William James, another prominent leader. Hall's contribution was to the science of adolescence to which he brought knowledge from many diverse sciences, and Clark University became a center for child study. Thorndike, like James and Hall, was particularly interested in the study of the individual, as is evident from the titles of his work on educational psychology: *The Original Nature of Man, The Psychology of Learning, Mental Work and Fatigue,* and *Individual Differences and Their Causes.* In addition to the works of these men, there have arisen the various schools of psychology: structuralism, functionalism, behaviorism, and Gestalt or organismic psychology.[4] These schools of thought have affected developments in educational psychology. The study of developmentalism has been furthered by the work of Dr. Arnold Gesell at the Clinic of Child Development of Yale University, and by other child development centers throughout the country.

[3]Newton Edwards and Herman G. Richey, *The School in the American Social Order* (New York: Houghton Mifflin Company, 1947), pp. 761–805.
[4]Adolph E. Meyer, *The Development of Education in the Twentieth Century* (Englewood Cliffs, N.J.: Prentice-Hall, Inc., 1949), pp. 455–74.

The fruits of the work of the educational developmentalists are found in improved classifications of students from kindergarten through college, the differentiated courses of study, broadened curriculum, adult education, and the many special programs for atypical, disadvantaged, and gifted children. Developmentalism has encouraged consideration of the child as having a personality of his own and to assure him treatment from the standpoint of his own special needs.

Just as educational developmentalism is closely allied with psychology, the movement for social education is closely allied with sociology. About 1900, Lester Ward, a pioneer sociologist, advocated universal education as the hope for social progress. The development of a social consciousness became an important consideration in educating children to live in a modern democratic society. Education, therefore, began to emphasize social purpose.

John Dewey led the way to social education with the publication of his book, *School and Society*, in 1899. He applied his ideas at the Laboratory School of the University of Chicago from 1896 to 1904 before beginning his long career at Teachers College, Columbia University. His work was carried on by other influential educators such as William Kilpatrick, Boyd Bode, and Harold Rugg. The principles of social education were an integral part of the whole progressive education movement, and they are still applied today.

The three types of education—scientific, developmental, and social education—complement each other to produce a better educational system. Developmentalism is aided by the adaptation of scientific procedures to the study of children. The aims or objectives set by social education become attainable when the fruits of scientific education and developmentalism are gathered and digested for use. Scientific education and procedures, at the service of developmentalism and social education, thus acquire a worthy direction and purpose.

Although scientific, developmental, and social education can all work in harmony, the military emphasis often conflicts with the others. Educational developmentalism and social education, in particular, may be at variance with the demands and goals of a military emphasis. This may force them into a period of eclipse during times of war emergency. Scientific education conflicts least with a military emphasis and can even be utilized in its service.

These are the movements that have had most significance in the development of modern education in the United States. The influence of each of these movements on the development of physical education will be specifically summarized and compared in the chapter previews of the next five chapters. It will be seen that physical education as well as general education owes much of its current philosophy and practice to these movements.

21

Physical Education
in
Education for Nationalism
1787-1865

When the United States came into existence following the Revolutionary War, there was a negative type of nationalism based on the opposition to British administration and policies. This nationalism had only been strong enough to provide the military victories of the war by a narrow margin, and it suffered a severe mauling in the political arenas of the Continental Congresses and the Constitutional Convention. The states were reluctant to yield any authority or power to the new federal government.

Nationalism burst into full flame following the War of 1812. This inconclusive conflict somehow developed a positive, distinctively American spirit. Congress authorized a national army and navy, and the traditional state militia was no longer the first line of defense. In the economic area, the Tariff Act of 1816 established rates designed to protect American industries from foreign competition. The desperate need for a stable currency after the war resulted in the Second U. S. Bank with power to issue a national currency. In the field of law, John Marshall, Chief Justice of the Supreme Court, was instrumental in molding the American constitutional system through his significant court decisions. In the same postwar era came the first budding of a national literature. Men such as Washington Irving, James Fenimore Cooper, and William Cullen Bryant broke away from English models and produced fresh works drawn from local sources. The *North American Review* was started in 1816 and played a leading role in developing a national culture.

Meanwhile, fur traders, explorers, and settlers penetrated the wilderness and pushed the frontier westward. The opening of the Erie Canal in 1825 facilitated the movement of people via the Great Lakes to Wisconsin and Illinois. Diplomatic maneuvers secured Florida from Spain and tightened the hold of the United States upon the Pacific Northwest. The Monroe Doctrine affirmed the intention of the United States to protect other countries in the Western Hemisphere from European interference.

The road to national unity was not easy, however. The problem of slavery in the South, the struggle of the industrial East for economic supremacy, the competition between the agricultural West and the South for markets, the settling of wilderness and prairie territories and establishing of law and order, and the wave of humanitarian idealism—all these combined to provide the severest tests for the fledgling republic.

The early national period was characterized by a gradual extension of democratic rights to more and more people. Suffrage was at first restricted to property owners, but these restrictions were gradually removed. In the early days, many poor children received their education from charitable organizations. Later, such children were educated at the taxpayer's expense. Women were slowly beginning to seek a more important role in social and governmental legislation. But the spirit of democracy was nowhere more evident than in the frontier regions of the West.

The popular concept of education during this period was expressed in the following constitutional provision carried over from the Northwest Ordinance of 1787: "Religion, morality and knowledge being necessary to good government and the happiness of mankind, schools, and the means of education shall forever be encouraged." Although statements may be found defining education in terms of the "physical, intellectual, and moral culture" of men, the idea of physical education had not yet become part of the school curriculum. The "faculty" psychology of the period concluded that the three attributes could be developed separately. The school was looked upon as the primary agency to provide mental instruction; the home and the church, for the most part, were to provide moral instruction; and the body, apparently, could take care of itself. When the term "physical education" was used, it meant a knowledge about the organs and functions of the body plus the various agents which affected it, including exercise, diet, ventilation, and clothing.

The masters of these schools were influenced by a strong carry-over of Puritanism besides their illfounded educational psychology. Acts that were merely playful seemed actually sinful. The First Continental Congress in 1774 called upon the colonies to "discountenance and discourage every species of extravagance and dissipation, especially all horse racing, and all kinds of gaming, cockfighting, exhibitions of shows, plays and other expensive diversions and entertainments." A common warning of teachers, pastors, and parents was that "the devil finds plenty of work for idle hands to do."

Furthermore, a large part of the country was wilderness. So much of the life of the early settler was spent in the open air, and so many of his activities demanded the use of big muscles, that there seemed no need to provide for physical exercise or even to teach habits of health. In the cities, where early effects of the Industrial Revolution were appearing in the establishment of new factories and industries, general sentiment favored useful work in mechanical or industrial pursuits that would contribute to the national economy.

Although the War of 1812 and the Mexican War helped to unify a people of diverse backgrounds and interests, emerging nationalism in the United States never was accompanied by the development of a powerful central government as was the case in many European countries. Local school boards and officials had almost complete responsibility in examining and certifying teachers, selecting textbooks, and administering the schools.[1]

Owing to this lack of centralization, physical education in the United States was not strongly influenced by nationalistic sentiment and the *military* emphasis, except in time of war. The advocates of military training have always supported their cause by an appeal to patriotism and nationalism. In 1790 President Washington proposed that youths of eighteen, nineteen, and twenty receive military education in special camps and that the right to vote be withheld pending receipt of a certificate of military proficiency. The House of Representatives in both 1817 and 1819 defeated a proposal that "a corps of military instructors should be formed to attend to the gymnastic and elementary part of instruction in every school in the United States." The opening of the military academy at West Point in 1802 and of the American Literary, Scientific, and Military Academy at Norwich, Vermont, in 1820 by Capt. Alden Partridge, formerly a superintendent at West Point, led to the founding of a number of military schools. Generally, however, public schools and colleges remained untouched by military training until the Civil War when military drill was instituted in many schools. The Morrill Act of 1862 required military instruction in all state colleges founded under its provisions.

The *scientific movement* during this period had not yet spread from the pure sciences to education or physical education. School curriculums and educational methods were largely based on tradition.

Some of the Pestalozzi's ideas concerning *educational developmentalism* were first brought to the United States in 1806 by Joseph Neef who had taught under Pestalozzi. Another source of ideas was the manual-labor movement of Fellenberg, a disciple of Pestalozzi. A number of Americans visited Fellenberg's school at Hofwyl and observed a regular daily program of play and exercise for children. However, most of the manual-labor schools established in the United States substituted agricultural and mechanical labor for the physical activities favored by Fellenberg.

[1]Edward H. Reisner, *Nationalism and Education* (New York: The Macmillan Company, 1923), pp. 410–12.

Social education received negligible attention up to the Civil War. The social values of wholesome play and recreation, as understood today, could not possibly have existed during the colonial period with its emphasis on family independence. Families were large and generally so busy with the basic necessities of life that they could not conceive of recreation as a social force. Occasionally, in the more populated centers along the Eastern Seaboard, references were made to the social values derived from physical activities. For example, a group of Harvard students in 1826 declared that not the least of the consequences of their new outdoor gymnasium was the social effect which "had brought into contact and friendly feeling, those who might have passed the whole period of college life without being more to teach other than mere strangers."[2] Another writer stated, "One invaluable merit of out-door sports is to be found in this, that they afford the best cement for childish friendship. Their associations outlive all others."[3] But these sentiments were only isolated examples, and the fuller exploration of social potentialities was not to occur until a later period.

During this period of emerging nationalism (from 1787 to 1865), the military emphasis was more pronounced in physical education than was scientific education, educational developmentalism, or social education. This emphasis was evident more in the efforts to achieve good health as a contribution to the national welfare than in a distinct accent on military training, which occurred only during the Civil War.

Aims of Education

Throughout the period of emergent nationalism, the main purpose of education was instruction in the three R's—reading, writing, and arithmetic. The dominant problem of the period was to extend this instruction to all children so that this democratic nation would survive. The War for Independence, the French Revolution, and the War of 1812 all exerted strong influences on the minds of settlers. They were still imbued with the fear of their narrow escape from tyranny and apprehensive lest their newly-found freedom dissolve through weakness as yet not manifest. The speeches of the early leaders expressed the thought: educate the people that they may never again be slaves to a tyrant on a throne; educate them that they may read, write, and think for themselves, because autocrats can rule only when the masses are ignorant. Consequently, education seemed of paramount importance to these first educators and political leaders. Freedom in instruction, in speech, in press, in assembly, and in religion— these were the qualities of existence that must be maintained if the people

[2]"Gymnasium in Boston." *American Journal of Education* 1 (July 1826): 444.
[3]Thomas W. Higginson, "Saints and Their Bodies," *Atlantic Monthly* 1 (March 1858): 589.

were to enjoy the liberty they had so recently won. Daniel Webster gave expression to these ideas in a speech in 1837:

> On the diffusion of education among the people rest the preservation and perpetuation of our free institutions. I apprehend no danger to our country from a foreign foe. . . . From the inattention of the people to the concerns of their government, from their carelessness and negligence, I must confess that I do apprehend some danger. I fear that they may place too implicit a confidence in their public servants, and fail properly to scrutinize their conduct; that in this way they may be made the dupes of designing men, and become the instruments of their own undoing. Make them intelligent, and they will be vigilant.[4]

Educators in the early nineteenth century had faith in the importance and the power of education. They maintained that every child had a right to a free public education, that education could raise the cultural and moral level of society, and that through education a person could rise to any social and economic level he desired to attain. The desire to widen educational opportunity led directly to the question of tax support for the public schools to enable poor children to attend. The idea of taxing everyone to support schools became reality only in the face of considerable opposition.

In general, education during this period showed little change in its aim to provide instruction in the three R's. The satisfaction of the American people with American things and the American way of life produced a state of mind that was not disposed to challenge the school curriculum. The basic principles of American education—free, tax-supported, nonsectarian—were established, but the serious questioning of the content and character of general education was not to come until the next period.

Aims of Physical Education

During this period of emerging nationalism, the emphasis in physical education was the development of health and strength. A few individuals perceived other possibilities in physical education, such as recreation and relief from mental toil, the development of mental qualities, character, grace, and beauty in movement. However, health and strength were dominant aims although the ways of achieving them varied considerably.

Benjamin Franklin was one of the first to express his views on physical education. In a 1749 pamphlet entitled *Proposals Relating to the Education of Youth in Pennsylvania*, Franklin expressed the value of exercise

---

[4]*The Writings and Speeches of Daniel Webster* (Boston: Little, Brown & Co., 1903), 2: 253–54.

in hardening the constitution. In 1790, Noah Webster observed the value of exercise in his "Address to Yung Gentlemen" and stated that it should be "the bizziness of yung persons to assist nature, and strengthen the growing frame by athletic exercises. . . ."[5] In a translation of Jahn's book on gymnastics, Dr. Charles Beck of the Round Hill School stressed that physical training was of great importance not only for the individual but also for the national safety and welfare. Dr. Charles Follen, a pupil of Jahn's, was instrumental in establishing the Boston gymnasium, and its purpose was "to furnish opportunity and means of exercise to the youth of the city. At the same time it would be open to persons of every age who might be inclined to embrace the opportunity for the regular practice of bodily exercise."[6] In a book published in 1856, Catherine Beecher defined calisthenics as "a course of exercises designed to promote health, and thus to secure beauty and strength."[7] Dr. George Winship made the aims of health and strength synonymous, and flatly expressed his firm conviction that everything that improved strength also improved health. Dio Lewis added the objective of body symmetry in his selection of exercises to goals of strength, flexibility, and agility.

Thomas Jefferson was one of those to observe other possible outcomes from physical education. He credited exercise as having some value for the body but felt it also should give boldness, enterprise, and independence to the mind. President Wayland of Brown University, in an annual report, noted that several students attributed increased body vigor and aptitude for study to exercises in the new gymnasium. Dr. A. B. Alcott, writing in 1836, believed that physical activity should also exercise and amuse the mind. Exercise should refresh the mind from its pursuit of studies. Other writers talked about the relation of mind to body and cited the ancient Greek education. Prevailing practice, however, was summed up by one physician who stated: "The importance of health to the regular exercise of the faculties of the mind, as well as those of body, is very well understood in theory, and very generally neglected in fact."[8]

It is important to bear in mind that during time of war in this early period, physical education was not modified to help prepare for military service. It was simply replaced by military drill and the question of retaining physical education (if it existed) hardly merited discussion. The advocates of military drill for schoolchildren claimed that it fostered habits of promptness and exactness; taught subordination; developed "erectness of carriage," clean appearance, and respectful behavior; and occupied time

[5]Noah Webster, *A Collection of Essays and Fugitiv Writings* (Boston: I. Thomas and E. T. Andrews, 1790), p. 388.

[6]"Gymnasium in Boston," *American Journal of Education* 1 (July 1826): 437.

[7]Catherine E. Beecher, *Physiology and Calisthenics for Schools and Families* (New York: Harper and Brothers, 1856), p. iv.

[8]John C. Warren, *Physical Education and the Preservation of Health* (Boston: William D. Ticknor and Company, 1846), p. 6.

that otherwise might be spent in harmful amusements.[9] They pointed out the need for schoolchildren to have some relief from long hours of toil. The supreme virtue of military drill, however, was the inculcation of patriotism. This association of patriotism and military drill automatically branded opponents as disloyal and unpatriotic, regardless of the validity of their arguments. Dio Lewis was one of the few to oppose military drill in the schools.

The only organized program of physical education in any college at this time was carried on by Dr. Edward Hitchcock at Amherst. He conducted classes for all students with emphasis on hygiene and recreation. The purpose of the class activities was to maintain health and to give the students some relief from the strain of their academic courses.

Promotion of Physical Education

During the period up to the Civil War, colleges had little to do with physical education. Between 1825 and 1830, some colleges provided an area or room for gymnastic apparatus. Any member of the faculty who supervised the exercises did so on his own time and the students participated voluntarily and on their own time. Harvard provided a typical example. Dr. Charles Follen came from Germany to join the faculty as an instructor of German. He began gymnastic exercises for students and attempted to duplicate with Harvard students what Jahn had done with German students. Harvard students met informally twice a week on the Delta, which was furnished with the apparatus of a Turnplatz, but interest in the exercises died out within three years.

President Wayland of Brown University was an exception to the general college administrator's apathy toward physical education. He stated, "By affording the means of pure and attractive social recreations, the students have sought and found their pleasure *at home*, and . . . with no risk of moral contamination and without a single explosion of unbecoming mirth."[10] But even the interest of President Wayland was unavailing and early gymnastics at Brown suffered the same fate as at other colleges. The University of Virginia maintained a large outdoor gymnasium from 1852 to the Civil War. A Frenchman was employed as the instructor, but he was paid by the students and obtained additional income by cultivating a kitchen garden and running a Russian bathhouse. The general situation was aptly summed up by Hartwell, who stated that ". . . there appears to have been no well considered and sustained attempt by the

[9]N. W. Taylor Root, *School Amusements* (New York: A. S. Barnes and Company, 1857), pp. xiii–xiv.

[10]Louis F. Snow, *The College Curriculum in the United States* (New York: Teachers College, Columbia University, 1907), pp. 125–26.

authorities of any American college to provide its students, either with instruction in gymnastics or adequate facilities for athletic sports, during the period extending from 1826 to 1860."[11]

In the late 1820s, a number of colleges and academies attempted to combine agricultural and manual labor with intellectual education, based on Fellenberg's school at Hofwyl. By 1829 the movement for manual labor schools had become quite influential and had spread to almost every state. The manual training idea was most popular in the new colleges of the West (Ohio, Indiana, and Illinois) because these institutions could more easily adapt to the new plan. Land was plentiful and fruitful, the forest had to be cleared away, little money was available, and prospective students were poor. Manual training in educational institutions reached its zenith about 1831 and supplanted gymnastic exercises which had been popular a few years earlier. But manual training in turn quickly faded. The expected financial gains from manual labor did not materialize, as it was found that the labor had to be continuous to make money, and that this would interfere with time devoted to study. Faced with these difficulties, the manual labor movement had entered a decline by 1835.

The first significant college program in physical education was that which started at Amherst in 1861 under the supervision of Dr. Edward Hitchcock. Amherst constructed a new gymnasium (which provided an area of 40 to 50 feet) and required all students to attend the gymnasium for half an hour four times a week. Dr. Hitchcock, a Harvard Medical School graduate, was appointed Professor of Hygiene and Physical Education, the first physical education instructor to have full faculty status. "Old Doc," as he was affectionately called by his many students, taught at Amherst for fifty years until his death and established a program that stood alone for twenty years but eventually served as an example for other colleges.

SCHOOLS: The academies and private schools for boys and girls were more receptive to physical exercises than the colleges, especially after the Revolutionary War. Timothy Dwight at Greenfield Hill Academy insisted on morning and afternoon recesses. An instructor at Dummer Academy halted classes in the middle of a period to take advantage of the right tide for swimming. Boys at these and other schools played various ball games while some of the girls took part in calisthenics and dancing.[12]

Joseph Neef came to the United States and opened a school in 1809 at the request of a philanthropic Philadelphian, William Maclure. He con-

[11]Edward M. Hartwell, *Physical Training in American Colleges and Universities*, Bureau of Education Circular of Information no. 5, 1885 (Washington, D.C.: Government Printing Office, 1886), p. 26.
[12]Harriet W. Marr, *The Old New England Academies* (New York: Comet Press Books, 1959), pp. 156–66.

ducted the school for several years and wrote a book on education which included a section entitled "Gymnastics or Exercise." Neef had little influence on American education, but his school may well have been the first to provide physical exercise on a systematic basis.

The most significant of these schools in the history of physical education was the Round Hill School founded in 1823 at Northampton, Massachusetts by Joseph Cogswell and George Bancroft, who later became America's first national historian. They were in the vanguard of many American scholars who went to Germany for graduate study in the nineteenth century. Cogswell visited Yverdun but was very critical of Pestalozzi; on the other hand he admired Fellenberg's school. In their first prospectus for the school, the two men declared their intent to "appropriate regularly a portion of each day to healthful sports and gymnastic exercises.[13] They also employed the first teacher of physical education, Dr. Charles Beck, in 1825. Beck, who was a Turner and friend of Jahn, had just arrived from Germany as a political refugee. He established an outdoor gymnasium which marked the introduction of German gymnastics to this country. Incidentally, Beck set an impressive precedent for subsequent teachers of physical education—he was an ordained Lutheran pastor and also held the Ph.D. degree.

The public schools showed little interest in physical education until the 1850s when some cities allowed a few minutes of calisthenics in the daily curriculum. In 1853 Boston became the first city to require daily exercise for school children. The Rincon School in San Francisco was notable not only for the time given to physical education but also for the quality of the program conducted by its principal, John Swett, who came from New Hampshire in the Gold Rush. In 1860, Brooklyn, Hartford, Toledo, and Cincinnati had school gymnasiums in the high schools and pupils were given physical exercises.

Two people in this period are outstanding for their attempts to popularize physical education—Catherine Beecher and Dio Lewis.

Catherine Beecher was one of the prominent Beecher family and a sister of Harriet Beecher Stowe. She conducted a girl's seminary at Hartford, Connecticut, in which daily calisthenics were given. Later she opened the Western Female Institute in Cincinnati. The following notice concerning this school is informative:

> To aid in Physical Education, Calisthenics are adopted as a means of relaxation and exercise, and instead of the practice of some schools . . . of allowing but *five minutes* to this daily session, we are gratified to learn that *half an hour* is devoted to it each half day. It is rendered

[13]Joseph C. Cogswell and George Bancroft, *Prospectus of a School to be Established at Round Hill, Northampton, Massachusetts* (Cambridge, Mass.: 1823), p. 17.

attractive by music and serves at the same time as a lesson in musical rhythm. We are assured by those who have tried both, that it is a far more efficient means than dancing, for improving the form and the manners, without any of its evils.[14]

Miss Beecher wrote one book in 1832 entitled *Course of Calisthenics for Young Ladies*, but her most influential work was *A Manual of Physiology and Calisthenics for Schools and Families*, published in 1856. This book marked a broadening of her efforts from merely advocating calisthenics for girls to working for the introduction of physical training in American schools. She spent the summer of 1856 visiting teachers and school boards in Cincinnati, Baltimore, and Philadelphia, and sent a communication to the annual meeting of the American Association for the Advancement of Education urging the adoption of physical training for all schoolchildren. She believed that each school should have one person responsible for health and physical training with a half-hour of each school session set aside for physical training.

Although many of Beecher's exercises were taken from European sources, she was perhaps the first native American to formulate a comprehensive gymnastic system adapted to American needs. She recognized the problem of securing support for the program and stated, "The great struggle will be to bring all the parties concerned—pupils, teachers, parents, and school committees—to take from the time now given exclusively to intellectual training, sufficient to secure the health, strength, and beauty of the physical system."[15] Catherine Beecher, despite her own poor health, was one of the first to participate actively in the struggle to establish physical education as part of the school curriculum in America.

The other person who popularized and promoted gymnastics was Dr. Dio Lewis, whose title is based on an honorary degree from an obscure homeopathic hospital. Depending largely on a magnetic personality and "such an inundation of animal spirits that he could flood any company, no matter how starched or listless,"[16] Lewis appeared before the annual meeting of the American Institute of Instruction in 1860 at Boston and completely captivated the group. In recording this meeting, the secretary rapturously wrote: "Over two hours were spent in witnessing the gymnastic exercises, and in the discussion of physical training, and it enlisted the most earnest attention of the large assembly. It was regarded as one of the most important and practically valuable subjects which has come before the meetings of this Institute."[17] Before adjourning, the Institute passed a resolution recommending the general introduction of Lewis' gymnastics into

[14]*American Annals of Education* 3 (August 1833): 380–81.
[15]Beecher, *Physiology and Calisthenics*, p. iv.
[16]Thomas W. Higginson, "Gymnastics," *Atlantic Monthly* 7 (March 1861): 300.
[17]*Massachusetts Teacher* 13 (October 1860): 383.

all the schools and for general use. A number of eastern cities incorporated his "New Gymnastics" into their school curriculums for not more than fifteen minutes daily.

BEGINNINGS OF TEACHER TRAINING: In view of the lack of teacher training for any subject in the public schools, the lack of recognition of teacher training for physical education was to be expected. Books on exercise such as Catherine Beecher's were written with the expectation that the reader could follow the instructions and imitate the illustrations. Only occasionally is there evidence that the need for qualified teachers was appreciated. When the new high school in New York City opened in 1825, gymnastic exercises were to be taught by older boys on the monitorial plan that was used throughout the school. Apparently difficulties soon arose because within a year it was recorded that gymnastic exercises were now under the superintendence of "an experienced and careful teacher."

Teacher training in physical education received its first genuine impetus from Dio Lewis when he established a Normal Institute for Physical Education in Boston in 1861. The first graduating class consisted of "seven ladies and six gentlemen" who practiced gymnastic exercises from six to twelve hours a day for nine weeks. This school existed for six or seven years and graduated some 250 pupils.

NONSCHOOL AGENCIES: An important agency was the German Turnverein.[18] Its clubs served as social and educational centers for the German immigrants who had come to the United States because of unsettled political conditions in their country. The new German residents tended to live together and preserve their old customs within the various cities where they settled. The entire family, from the youngest member to the oldest, went to the Turnverein for exercises, games, military drill, music, lectures, discussions, and social functions. The first Turnverein was formed in Cincinnati in 1848 as a result of the arrival of Friedrich Hecker, a popular hero in the Revolution of Baden. Many more societies came into existence following the wave of German immigration in 1848, thus leading to the formation of the National Turnerbund in 1850 and the first national festival, or Turnfest, the next year. By the time of the Civil War there were approximately 150 local societies with 10,000 members.[19] One contemporary writer observed: "The Turn Verein has been for some years endeavoring to teach us some good lessons in physical education, and we must say that we do not see that our American youth have benefited by the instruction imparted."[20] The Turnerbund became dormant during the Civil

---

[18]*Turnen* means gymnastic exercises; *Turner* means gymnast and a member of the *Turnverein* or gymnastic club. See Chapter 13.

[19]Emmett A. Rice, *A Brief History of Physical Education* (New York: A. S. Barnes and Co., 1929), p. 163.

[20]"The Turnfest," *Frank Leslie's Illustrated Newspaper*, 1 October 1864, p. 29.

War, as many of its members enlisted in the Union Army. Another national group, the Scots, held the Caledonian games, first at Boston in 1853, and later in New York and Philadelphia.

The example of Boston citizens in subscribing to and maintaining a public gymnasium appears to have had no imitators. This gymnasium was opened in 1826 and was supported by public subscription. Follen helped found the gymnasium and served as a supervisor for almost a year when he was succeeded by another German, Dr. Francis Lieber, personally recommended by Jahn. Lieber also opened a swimming school in connection with the Boston gymnasium. Such swimming schools had been established in a number of German and European cities, but the Boston swimming school was probably the first in the United States. The career of the swimming school was highlighted in 1837 by the personal appearance of President John Quincy Adams, an excellent swimmer, who dove off the six-foot springboard.[21] In the next two decades, some private gymnasiums, mainly for young males, were established in the larger cities.

EARLY PROGRESS IN PHYSICAL EDUCATION: During this period of emergent nationalism in the United States, two brief spans of time were most fruitful with respect to physical education. The first was between 1825 and 1830; and the second, from approximately 1850 to 1865. In between, was an interval in which physical education was overshadowed by an academic interest in physiology and hygiene.

The importation of Jahn's gymnastics and their appearance in eastern schools and colleges seemed a roseate beginning for physical education, but within a few years the movement languished. In an address in 1830 before the American Institute of Instruction in Boston, Dr. John C. Warren of the Harvard Medical School said: "The establishment of gymnasia throughout the country promised, at one period, the opening of a new era in physical education. The exercises were pursued with ardor, so long as their novelty lasted; but, owing to not understanding their importance, or some defect in the institutions which adopted them, they have gradually been neglected and forgotten, at least in our vincinity."[22]

There are a number of reasons for this precipitous decline in gymnastics. Part of the explanation is found in the temper of the times—times of many other ephemeral movements. Monitorial instruction, manual training, vegetarianism, temperance, phrenology, and various religious sects all received considerable popular, but short-lived, interest and support. German gymnastics, therefore, became just another fad that went the way of the others. Moreover, since no effort was made to modify or adapt them

---

[21]Thomas S. Perry, *The Life and Letters of Francis Lieber* (Boston: James R. Osgood and Co., 1882), p. 78.

[22]Quoted in Hartwell, *Physical Training in American Colleges and Universities,* p. 25.

for use, the spirit and purpose of the Jahn gymnastics was vitiated. No native teachers of German gymnastics were developed either. Even Beck, Follen, and Lieber depended for a living primarily on their academic capabilities, and their work in gymnastics was no more than an avocation. It is also likely that the German exercises proved rather strenuous for those who lacked the patience to develop needed strength and skill.

There are several reasons for the surge of interest in physical education in the 1850s. As the young nation matured and became urbanized, there were more people who did not have to engage in physical labor, and many people now had some time available that did not have to be used for maintaining existence itself. As for the schools, Boykin suggested that school officers were less absorbed with vital administrative questions and were therefore able to discuss physical training and give some thought to it.[23] He also believed the Turnerbund might have been influential, but German gymnastics were not prominent at this time. In fact, the Cincinnati Turners, who did their exercises in an open lot at first, soon put up a high board fence because of unfriendly spectators. A year later they were able to build a gymnasium.[24] Actually the Turner influence was confined largely to the German population until after 1880. Another contributing factor was that the textbooks in physiology from 1830 served the useful purpose of containing information on the value of exercise. The subject assumed more importance when, in 1843, an educational leader such as Horace Mann devoted the major part of his *Sixth Annual Report* to physiology and hygiene. The very title of Beecher's book, *Physiology and Calisthenics*, also caught the new spirit of the times by acknowledging the association of these two subjects. During the thirties and forties there was a growing popular interest in sports as reflected in the appearance of the first two important sporting weeklies: *The Spirit of the Times* and the *National Police Gazette*. Their columns contained news about horse racing, boxing, cricket, and baseball.

It must not be inferred that participation in sports and gymnastics became universal during the 1850s. A vast majority of the schools remained unaffected by Beecher's pleas and Boston's example. But enough progress had been made so that physical education finally established a foothold in American life.[25]

RECREATION: During the latter half of this period, educators also began to take some note of the undesirable recreations of the pupils. Commercial amusements were attracting the students then as now, with the

[23]James C. Boykin, "History of Physical Training," *Report of the Commissioner of Education for 1891–92* (Washington, D.C.: U. S. Government Printing Office, 1894) 1:514.

[24]Adolf E. Zucker, ed., *The Forty-Eighters* (New York: Columbia University Press, 1950), p. 92.

[25]Thomas W. Higginson, "Gymnastics," *Atlantic Monthly* 7 (March 1861): 288.

usual sensory and emotional appeal. Educators were sufficiently alarmed to point out that billiard rooms, grog shops, and bowling alleys were not the proper places for the education of youth. Some of the colleges sought to improve conditions by making rules against the use of intoxicating liquors, tobacco, narcotics, card-playing, and other games of chance. In brief, schoolmen of this early day attempted to suppress undesirable recreations, but at the same time they offered nothing socially constructive to replace the activities they so vigorously condemned.

Program of Physical Education

Benjamin Franklin was probably the first American to propose that physical training be made part of the educational curriculum. He suggested the desirability of such activities as running, leaping, wrestling, and in particular, swimming, which he had once taught and about which he later wrote a treatise. It is not known to what extent Franklin's ideas were carried out in the academy at Philadelphia which he helped found in 1749.

Noah Webster looked with favor on many activities. He preferred fencing, but running, football, quoits, and dancing were also good in his opinion, and he believed that all colleges should make daily provisions for exercise. However, he regarded these activities only as substitutes for labor in agriculture or mechanical arts.[26] Benjamin Rush saw some value in play for schoolchildren after classes, but he felt that play should help train the child for his future employment as a farmer, craftsman, doctor, or lawyer. Hence gardening, using a hammer and saw, or running a machine were most desirable and productive activities. Rush criticized "gunning" or hunting because it "hardened the heart," created habits of idleness, exposed one to fever and accidents, and aroused emotions leading to war rather than peace.[27] Thomas Jefferson, on the other hand, considered hunting to be an excellent exercise for both mind and body. In his plans for the University of Virginia, he regarded gymnastics as a proper object of attention but put most stress on military exercises and use of tools in manual arts.

Joseph Neef not only wrote about gymnastic exercises but also put them into practice. One of his pupils recalled: "We were encouraged in all athletic sports, were great swimmers and skaters, walkers and gymnasts. In the pleasant weather we went to bathe twice every day in the Schuylkill, with Neef, who was an accomplished swimmer, at our head."[28] Neef led the boys on long hikes and pointed out practical applications of agricul-

---

[26]Noah Webster, *A Collection of Essays*, p. 389.

[27]Benjamin Rush, *Essays, Literary, Moral, and Philosophical* (Philadelphia: Thomas and William Bradford, 1806), pp. 60–61.

[28]C. D. Gardette, "Pestallozzi in America," *Galaxy* 4 (August 1867): 437.

ture, botany, and mineralogy and thus was a pioneer in outdoor education. A former soldier in Napoleon's army, Neef also provided intensive training in riflery and military exercises.

Captain Partridge believed in physical education for health and vigor, but the program at his military academies had a distinct military flavor. The students hiked as many as forty miles a day, climbed mountains in New York and New England, and did mapping and surveying.

The gymnastics practiced at the Round Hill School, the Boston gymnasium, Harvard, and other colleges were characterized by the typical apparatus of the *Turnplatz*. Parallel bars, horizontal bars, ladders, swinging ropes, and jumping pits were standard equipment. Cambridge citizens were often treated to the sight of Dr. Follen leading a group of students single file, running through the streets "with the body thrown slightly forward, the arms akimbo, and breathing only through the nose."[29]

Round Hill School offered far more than gymnastics. These boys participated regularly in running, jumping, swimming, sledding, ice skating, baseball, football, archery, wrestling, horseback riding, and dancing. Considerable time was devoted to hiking, camping, and outdoor education. The students visited many historical places of interest, and Cogswell lectured on geology along the way. The boys themselves dug huts into the side of Round Hill where they cooked game which they had trapped or shot and ate roast corn and baked potatoes.[30]

Other institutions offered exercises on a more limited basis. One such school was the Thayer School in Boston where the principal took the elementary students outdoors for fifteen minutes of running, hopping, jumping with and without poles, tug-of-war, and walking on the edge of a plank. Any boy deficient in his day's lessons, however, could not participate in the exercises.[31]

The schools and colleges which adopted the manual labor plan provided scant facilities for physical education. Male students worked several hours a day chopping trees, constructing buildings, and planting crops. Females did housekeeping, light gardening, and sewing.

In view of the general status of women at the time, exercises for women received a surprising amount of attention. The girls attending the Boston Monitorial School probably had more strenuous activity than those at any other school. As described by the principal, William Fowle, "Besides the ordinary exercises of raising the arms and feet, and extending them in various directions, we have various methods of hanging and swing-

[29]Quoted in George W. Spindler, *Karl Follen, A Biographical Study* (Chicago: University of Chicago Press, 1917), p. 131.

[30]Bruce L. Bennett, "The Making of Round Hill School," *Quest* 4 (April 1965): 58–61.

[31]"Mr. G. F. Thayer's School, Boston," *American Journal of Education* 1 (September 1826): 562.

ing by the arms, tilting, raising weights, jumping forward, marching, running, *enduring*, etc."[32] Fowle even went so far as to maintain that walking and household labor could not completely replace gymnastics for girls.

Dr. John Warren recommended not only walking and dancing but also exercises on the triangle, ball games played with either hand, dumbbells, and parallel bars.[33] Other writers, however, tended to limit desirable activities for women to walking, riding, gardening, household duties, and possibly dancing, though the latter was sometimes declared to be immoral. Alcott described suitable exercises for women as an occasional ramble, a rapid walk "or even run, and clap your hands, and shout *Eureka*."[34]

Women educators themselves were rather conservative. Emma Willard in a pamphlet, "Plan for Improving Female Education," written in 1819, mentioned instruction in dancing.[35] At Mt. Holyoke Female Seminary, founded by Mary Lyon in 1837, the girls received twenty minutes of calisthenics and one hour of domestic work.[36]

A full exposition of Beecher's ideas is found in her *Physiology and Calisthenics*. In addition to the usual free exercises,[37] Beecher also described exercises using cotton bags filled with corn which were used as dumbbells and for playing catch. The only other apparatus was two parallel poles perpendicular to the floor and about a shoulder-width apart. All these exercises were for both boys and girls, and Beecher fervently desired to see them adopted for use in all public schools. She listed four advantages of her system:

1. Can be practiced in all schools or homes without a special room or apparatus.
2. Excludes severe exercises, yet contains all that either sex needs for perfect body development. Both sexes can do the exercises together.
3. Are based on scientific principles discovered by Ling.
4. The drawings make it possible to do exercises without aid from a teacher.[38]

Within a year after his arrival at the Rincon School in San Francisco in 1853, John Swett established a regular daily program of calisthenics,

[32]William B. Fowle, "Gymnastic Exercises for Females," *American Journal of Education* 1 (November 1826): 698.

[33]Warren, *Physical Education and Health*, pp. 37–38.

[34]William A. Alcott, *Letters to a Sister; or Woman's Mission* (Buffalo: George H. Derby and Co., 1850), p. 55.

[35]Willystine Goodsell, ed., *Pioneers of Women's Education in the United States* (New York: McGraw-Hill Book Company, 1931), p. 65.

[36]Ibid., p. 290.

[37]Free exercises refer to exercises without apparatus. Calisthenics means both free exercises and/or light gymnastics, which are exercises with light apparatus such as dumbbells.

[38]Beecher, *Physiology and Calisthenics*, p. iv.

light gymnastics, and free play. He also conducted boxing and organized student exhibitions to raise funds to buy needed equipment.[39] At the May festival in 1856, the boys led by Swett put on a gymnastic exhibition that included exercises on the horizontal bar, on the rings, and with clubs, wands, and dumbbells. Swett encouraged the boys to play ball and on Saturdays led them on hikes of ten to fifteen miles to the beach. The girls had daily drills in free gymnastics and wands.[40] Swett's early leadership in physical education has been obscured by the subsequent reputation he attained as an educator.

Dr. Winship's exercises consisted of the lifting of heavy weights, both with the hands alone and with a yoke or harness. Next best to lifting weights, in his opinion, were exercises with the heavy iron dumbbells that varied in weight up to one hundred pounds each.

Dio Lewis collected a variety of exercises that were performed with and without light apparatus. He denounced the German apparatus and the heavy weight-lifting appliances and used only light dumbbells and clubs, rubber balls, bean bags, wands, and rings. Lewis compiled numerous calisthenic exercises that could be accompanied by music and used a large number of simple games for children, men, and women. Lewis originated very few of these exercises but culled them from many sources, one of which was Catherine Beecher. He probably did originate the gymnastic crown. This device was an iron crown, weighing from five to thirty pounds, and padded so that it could be worn on the head. Wearing the crown twenty minutes a day (ten in the morning and ten at night) was supposed to straighten the spine. Lewis got the idea from watching people in other countries who carried loads on the head and had good posture.

The new Amherst gymnasium was provided with such apparatus as a horizontal bar, rack bars, vaulting horse, batule board, spool ropes, peg pole, incline board, perpendicular pole, various ladders, rings, lifting weights, and Indian clubs. Under Dr. Hitchcock's supervision, the typical class period consisted of about twenty minutes of light gymnastics with wooden dumbbells weighing less than a pound each. The exercises were done in unison to piano music. Wands and rings were occasionally substituted in place of dumbbells but were not so popular. Some marching by file and flank was done at quick time in the warm weather, double time in the cold. The remaining ten minutes of the period were occupied with voluntary exercises such as running, dancing, singing, somersaulting, or exercising with clubs or heavy apparatus. The gymnasium also had bowling alleys and rowing machines.

---

[39]Dudley S. DeGroot, "A History of Physical Education in California (1848–1939)" (Doctoral dissertation, Stanford University, 1940), p. 11.

[40]John Swett, *Public Education in California* (New York: American Book Co., 1911), pp. 121–24.

ATHLETIC SPORTS: Sports in the period from 1789 to 1865 became somewhat more popular, especially in the fifties. The game of nine pins (bowling), which had been banned in the 1830s because of its association with gambling, was changed to ten pins as a legalizing device, and the new game was destined to have an amazing growth. Women took up riding and ice skating. Swimming was enjoyed by both sexes. Cricket and rowing had many participants, but the former lost out to baseball because the "briskness and unceasing activity are perhaps more congenial, after all, to our national character, than the comparative deliberation of cricket."[41]

The commonly accepted notion that baseball was invented by Abner Doubleday at Cooperstown, New York, in 1839, has no basis in fact as shown by the painstaking research of Robert W. Henderson.[42] Baseball actually goes back to early eighteenth-century England where a game of that name was described in a book published in 1744. The game migrated to the United States, and a Revolutionary War soldier mentioned playing baseball in his diary. Early English baseball gradually became known as "rounders" while in America it was called "town ball" or "round ball." In the early nineteenth century, baseball in the form of one-old-cat, two-old-cat, and three-old-cat was generally played by children throughout the United States, although there were no standard rules.

The first printed rules for baseball in the United States appeared in Carver's *Book of Sports* in 1834. These rules were practically a reprint of rules for the English game of rounders given in an English volume that appeared five years earlier. Another book, published in New Haven in 1839, described the game of baseball in which four stones were arranged in a diamond shape with a home base for the batter. The batter was out if he missed the ball three times or if a fielder caught the ball after it was hit. The batter could also be put out if he was hit between bases by a ball thrown by a fielder.

In 1845, a group of New York gentlemen, who had been playing together informally for about three years, organized the Knickerbocker Base Ball Club and drew up a set of rules that marked a significant advance over the previous rules but still differed greatly from modern baseball. A game was over when one team scored twenty-one runs; a batted ball caught on a fly or first bounce was out; and the ball had to be pitched underhand to the batter. The size of the diamond was about the same as today except for a shorter pitching distance, and a baserunner could only be put out by being tagged. Throwing a ball at the runner was no longer permitted. Henderson credited the Knickerbocker Club with "first setting

41Thomas W. Higginson, "Saints and Their Bodies," *Atlantic Monthly* 1 (March 1858): 593.
42Robert W. Henderson, *Ball, Bat, and Bishop* (New York: Rockport Press, Inc., 1947), pp. 182–94. This book is the main source for the next two paragraphs.

up a reasonably stable organization, and in particular for drawing up a set of rules which may justly be called the foundation of the *modern* American game."[43]

During the 1850s, a number of baseball teams were formed in the New York area. However, baseball enjoyed only moderate popularity until the Civil War. It was played by soldiers of both armies and was carried to all parts of the country when they returned home. The first intercollegiate baseball game was played on the grounds of the Pittsfield Base Ball Club in 1859. Amherst defeated Williams, 73 to 32, in a game which took three and a half hours.[44] Football was also played during this period. It had come to the United States with the first colonists in New England and Virgina. During the seventeenth and eighteenth centuries there was little mention of the sport. One of the first references to football was to an interclass game at Harvard in 1827. In the 1840s, interclass games were also played at Yale and Princeton. However, at both Harvard and Yale, the game developed such roughness and violence that it was abolished for several years by faculty action. In 1862, the Oneida Football Club was formed in Boston by young high school graduates who played a number of games in the next few years.[45]

The first intercollegiate contest in any sport was a rowing match between Harvard and Yale in 1852. In view of all the problems of commercialism which have plagued college athletics through the years, it was prophetic that the first college athletic contest was sponsored by a railroad, at a site in New Hampshire far from both campuses, and in August during summer vacation. The crew race was only one of several festivities planned by railroad officials to promote the area as a summer resort.[46]

The Caledonian games of the Scots comprised many events such as hammer throwing, putting stones, broad jumping, running, walking, hurdling, quoits, and wrestling. Prizes were awarded and spectators admitted.[47]

In the rural areas and frontier settlements sports tended to be more primitive and crude. Cockfighting and bear- or bullbaiting attracted many rabid spectators. It was not unusual to see a man whose eye had been gouged out in a fight. Abraham Lincoln was a local champion in the style of wrestling similar to Greek wrestling, where the opponent was cleanly

[43]Ibid., p. 196.

[44]Frederick Rudolph, *Mark Hopkins and the Log* (New Haven: Yale University Press, 1956), p. 164.

[45]Henry L. Baker, *Football: Facts and Figures* (New York: Rinehart and Co., Inc., 1945), pp. 9–11.

[46]Robert F. Kelley, *American Rowing: Its Background and Traditions* (New York: G. P. Putnam's Sons, 1932), p. 100.

[47]Robert Korsgaard, "The Formative Years of Sports Control and the Founding of the Amateur Athletic Union of the United States," *67th Annual Proceedings of the National College Physical Education Association for Men,* p. 67.

thrown to the ground. Mountain men and fur traders at their remote rendezvous engaged in "hunting, fishing, target-shooting, foot-racing, gymnastics, and sundry other exercises," according to one participant.[48] These rugged individuals also engaged in a brutal, hand-to-hand combat with no holds barred. Such a fight between Boone Caudill and Streak is described in graphic detail by A. B. Guthrie in his brilliant novel, *The Big Sky*.[49]

As the frontier receded, and by the time of the Civil War, a number of sports were being practiced. Although participation at this time was still limited to individuals who had some economic means, social status, and leisure, nevertheless sports were beginning to find a place in American life.

Methods of Physical Education

Little was said about methods of physical education prior to the importation of German gymnastics in 1825. Franklin, Webster, Rush, and Jefferson did not elaborate their ideas on physical education sufficiently to go into details of instruction. Franklin did refer to the necessity of having both a safe place and a careful instructor for swimming. Jefferson recognized the need for teachers of gymnastics, music, dancing, and drawing at the University of Virginia, but they were to be paid by the students and not by the university. Neef taught calisthenics by personally demonstrating the motion to be performed. Then all the children responded upon command.[50]

There is a lack of information concerning the methods of instruction used for the German gymnastics, but it appears reasonable to assume that Beck, Follen, and Lieber continued the methods of Jahn without radical change. Follen at Harvard developed student leaders called monitors and vice-monitors with whom he met on Monday of each week to prepare for general exercises on Wednesday and Friday. These assistants seem comparable to the Vorturners developed by Jahn.

Catherine Beecher was the only American prior to Dio Lewis who worked out a system of exercises adapted to the schools. The teacher in charge of physical training was to train student or division leaders, who, in turn, would supervise and demonstrate the exercises. Each pupil had an

---

[48]T. D. Bonner, *Life and Adventures of James P. Beckwourth* (New York: Harper & Brothers, 1856), p. 69.

[49]A. B. Guthrie, Jr., *The Big Sky* (New York: William Sloane Associates, 1947), pp. 207–209.

[50]Joseph Neef, *Sketch of a Plan and Method of Education, Founded on an Analysis of the Human Faculties and Natural Reason, Suitable for the Offspring of a Free People and for All Rational Beings* (Philadelphia: Printed for the Author, 1808), pp. 102–103.

assigned place on the classroom or gymnasium floor. Each pupil should have a partner, and if boys and girls were present, they should be paired off as partners. Beecher suggested that the class should go over the exercises once to learn the method. The next time each exercise should be performed twice and done moderately. Gradually the exercises should be done with increasing speed and force. "In case of any delicate pupils, who are unfavorably affected by any of these exercises, the teacher should seek medical advice."[51] Pupils with personal defects were to be given additional special exercises to be done out of school.

Dr. Winship referred to the proper method of lifting: a person should lift as heavy a weight as he could handle and should never exercise more than a half-hour daily or one hour every two days. Contrary to many writers of that period, Winship recommended that a person should never leave the dinner table hungry, nor get up early in the morning unless "you retire early, or sleep with your windows closed, or have something to attend to which will not permit you to lie late."[52]

The exercises of Dio Lewis were adaptable for use by "the strongest man, feeblest woman, and frailest child" and could be done in a classroom or at home, individually or as a class. For class exercises, each person stood on marked spots on the floor. The teacher selected and demonstrated exercises and games. Lewis recommended musical accompaniment with either a drum, violin, piano, or, preferably, a hand organ; and he sought to maintain a spirit of joy and pleasure through the combined use of exercises and simple games.

At Amherst College each class met as a unit with a student captain who led the exercises. Rivalry was stimulated by an annual award of one hundred dollars given to the class that most faithfully discharged its duties in the gymnasium during the year. Students could also come to the gymnasium for volunteer work. Discipline was not strict, and the methods reflected the kindly personality of Dr. Hitchcock.

SUMMARY: Physical education enjoyed no general popular support or enthusiasm in this period, but tentative beginnings were made. Benjamin Franklin showed some appreciation of the value of exercise. The German gymnastics of Jahn were introduced into the United States in the middle 1820s, and various sports became moderately popular. John Warren, Catherine Beecher, George Winship, Dio Lewis, and others did a great deal to make the American public more receptive to the idea of physical education. The nature of their contribution is aptly stated by Betts: ". . . in the quarter century between 1820 and 1845 educators, physicians, and reformers had begun to develop a philosophical rationale concerning the

---

[51]Beecher, *Physiology and Calisthenics*, pp. 9–10.
[52]George B. Winship, "Physical Culture," *Massachusetts Teacher* 13 (April 1860): 132.

relationship of physical to mental and spiritual benefits derived from exercise, games, and sports."[53]

The results began to show up in the 1850s when baseball attracted a small following, and rowing achieved some prominence. Several cities initiated physical education in the public schools, although on a very modest basis, and Amherst instituted the first college program of physical education. The German Turnvereins nurtured a respect for physical education within their own group which proved beneficial to the non-German population in the 1880s. The foundation for the growth of sport and physical education which occurred after the Civil War had been laid prior to 1865.

[53]John R. Betts, "Mind and Body in Early American Thought," *The Journal of American History* 54 (March 1968): 805.

22

Physical Education
in
Education for Nationalism
1865-1900

Out of the destruction and anguish of the Civil War came a stronger American nationalism and an unshakable sense of national unity. The existence of this unity was strikingly apparent when the Spanish-American War broke out in 1898; the entire nation rallied to the cause despite the previous differences of opinion on the issues involved.

The years of 1865 to 1900 were primarily occupied with the nationalization of a people who lived in homes and farms spread out from "sea to shining sea." During these thirty-five years, the incredible total of 13,260,000 immigrants were admitted to the United States. From the standpoint of both geography and population, therefore, the effectiveness of the nationalizing process was all the more remarkable.

One aspect of nationalization was the growing centralized authority of the federal government in various affairs. The demands of the Civil War required that the government draft men and build railways. The rapid expansion and massive growth of business kept forcing the Federal Government to extend its authority. The Interstate Commerce Act of 1887 and the Sherman Anti-Trust Act of 1890 were two examples. In 1894 President Cleveland, without the consent of state officials, sent federal troops to break the Pullman strike.

A most necessary phase of nationalization was the reorientation of the South into the Union and the easing of wartime bitterness and postwar abuses. The increased intermingling of Northerners and Southerners in business and travel and the new literary works describing a romantic and chivalrous South helped overcome prejudices cultivated by the abolitionists. In addition, the South became tied in with industrial and agricultural problems that linked it to other parts of the country.

Underlying all these events were profound economic changes that contributed to the development of an American nationality. Foremost perhaps was the uniting of the Pacific Coast with the rest of the nation by transcontinental railroad in 1869. Within fifteen years three more railroads spanned the continent. Technological improvements fostered the growth and use of telegraph facilities, and the genius of Alexander Graham Bell provided the telephone. Another important factor in communication was the emergence of an efficient, modern postal service.

The growth of agriculture and industry created new problems and forces. Agriculture expanded with the settling of the vast lands west of the Mississippi and the use of mechanical power and labor-saving farm machinery. Industry boomed with the harnessing of steam for power and the tapping of seemingly inexhaustible sources of coal and iron. Factories spread from East to the Midwest and into the South. With the phenomenal growth of agriculture and industry came agrarian unrest and labor discontent. Representatives of these interests began to make their influence felt on political issues such as the tariff question.

This remarkable era also saw the end of the land frontier and the rise of cities, but the spirit of optimism and rugged individualism developed by frontier life remained part of the national heritage. The rise of the cities was accompanied by a host of problems resulting from a lack of knowledge and of experience in how to govern thickly populated areas. Political corruption, filthy slums, organized crime, poverty, juvenile delinquency, and disease epidemics were all painful characteristics of the shift of population from farms to cities and of the influx of immigrants. As cities expanded in population and became more congested, children were forced to use streets crowded with traffic for play space. As recorded by one contemporary writer, "Teams and traffic and the hungry builder have claimed all open spaces for their own."[1]

Education did not remain static while these trends were under way. Prior to the Civil War, free schooling became a fairly well established principle. Yet it was early recognized that this provision did not suffice to bring attendance up to expectations. Consequently, talk of compulsory education began to be heard in various quarters. At first this idea met with the most violent opposition, and it was felt that compulsory schooling was antirepublican and a flagrant violation of individual rights. Finally, however, judgment prevailed both against the violent opposition of the individualists and the indifference of those who constantly practiced laissez-faire in all matters. People began to say that the welfare of the nation was imperiled if too large a proportion of the people grew up in ignorance. Gradually the conviction grew that parents had no right, individual or otherwise, to deprive their children of the education that the state was will-

[1]Sadie American, "The Movement for Small Playgrounds," *American Journal of Sociology* 4 (September 1898): 159.

ing to provide. The famous Kalamazoo Case of 1872 established the legality of tax-supported high schools, thereby increasing the age limits for school attendance.

There was some expansion of the old style classical curriculum. Late in this period, the influence of Charles Darwin and Herbert Spencer was reflected in American education by a new interest in natural science. Darwin's doctrines aroused great controversy, and Spencer stimulated educational thinking by his arguments in favor of a more practical curriculum. The educational theories of Johann Herbart provided the impetus for introducing the social sciences in American education. This development occurred about the time when the sciences were competing with mathematics and the traditional classical subjects for a place in the curriculum. In order of sequence, the natural sciences were added to the curriculum first, then the social sciences, and finally such subjects as freehand drawing and industrial arts.

Education in general benefited from the changing economic conditions. As machine production made possible a higher standard of living, there was less necessity for children to supplement the family income. Furthermore, for humanitarian reasons, child labor was condemned and, as the machines grew more complex, it became unprofitable as well. Organized labor also sought to restrict the employment of children and vigorously encouraged public education. These developments contributed to the expansion of the free public schools, the passage of compulsory attendance laws, and a significant increase in the number of high schools. Although rural schools in general remained as poor as they were in the previous period, substantial improvements were noted in the urban schools of the East and Midwest. It was in these schools that physical education programs first began to get under way. Farm chores no longer provided all growing boys and girls with exercise for the physical upkeep of the body; particularly in urban centers, there was need for substitutions. These were found in consciously planned gymnastics and in informal athletics.

As mentioned in the preceding chapter, *military training* replaced physical training in many schools during the Civil War. After the war, some schools and colleges retained military training, though not without student protest. For example, at Bowdoin, the effort to require drill led to an open student rebellion that finally resulted in the compromise that students could take either military drill or physical education. The Spanish-American War lasted but 114 days and was not long enough to resurrect the question of military training. In 1899, it was estimated that less than 5 percent of the high schools gave military instruction.

The increasing influence of the *scientific movement* on physical education was felt with impressive effect in a number of ways: the taking of body measurements; the use of dynamometers to measure strength; athletic achievement tests; the ready acceptance of Swedish medical and pedagogical gymnastics based on physiological principles carefully worked out by Ling; the more extensive training of teachers; and the founding of the Association for the Advancement of Physical Education, an event that was motivated largely by a desire to determine the best methods of teaching physical training. The spirit of scientific inquiry was typified by Dr. William G. Anderson who questioned the value of the breathing exercises and slow leg work in the Swedish system even though he was an advocate of Swedish gymnastics.

Toward the close of this period, *educational developmentalism*, also known as the psychological movement, reappeared—this time to stay. Froebel's system of primary education was introduced from Germany and, with the principles of Rousseau and Pestalozzi, eventually revolutionized the current ideas on education. To apply Pestalozzi's new principles of learning and methods of teaching required special pedagogical training. After the Civil War, the Pestalozzian influence was in vogue in American education for the rest of the century.

Herbartism reached the United States in the 1890s. Herbart emphasized the social and moral aspects of education and thought that these objectives could be best achieved through a study of the great men and great events of history. Herbart's "scientific" procedure of teaching, called the "five formal steps of learning and teaching," was introduced at a time when the principal methods of teaching were reading, memorizing, and reciting. Herbart's systematic methods quickly became popular in normal colleges throughout the country.

G. Stanley Hall's influence in the child study movement was just beginning to be impressive as the last century came to a close. He popularized the "recapitulation" or the "cultural-epoch" theory (i.e., "ontogeny repeats phylogeny") and applied it to the mental life. His theory, though since fallen out of favor, stimulated interest and research in the interests of adolescents. He firmly believed in play as one of the best forms of education in modern civilization.

Developmentalism had little influence in American education until 1890, when, through the newly established kindergartens and playgrounds, it began to chip away at the old, ingrained association of play with idleness. This movement regarded play as an essential, even necessary, part of normal growth. The first state laws concerning physical education were passed in this period and, combined with the scientific movement, stimulated better teacher preparation.

Social education began to assume some significance through the greater participation in athletic sports. When it is considered that the entire impetus for athletic sports within educational institutions came from the student body, it is easy to recognize their social importance. They gave the student opportunities to operate outside the limited confines of the class-room, and furnished him with desirable activities to occupy his leisure hours and relax his mind. Although playgrounds were established at this time and might indicate a further social emphasis, they were largely maintained by private subscription and were only for young children. An important movement related to recreation and physical education was organized camping, which got its start at this time and served as an outdoor laboratory for social experiences.

In assaying the relative influence of these themes upon physical education from 1865 to 1900, one gains the impression that the scientific movement had the most impact. Almost all the leaders in physical education were men with medical degrees, who sought to apply to exercise the medical principles known at that time. The rise of athletic sports certainly underscored the increasing emphasis on social education. Developmentalism was just gathering momentum, while the military emphasis hardly existed except as an aftermath of the Civil War.

Aims of Education

In general, during this period from 1865 to 1900, the development of the schools was marked by material expansion and consolidation rather than innovation. In the last decade of the nineteenth century, new ideas were finding some application, but their full effect was reserved for the twentieth century.

There was a broadening of the scope of education; instead of being limited to the development of the intellect, education began to consider moral development as well. There were several factors leading to this change of the scope of education. In the first place, the growth of cities meant that the concentration of more people in restricted areas increased the probability of social maladjustment. Educators noticed that, as the population increased, the frequency of crime increased more than proportionately; also, that many of the wayward children came from hopeless home environments. As a result the feeling grew that schools should do all in their power to become an elevating influence.

In general, it was thought that the proper social ideals could be inculcated in the school children through the personal influence of the teacher, the atmosphere of the schoolroom, the teaching of social subjects, and by bringing up moral lessons from history and the lives of great men. Some schoolmen also believed that idleness caused sin and delinquency, and therefore proposed that the energies of children be sidetracked into wholesome industry. Unconsciously, many of these schoolmen, seeking substitutes for harmful activities, were arguing in favor of the modern directed playground and the school gymnasium.

The kindergarten was a significant innovation developed largely through the work of Froebel in Europe. The aim of the kindergarten was "to render the first schooling attractive, to connect learning with pleasure." It brought growth through self-activity, willing activity, and creative activity. Here is the germ of "play in education" which has pleased so many educators and disturbed so many others. In regard to this question, the followers of Froebel point out that *amusing* children is entirely different from *interesting* them, and the two should not be confounded.

The high school, meanwhile, acquired a dual purpose. In addition to its original function of providing further education for those who could not go to college, it now began to offer college preparatory work. In this period, the high school made but slow progress toward becoming a truly democratic institution for all people. The reactionary Committee of Ten, in 1893, believed that the high schools should be for "that small proportion of all the children in the country . . . who show themselves able to profit by an education prolonged to the eighteenth year, and whose parents are able to support them while they remain at school."[2] However, the principle of public taxation to support high schools had been established by court decision, and the schools were progressing toward the purpose of providing equal opportunity for all children.

Colleges and universities in the latter third of the nineteenth century exhibited a pronounced trend toward secularism, attributable in part to the spirit of nationalism and to the development of science and industry. This development led institutions of higher education to provide technical and scientific training accompanied by research facilities. Another cause of the trend toward secularism was the growth of democracy, which sought an extension of educational privileges for its citizens beyond the elementary and secondary school. The widespread establishment of state universities hastened the accomplishment of this aim.

These new purposes meant that the old concepts of "mental discipline" and "transfer of training"—alleged attributes of a classical education in Latin, Greek, and logic—had lost their efficacy. Colleges and universities sought character development and the acquisition of knowledge with the idea of preparing individual citizens for living in society and using their talents, whatever they might be. Two indications of this broadening of the functions of higher education were to be found in the admission of women in large numbers to colleges and universities and in the growth of the elective system whereby students no longer adhered to a prescribed curriculum but had a choice of a variety of courses.

[2]*Report of the Committee of Ten on Secondary School Studies* (New York: American Book Co., 1894), p. 51.

To summarize, higher education moved away from expensive, professional training for the few, with strong religious undertones, and advanced toward an inexpensive, secular education for the many, with recognition of their diverse occupational interests and purposes.

Aims of Physical Education

Physical education in the United States from 1865 to 1900 was characterized by the variety of systems or practices. These systems, coming from both European and American sources, continued to promote the objective of health, a dominant aim in the previous period of emergent nationalism. However, some systems had more far-reaching aims and, consequently, each deserves its own presentation.

Dr. Dudley Sargent, a pioneer physical educator, introduced some of his ideas on physical education when he came to Harvard in 1879. He listed four aims of physical training:

1. Hygienic: the consideration of the normal proportions of the individual, the anatomy and the physiological functions of various organs, and a study of the ordinary agents of health such as exercise, diet, sleep, air, bathing, and clothing.
2. Educative: the cultivation of special powers of mind and body used in the acquisition of some skillful trade or physical accomplishment, such as golf, swimming, or skating.
3. Recreative: the renovation of vital energies to enable the individual to return to his daily work with vigor and accomplish his tasks with ease.
4. Remedial: the restoration of disturbed functions and the correction of physical defects and deformities.[3]

In an article published in 1883, Sargent wrote that the purpose of muscular exercise was not to attain bodily health and beauty alone, "but to break up morbid mental tendencies, to dispel the gloomy shadows of despondency, and to insure serenity of spirit."[4] With particular reference to properly managed and regulated athletics, he declared, "The grand aim of all muscular activity from an educational point of view is to improve conduct and develop character."[5] Sargent did not regard an excellent physique in itself as a worthwhile objective of physical education. The basic purpose and the highest ideal of physical training was "the improvement of the individual man in structure and function."[6] This ideal supplied a constant in-

[3]Dudley A. Sargent, *Physical Education* (Boston: Ginn and Co., 1906), pp. 66–71.

[4]Dudley A. Sargent, "Physical Education in Colleges," *North American Review* 136 (February 1883): 177.

[5]Dudley A. Sargent, "Academic Value of College Athletics," *Education* 27 (February 1907): 323.

[6]Sargent, *Physical Education*, p. 296.

centive to right methods of living and led to "that prime physical condition called fitness—fitness for work, fitness for play, fitness for anything a man may be called upon to do."[7]

The German-American gymnastics sought to promote individual abilities as well as to provide the state with well-trained citizens ready to meet the emergencies of peace or war. As part of the school curriculum, physical exercises should be cultivated "not for their own sake only, not for the purpose of educating gymnasts, but for the purpose of making the body of the pupil healthy, strong, and agile; in other words, to preserve it and to train the pupil to discretion, resoluteness, courage, and endurance."[8] However, school gymnastic exercises were not intended to cure sickness or to be used as a general prescription to remedy ailments or deformity.

The aims of Swedish gymnastics were expressed by Baron Nils Posse, one of the first to bring Swedish pedagogical gymnastics to schools in this country: "Physical training should be one not only toward health, but toward skill as well, and hence it must assist in the education of attention for correct repression, impression, and expression; . . ."[9] Movements were chosen to "encourage Nature in her normal activity, and also to prevent and overcome tendencies to abnormal development, in fact, to counteract the evil effects of our modern civilization."[10] The value of a gymnastic exercise was determined by its effect on the body and by the simplicity and beauty of its performance.

The Young Men's Christian Association worked out its own system of physical education based on various sources. The aim of physical education in the YMCA was to contribute to the development of the all-round man. Such a man was conceived to be one "with his physical nature healthy, strong, evenly developed and well disciplined; his spiritual nature strong, well balanced and trained."[11] The YMCA sought to blend the physical, intellectual, and spiritual in young men, as symbolized by its triangle.

The aims of the short-lived Delsarte culture, based on the teachings of a French vocal and dramatic teacher, François Delsarte, were never clearly defined. His followers spoke vaguely of trying to relax, to energize, and to guide the nerve-force harmoniously in action.[12] Despite this lack of clearness of aims, however, the Delsartian system in its short period of

[7]Ibid., p. 297.

[8]Moritz Zettler as quoted in W. A. Stecher, ed., *Gymnastics, A Textbook of the German-American System of Gymnastics* (Boston: Lee and Shepard, 1895), p. 11.

[9]Nils Posse, *The Special Kinesiology of Educational Gymnastics* (Boston: Lothrop, Lee and Shepard Co., 1894), p. 2.

[10]Ibid., p. 3.

[11]Luther Gulick, "Physical Education in the Y.M.C.A.," *Proceedings of the American Association for the Advancement of Physical Education, 1891*, p. 43.

[12]Emily Bishop, "Americanized Delsarte Culture," *Proceedings of the American Association for the Advancement of Physical Education*, 1892, p. 85.

influence on American physical education served to bring the rhythmic and aesthetic aims of exercise into prominence.

In those colleges that had physical education, a great deal of emphasis was placed on the correction of physical defects through exercise. This was particularly true of the exercises and apparatus developed by Dr. Sargent and of the Swedish gymnastic exercises. The advocates of the Swedish system conceived correct posture as being straight-backed and square-shouldered, and the exercises were designed for the purpose of achieving this ideal.

The original emphasis on the athletic movement came from colleges and other institutions of higher learning where the majority of students lived away from home. The early schoolmen excused the games and sports of college students on the grounds that the latter did not have their regular chores and were thus deprived of exercise. In addition to being a substitute for chores, athletics provided an outlet for surplus energy. This reasoning was also used to promote the playground movement in its early days. The educational values of sports and play had scarcely yet been recognized.

As early as 1893, one person clearly expressed many of the aims and the philosophy that today guide the modern program of physical education. Dr. Thomas D. Wood, then Professor of Hygiene and Physical Training at Leland Stanford University, and later Head of the Department of Health Education, Columbia University, speaking before the Department Congress of the National Education Association, declared that systems of physical training should be replaced by the science of physical education. He continued, "The great thought in physical education is not the education of the physical nature, but the relation of physical training to complete education, and then the effort to make the physical contribute its full share to the life of the individual, in environment, training, and culture."[13] At that time, Dr. Wood was a voice in the wilderness, and the fruition of these thoughts was yet many years away.

Promotion of Physical Education

The pioneer work of Dr. Hitchcock and the precedent established by Amherst College in giving him faculty status as a professor remained unique until Dr. Dudley Allen Sargent became assistant professor of physical training and director of the new Hemenway Gymnasium at Harvard University in 1879. Launching into his chosen profession with zeal and energy, Dr. Sargent for the next forty years profoundly influenced all phases of physical education—teacher education, athletics, curriculum, tests and measurements, and gymnasium and apparatus construction. Furthermore,

[13]Thomas D. Wood, "Some Unsolved Problems in Physical Education," *National Education Association Proceedings* 32 (1893): 621.

motivated by a sense of broader responsibility, he endeavored to popularize physical exercise and hygienic living for the great mass of Americans.

Dr. Sargent's theory of physical education admirably fitted into the new pattern of general education at Harvard introduced by President Eliot. Eliot led the struggle to uproot the old-style classical education with its rigid curriculum; and, under his leadership, Harvard expanded its curriculum and allowed students to elect courses. Therefore, Sargent's concept of voluntary exercises based on individual examination was thoroughly consistent with the plan of general education at Harvard. Sargent's exact and professional approach to physical education through individual prescription for exercise contributed immeasurably to help physical education gain respectability and professional status. His insistence on professional training for teachers of physical education furthered the drive for status. He also demonstrated that women could engage in chosen gymnastic exercises and outdoor sports without physiological harm.

In was in this period that physical training became an established part of many colleges, some of whom followed Harvard's example in building a gymnasium and hiring a director of physical training. Most of these early leaders in college physical training were medical doctors, partly because of the emphasis on correction of defects and partly because of the then strong administrative tie between hygiene and physical training. Furthermore, a medical education was the only preparation for a physical educator who deserved faculty rank during this period. Physical training was only one of several new subjects: history, music, literature, psychology, art, and economics were others to come into the college curriculum.

At the same time, gymnastics found widespread acceptance in the public schools, and the place of physical education in the curriculum finally was established on a permanent basis. Major credit for this milestone in the history of physical education must go to the German Turnvereins and the Turnerbund. At their national convention in 1880, the Turners voted to work for the introduction of compulsory physical education in the public schools. A similar resolution was adopted by the American Association for the Advancement of Physical Education in 1887 at the instigation of a St. Louis Turner, C. G. Rathman. Many of the instructors in the Turnverein offered their services to the public schools. Carl Betz, for example, appeared before the Board of Education in Kansas City in 1885 and volunteered to teach for three months without pay. He proved his case and was then employed as director of physical training for the city. Other prominent Turner leaders in public school physical education were George Brosius (Milwaukee), Henry Suder (Chicago), William Reuter (Davenport), Carl Zapp (Cleveland), Alvin Kindervater and George Wittich (St. Louis), Robert Barth (Denver), Anton Leibold (Columbus), Robert Nohr (Dayton), Carl Burkhart (Buffalo), and William Stecher in Indianapolis and Philadelphia. In all, over fifty cities responded to Turner efforts before 1900.[14] Most of these Turner teachers did double duty—they taught in the public schools during the day and then continued at their Turn-vereins in the late afternoon, evenings, and weekends. These men developed courses of study and produced a number of books on physical education and games. The publication of a periodical, *Mind and Body*, in English, was started in 1894. Before 1880 virtually all Turner publications were in German and thus unknown to others. Turner leaders became active in the newly formed Association for the Advancement of Physical Education, and a member of the first Council was Herman Koehler, a Turner who directed physical training at West Point. Non-Turners were invited to attend the Turnfests.

The main rival to German gymnastics in the public school program after 1885 was the Swedish gymnastics of Ling. Although the Swedish movement-cure or medical gymnastics was used by Dr. Taylor in New York prior to the Civil War,[15] the Swedish school gymnastics were not generally introduced into the United States until Hartvig Nissen came from Sweden to Washington in 1883. Another countryman, Baron Nils Posse, came to Boston two years later, and these two men did a remarkable job of selling Swedish gymnastics to leading Americans. Mrs. Mary Hemenway, a Boston philanthropist, whose son gave the Hemenway Gymnasium to Harvard, agreed to give financial support to the new Boston Normal School of Gymnastics for the training of teachers in Swedish gymnastics. In addition to Mrs. Hemenway, other Americans who espoused the Swedish cause were Amy Morris Homans, Dr. William G. Anderson, and Dr. Edward M. Hartwell. The Boston schools adopted the Swedish system in 1890 and employed Dr. Hartwell as director. Other schools, primarily in Eastern cities, followed the example of Boston. The growth of the Swedish system was due mainly to the hard work of Nissen, Posse, and its American adherents, and was not related to the presence of a Swedish population.

During this period, the public schools were influenced very little by the college programs. Dr. Hitchcock's work and ideas were limited to colleges, and to Amherst in particular. Sargent's principles were not suitable for the public schools because of the cost of the apparatus, the need for a gymnasium, and the individual supervision that was required. A number of women's colleges used the Sargent principles, and his ideas and apparatus were also popular in athletic clubs and the YMCA. In the colleges, both the Swedish gymnastics and German gymnastics were taught. Women's colleges, in particular, adopted the Swedish exercises and also during the 1890s displayed a flurry of interest in the Delsarte system. Sargent

[14]Emil Rinsch, *The History of the Normal College of the American Gymnastic Union of Indiana University, 1866–1966* (Bloomington: Indiana University, 1966), pp. 146–50.

[15]David W. Cheever, "The Gymnasium," *Atlantic Monthly* 3 (May 1859): 538.

voiced a modern complaint of physical education administrators when he said that gymnasiums were built by architects who did not know what was needed and that carpenters built apparatus for appearance rather than use. With wry humor, Sargent observed, "This object is effected for they are never used twice by the same person."[16] A typical gymnasium of this time showed the validity of these complaints. The sand-bag (used for heavy bag-punching) weighed seventy-five pounds and was covered with heavy canvas that caused skinned knuckles. Mats weighed four-hundred pounds and were filled with excelsior or corn-husks. These soon became matted and lumpy and caused sprained ankles. The pulley weights banged, rattled, and erupted dirt and sawdust when they hit the trough. Parallel bars were broad at the base and narrow at the top, leading to insecure grip. Trapeze bars were two inches in diameter and poorly hung. The rough rungs of horizontal ladders raised blisters. Sargent's mechanical ability and keen attention to detail led him to correct many of these conditions in the Hemenway Gymnasium. Hand ropes were made of cotton, horizontal bars were reduced in diameter by inserting a steel rod through the wood, and parallel bars were shaped to the hand.[17]

BEGINNINGS OF STATE LEGISLATION: The rise of interest in public school physical education resulted in the passage of the first state laws regarding physical education. As early as the Civil War, the nation's leaders had expressed mild concern over the unsatisfactory physical condition of the young men examined for military duty. As time went on, this condition of the populace continued to deteriorate rather than improve. The rising tide of industrialism was making a radical change in the living habits of the people, particularly of the city dwellers. The children, who at one time were busily occupied with chores and odd jobs around the home, no longer had the opportunity to obtain exercise through such pursuits. Certain pressure groups agitated to obtain legislation making physical education a compulsory school offering.

Ohio is generally credited with being the first state to pass a physical education law. This occurred in 1892. Previously, however, the state of California had passed a law in 1866 providing that "Instruction shall be given in all grades of schools, and in all classes, during the entire school course in . . . the laws of health; and due attention shall be given to such physical exercises for the pupils as may be conducive to health and vigor of body, as well as mind."[18] It was further stated that in all primary

---

[16]Sargent, "Physical Education in College," *North American Review* 136 (February 1883): 174.

[17]Dudley A. Sargent, "The Apparatus of Hemenway Gymnasium," *Harvard Register* 1 (February 1880): 44–45.

[18]From *Second Biennial Report—State Superintendent of Public Instruction 1866–67.* Appendix E, Revised School Law, March 24, 1866, Section 55, as quoted in Dudley S. DeGroot, "A History of Physical Education in California (1848–1939)" (Doctoral dissertation, Stanford University, 1940), p. 23.

schools a minimum of five minutes, at least twice a day, should be used for free gymnastics and vocal and breathing exercises. This law was the first statewide legislation for physical education and was strongly supported by the state Superintendent of Public Instruction, John Swett, the former principal of Rincon School. The statute slipped out of existence in 1879 when a new state constitution removed the authority of the State Board of Education to create a statewide curriculum. During its lifetime the law was responsible for the inclusion of physical education in many public schools "in a modest but effective manner."[19]

The Ohio law of 1892 required that physical culture be taught in the larger schools throughout the state, and, in 1904, the law was amended to include all schools. Louisiana passed a state law in 1894, Wisconsin approved permissive legislation in 1897, and two years later North Dakota required physical education in all common schools to "develop and discipline the body and promote health through systematic exercise."[20] Strong efforts during the 1890s for a state law in Pennsylvania finally met with success in 1901.

Much of the credit for these early state laws concerning physical education goes to two groups—the Turnvereins and the Women's Christian Temperance Union. The Ohio law was proposed by Anton Leibold and introduced into the legislature by John Molter, both Turners, and it received firm support from the Cleveland, Columbus, and Cincinnati Turnvereins.[21] The Turners also seem to have been especially influential in Pennsylvania and Wisconsin.

The WCTU formed a Department of Physical Culture in 1890 to secure state legislation for physical education in the schools. The influence exerted by its efforts is difficult to determine, but it seems to have had some effect in North Dakota, Pennsylvania, and Ohio. This department of the WCTU also had a hand in the establishment of the Department of Physical Education in the National Education Association. R. Anna Morris, physical education supervisor in the Cleveland schools, was an associate in the WCTU, and she presented the petition requesting the establishment of a department of physical education to the Board of Directors of the NEA. The petition was approved and the department created in 1895.

TEACHER TRAINING: When the Institute of Dio Lewis folded up in 1868, there was only one other normal school in existence, and college gymnasiums were supervised by ex-prizefighters, weightlifters, and janitors. This school was a seminary started by the Turnerbund in New York City in 1866 with nineteen men enrolled. Plans for a teachers' seminary had

[19]DeGroot, "A History of Physical Education in California," p. 24.

[20]Anne S. Aller, "The Rise of State Provisions for Physical Education in the Public Secondary Schools of the United States" (Doctoral dissertation, University of California, 1935), p. 97.

[21]Rinsch, *The History of the Normal College of Indiana University*, p. 139.

been discussed six years before, but no action was taken and the Civil War intervened.[22] The seminary led a fugitive existence for its first decade, and one class was abruptly terminated by the great Chicago fire in 1871. Eventually it found a more stable home in Milwaukee under the competent leadership of George Brosius in 1875. The course ran for three to six months, and classes generally were held in the evening and on Sunday so that students could support themselves with fulltime jobs during the day. The students received both theoretical and practical work which was not limited to German gymnastics. In its first thirty-five years of existence, the Turnverein Seminary graduated only 221 persons, but they have made a vigorous impact upon physical education in the United States.

The cause of teacher training received a powerful boost when Dr. Sargent opened a private gymnasium, originally called the Sanatory Gymnasium, in Cambridge, Massachusetts, and offered to give his one-year normal course free to anyone who wished to teach. Six women enrolled but only one completed the course, the others leaving to take jobs. Dr. Sargent also projected a two-year course in theory and practice of physical education, but this plan was not realized until 1892 because of the demand for teachers and the difficulty of keeping students. Originally both men and women could attend, but the number of women predominated and soon only women were admitted.

Dr. Sargent's first gymnasium was quite unlike a modern gymnasium. It occupied the second floor of a carriage shed next to a blacksmith shop and across the street from a livery stable. At one end was a big, sliding barn door and at the other end a large stove. Many large windows furnished ample ventilation which was increased when the sliding door was opened. Dr. Sargent lectured to the girls around the great stove and then taught the practical work.[23] Classes were also held for children in the afternoon and for working girls and teachers in the evening. Normal school students occasionally assisted with these classes and also did practice teaching in nearby public schools. Although the early graduates of the school were few in number, many of them became very prominent and successful leaders in women's physical education. Among them were Dr. Delphine Hanna of Oberlin College, Miss Helen Blackwell, Director of Physical Training of Boston University, Dr. Carolyn Ladd and Dr. Alice B. Foster of Bryn Mawr, and Dr. Helen Putnam of Vassar. The ability of these early women leaders was praised by Dr. Leonard who said that "the

---

[22]Some sources maintain that the seminary actually did exist for a few months in 1861 in Rochester, New York. This contention is not supported by the most recent and authoritative work on the Turners. See Rinsch, *The History of the Normal College of Indiana University*, pp. 5–6.

[23]Bruce L. Bennett, "The Life of Dudley Allen Sargent, M.D., and his Contributions to Physical Education" (Doctoral dissertation, University of Michigan, 1947), p. 103.

most painstaking and satisfactory work is being done in the colleges for women."[24]

Subsequent to Dr. Sargent, other physical educators opened private normal schools. Dr. William G. Anderson began the Brooklyn Normal School for Physical Education in 1886 and moved it to New Haven when he went to Yale University. Dr. Watson L. Savage of Columbia founded the Savage School of Physical Education in New York. The Boston Normal School of Gymnastics was begun in 1889 under the benevolent sponsorship and financial assistance of Mrs. Hemenway for the purpose of training teachers of Swedish gymnastics. Amy Morris Homans served as director, and the first teacher was Baron Nils Posse, a graduate of the Royal Central Gymnastic Institute in Stockholm. After one year, Posse left to start his own school in Boston, the Posse Normal School.

Dr. Sargent and Dr. George Fitz in 1891 collaborated to establish a Department of Anatomy, Physiology, and Physical Training at the Lawrence Scientific School of Harvard University and a four-year program was offered. There were only nine graduates and the course was discontinued after a few years.[25]

Another important institution was the YMCA training school at Springfield, Massachusetts, which added a department of physical training in 1887 and established another training school in Chicago three years later. These eventually became known as Springfield College and George Williams College respectively. Men such as Robert J. Roberts, Dr. Luther H. Gulick, and Dr. James Huff McCurdy were particularly responsible for the creation and development of the excellent training program at Springfield.

It is apparent from this account of the origin of teacher-training institutions in the United States that private initiative and capital made them possible. This was consistent with the emphasis on private enterprise in the nation as a whole.

By 1883 gymnasia were reported in only 19 out of 119 public normal schools and in 16 out of 114 private normal schools.[26] It was nearly 1900 before any general college added a professional curriculum in physical education to its course offerings. Among the first such colleges were the University of Nebraska, the University of California, Oberlin College, the University of Missouri, Stanford University, and the Normal College at Ypsilanti, Michigan.

[24]Fred E. Leonard, "Physical Training in the Colleges," *National Education Association Proceedings* 36 (1897): 915.

[25]Walter Kroll and Guy Lewis, "The First Academic Degree in Physical Education," *Journal of Health, Physical Education, and Recreation* 40 (June 1969): 73–74.

[26]Edward M. Hartwell, "The Rise of College Gymnasia in the United States," *Special Report by the Bureau of Education of World's Industrial and Cotton Centennial Exposition, New Orleans, 1884–85* (Washington: Government Printing Office, 1886), p. 671.

The training of teachers for physical education has also been greatly facilitated by summer schools. Dr. Sargent early saw the value of summer school courses for teachers and students, and he asked President Eliot of Harvard about starting a summer school in physical training. Eliot approved the plan if Sargent would assume the financial risk. The first course, lasting five weeks, was given in 1887 and attended by a surprising total of fifty-seven men and women, only five less than the number enrolled in chemistry, the largest course. The success of this initial session was assured not only by the large number but also by the quality of the students, most of whom held regular teaching positions and came from all parts of the country. As the Harvard Summer School carried on year after year, the free mingling and association of students of diverse backgrounds and experiences served to temper the bitterness engendered by the "battle of the systems" which split the physical education profession near the end of the nineteenth century. The significance and effect of this conflict was evaluated by Boykin who stated: "All the history of the subject (physical education) shows that the conflict of systems and methods, not popular indifference, has been, next to the inefficiency of teachers, the most dangerous enemy with which physical training has had to contend."[27]

The Chautauqua Summer School of Physical Education also should be mentioned. This summer school began in 1886 and was conducted by Dr. William G. Anderson and Dr. Jay Seaver. The Chautauqua School of Physical Education was part of the much larger Chautauqua movement and had an important influence in training the early physical education teachers. Like the Harvard Summer School it too offered a variety of courses in gymnastics and athletics and endorsed no one system of physical training. The Turners started summer sessions in 1895 in Milwaukee which were designed particularly for public school teachers.

RISE OF PROFESSIONAL ORGANIZATIONS: Another indication of the growth of physical education was the founding of the first professional organization, now known as the American Association for Health, Physical Education, and Recreation. The original name, the Association for the Advancement of Physical Education, was selected at the first meeting held at Adelphi Academy in Brooklyn on November 27, 1885. Invitations to attend were issued by Dr. William G. Anderson, a twenty-five-year-old gymnastics instructor at the Academy. The sixty people who came comprised a diverse group: college physical educators, YMCA directors, school teachers, ministers, and one lawyer, among others. Forty-nine men and women became members, with Dr. Hitchcock of Amherst elected to be the first president. A year later the name was changed to the American

[27]James C. Boykin, "History of Physical Training," *Report of the Commissioner of Education for 1891–92* (Washington, D.C.: U.S. Government Printing Office, 1894), 1:524.

Association for the Advancement of Physical Education. Meetings in the first fifteen years centered around anthropometrical measurement and the rivalry between the partisans of the German and Swedish gymnastic systems, often referred to as the "Battle of the Systems." Ten proceedings were issued for each of the first conventions until 1896 when the *American Physical Education Review* was started as a quarterly. By 1900 sixteen local city societies and four state organizations (Ohio, Michigan, New York, and Nebraska) had been formed, and membership had risen from 49 to 1,076.[28]

The present National College Physical Education Association for Men was founded in 1897. Again, Dr. Anderson was largely responsible for calling the first meeting, which was held at New York University. Originally the organization called itself the Society of College Gymnasium Directors and was a rather exclusive group for college administrators of physical education.

A notable professional meeting was a "Conference in the Interest of Physical Training" held in Boston in 1889. It was financed by Mary Hemenway with the administrative assistance of Amy Morris Homans. The presiding officer was William T. Harris, the U.S. Commissioner of Education.

RISE OF ATHLETIC SPORTS: The popular interest in sports, which had been evident in the 1850s, gained impetus after the Civil War. Much initial work was necessary because athletic sports were not a part of daily life as they are today. The average newspaper of today has a one- to three-page sporting section, but one can scan any newspaper printed even as late as the 1890s without finding a single mention of athletics, professional or collegiate. The early references featured professional sports such as baseball, the turf, cycling, and boating. This initial emphasis caused many people to associate sports with loafers and those of low morals, thus tending to bring any type of athletic activity into disrepute. The founder of the modern newspaper sports section was William Randolph Hearst, who bought the *New York Journal* in 1895 and immediately expanded the sports section two to four times over his rivals, used banner heads across the page, ran cartoons and pictures, and paid prominent athletes for ghost-written articles.[29]

Original emphasis on athletic movements came from institutions of higher learning, mostly attended by students living away from home. Athletics was an original contribution by the student body. Beginning as free, spontaneous sports and games, athletics became organized by students

[28]Mabel Lee and Bruce L. Bennett, "This Is Our Heritage," *Journal of Health, Physical Education, and Recreation* 31 (April 1960): 26–33.

[29]William H. Nugent, "The Sports Section," *American Mercury* 16 (March 1929): 336–38.

apart from the school proper, largely in opposition to it. Later followed faculty advisory control and official adoption by educational authorities.

The modern, detailed system for regulation of athletic sports has been the result of trial-and-error solutions to various problems as they arose. Controls have evolved as a result of the experience of many individuals and institutions.

In a sense the first control of athletics was exercised before the Civil War at colleges where informal student sport activity was halted by faculty or presidential edict because of injuries, danger to property or pedestrians, or time taken from studies. Athletic regulation as it is known today had to await the beginning of organized intercollegiate competition, which began after the Civil War. It was appropriate that rowing, the first intercollegiate sport, became the first sport to be regulated. In 1870, the Rowing Association of American Colleges was formed and lasted six years.[30] In 1873, Columbia, Rutgers, Princeton, and Yale joined in the Intercollegiate Association for Football.[31] Two years later the Intercollegiate Association of Amateur Athletes of America was organized for track athletes; it is the oldest athletic association still in existence, known as the IC4A. The year 1876 marked the origin of the Intercollegiate Football Association with Princeton, Harvard, and Columbia as charter members. This organization replaced the former Intercollegiate Association.

These early associations were composed entirely of student representatives and were mainly concerned with setting rules for the respective sport, rather than eligibility of the participants. In 1881, Walter Camp, a Yale graduate of the previous year, continued to attend the meetings of the Intercollegiate Football Association, and from then on graduate representatives met with the undergraduates.

In the meantime a three-man faculty athletic committee was appointed at Harvard in 1882 because of the faculty complaint that the baseball team had played so many games away that its members had missed numerous classes. The committee, which included Dr. Sargent, was indirectly responsible for the meeting of the Intercollegiate Athletic Conference in December 1883, at New York. This conference marked the first joint attempt by college *faculty* representatives to impose some regulation on athletics, which were beginning to present problems that individual colleges could not solve alone. Representatives from nine colleges came, and three of the delegates were presidents. The conference wrote eight resolutions to prohibit college teams from playing against professional teams or from receiving coaching from professional athletes; to limit competition to four

[30]Howard J. Savage et al., *American College Athletics.* Bulletin No. 23, Carnegie Foundation (New York: The Carnegie Foundation for the Advancement of Teaching, 1929), p. 20.

[31]John A. Blanchard, *The H Book of Harvard Athletics, 1852–1922* (Cambridge: The Harvard Varsity Club, 1923), pp. 354–58.

years for each student; to have all games played on the home field of one of the competing institutions; and to have a standing faculty committee supervise all contests.[32] The conference failed, however, since only Harvard, Princeton, and Cornell ratified these resolutions.

The Intercollegiate Football Association was unable to weather this and subsequent storms concerning eligibility and finally disintegrated in 1893. It was succeeded by the American Football Rules Committee which confined its efforts principally to game rules and thus avoided many pitfalls. Regulation of athletics remained in the control of individual colleges with varying degrees of control vested in faculty, students, and alumni.[33]

Associations for baseball, lacrosse, and basketball existed before 1900. They had little to do with the regulation of athletics but concerned themselves primarily with standardizing rules and arranging schedules.

While Eastern colleges struggled with the problem of athletic regulation, the new institutions of the Midwest, profiting by the experience of the older institutions, had less difficulty in establishing faculty control. In 1895, President Smart of Purdue called together the presidents of seven universities to discuss regulation and control of intercollegiate athletics. The result was the creation of the Intercollegiate Conference of Faculty Representatives to "insure faculty control, the regulation of intercollegiate athletics as institutional activities, and harmonious intercollegiate relationships among member institutions," with one member each from Chicago, Illinois, Michigan, Minnesota, Northwestern, Purdue, and Wisconsin.[34] Thus originated the Western Conference, also known as the Big Ten. The conference adopted rules requiring players to be bona fide students; a six months' residence for transfers; loss of eligibilty for students delinquent in studies; and graduate students' eligibility limited to the minimum number of years necessary to obtain their degree.

The organization most closely connected with the beginning of athletics and one which today wields considerable authority is the Amateur Athletic Union (AAU). The various athletic clubs sponsored amateur athletics and the New York Athletic Club took the lead in 1879 in forming the National Association of Amateur Athletes of America to check the evils of professionalism and promote legitimate amateur sports. This association became the AAU in 1888 with fifteen athletic clubs as members. In its early days, the AAU claimed wide jurisdiction over more than forty sports. This number was reduced to sixteen by 1899 and thus possible conflict with colleges was avoided. The new sport of basketball soon became a

---

[32]Edward M. Hartwell, *Physical Training in American Colleges and Universities.* Bureau of Education Circular of Information No. 5, 1885 (Washington, D.C.: Government Printing Office, 1886), pp. 125–28.

[33]Savage, *American College Athletics,* p. 24.

[34]*Handbook of the Intercollegiate Conference of Faculty Representatives,* rev. (published by the Conference, 1949), p. 5.

sore point because colleges necessarily played athletic clubs and independent teams to complete their schedules. Some of these teams were not members of the AAU, and the colleges were therefore subject to AAU disapproval. The colleges preferred to keep their autonomy, however, and resisted centralized AAU regulation.

The development of regulation of high school athletics followed college practice in many ways. The high schools took up athletics after the manner of the colleges, and their teams even competed with each other. There was an utter lack of standards of eligibility and sportsmanship. Teachers, principals, and janitors were all eligible to compete on the school team, and some players only attended school during the football season, if at all. Early high school athletic supervision was begun by state associations. Wisconsin was perhaps the first to appoint a committee in 1896 to formulate rules for interschool athletic contests. Michigan, Illinois, and Indiana followed in the next four years.

Baseball was the professional sport that most quickly gained public favor. Professionalism began to creep into baseball following the Civil War; and in 1869 the Cincinnati Red Stockings embarked on a nationwide tour as a professional team, with the remarkable record of fifty-six victories and one tie for the season. The formation of the National League occurred in 1876. By 1890 there were about one hundred professional clubs. In 1900, the American League was formed as a rival to the National League. The definite organization of professional players also encouraged the growth of amateur baseball in schools, colleges, YMCAs, clubs, and sandlots.

NONSCHOOL AGENCIES: In addition to the Turners, four other nonschool agencies left their mark in the history of physical education—the YMCA, the athletic clubs and country clubs, the churches, and the Sokol. The "Y" did not develop a serious interest in physical education until the adoption of an 1864 resolution which stated: "Any machinery will be incomplete which has not taken into account the whole man. We must add physical recreation to all YMCAs."[35] This action paved the way for the first two complete YMCA gymnasiums, built in New York and San Francisco in 1869. The first physical directors were former circus performers or professional athletes. The quality of instruction was decidedly improved after the beginning of the physical training department at Springfield in 1887. Four years later, the YMCA had 348 gymnasiums which employed 144 men.[36] Further evidence of the professional growth of this agency was the issuance of the periodical, *Physical Education*, from 1892 to 1896. This publication was succeeded by the *Journal of Physical Training* in

---

[35]M. L. Walters, "The Physical Education Society of the Y.M.C.A.'s of North America," *Journal of Health and Physical Education* 17 (May 1947): 357.
[36]Gulick, "Physical Education in the Y.M.C.A.," p. 46.

1901, which in turn was followed by the *Journal of Physical Education* in 1928.

Along with the establishment of YMCA gymnasiums, a number of athletic clubs were constructed in the larger cities and became centers of physical activity for men. The most famous of these was the New York Athletic Club, founded in 1868, which built the first cinder track in America. In the 1880s country clubs began to appear and they provided sport facilities for the well-to-do. Three of the most elaborate were the Newport Casino, the Country Club in Brookline, Massachusetts, and the Tuxedo Park Club near New York City.

During this period a few Protestant churches began to move away from their traditional opposition to sport and physical education. An appeal for this action was sounded in an editorial in 1856 which stated: "Let religion recognize and restrain them [sports]. . . . but let it throw around them its gentle and holy bonds, to make them pure, cheerful, healthful— helpful to the great ends of life. What a blessed thing for the world were it, if its amusements could thus be rescued, redeemed, and brought into the service of its virtue and piety!"[37] A remarkable person and a leader in this change was Thomas Beecher, a stepbrother of Catherine Beecher. As minister of the Park Church in Elmira, New York, he supervised a new church building in 1875 which included a gymnasium and a romproom for dancing. This is considered to be one of the first of the so-called institutional churches which sought to minister not just to the spiritual needs, but to the social, physical, and intellectual needs of its members and the surrounding neighborhood. Another pioneer institutional church was St. George's Episcopal in New York City whose rector was Rev. William S. Rainsford. This church started a Boys' Club in 1884 and maintained both a gymnasium and a large vacant lot for sports. Other outstanding churches before 1900 were St. Bartholomew's and Judson Memorial Baptist in New York, Berkeley Temple in Boston, and Jersey City Tabernacle.[38]

Even the idea of allowing recreational activities on the Sabbath was becoming more palatable to some Protestant churches as the twentieth century approached. The institutional church realized that men who worked six full, long days a week needed some recreational outlet on Sunday. Many non-Germans began to think well of the Turner custom of having picnics and games on summer Sunday afternoons. Large scale immigration of Irish and Italian Catholics furthered the breakdown of the Sabbath as a day of worship and rest only.

In contrast to the Protestant denominations, the Church of Jesus Christ of the Latter-Day Saints, or Mormon Church, was never hampered by Puritanical restrictions. From its founding in 1830 Mormons enthusi-

[37]Editorial, "The Necessity of Recreation," *Spirit of the Times* 26 (27 December 1856): 546.
[38]Rufus R. Wilson, "Institutional Church and its Work," *Outlook* 54 (29 August 1896): 384–87.

astically participated in dancing and various sports which were incorporated into the ongoing program of the church.[39]

One other nonschool agency of lesser importance was the Sokols who formed their first society in St. Louis in 1865. More groups sprang up in other cities, mainly in the Midwest. The first *slet*, or national festival, was held in New York City in 1879.

NEGROES IN SPORTS: The early history of Negroes' efforts to participate in sports is an unpleasant chronicle. Harvard employed a Negro, A. Molineaux Hewlett, as director of its gymnasium from 1859 to 1871. Hewlitt previously ran a private gymnasium and was an excellent performer in boxing and gymnastics.[40] The first Negro major league baseball players were two brothers, Fleet and Welday Walker, who played for Toledo in the American Association in 1884. Their brief career was suddenly halted by the threat of mob violence on the first road trip to Richmond, Virginia.[41] The exclusion of Negroes from baseball goes back to a rule passed at the 1867 convention of the National Association of Base Ball Players. The rationale for this action was stated in these words: "If colored clubs were admitted there would be in all probability some division of feeling, whereas, by excluding them no injury could result to anybody, and the possibility of any rupture being created on political grounds would be avoided."[42] Negroes were effectively excluded from most other sports except boxing.

In college sports, a handful of Negroes achieved some success in northern institutions. Outstanding was William H. Lewis who came from Virginia and played football at both Amherst and Harvard. His play at Harvard as a center earned him All-American rating by Walter Camp in 1892 and 1893. He also served as an assistant coach at Harvard while playing.[43]

The first football game between two Negro colleges was played in 1892. Biddle University defeated Livingstone College, 4 to 0. Within the next two years Howard, Lincoln, Tuskegee, and Atlanta University began to compete also.[44]

Prejudice was not only directed against Negroes. Jewish citizens were barred from most of the country clubs and athletic clubs. Some Jewish baseball players changed their names to disguise their religious identity.[45]

[39]Bruce L. Bennett, "Religion and Physical Education," *Physical Educator* 19 (October 1962): 85–6.

[40]Edwin B. Henderson, *The Negro in Sports* (Washington, D.C.: The Associated Publishers, Inc., 1939), pp. 4–5.

[41]Robert H. Boyle, *Sport—Mirror of American Life* (Boston: Little, Brown and Company, 1963), pp. 102–3.

[42]Harold Seymour, *Baseball: The Early Years* (New York: Oxford University Press, 1960), p. 42.

[43]Henderson, *The Negro in Sports*, pp. 6–8.

[44]Ibid., p. 88.

[45]Bernard Postal and others, *Encyclopedia of Jews in Sports* (New York: Block Publishing Company, 1965), p. 16.

ORIGINS OF THE PLAYGROUND MOVEMENT.   The play movement in the United States achieved solid footing with the opening of the first playgrounds during this period, but vestiges of the play movement may be traced back to the New England town commons of the early seventeenth century. Although originally used for pasturage, the commons also were play areas for children.

After the Civil War, Boston forged ahead in the playground movement. In 1868, an outdoor playground was set up by the First Church in Boston in conjunction with a vacation school, but it had little influence. Organized play activities were conducted at several Boston vacation schools, supported after 1878 by the Women's Education Association and the Associated Charities.

Most authorities agree that the modern playground movement in America began with the two heaps of sand placed in the Parmenter Street Chapel and West End Nursery in Boston by the Massachusetts Emergency and Hygiene Association. This was done in the summer of 1885 at the suggestion of Dr. Marie Zakrzewska, who had recently returned from Germany where she had observed sand heaps in the public parks of Berlin. Within two years there were ten sand gardens in Boston. One of these was in a school yard, while the rest were situated in the courts of tenement buildings. Supervision at first was voluntary and done by interested mothers or neighborhood women. Paid matrons were then used and, in 1893, a superintendent of all the sand gardens was hired, and each sand garden had an assistant, or kindergartner, as she was called.

After 1887, most of the sand gardens were placed in school yards rather than in mission or tenement yards, although the schools had no connection with them except to furnish the area. Financial assistance from the city began in 1899 when the council gave $3,000 to the Massachusetts Emergency and Hygiene Association which, by that time, was sponsoring twenty-one playgrounds.

The association proved to be an effective force in promoting playgrounds in Boston. The construction of the famous Charlesbank outdoor gymnasium in 1889 by the Park Department was in large part a result of the work of a committee appointed by the association. It was the first play area to be landscaped, and this was capably done by the noted architect, Frederick Law Olmstead. The Charlesbank gymnasium also represented the earliest conscious effort by a park board to provide for play.[46] Daily attendance averaged about 1,500 individuals but there was only one instructor. Classes were held twice a day with individual instruction the rest of the time.

The valuable work of the Emergency and Hygiene Association came to a successful conclusion in 1901 when the Boston School Committee

[46]Clarence E. Rainwater, *The Play Movement in the United States* (Chicago: University of Chicago Press, 1922), p. 72.

opened sand gardens under its own supervision but following the procedures and methods used by the association. By this time, the School Committee realized that play was an integral part of education and should properly be a function and responsibility of the school.

In New York, the Society for Parks and Playgrounds was incorporated in 1890 and launched a campaign for playgrounds which was helped by many synagogues and churches. On one weekend 27 rabbis and 100 ministers preached on the need of playgrounds for children to their congregations.[47] The playground movement in New York also benefited extensively from the work of the Outdoor Recreation League and the secretary of a civic committee on small parks, Jacob Riis. In Detroit, the situation faced by determined fighters for playgrounds and recreational facilities was perhaps typical of most cities. A group of volunteer women raised some money and got a playground started in a school yard. Their problems and successes were summed up in this statement from an annual report: "Once more the playground demonstrated its need, and its benefits; and despite the continuous petty opposition of school janitors, the indifference of civic authorities, frequent hostile press notice, and the cry that the school premises were being ruined by turbulent children, the playground went serenely on, the police, shopkeepers and parents of the vicinity uniting in its praise."[48] As in other communities throughout the country, the Detroit playground maintained its precarious existence and eventually received public acceptance.

The first playground in Chicago was the model playground at Jane Addams' Hull House, which was set up in 1894 through the generosity of William Kent on land provided by the razing of tenements. The first municipal appropriation was for $1,000 in 1898, and it was given to the vacation school committee of local women's clubs. The Turnverein also expressed interest and loaned apparatus for use. School support for playgrounds in Chicago did not come until a later date.

In addition to these cities, Philadelphia, Providence, Pittsburgh, Brooklyn, Baltimore, Milwaukee, Cleveland, Minneapolis, and Denver all opened similar playgrounds before 1900. In general, these early playgrounds showed several common characteristics. They were only for the use of preadolescent children and were maintained only during the summer vacation period. The equipment was suitable only for outdoor use. Playgrounds were located in the densely populated sections of cities. The initiative and early financial support came from philanthropic sources, although public land was sometimes used. As the beginning efforts proved worthwhile, the municipal governments began to furnish financial aid. In a number of instances, policemen were either assigned or volunteered for play-

[47]"A Brief History of the Playground Movement in America," *The Playground* 9 (April 1915): 5.
[48]*The Detroit News*, 27 June 1926.

ground duty, because such supervision was effective in preventing juvenile delinquency associated with street play. The growing recognition of the right of children to play was one aspect of a nascent social philosophy that led to the passage of child labor laws.

It is clear that the playground movement in the United States is indebted to the efforts of many individual women and women's clubs who labored tirelessly on behalf of the children. It also seems evident today that churches, church members, and individual clergymen did far more for this cause than has been attributed to them in the past. The emphasis on "social gospel" and the development of the institutional church involved some urban congregations in the problems of the big cities before 1900.[49]

Finally, the beginnings of industry-sponsored recreation were apparent, although its first concern was to provide playgrounds for the children of employees. Two pioneer business firms in the nineteenth century in this endeavor were the Pullman Company starting in 1883 and the Ludlow Manufacturing Associates in Massachusetts.

ORIGINS OF SUMMER CAMPS: In addition to the playgrounds, another agency with rich potentiality for social education came into being. This was the organized summer camp, which, however, had its greatest growth in the twentieth century. The early work of Joseph Neef and Joseph Cogswell in providing camping experience and outdoor education for their pupils has been noted in the preceding chapter. These ideas were again put into practice by Frederick William Gunn, founder and headmaster of the Gunnery School for Boys at Washington, Connecticut. In 1861, as the Civil War began, the boys at his school wanted to live the life of soldiers by marching and sleeping out. That summer, Mr. and Mrs. Gunn took the whole school on a hike to a place on Long Island Sound for two weeks. The experience was repeated two years later and continued almost every year until 1879. The camping was a part of the school program for the boys and was not an independent, commercial enterprise. This close relationship between school and camp has been revived in recent years as a new trend in camping.

Joseph T. Rothrock, a Wilkes-Barre physician, opened the North Mountain School of Physical Culture in Pennsylvania in 1876. This was a summer camp for boys designed to provide exercise and study outside the usual academic lines. The camp survived three summers and then closed for lack of funds.

George Hinckley, pastor of a West Hartford church, took seven boys from his parish to a camp in Rhode Island in 1880. Three of the boys were Chinese, and the camp experience also proved to be a lesson in race relations. Hinckley later founded the Good Will Camp in Maine and continued his early interest in camping.

[49]See Richard A. Swanson, "American Protestantism and Play: 1865–1915" (Doctoral dissertation, Ohio State University, 1967), pp. 36–66.

These three camps all preceded the founding in 1881 by Ernest Balch of Camp Chocorua in New Hampshire, which is usually regarded as the first organized camp. Balch, although not first in point of time, deserves full credit for his careful planning and administration of the camp. The boys were encouraged to develop responsibility and to participate in the work of the camp. Camp Chocorua continued until 1889.

Another outstanding camping pioneer was Sumner F. Dudley, who took out small groups of YMCA boys to camp for one or two weeks each summer from 1885 to 1891, finally locating a permanent site on Lake Champlain. In 1903, the state YMCA accepted responsibility for the camp and, after the death of its founder, named it Camp Dudley. This is the oldest camp still in existence today. Dudley's initiative and faith started the YMCA on a camping movement that has spread throughout the world.[50] Meanwhile a type of camp experience known as "fresh-air" work had begun in New York City in 1872 as a philanthropic movement. The Children's Aid Society sent underprivileged children out of the city to a country home for a vacation of one or two weeks. This idea received considerable popular support through newspapers such as the *New York Times, New York Tribune*, and *Life Magazine*. The latter started a Fresh Air Fund in 1887 to send city children to rural homes and farms. Two years later a single camp was established. Although the fresh-air camps were motivated by human interest and strong social consciousness, the actual camp experience was not as yet carefully planned or supervised.

Program of Physical Education

The term, Sargent system, is often used to set the principles of Dr. Sargent apart from the Swedish and German systems and is a relic of the intense battle of the systems which characterized the early growth of professional physical education in this country. It is a misleading term because Sargent advocated not only the Swedish and German gymnastics, but also sports and athletics, along with his own principles and ideas. Sargent's distinctive contribution was the creation of appliances which had the basic and distinguishing feature of being adaptable to the strength of the user. By pulleys and weights, the apparatus could be adjusted for any individual and did not presuppose a certain amount of strength as did heavy gymnastic apparatus. Resistance could be increased as strength developed. Each machine was designed to develop specific muscle groups, and by proceeding from one machine to another a student could exercise most of his muscles. The most important appliance was the chest pulley weights which Sargent

[50]This history of camping is based largely on the series of articles by H. W. Gibson, "The History of Organized Camping," *Camping Magazine* (January to December, 1936). See also Porter Sargent, *A Handbook of Summer Camps* (Boston: Porter Sargent, 1934), pp. 33–109.

did not originate but did greatly improve in design and operation. Other appliances included machines for exercising specific muscle groups of the back, leg, wrist, finger, foot, abdominal region, neck, and shoulder.

The German and Swedish systems of physical education that were practiced in the United States did not deviate a great deal from their European antecedents, as described in Chapters 13 and 14. A typical class period in German gymnastics included exercises on several different pieces of apparatus, games for the whole class or for individuals, and occasionally some free exercises or light gymnastics. The Germans made a significant contribution to physical education through their many gymnastic games. The Swedish gymnastics used in the public schools of the United States stressed the free exercises, rather than apparatus exercises, because most schools provided only the classroom for a gymnasium. College programs of Swedish gymnastics, on the other hand, usually had both the free exercises and the apparatus exercises. The German exercises were often done to music, but teachers of Swedish calisthenics condemned it as a distracting influence.

The content of the YMCA physical education programs was rather eclectic with no particular allegiance to any system. One of the first YMCA physical directors, Robert J. Roberts, believed that exercises should be "safe, sane, easy, short, satisfying, and beneficial." The early program strove to attain some kind of balance in the use of vigorous, rapid calisthenics with dumbbells and light apparatus, some heavy apparatus, running, and sports. After the YMCA began to train its own physical education leaders, the program shifted to the use of calisthenics and gymnastics for conditioning, along with sports, athletics, aquatics, and recreational activities. The invention of both basketball and volleyball by "Y" personnel is ample evidence of its interest in sports.

The Delsarte system attempted to relate outer movements to inner states of feeling; in other words, motion to emotion. The movements were of a calisthenic type but characterized by graceful ease and relaxation.

ATHLETIC SPORTS: College football became dominant in the intercollegiate program during this period of nationalism and has remained so ever since. The first game of intercollegiate football was played on November 6, 1869, between Princeton and Rutgers at New Brunswick, New Jersey. The rules for the game were adapted from the London Football Association so that the contest closely resembled soccer. A round, inflated rubber ball was used, and the players wore no padding or protection. One player would advance the ball with short kicks while his teammates surrounded him and kept off the opponents. Defensive players smashed into the massed formation to get at the ball. A player could also reach up and bat a ball in the air with his hands, but apparently no catching or carrying of the ball was allowed. Goals were scored by kicking the ball into the goal. Rutgers won this first game, six goals to four, and intercollegiate football in this country had become a reality.[51] The following year Columbia also organized a team for competition.

Meanwhile a group of Harvard students in 1871 had started to play football, but in their game the ball could be picked up at any time. In May 1874, McGill University of Montreal came to Cambridge for a two-game series with Harvard students. The first game was played by the Harvard rules and the second by the rugby rules used by the Canadian team, in which running with an egg-shaped ball was permitted. The Harvard players liked the rugby version so well that they abandoned their own game. In 1875 Harvard played Yale in a game which largely followed rugby rules. The rugby game won the approval of the other colleges so that at a meeting in 1876, Harvard, Columbia, and Princeton formed the Intercollegiate Football Association and agreed on rugby rules. Yale did not join the association but played with the other teams anyway. These rules called for a field 140 yards by 70 yards with goal posts. A goal was scored by place-kicking or drop-kicking. A touchdown was scored by running the ball over the goal line, but it took four touchdowns to equal one goal. A player could run with the ball until downed and could pass laterally. Each side had fifteen men and a game consisted of forty-five-minute ha' es.[52]

These rugby rules may be considered the basis of our modern American game of football, and the history of football since 1876 has been a continuous modification of these rules. The present names for the different positions evolved out of the early terminology which designated the linemen as rushers and the backfield as quarterbacks, halfbacks, three-quarterbacks, and fullbacks.

The growth of football as a sport was marred by frequent incidents of slugging and fighting. In 1885, the Harvard faculty, upon recommendation of the Athletic Committee, banned football for one year because of such rough play. In 1892, E. L. Godkin, editor of the *Nation*, decried the professional spirit and gambling mania connected with college football, and a year later he condemned the practice of attracting athletically-gifted students to come to college.[53] These editorials contained criticisms that are still being voiced today.

Baseball continued its evolution toward the modern game through a number of significant rule changes. Gloves were worn, a base on balls was given for four balls instead of nine, restrictions were removed on the pitcher's throwing, and the present pitching distance was established. Baseball

---

[51]This account is taken from an article by Parke H. Davis, "Football," in Christy Walsh, ed., *Intercollegiate Football, 1869–1934* (New York: Doubleday, Doran and Co., Inc., 1934), pp. 25–35.

[52]Morris A. Bealle, *The History of Football at Harvard, 1874–1948* (Washington, D.C.: Columbia Publishing Co., 1948), pp. 21–22.

[53]*Nation* 55 (1 December 1892): 406–7; 57 (7 December 1893), 422–23.

was called the "national game" as early as 1872. Indoor baseball originated in 1887 when George Hancock at the Farragut Boat Club in Chicago playfully seized a broom and boxing glove and suggested a game of baseball to his friends. He then developed a larger ball for indoor use, but the game received little notice for many years.

A number of new games appeared in the years before 1900. Some of them, such as tennis and golf, were imported from Europe, while others, such as basketball and volleyball, were American inventions.

Modern tennis was first played in England and derived from the much older game of court tennis. The year 1873 is noteworthy in the history of modern or lawn tennis because Major Walter Wingfield in that year published an eight-page pamphlet entitled *Sphairistike* or *Lawn Tennis,* which contained the first rules.[54] Tennis was quickly taken to Bermuda by British Army officers and was observed there in the winter of 1873–1874 by a vacation visitor from the United States, Mary Outerbridge.[55] She obtained a set of equipment and marked out the first court in the United States at the Staten Island Cricket Club in the spring of 1874. A second court was laid out at Nahant, near Boston, in the following year. Tennis at this time was played on a court shaped like an hour-glass with the narrowest width of the court at the net. Local differences in rules and equipment led to the formation of the United States National Lawn Tennis Association in 1881.

Tennis was played at many cricket clubs where the well-kept grass areas afforded excellent courts. The two sports, tennis and cricket, competed for the favor of the members, but interest in the latter gradually waned. Tennis was played by women as well as men and became a popular outdoor sport for both sexes. A tennis game in 1880 was a rather leisurely affair in which the players wore ordinary street clothes and leather shoes. The pace of the game soon speeded up with the introduction of the overhand serve, the "kill" shot, and the net and baseline game.

Tennis spread rapidly during the 1880's. The first national tournament for men was won by Richard D. Sears in 1881 and a sectional women's tournament was held two years later. College students began tennis clubs in this period at a number of institutions such as Yale, the University of Pennsylvania, Harvard, and the University of North Carolina. The number of clubs joining the U. S. Lawn Tennis Association jumped from thirty-four in 1881, its first year, to seventy-six in 1890.

The game of golf in the United States dates its continuous growth from the late 1880s; although golf may have been played at Charleston, South Carolina as early as 1786, and there was a Savannah (Georgia)

[54]Malcolm B. Whitman, *Tennis Origins and Mysteries* (New York: The Derrydale Press, 1932), pp. 106–10.
[55]Ibid., pp. 112–13.

Golf Club in 1795.[56] Golf came to stay when Robert Lockhart, a business man of Yonkers, New York, visited his native country of Scotland in 1887 and brought back some golf clubs and balls. He showed them to a friend, John Reid, and these two men plus a few neighbors amused themselves in the summer of 1888 by playing on an improvised three-hole course. Upon Reid's initiative, these men formed the St. Andrews Golf Club at Yonkers in November, 1888. Three years later a 12-hole golf course was laid out at Shinnecock Hills (Long Island) by a group of wealthy businessmen who hired a Scotch professional for the job. The Chicago Golf Club was formed in 1892. Five clubs formed the present United States Golf Association in 1894 and by the end of the century there was the astonishing number of 1,040 golf clubs in operation around the country.[57] The first public golf course was laid out in New York's Van Courtlandt Park and quickly followed by others in Boston and Indianapolis. However, golf was essentially a sport for the country club set until after the first decade of the twentieth century.

Basketball was invented in the late fall of 1891 by James Naismith, an instructor at Springfield College, to provide an indoor game for the winter season.[58] In the spring of 1892 a conference of YMCA directors met at Springfield and two teams, with Naismith and Amos Alonzo Stagg as captains, demonstrated the game.[59] Peach baskets were nailed to the overhead running track for goals and a soccer ball was used. The players shot underhanded and did very little dribbling. There was a good deal of wrestling for the ball. The game shortly appeared at Cornell as a recreational sport, and a year later, Yale supported a team. Athletic clubs and independent groups quickly took up the new sport.

Volleyball might be considered a younger stepbrother of basketball. It was invented by William Morgan who was director of the "Y" at Holyoke, Massachusetts. In an effort to develop a gymnasium game that was not so strenuous as basketball, he combined elements from tennis and handball. According to the first published account of the game in July, 1896, a tennis net was suspended in the usual manner except that the top was six and a half feet above the floor. The ball was volleyed back and forth without hitting the floor or net. A player could dribble by bouncing the ball on the hand while moving, but he could not go within four feet of the net. A serve had to go at least ten feet and could be helped over the net by a player of the same side. A team ranged from one to an indefinite

[56]Harry B. Martin, *Fifty Years of American Golf* (New York: Dodd, Mead, 1936), pp. 46–47.
[57]Frederick W. Cozens and Florence S. Stumpf, *Sports in American Life* (Chicago: The University of Chicago Press, 1953), p. 162.
[58]James Naismith, "Basket Ball," *Triangle* 1 (15 January 1892): 144.
[59]Interview with George Meylan 27 March 1947. He was one of the visiting "Y" directors and played in the game.

number of players.[60] A basketball bladder was first used, then a basketball, and eventually a special ball was developed.

WOMEN'S ACTIVITIES: At this time, women were beginning to be interested in participating in sports and games. This was simply one phase of their struggle for greater freedom in society. Croquet, hiking, and bicycling were the first sports to attract women. These sports did not require any immodest form of dress. Tennis and archery were the next to attract women. The ladies' long full skirts and numerous petticoats dictated a leisurely fashion of playing at sports. In the middle 1880s, girls began to wear the divided skirts or bloomers and middy blouse. Dr. Sargent in particular vigorously championed greater freedom in dress and activity for women, and the girls at the Sargent School were among the first to wear the new costume.

Women were quick to take up the vigorous new sport of basketball. In 1892, the teachers of a Springfield elementary school began playing the game. In that same year, the young women at Smith College were playing interclass basketball, and shortly afterwards the girls at Dr. Sargent's Normal School took up the sport. Basketball for women spread across the country. In 1896, the first intercollegiate basketball game in California was played between two girls' teams from Stanford and California; in fact, basketball was primarily a girls' sport in that state until about 1910.[61] The first recorded modification of rules for girls' use was by Senda Berenson at Smith in 1894. Three changes were made: (1) a player could hold the ball for three seconds without having it snatched out of her hands; (2) the court was divided into three zones with no crossing from one zone to another; and (3) a player could not bounce the ball more than three times.[62] Basketball became so popular for women that, in 1899, a committee met to draw up standardized rules for women's basketball.

Women began to participate in track and field before 1900. Harriet Ballintine of Vassar attended the first class in track and field for women at the Harvard Summer School in 1896. She introduced track field days at Vassar, and other colleges soon followed the practice. Women were also competing in tournaments sponsored by national organizations. Twenty ladies joined 69 men in an archery tournament in 1879, and other sportswomen competed in a tennis tournament in 1887 and a golf tournament in 1896.

This trend in women's sports also held true in dancing. At this time girls did the so-called fancy steps which consisted of stylized movements with little action. The more vigorous aesthetic or classic dancing was de-

---

[60]"Volleyball," *Physical Education* 5 (July 1896): 50–51.

[61]DeGroot, "A History of Physical Education in California," p. 302.

[62]Senda Berenson, "Basketball for Women," *Physical Education* 3 (September 1894): 106–9.

veloped early in the 1890s by Melvin Ballou Gilbert at the suggestion of Dr. Sargent. From the physical educator's point of view, Sargent pointed out, dancing was weak because it involved only the legs and not the trunk and arms.[63] Gilbert then worked out a modified ballet which omitted toe dancing and the more intricate movements but exercised the body and arms as well as the legs. This new dance was first taught by Gilbert at the Harvard Summer School in 1893 and became exceedingly popular. Folk dancing also began to come into the curriculum, and the Swedish "day's order" occasionally included a folk dance.

The institutional churches, with an unusual variety of activities, attracted children and adults of both sexes. Physical culture classes were held regularly in the gymnasium, and many churches had bowling, pool, and billiard facilities.[64] St. George's Church offered wrestling and, with the financial aid of one of its members, J. P. Morgan, provided an outdoor area for track, cricket, and baseball.[65] Jersey City Tabernacle also offered outdoor sports. Even that old demon social dancing was no longer taboo. These activities show how some urban churches attempted to meet community recreation needs before municipal governments were ready to respond to the situation.

Brief mention should be made of the influence of technology on sport. Railroads made possible the organized leagues for baseball by providing rapid intercity travel after the Civil War. Within the cities themselves the electric street car in the 1890s enabled urban residents to flock to the ball park and the race tracks. Mechanical improvements and mass production techniques contributed to the widespread popularity of bicycling after 1880. The electric light added many hours to gymnasium use in colleges, YMCAs, armories, and athletic clubs and thereby stimulated participation in basketball and volleyball.[66] And in 1899, the international yacht race between England and the United States was the first story reported by wireless. A new age of international communication about sports had begun!

PLAYGROUND AND CAMPING ACTIVITIES: The early playgrounds centered around the sand pile or sandbox. Shovels, pails, wagons, wheelbarrows, and other tools were supplied for use when the sandbox was not exposed to the hot rays of the sun. Other equipment used by the children included blocks, drums, picture books, small blackboards, horse reins, skipping ropes, toy brooms, and plenty of seats. Sewing cards and cut-out

[63]"Our Tribute to the Late Mr. Gilbert," *Mind and Body* 17 (June 1910): 142.

[64]Wilson, "Institutional Church and its Work," pp. 384–87.

[65]William S. Rainsford, *The Story of a Varied Life* (Garden City, New York: Doubleday, Page and Company, 1922), p. 302.

[66]John R. Betts, "The Technological Revolution and the Rise of Sport, 1850–1900," *Mississippi Valley Historical Review*, 40 (September 1953): 235–52.

figures were very popular. Many of the playgrounds used kindergarten games and songs. Swings, see-saws, and giant strides appealed to the child of 1900 just as they do to the child of today.

The playgrounds in cities with active Turner societies such as New York and Chicago were apt to have parallel bars, horizontal bars, and other German apparatus. In some of the New York schools with no school yard, playgrounds were put on the roof. By 1898, games such as shuffle-board, handball, hop-scotch, prisoners' base, hand tennis, and the new game of basketball were played on New York playgrounds.[67]

The Charlesbank outdoor gymnasium in Boston deserves special mention because of its size and completeness. The men's gymnasium was 450 by 150 feet and was fully equipped with all kinds of gymnastic apparatus, both Swedish and German, and included the chest pulley weights popularized by Sargent. A running track and areas for high and broad jumping, pole-vaulting, and shot-putting were supplied. The only game equipment was two sets of quoits. Most remarkable, however, was the fact that the gymnasium was open fourteen and a half hours daily except Sunday from 6:30 A.M. to 9:00 P.M.; arc lights were turned on after dark. The gymnasium was open from April to December when the apparatus was removed and the grounds flooded for skating.[68] The Charlesbank gymnasium included not only playground facilities for children but anticipated the coming recreation movement by providing public facilities for older children and men and women. It showed how an attractive park area could be put to functional use.

The small parks that were put to recreational use in 1900 generally provided facilities similar to those of the Charlesbank. The parks, however, responded to the popular interest in sports, which had increased greatly in the decade after the opening of the Charlesbank, by providing an open space for athletics. One New York park had a baseball diamond, others had areas for golf, basketball, and tennis.

The boys from Gunnery School enjoyed boating, sailing, fishing, and tramping at their Long Island Sound camp. Camp Chocorua offered these activities plus baseball, tennis, rowing, running, and swimming, and was probably the first camp to offer organized sports.

Methods of Physical Education

The methods used by Dr. Sargent were best described in an early pamphlet for his Hygienic Institute and School of Physical Culture which he conducted in New York City the year before he went to Harvard. The following steps were taken:

[67]Sadie American, "The Movement for Small Playgrounds," *American Journal of Sociology* 4 (September 1898): 159.
[68]Ibid., pp. 168–69.

1. Solicit information on personal history, family diseases, etc.
2. Thoroughly examine the heart and lungs.
3. Accurately test muscular strength of arms, chest, back, etc., with dynamometers.
4. Take extensive list of physical measurements, note differences in growth between two sides and the deviations from a fixed standard of comparison.
5. Prescribe exercise to fit in with occupation and muscles already used.
6. Strengthen weak muscles on specially designed apparatus in accordance with prescription.
7. Enter patient in developmental class after weaknesses have been strengthened.

Because the program at Harvard was voluntary, students exercised or not as they wished, even after having a physical examination and exercises prescribed for them. Hence, it was an important part of Dr. Sargent's duties to develop in each student a desire to improve his own physical condition so that he would exercise regularly. For this purpose, Sargent designed his individual charts of anthropometric measurements which showed how the individual compared with others of his age and sex. He later urged a required physical education program for students because he realized that many students who needed exercise the most never came to the gymnasium.

German-American gymnastics were characterized by the class method developed by Spiess. Swedish gymnastics in the United States adhered to the procedure worked out by Ling. Both systems stressed the formal method whereby one teacher could handle a large group in a comparatively small area. Although modern physical educators may deplore this formality, it was necessary for the acceptance of physical education in the school curriculum in the late nineteenth century.

The methods of instruction used in the YMCA were generally less formal because of the fact that membership was voluntary and attendance depended on the interest of the participants. Furthermore, the "Y" drew its membership from out-of-school age groups as well as school age groups. Therefore, class gymnastics lacked the austerity of the Swedish system; in addition, games received considerable attention.

TESTS AND MEASUREMENTS: Probably the most important development in methods in this period was that of tests and measurements. Anthropometric measurements and strength testing were the two areas in which most work was done, and each will be discussed briefly.

The first person to take anthropometric measurements was Dr. Hitchcock of Amherst College who recorded the age, weight, height, finger reach, chest girth, lung capacity, and strength of each student five times during his college course. Strength was measured by the number of pull-ups performed. The measurements that Dr. Hitchcock took were secured "mainly for anatomical and physiological science, and to allow the student by annual comparisons to see what his development might be."[69]

When Dr. Sargent went to Harvard in 1879, he had formulated a series of over forty measurements of the human body and included such data as height of pubic arch and sternum, girth of the elbow and instep, and the distance from the shoulder to the elbow. It is certain that Sargent was influenced by the work of the English physical educator, Archibald Maclaren. However, primary credit for anthropometric measurements goes to an anthropologist, William T. Brigham, a Harvard graduate. Brigham first became interested in measuring the human form in 1865 when he was crossing the Pacific on a ship with a number of Chinese. He observed the differences in stature and physique of these people and devised a complete system of measurements for various parts of the body that would also mark changes in muscular growth.[70]

Dr. Sargent vigorously promoted and aroused popular interest in measurements. He sought to determine what the ideal proportions should be for the harmoniously developed man. He published a manual on the method of measuring and testing in 1887, wrote a number of magazine articles on the subject, conducted a popular contest with cash prizes for the most nearly symmetrically proportioned man and woman, and personally measured leading professional athletes such as John L. Sullivan, the heavyweight boxing champion, and Eugene Sandow, the Prussian strong man. Sargent exhibited life-size statues of the typical American college man and woman, based on the measurements he had collected, at the World's Columbian Exposition in Chicago in 1893.

The period from 1885 to 1900 was truly the golden age of anthropometric measurements. Sargent's list of measurements was adopted by the American Association for the Advancement of Physical Education for use in schools and colleges. The YMCA consulted Sargent and used his list as a basis for their international physical examination but changed to a shorter form after a few years. In this period, Seaver charted 2,700 students at Yale; Wood, 1,500 at Wellesley; Hanna, 1,600 at Oberlin; and Clapp, 1,500 women at the University of Nebraska.[71] The interest in measurement extended from the colleges down into the public schools; studies were made of public school children by Porter in St. Louis, Hastings in Omaha, Christopher in Chicago, and others.

[69]Edward Hitchcock, "Athletics in American Colleges." *Journal of Social Science* 20 (June 1885): 41.

[70]Edward Hitchcock, Jr., "Physical Examinations," *Physical Education* 1 (February 1893), 221–28; also a letter from D. A. Sargent to W. T. Brigham, dated January 20, 1879, in the Harvard University Archives.

[71]John F. Bovard and Frederick W. Cozens, *Tests and Measurements in Physical Education* (Philadelphia: W. B. Saunders Co., 1938), p. 59.

Interest in strength testing was inaugurated by Sargent who was convinced by his empirical observations that the tape measure alone was not a sufficient measure of strength and performance. He therefore evolved a series of strength test items in 1880 using the dynamometer that Brigham had first brought over from Paris eight years earlier. Brigham experimented with strength tests for only a short time, but Sargent continued the work. He originated his own strength test which measured strength of back, legs, gripping strength of the hands, strength of upper arms, and a non-strength item, lung capacity. In 1898 Sargent standardized these tests for large-scale intercollegiate competition. However, intense rivalry led to so many violations of the rules, fake records, and juggling of the instruments that Sargent felt it had lost its special value.[72] Interest in strength testing diminished after 1900 but revived again in the 1920s.

Although anthropometric measurement and strength testing received the greatest attention prior to 1900, note should be taken of the first athletic achievement tests. Luther Gulick advocated a pentathlon for the Athletic League of the YMCA in 1890, and a pentathlon was also conducted at the Cleveland Turnerbund festival in 1894. At Cleveland, achievement tests were given for the 100-yard dash, running high jump, hop-step-jump, 16-pound shotput, and hand-over-hand rope climbing.[73] It was another decade, however, before the example of these nonschool agencies was followed by either the public schools or the colleges.

SUMMARY: Thus were the main lines of development of physical education during the last third of the nineteenth century. A cross-section of physical education practice in the United States around 1900 showed a conglomeration of activities drawn from German gymnastics, Swedish gymnastics, Dr. Sargent's exercises, the YMCA, athletics, and the new play and recreation movement. School physical education was largely physical training with its emphasis on health, correction of physical defects such as poor posture, and mental discipline through gymnastics and calisthenics. School administrators allotted fifteen to thirty minutes daily for physical exercises in some schools while many children had no physical education at all. College programs were similar, although here and there eager students were being offered a few sports such as track, wrestling, and boxing. College athletics moved from student clubs to faculty-supervised athletic associations. The formation of conferences began in response to the need for standards for intercollegiate competition.

The progress made in all areas of physical education during these thirty-five years furnished a stable foundation for the expansion that was to occur in the twentieth century.

[72]Dudley A. Sargent, "Twenty Years' Progress in Efficiency Tests," *American Physical Education Review* 18 (October 1913): 453.

[73]Helen Petroskey, "A History of Measurement in Health and Physical Education in the United States" (Doctoral dissertation, University of Iowa, 1946), p. 246.

23

Physical Education
in
Education for Nationalism
1900-1930

The amazing energy and vitality displayed by the United States between 1865 and 1900 not only produced a vigorous nationalism but also pushed the country into the circle of world politics and power. In fact, the international activity of the United States during this period manifested the spirit of nationalism that evolved as the new nation gained confidence and strength. The United States signed more than fifteen treaties including the International Red Cross agreement, annexed Hawaii and fifty other islands in the Pacific, and arbitrated several conflicts in South America. The acquisition of Cuba, Puerto Rico, and the Philippines as a result of the Spanish-American War made the United States a colonial power both in the Western Hemisphere and in the Pacific area.

These events before 1900 were only shadows of the internationalism that was to emerge in the early twentieth century. A national spirit that could no longer express itself in continental expansion began to seek new areas. The domestic market for products was so fully supplied that industrialists sought new markets and capitalists cast about for new investments. The total value of American foreign investments rose from a negligible amount in 1870 to half a billion dollars in 1900 and two billion dollars in 1909. American economic interest was an important factor behind the United States' support of the "open-door" policy in China and the preservation of Chinese independence. Moreover, philanthropic and religious groups took an active part in promoting internationalism through overseas missionary activities.

In the years from 1900 to 1917, the United States was drawn into the orbit of an unorganized international community as yet dominated by the nationalistic interests of each country. On occasion the United States exhibited a similar self-interest especially when President Theodore Roosevelt, through a series of aggressive actions, cleared the way for the construction of the Panama Canal and aroused the Latin American countries' fear of the "Colossus of the North." Roosevelt, in a corollary to the Monroe Doctrine, asserted the responsibility of the United States to guarantee the financial good faith of Latin American republics when needed to forestall intervention by European creditors. This principle led to direct intervention by the United States in the internal affairs of other countries and, on various occasions, American troops were dispatched to the Philippines, Panama, the Dominican Republic, Haiti, Nicaragua, and Mexico.

Prior to the war, this country participated with other nations seeking international cooperation and peace. The two Hague Conferences of 1899 and 1907 sought to limit armaments and promote peace, and as a result of their deliberations a Permanent Court of Arbitration was created. President Roosevelt persuaded Russia and Japan to end their war in 1905, and a year later the United States took part in the settlement of the Moroccan dispute, which threatened to ignite a European War. In 1913, the United States invited governments to sign reciprocal treaties requiring the arbitration of all controversies and to abstain from hostilities until after the arbitration report.

The outbreak of war in Europe, however, marked a return to nationalism and narrow-minded patriotism. Popular suspicion arose against the Hun and also European diplomacy.[1] The Senate rejected the Treaty of Versailles in 1920 and President Wilson's efforts created a League of Nations which attracted fifty-four members, but not the United States. This country helped found the World Court but failed to join it. During the 1920s the United States signed a series of treaties with other nations renouncing war as an instrument of national policy, but this was an expression of pacifism, not internationalism. The Ku Klux Klan became active as an agent of "Americanism" opposed mainly to the Negro, but also to the Jew and the Catholic. Congress drastically limited immigration by a national quota system favoring western Europeans.

The return of good times in 1922 signalled a period of unparalleled benefits and a new standard of living. The budding idealism of the previous decade—entering a "war to end all wars" and Wilson's dream of a League of Nations guaranteeing peace—became submerged in material concerns such as acquiring automobiles, radios, higher wages, playing the stock market, belonging to clubs, and going to the movies.

Education between 1900 and 1930 underwent tremendous growth and change which affected the entire system. The drive for universal, free public education continued unabated, and attendance during this period increased 11 percent in elementary schools and 66 percent in high schools.

---

[1]Dixon Wecter, *The Age of the Great Depression* (New York: The Macmillan Company, 1948), pp. 287–88.

The 1920s saw an unprecedented number of school buildings constructed. Aided by the school bus and good roads, the consolidation movement for rural schools made a substantial start and the little red schoolhouse became obsolescent. College enrollments jumped 75 percent, and the development of the junior colleges extended educational opportunities for many who could not go away to college.

This expansion of the school systems was accompanied by far-reaching changes that dwarfed the school achievements of previous periods. The influence of William James, G. Stanley Hall, Charles Eliot, Edward L. Thorndike, William Kilpatrick, and John Dewey was reflected in a new understanding of child nature, in an enthusiasm for "interest versus effort" in the learning process, and in the beginnings of an appreciation of individual differences. These interests led to organizational changes in the schools, as a result of which the junior high school emerged as a separate institution. The advent of *interest* subjects brought new emphasis to art, music, manual training, domestic science, commercial subjects, literature, and modern languages. The new biological sciences gained momentum by the discoveries of Weissman and Mendel. Early in the period, increased emphasis was given to history and government. Manual training became the vogue in some cities. Night schools, trade schools, and part-time schools for working boys and girls were also instituted at this time.

The new education encouraged extracurricular activities and club movements of all types; provided for vacation schools, playgrounds, and social centers; brought the advent of special classes for the crippled, tubercular, and retarded; promoted the development of testing programs to assist in individual placement and guidance; and encouraged closer school-community contacts by the inauguration of such groups as the Parent-Teachers Association. The result of all these developments was evidenced in an enhanced community interest in the schools and by increased enrollments. From 1900 to 1930 there was continued emphasis and further expansion of physical education and athletics, particularly after World War I. The rather dismal picture of the nation's health, revealed by draft statistics, aroused popular interest in health and physical education as did increasing spectator interest in athletics throughout the 1920s. College football became big business and huge stadiums were built. A number of factors contributed to these developments: an abundance of spending money, increased publicity through newspapers and radio, and—most important—the convenient transportation offered by the automobile and paved roads. Not only the rabid rooter but the whole family could make a holiday occasion of the big football game. The crowds at basketball, too, began to tax the available indoor facilities. Increased leisure time because of shorter working hours in industry, the elimination of child labor, and an earlier retirement age, as well as the longer life expectancy were all factors which favored the extensive growth of recreation.

When the United States entered the world conflict in April 1917, the *military emphasis* was revived. The old question of military training, of the *nationalistic* theme, dormant since the Civil War, came to the fore once again. A serious effort was made at the meeting of the National Education Association in 1918 to introduce military drill into elementary schools. The *Journal of the American Medical Association* observed that physical training had not produced anything like the remarkable physical development seen in the military training camps.[2] In some high schools military drill replaced physical training. However, Newton D. Baker, the Secretary of War, declared that military drill made little contribution to immediate military strength, and that vigorous, disciplined physical training furnished excellent preparation for either civil or military usefulness.[3] Baker also affirmed the importance of college athletics, arguing that sports helped men adjust to military life and provided a means of recreation. However, he decried overemphasis on varsity teams and pleaded for wider participation by all college men. Following the war, military training was dropped from the curriculum, and athletic competition resumed with renewed eagerness.

The *scientific movement* first felt in physical education during the preceding period, gained momentum and force. Physical education programs began to feature the development of athletic achievement tests, the compilation of achievement scales, the measurement of posture, the use of new statistical techniques and objective tests, cardiovascular research, and the determination of factors involved in motor performance. The need for more carefully trained teachers of physical education was recognized. Four years of college work became a desirable minimum and graduate programs were offered for advanced students. The formation of research societies indicated a growing coterie of science-oriented personnel. School buildings and gymnasiums were constructed in accordance witn scientifically-determined standards and furnished with scientifically-tested equipment. In short, teachers, pupils, facilities, and curriculum were all influenced by the scientific movement.

Educational developmentalism became a powerful force in this period and was directly applied to physical education through the "New Physical Education" developed by Dr. Thomas Wood and Clark Hetherington. The first extensive formulation of their ideas appeared in two publications in 1910. One was *Health and Education*, by Wood, (Part I of the Ninth Yearbook of the National Society for the Study of Education), and the other was an article, "Fundamental Education," by Hetherington in the NEA *Proceedings*. It was in this article that Hetherington first used the phrase, "New Physical Education," which has become the accepted name for this movement. In 1922, Hetherington wrote a book, *School Pro-*

---

[2]"Universal Training vs. Physical Training," 70 (12 January 1918): 95.
[3]*American Physical Education Review* 23 (April 1918): 251.

gram in Physical Education, for the Commission on Revision of Elementary Education of the NEA. Five years later, Wood and Rosalind Cassidy wrote *The New Physical Education.* The pioneer leadership of Wood and Hetherington was carried on in the 1920s by two able younger proponents, Dr. Jesse F. Williams and Dr. Jay B. Nash.

Developmentalism contributed new ideas and attitudes toward play that were important to the promotion of the playground and recreation movement in the present century. According to developmentalism, play was an essential part of normal growth. As stated by Hall, "Play is the best kind of education, because it practices powers of mind and body which, in our highly specialized civilization, would never otherwise have a chance to develop."[4] In his book, *Growth and Education,* J. M. Tyler stressed the valuable results of exercise to the growing child. This justification for play made it possible to seek financial support for playgrounds on other grounds than preventing juvenile delinquency or keeping children off busy streets.

Developmentalism also led to an emphasis on health service and health education. As attention shifted from the subject matter to the child, it was realized that the health status of the child had an important effect on learning. Developmentalism was therefore of considerable value in extending the medical examination from mere inspection for communicable disease to a more comprehensive examination of eyes, throat, heart, lungs, and so forth. Health education was adjusted to the interests and needs of the child, with increased interest in the problems of handicapped children.

Developmentalism also led to the passage of state laws concerning physical education—a recognition of the need for physical education as a planned part of each child's school experience.

The *social trend* in education flourished with the continued popularity of athletic sports and the prodigious growth of the new recreation movement, particularly in the 1920s. Luther Gulick, writing in 1910, anticipated the trend when he stated that exercise and recreation must be a social experience in order to induce people to use facilities and to continue to use them. In his opinion, adults did not need large amounts of exercise, but they did need relaxation from work, open air, and the pleasures of social relations.[5] As athletic sports gradually became part of the physical education program, physical education contributed to social education in three main ways: (1) development of such qualities essential to social living as cooperation, self-sacrifice, friendliness, and others, (2) development of habits and attitudes conducive to good citizenship in a

[4]G. Stanley Hall, "Play and Dancing for Adolescents," *The Independent* 62 (14 February 1907): 355–56.

[5]Luther Gulick, "Physical Education from the Standpoint of Health," *Journal of Proceedings and Addresses of the National Education Association* 48 (1910): 349–50.

democracy; and (3) development of the ideals and practices of good sportsmanship and ethical conduct.

The growth of social education was also furthered by a closer alliance between physical education and recreation. Physical education supplied many sports, activities, and facilities for recreation programs; and prominent physical education leaders furnished leadership and support to the recreation movement. On the other hand, recreation contributed to physical education by adding informal activities to the required program; by adding social and moral objectives to those of health; by making play activity a natural part of the child's growth and an integral part of education; by placing emphasis on leisure education in the schools; and by providing ideas for tournaments, point systems, and badges which were adopted by intramural programs in the early 1920s.[6]

Social education was also effectively promoted through the organized camp, a movement that spread throughout the country after 1900. In the words of President Eliot of Harvard, "The organized summer camp is the most important step in education that America has given to the world."[7] The camping movement was generated by three main forces: the industrialization and urbanization of society which separated people from the natural world; the marked increase in leisure; and a recognition of the need of children and youth for those experiences of freedom and spontaneity which a camp is particularly able to provide.[8]

To conclude, it would be difficult to ascribe the relative emphasis of each of the themes of scientific, developmental, or social education. For the first time important effects of all three of these themes were observed in physical education theory and practice. The military (nationalistic) emphasis was confined to the brief period of participation in World War I.

Aims of Education

The aims of education for the first thirty years of this century were influenced most by the social education movement and educational developmentalism. John Dewey, the spokesman for social education, is generally conceded to have had a wider influence on education in this country than any other person, although G. Stanley Hall and Edward L. Thorndike also made significant contributions.

Dewey believed that children could learn as much from experience and *doing* as they could from book drills. He therefore felt that the school

[6]Elmer D. Mitchell, "Contributions of the Recreation Movement to Physical Education," *Recreation* 25 (May 1931): 90–92, 100.

[7]H. W. Gibson, "The History of Organized Camping," *Camping Magazine* 8 (December 1936), reprint.

[8]*Social Work Yearbook*, 1949, p. 73.

should be a miniature society with an elastic curriculum. Education should be living, and not a preparation for a future living that might be impossible to predict.[9] "The school is primarily a social institution," Dewey wrote. "Education being a social process, the school is simply that form of community life in which all those agencies are concentrated that will be most effective in bringing the child to share in the inherited resources of the race, and to use his own powers for social ends."[10]

Dewey's concepts were not new. Froebel had used many of them in his kindergarten, but Dewey extended these principles to all grades. He performed the task of reorientating American schools toward social living and social efficiency. This led to an emphasis on social studies. Teachers and others who concerned themselves with society and its problems were aware of the contrast between man's mastery of his physical environment and his mastery of himself.

The ideas of Hall concerning the basis of the educational process are summed up in the following four principles:

1. The continuance of the race is supremely important; the individual is incidental. Preparation for sex life, reproduction, and raising a family become important functions of education.
2. The emotional life is far more fundamental than the intellectual. Genetically, man's emotional life preceded his intellectual development; and, in fact, emotion supplied the motive for intellectual growth.
3. Human development is a process of recapitulating the racial developments. Education must proceed from the fundamental movements of the body to the finer accessory movements, and from presenting general, simple ideas for intellectual understanding to the more detailed, complex ones. (This theory is now no longer accepted.)
4. Education must develop the child's own nature and include activities, capabilities, and interests that would lead to a well-balanced personality.[11]

Thorndike, like Hall, was interested in the study of the individual. His aims of education were "to give boys and girls health in body and mind, information about the world of nature and men, worthy interests in knowledge and action, a multitude of habits of thought, feeling, and behavior, and ideals of efficiency, honor, duty, love and service."[12]

[9]John Dewey, *The School and Society* (Chicago: University of Chicago Press, 1899), pp. 116–17.
[10]John Dewey, *My Pedagogical Creed*, Article II, as quoted in Frederick Eby, *The Development of Modern Education*, 2d ed. (Englewood Cliffs, N.J.: Prentice-Hall, Inc., 1952), p. 622.
[11]Eby, *The Development of Modern Education*, pp. 607–8.
[12]Edward L. Thorndike, *The Principles of Teaching* (New York: A. G. Seiler, 1906), pp. 3–4.

The doctrine of individual differences received general approval. There was a growing realization that each child should be allowed to develop his own peculiar aptitudes and talents. In the problem of recognizing these individual differences, recourse was had to many new types of tests —physical, intelligence, and temperament—which had been developed and used so extensively during World War I.

Education was reoriented to provide the child with creative experiences through the "natural" program, a democratic approach, and the project method. "Interest" as opposed to "effort" was applied to teaching. New importance and dignity were ascribed to the "play" method in education.

Greater emphasis was placed on preparing pupils for vocations and for citizenship. Congress passed the Smith-Hughes Act in 1917. It authorized federal appropriations for vocational education.

The aims of education were summarized and set forth in 1918 as the Seven Cardinal Principles of Education. They were the following:

1. Health and safety
2. Mastery of tools, techniques, and spirit of learning
3. Worthy home membership
4. Vocational and economic effectiveness
5. Citizenship
6. Worthy use of leisure
7. Ethical character

The expression of these aims, though not universally achieved in practice, indicated that American education in the first thirty years of the twentieth century had moved far beyond the three R's of the nineteenth century.

Aims of Physical Education

In the early years of this period, there was increasing dissatisfaction with a physical education that was dominated by the German and Swedish systems of gymnastics. Dr. Wood indicted the traditional program on three counts:

1. It sought postural and corrective results that are not satisfactorily obtained in class exercises by formal movements involving consciousness of muscle and body. Except for individuals needing remedial gymnastics, these results may be gained as well or better through exercises that are more natural, spontaneous, and enjoyable.
2. It concentrated too much upon the body and lacked sufficient regard for the attitude of the mind and the effects upon disposition and personality.

3. It developed various forms of ability that are not closely enough related to activities of human life to justify the time and effort given to them.[13]

Wood believed that exercises which only aim at bodily health may fail to accomplish their goal. Health should be a by-product of activity rather than the main aim. He pointed out the necessary dependence of physical education on other sciences and its relation to education in writing: "When physical education presents a programme which is psychologically and physiologically sound, and therefore, pedagogically acceptable, it will find itself in organic relationship with education as a whole and to the other subjects or departments represented."[14]

Clark Hetherington provided an excellent statement of the change of emphasis: "The interpretation given might be called the new physical education, with the emphasis on education, and the understanding that it is 'physical' only in the sense that the activity of the whole organism is the educational agent and not the mind alone. . . . Back of the thesis maintained is the general idea that education is neither for body nor for mind alone, but for all human powers that depend on educational activities for development."[15]

Hetherington then went on to define four phases of the educational process for the new physical education as follows:

1. Organic education—the process that develops vital vigor. This refers not only to skeletal muscular development but perfect elimination and high nutrition. It is the development of power in the organs of vegetative life with a hygienic background during the period of growth and development.
2. Psychomotor education—the process that develops power and skill in neuromuscular activities. Its main function is to develop the fundamental nervous centers by exercising fundamental muscles until the nervous system can carry the burden of civilization. Power in the fundamental centers is necessary to give nervous stability.
3. Character education—the development of moral, social, and spiritual powers. This is done by the school, home, Sunday school, and play. "The outside play life is the only agent that touches all children and youth, which lasts through the entire period of growth and development, which is naturally character-forming, good or bad." The character education of children continues into the athletics of adolescence.

[13]Thomas D. Wood, *Health and Education*, Part I, Ninth Yearbook of the National Society for the Study of Education (Chicago: University of Chicago Press, 1910), pp. 81–82.
[14]Ibid., p. 82.
[15]Clark Hetherington, "Fundamental Education," *Journal of Proceedings and Addresses of the National Education Association* 48 (1910): 350.

4. Intellectual education—the child learns by doing, especially through play. The natural incentives to intellectual education are the hunger for experience and for expression, developed through play and activity. The child builds up insights, sympathies, understandings, and habitual reactions which become the foundation for social thinking.[16]

These aims show the definite influence of educational developmentalism, and Hetherington's emphasis on play indicates his indebtedness to Hall, with whom he studied at Clark University.

It should be noted that the aims of the New Physical Education found acceptance in the minds of some of the older physical educators. Even the conservative Dr. Leonard, who had considerable respect for the Swedish and German systems, approved the new idea when he wrote: "A better usage, and one more in conformity with the present conception of man's nature as a unit, is that which regards his motor activities as a means of influencing for good the entire individual —in mind and character as well as in body; it employs the word *physical* to denote the means, and not the end."[17]

As an aftermath of World War I, social values and good citizenship became important aims for physical education. Dr. William Burdick, in his presidential address to the American Physical Education Association in 1919, declared that physical training would help many soldiers become better citizens. The following year the new president, Dr. Dudley B. Reed, expressed the need to "work more wholly together toward the ultimate end which we all have in view, the betterment of the citizens of our country."[18] In 1920, a committee of the Society of Directors of Physical Education in Colleges reported four aims of physical education:

1. If the perfection of the individual in his social relations is of greater importance than purely personal values, then the first aim is the development of habits of obedience, subordination, self-sacrifice, cooperation, friendliness, a spirit of fair play, and sportsmanship.
2. Other character traits of indirect significance to community life are self-confidence and self-control, mental and moral poise, good spirits, alertness, resourcefulness, courage, aggressiveness, and initiative. These traits were formerly developed by farm life and the home. Now other means have to be used.
3. There is the underlying purpose of promoting normal growth and organic development, conserving health, and providing strength and endurance, good posture, and neuromuscular control.

[16]Ibid., pp. 350–57.
[17]Fred E. Leonard, "The Relation of Motor Activity to Health and Education," *American Physical Education Review* 20 (November 1915): 516.
[18]"Presidential Address," *American Physical Education Review* 25 (June 1920): 226.

4. It is important to engender intelligent and healthful interest leading to lifelong practice of active exercise for physical efficiency, mental sanity, and stimulating social contacts.[19]

The concern of educational developmentalism for individual differences and the recognition of the need and value of educating the handicapped to useful citizenship brought about a significant change in attitude toward the handicapped. It was now realized that the previous emphasis on corrective and remedial physical education was of little help to those whose handicaps could not be corrected. A clear statement of the new objectives for the handicapped was made in 1926 by Harry A. Scott, then at the University of Oregon. Scott believed that the handicapped person should acquire skills in recreational activities which he could enjoy in later life; he should participate in as many competitive sports as possible in order to acquire social and emotional control; and he should have a thorough knowledge and understanding of his defect as it concerned his physical and social well being.[20] Lillian Drew of Teachers College in her book *Individual Gymnastics* (1922) approved the name "individual gymnastics" as being much more suitable than the former one of "corrective gymnastics." Harlan Metcalf, then at Ohio State, shortly afterward suggested the name, "individual physical education," as more descriptive than the older ones. He believed that the individual program should be more concerned with education and less with correction.[21] Individual physical education, therefore, sought the same aims and objectives for the handicapped as for other children.

The aims of physical education from 1900 to 1930 showed a close affiliation with the purposes of educational developmentalism, social education, and scientific education. Thus the groundwork for the modern physical education program was completed.

Promotion of Physical Education

The theory and philosophy of the New Physical Education had little effect on school and college physical education before World War I, but pressure for change came from another source. The athletic and playground movements indicated a rising revolt against formalism in educational training. As a result, the older gymnastic systems began to decline in popular interest. The favorite activities of the recreation and athletic programs

---

[19]"The Aims and Scope of Physical Education," *American Physical Education Review* 25 (June 1920): 259–60.

[20]Harry A. Scott, "Supervised Exercise Corrects Defects of College Men," *Nation's Health* 8 (October 1926): 660–62, 722.

[21]Harlan G. Metcalf, "Objectives of Individual Physical Education for College Men," *Journal of Health and Physical Education* 1 (November, 1930): 10–11, 60.

started to find a place in physical education. Games that were taught wholesale on the playground also began to be used in school yards and gymnasiums. The net result was in the long run desirable, as it was to lead to a combined program of formal and informal activities.

With the outbreak of war, physical education programs in many schools and colleges were set aside for military training, in spite of opposition by the organized physical education profession and some military leaders. The military services called on a number of physical educators to help develop a physical training program in the military camps. Dr. Joseph Raycroft was chairman of the Athletic Division of the War Department Commission on Training Camp Activities, and Walter Camp did a similar job for the navy stations. John L. Griffith directed the Athletic Division of the War Camp Community Service, which was proposed by the Playground and Recreation Association to help communities meet problems of recreation arising from the presence of large numbers of military personnel or war workers. Dr. James McCurdy of Springfield College and Dr. James Naismith, the inventor of basketball, worked with the American Expeditionary Force in France. Dr. George Meylan of Columbia worked directly with the French army, and Dr. R. Tait McKenzie of the University of Pennsylvania, also a famous sculptor of athletic youth and war memorials, did significant rehabilitation work with the English army. Physical education teachers and coaches were utilized for physical training, and the YMCA provided recreational activities in areas were soldiers were on leave.

The draft examinations during the war revealed the shocking news that one-third of the men examined were unfit for military service because of poor physical condition and another one-third had pathological deficiencies. These facts gave health education a powerful stimulus and caused some schools to take time from physical education activities for health instruction. In certain localities the term "health education" was used to include both physical education and health education. This appellation proved expedient in securing tax appropriations.

In the 1920s physical education capitalized on the growing popularity of informal play and athletics. The public was willing to provide money for larger gymnasiums, greater outdoor field areas, and swimming pools, since these could also serve as centers for community activities. New gymnasiums stressed functional design with maximum floor area, good lighting, and adequate ventilation. The old balcony running track became obsolete, and ceilings were made high enough for ball activities. Locker and shower room facilities were enlarged. Equipment was selected with a view to safety and utility in the new physical education program.

PROGRESS IN STATE LEGISLATION: One significant effect of the First World War was improved state legislation on physical education. Prior to

1900, five states had passed some type of physical education law. Between 1900 and 1914, only three states enacted legislation: Pennsylvania in 1901, Michigan in 1911, and Idaho in 1913. In the four years following the start of World War I, eight more states passed physical education laws. Seventeen states enacted legislation in the postwar period from 1919 to 1921 and other states revised earlier laws.

In February 1918, sixty national leaders met in Atlantic City at the invitation of the U. S. Commissioner of Education to discuss ways and means of securing a nationwide movement for health and physical education. Dr. Thomas D. Wood prepared proposals for discussion and a National Committee on Physical Education was formed. The committee asked the Playground and Recreation Association to take over, and the National Physical Education Service was formed in November 1918. The Playground and Recreation Association appropriated $10,000 to get the Service under way. Its purpose was twofold: (1) the promotion of federal and state legislation requiring physical and health education for all school children; and (2) assistance to state departments of education in developing statewide programs under trained leadership of state directors on the staff of state superintendents of public instruction.[22] The efforts of the service helped to continue the promotion of statewide physical education after the original wartime impetus had dissipated. Seven states enacted new legislation between 1922 and 1931, and ten states revised existing legislation.

As a general rule, the state laws passed prior to 1914 made the teaching of physical culture and calisthenics mandatory in the larger schools and permissive in the smaller. After 1914, several definite trends characterized state legislation. One was the inclusion of more specific provisions concerning time allotment, financial support, teacher training, special or modified courses for handicapped children, and requirement for graduation. A second trend was a shift in emphasis away from calisthenics and formal gymnastics for health and discipline in favor of the educational results of sports, games, athletics, and rhythmic activities. A third trend was the use of the title "health and physical education" rather than "physical culture" or "physical training."[23] In some cases the law was ineffective, as in Tennessee where school officials could not be required to appropriate money for physical education.

Even in states that had model legislation, experience showed that a state supervisor was necessary to achieve the best benefits possible under the law. The first state supervisor was Dr. Thomas Storey in New York,

22"Twentieth Anniversary of the National Physical Education Service of the National Recreation Association," *Journal of Health and Physical Education* 9 (September 1938): 424.

23Anne S. Aller, "The Rise of State Provisions for Physical Education in the Public Secondary Schools of the United States" (Doctoral dissertation, University of California, 1935), p. 163.

appointed in 1916. Clark Hetherington was given a similar position in California a year later. By 1930, thirty-six states had laws and twenty states had a supervisor. The passage of legislation helped school administrators to think of physical education as a part of general education rather than as a special subject in the curriculum.

TEACHER-TRAINING DEVELOPMENTS: A cultural lag was evidenced as a result of the compulsory physical education laws. Teachers were not available when the legislation was passed, and it took time to set up necessary machinery for training them. The lack of trained teachers was a heritage from the preceding period when there was little felt need for professional personnel.

Up to World War I, the great majority of physical education teachers were graduates of the private teacher-training schools, many of which bore the names of the early leaders who founded them. In the East were Arnold College for Hygiene and Physical Education, the Bouvé School, the International YMCA College, Ithaca School of Physical Education, Panzer College, Posse-Nissen School of Physical Education, Russell Sage College, Sargent School for Physical Education, Savage School of Physical Education, and Wellesley College. In the Midwest, the private school movement in teacher preparation was less pronounced, but the Normal College of the American Gymnastic Union, the American College of Physical Education (Chicago), the Chicago Normal School of Physical Education, and George Williams College were important in the early developments. In the South, George Peabody College at Nashville, Tennessee, similarly pioneered in teacher preparation. The important place of the private normal schools declined, however, as the state and denominational colleges began to introduce major physical education curriculums leading to the A.B. or B.S. degree. Between 1914 and 1921 the number of state normal schools preparing teachers of physical education jumped from three to twenty-eight, the number of state universities from four to twenty, and endowed colleges from eight to twenty-two.[24] It became increasingly difficult for the private normal schools to maintain their financial security. Some of them continued, while others either dropped out of existence or became affiliated with colleges and universities, e.g., the Boston Normal School of Gymnastics with Wellesley, Posse School with Tufts, Arnold College with the University of Bridgeport, and Sargent School with Boston University.

Geographically, the East yielded its early dominance in teacher training to the Midwest. One of the new leaders in teacher training was Professor Wilbur P. Bowen who taught at the Michigan State Normal College in Ypsilanti from 1903 to 1928. Owing to his influence, one of the first state syllabuses for use by teachers was prepared in 1915. Bowen wrote half a

[24]W. P. Bowen, "Seven Years of Progress in Preparing Teachers of Physical Education," *American Physical Education Review* 27 (February 1922): 64.

dozen books, the best known of which were *Applied Anatomy and Kinesiology* and *The Theory of Organized Play*, the latter with Elmer D. Mitchell. The number of teacher training schools reached 150 by 1930, and they were located in all parts of the country.

The Turnverein Seminary moved to Indianapolis in 1907 and changed its name to the Normal College of the American Gymnastic Union. Emil Rath became director two years later and provided outstanding professional leadership for the next twenty-five years. The school was accredited under Indiana law, and the curriculum was gradually lengthened from two to four years. The Phi Epsilon Kappa fraternity originated at the Normal School in 1913. Two women's organizations, Delta Psi Kappa and Phi Delta Pi, began in 1916 and 1917, respectively. Rath wrote books on apparatus, track and field for girls and women, and dancing, and founded the Indiana state association in 1917.[25] The Turner publication *Mind and Body*, in 1907 acquired a new editor, William Stecher, and he served with distinction for a quarter of a century.

Many leaders in the YMCA program were products of the International Young Men's Christian Association College at Springfield, Massachusetts (later called Springfield College) which had many competent and devoted teachers such as Robert J. Roberts, Dr. Luther Gulick, Dr. James Huff McCurdy, Dr. John Brown, Jr., George B. Affleck, and Harold Friermood. A sister institution, the YMCA Training School at Chicago (later known as George Williams College), achieved recognition through the work of men like George Ehler, Dr. Henry Kallenberg, Martin Foss, and Arthur H Steinhaus.

The training of leaders for the YWCA program was originally carried on at the Central School of Hygiene and Physical Education. It later became the School of Physical Education and Hygiene of Russell Sage College under the directorship of Helen McKinstry.

A remarkable leader of youth in three national agencies was Dr. George J. Fisher. He first served as national director of YMCA physical education from 1903 to 1919 and was an editor of the official "Y" publication, *Physical Training*. In 1919 he became Deputy Scout Commissioner of the Boy Scouts of America for twenty-four years until his retirement. In addition, he helped to found the U.S. Volleyball Association in 1928, served as its first president for twenty-four years, and edited the *Official Volleyball Guide* for twenty-one years.[26]

Summer schools increased in numbers and size, particularly during the 1920s when colleges and universities initiated course work in the summer. As a result of this competition and other factors, the Chautauqua

[25]W. K. Streit, "Normal College of the American Gymnastic Union," *Physical Educator* 20 (May 1963): 54.

[26]J. Edmund Welch, "George J. Fisher, Leader of Youth," *Journal of Health, Physical Education, and Recreation* 39 (May 1968): 37, 86.

Summer School declined rapidly after World War I and the Harvard Summer School was forced to close in 1932. A curious phenomenon of the early 1920s was the so-called coaching school, which first started at the University of Illinois in 1914. These schools were first designed to help the coaches in their work, and then were extended to prepare them to teach the physical education classes required by the new state laws. These schools were destined to a short existence, as the colleges soon began to turn out four-year products with a well-rounded training for physical education and coaching. Such coaching schools as now exist are of the short-term, institute type and grant no credit.

Graduate programs started at Teachers College of Columbia University under Thomas Wood, and the first master's degree in physical education was granted in 1910.[27] Teachers College and New York University first offered study for the Ph.D. degree in 1924 and became influential centers in graduate education for a number of years. The YMCA established a graduate school in Nashville, Tennessee to train state directors for the "Y." This was a cooperative program involving Vanderbilt University, George Peabody College for Teachers, and Scarritt College for Christian Workers. Four men earned the Doctor of Physical Education degree between 1925 and 1929.[28] By 1933 over thirty colleges in the United States offered graduate courses.

PROFESSIONAL ORGANIZATIONS: The American Association for the Advancement of Physical Education acquired a new name and a new constitution in 1903. Its new name was the American Physical Education Association, and the new constitution permitted the formation of national sections based on interest as well as geographical areas. Among the first sections were anthropometry, elementary schools, normal schools, college directors, and secondary school physical directors. The Association experienced a painful struggle to become a representative national organization. For the first time, in 1922, the APEA could claim membership from every state in the Union, but it was not until 1920 that a president was elected who did not come from an eastern state. He was Dr. Dudley B. Reed of the University of Chicago. By 1930 three districts had been formed—the Eastern, Middle West, and Southern. The growth of the profession after the First World War is evident from membership figures. In 1915 there were 1,367 members, a modest gain of 27 percent since 1900. In the next fifteen years there was a spectacular rise of 4,366 members, a 320 percent increase!

[27]George W. Averitte, Jr., "A History of the Department of Health Education and Physical Education, Teachers College, Columbia University" (Doctoral dissertation, Columbia University, 1953), p. 55.

[28]J. Edmund Welch, "The YMCA Graduate School of Nashville," *Forum* 50 (March 1969): 13–16. This is published by the Association of Professional Directors of the YMCA.

The Association started a useful service in 1911 by selling books to members. This continued until 1928 when the development of several large companies specializing in physical education books made the service unnecessary. In response to urgent problems in teacher training during the twenties, the Association cooperated with Dr. James F. Rogers of the U.S. Bureau of Education to sponsor two national conferences in 1925 and 1927. Furthermore, two committees of the APEA were concerned with curriculum matters. One dealt with state curriculum requirements and was headed by Allan Ireland, state director for Connecticut. The other reported on junior and senior high school curriculums under the chairmanship of Carl Schrader, state supervisor for Massachusetts. This report was published in the 1928 Yearbook of the Department of Superintendence of the NEA.

The national influence of the APEA was greatly enhanced by the publication of the *American Physical Education Review* which changed from a quarterly to nine issues in 1908. The *Review* reported local, state, district, and national meetings, published articles by leaders in the field, provided book reviews, and served as a strong influence in the growth of the profession. Its success was due mainly to the talent and energy of Dr. James Huff McCurdy of Springfield College, who was editor from 1906 through 1929. During the same period Dr. McCurdy was also secretary and treasurer of the Association; his wife, Persis McCurdy, held the office of assistant secretary-treasurer-editor for more than ten years; and their house served as an office. Seldom has any professional organization owed more to one family!

The Society of College Gymnasium Directors became the Society of College Directors of Physical Education in 1908 and formed committees to explore pertinent problems. The titles of some committees give an insight into problems of the times: Committee on the Advisability of Determining the Physical Condition of a Candidate for Gymnastic and Athletic Exercise; Committee on Credit for Gymnastic Training in College Work; Committee on the Relationship Between the Department of Gymnastics and Athletics; Committee on Construction and Material Equipment; and Committee on Curriculum Research.[29] Since 1908 the society has grown under a succession of strong presidents and has had continuity with the following secretaries serving long terms of office: Dr. Paul C. Phillips of Amherst; T. N. Metcalf, then of Iowa State; Harry Scott of Columbia; and Glenn Howard of Queen's College.

A similar organization for women was the National Association of Physical Education for College Women, initiated by Amy Homans in 1909. Meetings were held by local groups meeting independently until

---

[29]Glenn W. Howard, "The College Physical Education Association," *Journal of Health and Physical Education* 17 (September 1946): 411.

1924 when the present national association was formed.[30] This group originally consisted of women directors of physical education but was enlarged to include others associated with college physical education for women.

The new interest in research was reflected in the founding of organizations for that purpose. The American Academy of Physical Education was conceived by Luther Gulick and formed in 1904–05 to "bring together those who were doing original scientific work in the field of physical training, and to aid in the promotion of such work."[31] The group met annually at Dr. George Meylan's camp on Sebago Lake in Maine until the outbreak of World War I. The Academy was revived in 1926 by Hetherington, Jay B. Nash, R. Tait McKenzie, Thomas Storey, and William Burdick. McKenzie was elected the first president, and a constitution was adopted in 1930 which limited membership to fifty active fellows.

ATHLETIC GROWTH AND THE NCAA: The institution of athletics in the 1920s underwent an enormous expansion in all its aspects. The number of participants increased as the number of teams multiplied. To the traditional varsity sports of football, baseball, track, and basketball were added teams in swimming, tennis, wrestling, cross-country, fencing, soccer, gymnastics, and golf. The expanded player interest encouraged the expansion of facilities for the various sports. Enlarged staffs followed as a matter of course. The incredible growth in spectator interest led to larger stadiums, larger gymnasiums or fieldhouses, and in many cases, rented auditoriums. The most remarkable development occurred in football. Although the first of the modern steel stadiums was built by Harvard in 1903 with seats for over 23,000 people, the decade from 1920 to 1930—a period of national prosperity—was truly the stadium era. During these years the seating capacity of 135 college and university stadiums jumped from 929,-523 to 2,307,850. Most of this construction occurred in the Midwest as exemplified by Michigan's stadium seating 87,500 and Ohio State's stadium for 77,000.[32] College football attendance soared above ten million in 1930. The problems of handling large sums of money and of indebtedness for expanded facilities caused athletics to assume the proportions of big business. These changes all had their effects on the administration of athletics.

College athletics, especially football, increasingly captured public attention but also aroused concern among educators. A group of private school headmasters asked President Theodore Roosevelt to call together the coaches of Yale, Harvard, and Princeton to "persuade them to under-

[30]Dorothy Ainsworth, "National Association of Physical Education for College Women," *Journal of Health and Physical Education* 17 (November 1946): 525.

[31]Luther Gulick, "Academy of Physical Education," *American Physical Education Review* 15 (May 1910): 342.

[32]The capacities of these two stadiums were later raised to 101,000 and 85,000 respectively.

take to teach men to play football honestly."[33] This meeting was held early in October of 1905. The season of 1905 was marred by a large number of injuries and sharp dissension over eligibility. The game was abolished at Columbia, one of the leading powers in intercollegiate football. Northwestern and Union College prohibited football for one year; Stanford and California substituted rugby for football, a change that lasted ten years. Severe restrictions were also levied at other prominent institutions. The death of a Union College player late in the season prompted Henry McCracken, Chancellor of New York University, to call a meeting of the nation's colleges to determine whether college football was worth keeping, and, if so, what could be done to improve it. Thirteen colleges were represented at the meeting in New York early in December 1905. After long debate, the delegates agreed to keep football as a college sport and to organize an agency for college athletics. Another conference was called late in December which was attended by sixty-two colleges and resulted in the establishment of the Intercollegiate Athletic Association of the United States. It assumed its present name, the National Collegiate Athletic Association (NCAA), in 1910.

From the beginning, the NCAA assumed no legislative or executive powers and served primarily as an educational body. Conduct of college athletics was left in the hands of the academic authorities of each institution. Minimum eligibility rules similar to those of the Western Conference were adopted but without any method of enforcement. In the first year, thirty-eight institutions became members, and Palmer E. Pierce of West Point was elected president.[34]

There were five main contributions of the NCAA to the development of college athletics.

1. Faculty control. The NCAA stood for faculty control of athletics and its example was undoubtedly a key factor in promoting the change from student and alumni supervision in many institutions.
2. Growth of conferences. The NCAA consistently encouraged the formation of new conferences among its members. In the period between 1906 and 1915, twenty-nine conferences were formed which regulated all sports of the member institutions and became popular in the Midwest, Far West, and South. The East largely adhered to its traditional leagues for each sport.
3. Elimination of seasonal coaches. In 1910 the NCAA passed a resolution favoring employment of coaches on a full-time basis as regular members of the teaching staff.

[33]Letter from Endicott Peabody to Theodore Roosevelt, Sept. 16, 1905, quoted in Guy M. Lewis, "The American Intercollegiate Football Spectacle, 1869–1917" (Doctoral dissertation, University of Maryland, 1964), p. 224.

[34]Paul Stagg, "The Development of the National Collegiate Athletic Association in Relationship to Intercollegiate Athletics in the United States" (Doctoral dissertation, New York University, 1946), pp. 24–32.

4. Rules committees and national tournaments. One important function of the NCAA since its inception has been the creation of rules committees for various sports. Much of this work was done jointly with the Amateur Athletic Union, the YMCA, the National Federation of State High School Athletic Associations, and the Canadian Physical Education Association. The rules standardization for college sports was influential in the establishment of a program of national championships conducted by the NCAA in many sports, beginning with track and field in 1921. Swimming was added three years later, and in time other national sports championships were instituted.

5. Subsidization and recruitment. In 1926, the NCAA was one of several agencies to request a survey of college athletics by the Carnegie Foundation. This report, *American College Athletics*, published in 1929, revealed serious conditions of proselyting and professionalism. It was effective in creating public awareness of athletic evils but led to little actual change.

The progress of intercollegiate athletics was temporarily slowed during the time of America's participation in World War I. The NCAA called a meeting of college representatives in Washington to discuss the continuance of athletics. After hearing the Secretary of War advocate college athletics for as many students as possible, the NCAA passed resolutions recommending that colleges continue athletic sports, extend athletics to all men, and reduce expenses of the intercollegiate program. Nevertheless, many colleges and high schools dropped varsity sports or abbreviated their schedules. Athletic departments turned over their services to the ROTC divisions and carried out athletic practices under the direction of the school commandants. This arrangement terminated with the Armistice.

THE AAU AND THE NCAA: The formation of the National Collegiate Athletic Association demonstrated the desire of the colleges for autonomy in the control of their own sports, and it provided leadership in the areas of dissension with the Amateur Athletic Union. The relationship between the NCAA and the AAU is complex.[35] By 1912 the AAU had jurisdiction over 538 athletic clubs and 19,000 registered athletes.[36] It claimed to be the national controlling body for a number of sports, especially basketball and track and field. On the other hand the colleges, YMCAs, and Turners —all of whom had experienced accelerated growth—resented efforts by the AAU to determine eligibility and collect fees for competition without

[35]For an excellent factual discussion see Arnold W. Flath, *A History of Relations Between the National Collegiate Athletic Association and the Amateur Athletic Union of the United States, (1905–1963)* (Champaign, Ill.: Stipes Publishing Company, 1964).

[36]Henry F. Kallenberg, "The Present Situation in the Administration of Athletics and What to Do," *American Physical Education Review* 17 (June 1912): 504.

representation. Clark Hetherington and the Athletic Research Society tried to ease differences by establishing the National Federated Committee in 1911. The NCAA and a dozen other organizations supported it, but not the AAU. This fact and the outbreak of the war caused the plan to fail.[37] Some success was achieved in basketball when a joint basketball rules committee of the YMCA, NCAA, and AAU was formed in 1915 and lasted for twenty years.

Trouble arose again over the selection of representatives for the 1920 Olympic Games by the AAU-dominated American Olympic Committee. Secretary of War, John W. Weeks, stepped in with a proposal which culminated in the formation of the National Amateur Athletic Federation (NAAF) in 1922. The Federation was composed of a number of national athletic groups who each determined the eligibility of their own members. In the meantime, the AAU created a new American Olympic Association with changes acceptable to the NCAA and other interested groups so that the 1924 Olympic Games were free of bickering. This truce, however, only lasted until 1926. This time General Douglas MacArthur took over as president of the American Olympic Committee, and he patched things up in time for the 1928 Olympic Games. There was further progress in 1930 when the American Olympic Association established Olympic game committees for each sport and made other changes which met with NCAA approval.[38] These changes contributed to the demise of the Men's Division of the NAAF in the 1930s.

SCHOOL ATHLETICS: Some of the problems faced by early state high school associations were pointed up by McCurdy's questionnaire study of 555 communities in 1905. He concluded that the sports competition was managed largely by students without the help of the physical directors and that the regular gymnastic work was not a substitute for athletics. McCurdy wrote that in many cases competitive sports grew up almost in spite of the school authorities.[39] The state high school athletic associations by 1925 had spread rapidly to every state in the Union. The beginning of a national organization occurred with the founding of the Midwest Federation of State High School Athletic Associations. This Federation was organized at the suggestion of L. W. Smith, secretary of the Illinois state association, who met in 1920 with representatives from Indiana, Iowa, Wisconsin, and Michigan to discuss problems arising from high school tournaments conducted by outside groups. Two years later, representatives from eleven states showed up at the annual meeting and the present name, the National Federation of State High School Athletic Associations, was

[37]Flath, *A History of Relations Between the NCAA and the AAU*, pp. 30–36.
[38]Ibid., pp. 97–98.
[39]J. H. McCurdy, "A Study of the Characteristics of Physical Training in the Public Schools of the United States," *American Physical Education Review* 10 (September 1905): 211.

adopted. Twenty-eight states joined the national organization prior to 1930. The purpose of the Federation was to protect and regulate interstate interests of its member schools. In 1929, the Federation adopted a set of "Recommended Minimum Eligibility Requirements" which served as a valuable guide to states in raising athletic standards.[40]

One short-lived but noteworthy innovation occurred in New York State. Proposed by the state director, Frederick Rand Rogers, a statewide program was started in 1928 whereby coaches were not allowed to sit on the bench or to direct play in any way during a game. They could act only in case of injury. The plan was in effect for two years before being abandoned. Vaughn Blanchard adopted Rogers' plan for the Detroit schools in football and basketball, but it drew sharp criticism from sports writers and was soon terminated.[41]

Another impressive organization for athletic participation was the Public School Athletic League in New York City, commonly referred to as the PSAL. The league was a product of the creative mind and organizational genius of Luther Gulick, the Superintendent of Physical Instruction. Activated by a concern for the physical welfare and morals of the school children during the school year,[42] Gulick formed the PSAL in 1903 and enlisted support and financial assistance from such people as President Roosevelt, James Sullivan, president of the AAU, Andrew Carnegie, John D. Rockefeller, the superintendent of schools, and many other leading citizens, as well as the newspapers. The city was divided into twenty-five districts to provide mass competition for elementary and high school boys in more than a dozen activities. District winners competed for the league championship. Boys were classified by weight.[43] In 1909 over 7,000 buttons were given to successful participants, and the championship baseball game in 1907 drew a crowd of 15,000 to the Polo Grounds. The success of the League encouraged the Board of Education to spend half a million dollars to establish and equip four parks for competition.[44] The plan of the PSAL in New York was adopted by numerous other cities.

INTRAMURAL SPORTS: Even the phenomenal growth of varsity football did not obscure the new intramural development in athletics. Although informal intramural sports existed at colleges in the early nineteenth century and actually preceded varsity sports, the conscious direction and organization of intramural athletics began just before World War I. Intra-

---

[40]Charles E. Forsythe, *The Administration of High School Athletics* (Englewood Cliffs, N.J.: Prentice-Hall, Inc., 1948), pp. 10–13.

[41]Letter to author from Vaughn Blanchard, January 18, 1969.

[42]Recreation programs at that time operated only in the summer.

[43]George W. Wingate, "The Public Schools Athletic League," *Outing* 52 (May 1908): 165–71.

[44]Arthur B. Reeve, "The World's Greatest Athletic Organization," *Outing* 57 (October 1910): 114.

mural programs first developed in the colleges, and, in 1913, both Ohio State and the University of Michigan appointed an intramural director from the athletic staff. The NCAA gave its support to the intramural movement by appointing a Committee on the Encouragement of Intra-Collegiate and Recreative Sports. The committee made a national survey in 1913–14 and estimated that half the college men had no regular or systematic exercise. They believed that ninety percent of the students would participate and urged all colleges to appoint a "capable and enthusiastic" director to supervise the program.[45] A survey in 1916 showed that some type of intramural programs, usually student-administered, existed in 140 institutions.[46]

Expert direction and leadership for the new intramural sports movement in the first twenty years was provided by Elmer D. Mitchell. He was appointed intramural director at the University of Michigan in 1919 and exercised great influence through his book, *Intramural Athletics*, first published in 1925. Three years later, the University of Michigan opened its superb Intramural Sports Building, a salient landmark in the history of intramural sports, and the program at Michigan became a nationally recognized model.

The first intramural programs were conceived primarily as a feeder for the varsity teams, but gradually a sounder justification was worked out and intramural departments in the 1920s were concerned with (1) promoting a wider variety of sports to take care of individual needs and interests, (2) expanding facilities for the many desirable forms of physical recreation, (3) offering skilled instruction in the recreative sports to those desiring such opportunity, (4) increasing encouragement to informal as well as organized participation in sport, (5) improving the health requirements in connection with athletic competition; and (6) devising improved techniques for the stimulation of student interest in physical exercise and the administration of programs involving large numbers of participants.

Intramural programs were not established in high schools until about 1925. In general, high school intramural programs tended to follow the pattern and policies laid down by the colleges. Junior high schools were particularly suited to carry on intramural sports, partly because of the lack of interscholastic competition.

WOMEN'S SPORTS AND ORGANIZATIONS: As the nineteenth century ended, girls and women had made considerable progress in shedding restrictive clothing for physical activity and were enthusiastic about the new sport of basketball. Women at eastern colleges enjoyed field days and inter-

[45]H. Shindle Wingert and others, "Report of the Committee on the Encouragement of Intra-collegiate and Recreative Sports," *American Physical Education Review* 19 (May 1914): 368.

[46]Athletic Research Society, "Report of the Committee on Intramural Sport," *American Physical Education Review* 23 (April 1918): 189–212.

class competition in tennis, golf, field hockey, basketball, track, and, at Wellesley, rowing. This competition was usually under the supervision of the Women's Athletic Association. However, according to a survey in 1909, nearly half the colleges in the Midwest and West engaged in women's intercollegiate competition but generally with desirable controls such as women officials, audience by invitation, financial support by the colleges, and the absence of a professional spirit.[47] There was some question about admitting male spectators for women's sports. The faculty of one Ohio college feared that "the bloomers were more of an attraction than the game itself." In 1915–16 women on interclass teams in basketball and tennis at Stanford and California climaxed their intramural season by playing against each other.[48]

It seems apparent, however, that the most serious problems were found at the high school level. When the high school girls' team of Marshall, Michigan returned home in 1905 after winning the state basketball championship, they were greeted by "bonfires, 10,000 Roman candles, crowds, noise, Supt. Garwood, ex-mayor Porter, and all red-corpuscled Marshall." The first meeting of the Public School Training Society of the APEA in March, 1906 centered on the topic, "Athletics for Girls." The society passed resolutions addressed to the prevailing situation: coaches should be responsible to the schools, the general public should not be admitted to games, sensational written and illustrated newspaper reports were disapproved, and interschool games should be replaced by intra-school competition.[49] Even Dr. Sargent, who had long advocated the right of women to enjoy vigorous activity, felt constrained to caution against excessive competition.[50] On the other hand, supporters of girls' interscholastic sports claimed that the girls would not play at all without this competition and that they would lose interest in basketball if they could not use boys' rules.[51] In New York City a girls branch of the Public School Athletic League was started in 1905 which offered basketball, relay teams, and Indian clubs. However, most emphasis was placed on folk dancing in which Elizabeth Burchenal played a leading role.

The first attempt at regulation was made by a committee of women which was appointed at a conference on physical training in 1899 to draw up standardized rules for women's basketball with desirable modifications

[47]Gertrude Dudley and Frances A. Kellor, *Athletic Games in the Education of Women* (New York: Henry Holt and Company, 1909), pp. 99–100.

[48]Florence C. Burrell, "Intercollegiate Athletics for Women in Co-educational Institutions," *American Physical Education Review* 22 (January 1917): 18.

[49]"Report of the Convention of the Public School Physical Training Society," *American Physical Education Review* 11 (September 1906): 151–52.

[50]Dudley A. Sargent, *Health, Strength, and Power* (New York: H. M. Caldwell Company, 1904), p. 74.

[51]Elma L. Warner, "Inter-School Athletics," *American Physical Education Review* 11 (September 1906): 186.

of the men's rules. A basketball guide was published in 1901, and four years later a permanent committee was organized with Senda Berenson as chairman. In 1917, Dr. Burdick, president of the APEA, appointed a Committee on Women's Athletics to set standards for activities for girls and women. Elizabeth Burchenal was appointed chairman, and within five years there were subcommittees on hockey, swimming, track and field, and soccer, in addition to the original one on basketball. The work of the Women's Athletic Committee increased in scope and significance and, in 1927, it became a section of the APEA and was known as the Women's Athletic Section. Many problems in officiating were solved by the formation of the Women's National Officials' Rating Committee (WNORC) in 1928, due in considerable part to the efforts of Grace E. Jones and Elise Nelson.

In 1917 Blanche Trilling of the University of Wisconsin brought together twenty-three student presidents of college women's athletic associations and thereby created the Athletic Conference of American College Women (today called the Athletic and Recreation Federation of College Women). In its early years the ACACW went on record as opposing intercollegiate competition for women and favoring girls rules for basketball. It sought to align the Women's Athletic Association on each campus with the Department of Physical Education, and it also encouraged sports activity and outing clubs.[52] The emphasis on student participation remains an unusual feature of this organization.

Another important agency for control of women's athletics was the Women's Division of the National Amateur Athletic Federation, which was the counterpart of the Men's Division. Mrs. Herbert Hoover assumed leadership for the women's and girls' side of the NAAF, and the first meeting was held in 1923.[53] Lillian Schoedler became the first executive secretary. The Women's Division was nearly identical in purpose with the co-existent Committee on Women's Athletics, and a number of women such as Blanche Trilling, Elizabeth Burchenal, and Katherine Sibley were prominent in both organizations. However, although the membership of the Committee on Women's Athletics was entirely on an individual basis, the membership of the Women's Division was by individuals or groups such as colleges, secondary schools, athletic associations, YWCAs, women's clubs, and church organizations. Members paid dues and subscribed to the platform of the Women's Division, which sought to promote sports for all women and to establish principles for the wise selection, promotion, and supervision of women's sports. The Women's Division itself did not conduct or organize activities.

[52]Marguerite Schwarz, "The Athletic Federation of College Women," *Journal of Health and Physical Education* 7 (May 1936): 345–46.

[53]Alice A. Sefton, *The Women's Division, National Amateur Athletic Federation* (Palo Alto, Cal.: Stanford University Press, 1941), pp. 1–5.

Thus by the middle 1920s, three national women's organizations were working to control women's athletics. They achieved considerable success. For example, the number of colleges sponsoring varsity competition throughout the country dropped from 22 percent in 1923 to 12 percent in 1930.[54] The Committee on Women's Athletics and the Women's Division of the NAAF opposed international competition by women under AAU auspices. All three groups vigorously encouraged play days and sports days which became very common for both high school girls and college women. These started on the West Coast in 1926 at the University of Washington with a sports day for high school girls. The women at Stanford, California, and Mills College, guided by Rosalind Cassidy, began an annual Triangular Sports Day in November of the same year which replaced interclass and intercollegiate competition.[55] Telegraphic meets were another common method of competition. Nevertheless, these efforts for control were considerably more effective among the colleges than the high schools. At a general conference initiated by Helen Coops at the University of Cincinnati in 1925, some two hundred participants reported a good deal of girls' varsity high school competition in Ohio and Kentucky with emphasis on winning.[56] A survey of Pennsylvania high schools in 1928 revealed that 82 percent of the schools had interscholastic sports for girls, 22 percent did not require a health examination, 26 percent had a man in charge of girls' athletics, and 77 percent used the girls' game as a preliminary to the boys' game. These were some of the practices which caused so much of the opposition to interscholastic competition by women physical educators.[57]

NONSCHOOL AGENCIES: Opportunities for out-of-school participation in sports and physical activities multiplied after 1900. More YMCA buildings included a gymnasium, a pool, handball courts, and other facilities. Athletic clubs continued to flourish, and the number of country clubs climbed to a peak of 4,500 in 1929. Most of the latter had golf courses. Churches moved ahead on a large scale to provide facilities and supervision for sports competition. Church and Sunday School Athletic Leagues sprang up before World War I. When the National Federated Committee was formed in 1911, Elbert Beeman represented the Protestant Sunday Schools. In 1916 the Catholic Boys' Brigade was created to sponsor athletic games. Providing desirable leadership was a problem for the churches, and they

[54]Mabel Lee, "The Case For and Against Intercollegiate Athletics for Women and the Situation Since 1923," *Research Quarterly* 2 (May 1931): 93.

[55]Margaret M. Duncan and Velda P. Cundiff, *Play Days for Girls and Women* (New York: A. S. Barnes, 1929), pp. v-vi, 79.

[56]"Outstanding Problems of Girls' Athletics," *American Physical Education Review* 31 (May 1926): 846–47.

[57]"Detailed Report of Answers to Questionnaire, State Department of Public Instruction, Harrisburg, Pa.," *American Physical Education Review* 33 (May 1928): 308–13.

sought assistance from the YMCA, the YWCA, and the National Recreation Association. In rural areas many ministers accepted the role of recreational leader by default. These men saw that the old forms of recreation —the husking and quilting bees, barn raising, and others—were gone, and the church suppers, strawberry festivals, and Sunday school picnics were not appealing to youth. Thus, a Pennsylvania minister got one floor of a neighborhood house for a gymnasium; another minister and former player organized a football team among his young parishioners.[58]

Three new youth agencies came on the scene and exerted a beneficent influence on millions of children—the Boy Scouts, the Girl Scouts, and the Campfire Girls. The Boy Scouts of America started in 1910 modelled after its English predecessor begun by Lord Baden-Powell. The movement quickly spread through the efforts of Luther Gulick, Lee Hamner of the Russell Sage Foundation, Colin Livingstone, Ernest Thompson Seton, Dan Beard, James E. West, and various churches who sponsored ninety percent of the 6,868 troops started in the first three years. The Mormons adopted scouting on a churchwide basis in 1913.[59] Mrs. Juliette Low started the Girl Scouts in 1912 as a national nonsectarian, nonpartisan movement, patterned after the English Girl Guides. The Campfire Girls, established the same year, reflected the distinctive personalities and character of its founders, Dr. and Mrs. Luther Gulick.

Professional sports profited from public enthusiasm and the economic prosperity of the 1920s. This was the era of the million-dollar gate in boxing, and the second Tunney-Dempsey fight in 1928 drew nearly three million dollars, a record which has never been approached. Professional football started in Pennsylvania just before 1900 and other teams emerged from various cities of the Midwest in the next twenty years. Eleven teams organized in 1920 to form the American Professional Football Association which, two years later, became the present National Football League.[60] Professional ice hockey began in the United States in 1924 when Boston joined the National Hockey League which heretofore had included only Canadian teams. Hockey came to New York following the opening of the new Madison Square Garden in 1925 at a cost of $5,500,000. Olympia Stadium in Detroit and the Chicago Stadium were also constructed about this time, and these cities soon had teams in the National Hockey League. Bobby Jones, who remained an amateur, captured popular fancy in golf by winning thirteen national championships in eight years between 1923 and 1930. The American Bowling Congress sponsored its first national

[58]F. E. Eastman, "Rural Recreation Through the Church," *Playground* 6 (October 1912): 233–36.
[59]Frederick W. Cozens and Florence S. Stumpf, *Sports in American Life* (Chicago: The University of Chicago Press, 1953), pp. 98–100.
[60]Harold Classen, *The History of Professional Football* (Englewood Cliffs, N.J.: Prentice-Hall, Inc., 1963), pp. 32–4.

tournament in 1901. National bowling tournaments for women started in 1917 when women began to display interest in this sport. Baseball, on the other hand, suffered a relative decline. An 11 percent gain in major league attendance between 1920 and 1930 did not keep pace with a 20 percent gain in the general population.[61] Baseball, by this time, was affected by the competition of the many newer sports.

Boyle contended that the sporting boom of the 1920s was primarily one of spectators, not participants, and he cited the record crowds, new stadia, and radio broadcasts as evidence.[62] Stuart Chase, a contemporary observer and economist in 1928, made the same observation and condemned the commercialism involved in so much of the recreational activities.[63] This is probably a relative matter. Compared with the preceding period, there was a great increase in both spectators and participants. In the decade after 1930, there was an indisputable shift from observation to participation.

NEGROES IN SPORTS: During this period intercollegiate competition developed at many Negro colleges as in the mainly white colleges. In 1912 the Colored Intercollegiate Athletic Association, now the Central I.A.A., was founded by representatives from Hampton Institute, Howard University, Lincoln University, Shaw University, and Virgina Union. An early leader in the Association was Charles H. William of Hampton Institute.[64] Further south, another strong league was the Southern Intercollegiate Athletic Association started at Morehouse College in 1913. There were few Negro athletes in northern colleges, particularly outside New England. Many white college coaches did not want to deal with the problem of making separate arrangements for the meals and housing of Negro players on trips.

Negro youth generally were exposed to basketball later than white youth. Edwin Henderson, for example, found out about the game at the Harvard Summer School in 1904 and taught it to boys in Washington, D.C., that winter. In two years' time a league ·of teams was established.[65] Basketball started about 1910 in Negro colleges.

Barred from participation in most organized sports, Negroes were forced to found their own groups. The National Negro Baseball League started in 1920 with six teams and a World Series was held four years later. The New York Renaissance professional basketball team organized

[61]Jesse F. Steiner, *Americans at Play* (New York: McGraw-Hill Book Company, 1933), p. 84.

[62]Robert H. Boyle, *Sport—Mirror of American Life* (Boston: Little, Brown and Company, 1963), pp. 39–42.

[63]Stuart Chase, "Play," in Charles A. Beard, ed., *Whither Mankind* (New York: Longman's Green and Company, 1928), p. 353.

[64]Edwin B. Henderson, *The Negro in Sports* (Washington, D.C.: The Associated Publishers, Inc., 1939), p. 247.

[65]Ibid., p. 127.

in 1923 and soon became the best quintet in the country. The American Tennis Association began in 1916 in Washington, D.C., and held the first national championship a year later. The United Golfers Association sponsored the first national tournament for Negro players in 1926. The use of Negro boys as caddies aroused more interest in golf but chances to play were limited until public courses became more common.[66] The first Negro Olympic winner was DeHart Hubbard of the University of Michigan who won the broad jump in 1924. In professional football two former college All-Americans, Fritz Pollard and Paul Robeson, played for several years beginning with Hammond and Akron in 1920.[67] Robeson later received national acclaim as a singer.

EXTENSION OF THE PLAY AND RECREATION MOVEMENT: Further opportunities for activity arose out of the expanded playground and recreation movement. An important step occurred in April 1906, with the founding of The Playground Association of America, largely through the efforts of Dr. Luther Gulick and of Dr. Henry Curtis, a pioneer playground worker in Washington, D.C. Eighteen delegates attended the first meeting and enjoyed having one session in the White House upon the invitation of President Theodore Roosevelt. President Roosevelt was chosen an honorary president, Gulick was elected president, and Curtis became secretary of the new association.

The organizers of the association lost no time in getting under way. Various pamphlets were written to arouse public interest in the right of children to play. The publication of a monthly official magazine, *The Playground*, began in 1907. The *Normal Course in Play*, prepared in 1910 by a committee under Clark Hetherington, represented the first attempt to outline a scientific, comprehensive training for recreation workers. The association also served as a clearing house for recreation information, collecting data from all over the country, and distributing this material for effective use. The purposes of the Association were further carried out by the appointment of Lee Hamner as field secretary in 1907, through the generosity of the newly-formed Russell Sage Foundation. Because of the evident interest, district institutes of several days' duration were held by experienced play leaders to train other instructors and improve the quality of local leadership. The name of the Association was changed in 1911 to The Playground and Recreation Association of America. This new title was a clear indication that playgrounds had become just one part of a broader movement—recreation for older children and adults.

The close relation between physical education and recreation existed from the beginning. The first constitution of the Playground Association

[66]Ibid., pp. 194–98.
[67]Roger Treat, *The Official Encyclopedia of Football* (New York: A. S. Barnes and Co., Inc., 1967), pp. 27, 415, 424.

declared its intent to "further the establishment of playgrounds and athletic fields in all communities and directed play in connection with the schools." Many physical education leaders were prominent in aiding the new movement. Dr. Gulick served as president of the association for three years, and men such as Clark Hetherington, E. B. DeGroot, George W. Ehler, Joseph E. Raycroft, George Meylan, George Fisher, and James McCurdy were particularly active in playground and recreation promotion. Gulick was deeply convinced of the significance of play as a social force in education and also recognized its character-educating significance. Joseph Lee, philanthropist, pioneer social worker, and author of one of the first American books on play, *Play in Education*, became president of the Playground Association in 1910 and Howard Braucher, another social worker, became secretary. These two men served the association continuously in these capacities throughout this period and later, and through their direction and the financial support they secured, advanced the growth of playgrounds and public recreation in the United States.

A most important development in the playground movement occurred in 1903. In that year the voters of the Chicago South Park District approved a $5,000,000 bond issue that was used to open ten parks two years later. In this planning, the park commissioners saw the need of both outdoor and indoor park facilities for the promotion of health, sociability, morality, and art, combined with beauty and cleanliness, accessible for public use day and evening all year round. The commissioners realized the need for trained leadership and employed an experienced physical educator, E. B. DeGroot, as Director of Gymnastics and Athletics. Each park was supervised by two year-round instructors, a man and a woman, most of whom had had college or normal school training in gymnastics and athletics.[68] It was quite appropriate that the Playground Association of America held its first convention at Chicago in 1907 so that the delegates could see the South Park system and carry the information back to their communities.

On a smaller, less expensive scale, Los Angeles duplicated Chicago in providing all-year facilities for all ages in a variety of activities with trained leadership. The first center in 1905 was followed by five more in the next seven years. By 1912, Pittsburgh, Philadelphia, Minneapolis, St. Paul, Oakland, and Louisville also had opened field houses.

Along with the development of municipal centers in these cities, other municipalities began to use existing school buildings as community recreation centers. New York City first used schools for this purpose in 1898, but the example of Rochester, New York, in 1907 attracted national attention. Not only did this use of existing facilities eliminate the cost of con-

[68]Elizabeth Halsey, *The Development of Public Recreation in Metropolitan Chicago* (Chicago: Recreation Commission, 1940), pp. 31–32.

structing field houses, but by restoring the schoolhouse to its traditional place as a neighborhood social center, community participation and better citizenship were encouraged.

The number of cities using schoolhouses as recreation centers multiplied rapidly after Rochester's initial effort. Additional stimulus came from the resolution of the National Education Association in 1911 approving the use of school buildings for recreation centers. Six years later 639 cities supported 3,500 such centers, with Milwaukee achieving special recognition as "the city of the lighted schoolhouses." An important outcome of this development was the change in school architecture. The newer school building was designed to provide the features of a recreation center in addition to meeting its traditional curriculum demands.

Throughout this period of expansion in public recreation, the Playground and Recreation Association continued its effective work of promotion and encouragement. The Association helped civic groups plan campaigns to secure a tax-supported municipal recreation program, especially after World War I, through its Community Service organization, created in 1919. Community houses were constructed as war memorials in many cities and towns. The number of employed recreation leaders more than doubled between 1920 and 1930. Inasmuch as the colleges only offered a course or two for recreation leaders, the Association, in 1926, opened a one-year graduate school in New York City to train recreation administrators. One feature of this training was the apprenticeship the students served by working part-time in settlements, clubs, and recreation centers. After ten years this school closed during the depression.

The number of cities which established recreation programs grew from 41 in 1906 to 350 in 1914 and to 945 in 1929. The annual reports of the association between 1920 and 1930 showed an increase in all recreation facilities. New municipal park acreage was acquired by cities in huge amounts. Expenditures for recreation jumped nearly fivefold. In 1930, in recognition of the growing attention to recreation for people of all ages, the Playground and Recreation Association changed its name to the National Recreation Association.

THE GROWTH OF CAMPING: The camping movement met with no general acceptance before 1900, and the existing camps had been carried on, for the most part, by idealists or philanthropists. The real development of camping began early in the twentieth century when a hundred camps were started, most of them by school teachers interested in utilizing their summer vacation. The first camps for girls also appeared in this period. In addition to the YMCA, the camping movement was promoted by the Boy Scouts, Girl Scouts, Campfire Girls, YWCA, Woodcraft League, social settlements, churches, and industries. In 1910, twenty camp directors organized the Camp Directors' Association, which later became the American Camping Association.

As the number of camps increased, the problem of trained leadership became more acute. Columbia University and Boston University offered special courses in camping in 1921, and the Camp Directors' Association conducted special courses for intensive training of camp counsellors.

Three significant occurrences in camping in the latter part of this period were the forerunners of new developments which, however, were not fully exploited until the next period. One was the first public-school camp at Camp Roosevelt, a venture which was associated with the Chicago public schools and begun in 1919 with the cooperation of the War Department.[69] A second event was the beginning of day camps by the Girl Scouts in 1921. The third event was a four-year experiment in the Life Camps, conducted by Lloyd Sharp from 1925 to 1928, which demonstrated the value of a camping program based on sound educational principles. The success of his work in applying scientific research to camping was destined to raise the level not only of welfare camps but of camps in general.

Program of Physical Education

During the first ten years of the twentieth century, informal types of activity were included in the required gymnasium class. The classroom was becoming more closely related to life outside the school, and physical education, in trying to make its program more meaningful and interesting, followed this trend.

The first sports to be included in the gymnastic program were track and field events such as running, jumping, and climbing, and the combative sports of fencing, wrestling, and boxing. These lent themselves to class drill and mass exercise. It was easy, for example, to send a class up to the running track for so many laps as a "conditioner." Jumping over a bar could be practiced by one group while other squads worked on the horse or horizontal bar. Fencing, which early had an association with the foreign gymnastic programs, was another sport that could be carried on in class in unison, with wands as make-believe swords. The other combative sports —wrestling and boxing—were favored because of their value in producing strength and increasing muscle.

Gradually, basketball and volleyball began to be found in class programs, in spite of die-hard formalist opposition. It was claimed, with some justification, that these sports did not develop the upper part of the body, and that the amount of participation in them could not be scientifically

[69]Marie M. Ready, *The Organized Summer Camp*, Physical Education Series no. 7, Bureau of Education, Department of Education (Washington, D.C.: Government Printing Office, 1926), pp. 3–5.

regulated as in gymnastics. Basketball was criticized because of its bad effect on posture.

In the first year of intramural competition at Ohio State University in 1913–14, students from thirteen departments and colleges played basketball, baseball, tennis, and ran indoor and outdoor track. All these were also varsity sports, and early intramural competition provided an outlet for students who lacked the ability or inclination for intercollegiate competition. During the 1920s more attention was given to sports which could be played at leisure or in later life such as swimming, handball, golf, squash, and tennis. These sports also began to appear in the physical education class curriculum.

The newer concept of physical education fully recognized the popular movements of play and athletics. As outlined by Wood, the content of physical education was to be found in play, games, dancing, swimming, outdoor sports, athletics, and gymnastics. For physiological reasons, the New Physical Education condemned the practice of toeing out as required in all formal gymnastics, the excessive stamping of the feet, and the backward bending of the spine. The new or natural gymnastics replaced the rigid, jerky, and artificial movements of the old systems with natural, meaningful movements that either expressed a worth-while idea, feeling, or emotion, or else had a definite objective such as hitting a ball, swimming across a pool, shooting a basket, and so forth. The gymnastic movements closely simulated actions used in games and athletics or in actual performance in life activities. Physical education activities were correlated with other school subjects and activities such as folk dances during the harvest or Christmas season, festivals, and others. The value of specific activities for the correction of physical defects was recognized, but such activities were prescribed and performed on an individual basis and not given to a whole class.[70]

During World War I, physical education was replaced in a number of schools by military training. The military services themselves had no adequate plan for achieving physical fitness on the large scale that suddenly confronted them. Two types of programs developed. One was physical training, which included a program of developmental and combative activities. The other was the recreation program, which consisted of mass activities, sports, and games, Army officers at first were dubious about the need for recreational sports; however, their value was gradually recognized.

During and after the war, calisthenics in the form of the "daily dozen" experienced a revival of interest. This type of exercise was not only part of the gymnasium routine, but became a part of the hygienic routine of thousands of families throughout the country. A physical in-

[70]Wood, *Health and Education*, pp. 75–108.

structor was hired by a well-known insurance company to lead these exercises over the radio. Thousands of exercise charts were furnished to users. A new intercollegiate activity, rifle shooting, began during the war and continued in some schools afterwards.

Following the war, physical educators were reluctant to consider military drill as an adequate substitute for the wide variety of activities that should be included in a program for all-round growth and development. To them, military drill did not offer the opportunity for the self-expression, independent thinking, sociability, and sportsmanship that were offered in a program of games and sports. Moreover, military activities were not graded to age interests, nor were they contributive to healthy and happy use of leisure time. In spite of these objections from physical education sources, many colleges continued to permit military drill to be substituted for the requirement in physical education.

Shortly after 1920, another European system of gymnastics made a brief appearance. This was the Fundamental Danish Gymnastics developed by Niels Bukh. American interest in the Danish gymnastics was stimulated by a group of Danish students who toured the United States with Bukh in 1923. The Danish exercises were mostly popular among high school and college women from 1925 to 1930, and also among some athletic coaches for early season conditioning of their squads.

Up to the time of World War I, corrective physical education consisted of formal exercises that had little intrinsic interest for the individual, unless he was strongly motivated by a desire to improve his condition. In the years that followed, thoughtful educators began to consider the value of games and sports for students with defects which could not be corrected, such as amputees, the hard of hearing, mental defectives, cardiacs, and others. One of the first sports programs for the handicapped was conducted by Harry A. Scott at the University of Oregon in 1921. This program offered swimming, handball, tennis, golf, tumbling, wrestling, hiking, squash, basketball, volleyball, fencing, boxing and track.[71] This trend toward natural activities and games was confirmed by a survey of twenty-nine institutions in 1929.[72] A comprehensive presentation of group games and athletic activities for the handicapped was made by Lowman, Colestock, and Cooper in their book, *Corrective Physical Education for Groups*, which was published in 1928.

ATHLETIC SPORTS: Specific games and sports underwent modification and some innovations were made. Football changed several rules that established most of the features of the modern game. At the meeting in

[71]Harry A. Scott, "Supervised Exercise Corrects Defects of College Men," *Nation's Health* 8 (October 1926): 722.
[72]Harlan G. Metcalf, "Status of Special Adaptive Corrective Procedures in Colleges and Larger Universities," *American Physical Education Review* 34 (April 1929): 208.

1905 that marked the origin of the NCAA, the forward pass was legalized although at first hemmed in with many restrictions. Other rules changes made in the interest of safety of the players, effectively outlawed the flying wedge, V formation, tandem, and other types of mass play. This was done by prohibiting members of the offensive team from using hands or arms to assist the ball carrier and from interlocking arms or bodies for interference.[73] In this expansion of college football during the years 1900–1930, Alonzo Stagg of Chicago, Fielding Yost of Michigan, Knute Rockne of Notre Dame, Glenn Warner of Stanford, Percy Haughton of Harvard, and Robert Zuppke of Illinois were prominent.

In 1928, night football was tentatively begun by several California high schools and colleges. Primary reasons for the experiment were a desire for larger gate receipts and the better playing conditions afforded by the cooler evenings.

Although baseball changed little, the game of indoor baseball began to evolve as an eventual rival to its parent game. Around 1907, the outdoor game of playground ball was developed on the Chicago South Park Playgrounds. Rules were drawn up by E. B. DeGroot, the director, and provided for a ball 12 to 14 inches in diameter, bases 35 feet apart, a pitching distance of 30 feet, and 10 players on a side. The extra player served as a second shortstop. The batter, upon hitting the ball, could run to either first or third and continue in that direction.[74] The game spread rapidly, but much confusion followed when different sets of rules were set up in different localities. The name, *softball*, was first suggested by Walter Hakanson, a YMCA director in Denver, Colorado, in 1926, but it was not widely used until the mid-thirties, when the game finally became standardized.

Basketball went through a period of roughness comparable to that of football. An editorial in 1909 declared that basketball "has gradually degenerated until it is now a cross between a wrestling match and a pugilistic encounter."[75] Officials, hesitant to slow up the game, were lax in calling fouls; not until 1911 were two free throws given for a foul in the act of shooting. The rule permitting a player to use a series of dribbles caused the defense to resort to tackling and body-checking. Several sets of rules also aggravated the situation. Furthermore, many courts were no larger than a volleyball court, and in some cases completely enclosed by a wire screen so that the ball was always in play. Elbows and fists were used freely, and mouth pieces and nose guards were standard equipment for players, especially in the early professional and semiprofessional games.

[73]Parke H. Davis, *Football: The American Intercollegiate Game* (New York: Charles Scribner's Sons, 1911), pp. 109–17.

[74]E. B. DeGroot, "Two New Games," *Playground* (March 1908): 3–5.

[75]"Editorial Note," *American Physical Education Review* 14 (March 1909): 179.

College basketball was greatly improved by the action of the new basketball committee of the NCAA. In 1908, a five-foul limit on a player was put in effect, and in 1910 charging was made a foul whether a player had the ball or not. The formation of a Joint Rules Committee in 1915 also served to reduce confusion and improve the game. The tempo of play accelerated as the court area was increased, but under the rules of that day scoring totals remained modest by present-day standards. In a typical game the combined score of both teams was usually less than fifty points.

During the first half of this period, tennis and golf became more common and, with public facilities, these games were no longer restricted to the well-to-do. Tennis owed its popular growth to the public tennis courts constructed by the park systems of the larger cities. These public facilities in turn led schools and colleges to provide tennis courts for their students.

Golf remained a rich man's sport for several years longer, and in 1910 there were only twenty-four public golf courses. When Francis Ouimet, a 20-year old ex-caddie, won the National Open in a playoff match against two British professionals in 1913, golf caught the imagination of the common man almost overnight. By 1930 there were 6,000 golf courses in the country and over 200 cities had municipal links. The automobile enabled golf lovers to drive to courses built on cheaper land away from urban centers. The democracy of golf was extolled by the noted sports writer, Grantland Rice, when the city championship match in Cleveland was played between a young millionaire and one of his gardeners. Rice also glowingly told of the caddies who had become wealthy pros in the fulfillment of the American dream.[76]

Volleyball became known through the national and international organization of the YMCA and was particularly promoted through the efforts of Dr. George Fisher. Between 1910 and 1920, the game received widespread acceptance, especially during the war years when it was played by soldiers in military camps. Volleyball then became part of school and recreational programs. The first national YMCA volleyball tournament was held in 1922, and six years later the U.S. Volleyball Association was formed.

A native contribution was the game of speedball developed in 1921 by Elmer D. Mitchell at the University of Michigan. Speedball was a combination of soccer, football, and basketball designed to provide an outdoor fall activity for the average student not playing football. It found its widest use in elementary schools and in the physical education classes and intramural programs of high schools and colleges.

Girls and women during this period flocked to the basketball courts, but some new activities acquired their adherents also. Field hockey was

[76]Grantland Rice, "The National Rash," *Collier's* 82 (20 October 1928): 10.

brought to this country in 1901 by Constance Applebee, an Englishwoman attending the Harvard Summer School. The first game was played in a small concrete yard by a group of men and women, teachers and students. Harriet Ballintine invited Miss Applebee to teach the game to Vassar students in the fall, and she continued on to other eastern women's colleges.[77] The next year Miss Applebee published a book on field hockey which helped to spread the game to other parts of the country. It is unfortunate that this excellent game has been ignored by men in the United States. Swimming and playground ball began to attract women during this time; modified rules in volleyball were adopted, and shortly after the invention of speedball, Alice Frymir at Battle Creek (Michigan) College developed speedball rules for girls. In 1930 speedball was adopted by the National Section on Women's Athletics and an official girls' rule book was regularly issued. Sports for high school girls developed much more slowly than in the colleges, and basketball for many years remained the only high school sport for girls.

THE FIELD OF THE DANCE: Popular dancing found a rival in folk dancing, which represented a concession to the play spirit. National and folk dances were taught by Louis Chalif, a Russian, who came to New York in 1904 and accepted an offer by Luther Gulick to give a teachers' course in the dance at New York University the next year. Chalif devoted himself wholeheartedly to the encouragement of dance in education and published five dance textbooks. He also modified and adapted ballet for use in schools and colleges. Elizabeth Burchenal organized and served as first chairman of the Folk Dance Committee of the Playground and Recreation Association and published ten volumes on folk dancing, based on much original research in the United States and other countries. The teaching of folk dancing in schools offered excellent opportunities for developing better attitudes toward peoples of other countries and thereby contributed to international understanding. Vigorous clog and tap dancing were also found in school programs in the 1920s, owing to the particular efforts of Mary Wood Hinman, Helen Frost, Marjorie Hillas, and Anne Schley Duggan.

The prime instigator of the modern dance movement was Isadora Duncan who rejected the artificial, conventional methods of the traditional dances and used only natural movements for personal expression. She shocked her contemporaries by dancing barefooted in a simple Greek tunic. Although Duncan began her dance revolution about 1900, her ideas had little effect in the United States for some years. Many of her ideas came to the United States from Germany after World War I through the tours of Mary Wigman.

[77]Constance M. K. Applebee, "Early Landmarks of American Hockey," in Caryl M. Newhof, ed., *Selected Field Hockey and Lacrosse Articles* (Washington, D.C.: National Section for Girls' and Women's Sports of the AAHPER, 1955), p. 10.

Another pioneer was Ruth St. Denis who began her dance career in 1904 and made a special study of Oriental dances. She joined with Ted Shawn to form the Denishawn school in Los Angeles in 1915 which spawned Martha Graham, Doris Humphrey, and Charles Weidman. Shawn demonstrated that dancing was a worthwhile educational activity for men.

Three women—Gertrude Colby, Bird Larson, and Margaret H'Doubler—helped to overcome the barriers between the professional dancers and dance educators. Gertrude Colby came to Columbia University in 1913 with the encouragement of Dr. Wood and began experimentation in dance based on the interests of children and using natural, rhythmic movements. She believed that one should "dance ideas, not steps." She published a book, *Natural Rhythms and Dance*, in 1922 and was on the staff at Teachers College until 1931.

Bird Larson taught at Barnard College and was a close friend of Colby. She emphasized natural, rhythmic expression and took a scientific approach to dance based on a study of anatomy, kinesiology, and physics. She taught a science of movement based on the needs, capabilities, and limitations of each student.

Margaret H'Doubler came to Columbia for graduate work in 1916 and observed the work of Colby and Larson. She reflected Larson's influence by clarifying the educational principles underlying dance. She returned to the University of Wisconsin and developed the first major program in dance in 1926. H'Doubler was a prominent leader in encouraging the acceptance of dance in college curriculum.[78]

The natural dance originated by Colby was an integral part of the New Physical Education, and it took the area of dance away from the older aesthetic dancing originated by Gilbert. It opened the way for the modern dance which was to follow in the 1930s, led by many of Miss Colby's pupils such as Martha Hill, Mary O'Donnell, Martha Deane, and Ruth Murray.

Just before World War I the eurhythmics of Jacques Dalcroze came to the United States from Germany. This system emphasized rhythmic accuracy with body movements based exactly on the music. The arms beat the time and the feet expressed the note value.[79] It was first taught at Bryn Mawr in 1913 and spread to other colleges in the twenties and early thirties.

PLAY AND RECREATION: The great expansion in recreation was based on an enlarged program of activities that would appeal to all ages. Such a program was provided by the South Park system in Chicago and

[78]The information on Colby, Larson, and H'Doubler is drawn from Mildred C. Spiesman, "Dance Education Pioneers: Colby, Larson, and H'Doubler," *Journal of Health, Physical Education, and Recreation* 31 (January 1960): 25–26, 76.

[79]Florence E. Goold, "The Eurhythmics of Jacques-Dalcroze," *American Physical Review* 20 (January 1915): 36.

was indicative of the general trend. Each park had an indoor plant with a men's and women's gymnasium. The outdoor area had a playground and space for baseball, football, soccer, hockey, ice skating, and a swimming pool.[80] The expanded recreational program of the South Park system also included manual training activities, social dances, parties, banquets, and clubs; civic meetings and lectures on public questions and child welfare; and theatrical, choral, orchestral, and dance programs. Thus, the scope of municipal recreation programs was broadened and the outline for present-day public recreation was sketched.

Industrial recreation programs made significant headway during this time. The founder of the National Cash Register Company made part of his wooded estate available to factory workers in 1904. An example for labor unions was set by David Dubinsky, president of the International Ladies Garment Workers Union, who purchased a 1,000-acre recreational area in the Pocono Mountains. Three-fourths of the members of this union were female.[81]

CAMPING: The programs of organized summer camps also showed a broad array of new activities which helped to contribute to their growth. The traditional camp activities of boating, swimming, sailing, fishing, and hiking were soon supplemented by sports and games such as baseball, tennis, softball, golf, track, basketball, and volleyball. Seton and Beard did much to promote the value of Indian lore and woodcraft. A few of the activities added later were riding, rifle marksmanship, nature study, music, dancing, arts and crafts, and an enlarged program of swimming and water activities. Later, some camps began to specialize in a particular activity such as canoeing, horseback riding, athletics, swimming, dance, or music.

Methods of Physical Education

In accordance with the tenets of educational developmentalism, modern physical education worked out methods that were to be determined by the child's abilities and interests and based on sound psychological principles of learning. The basic steps in conducting the new physical education were outlined as follows:

1. A felt difficulty. Children should themselves see that a problem or difficulty exists.
2. Analysis. Children should analyze the problem or felt difficulty and see what should be done to meet it. This will often lead to a study of what is the best form of movement and why.

[80]Henry S. Curtis, "The Playgrounds of Chicago," *Playground* (June 1907): 3–6.

[81]Cozens and Stumpf, *Sports in American Life*, pp. 55–58.

3. Slow practice of elements. Children go slowly through the desired movement. This may be done in mass formation with an informal rhythm that approximates the rhythm of the skill in the game situation and the rhythm of the individual.
4. Practice in game forms of lower organization. The action is speeded up and approximates the original situation in which the difficulty occurred. Relays are excellent here.
5. Participation in the final form worked· for. This is the desired goal of the children for which the preceding steps were used.[82]

It should be observed that drill and repetition had a legitimate place in teaching the new physical education. However, in accordance with the principles of learning, the teacher was to be sure that the activities were practiced with accuracy. Mere practice of skills would not make them perfect, but correct practice would. The activity was also to be satisfying, rather than annoying, to the participant in order to secure the most effective learning. The possibilities of participating in exercise with a joyous exuberance would be enhanced by the acquisition of skill and the reasonable assurance of success.

In the early days of the movement from gymnastics and apparatus work to plays and games, there was almost complete absence of teaching methods in the class program. The program was frequently a play program with little or no attention paid to instructional methods or progression in graded experience. Emphasis on instructional methods came when teachers of physical education were specifically trained for their work, with adequate knowledge of physiology, psychology, education, sociology, and their application to teaching. On the other hand, the teaching methods of formal gymnastics were highly developed. Even an outspoken critic of formal gymnastics, Jesse Feiring Williams, paid tribute to their teaching technique. He wrote:

> Whatever one might wish to say about formal gymnastics, . . . it should never be forgotten that one item of excellence was teaching technic. The teachers of formal gymnastics knew how to begin a lesson, how to proceed, what to look for, and how to judge performance. . . . these values in method were often overlooked or forgotten. They are abiding values in all teaching, in all times, and in all places.[83]

The old quarrel between formal and informal activities and teaching methods disappeared when it was realized that a program should include various types of activity, and that it was largely teaching method that de-

---

[82]Adapted from Thomas D. Wood and Rosalind Cassidy, *The New Physical Education* (New York: The Macmillan Company, 1927), pp. 217–31.
[83]Bonnie Cotteral and Donnie Cotteral, *The Teaching of Stunts and Tumbling* (New York: A. S. Barnes and Co., Inc., 1936), p. xii.

termined whether an activity was formal or informal. Moreover, whether an activity was formal or informal, it should be invested with meaning and related to purposeful living. As Sargent observed, "Wherever there is organized effort either in gymnastics or athletics, much of the work will be more or less formal."[84] In other words, there is nothing informal about a football team going through an hour of dummy tackling practice. At the same time, a gymnast trying out new stunts or developing his routine is enjoying excellent informal activity.

There was an extension of mass instruction in teaching the fundamentals of sports such as wrestling, swimming, football, baseball, basketball, and track. This mass instruction was developed by the army to teach boxing in 1917, and the method was extended to other sports by schools and colleges in postwar years. Many schools with very large classes required techniques for mass instruction.

The corrective or orthopedic classes that became established after the war were organized to accommodate all students with defects ranging from round shoulders and flat feet to hernia. Each student was provided with formal exercises that were designed to improve his condition. Although some good work was accomplished, the members on occasion suffered the stigma of being set apart from the students in the regular program. Furthermore, in many schools there was little medical supervision or cooperation, and the physical education teacher tried to assume too much responsibility. In his pioneer work at the University of Oregon, Scott permitted students with minor defects to enroll in regular classes and only those with more serious physical or organic disorders were placed in the restricted exercise program. He also encouraged the student to develop a better understanding of his condition through discussion and conferences.[85]

TESTS AND MEASUREMENTS: During the twentieth century and particularly after 1920, methods in physical education were enriched by the widespread use of tests and measurements and tools of evaluation. As explained by Clarke, testing is "a particular phase of administration, as tests should be used to obtain essential information about pupils so that programs can be planned effectively and conducted efficiently."[86]

Tests and measurements as used in physical education at this time had two basic functions:

1. To provide accurate data regarding the health, abilities, and capacities of pupils in order to ascertain individual needs.
2. To measure progress or achievement of pupils according to the

---

[84]Dudley A. Sargent, "The Biological Significance of Physical Education," *American Physical Education Review* 23 (December 1918): 529.

[85]Scott, "Supervised Exercise Corrects Defects of College Men," p. 661.

[86]H. Harrison Clarke, *The Application of Measurement to Health and Physical Education* (Englewood Cliffs, N. J.: Prentice-Hall, Inc., 1946), p. 321.

objectives of the physical education program. The results could be used both as a basis for grading and for evaluating teaching efficiency.

The application of tests and measurements to health and physical education helped in the struggle to obtain status in the curriculum for these subjects. As the possibilities for sounder grading developed through the use of scientific tools, administrators were more inclined to grant academic credit for health and physical education.

As this period opened, strength testing was on the decline, partly because of the increasing interest in athletic sports. Strength tests were not very popular with athletes because many skilled performers had only mediocre strength test scores. Sargent expressed his own dissatisfaction with strength tests because of their failure to test endurance and speed, the expense of the instruments, and the strain on small groups of muscles. He helped to divert attention from strength tests with his own Universal Test for Strength, Speed, and Endurance, devised in 1902, which used calisthenic-type exercises.

The first use of athletic achievement tests by nonschool agencies— the YMCA and the Turnerbund—was mentioned in the last chapter. Schools and colleges did not use them until after 1900. The Public Schools Athletic League in New York used achievement tests starting in 1904, and buttons were awarded for successful performance. A similar league and tests were started four years later in Baltimore. In 1913, The American Playground Association developed the well-known Athletic Badge Tests which established minimum standards for every boy. A 1920 survey of tests used in high schools showed that the tests most frequently used for boys were the running high jump, pull-ups, short dashes, standing and running broad jump, rope climb, push-ups, three standing broad jumps, and shot put. For girls, the tests used were basketball distance throw, short dashes, rope climb, and vaulting.[87]

The first report on college achievement tests was made by Dr. George Meylan at Columbia in 1907. He was concerned with the problem of grading students in physical education on a basis similar to academic subjects. He used five tests: (1) written examination on personal hygiene and sanitation; (2) subjective control as manifested by good carriage and graceful movements; (3) objective control as measured by the high jump, bar vault, and swinging jump; (4) endurance; and (5) swimming.[88] Kleeberger at the University of California administered a testing program for

[87]Abner P. Way, "Present Status of Physical Efficiency Tests in High Schools," *Proceedings of Athletic Research Society*, 1920–21, pp. 13–21, as quoted in Helen Petroskey, "A History of Measurement in Health and Physical Education in the United States" (Doctoral dissertation, University of Iowa, 1946), pp. 286–87.

[88]George L. Meylan, "The Place of Physical Education in the College Curriculum," *American Physical Education Review* 12 (June 1907): 105.

health; agility, as measured by the hand vault, high jump, broad jump, and 100-yard dash; defensive ability in wrestling, boxing, and fencing; swimming; and sportsmanship.[89] Dr. J. H. Nichols, then at Ohio State, gave physical efficiency tests consisting of the rope climb, 118-yard dash, and bar vault.[90] At Oregon a pentathlon consisting of the running high jump, bar vault, rope climb, 196-yard run, and 100-yard swim was given.[91]

Meylan, Kleeberger, Nichols, and Scott all used test performance as a basis for classification. Meylan barred men from varsity competition who had a poor test performance. Failure on any test at California resulted in assignment to an activity that would correct the student's deficiency. At Ohio State, men with highest scores could elect a sports activity. Oregon students who had acceptable scores in the pentathlon could choose a supervised sport in place of regular class work.

Agnes Wayman devised a physical efficiency test for college women in the early 1920s which included a medical test, an anthropometric test, and a motor ability test using the high jump, basketball throw, 25-yard dash, rope climb, vaulting the buck, balance beam, tumbling, and gymnastics. Based on data obtained from a number of women's colleges, she set up a point system for evaluating the results.[92]

The previous dominance of strength testing was also weakened by a new interest in cardiovascular research. This area was opened up through the invention of the ergograph in 1884 by the Italian physiologist, Angelo Mosso, and the new contributions of physiology to knowledge of the heart and blood circulation in the 1890s. In 1905, Dr. Ward Crampton devised a blood ptosis test which served as a model for further research in cardiovascular tests. In 1910, McCurdy established standards of heart rate and blood pressure, and Meylan worked out tests of cardiovascular efficiency in 1913. During World War I, Schneider developed his test of cardiovascular efficiency, and just as this period ended, Tuttle developed his pulse-ratio test, which proved of value in evaluating general athletic condition and detecting pathological conditions of hearts.

During the 1920s new statistical methods were applied to physical education. These methods contributed to the development of achievement scales as explained by Charles H. McCloy in an article published in

[89]F. L. Kleeberger, "Physical Efficiency Tests as a Practical Method of Popularizing Physical Education at the University of California," *American Physical Education Review* 23 (January 1918): 27.

[90]J. H. Nichols, "Report of Physical Examinations and Physical Efficiency Tests at Ohio State," *American Physical Education Review* 25 (May 1920): 212.

[91]"The Pentathlon, A Physical Ability Test," *American Physical Education Review* 29 (January 1924): 30–32.

[92]Agnes R. Wayman, "A Scheme for Testing and Scoring the Physical Efficiency of College Girls," *American Physical Education Review* 28 (November 1923): 416–19.

1921.[93] The National Recreation Association computed its National Physical Achievement Standards for boys in track and field, games, gymnastics, and aquatics, and published the results in 1929. David Brace developed a battery of tests for women's basketball in 1924 and used McCall's new T-score techniques for scoring the results.[94] A year earlier, he made the first application of the new objective-type tests when he constructed an eighteen-question true-false test on basketball rules.[95] Elizabeth Beall set up a battery of tests for tennis in 1925.

A number of physical educators endeavored to develop various tests for other factors involved in motor performance. Dr. Dudley A. Sargent orginated the Sargent Jump in 1921 to measure a factor contributing to power and efficiency in performance. In 1927, Brace devised his motor ability test of twenty stunts. Two years later Cozens developed a test of general athletic ability of college men.

Measurement and evaluation of posture engaged the attention of physical educators for many decades, and each presentation of standards for posture evoked considerable debate and criticism. Individuals such as Dr. Jay Seaver and Dr. Eliza Mosher in 1900 believed that poor posture was the cause of many human ailments, but later research tended to discredit this belief.

Interest in strength testing was revived in the twenties, largely attributable to Frederick Rand Rogers who became interested in testing when he took the Harvard Strength Test as a prep-school student. Rogers borrowed the items of Sargent's old strength test and refined the use of the scores by computing a Strength Index and a Physical Fitness Index.

Scientific experimentation and research contributed to the problem of improving the classification of students in physical education. The insufficiency of weight alone as a basis for classification was demonstrated and new formulas were developed. One of the first was calculated by Reilly in 1917, using age, weight, height, and grade.[96] This formula was widely used for ten or fifteen years. In the late 1920s McCloy developed a classification index from a weighted formula of age, height, and weight. The Brace Motor Ability Test and Rogers' Strength Index were also used for homogeneous grouping.

Just before this period drew to a close, the first efforts to measure some of the more intangible values of physical education appeared. The need for such measurement arose out of the emphasis on character out-

[93]C. H. McCloy, "A Statistical and Mathematical Method of Devising Athletic Scoring Tables," *American Physical Education Review* 26 (January 1921): 1–12.

[94]David K. Brace, "Testing Basketball Technique," *American Physical Education Review* 29 (April 1924): 159–64.

[95]David K. Brace, "A True-False Test on the 1922 Basketball Rules," *American Physical Education Review* 28 (March 1923): 134.

[96]Frederick J. Reilly, "A Rational Classification of Boys and Girls for Athletic Competition," *American Physical Education Review* 23 (January 1918): 13–24.

comes and social values which were proclaimed as objectives of physical education. In 1928, Luther Van Buskirk employed a new psychological technique, the rating scale, and sought to evaluate moral qualities and social traits resulting from physical education by listing the various types of behavior to be rated.[97] Two years later, one of the first studies on character rating was reported by McCloy.[98] These studies were the first of many similar efforts which were to come in the next twenty years.

RECREATION AND CAMPING: In planning recreation and camping programs, the emphasis was on creating and sustaining interest. As participation was also voluntary, the school and college intramural program had much in common with the recreation movement and many of the same methods were used, such as classification of participants and various types of tournaments for competition. Different point systems were conceived and effected. The use of these and other types of awards raised issues as to their nature, value, and when they should be given. Some of the new methods for teaching physical education, which were outcomes of educational developmentalism, were equally applicable to activities in recreation and camp programs.

SUMMARY: A summary of the history of physical education between 1900 and 1930 shows that the greatest progress occurred after World War I. The new gymnasiums and outdoor areas constructed during the prosperous 1920s provided facilities far superior to those existing before. The number of physical education teachers decidedly increased as more colleges and universities offered a professional curriculum. The quality of teacher training showed improvement, and the four-year curriculum was more generally required. The net effects of these and other developments upon the physical education program were observed by James E. Rogers who noted the following main trends:

1. Programs were better organized; lesson plans and modern curriculum procedures were being used.
2. Programs were graded with better selection, classification, and adaptation; activities were placed at the proper age and grade level according to newest psychological, physiological, educational, and recreational values.
3. Programs were adapted to individual needs based on health and physical examinations, physical fitness tests, and others; homogeneous groups were used in physical education as in other subjects.
4. Programs were evaluated by the use of tests and measurements.[99]

[97]Luther Van Buskirk, "Measuring the Results of Physical Education," *Journal of Educational Method* 7 (February 1928): 221–29.

[98]C. H. McCloy, "Character Building Through Physical Education," *Research Quarterly* 1 (October 1930): 41–61.

[99]James E. Rogers, "Trends in Physical Education," *Journal of Health and Physical Education* 2 (October 1931): 47–48.

School and college athletics meanwhile became an accepted part of education. Restrictive and regulative standards were established by school authorities. Restrictive standards discouraged intercollegiate competition for women and interscholastic athletics for girls and junior high boys. Regulative standards dealt with matters of health, eligibility, awards, and the like. Attention was given to the standards of sportsmanship and ethical conduct in relations with rival schools. Many state athletic associations were active in this field, and a national group drew up the Sportsmen's Code that was widely circulated in poster form. Participation in many activities for students of all ages and both sexes was tremendously stimulated by the new intramural programs and the sports and play days.

Physical education and sports by 1930 had acquired a firm educational status which commanded considerable respect for their potential accomplishment in the preparation of youth for life in the American society.

24

Physical Education

in

Education for Nationalism

1930-1950

The years between 1930 and 1950 witnessed striking contrasts to the prosperity and peace of the 1920s. The first decade was marked by the Great Depression which became worldwide. In the second decade the United States participated in the greatest war in history to combat Fascism and Nazism, and then, just as this second decade drew to a close, again took up arms as a member of the United Nations to check the spread of Communism. Yet, during these tense and unsettled years, many developments of unusual significance were taking place in the educational and social world.

The internationalism of the United States in 1950 was not the product of a steady, consistent development from the 1920s. Actually, the United States in the mid-thirties had an isolationist attitude and showed indifference and cynicism toward European affairs. But fast-moving events prodded the United States into a new type of internationalism that transcended the previous emphasis on economic considerations. This change of foreign policy was heralded when President Franklin D. Roosevelt announced the Good Neighbor policy toward Central and South America which was followed by an impressive series of actions: reciprocal trade agreements and reduced tariffs; a cultural-exchange program; the pledge to refrain from armed intervention and aggression; and loans by the Export-Import Bank to Latin American countries. These actions meant the end of the old Monroe Doctrine and the beginning of a Pan-American doctrine based on equality and mutual understanding among all the nations of the New World.

Unfortunately, these idealistic steps toward understanding between nations were not duplicated in other parts of the world. Japan's invasion of China and Italy's attack on Ethiopia undermined the League of Nations, and the Kellogg-Briand Treaties outlawing war led nations to wage war without a formal declaration. These outbreaks of international banditry generally convinced American authorities that this country should not meddle in foreign matters that were not directly its concern, and Congress, in the mid-1930s, passed a series of neutrality laws designed to avoid incidents such as those that led to participation in World War I.

The Nazi aggressions in Europe soon led to the modification of this neutrality legislation. The repeal of the arms embargo, the furnishing of naval escorts, and the arming of merchant ships all indicated the growing United States involvement in foreign affairs, culminating in the all-out war effort following the attack on Pearl Harbor.

The groundwork for United States participation in postwar efforts to preserve peace occurred long before the fighting was over. The first step was the Atlantic Charter of 1941 in which certain principles for peace were promulgated and agreed to by both England and the United States. Early in 1942, all of the Axis-resisting powers banded together as the United Nations and pledged full cooperation.

The actual formation of the United Nations in 1945 was preceded by several international organizations such as the Food and Agriculture Organization, the United Nations Relief and Rehabilitation Administration, and the World Bank, all created during the war. After the United Nations came into existence, these agencies were continued and other ones added such as the World Health Organization (WHO) and the United Nations Educational, Scientific, and Cultural Organization (UNESCO).

The United States showed itself willing to accept responsibilities as a world citizen and a member of the United Nations by defending South Korea when that country was attacked by the North Korean communists in June 1950. For the first time in history, the United States took military action for collective security before being attacked itself and thereby contributed to the concept of maintaining order in the international community by means of an international force. The changed American attitude toward international affairs is summarized by Arthur Schlesinger in these words:

> In the course of these developments the line between 'domestic' and 'foreign' affairs has grown increasingly dim until in the aging twentieth century it has become almost a distinction without a difference. Today the intelligent citizen must be informed about Ethiopia and Manchuria, Iran and Israel, India and Pakistan, French Indo-China and Korea, as well as about his own land, since what goes on in far corners of the globe may immediately affect his own welfare and happiness.[1]

The spread of education among the American people is strikingly illustrated by comparing the armies that fought in two wars. The typical

[1]Arthur Meier Schlesinger, *The Rise of Modern America, 1865–1951* (New York: The Macmillan Company, 1951), pp. v–vi.

enlisted man in 1917–1918 had finished seven years of school; his counterpart in 1944 had completed ten years. In World War I, 4.1 percent of the enlisted men had finished high school as compared with 23 percent in World War II. Similarly, 5.4 percent of the enlisted men in the first war completed at least one year of college, but for the second war, the figure was nearly 16 percent.

Public education, however, was directly affected by the Great Depression. During the years 1931 and 1932, there were a series of sharp curtailments in school budgets, and by 1933, the situation was desperate. Many schools were forced to close, the school year was shortened, improvements and upkeep of the school plant were neglected, and teachers found themselves faced with sharp salary reductions, long continued nonpayment for service, and only too frequently, with unemployment. The result was a great surplus of teachers, aggravated by the return to the teaching field of those who, in the days of prosperity, had gone into more lucrative positions and by the addition to the teaching ranks of recent college graduates. Conditions improved by 1936, with a short period of unemployment again during the 1939 recession.

Throughout the educational crisis, the teaching profession made valiant efforts locally, in state associations, in district groupings, and in the national association to prevent the undermining of the school system and to enlighten public opinion on modern educational needs. Conservative critics demanded a return to the three R's. Special subjects such as art, music, shopwork, and physical education were questioned and, in many schools, were curtailed or eliminated. The question had to be settled whether the people would be content with an impoverished public school curriculum when, at the same time, an enriched private school curriculum was available to privileged children. Educators and public-spirited community groups, particularly the Parent-Teachers Associations, rallied to respond to this challenge. They mounted educational campaigns to demonstrate that the new school programs were designed to meet radically changed social conditions.

Two or three beneficial effects of the depression should be noted. One was the definite upgrading of educational requirements for teachers. Before 1930, few states required more than a year of college for elementary teachers; ten years later, all but a few states required two to four years of professional preparation. During the depression, the federal government not only created special agencies for adult education, but hired 44,000 unemployed teachers who taught some 1,725,000 persons. The depression focused attention on youth problems, which the federal government sought to alleviate by such agencies as the Civilian Conservation Corps and the National Youth Administration. The American Youth Commission of the American Council on Education and special commissions of the Progressive Education Association contributed a number of valuable studies.

While education was still recovering from the depression, it was catapulted into another world war situation. During the war, needed improvements and facilities could not be constructed because of the demands of war production. Teachers were called into service or entered high-paying war industries while college enrollments in teacher education dropped precipitously.

The postwar period saw boards of education struggling to make material improvements in the face of soaring costs. The shift of population to suburban communities, the construction of complete new villages, and a greatly accelerated birth rate all had tremendous effects on education. Elementary education in particular suffered acutely from lack of facilities and teachers. Colleges literally burst at the seams after the war as a swelling influx of veterans rushed in to take advantage of the generous provisions of the G.I. Bill of Rights.

Health and physical education programs had difficulty surviving the depression. Some programs were retained through the support of outside organizations such as the American Federation of Labor, the American Legion, and groups such as the Turnvereins and Sokols. These two groups, because of strongly organized political influence, were able to restore the physical education programs in the Chicago schools where they had been almost eliminated because of drastic curriculum retrenchments. The American Legion was instrumental in Michigan in saving the state physical education law and also passed a resolution to continue the health, physical education, and recreation programs. The American Federation of Labor, influenced by the value of organized recreational programs in improving the morale of the unemployed, advocated public recreational movements. Similar support came later from the Congress of Industrial Organizations. The Federal Government, through agencies such as the CWA, PWA, and WPA, provided money and materials so that many communities were able to construct and staff new gymnasiums and community centers.

The exigencies of World War II placed special responsibilities and demands upon physical education, and for a period of four years the *military emphasis* shaped and dominated physical education programs in the United States. However, the usual clamor for military drill was conspicuously muffled. Both civilian and military leaders agreed that the schools and colleges would contribute most to the war effort by developing physical fitness rather than giving military training. The official attitude of the War Department was stated by the Secretary of War, Henry L. Stimson, in a letter to the U.S. Commissioner of Education, Dr. John W. Studebaker, as follows:

> The amount of military drill which can be given in schools and colleges can also be given after induction into the Army, in a relatively short period of time, and under the most productive circumstances. A good

physical condition, however, cannot be developed in so short space of time. . . . The War Department therefore does not recommend that military drill take the place of physical education in the schools and colleges during this war period.[2]

In general, therefore, World War II was characterized by the general retention of athletics and physical education in schools and colleges. Wartime needs focused attention on related aspects of the physical education program such as medical examinations and their follow-up, first aid, immunization and control of communicable disease, nutrition, and better health education and guidance. For the first time, the armed services themselves made sports an integral part of both their training and recreational program.

During this period the *scientific movement* became an established part of the profession of physical education. Research in tests and measurements pervaded the profession and provided data for the determination of individual differences, the improvement of teaching, and the measurement of outcomes. For the first time physical educators were encouraged to specialize in research. The development and application of scientific knowledge and method demanded trained personnel, and the proliferation of graduate programs throughout the country helped to meet this need. During the war, physical educators performed considerable research for the armed forces on physical fitness and rehabilitation techniques.

Educational developmentalism continued as a dominant force in physical education from 1930 to 1950 with a momentous shift of attention from the environment to the individual. A wide range of physical education activities encouraged the individual to find those sports in which he could excel or at least play with sufficient proficiency to enjoy. Within the limits of a physical education requirement, students often were permitted to elect the sports which they wished to learn. This concept was expressed in a Platform of Physical Education prepared by national leaders: "Everyone should be encouraged to take part regularly in a variety of activities appropriate to his age, physical condition, abilities and social interests."[3]

Individual health received greater scrutiny. Contestants in athletics were given closer supervision by health authorities. A physician was usually available at varsity football games. Trainers were better prepared to assist in the prevention and treatment of injuries. Intramural departments set up a physical examination as a prerequisite to participation in the more exacting sports. Physical education instructors showed more concern for the safety of their students.

[2] "A Letter from Mr. Stimson," *Journal of Health and Physical Education* 14 (September 1943): 368.

[3] W. K. Streit and Simon A. McNeely, "A Platform for Physical Education," *Journal of the American Association for Health, Physical Education, and Recreation* 21 (March 1950): 137.

Another aspect of developmentalism was interest in the handicapped. Physical recreation was found to have a great deal to offer in helping handicapped veterans adjust to their return to civilian life. Within the schools and colleges individual physical education programs stressed education and preparation for living as a well-adjusted member of society.

Social education was firmly established in the early 1930s when acceptance of the educational value of recreation in the schools was realized. Because of shorter working hours in industry, the elimination of child labor, earlier retirement age, and longer life expectancy, increased leisure time had become part of the fabric of the American way of life. Hence, schools began to assume responsibility to assist in preparation for leisure time. The theme of American Education Week for 1930 was "The Wise Use of Leisure, the Enrichment of Human Life, and Adult Education." Recreation was broadened to include the philosophical aspects of leisure time and the cultivation of healthful, cultural, and satisfying avocations. The educational aspects involved not only the inculcation of skills and interests for active participation, but also improvement in the standards and appreciation for vicarious forms of recreation.

In reviewing these eventful decades, all four themes received considerable emphasis although the military or nationalistic theme was limited to the duration of World War II. The scientific, the developmental, and the social themes each shared in determining the philosophy and substance of education and physical education.

Aims of Education

The ideas of John Dewey, Edward L. Thorndike, and G. Stanley Hall described in the preceding chapter continued to shape American education from 1930 to 1950. Their influence was particularly evident in the emphasis on social education and educational developmentalism which was found in many modern American schools. Scientific education contributed little to the aims of education but rather raised the question of usefulness or utility in regard to education content and directed its energies toward the development of efficient methods and effective measurements.

Education during the depression was discussed and evaluated by many individuals and groups. To clarify the situation, the National Education Association created the Educational Policies Commission, which formulated the following four groups of educational objectives:

1. *Self-realization*, which includes the skills of speaking, reading, writing, and arithmetic; desirable health knowledge and action; participation and observation of sports and pastimes; mental resources for use of leisure; and responsible direction to one's own life.

2. *Human relationships*, which include those practiced as a friend and neighbor and in the home and family.
3. *Economic efficiency*, which includes the individual both as a consumer and a producer.
4. *Civic responsibility*, which includes defenses against propaganda, unswerving loyalty to democratic ideals, respect for honest differences of opinion, and co-operation as a member of the world community.[4]

After World War II certain groups disturbed by mounting taxation and lawlessness among teen-agers, again advocated a return to the three R's and more discipline in the classrooms.

A basic cause of criticism and doubt, in the opinion of historian Henry Steele Commager,[5] was the lack of defined objectives for the schools. The nineteenth century schools, for example, faced the job of "Americanizing" their students. But the school of 1950 had no clear mandate as to whether its teaching should reinforce nationalism or inspire internationalism. Likewise, the school was in a dilemma because of increased demands upon its services. It was expected to prepare good citizens and train for democratic living; but the new demands of industry, the professions, the government, and the military services sought narrower technical training for specific jobs. At the same time high schools were expected to prepare students for college.

This basic problem of specialization versus general education received serious attention from educators. A committee of the Harvard University faculty prepared a report, *General Education in a Free Society*, which pointed out two main functions of education. "(1) To help young persons fulfill the unique, particular functions in life which it is in them to fulfill; and (2) to fit them so far as it can for those common spheres which, as citizens and heirs of a joint culture, they will share with others."[6] To accomplish the second objective, the committee recommended that one-half of the high school courses and approximately three-eighths of the college courses should be concerned with a core of general education spread out during the four years. Most of the remaining time would be available for the achievement of the first objective.

Much has been written on the problems facing American education during this period. The Harvard committee identified three main reasons for some of this concern and confusion: (1) the staggering expansion of knowledge, produced largely by specialization, (2) the phenomenal growth

---

[4]Educational Policies Commission, *The Purposes of Education in American Democracy* (Washington, D.C.: NEA and the American Association of School Administrators, 1938), pp. 50–123.

[5]"Our Schools Have Kept Us Free," *Life*, 16 October 1950, pp. 46–47.

[6]Harvard Faculty Report, *General Education in a Free Society* (Cambridge, Mass.: Harvard University Press, 1945), p. 4.

of educational systems; and (3) the ever-growing complexity of society itself. In appointing the committee, President Conant stated, "Our purpose is to cultivate in the largest possible number of our future citizens an appreciation of both the responsibilities and the benefits which come to them because they are Americans and are free."[7]

Aims of Physical Education

The philosophy and concept of physical education that was developed by Wood and Hetherington in the previous period gradually gained acceptance and support. Two of the most active proponents of these ideas were Dr. Jesse Feiring Williams of Columbia, and Jay B. Nash of New York University, both of whom made further contributions of their own.

Wood's insistence on considering physical education as part of education was echoed by Williams in his well-known statement that physical education is education *through* the physical, rather than education *of* the physical.[8] Williams summed up the purpose of physical education:

Physical education should aim to provide skilled leadership and adequate facilities which will afford an opportunity for the individual or group to act in situations which are physically wholesome, mentally stimulating and satisfying, and socially sound.[9]

Nash carried forward some of Hetherington's concepts when he described the four levels of human life. They are the following:

1. Organic powers, which are basic to the other three levels.
2. Neuro-muscular, which corresponds to Hetherington's psychomotor education.
3. Interpretive-cortical, by which Nash meant the accumulation of meanings through activity. This is essentially Hetherington's intellectual education.
4. Emotional-impulsive, which is Hetherington's character education.[10]

Nash stressed the interrelationship of these levels in the human organism and stated that every activity contributed to all four levels. Thus education and physical education had a significant effect on the development of all levels and therefore upon the integrated individual.

[7]Ibid., p. xv.

[8]Jesse F. Williams and Clifford L. Brownell, *The Administration of Health and Physical Education* (Philadelphia: W. B. Saunders Company, 1947), pp. 25–26.

[9]Jesse F. Williams, *The Principles of Physical Education* (Philadelphia: W. B. Saunders Company, 1948), p. 242.

[10]Jay B. Nash, *The Administration of Physical Education* (New York: A. S. Barnes and Co., 1931), pp. 103 *et seq.*

During the 1930s, a new aim ˙ ᶜ physical education moved rapidly into the foreground. This aim was preparation for leisure time, and its coming was hastened by the adverse economic conditions which enforced leisure for millions of Americans. An analysis of eighteen courses of study in physical education for secondary schools (most of which were dated 1929 or later) showed that the objective listed most frequently was "Teach games and exercises for leisure in later life." Other objectives were "Establish desirable and applicable habits of health conduct"; "Develop citizenship and upright character"; "Improve posture and prevent, detect, and correct physical defects"; "Develop and promote normal growth and organic development"; and "Coordinate effectively mental and motor activity."[11]

A change occurred in assessing the value of participating in athletic sports. Participation was urged not so much for developing moral qualities (though this was still essential) as for giving young people experience in adjusting to social situations. Sports offered a laboratory for genuine democratic action where a person was measured by his skill and sportsmanship.

The aims of the individual physical education programs were discussed, and Dr. George Stafford suggested that the handicapped individual be given the opportunity to develop leisure-time activities adjusted to his abilities, rather than to his disabilities.[12]

During the war, the primary objective of physical education became physical fitness, which emphasized the development of strength, endurance, coordination, and physical skills for military service or civilian war work. Furthermore, a school physical education program for all students and accompanied by medical examinations and health supervision was advocated because it would enable more individuals, both men and women, to qualify for military service.

In the postwar period, the purposes and functions of physical education were again subject to examination. One competent and authoritative evaluation was made by a joint committee of the AAHPER and the Society of State Directors of Health, Physical Education, and Recreation. In preparing a platform for physical education, this committee declared:

> Physical education is a *way* of education through physical activities which are selected and carried on with full regard to values in human growth, development, and behavior. Because it is a phase of the total educational program, physical education aims for the same general goal that gives purpose to all the other learning experiences of the school—the well rounded development of all children and youth as responsible citizens in our democratic society.[13]

[11]P. Roy Brammell, *Health Work and Physical Education.* U.S. Office of Education, Bulletin 1932, no. 17. National Survey of Secondary Education, Monograph no. 28 (Washington, D.C.: Government Printing Office, 1933), p. 69.

[12]George T. Stafford, *Sports for the Handicapped* (Englewood Cliffs, N.J.: Prentice-Hall, Inc., 1939), p. 46.

[13]Streit and McNeely, "A Platform for Physical Education," p. 136.

To summarize, the emphasis in physical education shifted from *physical* to *education,* and, at midcentury, physical education thus moved into close harmony with the aims of education.

Promotion of Physical Education

The New Physical Education during this period had great influence on elementary and secondary school programs. Its effective implementation depended upon trained teachers, adequate time, and ample facilities. These factors varied considerably from one school to the next, but overall progress could be observed. In the matter of facilities, for example, scientific ingenuity developed the folding or telescopic bleachers which solved seating problems and yet allowed floor space vital for class physical education activities. A new trend developed of locating schools adjacent to community park and recreation facilities to provide greater area for physical education activities. The new unit plan, by which the recreational areas of the school could be available for evening use, without opening the entire school building, became increasingly popular. Even so, many schools and colleges were still using gymnasiums that were thirty-five or more years old, and many older city schools were located in crowded areas where play space was extremely small and impossible to enlarge.

The role of educational institutions during World War II was of great significance. The facilities of many colleges were used by the armed forces for training military personnel. For example, the Universities of North Carolina, Georgia, Iowa, and St. Mary's College were used for the Navy Pre-Flight Schools. The Navy V-12 training for officers was carried on at many colleges. The Army likewise took over large parts of other institutions to train specialized personnel. In all these programs, the physical education facilities and athletic fields were heavily used. This arrangement between the armed services and the colleges was mutually advantageous because it enabled military training programs to get under way quickly by using existing facilities, and the assignment of service personnel to colleges took up the slack in enrollment of civilian students. For civilian students, physical education classes and intramural programs were maintained as much as possible with special emphasis on developing physical fitness. College staffs were reduced as many coaches and teachers entered the service. Most of the new athletic equipment produced went to military installations. Following the war, returning veterans were almost universally excused from physical education requirements. This policy was based on a recommendation of the American Council on Education, but only a few physical educators questioned its wisdom.

The war resulted in a number of changes in the nation's high schools. These changes included increased time allotment for physical education, increased percentage of boys and girls enrolled in physical education, improved interest in physical education by school administrators, and the granting of academic credit.[14] The revision of high school instruction was in large part guided by the booklet, *Physical Fitness Through Physical Education for the High School Victory Corps*, which was the product of a joint committee of professional physical educators and representatives of the armed forces. It recommended that every high school pupil should have physical education five days a week. Its publication and distribution were carried out by the U.S. Office of Education, and more than thirty states used this program.

In spite of the unmistakable interest in physical education, a survey of the nation's schools by the Office of Education for 1943–1944 showed that only one-half of the boys and girls in the last two years of high school were enrolled in physical education. Most of the students not receiving physical education were in small high schools of less than three hundred enrollment where physical education facilities and staff were inadequate. This situation improved considerably in the next five years. A national survey by the NEA for 1948–49 revealed that 92 percent of all public school students had physical education for an average of 132 minutes per week.[15]

Selective service statistics for World War II showed that out of 4 million men rejected for military service, about 700,000 had remediable defects which had not been corrected. In addition, many men were accepted for military service with defects which were corrected by army and navy doctors and dentists. In some quarters, physical education was charged with the responsibility for the poor record of Americans on the draft examinations. Oberteuffer cited five reasons why such criticism was unwarranted:

1. The vast majority of rejections—eyes, hearing, hernia, teeth, disease, illiteracy, psychological, nutritional, orthopedic—had nothing to do with physical education.
2. Failure to correct remedial defects was due to the inadequacy of correlation between school appraisal services and home or community corrective efforts.
3. Many rejections were the by-products of imperfect genetic matching and would appear unless mating was done arbitrarily on a genetically scientific basis.
4. Methods of examinations in the last war were more searching.
5. Physical education under conditions of an ideal setup might be blamed for musculoskeletal deficiencies that were found. But until

[14]David K. Brace, "Physical Fitness in Schools and Colleges," *Journal of Health and Physical Education* 15 (November 1944): 490.

[15]National Education Association, *Personnel and Relationships in School Health, Physical Education, and Recreation.* Research Bulletin 28, no. 3 (October 1950): 90–92.

all schools permit an hour of activity daily through all twelve years, physical education cannot be held entirely responsible.[16]

During these twenty years, more funds for the care of crippled children were made available by the provisions of the 1935 Social Security Act which authorized the Federal Government to match state money for this purpose. Federal agencies such as the WPA and PWA constructed up-to-date facilities which were new in some areas or replaced old structures in others. The new schools had ramps and elevators, floors were covered with heavy linoleum to withstand crutches and wheelchairs, and special equipment included sun lamps, solariums, and therapeutic pools.[17]

STATE LEGISLATION: A few new states passed legislation regarding physical education, so that by 1949, a total of forty-one states reported a physical education law. Most of the states employed state directors or supervisors.

State administration and legislation in physical education showed a growing tendency to unify administrative responsibility for all phases of school health, physical education, and recreation in one division. The state director of health and physical education assumed responsibility not only for health education and physical education, but also for recreation, safety education, driver training, school lunches, and education for the handicapped or exceptional children. Furthermore, many states established specific requirements through codes, standards, and regulations. Another significant trend was that of increased co-operation between state departments of health and education. This trend first appeared about 1935 when Indiana, North Carolina, and Tennessee initiated co-operative arrangements between the respective state departments.

TEACHER EDUCATION: The general effect of the depression in raising the requirements for teachers in general, also applied to physical education. However, this progress was halted by the war when a shortage of teachers developed because of mobilization. Twenty-eight states issued emergency certificates to people with no professional training in physical education. This situation continued after the war when the demand for teachers increased because of larger school enrollments. Many colleges instituted a major program in physical education for the first time, and by 1950 over 400 colleges and universities offered this major. In June, 1950, more than 10,000 physical education men were graduated, an increase of 37 percent

[16]Delbert Oberteuffer, *School Health Education* (New York: Harper & Brothers, 1949), p. 356.
[17]Corinne R. Frazier, "Special Schools for Physically Handicapped Children," *The Nation's Schools* 26 (August 1940): 18–20.

over 1949 and of 600 percent over 1941.[18] By 1950 supply had caught up to demand and some graduates could not find employment except in the field of recreation. Women graduates in physical education had no difficulty finding positions.

Teacher education curriculums were characterized by a lack of similarity in courses, staff, and facilities. One of the first attempts to standardize teacher-training programs was made by a committee of the Department of School Health and Physical Education of the National Education Association, appointed in 1931, under the chairmanship of Dr. N. P. Neilson. A more recent effort was that of the National Conference on Undergraduate Professional Preparation in Health Education, Physical Education, and Recreation, held at Jackson's Mill, West Virginia, in May 1948. The report published by the conference outlined recommended programs and guiding principles for undergraduate teacher preparation in each of these three fields.

The period 1930 to 1950 was significant for the development of graduate curriculums in physical education. Over seventy institutions inaugurated a master's degree program and approximately twenty began to grant the doctorate. The rapid increase in the number of these degrees is evident from a 1945 study of the graduate faculties of 49 institutions which disclosed that 54 percent of the staff members had the master's degree and 22 percent the doctor's degree. Furthermore, 39 percent of those with the master's degree were working on their doctorates.[19] The summer schools particularly profited from the demand for graduate work.

The graduate programs, like the undergraduate, exhibited tremendous differences in the quality and the quantity of the work offered. Dr. Seward Staley of the University of Illinois called a meeting of representatives of midwestern universities in 1946 to discuss problems in graduate education. Successive meetings led to the National Conference of Graduate Study in Health Education, Physical Education, and Recreation, which met at Pere Marquette State Park in Illinois in January 1950. This conference attempted to do for the graduate program what the Jackson's Mill conference did for the undergraduate program.

Toward the end of this period, many of the larger secondary schools demanded that their teachers have a master's degree. A doctor's degree became a prerequisite for those interested in teacher education. Sentiment also grew for a five-year undergraduate curriculum. These conditions in 1950 were eloquent testimony to the progress made in teacher education from the nine-week training course given by the Dio Lewis Institute less than ninety years before.

---

[18]Charles A. Bucher, "1951 Employment Outlook," *Journal of the American Association for Health, Physical Education, and Recreation* 22 (March 1951): 42.

[19]Jack E. Hewitt, "Status of the Graduate Faculty," *Research Quarterly* 16 (October 1945): 236–37.

PROMOTION OF RESEARCH: The quality of teacher education was considerably enhanced by a phenomenal outpouring of numerous research studies—evidencing the scientific emphasis in physical education. At some institutions, physical education personnel used the research facilities of other departments, such as the physiological and anthropometrical laboratory of the Child Welfare Station at the University of Iowa, the Laboratory of Physiological Hygiene at the University of Minnesota, and the Medical Physiological Laboratories at Indiana University and the University of North Carolina. In other institutions, separate laboratories were created in the physical education department. A survey in 1950 indicated that this was the case in sixteen colleges and universities.[20] The institutions with research laboratories in the graduate department of physical education were Springfield College, George Williams, the University of Illinois, U.C.L.A., and New York University. Some universities designated certain physical education staff members as research personnel and freed them from some teaching and administrative duties.

The collaboration of workers in other departments has helped in these research developments. In Departments of Physiology, Dr. D. B. Dill of Harvard University, Dr. Eugene Howe of Wellesley College, Dr. Sid Robinson of Indiana University, Dr. Percy Dawson of the University of Wisconsin, Dr. W. W. Tuttle of the University of Iowa, and Dr. E. C. Schneider of Wesleyan University assisted in conducting researches of import to physical education workers. In the psychological laboratory, Drs. Coleman Griffith (Illinois), Clarence Ragsdale (Wisconsin), and John Lawther (Penn State) have made studies in motor learning, attitudes, and psychology of athletic coaching.

A milestone in the development of research in health and physical education was the new *Research Quarterly*, first published by the APEA in 1930. This periodical transmitted information of new research by printing reports of the best studies and thereby stimulating further studies. It published summaries of many excellent master's theses and doctoral dissertations that otherwise would have been little known. Another valuable step forward in the encouragement of scientific research was the publication of *Research Methods Applied to Health, Physical Education, and Recreation* under the sponsorship of the Research Section of the AAHPER in 1949. The preparation of this book involved contributions from forty authors, showing that the day of the specialist had arrived.

PROFESSIONAL ORGANIZATIONS: During the 1920s the American Physical Education Association was faced with a number of problems which resulted in several important changes in 1930. The most apparent change was the publication of the first issue of the *Journal of Health and Physical*

[20]Paul A. Hunsicker, "A Survey of Laboratory Facilities in College Physical Education Departments," *Research Quarterly* 21 (December 1950): 420–23.

Education which succeeded the *American Physical Education Review*. The new editor was Elmer D. Mitchell of the University of Michigan who had handled a similar publication, *The Pentathlon*, for the Middle West Society in 1928 and 1929. At the same time Mitchell served as editor for a completely new publication, *The Research Quarterly*. In this way the Association solved McCurdy's dilemma of trying to cater to the interests of the teaching practitioner and the research specialist through the pages of the *Review*. Mitchell edited both periodicals for thirteen years and concurrently was secretary of the Association for eight years. Also in 1930 Mabel Lee of the University of Nebraska became the first woman president of the APEA. Furthermore a number of constitutional changes were effected which strengthened state and district organizations and made the Association more democratic and representative of the country as a whole.

The widening scope of the American Physical Education Association was shown in its changing name. In 1937 it became the American Association for Health and Physical Education, in recognition of the growth of health education. One year later the recreation movement found a place in a new title, American Association for Health, Physical Education, and Recreation (AAHPER). A major step was taken in 1937 when the Association became a department of the National Education Association. This action reflected, at the professional level, the integration of physical education with the total school curriculum.

In 1938 the Association employed Neils P. Neilson of Stanford University as executive secretary-treasurer, the first full-time officer. The national headquarters was moved to the NEA building in Washington. Neilson was succeeded in 1944 by Ben W. Miller, and he was followed in 1948 by Carl A. Troester, Jr., of Syracuse University.

The Association under Mitchell's prudent management came through the depression remarkably well. In various ways it supported the retention of physical education in hard-pressed school programs. One effort was the preparation of an enlarged *Journal* for March 1933 with special articles emphasizing the relation of health, physical education, and recreation to modern life. Twenty thousand copies of this issue were sent free of charge to school administrators and boards of education.[21]

During World War II, the Association suffered as officers and members were drawn into service for their country. In the postwar period, however, the Association dealt with major problems and inaugurated the first of many conferences with other related organizations. The first conference met in 1946 and produced a widely used book, *A Guide on Planning Facilities for Athletics, Recreation, Physical, and Health Education*. The Association also participated in planning the two conferences on professional

[21]Mabel Lee and Bruce L. Bennett, "This is Our Heritage," *Journal of Health, Physical Education, and Recreation* 31 (April 1960): 63, 66.

undergraduate and graduate education described previously. It embarked upon an ambitious program of publications in 1949 by taking over all the sports guides of the National Section on Women's Athletics, which the A. S. Barnes and Company had printed for many years. This was quickly followed by the book on research methods and a second volume, *Measurement and Evaluation Materials in Health, Physical Education, and Recreation* in 1950. Membership in the national organization reached a new high of 18,000 in 1950 and it became the largest department of the NEA.

The Society of College Directors of Physical Education changed its title in 1933 to the College Physical Education Association (CPEA) and broadened its membership requirements to include teachers as well as administrators of college health or physical education. The association sponsored several important publications. One was *The Physical Education Curriculum—A National Program*, prepared by the Committee on Curriculum Research under the chairmanship of William Ralph LaPorte. This book presented a recommended program for all grades. Another useful reference was *College Facilities for Physical Education, Health Education, and Recreation*, published in 1947 and edited by Karl Bookwalter of Indiana University.

Some of the other professional organizations affiliated with the AAHPER were the Physical Education Society of the YMCAs of North America; the Society of State Directors of Health, Physical Education, and Recreation; Phi Epsilon Kappa (for men); Phi Delta Pi (for women); and the Canadian Physical Education Association.

COLLEGE ATHLETICS: In the area of athletics, problems of subsidization and recruitment continued to demand attention, and the NCAA made two more attempts to improve the situation. In 1933, it appointed a committee, headed by Z. G. Clevenger of Indiana, to determine legal recruiting. The committee presented a code of justifiable and unjustifiable acts which was sent to the presidents of member institutions for earnest consideration and later incorporated in the NCAA constitution. About the same time the North Central Association published a report of its Committee on Physical Education and Athletics which indicated that the practice of favoring athletes through the media of scholarships, loans, and jobs was not so serious as was generally believed. The report also urged the raising of academic qualifications of athletic staff members and recommended the unified direction of athletic facilities and programs.[22]

The second attempt of the NCAA to improve athletic standards was through the so-called Sanity Code. The idea for the code developed out of a meeting called by the Executive Committee of the NCAA in July 1946.

[22]"Report of the Committee on Physical Education and Athletics," *The North Central Association Quarterly* 8 (June 1933): 26–69.

A code for the conduct of intercollegiate athletics was worked out and approved as a part of the constitution at the annual convention in January 1948. The first test of the widely-discussed Sanity Code came at the convention in January 1950, when seven member institutions were cited for noncompliance. A vote to expel these institutions from the Association fell short of the required two-thirds. A year later the charges against the code violators were dropped, and the Sanity Code was in effect abandoned. The problems of recruiting and subsidization remained unsolved.

College football attendance dropped off somewhat after 1930 because of the depression and the radio broadcasts of games. Some colleges played games for charity where the receipts were given to agencies for assisting the millions of unemployed and their families. During the war, attendance was hurt by travel restrictions. A decline in 1949 was blamed by athletic leaders on television. The Western Conference banned live television of all its football games for the 1950 season, and the NCAA formulated plans to make a careful study of the possible effects of television on college athletics.

Throughout World War II, college athletics fared much better than in 1917–1918. The administration of athletic programs remained in the hands of the civilian staff even though military units were stationed on the campus. Intercollegiate athletics were generally maintained in spite of transportation restrictions and reduced enrollment. In fact, many colleges expanded their schedules to play extra games with service teams. Eligibility rules were relaxed to permit freshman participation, and transfer students were immediately eligible without the usual year of residence. The military officials cooperated by securing large quantities of athletic equipment. In brief, athletic competition played an integral part in the training of America's fighting men in World War II.

Meanwhile, the NCAA extended its national tournaments to embrace many new sports. Boxing was started in 1932; gymnastics, tennis, and cross country in 1938; basketball in 1939; golf in 1940; fencing in 1941; baseball in 1947; and ice hockey in 1948. In the Olympic years some of these national tournaments are used to help select America's representatives to the Games.

THE AAU AND THE NCAA: Compared with the tempestuous times of the 1920s, relations between the AAU and the NCAA entered a period of relative calm. The 1932 Olympics held in Los Angeles went very well, but an angry fight erupted over whether the United States should send a team to Nazi Germany in 1936. The NCAA favored participation and the AAU was closely divided, but a team finally was sent. After the war the two organizations buried the hatchet and agreed upon the Articles of Alliance whereby each group recognized the jurisdiction of the other over its own members. The 1948 Olympic Games were marked by a spirit of cooperation, and the AAU and NCAA each raised $190,000 for the U.S. Olympic Committee.[23]

The AAU continued as an important force in amateur athletics outside the colleges. It supervised the activities of several million men and women and had jurisdiction over fifteen sports. Some of its allied organizations were the Amateur Fencers' League of America, the Amateur Softball Association, and the U.S. Amateur Baseball Congress. The AAU itself was allied with the various International Amateur Sports Federations.

SCHOOL ATHLETICS: The National Federation of State High School Athletic Associations, under the direction of H. V. Porter, Executive Secretary, demonstrated its merit and added sixteen states to its membership rolls. The work of the national federation and the various state associations was largely responsible for the establishment of sane standards in the conduct of interscholastic sports and the avoidance of some of the abuses found in intercollegiate athletics.[24] Nevertheless, school authorities were beset with their own particular problems. Some of these arose from the demands of overzealous partisans for interscholastic competition for boys at the junior high level and even in the upper grades of the elementary school. Continuing pressures were also exerted to provide interscholastic competition for high school girls, especially in rural communities. Although most professional organizations opposed these kinds of competition, other groups and individuals vigorously supported them.

INTRAMURAL SPORTS: Intramural sports after 1930 stressed the recreational aspects of sports and in some institutions the title of Intramural Director was changed to Recreation Director. There was also a change in the attitude of students toward their intramural play. Intramural participation became less forced than it was in the earlier stages of the movement when aggressive organizing measures were needed to popularize the new program. Students began to form sporting interests with few external attractions in the way of publicity and prizes. Sports were enjoyed more for their own sake.

It was recognized that a good physical education program was the most important factor in motivation for the intramural program. Many students were introduced to certain sports in gymnasium classes and, liking them, participated in them intramurally.

Intramural departments used various techniques to publicize intramural sports and increase the number of participants: sports clinics, annual

[23]Arnold W. Flath, *A History of Relations Between the National Collegiate Athletic Association and the Amateur Athletic Union of The United States,* (1905–1963) (Champaign, Ill.: Stipes Publishing Company, 1964), pp. 115–17.
[24]Charles E. Forsythe, *The Administration of High School Athletics* (Englewood Cliffs, N.J.: Prentice-Hall, Inc., 1948), pp. 13–20.

open houses, freshman orientation, and printed handbooks. In general, college intramural programs throughout the country showed a surprising uniformity in their organization and administration.

WOMEN'S SPORTS: Following a reorganization of the Women's Athletic Section of the APEA in 1932, the promotion of women's athletics was taken over by the National Section on Women's Athletics (NSWA). The Women's Division of the NAAF had previously become affiliated with the APEA in 1931 and thus moved closer to the eventual merger with the NSWA, which occurred in 1940. The NSWA outlined a fourfold program:

1. The stating of guiding principles and standards for the administrator, leader, official, and player.
2. The publication and interpretation of rules governing sports for girls and women.
3. The dissemination of accurate information in various types of periodicals and special publications and through convention programs.
4. The stimulation and evaluation of research in the field of women's athletics.[25]

The work of the NSWA was carried out by national standing committees, one of which was the Rules and Editorial Committee that published the following official guides in 1949: aquatics, winter sports, and outing activities; basketball; tennis and badminton; field hockey and lacrosse; individual sports of archery, bowling, fencing, golf, and riding; recreational games and volleyball; softball and track and field; soccer and speedball.

The NSWA operated through the medium of education and wielded no legislative or executive power. Membership was on an individual basis, consisting of all women who were members of the AAHPER. In 1936, the plan of appointing state representatives was inaugurated so as to make the contact between teachers in the field and the national section more effective. Eventually, the NSWA became the leading authority on questions and problems concerning athletic activities for girls and women, in community recreation programs, industrial plants, private clubs, and the military service, as well as in schools. The organization continually promoted the objective of "A sport for every girl, and every girl in a sport."[26]

The Athletic Conference of American College Women continued its activities under a new name adopted in 1933—Athletic Federation of College Women.

A comprehensive survey made in 1943 showed that little change had

[25]Eline von Borries, *The History and Functions of the National Section on Women's Athletics* (Washington, D.C.: American Association for Health, Physical Education, and Recreation ,1941), p. 13.

[26]This was originally the motto of the Women's Division of the NAAF.

occurred in women's athletic competition since 1930. About sixteen percent of the colleges had varsity teams, mainly in the East. Eighty-one percent had some form of extramural competition, largely as play days or by telegraph. The latter was especially popular in the West.[27] Varsity competition at the high school level possibly showed some decline, but it remained strong in local areas. Eight states held girls' basketball tournaments but fifteen states prohibited them.[28]

In spite of prevailing practice, there were some signs of a mounting demand for more competitive opportunities for college women. In 1941 Gladys Palmer of Ohio State University proposed a Women's Collegiate Athletic Association, similar to the NCAA, to provide intercollegiate competition for women. She also announced that a women's collegiate golf tournament would be held at Ohio State in June. Both ideas were strongly disapproved by the National Association of Directors of Physical Education for College Women.[29] In spite of this opposition, the golf tournament went on as scheduled and, after a war-induced hiatus, was resumed in 1946 on an annual basis.

NONSCHOOL AGENCIES: Physical education has received considerable help from The Athletic Institute which was founded in 1934 as a nonprofit organization by a group of athletic goods manufacturers. In the early years its activities were limited to the promotion of interest and participation in sports, mainly baseball and softball. During the Second World War the Institute encouraged activity in other sports and recreational activities. It paid for a full-time secretary when the National Industrial Recreation Association was getting started. It established a chair of Industrial Recreation at Purdue University in 1942. Colonel Theodore Bank became president in 1945 and an advisory board of professional people in physical education, athletics, and recreation was created. The Institute then began to make substantial donations of money to support important conferences, such as the one on facilities in 1946, and the two professional education conferences at Jackson's Mill and Pere Marquette. It contributed towards the publication of the conference proceedings which were eagerly received by many people in the profession.

During the war, the various training stations and camps of the armed services provided considerable physical education and sports for their personnel. Athletics and calisthenics were used to train recruits, maintain physical fitness, and supply recreational activities. Recreation was the major

[27]M. Gladys Scott, "Competition for Women in American Colleges and Universities," *Research Quarterly* 16 (March 1945): 70–71.

[28]H. V. Porter, "Revival of the Interest in Athletic Activities for Girls," *The Progressive Physical Educator* 30 (May 1948): 42.

[29]*Record of the 1941 Conference of the National Association of Directors of Physical Education for College Women* (Northfield, Minnesota: Mohn Printing Company, 1941), pp. 42–43.

need at overseas bases. Many military stations had a physical training or athletic officer who supervised the program. The most extensive use of physical education and athletics occurred at the Navy Pre-Flight schools where every cadet had two hours of instruction and two hours of intramural competition daily. This excellent Navy program was headed by Commander Tom Hamilton and the Navy gave commissions to 2,000 coaches and physical education instructors to obtain the necessary leadership.

The YMCAs throughout the country opened their facilities and staff for the service of military and civilian personnel alike. Soldiers and sailors were admitted without membership cards; and classes were held for war-workers, teenagers, businessmen, and preinduction groups. The aquatic program of the "Y" was particularly valuable.[30]

Several physical educators played key roles in developing new reconditioning programs for the armed services. These programs used a revolutionary concept of starting physical activity even for bedridden patients, to prevent muscle atrophy and to promote recovery and return to duty. The first Army officer in charge of this program, Colonel Walter Barton, a psychiatrist, called upon Arthur Esslinger and Charles McCloy for professional assistance. Arthur Daniels and George Stafford served in similar capacities for the Air Force and Navy respectively. Many other physical educators carried out the program in military hospitals. After the war, hospitals under the Veterans' Administration adopted the principles of physical reconditioning but with a new name, corrective therapy.

Professional sports were unquestionably slowed down by the depression and the various restrictions imposed by the war effort in the 1940s. Some development got under way after the war. Professional football expanded in 1946 with the founding of the All-American Conference, which lasted for four seasons and was absorbed by its older rival, the National Football League. Organized professional basketball was started on a large scale with two leagues operating in 1946. Public support proved inadequate, however, and a merger of the two leagues in 1949 resulted in the formation of the National Basketball Association. The Harlem Globe Trotters regaled audiences throughout the entire period and earned international recognition for their skillful and entertaining play.

Skiing became prominent during this era, with assistance from private business. The first ski train was run by the Boston and Maine Railroad from Boston to New Hampshire in 1931. The Union Pacific Railroad spent four million dollars to develop Sun Valley, Idaho in the mid-1930s. Skiing and other winter sports received further emphasis from the 1932 Olympic Winter Games held at Lake Placid, New York. The number of ski enthusiasts grew steadily even during the worst of the economic hard times.

[30]Harold T. Friermood, "Wartime Physical Education in the YMCA," *Journal of Health and Physical Education* 15 (April 1944): 185.

NEGROES IN SPORTS: Prior to World War II, little progress could be observed in the acceptance and recognition of Negroes in sports. Athletics in Negro colleges flourished, and these schools competed vigorously for outstanding performers. The Middle Atlantic Athletic Association was formed in 1931 and the Mid-Western Association started the next year. The war itself began to produce some rumblings in America's social structure and doubtless contributed to some revolutionary events which followed.

The appearance of Jackie Robinson in a Brooklyn Dodgers uniform in 1947 was described as "one of the most dramatic and fruitful steps the American Negro had taken since the Civil War toward social integration."[31] This introduction of a Negro into major league baseball was a deliberate action by Branch Rickey, president of the Dodgers. He was advised by Dan W. Dodson, a sociologist and executive director of the Mayor's Committee on Unity for the city of New York.[32] Rickey's courageous move was successful, and it cleared the way for other Negro players. Another major breakthrough occurred in bowling when the discriminatory policies of the American Bowling Congress were ended in 1949. Organized labor, represented by the UAW-CIO, was in the forefront of this fight.[33]

A few Negroes played professional football through the 1920s and up to 1933. However, there was no further participation until 1946 when Kenny Washington and Woody Strode joined the Los Angeles Rams. In that same year Paul Brown signed Bill Willis and Marion Motley to play for the Cleveland Browns of the new All-American Conference.

ORGANIZED RECREATION: The organized recreation movement, which had thrived in the prosperous 1920s, quickly wilted in the financially stringent 1930s. For example, Detroit's recreation budget was reduced from $1,000,000 to $200,000. Paid staffs were drastically cut in both numbers and salaries; they bore the brunt of reduced appropriations. The construction of new facilities slowed down, although there were increased numbers of buildings and centers used for recreation.[34]

Following 1933, the recreation movement profited immensely through Federal relief projects. In the first place, many unemployed teachers were chosen to conduct institutes which trained newcomers in recreational leadership. Thus a body of Federal relief (WPA) workers in recreation was developed. Their importance was especially felt in the fields of arts and crafts, music, dramatics, and activities in other areas that previously had

[31]Richard L. Tobin, "Sports as an Integrator," *Saturday Review*, 21 January 1967, p. 32.

[32]Dan W. Dodson, "The Integration of Negroes in Baseball," *Journal of Educational Sociology* 28 (October 1954): 73–75.

[33]Frederick W. Cozens and Florence S. Stumpf, *Sports in American Life* (Chicago: The University of Chicago Press, 1953), pp. 255–56.

[34]E. C. Worman, "Trends in Public Recreation," *Recreation* 32 (August 1938): 267–69.

not received specialized instruction. Also, many recreation surveys of cities were made with the help of these workers. In the second place, recreational projects were approved for relief labor. Through CWA, FERA, and NYA labor, many clearance projects took place; consequently playground areas, athletic fields, golf courses, tennis courts, skating rinks, swimming pools, and wading pools were made available for community recreation. Up to 1938, a total of about one-and-a-half billion dollars was spent by Federal agencies for the construction of recreational facilities. This included an estimated 13,700 parks, 22,100 playgrounds and athletic fields, 670 golf courses, 1,510 swimming pools, and 7,930 recreational buildings that were repaired or built.

The WPA recreation program gave the publicly sponsored recreation movement a substantial boost. Even though leadership was weak in some cases, it enabled many people for the first time to see the possibilities of a broad recreation program. It planted the idea of publicly-paid recreation leadership in many areas.[35] During the years 1936 and 1937, the number of federal workers was reduced, but frequently their activities were taken over and continued by communities. In spite of the initial effect of the depression, public recreation moved forward during the 1930s.

The outbreak of war in 1941 forced recreation agencies to adjust to meet wartime needs and demands. Because war industries worked around the clock, recreational facilities were made available at all hours. Particular emphasis was given to youth centers. The National Recreation Association reported that 40 percent of all buildings and centers in 1944 were operated particularly for youth. For the first time since 1930, women recreation leaders outnumbered men, and they made possible the continuance of recreational services.[36] Since there was little new construction of facilities, the major expenditure was for leadership. The United Service Organizations (USO) was a wartime agency to direct and provide for the needs of enlisted men and to serve as a "home away from home." The American Red Cross distributed recreation kits to servicemen, gave instruction in life-saving and first aid, and collected blood as well. The multitude of commercial recreational agencies that operated golf courses, bowling alleys, athletic clubs, swimming pools, and other facilities played important roles in meeting recreational needs.

Following World War II, community recreation began a period of further development similar to that after the first war. Total expenditures for community recreation soared from $51,800,000 in 1946 to $93,800,000 just two years later.[37] The Yearbook of the National Recreation Associa-

[35]A. F. Wileden, "Recreation Trends in the Rural Community," *Recreation* 42 (December 1948): 413.

[36]*Recreation* 38 (June 1945): 172–73.

[37]*Recreation* 40 (June 1947): 108; also 42 (June 1949): 100.

tion reported that nearly one-third of the amount spent in 1948 was for capital expenditure on land, buildings, and permanent improvements, indicating that cities once again were expanding recreational resources after a lull of several years. Many war memorials were dedicated to purposes of community recreation. The growing use of schools as recreation centers was revealed by the fact that 4,478 or 75 percent, of all recreation centers in 1948 were school buildings.[38]

Another factor in these gains was the population increase in the United States beginning in 1941. Moreover, with the increased life expectancy, the elderly made up a larger percentage of the population. The recreational needs of these older people were met by organizing Golden Age clubs of Senior Citizen groups which often used municipal recreation facilities.

The growth of public recreation created a demand for trained leaders and administrators. Gradually, some colleges began to develop a separate curriculum in recreation. By 1949, forty institutions offered a major in recreation and several gave an advanced degree. The Jackson's Mill Conference in 1948 outlined a recommended training program for recreation, as well as for health and physical education.

Industrial recreation progressed during this period and achieved professional status through the able leadership of Floyd Eastwood of Purdue University. Just before the war, he developed the first degree program in industrial recreation. In 1940 he brought together twelve individuals who formed the Recreation Association for American Industry. The name, National Industrial Recreation Association, was assumed in 1949. Eastwood was elected the first president and held that office for four years.[39]

By 1948 there were an estimated 200 full-time industrial recreation directors. Labor unions were alert to needs in this area also, and the UAW-CIO set up a Recreation Department in 1937 headed by Olga Madar.[40] As schools, communities, industry, labor, government, private enterprise, and various voluntary agencies took over responsibility for meeting the nation's recreational needs, the activity of the church in this area diminished. The following appraisal by the Institute of Social and Religious Research described the situation: "When it comes to recreation, there is more than an even chance that this will be done, if it is done at all under religious auspices, in a non-church agency rather than in a church."[41] Organized religion could reflect with legitimate pride on the early efforts of individual

[38]*Recreation* 42 (June 1949): 101–4.

[39]Floyd Eastwood, "NIRA's First Twenty-Five Years," *Recreation Management*, 9 (May 1966): 12–14.

[40]Charles E. Doell and Gerald B. Fitzgerald, *A Brief History of Parks and Recreation in the United States* (Chicago: The Athletic Institute, 1954), pp. 112–14.

[41]H. Paul Douglass and Edmund Brunner, *The Protestant Church as a Social Institution* (New York: Harper and Brothers, 1935), p. 141.

churches and ministers to develop a national conscience about serving the recreational needs of all citizens.

ORGANIZED CAMPING: Camping from 1930 to 1950 moved steadily toward integration with education. Early in the period such writers as Mason in his *Camping and Education* and Dimock and Hendry in their *Camping and Character* were expressing an educational philosophy of the camping movement. The comprehensive programs developed by the Civilian Conservation Corps (CCC) camps, the growth of the Youth Hostel movement which was introduced to the United States in 1934, and foundation grants to carry on experimental programs with individuals needing physical and social adjustment, were all important factors in bringing the camping movement to the attention of educators as another way of education. In 1947, the New York City Board of Education, in cooperation with Life Camps, Inc., conducted an interesting experiment with public school children which indicated that the camping experience was more conducive to certain learning than the schoolroom.[42] The rapprochement of camping with education was also apparent from the introduction of courses for camp counsellors in over 400 colleges and universities.

Day camps, which started on a small scale in the 1920s, appeared in large numbers during the 1930s because they were less expensive than the regular camps. The Girl Scouts especially promoted day camping and in 1939 conducted 453 camps with an attendance of 729,000 girls. In the same year, eighty-one cities operated one or more day camps.[43] Day camps demonstrated their value during World War II because they were used during the summer months for the schoolchildren of mothers who were working in war industries or business.

Public school camps became more common and furnished administrative proof of the growing alliance of camping with education. In 1934, the New York City public schools began "day-outing camps" for children in the summer play schools. Ten years later, the U.S. Office of Education estimated that more than fifty school systems had camp programs as one of their education-recreational activities, and the Office urged the extension of education into outdoor living. The National Association of Secondary School Principals published a monograph on *Camping and Outdoor Education* in 1947. Some states passed legislation authorizing school boards to make camping a regular part of the school curriculum; Michigan, New York, and California furnished pioneer leadership in school camping. In the former state, much of the experimentation in camping was made possible by the Kellogg Foundation in collaboration with the State Department

[42]Board of Education, New York City, *Extending Education Through Camping* (New York: Life Camps, Inc., 1948).
[43]Weaver W. Pangburn, "Play and Recreation," *Annals of the American Academy of Political and Social Science* 212 (November 1940): 126.

of Public Instruction. The pilot project in outdoor education of the City and County of San Diego, California, established in 1946, is one that is recognized as outstanding in school-community camping.

The American Camping Association kept pace with the rise of the camping movement. It published a monthly magazine, *Camping*, and in 1949 boasted a membership of 2,000 camps and 4,000 individuals. The 1948 convention of the ACA formally approved a set of standards for camps.

During the summer of 1949, an estimated ten million American youth spent at least one weekend at one of more than ten thousand camps. Millions more of American adults and family groups enjoyed informal camping in the numerous national, state, and local parks and forests. The widespread enjoyment in camping experienced by so many people was fitting tribute to the work and spirit of men such as Dan Beard, Luther Gulick, and Ernest Thompson Seton who sought to bring the joy of camping to all. In a sense, the adventure of camping was substituted for the open frontier and the wilderness which lured the early pioneers westward.

Program of Physical Education

The physical education program from 1930 to 1950 showed considerable diversity. It featured some of the older traditional activities as well as some of the newer recreative sports. Calisthenics, rhythmic movements, apparatus and tumbling, athletic contests, team games, swimming, life saving, mass games, dance, tennis, golf, handball, and others were all properly included in the program. They offered the means to explore and reach the wide range of individual differences of interest that were found in every physical education class.

During the war years, physical education programs were modified to meet the primary objective of physical fitness. Activities stressed were aquatics, gymnastics, relays, calisthenics, tumbling, boxing, wrestling, group games, and team sports, as well as road work, hard physical labor, and camping. Aquatics emphasized the ability to stay afloat fully clothed and to swim long distances. The side-stroke and back-stroke were taught as well as the crawl. Obstacle courses with walls, ladders, pits, hurdles, and balance beams became a familiar sight on many school athletic fields. Running games such as soccer, speedball, and touch football were played with considerable gusto. The NCAA urged its member schools to require at least three hours of physical education per week for all students.

In military training programs, attention was given to many of the above-mentioned activities plus others such as judo, rough-and-tumble wrestling, hand-to-hand combat, cross-country hiking, and land-or-sea-survival. These activities were specially required because of the nature of warfare in the Pacific.

Physical fitness for women received a major share of attention. For the first time in the history of the country, women were accepted into the armed forces, and this served as an additional incentive for many women to participate in a physical education program. Women also played a vital role in war production and filled many jobs previously performed only by men, as illustrated by the title of one popular song, "Rosie the Riveter." Activities for women included aquatics, gymnastics, relays, calisthenics, rhythmical activities, team sports (fieldball, field hockey, soccer, speedball, basketball), and individual sports (hiking, skating, bicycling, skiing, and horseback riding).

Wartime casualties within the physical education program were recreational sports and co-recreational activities. The leisure-time sports of golf, badminton, tennis, and others were forced out of the curriculum by the demand for rugged physical fitness. The programs for boys and girls were usually completely separated, and co-recreational activities were limited for the duration. Military drill in schools and colleges, while not quite neglected, generally comprised only one part of a total program for physical fitness; it did not replace physical education.

A new apparatus to come into use was the trampoline, a raised, rigid frame to which a canvas bed is attached by means of rubber or nylon cords. Originally a circus prop, the trampoline was standardized and used during the war in military training programs, especially in naval aviation. After the war, it was generally accepted as an additional event for intercollegiate gymnastic meets.

When the war ended, the emphasis on physical fitness declined and programs stressed a variety of sports. Instruction in ten or twelve sports at a given school or college was no longer unusual. To illustrate, the service class program in physical education for men at Ohio State University for 1949–1950 consisted of the following activities: archery, badminton, basketball, boxing, fencing, golf, gymnastics and tumbling, handball, lacrosse, sailing, soccer, social dancing, squash, swimming and diving, tennis, touch football, track, volleyball, and wrestling.

The idea of spending part of the time for required physical education in the classroom occurred around 1930. An early innovator was Glenn Howard who, with his colleague, Gordon Ridings, at the Seth Low Junior College, met their students for a lecture course one period each week beginning with the 1932–33 academic year. The classroom time was supplementary to the time spent in the gymnasium. The purpose of the lecture period was to discuss reasons for the physical education requirement; to acquaint students with unfamiliar activities both within and outside the program; to relate the intercollegiate program to the objectives of physical education; and to create an appreciation of the outcomes of participation in desirable physical activities. They used a textbook, showed movies, and gave a written examination. A similar orientation course was given at Pennsylvania State University and also by a few women's departments at about the same time.[44]

Programs for the handicapped tended to become similar to the program for normal students. The formal corrective exercises were still useful in a supplemental role for specific conditions, but the individual was also encouraged to be successful in some sports activity. A trend toward emphasis on fatigue and relaxation was noted later in the period in the programs of Josephine Rathbone at Teachers College and in her writings.

DEVELOPMENTS IN SPORTS: Football rules underwent only minor changes, most of which were designed to reduce injuries. For example, helmets were required, and a ball carrier could not get up and run after one knee touched the ground. A postwar experiment was the two-platoon system, in which separate offensive and defensive teams were used. The forward pass was heavily emphasized. Night football became firmly established in both high schools and small colleges, but most large universities still played in the afternoon.

One offshoot of football was six-man football, invented by Stephen Epler in 1934 for smaller high schools which had neither the student personnel nor the money to support a regular eleven-man team. The first game was played by the students of four high schools at Hebron, Nebraska. The game seemed to fulfill a real need and within four years had spread to 1,233 high schools in forty states.[45]

Another variation of football was touch football, which found its loyal adherents in intramural and informal competition. The game provided an opportunity to utilize football skills with less chance of serious injury and without the cost of expensive equipment. It did not become a varsity sport.

Baseball underwent no significant change in its rules, but the number of players coming from colleges to the major leagues increased substantially. Night baseball was first played by the Des Moines team of the Western League in 1930, and five years later the Cincinnati Reds became the first major league team to play under lights. This innovation proved to be such a financial success that eventually all major league teams played some night games.

A college baseball game between Columbia and Princeton on May 17, 1939 achieved historical distinction as the first sporting event ever to

[44]William L. Hughes, "Orientation Courses in Physical Education for College Freshmen," *Journal of Health and Physical Education* 5 (December 1934): 22–23.
[45]Stephen Epler, *The Official Six-Man Football Guide and Rulebook* (Lincoln, Nebraska: The University Publishing Company, 1939), pp. 42–47.

be televised. The single camera, placed on a large platform close to home plate, was focused on the batter, catcher, and umpire because its range was limited to fifty feet. Only four hundred sets could pick up the game.[46]

Softball rapidly pushed its way into national prominence. The Amateur Softball Association, organized in 1933, assumed general direction of state and national competition in softball. Standard rules were finally agreed upon in 1934 by a Joint Rules Committee on Softball of the National Recreation Association, the YMCA, the NCAA, and the APEA, in cooperation with softball organizations. The depression years served as a tremendous stimulus because unemployed workers, who had time to play but could not afford baseball equipment, were attracted to the game. The addition of lights for softball fields and the smaller space requirements contributed heavily to its growth. In 1936, over ten million people were reported to be playing the game, which probably included a greater number of adult players than any other sport, and the Amateur Softball Association of America had become the largest amateur sports body in the world.[47] Inasmuch as the game could be played rather well with little practice or training and resulted in few injuries, it found solid popularity in industrial recreation programs, intramural leagues in schools and colleges, and thousands of independent teams for people of all ages and both sexes. For some reason softball was never played as a varsity sport in high school or college.

Basketball from 1930 to 1950 became faster and more exciting, with the emphasis shifting to offensive play and point scoring. Several rules changes speeded up play. In 1932 the ten-second rule was adopted; three years later the center jump was eliminated after a successful free throw, and in 1937 after a field goal as well. These changes caused an increase in the average total points scored in college games from 60.7 in 1934–35 to 75.4 in 1937–38.[48] The scoring rate continued to climb with the widespread use of the running one-hand shot and the fast-break style of offense so that a combined game score of over one hundred points was commonplace in 1950. Basketball spread to every hamlet in the United States and was played by boys and girls from grade schools through college and into adult life. College games attracted capacity crowds at Madison Square Garden and the Chicago Stadium. Intersectional contests, rare before 1935, became frequent events and helped to standardize the game.

Tennis became a popular sport at all levels—varsity, intramural, and class. The East no longer had a monopoly on the best players, and California particularly contributed many excellent players. Most important, per-

[46]Leonard Koppett, "A Little Game That Turned TV Loose on Sports," *Sports Illustrated* 22 (10 May 1965): M3–4.

[47]*Literary Digest*, 11 September 1937, p. 32.

[48]Paul Stagg, "The Development of the National Collegiate Athletic Association in Relationship to Intercollegiate Athletics in the United States" (Doctoral dissertation, New York University, 1946), p. 199.

haps, was the fact that tennis had its major appeal as an activity sport rather than as a spectator sport.

Golf offered the same possibilities as tennis for carry-over and co-recreational values. During the depression, many private golf clubs were forced to close and fewer people could afford to play. There was a consequent demand for more municipal courses, and federal money and labor helped to meet the situation by constructing new courses or maintaining old ones. Many private clubs became daily fee courses. In the summer of 1941 there were over 5,200 courses in the country, of which 2,000 were either daily fee or municipal. Golf at the country club began to revive from the disastrous effects of the depression and war, and new clubs appeared for the first time in years. Golf was a game suitable for older men and women as well as youths; in the opinion of one historian it did more than any other sport to get grown men to play.[49]

Volleyball appeared almost everywhere except in interscholastic and intercollegiate competition; a few colleges, such as Springfield and Florida State University, sponsored a varsity squad. Volleyball, like tennis and golf, owed its status to player rather than spectator interest and thus found its enthusiasts in athletic clubs, YMCAs, community centers, school and college intramural programs, on playgrounds and beaches, and at military camps during the war.

Another recreational sport was badminton. First brought to the United States in 1878, it was confined to a small exclusive group in New York City for half a century. During the 1920s, badminton swept through Canada, and the enthusiasm spilled over the border into northern cities of this country in the early 1930s.[50] English and Canadian experts toured this country and helped engender interest in the sport. In 1936, sixty-five clubs formed the American Badminton Association. The number of member clubs jumped to 155 in one year, and a national tournament was conducted. Although it was primarily an indoor game, outdoor sets for the backyard further enhanced its popularity.

Following the war, the sports of lacrosse and soccer were added to the intercollegiate programs of many colleges, either on a club basis or as a regular varsity sport. Most foreign students were well acquainted with soccer, so they played the game with interest and enthusiasm. They also shared their skills and knowledge with American players.

Postwar trends in intramural sports reflected an ever-broadening program to interest students in many less vigorous activities, such as archery, billiards, riflery, dart baseball, lawn bowling, shuffleboard, and table tennis. Other students were drawn to more active sports such as ice skating,

[49]Herbert Manchester, *Four Centuries of Sport in America, 1490–1890* (New York: The Derrydale Press, 1931), p. 231.

[50]John R. Tunis, *Sport for the Fun of It* (New York: A. S. Barnes and Company, 1940), p. 20.

hockey, badminton, crew, lacrosse, weight lifting, rugby, and bicycling. More co-recreational participation was offered after the war as colleges attempted to meet the interests of married veterans. Table tennis, volleyball, tennis, badminton, golf, bowling, and swimming were particularly appealing to both sexes.[51]

The program of sports for women expanded to include golf, tennis, badminton, volleyball, softball, bowling, and others. The most popular sports for extramural competition were archery, basketball, hockey, swimming, tennis, and badminton.[52] The movement for co-recreation grew as women developed interest in those sports in which they could attain skill comparable to that of men. High school girls were given many opportunities to learn a variety of sports.

THE DANCE: The modern dance, which began in the late 1920s, grew rapidly during the following decade. Martha Graham, Doris Humphrey, Charles Weidman, and Hanya Holm were important early leaders in the modern dance movement in America. The work of the first three has been discussed in the previous chapter. Hanya Holm, a pupil of Mary Wigman, came from Germany in 1931 and remained in this country as a teacher and leader. Mary Wigman herself made three tours of the United States. In 1932, the Dance Section was organized as part of the American Physical Education Association. Another important step in the history of the modern dance was the opening of the Bennington School of the Dance at Bennington College in Vermont in the summer of 1934. This annual summer school began under the direction of Martha Hill of New York University and Mary Josephine Shelly of the University of Chicago and continued until 1942. The Bennington School of the Dance was a meeting place for modern dance teachers and students from all over the country. In the summer of 1948, a new Summer School of the Dance was begun at Connecticut College. Three years later a department of dance was established at the famous Juilliard School of Music in New York City with Martha Hill as director.

A survey of the dance in American colleges, exclusive of teacher-training institutions, in 1947 showed that 42 percent of 526 colleges taught at least one course in modern dance. Folk dance courses were second in frequency, followed by tap, social, and square dance. Ballet had practically disappeared. The same survey revealed that seventeen colleges offered a major in dance. The modern dance movement still lacked standardization of the curriculum and an adequate bibliography.[53] A special feature of the dance movement was the enthusiasm for square dancing. Interest developed in the late 1930s encouraged by the automobile manufacturer, Henry Ford,

[51]Arthur A. Esslinger, "Extending Intramural Services," *College Physical Education Association Proceedings of the 51st Annual Meeting*, 1948, p. 17.

[52]Scott, "Competition for Women," 70–71.

[53]Phyllis Pier Valente, "The Dance in American Colleges," *Journal of the American Association for Health, Physical Education, and Recreation* 20 (May 1949): 312–13.

who maintained an institute at Greenfield Village in Michigan. After the war, square dance clubs were found in the city as well as the country, and young and old alike swung their partners with unrestrained exuberance.

Modern dance earned its place in the school and college curriculum because of its contributions to the general purposes of education and physical education. It was an extremely valuable medium for the development of strong and vigorous bodies. The steps in creating modern dance afforded opportunities for democratic experiences and social interchange. Modern dance was not primarily a display of personal skill, but it was a means of communicating and sharing with others something that was worthwhile.[54]

RECREATION AND CAMPING: Some idea of the progress of recreation may be gained from the annual report of the National Recreation Association for 1948. Community recreation programs embraced seventy-five activities which were classified into nine groups: arts and crafts, athletics and games, dancing, drama, music, outing activities, water sports, winter sports, and miscellaneous, such as gameroom activity, motion pictures, community celebrations, and hobby clubs.

Of these nine groups, athletics and games were the most popular and comprised nine out of the ten most popular activities, which were as follows: softball, baseball, basketball, horseshoes, volleyball, table tennis, swimming, tennis, storytelling, and badminton.

Some of the newer activities listed were boating, fishing, day camping, and winter sports. Since 1946, the greatest relative increase was reported in activities for older people and square dancing. Arts and crafts assumed new importance, particularly clay modeling and ceramics, leathercraft, needlecraft, weaving, and woodwork.[55] This expanded program content and the increased use effected by the lighting of outdoor facilities indicated that progress was made toward one purpose of the National Recreation Association: "That everybody in America, young or old, shall have an opportunity to find the best and most satisfying use of leisure time."

Some of the other informal recreation and outing activities that occupied millions of Americans and involved the expenditure of millions of dollars would include fishing and hunting, motorboating and sailing, bowling, skiing, and pool and billiards. These activities rounded out a recreational program available for all people, year round, indoors or outdoors.

Methods of Physical Education

The trend of physical education towards sports and athletics was positive and unmistakable. The teaching and supervision of these various activities

---

[54]Anne Schley Duggan, "The Place of Dance in the School Physical Education Program," *Journal of the American Association for Health, Physical Education, and Recreation* 22 (March 1951): 26–29.

[55]*Recreation* 42 (June 1949): 110–11.

reflected the philosophy which was striving to lessen competition in societal life and correspondingly build up co-operation. This tendency was being realized in practice in a number of ways: in athletic tests in which the individual competed against his own record instead of against his fellows; in activities in which man competed against nature; in play days and sports days in which there were enough activities for everyone to be a participant —including many novelty games and relays—which emphasized the joys of playing rather than achieving; and, in the case of intramural programs, in the favoring of sports enjoyed informally as well as in organized competition.

Teachers in the field placed less emphasis than previously on precept and preaching as factors in the development of character. Instead, they attempted to provide wholesome situations in which socially desirable habits could grow and in which the qualities of both leader and follower could be developed. Student leaders were utilized as never before and in such a way as to bring out the potentialities of programs in physical education.

Early in this period, physical education classes were generally large, sometimes having as many as a hundred students. To help with this situation, many classes were organized into teams representing various squads into which the class was divided. This competition not only added interest to the program but provided each student with experience in sharing group loyalties and leader-follower responsibilities. Unfortunately, this useful technique was abused in cases where it was not accompanied by good skills instruction. Furthermore, it was eventually realized that desirable outcomes were not automatic results of athletic participation. Psychology taught that the achievement of desirable outcomes depended on specific teaching directed toward such results.

Modern educational practice recognized that the atypical student liked to be treated the same as a normal student and that he desired normal group recognition. In the words of Stafford, "Segregation is not recommended unless the student cannot receive as good or better training with the normal group, or unless the group suffers because of his presence."[56] Segregation might be advisable for a short time to build up confidence and security, but the sooner the atypical student could engage in regular sports with the regular class, the better. Progress was evaluated by means of various tests of knowledge, achievement, and skill plus individual conferences.[57]

In this period, increased emphasis was given to the teaching of "fundamentals," i.e., the breaking up of games into fundamental or basic skills

---

[56]George T. Stafford, *Sports for the Handicapped* (Englewood Cliffs, N.J.: Prentice-Hall, Inc., 1947), p. 77.

[57]Arthur S. Daniels, "New Opportunities and Responsibilities in Physical Reconditioning," *Journal of Health and Physical Education* 17 (November 1946): 513–14.

for group instruction. The women teachers applied this type of instruction both to sports fundamentals and to rhythmic fundamentals. The mechanics of game skills were analyzed to discover if some movements or rhythms might not be basic to whole groups of skills. The acquisition of skill in these basic movements should therefore speed up learning in all skills.[58]

WARTIME PHYSICAL FITNESS EMPHASIS: Physical fitness testing received considerable emphasis and, for the first time, many high schools and colleges kept records of individual performance over a period of time. Although the value of some of the tests used was questionable, nevertheless the record-keeping reflected an interest in individual students and stimulated ways of improving their performance. Various achievement tests were used and performance was compared with achievement standards. Popular testing activities included chins, push-ups, dips, rope climb, bar vault, and running events. The obstacle course had a temporary vogue. The Navy V-12 Test, by continually raising its passing standards, showed that physical fitness could be set at a higher level. Testing for girls was less satisfactory, but the jump-reach, potato race, and swimming tests were of some value.

During World War II, mass calisthenics were commonly used, not only for their conditioning value but also because they developed a quick response to command. Students in the class often led the exercises in order to develop their ability to lead and give commands. On the whole, however, instruction in sport skills in schools and colleges was probably poorer during the war than either before or after. This was partly due to less time being allocated for instruction in skills and more time for calisthenics and conditioning and partly due to the loss of many physical education teachers to the military services.

Various insignia were used to motivate students toward physical fitness. Many of these were part of the program of the national Victory Corps organization, but some of the states gave awards or certificates for passing physical achievement tests and having health examinations.[59]

An example of the methods used by schools to develop physical fitness is provided by the recommendations in 1942 of an Indiana State Physical Fitness Committee, headed by the State Director of Health and Physical Education:

1. Every school should have a physical fitness committee to direct the physical fitness program.
2. Every boy and girl in the eleventh and twelfth grades, or sixteen years of age, shall have a physical, medical, and dental examination.

[58]Agnes Wayman, "Trends and Tendencies in Physical Education," *Journal of Health and Physical Education* 4 (February 1933): 62.
[59]Rosalind Cassidy and Hilda K. Kozman, "Trends in State Wartime Physical Fitness Programs," *Journal of Health and Physical Education* 14 (September 1943): 392.

3. A minimum of fifteen hours instruction shall be given in first aid and fifteen hours in health. One period per week should be devoted to this instruction.
4. Every pupil in the eleventh and twelfth grade should have one fifty-minute period of physical education four days a week and receive credit. Pupils in the first ten grades should have daily physical education.
5. Interschool activities should be maintained as long as possible or replaced by an extensive intramural program.
6. All school facilities should be available after school hours and during vacations for recreational activities by community groups of children and adults.
7. Regular in-service training in health, physical education, and recreation should be provided by each school for other faculty members so that they might share in the additional load or provide replacements when needed.

These recommendations were adopted by the school administrators, and the State Department of Public Instruction was requested to make them mandatory. Two physical fitness manuals were published, one for boys and one for girls.[60] A statewide survey a year later showed that most of the recommendations had been put into practice by over 75 percent of the schools. The last two recommendations were the ones least put into effect.[61]

POSTWAR TRENDS: Physical education made further advancement after the war toward standardizing programs. At some colleges and universities, the departmental staff prepared a syllabus or manual which outlined the skills, knowledge, and attitudes to be taught in each course. Furthermore, courses were planned in sequence so the individual could progress in his work in the same way that he advanced to more difficult material in academic subjects. Greater use was made of some excellent instructional movies, film strips, loop films, and records. There was some evidence, too, that the teacher of 1950 was more concerned about class size than he was in 1930 and that he preferred a class of less than forty students in order to give individual instruction and specific assistance.

TESTS AND MEASUREMENTS: The development of tests and measurements was so extensive that it will be impossible to do more than simply indicate some of the major areas of study. It was natural that the interest in sports and athletics should lead to many efforts to measure achievement in specific sports. The usual technique was to pick out one or two particular

[60]Frank S. Stafford, "The Development of a Physical Fitness Program in Indiana Schools," *Journal of Health and Physical Education* 14 (February 1943): 79–80, 125–126.

[61]Frank S. Stafford, "Indiana's Youth is Keeping Fit," *Journal of Health and Physical Education* 15 (March 1944): 127, 164.

skills that seemed to correlate well with ability to play the game and devise a short, simple test to measure these skills. Elizabeth Rodgers and Marjorie Heath developed knowledge and playing ability tests for both softball and soccer in the early 1930s.[62] These tests for many sports became so numerous that, by 1938, Glassow and Broer compiled a book of achievement tests alone.[63] Gladys Scott and Joanne Dyer also did excellent work in this field. Probably the most valid technique for evaluating athletic achievement was available only to varsity coaches who filmed football and basketball games and spent hours observing and evaluating the play of each individual.

The value of athletic achievement tests was enhanced by the computation of norms for various ages and groups, based on thousands of cases. McCloy constructed such norms for track and field events in 1932. The National Recreation Association, which had published standards for boys in track and field, games, gymnastics, and aquatics in 1929, published similar standards for girls in games, athletic events, and self-testing activities in 1935. An extensive five-year research program in the state of California resulted in the construction of achievement scales for boys and girls from the elementary grades through college. N. P. Neilson, Frederick Cozens, and Hazel Cubberley were the leaders in this tremendous task.

Problems related to classification continued to receive attention. Neilson and Cozens worked out a weighted formula using age, height, and weight, which varied from McCloy's earlier formula. McCloy developed the shorter Iowa Revision of the Brace Motor Ability Test. Granville B. Johnson also developed a test of motor educability which was useful for grouping students into homogeneous units and which gave more than the usual emphasis on stunts. Other research workers, such as Joy W. Kistler, Leonard Larson, and T. K. Cureton, developed test batteries for classification. Larson developed his battery in 1940 and then continued its use in the Army Air Force during the war. In 1944, Cureton developed the Illinois 14–item Motor Fitness Test for use in classifying postadolescent boys.

A great deal of cardiovascular research was done during the war. The Schneider test was adopted for use to help determine the fitness of aviators for flight duty. The naval aviation physical training program used the strenuous pack step test which was developed at Harvard by Lucien Brouha and others.

As physical education sought to draw closer to education in its purpose and methods, grading was no longer based solely on athletic ability or skill. In teaching activities for leisure-time use, educators expected stu-

---

[62]Elizabeth G. Rodgers and Marjorie L. Heath, "An Experiment in the Use of Knowledge and Skill Tests in Playground Baseball," *Research Quarterly* 2 (December 1931): 113–31; and "A Study in the Use of Knowledge and Skills Tests in Soccer," *Research Quarterly* 3 (December 1932): 33–53.

[63]Ruth B. Glassow and Marion R. Broer, *Measuring Achievement in Physical Education* (Philadelphia: W. B. Saunders Company, 1938).

dents not only to develop some skills but also to learn about rules, courtesy, attitudes, sportsmanship, and other concomitant outcomes. This changing philosophy led to the development of written objective-type tests of which Esther French and Gladys Scott constructed several for different sports. The measurement of personal and social qualities challenged investigators. The pioneer work of Van Buskirk and McCloy was followed by the 1932 publication of *Character Education Through Physical Education,* edited by Jay B. Nash. Charles Cowell at Ohio State and Purdue conducted studies to determine the attitudes and interests of students in physical education and stressed the contributions of physical education to social acceptability. William Lauritsen developed tests to measure sportsmanship and conceived some useful paper-and-pencil problem situations for determining attitudes.[64]

A careful evaluation of the status of tests and measurements in physical education was presented in the *Encyclopedia of Educational Research* for 1950 and is reproduced in part here:

> Although much research is still needed, we can now make a reasonably accurate appraisal of the individual's status in relation to (a) general motor or athletic ability, (b) motor fitness (sometimes designated as physical fitness), (c) specific skills, and (d) certain phases of knowledge. Classification devices used to equate performance on the basis of age, height, and weight are fairly effective, particularly for boys and girls of elementary-school age and for boys of secondary-school age. Progress has been made in measuring posture, but further research is necessary to produce more efficient and economical methods. . . . While the laboratory offered in the physical-activity classes affords an exceptional opportunity for observing behavior, we have a long road to travel in refining our measuring instruments in this area.[65]

SOME RECENT EMPHASES IN RESEARCH: After 1930, a growing number of psychological studies were made that had direct value and meaning for physical education. Problems of learning, transfer, attention, motivation, emotion, muscular tension, vision, rhythm, and reaction time were all investigated by either physical educators or psychologists. Attention was also directed to sociological studies and data that had direct bearing on physical education. A new area of interest for physical educators was cultural anthropology with its emphasis on the effect of cultural patterns upon the individual. As this period drew to a close, the trend toward psychological and sociological research was quite apparent.[66]

[64]William H. Lauritsen, "Some Techniques for Measuring Achievements of Objectives of Physical Education" (Doctoral dissertation, Ohio State University, 1939).

[65]Willard P. Ashbrook, Anna Espenschade, and Frederick W. Cozens, "Physical Education Measurement," *Encyclopedia of Education Research,* ed., Walter S. Monroe (New York: The Macmillan Company, 1950), p. 839.

[66]Harry Scott, "Graduate Instruction in Physical Education," *Teachers College Record* 50 (January 1949): 247–257.

RECREATION AND CAMPING: In this period, the recreation and camping movements developed such close relationships with physical education in respect to aims and objectives, programming, and promotion, that the methods of instruction were also similar. More and more dependence was placed on psychology and sociology in planning methodology. The relationship of recreation to mental health was more clearly expressed by writers such as John Eisele Davis. He stressed the need for setting standards of performance in relation to the individual capacity of the child himself rather than upon the ability of someone else.[67]

A growing identity between education and recreation was increasingly recognized. L. P. Jacks, the English philosopher, expressed this synthesis: "To understand the meaning of education and of recreation we must see the two in unison and not in separation."[68] With this "unison" in mind, the methods of instruction were reshaped. There was more emphasis on education for leisure, more emphasis on education in the tools, skills, and appreciations of the wider arts of living, and guidance programs for recreation were developed.

Camping showed the effects of these changed methods. There was a definite trend away from regimentation, away from enforced regulations, except where general safety was at stake, and a decreasing emphasis on competition and awards. Conversely, there were more diversified activities with more emphasis on companionship and leisurely living; more emphasis on the camp as a unit rather than an association of competing groups; and more emphasis on rest and relaxation. The camp experience of the boy or girl in the summer was more than just health-building or spending a carefree vacation: it was an educational process that supplemented school education in a number of ways. This realization encouraged the new movement of school camping and outdoor education which sought to provide a camping experience for all children in school.

SUMMARY: With the emphasis on the individual and with the stress placed on research, physical education achieved a recognized place in general education. This was reflected in various ways: teacher education courses were placed in the school of education; academic rank was bestowed upon the physical educator; students in physical education courses earned academic credit; universities offered master's and doctoral degree programs in physical education; and the national association became affiliated with the National Education Association. Furthermore, the leaders of the profession were no longer exclusively trained in medicine, but held advanced degrees in physical education. The graduate centers, started in the 1920s,

[67]John Eisele Davis, *Play and Mental Health* (New York: A. S. Barnes and Co., 1938), pp. 196–97.
[68]L. P. Jacks, *Education Through Recreation* (New York: Harper & Row, Publishers, 1932), p. 2.

began to produce professional physical educators with doctoral degrees in sufficient numbers so that by 1950 only a handful of physicians remained active.

Physical education adapted to meet the particular challenges of the depression and World War II. However, it could not look ahead to a period of normalcy and status quo. With the arrival of the nuclear age, and with the world suddenly becoming smaller and more threatening, changing conditions confronted society, the educational system, and the profession of physical education.

Physical Education
in
Education for Nationalism
Since 1950

The twenty years following 1950, unlike previous periods, were free from a prolonged depression and a total commitment to war. Citizens of the country started with the Fair Deal of President Truman, changed to Modern Republicanism under President Eisenhower, faced the New Frontier with President Kennedy, and moved into the Great Society envisioned by President Johnson. The new administration of President Nixon in 1969 was marked by caution and deliberation in its early months.

It was a period full of contrasts. The shock of three assassinations—President Kennedy, Martin Luther King, and Robert Kennedy—was tempered by national pride in the success of American astronauts and the first moon landing. Sweeping gains in social legislation and civil rights were obscured by mob violence and revolutionary reactions. The calm conformity of the fifties was swept aside by the intense individuality of the sixties which affected everything from hair styles and dress to morals and education. The Korean settlement in 1953 contrasted with the seemingly interminable military involvement in Vietnam.

Each President faced a series of international crises. In some cases the United States responded with material assistance of men and supplies, and in other cases it could only respond with words and anguish. The Hungarian revolt and the Suez Canal conflict in 1956, the Lebanon situation in 1958, the Congo revolution, the Bay of Pigs and the Berlin Wall confrontation in 1961, the Cuban missile crisis in 1962, the Dominican Republic revolt in 1965, the Arab-Israeli War of 1967, and the Russian invasion of Czechoslovakia in 1968 all posed difficult decisions and tested national policy. Yet none of these incidents so concerned the populace as did the intervention in Vietnam which dragged on year after year, involving a force of 550,000 servicemen and producing a casualty total which, in early 1969, was exceeded only by World War II and World War I. However, a significant change occurred in relations with Russia. The national anti-Communist obsession, which spawned McCarthyism and governed U.S. policy in the 1950s, shifted toward peaceful coexistence under President Kennedy. The agreement on a nuclear test ban treaty in 1963 was of immense importance and followed Russia's action in removing the missiles from Cuba. The sale of American wheat to the Soviet Union was approved with some congressional opposition, but it paved the way for increasing trade, cultural, and educational exchanges with the Russian people. Another promising sign was the start of strategic arms limitations talks in 1969 between Russian and the U.S.

In the latter part of the 1960s, many Americans began to question the extent of national involvement abroad. The maintenance of American civilian and military personnel around the world was a substantial drain on the national budget and unfavorably affected the balance of trade. On the domestic scene, many problems clamored for solution. Most urgent were the needs of the inner city and the ghetto for housing, education, and employment. In spite of the affluence, millions of Americans were found living in real poverty and severe cases of malnutrition actually existed. Adequate medical care was denied to many citizens, the growing number of elderly required attention, and air and water pollution became an increasingly greater threat to the nation's health. These were some of the reasons why the nation felt its economy could not sustain the Vietnam war and also cope with vital domestic needs. Added to these problems was a mounting inflation which developed in the late 1960s.

If it is possible to condense events in education since 1950 into a few words, one might say that an attempt was made to achieve quality and equality, but not always at the same time.

The motivation for improving the quality of education was supplied by Russia's successful launching of Sputnik in October 1957. Our national pride was hurt and our educational system was blamed for our loss of status. Many American leaders charged our educational system with these faults: it was geared primarily to the ability and needs of the average child; it did not motivate all children to develop their full potential; it placed too much emphasis on social skills; it failed to keep the curriculum content abreast of advances being made in knowledge; and it did not give teachers sufficient in-depth knowledge of their subject matter. To overcome the apparent technological superiority of Russia, demands were made to place more emphasis on the academic subjects and to give intellectually-gifted students a greater opportunity to develop their talents for the national welfare. Leading spokesmen for these demands were Vice-Admiral Hyman Rickover, John Fischer, Dean of Teachers College at Columbia University, and James Conant in his *Report on the American High Schools.* Congress gave support by passing the National Defense Education Act in 1958 which granted millions of dollars to promote the study of science, mathematics, and foreign languages.

At the same time, however, pressure for equality was growing. The old and erroneous doctrine, "separate but equal facilities," which buttressed a segregated educational system for many years, was finally declared unconstitutional by the Supreme Court in 1954. Public schools were ordered to integrate with "all deliberate speed." Progress toward this objective was slow and, at times, depended on the use of force.

The idea of academic quality for the gifted pupils, which in practice largely excluded the poor, was severely shaken during the 1960s as city after city was torn by violence and riots. The schools were called upon to reexamine the relevance of their programs for underprivileged children. The federal government provided $2300 million to local school districts through the Elementary and Secondary Education Act of 1965 to better the education of low income families. The Economic Opportunity Act provided a Job Corps program for youths between the ages of 16 and 24, many of whom were school dropouts. The Head Start program was conceived to give deprived children the preschool experiences enjoyed by middle-class youngsters. The Higher Education Act provided substantial financial assistance to colleges and their students. Administrators made a more strenuous effort to recruit minority students and to subsidize their education, and minority students placed strong pressures on administrators to expand these programs. This massive infusion of money by the federal government into education at all levels was a distinctive characteristic of this period. The problem of burgeoning enrollment alone faced by educators and the public was a Gargantuan task. Between 1950 and 1969 the number of pupils in the first twelve grades increased from 28.4 million to 51.4 million; the total of college students, from 2.7 million to 7.1 million. The estimated national expenditure for all education in 1969 was 60 billion dollars.

The sixties seemed to be a time of turbulence throughout the educational system in the United States. Parents and school boards fought over *de facto* segregation, school bussing, decentralization of authority, sex education, and religious practices. Public school teachers exercised new-found militance by picketing and striking. The American Federation of Teachers contested vigorously with the National Education Association in its effort to organize teachers' unions.

Rebellious college students expressed their dissatisfaction with the structure of society in nonnegotiable demands, protest marches, underground newspapers, strikes, riots, sit-ins, ghetto programs, political activity, long hair and hippie attire, and revolutionary rhetoric of four-letter words and verbal overkill. They were concerned about the war in Vietnam, minority student recognition, civil rights, the liberation of women, dormitory regulations, the existing morality and value systems, the relevance of the curriculum to student needs, aspirations, and problems, and greater student participation in policy making. The youths who participated in the "revolutionary movement" were not all catalyzed by the same issues and did not all belong to the same subculture. Some were destructive anarchists; some were primarily concerned with seeking excitement and adventure; some were dupes of cynically manipulative leaders; some peddled dope for profit; but others were lofty idealists who were deeply concerned about their fellow man, outraged about injustice and oppression, and committed to establishing joyful and humane styles of work and play. Many college students around the country took no part in this movement and were, in fact, critical of these actions by their peers.

The observer of American education and society could easily become discouraged and pessimistic. The problems at times seemed insurmountable, but the judgment of a contemporary historian provides some encouragement:

> "Let us not forget that, in scope, content, and universal application, American education is one of the noblest single cultural achievements of our society and, indeed, of all mankind."[1]

Perhaps the protests and criticisms were healthy indications that American education will continue to justify this praise in the years ahead. At any rate, the traditional concept of the common school serving as a unifying element in society was put to a severe test.

The undeclared war in Korea was not accompanied by a pronounced *military emphasis* or trend toward physical fitness. Yet, three years after the fighting ended, the entire nation started on a physical fitness movement which continued with little abatement through the 1960s. What the war failed to do was accomplished by an article entitled "Muscular Fitness and Health" which appeared in the *Journal of the AAHPER* in December, 1953. In this article Dr. Hans Kraus, an orthopedic surgeon, and Ruth Hirschland reported on a muscle-testing study which showed that American children were considerably inferior to European children. The report received nationwide publicity and eventually was called to President Eisenhower's attention by John B. Kelly, a prominent amateur sportsman from Philadelphia. Eisenhower then invited thirty-two sport celebrities to a White House luncheon in 1955, a President's Conference on Physical Fitness followed a year later, and the President's Council on Youth Fitness was created with Vice-President Richard Nixon as chairman. The AAHPER gave full support to the movement which rapidly picked up

[1]Mehdi Nakosteen, *The History and Philosophy of Education* (New York: The Ronald Press Company, 1965), p. 684.

momentum and later was augmented by the enthusiasm and example of President John Kennedy.

Why did physical fitness command this popularity without wartime circumstances? It was unquestionably a matter of national pride during the Cold War period. The assumption of U.S. superiority in science was shaken when the Russians orbited their first Sputnik, and evidence of the inferiority of American children in physical fitness was more than the national conscience could bear. As the political atmosphere changed from the Cold War to peaceful coexistence, the physical fitness emphasis continued to have nationalistic overtones, but an additional rationale came from medical research which began to document the contributions of physical activity to the health and efficiency of the heart and circulatory system. Thus, for the first time in the history of American physical education, programs reflected a strong physical fitness theme without the stimulus of a war.

The *scientific emphasis* continued into this period with undiminished force. An effort was made to define physical education as a scientific discipline. The scientific emphasis of the profession after 1950 was carried out in an ever-increasing number of university graduate programs. As 1970 approached, a trend toward preparing research specialists was noticeable. The area of exercise physiology dominated research efforts by physical educators and monopolized the pages of the *Research Quarterly*, due in part to the availability of grants of money from the federal government and private sources. There also developed a much closer association with the medical profession. Physical educators and physicians enjoyed a common association in the American College of Sports Medicine founded in 1954. The value of regular physical activity for good health was observed by an increasing number of physicians and scientists such as Wilhelm Raab, Paul Dudley White, Hans Kraus, and Jean Mayer. The prominence of testing was reflected in the widespread use of the Kraus-Weber Test and the AAHPER Youth Fitness Test. The AAHPER in 1962 began three important projects: the Sports Skills Tests, the Kindergarten-Fourth Grade Skills Progression, and the Sports Knowledge Tests.

Educational developmentalism was a basic theme throughout the period as physical educators sought to expand programs according to student needs and to develop the potential of each student. Physical education programs for elementary school children showed unmistakable progress as time allotments were increased. Movement education stressed the technique of individual problem-solving and encouraged each child "to rely on his own ability to adapt his physical and emotional potentials for mastering the set objective."[2] Special programs with government assistance were begun in the 1960s for underprivileged children, the handicapped, and the

---

[2]Werner Haas, "Natural Gymnastics," *Journal of Health, Physical Education, and Recreation* 31 (January 1960): 39.

mentally retarded. Girls and women rejoiced in newfound opportunities to play on interscholastic and intercollegiate teams as leaders now felt that highly skilled girls should no longer be deprived of the opportunity to achieve their highest potential through competitive sport.

The problems of slow learners in the classroom were attacked by Newell Kephart of Purdue University who felt that their difficulties were due to deficiencies in certain perceptual-motor skills. He developed a rating scale for measuring a child's perceptual-motor performance and prepared a variety of training activities which could be used to strengthen these weaknesses.[3] The whole area of perceptual motor learning was studied by physical educators in the May 1966 issue of *Quest* magazine, at the American Academy of Physical Education meetings in 1967, and by the AAHPER Symposium in 1968.

The ideas of the Harvard psychologist, Jerome Bruner, influenced many physical educators. Bruner underscored the need for relating specific skills or topics to a broader field of knowledge in order for learning to be most effective. The best way to create interest in a subject was "to render it worth knowing which means to make the knowledge gained usable in one's thinking beyond the situation in which the learning has occurred."[4]

The value of *social education* reached a new peak of relevance in the 1960s as disorder, demonstrations, and physical confrontations became commonplace in American life. The Chicago riots of 1966 exploded when police turned off fire hydrants on a hot July night in a Negro section of the city. In only one of four nearby municipal swimming pools were Negroes allowed to swim. Similarly, deprivation in the area of public recreation was a cause of rioting in Jersey City, Cleveland, New York, Omaha, and elsewhere.[5] Much effort and money was expended to better meet the social and recreational needs of urban residents. The teaching of sports for leisure time, which was accepted in the previous period, received encouragement through the Outdoor Education Project started in 1955 and the Lifetime Sports Foundation organized in 1965. Both projects were supervised by the AAHPER but financed by private industry. Leaders of interscholastic and intercollegiate competition for girls and women emphasized social outcomes for the participants. Coeducational programs and school camping found much wider acceptance and practice.

In summarizing the influence of the four themes on physical education since 1950, no one theme was dominant. In fact, this was the only period in which all four themes were so equal in their importance, particularly

[3]Newell C. Kephart, *The Slow Learner in the Classroom* (Columbus, Ohio: Charles E. Merrill Books, Inc., 1960).

[4]Jerome S. Bruner, *The Process of Education* (Cambridge, Mass.: Harvard University Press, 1960), p. 31.

[5]Richard Kraus, *Public Recreation and the Negro* (New York: Center for Urban Education, 1968), pp. 17–19.

after 1955, and they all materially shaped the purposes, programs, and methods of the profession.

Aims of Education

During the early 1950s education was considerably influenced by the Life Adjustment Movement. This was formally started in 1947 with the appointment of a Commission on Life Adjustment Education for Youth by the U.S. Commissioner of Education, John Studebaker. The purpose of the movement was to "better equip all American youth to live democratically with satisfaction to themselves and profit to society as home members, workers, and citizens."[6] The Commission recognized that this objective had been stated many times before, beginning with the Seven Cardinal Principles in 1918, and therefore considered its prime function to be one of stimulating action to reduce the lag between pronouncement and practice. The Life Adjustment curriculum embraced guidance services, citizenship education, home and family life education, health and safety, use of leisure time, consumer education, ethical and moral living, and work experiences.

The life adjustment concept was attacked by critics such as Arthur Bestor, Albert Lynd, and others who urged an emphasis on intellectual development and scholarship. The space race with Russia gave a rationalization for these critics and further validation came from a report by the Educational Policies Commission in 1961 which narrowed the aims of education to one: the development of the ability to think.[7]

Within a short time, however, the expression of long-standing frustration of minority groups by boycotts, freedom rides, sit-ins, and eventually rioting forced educators and leaders to recognize that the schools were not meeting the needs of many students nor playing a wholly pertinent role in society. The U.S. Commissioner of Education, Harold Howe II, advocated job training for every non-college-bound student as an essential step in combating crime and delinquency.[8] Ralph Tyler added two new purposes to the traditional ones—"reaching the disadvantaged and making the high school effective for a large proportion of the population."[9] The newer community schools aimed for firsthand learning, a life-relevant curriculum, and social improvement. Thus, the new aims of education at the end of the

[6]U.S. Office of Education, *Life Adjustment Education for Every Youth* (Washington, D.C.: Federal Security Agency, n.d.), p. 4.

[7]Educational Policies Commission, *The Central Purpose of American Education* (Washington, D.C.: National Education Association, 1961), p. 12.

[8]Harold Howe II, "Education and Social Reconstruction," *Educational Leadership* 25 (January 1968): 321–22.

[9]Ralph W. Tyler, "Purposes for Our Schools," *Bulletin of the National Association of Secondary-School Principals* 52 (December 1968): 10.

1960s resembled those stated twenty years earlier by the proponents of life adjustment education.

Aims of Physical Education

Previously stated aims of physical education carried over into the post-1950 period with no marked change in substance. There was some debate about how much emphasis should be given to achieving organic development and physical fitness. McCloy believed that the physical aspects are primary to our field and should be a major responsibility. Oberteuffer contended that physical education is concerned with the whole person and that it is impossible to deal "primarily" with any one aspect. The AAHPER Fitness Conference in 1956 agreed that fitness is the degree to which a person is able to function and that it has physical, mental, emotional, social, and spiritual components which are mutually interdependent.

The intellectual content of physical education received more attention. The purpose was stated as follows: "To develop an understanding and appreciation of certain scientific principles concerned with movement that relate to such factors as time, space, force, and mass-energy relationships."[10] Additional aims were to teach people to become more sophisticated spectators, to be knowledgeable consumers in purchasing equipment, and to understand the relationship between physical activity and good physical and mental health.

The purpose of movement education was stated by Naomi Allenbaugh as education "for efficiency of movement and for self-discovery, self-direction, and self-realization."[11] The phenomenologist sought the understanding of self with the ultimate goal for the student to "create on his own an experience through movement which culminates in meaningful, purposeful realization of the self."[12]

As a final point, the older objective of leisure-time preparation gained renewed urgency as industry moved toward more automation and a 30-hour work week.

Promotion of Physical Education

The effects of the national concern for physical fitness were felt in school programs throughout the country and at all grade levels. A report in 1963

[10]American Association for Health, Physical Education, and Recreation, *This Is Physical Education* (Washington, D.C.: AAHPER, 1965), p. 3.

[11]Naomi Allenbaugh, "Learning About Movement," *National Education Association Journal* 56 (March 1967): 48.

[12]Seymour Kleinman, "The Significance of Human Movement: A Phenomenological Approach," in *National Association of Physical Education for College Women Report* (Washington, D.C.: AAHPER, 1964), p. 126.

stated that 20 million public school children out of 26 million in grades 4 to 12 took part in regular physical fitness programs, a gain of 2.1 million over the previous year. Eight states required daily physical education for elementary schools, and California required daily physical education for all students for several years. Thirty states had a state fitness council or commission.[13] The United States Office of Education found that 56 percent of 108,000 public schools had strengthened their programs of physical education in one year. Also 11,000 boys and girls who took the Youth Fitness Test in 1964–65 had higher mean scores for every event and at all ages, except one, than those who took the test in 1957–58. The lone exception was for 16- and 17-year-old girls in the softball throw.[14]

These and other tangible results were produced by many factors. Some of the most influential were the following:

1. The AAHPER Youth Fitness Test. This seven-item test was drawn up under the direction of Paul Hunsicker of the University of Michigan in 1957–58 with norms for boys and girls from the fifth through the twelfth grades. It was officially adopted by forty-three states and was administered to over twenty million children in the first two years alone.

2. The President's Council on Youth Fitness. This group was most effective in the early 1960s when it had the full backing of President Kennedy, the leadership of Charles (Bud) Wilkinson, the highly successful football coach from the University of Oklahoma, and the assistance of Simon A. McNeely from the Office of Education. The Council received excellent publicity in promoting a minimum of fifteen minutes a day of vigorous activity for all children. The Council sold or distributed half a million copies of a booklet, *Youth Physical Fitness: Suggested Elements of a School-Centered Program.* It also prepared six movies with the cooperation of private industry.

3. Operation Fitness—U.S.A. This was a massive campaign launched in 1958 by the AAHPER to stimulate fitness nationally. It included the Youth Fitness testing program, a track and field project for thirty million youths, the Sports Skills Test project, and an array of promotional materials such as certificates, emblems, and uniforms.

4. President John F. Kennedy. President Kennedy used his personal appeal and high office to encourage the development of fitness for all Americans. He wrote an article, "The Soft American," for a national sports magazine in which he declared: "The President and

13"Progress Report from the President's Council on Physical Fitness," *Journal of Health, Physical Education, and Recreation* 34 (October 1963): 10.

14Paul A. Hunsicker and Guy G. Reiff, "A Survey and Comparison of Youth Fitness, 1958–1965," *Journal of Health, Physical Education, and Recreation* 37 (January 1966): 23–25.

all departments of government must make it clearly understood that the promotion of sports participation and physical fitness is a basic and continuing policy of the United States."[15] He also sent a message to all schools in the country urging them to follow the recommendations in *Youth Physical Fitness.*

Some professional leaders deplored the passion for physical fitness because they feared it would limit programs to calisthenics and fitness tests. However, Ray Duncan spoke for those holding a different view when he wrote:

> The national interest in physical fitness has established the most favorable climate for health, physical education, and recreation that has ever existed in the history of American education. . . . I am convinced that we should applaud this situation, accept it with pleasure, and set about to interpret to the pupils, parents, and patrons of our schools what physical fitness means.[16]

In recalling the American drive for academic excellence in the late 1950s and the strong push for concentration in science, one realizes that the physical fitness movement served as an important balancing and countering force.

A definite beneficiary of the fitness activities was elementary school physical education. The self-contained classroom, which was common in the 1950s, had reduced the need for special teachers, including physical education. In the 1960s for the first time there was an insistent demand for elementary school teachers of physical education. Schools began to allocate time for physical education in addition to the recess period. Federal money was used for the extension and enrichment of elementary programs in such cities as New Orleans, Plattsburg, New York, and Ellensburg, Washington.

College physical education generally held its own and a 1969 nationwide study showed that only six percent had no required physical education. Within the past five years fifteen percent of the colleges had increased their requirement and fourteen percent had decreased it.[17] During the mid-1950s the physical education requirement was questioned at over fifty institutions—notably the University of Illinois, the University of California at Los Angeles, and the University of Wyoming—but in most cases it was successfully defended. However, in the late 1960s there was an indication

[15]John F. Kennedy, "The Soft American," *Sports Illustrated* 13 (26 December 1960): 17.

[16]Ray O. Duncan, "Fundamental Issues in Our Profession," *Journal of Health, Physical Education, and Recreation* 35 (May 1964): 21.

[17]Joseph Oxendine, "Status of Required Physical Education Programs in Colleges and Universities," *Journal of Health, Physical Education, and Recreation* 40 (January 1969): 32.

that some colleges were changing to an elective program and, surprisingly perhaps, without great opposition from the department of physical education. College physical educators in a joint committee of the CPEA, AAHPER, and NCAA headed by Delbert Oberteuffer, recommended that veterans should receive credit for physical education only on a basis of equivalent experience in the service, not automatically or on a blanket basis. The Committee also opposed the substitution of military science for physical education.[18] One trend during this time was a tendency for departments of physical education to separate from intercollegiate athletics in the larger institutions because of a growing incompatibility in philosophy and principle between physical education and the conduct of a bigtime athletic program.

PROFESSIONAL PREPARATION: In June 1969, prospective teachers of health, physical education, and recreation were graduated from about 650 institutions of higher learning. Master's degrees were conferred at 200 colleges, and doctoral degrees were awarded at 50 universities. The postwar baby boom began to reach the country's graduate schools in 1968 and greatly increased enrollments were forecast for the next five years.

During this period of spectacular growth, the teacher preparation programs were closely scrutinized by legislatures, university administrators, and professional organizations. The conclusion was reached that prospective teachers devoted considerable time learning how to teach and too little time pursuing in-depth, up-to-date knowledge about their subject matter. As a consequence many institutions revised their teacher-preparatory programs. In most instances a two-year liberal arts background was made a prerequisite for a two to three-year program of specialization. Some of the previous physical education courses were consolidated or dropped, the amount and depth of knowledge in the academic physical education courses were increased, and a somewhat greater degree of specialization was encouraged than in the past. As a result, the preparation of general practitioners of health education, physical education, safety education, and recreation may gradually be replaced by specialists within each of these areas. The separation of health education and recreation from physical education is taking place both at the undergraduate and graduate level.

The preparation of athletic trainers moved from an apprenticeship service to a professional program during this period. This change was sparked by the National Athletic Trainers Association (NATA), established in 1951 through the work of William (Pinky) Newell, Charles Cramer, and others. By 1969 the first four schools were approved by the NATA to offer a curriculum leading to certification as an athletic trainer.

[18]College Committee on Physical Education and Athletics, "College Physical Education for Peace and Defense," *College Physical Education Association 53rd Annual Proceedings, 1950,* pp. 134–35.

To meet the need for coaches in expanding interscholastic programs, pressures had developed for recognizing a minor in coaching for students who majored in subjects other than physical education. A coaching minor was recommended by the Ohio Green Meadows Conference in 1965 and again by the AAHPER Task Force in 1968. Florida State University and the University of California at Santa Barbara were among the first to offer this minor.

Long-standing efforts to improve teacher education made definite forward strides between 1950 and 1970. The leadership of Carl Nordly in developing evaluative criteria and working with the National Council for the Accreditation of Teacher Education (NCATE) in the 1950s was a firm foundation for the important contributions of the AAHPER Professional Panel in the 1960s. This 12-man panel was appointed in 1963 with Arthur Esslinger as chairman. Its major accomplishments were the following:

1. Publicized the work of the Professional Preparation Conference of 1962. Two conference recommendations were for a five-year undergraduate program and for devoting half of a four-year program to general education.
2. Developed self-evaluation checklists which were sent to the presidents of all colleges in the country with a major program.
3. Established effective working relationships with NCATE.
4. Set up a nationwide organization with district and state representatives to assist institutions in improving programs.
5. Initiated the 1967 Conference on Graduate Education in Washington.[19]

The panel also publicly challenged the views of James Conant as expressed in his book, *The Education of American Teachers.* He was critical of accreditation and certification and believed that graduate programs in physical education should be abolished.

The passage of the Fisher Bill in California in 1961 caused educators in many fields to reexamine the content of their teacher education programs. This bill defined academic and nonacademic areas of study and stipulated that teachers could not hold administrative positions unless they had majored in an academic area. Physical education was identified as a nonacademic area which could qualify for academic status by meeting certain criteria. Some institutions attained this status because they could demonstrate that their programs were drawn from concepts and principles in anatomy, physiology, cultural anthropology, history, sociology, psychology, and physics that would give students in-depth knowledge about human movement.

[19]Raymond A. Snyder, "Work of the Professional Preparation Panel," *Journal of Health, Physical Education, and Recreation* 39 (January 1968): 73.

The academically oriented physical education program is quite different from the education oriented program. At the University of California at Berkeley, for example, the Department of Physical Education is in the College of Letters and Science and offers an A.B. major in physical education which is considered an academic discipline. Students who intend to teach activities take some elective activity and education courses, but the required courses are basically academic. Graduates of the program may obtain a teaching credential, not a master's degree, by taking a fifth year of study; or they may pursue an academic M.A. program which is research oriented; or they may take a somewhat longer time to pursue a M.A. and a teacher credential program concurrently.

In the 1960s the curriculum, professional journals, and new textbooks began to reflect the impact that had been made by a number of professional meetings which sought to establish physical education as an academic discipline. At the National Conference on Interpretation of Physical Education in 1961, Ruth Abernathy spoke of a mounting concern in some colleges to try to determine an identifiable body of knowledge justified by basic, rather than applied, research.[20] The identification of a body of knowledge relating to physical education was the subject for informal discussion at meetings of the American Academy of Physical Education beginning in 1962 and leading to the Design Conference in 1965 which was financed by the Athletic Institute and cosponsored by the national Association and the Academy. Physical education personnel from the Western Conference schools started a similar study in 1964 and identified six areas of knowledge: sociology of sport and physical education; administrative theory; history, philosophy, and comparative physical education and sport; exercise physiology; biomechanics; and motor learning and sports psychology.[21] The AAHPER furthered the movement by sponsoring the Conference on the Theoretical Structure of Physical Education at Zion, Illinois in 1969 which attempted to structure a unified theory of human movement that would give a complete and interrelated description of human movement phenomona and would separate physical education from the disciplines upon which it now draws. Some of the leaders in the academic discipline movement were Eleanor Metheny, Franklin Henry, Leonard Larson, Celeste Ulrich, Louis Alley, D. B. Van Dalen, Warren Fraleigh, and John Nixon.

During the period of transition in the 1960s, some institutions continued to prepare general practitioners exclusively, some developed programs for teachers or coaches in specific areas, some trained scholars and researchers to advance knowledge in the field which might or might not be

[20]*Report of the National Conference on Interpretation of Physical Education* (Chicago: The Athletic Institute, Inc., 1962), p. 34.

[21]Earle F. Zeigler and King J. McCristal, "A History of the Big Ten Body-of-Knowledge Project in Physical Education," *Quest* 9 (December 1967): 83.

followed by a teacher credential program, and some institutions, such as the Universities of Iowa and Wisconsin, developed a two-track program to prepare practitioners as well as scholars. Some of the institutions that have established discipline-oriented programs are now in the process of retitling their departments with such names as Department of Ergonomics and Physical Education, Department of Kinesiology, and Department of Human Movement.

The graduate program expanded rapidly after 1950 because of the demand for highly qualified teachers and administrators to deal with the expanded enrollment, government grants to institutions and to students, draft deferment for students, and teacher internships, scholarships, and loans which were widely offered. Because the federal government recognized the importance of research, federal funds were made available to equip research laboratories and to conduct research studies. As a result, 151 institutions had research facilities in 1966. Fifty-eight of them were for exercise physiology, 40 for measurement, 27 for motor learning, 24 for kinesiology, and 12 for growth and development.[22] Graduate students began to concentrate in special areas of study more than students had in the past. Computers, telemetry, and a new array of research tools and techniques enabled them to investigate problems that could not be undertaken previously. The research became more theoretically oriented and more experimental research was reported than in the past when most doctoral dissertations were descriptive studies. The number of doctoral candidates increased, and some universities dropped the requirement for a master's thesis.

The dissemination of research information is always essential for scientific progress. One source was the microcard project begun about 1950 and carried on since then by H. Harrison Clarke of the University of Oregon. Another valuable aid was the Dissertation Abstracts series which published abstracts and sold microfilms of completed dissertations. The American College of Sports Medicine served to bring together research specialists from several disciplines and shared in the publication of the *Journal of Sports Medicine and Physical Fitness* started in 1961. A significant conference was the Colloquium on Exercise and Fitness held at Monticello, Illinois in 1959.

It would be impossible to name all those who have provided distinguished leadership in research but among those who had retired or were near retirement at the end of this period were Arthur H Steinhaus of George Williams College, Thomas K. Cureton of Springfield College and the University of Illinois, David K. Brace of the University of Texas, Anna

---

[22]Ben W. Miller, "Physical Education Programs in the United States," *International Council on Health, Physical Education, and Recreation, 10th International Congress, 1967* (Washington, D.C.: ICHPER, 1968), p. 117.

Espenschade and Franklin Henry of the University of California at Berkeley, Karl Bookwalter at Indiana University, Frances Hellebrandt and Ruth Glassow of the University of Wisconsin, and John Lawther at Pennsylvania State University. A great loss occurred with the death of the versatile Charles Harold McCloy in 1959. But it is certain that other competent young men and women are stepping forward to carry on their work.

PROFESSIONAL ORGANIZATIONS: The American Association for Health, Physical Education, and Recreation kept the same name and employed the same executive-secretary, Carl A. Troester, Jr., during this twenty-year period. The total Association income jumped from $126,000 in 1950 to $2,430,000 in 1968, and the membership climbed from 17,000 to almost 49,000. The Association paused in 1960 to observe its seventy-fifth anniversary at Miami Beach, and for this occasion its history was recorded by Mabel Lee and Bruce L. Bennett in a special anniversary issue of the *Journal*.[23] More important, however, were the services and work of the Association, and this story may be told under these headings:

1. Consultant services. The AAHPER employed twelve full-time consultants in 1970 compared with two in 1950. They worked in the areas of girls' and women's sports, men's athletics, recreation and outdoor education, health and safety education, elementary education, international development, Western states, programs for the handicapped, dance, school nursing, and student services.
2. Publications. These became a major part of Association business and produced an income of over $700,000 in 1968 which was nearly thirty percent of total income. Twenty to thirty new titles were published each year.
3. Conferences. Each year the Association called about a dozen conferences, symposiums, and committee meetings, for special interest groups of all kinds.
4. Special projects. A distinctively new operation during this period was the work of the Association in getting grants of money outside the organization to support special projects. Supervision was provided by AAHPER personnel. This added up to $823,000 for 1968. The first one, the Outdoor Education Project, started in 1955. Others included the Peace Corps, College Scholarship Awards, Lifetime Sports, Bowling, Recreation and Fitness for the Mentally Retarded, and Operation Fitness. A number of physical educators served in the Peace Corps in various parts of the world.
5. Legislation. From its central location in the nation's capital, Association officers attempted to support federal legislation desirable for the profession and to work with members of Congress and other government officials.

[23]See Mabel Lee and Bruce L. Bennett, "This Is Our Heritage," *Journal of Health, Physical Education, and Recreation* 31 (April 1960): 25–85.

6. The National Foundation for Health, Physical Education, and Recreation. This was started in 1966 by the Association as a private, nonprofit corporation to receive contributions for various professional enterprises. One of its first actions was to provide rental for the new Association archives in Washington.

7. Negroes. In 1961 the AAHPER appointed a committee to study methods of improving services to Negro members. Four years later, all state associations were asked to accept members regardless of race. The first Negro to occupy a staff position was John C. Mitchem who succeeded Carolyn Bookwalter as professional editor of the *Research Quarterly* in 1969.

Much of the success of the Association over the years has been due to the voluntary efforts of its presidents who have uniformly exhibited leadership of a high caliber. Their names and years in office are given below:[24]

Edward Hitchcock	1885–87	Strong Hinman	1934–35
William Blaikie	1887–90	Agnes R. Wayman	1935–36
Dudley A. Sargent	1890–91	William G.	
Edward M.		Moorhead	1936–37
Hartwell	1891–92	Charles H.	
Dudley A. Sargent	1892–94	McCloy	1937–38
Jay W. Seaver	1894–95	Neils P. Neilson	1938
Edward M.		Frederick W.	
Hartwell	1895–99	Cozens	1938–39
Dudley A. Sargent	1899–01	Margaret Bell	1939–40
Watson L. Savage	1901–03	Hiram A. Jones	1940–41
Luther H. Gulick	1903–07	Anne Schley	
George L. Meylan	1907–11	Duggan	1941–42
R. Tait McKenzie	1912–15	Jay B. Nash	1942–43
Ernst H. Arnold	1915–16	August H. Pritzlaff	1943–44
William H.		William L. Hughes	1944–46
Burdick	1917–19	Helen Manley	1946–47
Dudley B. Reed	1920–22	Vaughn S.	
Carl L. Schrader	1923–25	Blanchard	1947–48
Charles W. Savage	1926–28	Ruth Evans	1948–49
Frederick W.		Carl L. Nordly	1949–50
Maroney	1929–30	Dorothy S.	
Mabel Lee	1931–32	Ainsworth	1950–51
Jesse Feiring		Frank S. Stafford	1951
Williams	1932–33	Bernice R. Moss	1951–52
Mary Channing		Clifford L. Brownell	1952–54
Coleman	1933–34	Ruth Abernathy	1954–56

[24]Mabel Lee, "Of Historical Interest," *Journal of Health, Physical Education, and Recreation* 39 (January 1968): 29.

Ray O. Duncan	1956–58	Catherine L. Allen	1964–65
Pattric Ruth		Reuben B. Frost	1965–66
O'Keefe	1958–59	Leona Holbrook	1966–67
Arthur A. Esslinger	1959–60	Joy W. Kistler	1967–68
Minnie L. Lynn	1960–61	Mabel Locke	1968–69
Arthur S. Daniels	1961–62	John M. Cooper	1969–70
Anita Aldrich	1962–63	Laura Mae Brown	1970–71
Ben W. Miller	1963–64		

The American Association for Health, Physical Education, and Recreation has moved into a strong position of action and leadership in the profession, but some individuals feel that the organization has grown too big and unwieldy and that it has tried to cover too many areas. Significant organizational changes may be forthcoming which could result in a federation plan or a splitting-off of some groups. Separate areas, such as health and recreation, are motivated by a desire for professional status and better recognition. They also prefer more autonomy in handling their own business.

The College Physical Association became the National College Physical Education Association for Men (NCPEAM) in 1964. A western division covering eleven states developed during this period. A most notable accomplishment was the cooperation of the NCPEAM and the National Association of Physical Education for College Women in starting *Quest* magazine in 1963. Elwood Craig Davis and Donna Mae Miller served as first editors. This twice-a-year publication has more than lived up to its editorial hope of providing "a creative literary journal for the members of our profession" and its commitment to publish "scholarly papers of philosophical and scientific interest."

Another professional publication is *The Physical Educator*, a quarterly magazine of Phi Epsilon Kappa, a professional fraternity for men. This publication favors articles of a more practical nature. R. R. Schreiber has been either editor or general manager since it started as *The Black and Gold* in 1940. C. O. Jackson has been editor since 1950. There are three active professional sororities for women—Pi Lambda Theta, Phi Delta Pi, and Delta Psi Kappa. The latter makes an annual research award to a graduate student.

The Athletic Institute continued its fine program of enlightened financial support for many worthy professional enterprises. A major part of its success was due to the excellent leadership of Colonel Ted Bank who retired in 1966 after being president for twenty-one years.

COLLEGE AND SCHOOL ATHLETICS: Intercollegiate athletics enjoyed a period of lusty growth in spite of some betting scandals, slush funds, and other illegal operations. Two major educational organizations—the American Council on Education and the North Central Association—offered their solutions for the problems of college athletics in 1952 with no apparent effect. College football players performed before a new record of 27.6 million spectators in 1969. This was an era when many attractive new arenas were constructed on college campuses for the fans of basketball. Huge fieldhouses provided facilities for a variety of sports. A number of colleges added indoor ice rinks to their facilities, but none surpassed that at Bowling Green State University in Ohio which has separate ice sheets for hockey, figure skating, and curling. Engineering advances in ice manufacturing enabled even southern colleges, such as the University of Tennessee, to have a hockey team.

The most striking change in interscholastic athletics was the addition of new sports. The executive secretary of the National Federation of State High School Athletic Associations found that the average number of sports sponsored by a high school increased from three in 1946 to eight in 1969.[25] Junior high school athletic competition stubbornly refused to yield any ground to its numerous and eminent critics, including James Conant. A thorough study in 1958 confirmed that eighty-five percent of the junior high schools had some interscholastic competition. Of the schools planning to make changes, two out of three were going to broaden the program.[26]

Both high school and college athletic programs felt the growing tensions and financial problems of the inner city, the pressure for bringing minority groups into the mainstream of American life, and many other cultural changes. Many high schools eliminated night games because of the disruptions and violence that occurred during or after these events. Some high school athletic programs were curtailed or had to find support from other sources because of the many demands on the tax dollar. Some student governments in the colleges curtailed the funds they had previously allotted for athletic activities and used the money to develop social action or ghetto programs. Coaches had to cope with intensive competition in recruiting, the increased use of college sports programs as a stepping-stone to professional athletics, the number of married college athletes, the emergence of a drug culture among the student body, and the right of athletes to grow beards and wear long hair. There were strong pressures from the black community to eliminate racial attitudes and practices, to boycott contests in which racial discrimination was practiced, and to employ black coaches.

[25]Clifford B. Fagan, "Increased Participation in Interscholastic Athletics—A Sport for Every Boy—Every Boy in a Sport," *Ohio High School Athlete* 38 (February 1969): 128.

[26]Ellsworth Tompkins and Virginia Roe, "A Survey of Interscholastic Athletic Programs in Separately Organized Junior High Schools," *Bulletin of the National Association of Secondary-School Principals* 42 (November 1958): 3–4.

NCAA, NAIA, AND NJCAA: After the Sanity Code was abandoned, the NCAA membership settled for a three-man fact-finding committee to study alleged infractions and report them to the NCAA Council for punitive action. The national tournament championships were enlarged by adding wrestling, track, skiing, soccer, trampoline, water polo, and volleyball. Boxing was eliminated. The NCAA established the College Division in 1957 to better meet the needs of the smaller institutions who resented the dominance of the large universities. The College Division had 390 members out of the total active membership of 613 in 1969.

The formation of the College Division was undoubtedly a response to the success of a rival organization, the National Association of Intercollegiate Athletics. The NAIA began in 1940 as the National Association of Intercollegiate Basketball, thanks to the efforts of Emil S. Liston of Baker University in Kansas. After Liston's death, A. O. Duer became executive secretary in 1949 and the association soon began to move away from its singular promotion of basketball. It assumed its present name in 1952 and added national tournaments in track, golf, and tennis to the basketball. The NAIA in 1969 has competition in fifteen sports for its 520 member colleges who are drawn mainly from institutions with less than 3,000 students. Unlike the NCAA, the NAIA has consistently supported the AAU, and it has stressed the Olympic sports.

After a period of relative calm, relations between the NCAA and the AAU became strained once again. President Kennedy appointed General Douglas MacArthur as an arbitrator in 1962 to insure a representative team for the 1964 Olympic Games. The U.S. Senate intervened in 1965 and created a sports arbitration board headed by a labor arbitrator, Theodore W. Kheel. After two years of study, the board came up with a set of recommendations which pleased the AAU but was rejected by the NCAA. In the meantime the NCAA took the lead in organizing separate federations for track and field, gymnastics, basketball, and wrestling without the cooperation of the AAU. Thus the matter stands, with athletes caught in the middle of this continual tug-of-war which may achieve final settlement only in Congress or the federal courts.

The NCAA collaborated with the federal government in a plan to meet one of the urgent problems of the period through a National Summer Sports Program first conducted in 1969. One hundred colleges in fifty-four metropolitan areas opened their facilities and used their staffs to provide sports activity for thousands of inner city youth.

Athletic competition for junior colleges is supervised by the National Junior College Athletic Association (NJCAA) which started in 1938 with thirteen members, all from California. Membership grew at a modest pace to 260 by 1960 but then accelerated to 462 schools in just eight years. The NJCAA conducted national tournaments in twelve sports during the 1968–69 school year. It joined with the NFSHSAA and the NAIA in 1957 to form the National Alliance. The first full-time executive director took office in 1969 at the national headquarters in Hutchinson, Kansas.

INTRAMURAL SPORTS: The founding of the National Intramural Association in 1950 and the development of graduate programs for intramural directors marked another step toward greater specialization within the field. The director of intramural sports was more likely to be a full-time job and not a part-time responsibility assigned to a coach in his off-season. Intramural sports also derived some benefits from the new facilities constructed for varsity teams, and some institutions, such as Purdue, Illinois, and Michigan State universities, erected impressive structures primarily for intramural activities.

One pronounced development was the formation of sports clubs in a limitless variety of activities. In some cases these student group activities later became varsity sports, but more often than not they remained as clubs, providing informal activity and frequently some extramural competition for the members. The clubs were attractive to those students who disliked the regimentation of varsity competition or who did not meet the restrictive eligibility rules, and they met the social needs of other students who did not care for the traditional intramural competition. These sports clubs, which were largely student-directed, were ideally suited to the prevailing mood of the student generation.

There was some tendency on large campuses to separate the administration of the intramural program from the department of physical education and to combine it with other recreational programs under one head located in the top administrative echelon of the university. As an example, intramural sports at UCLA were handled by the Office of Cultural and Recreational Affairs.

GIRLS' AND WOMEN'S SPORTS: The specter of interscholastic and intercollegiate competition, which had long been viewed with mixed feelings by women leaders, was greeted in the late 1960s with unabashed enthusiasm. In analyzing reasons for the opposition, Phebe Scott pinpointed the following:

1. Belief that competition might be harmful physically.
2. Undesirable examples from the boys' programs.
3. A philosophy of mass participation.
4. Cultural belief that girls should be homemakers, not sportswomen.[27]

[27]Phebe Scott, "Secondary School Athletic Programs for Girls," *Theory Into Practice* 3 (June 1964): 99. This is a publication of the College of Education, Ohio State University.

An outcome of the restrictions on school and college participation was that girls sought outside competition under less than satisfactory conditions in many cases.

The first specific organizational step in this direction was the formation in 1960 of the National Joint Committee on Extramural Sports for College Women by representatives of the Division for Girls' and Women's Sports of the AAHPER, the NAPECW, and the Athletic and Recreation Federation of College Women. This committee's operation proved to be as cumbersome as its title, and it was dissolved five years later. It was succeeded in 1966 by the Commission on Intercollegiate Athletics for Women (CIAW) under the DGWS. The first members were Phebe Scott, Maria Sexton, and Katherine Ley, chairman. The Commission set about to develop guidelines for intercollegiate competition, establish a sanctioning service, and sponsor national tournaments. The first national championships were in gymnastics and track and field in 1969 while the Commission also took under its wing the existing tournaments in golf and tennis.

Women's competition received further encouragement from the U.S. Olympic Development Committee which appointed a Women's Advisory Board in 1961. The purpose was to broaden the base of participation for girls and women in Olympic sports and to provide better experience for the skilled athlete. Sarah Staff Jernigan of Stetson University was instrumental in setting up a series of five National Olympic Institutes on Girls' Sports between 1963 and 1969. Hundreds of teachers and coaches attended them and returned home to conduct workshops for others in their areas.

It should be mentioned that the National Section on Women's Athletics became the National Section for Girls' and Women's Sports (NSGWS) in 1953. This was changed to the Division of Girls' and Women's Sports (DGWS) four years later. The Athletic Federation of College Women broadened its title to the Athletic and Recreation Federation of College Women (ARFCW) in 1959. It made a major move three years later when it affiliated with the DGWS and opened a permanent office at AAHPER headquarters with a consultant in charge. The ARFCW publishes the *Sportlight* three times a year.

The supervision of interscholastic sports for girls was turned over to the state high school athletic associations which, in most instances, involved women physical educators in developing policies and regulations. It was also evident that extramural competition was dropping down to the junior high level, and the DGWS published standards for these grades in 1966. The latest wave of the future may come out of a one-year experimental project in New York state which allowed high school girls to participate on boys' team in non-contact sports.

Women leaders express confidence that they can provide high level competition and still avoid the snares and pitfalls which have littered the path of athletics for men. CIAW stands opposed to athletic scholarships for women athletes, but McCue found 21 colleges already granting athletic scholarships in 1962.[28] The success of the CIAW and the DGWS will have to be judged by a future historian.

NONSCHOOL AGENCIES: The sight of children playing pick-up games on vacant lots or in the streets often observed in the 1930s was a rare occurrence in the 1960s. In its place were youngsters in resplendent uniforms playing scheduled games under adult supervision and disrupting family suppertimes and vacation schedules.

Little League baseball was started in Williamsport, Pennsylvania by a businessman, Carl Stotz, in 1939. Not much happened until after the war, but then it really caught on and by 1953 over 11,000 teams were playing in 46 states. Older boys played baseball in the Pony League, the Little Bigger League, the Babe Ruth League, and the American Legion League. Boys and girls also played Biddy Basketball, started in 1950 by Jay Archer, a youth center director in Scranton, Pennsylvania. Pop Warner football originated with Joe Tomlin, a businessman and former Swarthmore football player, in 1930. He hoped to use football as an outlet for street gangs in Philadelphia. It too grew slowly until the later 1940s. An additional mass promotion of sports for children was made by the U.S. Junior Chamber of Commerce and the Athletic Institute in golf, tennis, basketball, softball, track, and bowling.

Another major sport development was age-group swimming, started by the AAU in 1950. Over half a million boys and girls of nine years and older got up in the early hours of the morning for practice in the summer of 1969. This movement began in California with its early leaders including George Haines at Santa Clara, Finn Ruuska at Berkeley, Mrs. Beth Kaufman, and Peter Daland in Los Angeles.[29]

The AAU also played an active part in the national emphasis on physical fitness. In 1948 it embarked on a Physical Fitness and Proficiency Test program for boys and girls from six to eighteen years of age. Three physical educators, Leonard Larson, David K. Brace, and Ben Miller, were members of the committee which devised the test. Certificates of Achievement were given to millions of youth who met established standards for their age group and sex. The AAU also began a Junior Olympics program with national championship competition starting in 1967. As of 1969, the Amateur Athletic Union maintained jurisdiction through 57 district associations over 17 sports—basketball, baton twirling, bobsledding, boxing, gymnastics, handball, horseshoe pitching, judo, luge, skibobbing, swimming and

[28]Betty F. McCue, "Athletic Scholarships for Women," *Journal of Health, Physical Education, and Recreation* 33 (April 1962): 18.
[29]Keith Monroe, "Johnny Weissmuller was a Slow Swimmer," *New York Times Magazine*, 18 December 1966, pp. 33–36.

diving, synchronized swimming, track and field, trampoline, water polo, weightlifting, and wrestling. Its program used 100,000 volunteer workers to reach an estimated 16 million people of all ages.

The immense popularity of these and other sponsored sports for youth was attributed to several factors: (1) effect of radio and television in communicating sports; (2) support of parents; (3) desire of many service clubs, veterans' groups, and business organizations to benefit children; and (4) inadequacy of elementary school programs.[30]

The insatiable appetite for sports competition extended to the severely handicapped as well. Timothy Nugent organized the first annual wheelchair basketball tournament at the University of Illinois in 1949. The idea of wheelchair sports came out of the Veterans' Administration hospitals after the Second World War. Benjamin Lipton of the Bulova Watch Company spearheaded efforts resulting in the first National Wheelchair Games in 1957, modelled after the Stoke Mandeville games in England. These games have since become annual events, under the auspices of the National Wheelchair Athletic Association. Events include bowling, swimming, weightlifting, table tennis, archery, discus throwing, and wheelchair racing, shuttle relays, and slalom racing.[31] One thousand mentally retarded children recevied their opportunity to compete at the Special Olympics held in 1968 at Chicago.

NEGROES IN SPORTS: Integration in professional baseball and football moved slowly at first. Seven years after the precedent set by Jackie Robinson, there were only twenty-two Negro players in the major leagues, and it was 1959 before all teams had Negro players. The first Negro to play in the professional National Basketball Association was Charles Cooper for the Boston Celtics in 1950.[32] Professional basketball was ahead of the other sports in selecting Negro coaches, however. John McLendon coached the Cleveland Pipers of the American Basketball League in 1961, and Bill Russell became player-coach of the Boston Celtics of the NBA in 1966. By the end of the decade, over half of the professional basketball players, thirty-two percent of the football players, and twenty-five percent of the baseball players were black.

The more exclusive sports of tennis and golf grudgingly gave way to the inevitable. Althea Gibson competed in an USLTA tournament in 1950 although Reginald Weir had played in a tournament two years before. Arthur Ashe also broke tradition and made the Davis Cup team in 1965.

[30]Arthur A. Esslinger, "Out-of-School Athletics for Children," *American Academy of Physical Education, Professional Contributions*, no. 3 (Washington, D.C.: American Academy of Physical Education, 1955), pp. 32–33.

[31]"The History of Wheelchair Sports" (Woodside, N.Y.: Joseph Bulova School of Watchmaking, n.d.), mimeographed, pp. 1–4.

[32]Andrew S. Young, *Negro Firsts in Sports* (Chicago: Johnson Publishing Company, 1963), p. 239.

The Professional Golfers' Association admitted Negro members in 1961 under legal pressure from the state of California, and forty-six-year-old Charlie Sifford became the first Negro to win a major tournament (the Los Angeles Open) in 1969.[33]

The number of Negro athletes appearing on college teams grew steadily during this time, even among southern schools. There was some encouragement in the fact that 6 percent of all athletic scholarships in seven major conferences went to Negroes although only 1.5 percent of the students were black.[34] A great forward step in high school athletics occurred in 1968 when a federal judge ordered the merger of the separate white and Negro high school athletic associations in Alabama.[35]

The acceptance of Negro athletes has done far more than open some locker room and clubhouse doors. Increased numbers of Negro spectators helped to eliminate a great deal of segregation in seating at games, in restaurants, and in hotel accommodations, even in the South. This progress gives promise and hope to the prediction of one observer who stated: "Many Southerners will not cling to segregation if it means giving up popular sports."[36]

RECREATION, CAMPING, AND OUTDOOR EDUCATION: Public and private recreation in the United States achieved new heights of popularity and participation in the 1960s. For the first time in history, as the work week diminished to forty hours, the average worker had more time (forty-four hours) for leisure. The recreation boom was also a result of population growth, greater mobility through airplane travel and automobile travel aided by the interstate highway system, longer vacations and earlier retirement age, increase in income, philosophical acceptance of play and recreation, and higher levels of education which broaden recreational interests.[37] Yet it was paradoxical that those with the most money and resources for leisure had the least time and those with the most time had the least resources.[38] The use of municipal parks and playground facilities, long denied to most black citizens, was guaranteed by a 1963 Supreme Court decision, but in practice, discrimination still existed.

[33]William Johnson, "Call Back the Years," *Sports Illustrated* 30 (31 March 1969): 58.

[34]"In Black and White," *Sports Illustrated* 28 (19 February 1968): 10.

[35]Severne A. Frazier, "A History and a Comparative Analysis of the Alabama Interscholastic Athletic Association and the National High School Athletic Association" (Doctoral dissertation, Ohio State University, 1969), pp. 96–113.

[36]Howard Zinn, "A Fate Worse Than Integration," *Harper's Magazine* 219 (August 1959): 55.

[37]O. N. Hunter and Clayne R. Jensen, "Recreation and a Changing World," *Journal of Health, Physical Education, and Recreation* 36 (September 1965): 32–33, 70.

[38]Richard G. Kraus, "Recreation for the Rich and Poor: A Contrast," *Quest* 5 (December 1965): 49.

The role of the school in public recreation began to weaken after 1950, especially in communities with a population over 10,000. One administrative study showed that there were 1,009 combined park and recreation authorities, 949 with recreation separate, and only 274 school-sponsored. This reflected an extension of recreation programs beyond children's sports and games and a strong trend toward outdoor recreation.[39] Park and recreation groups, which had previously stood aloof from each other, began to combine their efforts. This occurred at the professional level in 1965 when the National Recreation Association, the American Recreation Society, and three park associations merged into the new National Recreation and Park Association (NRPA). The title of its official publication changed from *Recreation* to *Parks and Recreation*. The NRPA also initiated a quarterly publication in 1969, the *Journal of Leisure Research*. Professional preparation of recreation personnel was offered in over a hundred colleges through a major in recreation. Fifty-three colleges conferred a master's degree and twenty-seven gave the doctorate in recreation.[40]

Industrial recreation turned in a new direction. Before World War II, many companies recruited star athletes and assembled a strong team to advertise the organization and entertain the employees. After the war, when people could watch professional teams on television, companies could not justify expensive teams. Their primary objective changed to active participation in many activities by a maximum number of employees in an intramural-type program. In the late 1960s some plants were beginning to schedule games with other companies, and the National Industrial Recreation Association sponsored national tournaments in golf, archery, and bowling.[41]

A remarkable development after 1950 was the outdoor education movement which added a new dimension to camping. John J. Kirk defined outdoor education as "the method which utilizes the natural environment to cultivate in students a reverence for life through an ecological exploration of the interdependence of living things and we aim to form in our students a land ethic illustrating man's temporary stewardship of the land."[42] Outdoor education was first identified with school camping in the 1930s and 1940s and was used to enrich the curriculum and provide recreation. President Kennedy's concern for conservation was transmitted to outdoor

[39]Richard Kraus, "Which Way School Recreation?" *Journal of Health, Physical Education, and Recreation* 36 (November–December 1965): 26.

[40]Jackson M. Anderson, "Professional Preparation for Recreation and Park Personnel," *Journal of Health, Physical Education, and Recreation* 39 (March 1968): 85–86.

[41]Bil Gilbert, "Sis-Boom-Bah! For Amalgamated Sponge," *Sports Illustrated* 22 (25 January 1965): 56–64.

[42]John J. Kirk, "Trends in Outdoor Education," *International Council on Health, Physical Education, and Recreation, 11th International Congress, 1968* (Washington, D.C.: ICHPER, 1969), p. 82.

education programs as an additional objective. New outdoor land areas were set aside for the public welfare through the federal Land and Water Conservation Fund, the Open-Space Land Program, the National Sea Shore Act, and the active leadership of Stewart Udall, Secretary of the Interior. The Bureau of Outdoor Recreation was established in 1962 in the Department of the Interior, and outdoor education programs qualified for significant federal support under the Elementary and Secondary Education Act. The Outdoor Recreation Resources Review Commission issued reports on the nation's future needs and desirable policies in 1962 and 1967. An outstanding facility was the New Jersey State School of Conservation directed by John J. Kirk. Many public schools developed school-site laboratories to provide daily experiences for children in the out-of-doors.

The AAHPER contributed by undertaking its Outdoor Education Project in 1955 with the financial backing of various sporting goods manufacturers. Under the productive leadership of Julian W. Smith of Michigan State University, the project engaged in a multitude of activities. Its most effective work was accomplished through numerous state and regional workshops and clinics for teachers, administrators, and leaders in recreation and conservation agencies.

Program of Physical Education

The national urge for physical fitness did not bring back the obstacle course of World War II days to school programs. In its place were activities drawn more from the various physical fitness tests such as the AAHPER Youth Fitness Test which consisted of pull-ups, sit-ups, shuttle-run, 600-yard run-walk, standing board jump, 50-yard dash, and softball throw for distance. The six parts of the Kraus-Weber Test were frequently used also. Strenuous calisthenic activities were incorporated into many physical education class periods as a part of the lesson. Weight training became very popular among older boys and college students. A new activity in the fitness curriculum was circuit training which was imported from England and Canada around 1960.[43]

Many boys and girls outside of the schools took the AAU Physical Fitness and Proficiency Test. They worked in five events—a sprint, walk and run, sit-ups, push-ups, and standing long jump—plus one elective selected from pull-ups, softball throw, distance hike, or running high jump. In 1968, pull-ups became a required activity and push-ups were made optional.

Classroom work was also introduced in many institutions, either as a part of the activity course or as a separate course under some such title as

---

[43]Maxwell L. Howell and W. R. Morford, "Circuit Training," *Journal of Health, Physical Education, and Recreation* 32 (November 1961): 33.

"Foundations of Physical Education." These courses generally had three objectives: (1) to discuss the value of physical activity and its contributions to good health and modern living; (2) to evaluate the student's own status and potential through a series of tests and measurements; and (3) to work out a program of activities best suited to the student's individual needs. Michigan State University offered one of the early courses of this type in 1957, and by 1960, about one-third of the colleges gave similar courses. Toledo University particularly stressed this approach.

MOVEMENT EDUCATION: A new direction in physical education was explored during this period, known variously as movement exploration, basic movement, or movement education. This was an import from England, probably first introduced by Betty Meredith-Jones who came to this country in 1952. She lectured at many colleges across the country and spoke at the 1954 AAHPER convention. An article by her, "Understanding Movement," appeared in the May-June 1955 issue of the *Journal*. In the meantime, Elizabeth Halsey observed movement exploration on a trip to England in 1954 and made arrangements with Ruth Foster, chief inspector of physical education for women, for the first Anglo-American Workshop which was held in England in the summer of 1956. Fifteen Americans attended. Shirley Howard sponsored a second workshop ten years later for twenty-one teachers from the U.S.

Movement education encouraged a variety of activities and sought to apply the elements of space, force, time, and flow. Movements were performed with and without apparatus. Some of the equipment used were ropes, different-sized balls, hoops, bean bags, wands, and fixed apparatus for hanging, balancing, jumping, climbing, and swinging. The Lueneburger Stegel apparatus, particularly designed for these activities and invented in Germany, was brought to the United States in 1960, where it was also known as the Lind Climber. Children exposed to this program in the lower grades were supposed to develop the fundamental motor skills which later would facilitate performance in sports, dance, and games. Movement education was most applicable to the elementary school child. Many movement education devotees backed Rosalind Cassidy's belief that the term, "physical education," was no longer appropriate for the profession and that it should be replaced by "the Art and Science of Human Movement."[44] The following effects of movement education upon school programs might be noted:

1. It caused greater emphasis on pre-school and primary school programs.
2. It got many more children interested and active in versatile programs.

[44]Rosalind Cassidy, "The Cultural Definition of Physical Education," *Quest* 4 (Spring 1965): 14.

3. It kept the competitive element from taking away the joy of physical activity from slow developers.
4. It started a movement toward more extensive and more progressive programs.[45]

It is difficult for the objective observer to really see much new in the actual content of movement education programs. Dance educators started teaching these movements in the 1930s. At that time also as mentioned in the preceding chapter, Agnes Wayman led a group of women physical educators who sought to break down various games into their fundamental skills or basic movements. Certainly, the old German and Swedish apparatus was designed precisely to let children hang, climb, jump, and swing. Dio Lewis would applaud the use of bean bags. However, movement education does have its own technique which will be discussed in the next section on Methods.

SCHOOL AND COLLEGE SPORTS: It would be erroneous to conclude that recreational sports lost ground in the schools and colleges to the fitness drive or movement education. The Outdoor Education Project of the AAHPER gave real assistance to the teaching of flycasting, fishing, shooting, archery, and boating. The Lifetime Sports Foundation was created in 1965 by two private manufacturers and directed by Bud Wilkinson to promote lifetime sports, especially archery, bowling, badminton, golf, and tennis. College physical education offerings were enriched by adding courses in SCUBA (self-contained underwater breathing apparatus) diving, ice skating, figure skating, ice hockey, the combative sports such as fencing, judo, and karate, conditioning and weight training, and even bicycle riding. Instruction in skiing became feasible in a larger area of the country because of the development of the artificial snow-making machines. Some colleges built their own slopes and others used commercial facilities to meet a strong student demand. The number of ski resorts in the Midwest alone jumped from 4 in 1954 to 141 in 1961.[46]

Students enlarged their opportunities for participation by organizing clubs. According to a recent study, the twelve most common sports clubs in order of rank were soccer, karate, water and snow skiing, sailing, judo, fencing, gymnastics, rugby, ice hockey, volleyball, weight training, and handball.[47] Less common but more exotic sport clubs existed for skydiving, spelunking, and rock climbing.

[45]John D. Lawther, " 'Movement Education' and Skill Learnings," *Gymnasion* 6 (Spring 1969): 14.
[46]Ray Cave, "The Fresh Face of Sport," *Sports Illustrated* 15 (21 August 1961): 14.
[47]Mimeographed report of questionnaire study received from Richard E. Jamerson, 14 February 1969.

It may be worthwhile to compare the most common varsity sports for high schools and colleges as shown in the table below.[48]

Rank	High School	College
1	Basketball	Basketball
2	Football	Baseball
3	Track and field	Tennis
4	Baseball	Track and field
5	Wrestling	Golf
6	Cross country	Football
7	Swimming	Cross country
8	Tennis	Wrestling
9	Soccer	Swimming
10	Volleyball	Soccer

The lower rank for college football bears out the fact that it was dropped by some institutions because of the high cost of maintaining a team plus competition from television. Eighty-one colleges abandoned football between 1948 and 1954.[49] Some of the newer colleges in the 1960s chose to have soccer and other sports rather than football. Soccer and wrestling have shown especially rapid growth in the last ten years. The Catholic Youth Council program in St. Louis has produced high-quality soccer players for colleges all over the country, and St. Louis University has a stranglehold on the NCAA soccer championships. The inauguration of two professional soccer leagues in 1967 helped spread the game to all parts of the country. Wrestling zoomed into popularity for both participants and spectators. The 1969 Ohio high school state wrestling tournament drew over 10,000 fans on the final night.

A few highlights in several sports deserve mention. In the 1950s basketball players began to go to the one-hand shot and then the jump shot. The result was an unbelievable improvement in accuracy. A team's shooting average was often fifty percent or better whereas thirty-five percent used to be considered excellent. Softball players began to flock to the new slo-pitch variation about 1960. This game proved exciting because it resulted in better hitting and more action in less time. Volleyball became a hard-hitting, sophisticated game with complicated patterns for setting up the ball and blocking.

[48]Data for high schools are for 1968 and taken from Clifford B. Fagan, "Increased Participation in Interscholastic Athletics," *Ohio High School Athlete* 28 (February 1969): 128. College data are for 1966 from the NCAA, *The Sports and Recreation Programs of the Nation's Universities and Colleges*, Report no. 3 (Kansas City, Missouri: NCAA, n.d.), p. 4.

[49]George Van Bibber, "The NCAA's Sanity Code and Its Effect on Intercollegiate Athletics," *Physical Educator* 13 (December 1956): 140.

POPULAR AND PROFESSIONAL SPORTS: The clamor of tennis buffs to watch competition between professional and amateur players finally resulted in the first U.S. Open Tennis tournament at Forest Hills in 1968. Country clubs rebounded from wartime troubles and added swimming pools and tennis courts to entice the whole family while Dad played golf. Automatic pin-setters contributed to an increase in the number of bowlers from seventeen million in 1954 to about thirty million in 1960. Skiers raced down slopes on artificial snow in the winter and practiced on artificial turf in the summer. The fifty-mile hiking craze of 1963 fortunately was very brief, but more lasting was the jogging movement later in the decade. The National Jogging Association was organized in 1968 and Mr. and Mrs. jogging shoes sold for $17.95 per pair. People of all ages and shapes were often seen plodding along the roads of cities and suburbia day and night.

Professional teams multiplied. Baseball changed from the traditional two leagues of eight teams to four divisions of six teams each. The National Football League went from twelve teams to sixteen teams and competed for player talent with the ten-team American Football League before a compromise was arranged. The hidebound National Hockey League enlarged from six to twelve teams. The National Basketball Association grew from nine to fourteen members and faced serious competition from the eleven-team American Basketball Association. This expansion, of course, was dependent upon a growth of population to over 200 million people, the development of new metropolitan areas, jet travel, and the construction of a dozen beautiful new stadia such as the completely enclosed Astrodome in Houston in the 1960s.

The sale of radio and television rights for sporting events poured money into the professional club coffers and to the NCAA. For example, radio and television stations and networks paid $55 million to broadcast professional and college football games for the 1967–68 season alone— $6 million more than for the previous year.[50] Television rights for the Olympic games soared from $660,000 in 1960 to $13,500,000 for the 1972 games in Germany. This money has boosted the salaries of professional athletes and enabled many of them to become businessmen also.

A concerned writer in 1915 declared: "The disease of *spectatoritis* is abroad in the land."[51] Jay B. Nash expressed the same fear in his book, *Spectatoritis*, in 1932. The disease would seem to be even more serious in the 1960s with huge crowds watching more teams in larger stadia, viewing color television, and attending horse racing, which was the leading spectator sport. Nevertheless, other facts supported the contention that since the 1930s Americans had become increasingly more active and were spending

[50]"Cost of Football is Going Up," *Broadcasting*, 12 August 1968, p. 23.
[51]Richard H. Edwards, *Christianity and Amusements* (New York: Association Press, 1915), p. 14.

more time outdoors. Boyle estimated in 1964 that people spent ten times as much money on participant sports as spectator sports.[52] The Outdoor Recreation Resources Review Commission recorded an increase of almost fifty percent in summertime outdoor recreation activities between 1960 and 1965.[53] Swimming, boating, fishing, surfing, water skiing, skin diving, and other water activities particularly showed remarkable growth. Evidently millions of people in the United States had the time and the money to be both spectators and participants.

The acceptance of sports by society became complete and official when the 1969–70 edition of *Who's Who In America* listed professional athletes—Bob Gibson, Mickey Mantle, Arnold Palmer, Johnny Unitas, and Carl Yastrzemski—for the first time. Sport also penetrated the cultural circles of art with the founding of the National Art Museum of Sport in 1959. *Sports Illustrated*, a high quality weekly sports magazine for the general public, made a successful debut in 1954.

PROGRAM FOR GIRLS AND WOMEN: Programs for girls and women in the 1960s began to respond to a planned effort to improve our showing in the Olympic games. This was an influence of the five National Institutes on Girls' Sports which dealt with gymnastics, track and field, fencing, diving, kayak paddling, figure skating, skiing, advanced basketball, volleyball, advanced coaching and officiating of basketball and track and field, and officiating in gymnastics. By 1970 the Commission on Intercollegiate Athletics for Women planned to hold national championships in gymnastics, track and field, swimming, badminton, volleyball, golf, and tennis. The CIAW sponsored a national invitational basketball tournament at Westchester State College in 1969.

The Olympic influence and the desire for varsity competition produced a marked tendency toward more vigorous activities for girls and the adoption of boys' rules. Basketball went through a period of confusion and conflict over suitable rules. The NSWA rules were rejected by a group from twelve states who, in 1952, formed the National Girls' Basketball Committee for Secondary Schools and adopted rules similar to boys' except that the sixth player was retained. This was partly to reduce confusion for the men who often coached and officiated both boys' and girls' games.[54] Eventually, in 1969, a joint DGWS-AAU basketball rules committee voted to try a five-woman team for two years. The DGWS and the U.S. Volleyball Association agreed on the same rules in 1957 for the skilled player in

[52]Robert H. Boyle, "The New Wave in Sports," *Sports Illustrated* 21 (21 December 1964): 41.

[53]ORRRC, *Outdoor Recreation Trends* (Washington, D.C.: U.S. Government Printing Office, 1967), p. 7.

[54]LeOra M. Lipe, "A Comparative Study of Existing Basketball Rules as Used by Amateurs in the United States and Canada" (Master's thesis, Ohio State University, 1952), pp. 115–17.

volleyball. Women leaders first discussed the problem of touch football in 1950 and finally, in 1969, the DGWS officially approved (by a one-vote margin) a noncontact football game for girls and appointed a committee to draft appropriate rules.

In the late 1960s courses in self-defense for women began to appear. They arose out of people's fears for their personal safety in the streets of the nation. The value of this instruction was questioned by one physical educator on the basis that it generated negative learnings and that ninety percent of the students could not learn the techniques well enough to apply them effectively anyway."[55]

DANCE: In the earlier part of this period, modern dance discarded black leotards and somber expressions for colorful costumes and pleasant smiles. More variety was tolerated in the accompaniment, the setting, the subject matter, and the movement techniques.[56] It was often referred to as "creative dance."

The contemporary dance of the 1960s was something else, influenced by Alwin Nikolais, Erik Hawkins, Merce Cunningham, and, in modern ballet, George Balanchine. Dance turned to a technical study of movement rather than mere self-expression. Contemporary dance was abstract and cerebral without logic or continuity. Choreographers used some of the techniques of the abstract painter. The music for dance was completely unconventional and used unorthodox sounds from all kinds of mechanical instruments. The general approach was intellectual, objective, and unemotional which made modern dance seem more like a science than an art.[57]

In most educational institutions, modern dance found its home in the department of physical education, but in the late 1960s at some colleges dance moved into a new administrative unit encompassing all the performing arts. A new school of dance, comparable to Connecticut College, started at California State College in Long Beach. The Dance Notation Bureau moved from New York City to the educational setting of Ohio State University. Illinois State University made a worthy effort to stimulate male participation by sponsoring the First Institute in Dance for the American Male in 1968. Dance was made a division of the AAHPER in 1965. The secure status of dance on college campuses today is a credit to the competent leadership and hard work of many women such as Ruth Murray, Esther Pease, Alma Hawkins, Miriam Gray, Helen Alkire, Elizabeth Hayes, Virginia Moomaw, Frances Dougherty, Mary Ella Montague, Lucile Czarnowski, and Margaret Erlanger.

[55]Roger K. Burke, "Physical Education Can Teach Self Defense But Shouldn't," *Ohio High School Athlete* 28 (April 1969): 184.

[56]Delia P. Hussey, "Dance in Education," *Journal of Health, Physical Education, and Recreation* 25 (November 1954): 44–45.

[57]See Olga Maynard, *American Modern Dancers: The Pioneers* (Boston: Little, Brown, and Company, 1965), pp. 164–76.

The folk dance movement also gained momentum during the fifties and sixties. During this era of extensive mobility and impatient student confrontations with the establishment, the guitar, the social protest songs, and the rock bands became the social action and psychological tools of the young. Through folk music, folk dancing, and free body movement youths found means of expression. An upsurge of interest in ethnic dances was experienced on all campuses; the minority groups utilized the dance as a means of inculcating cultural pride. Besides the introduction of the folk mass, a few churches experimented with using the dance as a means of giving expression to religious feelings and interpreting religious concepts.

Methods of Physical Education

During the fifties and sixties educators focused their attention not only on what to teach but also on how to teach more effectively. They experimented with team teaching, programmed instruction, television and videotapes, nongraded classes, year-round schools, modular scheduling, teacher assistants, computer scheduling, independent study, mechanized language laboratories, and new mathematics curriculum.

PHYSICAL FITNESS AND TESTING: In the field of physical education considerable attention was focused on physical fitness and testing. The President's Council on Youth Fitness recommended a four-step program for improving the physical fitness of the nation's youth:

1. As part of a health appraisal, identify pupils with a low level of muscular strength, agility, and flexibility, and provide a required program to raise their performance to desirable levels.
2. Include at least fifteen minutes of vigorous activity in the daily physical education period.
3. Use objective physical achievement tests to determine pupil status, measure progress, and motivate pupils to better physical fitness.
4. Provide a comprehensive program of health education and physical education for all pupils although priority should be given to the first three recommendations.[58]

The third step was implemented by the widespread use of the AAHPER Youth Fitness Test. Norms were originally developed for grades five through twelve but were later obtained for college men and women. Comparative studies were made with English, Danish, and Japanese children, as well as others. The Kraus-Weber Tests were also commonly given although some teachers erroneously considered them to measure physical fitness rather than to be a test of minimal muscular strength and flexibility.

[58]*Youth Physical Fitness: Suggested Elements of a School-Centered Program* (Washington, D.C.: Government Printing Office, 1961), p. 14.

Many teachers, pupils, and adults were introduced to testing through the physical fitness movement. The overall results have been good, in spite of some criticism here and there. The achievement of fitness was encouraged by various emblems and awards. President Johnson initiated the Presidential Physical Fitness Award in 1966 for students who scored at or above the eighty-fifth percentile on the AAHPER Test. In the first four years, over 300,000 boys and girls qualified for the award with the largest number living in California.

COACHING METHODS: Another aspect to the development of physical fitness was a radical change in coaching methods toward using weight training as an adjunct to the program. Prior to the early 1950s coaches of almost all sports viewed weight training with anathema. Furthermore, athletes were not supposed to mix their sports: track men would soften their muscles if they swam; bicycle riding would harden their muscles; swimmers should avoid boxing, wrestling, and gymnastics; most taboo of all was weight lifting because it was thought to cause muscleboundness and slow reaction time. The accepted theory was to only practice one's own sport and to conserve energy. In the early 1930s Charles McCloy, Frederick Rand Rogers, and Bob Hoffman emphasized the need for strength in athletic performance. Several studies in the *Research Quarterly* in the early 1950s showed that weight lifters had as much flexibility and speed of movement as other athletes. Moreover, there were some well-known athletes who lifted weights— Bob Richards, Parry O'Brien, and Fortune Gordien in track; Dick Cleveland in swimming; and Frank Stranahan in golf. Finally, in 1956, Jim Murray and Peter Karpovich published the first book to directly apply a weight training program to sports.[59] By the end of the 1950s, weight training was extensively used by coaches of almost all sports throughout the country.

Along with weight training, a great deal was also heard about isometric exercises based on the research of two German scientists, Müller and Hettinger, in 1953. An isometric or static contraction creates tension in the muscle without movement of the muscle. No work is accomplished. Isometric exercises were found to develop strength and could be used to restore strength to injured muscles. These facts led to a marketing of all kinds of commercial apparatus, and isometrics were used as a supplement to the training programs of many sport teams.

Another technique which came into common use during this period, particularly for swimming and track, was interval training. This method consisted of four factors: (1) the distance to be covered; (2) the number of times to be done; (3) the pace or time; and (4) the recovery or rest interval. Interval training developed endurance based on the overload prin-

---

[59]Jim Murray and Peter V. Karpovich, *Weight Training in Athletics* (Englewood Cliffs, N.J.: Prentice-Hall, Inc., 1956).

ciple and concentrated more work in a short period of time. It proved tremendously effective and is generally acknowledged to be the primary reason for the phenomenal record-breaking performances of modern competitors in swimming and track. For example, at the 1964 NCAA swimming championships a new record was set in every single event.

Track coaches also have made use of *fartlek* as a training procedure. This is a Swedish word meaning speed play. *Fartlek* develops endurance by long distance runs interspersed with easy jogging and short sprints. It is done in the natural environment running over hills and valleys, in the woods, and across sand, dirt, snow, or pine needles. The runner gets tired but does not feel tired.[60] *Fartlek* differs from interval training in that it is not done on a level track and the workouts are not timed. A combination of *fartlek* and interval training was used in this country prior to 1940 by Billy Hayes of Mississippi State University and later Indiana University and Dink Templeton of Stanford University.

MOVEMENT EDUCATION: The elementary schools particularly utilized movement education, which is dependent upon an ample supply of equipment for each child with sufficient space for all children to be active at the same time. The teacher makes suggestions to each child and generally avoids a personal demonstration of what is to be done, at least in the earlier stages. The basic idea is expressed in this quotation:

> They run, they jump, they bend, they stretch, and explore the different possibilities of movement. The teacher guides and the children are free, without the restrictions of monotonous commands, to find and to create movements adequate to their own motor pattern. This kind of work develops all the potentialities of the child as a whole.[61]

The emphasis is on problem-solving, rather than teacher-direction. This is often referred to as guided discovery or exploration. A class may be divided into several small groups, each doing a different activity. Games and rhythmic activities should be freely modified by the teacher to encourage more movement and creativity.[62] The skillful teacher must be adept at arranging a suitable progression of activities appropriate to the movement abilities of the class.

TECHNOLOGICAL DEVELOPMENTS: A number of technological developments had an impact on physical education programs. The introduction of artificial turf and other all-weather surfaces were important innova-

[60]J. Kenneth Doherty, *Modern Track and Field* (Englewood Cliffs, N.J.: Prentice-Hall, Inc., 1963), p. 166.

[61]Elly Friedmann-Wittkower, "Fitness Through Creative Gymnastics," *Journal of Health, Physical Education, and Recreation* 28 (September 1957): 70.

[62]Heidie Mitchell, "Upgrading Elementary School Physical Education," *Croft Physical Education Newsletter, Supplement,* 15 April 1968, n.p.

tions. The use of fiberglass, nylon, aluminum, styrofoam, and plastic made it possible to produce sports equipment and apparel that was lighter, more durable, and easier to keep clean.

Another offshoot of modern technology was the development of teaching machines for programmed instruction. A program for college physical education was first worked out by Kenneth Penman of Arizona State University in 1964.[63] This was a scramble book in which the material to be learned does not follow the page sequence. Alternate-choice responses to questions direct the reader to new or review material.

Since 1950, teachers and coaches have used television as a teaching aid. Educational television was assured by the action of the Federal Communications Commission in reserving 259 channels for educational television in 1952. In the first ten years, 70 educational stations went into operation. According to a national survey by Hixson in 1964, 107 out of 473 colleges in 28 states used television for health, physical education, or athletics. The largest group was for athletic events.[64] In 1969 a new series for teaching physical education to first graders appeared on television entitled "Ready? Set . . . Go!" It consisted of thirty lessons and a manual for teachers prepared by a committee of physical educators. The recent invention of videotape was a big boon to the use of television for class instruction as a teaching and evaluative device. An unusual application of this technique was for a gymnastic meet between the University of Washington and the University of Illinois in 1968. Each team's performance was videotaped at separate meets with other schools, and then the tapes were sent to a panel of judges who scored the routines and determined the winner.

Other technological improvements have contributed to better teaching. One of the best was an inexpensive special projector which could easily be loaded with a film cartridge and run repeatedly as a loop film. The Athletic Institute offered these for seven sports in 1969 with nine more in production. The Institute's pioneer project of slide filmstrips and records was enlarged to cover thirty-five different activities. Instructional books for various sports have grown from the single-volume effort, such as the AAHPER's *Physical Education for High School Students* (1955), to a separate book for each sport in a series which could be purchased from half a dozen different book publishers.

SUMMARY: As physical education stands on the threshold of the 1970s, its status in American society appears to be the highest it has ever enjoyed, and its justification on educational grounds has been maintained. Physical education has contributed in developing techniques for teaching

[63]Kenneth A. Penman, *Physical Education for College Students* (St. Louis: The C. V. Mosby Company, 1964).
[64]C. G. Hixson, "Educational Television Committee," *National College Physical Education Association for Men, 67th Annual Proceedings, 1964*, p. 153.

the slow learner and the brain-damaged child, according to the work done by Newell Kephart and Carl Delacato. The relationship of the growth of intelligence to motor and sensory experience as conceived by Jean Piaget has far-reaching significance for every physical educator. There is some evidence that the development of vision and intelligence is related to motor activity. In short, few people today seriously accept the old concept of the dualism of man.

In addition to this, the cause of physical education has found support from the scientific world which it never previously enjoyed. At the first International Conference on Preventive Cardiology at the University of Vermont in 1964, many experts from all over the world gave convincing testimony for the role of physical activity in maintaining the health and efficiency of the heart and cardiovascular system in adult life. Many authorities now regard exercise to be an important factor in controlling weight, whereas twenty years earlier, it was considered to be of negligible value. Some scientists think that regular exercise over a long period of time helps to keep down the serum cholesterol level in the blood.

The term, Golden Age of Sports, was first applied to the 1920s and then to the post-World War II years. But sports participation and interest at all levels during the decade of the 1960s, indisputably has surpassed any previous period. This era is truly the Golden Age of Sports although the term now seems a bit hackneyed.

The honest historian must point out some dark spots in this bright picture. The trend toward professionalism may parallel the tragic decline of the ancient Greek and Roman society. President Kennedy publicly viewed this professionalism in sports "without enthusiasm."[65] The pressure to win and set records has placed fantastic claims upon the time of participants from the nine-year-old girl swimmer to the college senior basketball player. Does this time expenditure rob children of other valuable experiences in growing up? Does the college athlete achieve his skill at the cost of a lower quality education because he spends so much time on the playing field, in the pool, or at the gymnasium? Competitive athletics for children snowballs in spite of expressed concern by the medical profession. Besides damaged knees, concussions, and other injuries, football exacts a costly toll of twenty-five lives each year—a price which is willingly paid. The undeniable use of drugs, pain-killers, and other pharmaceuticals by athletes raises some serious questions. Undesirable elements of society are attracted to sports and athletes as the repeated gambling scandals have shown. Will female athletes fall prey to the same problems as they seek higher levels of competition? The impressive figures on sports participation must be viewed with some dismay by the professional physical educator when he sees a

---

[65]"Kennedy is Concerned at Nation of Spectators," *Washington Post*, 6 December 1961, p. 7.

golfer jumping into his motorized cart to drive on for his next shot. Money spent for power boats, snowmobiles, and luxurious camping equipment contributes little to developing a more vigorous people even though they are out of doors.

These are some of the problems faced by the profession of physical education. The profession is challenged to make itself effective in dealing with these and other problems. It is challenged, as are the schools, to make itself relevant to the needs of the inner city community, the deprived, the elderly, the poor, and other disadvantaged minorities, whether they be Negro, Indian, or Mexican. The profession must be sure that it does not become exclusively an academic discipline and lose its contact with reality —with boys and girls and with men and women.

Finally, an ominous sign ever reminds us that the future of physical education is inextricably linked with other problems of our modern society. It is the announcement that students in Los Angeles County will be excused from strenuous activities during periods of smog alerts when air pollution reaches a certain concentration. Physical education classes will obviously be affected, and major athletic events may also be interrupted. This chilling prospect, added to others arising from water pollution and wasteful use of land resources, should clearly warn modern physical educators that they cannot afford an attitude of professional parochialism. Physical educators and all people of the United States must come to grips with the urgency of present-day reality. The decade of the 1970s looms as a crucial one for determining the quality of man's future existence on earth.

part five

Physical Education
in

OTHER MODERN COUNTRIES

26

Physical Education in Education in the Pan-American Nations

Although the Pan-American nations are hemisphere neighbors, until relatively recently they have maintained closer relationships with Europe than with one another. Because of their geographical location and the nature of their European ties, Canada and the Latin American countries are quite different. The Latin American countries also differ from one another in many respects, but they share some common problems and cultural characteristics. In the following discussion, the development of physical education in Canada is presented, followed by general background information about the Latin American countries and the development of physical education in eleven of them.

PHYSICAL EDUCATION IN CANADA

Canada, a member of the British Commonwealth, was the scene of prolonged British-French rivalry until it was ceded to Great Britain by the Treaty of Paris in 1763. The four colonial provinces were united politically by the British North American Act of 1867. Over the years, the Confederation expanded from ocean to ocean and peacefully moved toward full independence.

Larger than continental United States in territory, Canada has many fewer people (twenty million), half of whom live in the Great Lakes-St. Lawrence Valley region. Because of the wealth produced by the vast forests and wheat fields, the rich mineral and fishing resources, and the spectacular industrial and urban growth of recent years, the Canadians enjoy a standard of living that is second only to that of the United States.

In Canada, where about forty-four percent of the people are of British stock and thirty percent of French origin, the schools have not served as an ethnic melting pot. Because of sectarian differences, the Canadians have established separate public school systems. Quebec has a French-speaking Catholic school system and an English-speaking Protestant school system; Newfoundland has seven school systems. The control of education is vested in the provincial governments. The national government has no department of education and few educational powers, but through legislation and grants, it has stimulated the development of sports and fitness and has encouraged the provinces to establish divisions to promote physical education in their departments of education, recreation offices, or other agencies.

As early as 1852, Dr. Egerton Ryerson, the superintendent of schools for Upper Canada (Ontario) published articles in the *Journal of Education* in which he described a course of physical exercises, urged schools to initiate programs, and promised government aid for the purchase of equipment. A decade later, the Toronto Normal School for Upper Canada opened a gymnasium, probably the first in Canada, and about this time a cadet training program, which was closely associated with the schools, was also established. Between 1865 and 1900, some grants were made to encourage the promotion of gymnastics, drills, and calisthenics in the schools, and, in the 1890s, physical education was made compulsory in some grades in Ontario. Little instruction was provided until after the turn of the century, but by 1930, all of the colleges and about half of the high schools were built with a gymnasium.

The physical education movement was led by dedicated pioneers, such as Mary Hamilton at the Margaret Eaton School in Toronto (1910–1934) and F. S. Barnjum, who was employed as Drilling and Gymnastic Master of the new gymnasium at McGill University in 1862; James Naismith, who filled the position in 1888; and their distinguished successors at McGill University, Dr. R. Tait McKenzie (1890–1903), Dr. Arthur Lamb (1912–17; 1920–49), and Ethel Mary Cartwright (1906–1927). National impetus was given to the physical education movement when the Strathcona Trust Fund was established in 1909. The Fund, which was administered by the National Department of the Militia, allotted annual grants to the provinces that made physical education a part of the curriculum above the elementary level, provided teacher training in physical education, and formed cadet corps.

The physical education movement experienced modest growth until the depression of the 1930s when many schools dropped their programs and few gymnasiums were built. But because of the amount of enforced leisure, the Youth Training Act of 1939 was passed which encouraged many provincial and local governments to develop or expand recreation and leadership training programs, such as the British Columbia Pro-Rec program. By 1947, most provinces had functioning recreation programs.

With the outbreak of World War II, the National Physical Fitness Act of 1943 was passed which provided graduate study grants and stimulated provinces to initiate or to improve their physical education and/or recreation programs. The Act was rescinded in 1954, but the Physical Fitness Division of the Department of National Health and Welfare continued to function, and Dr. Doris Plewes, who served as consultant until 1962, continued her energetic work on behalf of physical fitness.

In 1961, The Fitness and Amateur Sport Act (Bill C–131) was enacted as a result of the concern about Canada's mediocre performance in international competitions and the intensive drive mounted by physical education and sports organizations. Since its enactment, this significant bill, which established the National Advisory Council on Fitness and Amateur Sport, has provided for the training of coaches, has assisted participants in national and international competitions, and has given substantial financial aid to voluntary bodies, to amateur sports organizations, to university research projects, and to graduate students. The directors of Fitness and Amateur Sport have been Gordon Wright, Roger Dion, and L. E. Lefaive.

In French Canada, where the Roman Catholic school system is patterned after the French tradition, the physical education movement has developed very slowly. The *Collèges Classiques*, private schools, have paved the way for other schools to follow, and private organizations, such as *L'Oeuvres des Patronages* (Les Patros) and *La Conféderation des Oeuvres de Loisirs* (COP) have developed a complex of out-of-school programs. In the past decade, greater interest in physical education has been exhibited in Quebec. A provincial supervisor was appointed in 1964, and improvements have been made in the facilities, the teaching personnel, and the curriculum.

The objectives of the Canadian physical educators are to develop: (1) a level of organic and emotional fitness that enables a person to function at his physical and mental optimum; (2) the skills, coordination, and safety practices that are necessary to perform and to enjoy vigorous physical activities; and (3) the health practices, efficient movements, posture habits, and behavior patterns that enable a person to live in a socially useful and personally satisfying way.

Postwar prosperity, the consolidation of rural schools, and the increased number of teachers with college degrees and a few with a major degree in physical education have done much to improve the elementary school programs and facilities. Physical education is included in all elementary school courses of study, but it is not required. The time allotment is usually twenty-five minutes per day plus recess periods. Classroom teachers conduct the classes, but specialists supervise the program in some large cities. Since World War II, impressive progress has been made in upgrading the secondary school program. The subject is usually compulsory and consists of three activity classes and one health period a week. In some universities physical education is a required, noncredit subject, usually for two periods a week during the first two years. A wide choice of activities is offered, but swimming is usually compulsory.

Through the years, the British Syllabi of Physical Training have had a major influence on the curriculum. In the early days, the Ling gymnastics, the Turnverein societies, the army and ethnic groups, and some American leaders, such as Dio Lewis, Dudley Sargent, William Skarstrom, and Luther Gulick have influenced the curriculum. The YMCA leaders and the American-trained Canadian teachers were partly responsible for the inclusion in the curriculum of more sports, play, and recreation activities. Medau and others of the German school, the Sokol program, the Dalcroze eurythmic movement, and the tours made by Niels Bukh's gymnasts in 1931 had an effect on the program. In recent years, the influx of teachers from England has spurred interest in physical education, and the movement education approach, which was introduced in the United Kingdom by Rudolph Laban for the dance, has been adapted to fundamental movement training and to gymnastics. Public interest in the military 5BX and XEX exercise programs and the Kraus-Weber Test findings have resulted in increased emphasis being given to fitness-centered activities. Cadet work is still carried out in some schools, but is usually separated from the physical education program.

Play days, sports afternoons, and intramural programs are becoming increasingly popular. In some provinces, interscholastic associations coordinate the local or regional leagues and organize championships in a number of sports. The interscholastic programs are broadened by having two or three teams represent a school in a sport. The coaches are qualified teachers, and most of them receive no extra remuneration for coaching.

The intercollegiate program in Canada is somewhat curtailed by the shortness of the academic year (late September through early May), by the time and expense of traveling great distances, and by the suspicion that athletics are a threat to scholastic performance. Few full-time coaches are employed, and prior to the announcement of Simon Fraser University in 1964, no athletic scholarships were provided. The regional governing bodies that were organized early in the century united in 1961 to form the Canadian Intercollegiate Athletic Union. The intercollegiate program for women, which is developing rapidly, is still governed by regional bodies.

The army men who were provided by the Strathcona Trust Fund to teach in the normal schools in the early years were replaced gradually by professional educators. The first diploma course for physical educators was organized in 1910 at the Margaret Eaton School of Literature and Expression, which eventually became a physical education school within the University of Toronto. Shortly thereafter, McGill University organized a program. Many students went to the United States for their undergraduate and graduate work until the right to establish degree programs was finally won in Canada. The first undergraduate degree program was established at the

University of Toronto in 1940. By 1967, when the University of Alberta established the first doctoral degree program, twenty-two universities had an undergraduate degree program and some had a master's degree program. During the 1960s research facilities were established at some universities; the grants provided by the Fitness and Amateur Sport Act have given considerable impetus to this movement.

The Canadian Physical Education Association was organized in 1933 through the efforts of the professional organizations that had been formed in Quebec and Toronto in the 1920s. Under the guidance of Australian-born Dr. A. S. Lamb, the "father of Canadian physical education," and others, the Association grew slowly. The *Bulletin* which was published in the early years was suspended in 1951, but in 1957 the decision was reached to publish the *Journal of Canadian Association for Health, Physical Education and Recreation* which contains curricular and research articles. In French Canada, *L'Association des Diplômés en Éducation Physique et Récréation* (ADEPR) was organized in 1960. In the same year, the organization which is now known as the *La Ligue Canadienne-française de l'Éducation Physique* was founded as a branch of FIEP.

In the pioneer days in Canada, hunting, fishing, canoeing, and horseback riding were a part of the normal work activities. Land-clearing, corn-husking, and barn-raising bees were often followed by an evening of dancing. Plowing matches, logrolling and hurling contests, horse races, and snowshoe races were common pastimes. Scotch settlers organized Highland Games which included foot racing, jumping events, and tossing the caber.

During the nineteenth century, men from the military, university, and business world formed a number of sports clubs. Three of these clubs affiliated in 1881 to form the Montreal Amateur Athletic Association which, in turn, instigated the formation of the association which is now known as the Amateur Athletic Union of Canada (AAUC). The Women's Amateur Athletic Federation of Canada, formed in 1925, became a part of the AAUC in 1954. To provide a forum for discussing their problems, the sports governing bodies organized the Canadian Sports Advisory Council in the 1950s and changed its name to the Canadian Amateur Sports Federation in 1963. The Canadians have participated in the Olympics, the Pan-American Games, and the British Empire and Commonwealth Games. They served as host for the 1967 Pan-American Games, and in 1934 and 1954 for the British Empire and Commonwealth Games. In international competitions, the performances of Canadian athletes has been particularly outstanding in ice hockey and figure skating.

In summer, there is a flow of traffic in Canada to cottages, campgrounds, beaches, and the unsurpassed beauty of the wilderness areas and the national and provincial parks. A gun and fishing pole are standard equipment in the average home, and most children can ice-skate before they go to school. The claim is made that the Canadians originated ice hockey, which is their major amateur and professional sports' attraction, but the sport has an ancient ancestry through shinty, hurly, and bandy. Hockey, curling, and skiing are included in the curriculum in an increasing number of schools; competitions are held between schools, sometimes on a provincial basis. Curling is the only sport in which a national student championship is held.

The Canadians play four types of football: association, rugby, American, and Canadian football. Basketball and baseball are growing in favor. Four of the youths on the original basketball team organized by James Naismith at the YMCA college in Springfield in 1891–92 were Canadians, and two of them returned home to introduce the game. Girls adopted the sport at McGill in 1902, and many successful women's teams have been developed. Lacrosse is derived from the ancient Indian game of baggataway, which was played after a feast, powwow, or religious ceremony. White men adopted lacrosse about 1840, and, by 1867, rules had been established and play was organized into leagues.

PHYSICAL EDUCATION IN LATIN AMERICA

The advanced cultures of the Aztecs, Mayas, Incas, and most of Latin America came under the military and cultural domination of the Spanish conquistadores soon after their initial explorations in the New World. The Spanish tradition of centralized control by the state and church prevailed; the highest leadership roles were reserved for the Spanish-born colonists; secondary administrative positions were held by colony-born Spaniards. In Brazil, which was colonized by the Portuguese, the influence of the Crown and the political activity of the Church was not as strong as in the Spanish colonies. But in both Spanish and Portuguese America, the white landowners, churchmen, and professional soldiers controlled the wealth and the *mestizos* (white-Indian), Indians, Negroes, *zambosi* (Indian-Negro), and mulattoes were relegated to low-status roles in a feudal society.

The nineteenth-century struggle for independence in Latin America was nourished by several forces: the political and economic restrictions imposed by Spain, the secondary position assigned to colony-born whites, the new social philosophies of the Age of Enlightenment, and the examples of the French and American Revolutions. After Bolivar, San Martin, O'Higgins, Hidalgo, Morelos and other leaders succeeded in liberating their homelands from Spain, the Latin Americans drafted idealistic constitutions, but failed to establish representative democracies and political stability. The wealthy *criollos* who assumed political power perpetuated the rigid social stratification and remained aloof from the Industrial Revolution which helped incorporate the masses into the political process in Europe and the United States. During the postcolonial era of regional hacienda control, strongman rule, chronic revolutions, and economic chaos, the status of the disadvantaged masses did not improve. The Indians were actually placed in a less favorable position, for they lost the benefits of Spanish legislation which previously had given them some protection.

Latin America is a land of contrasts and paradoxes. Nations still struggle with a staggering array of traditional problems; they enjoy the benefits of some spectacular successes, but some advances have given birth to new problems. In Argentina, Uruguay, and Chile, the standard of living and literacy rates are quite high, but in Bolivia, Haiti, and some Central American countries the people are plagued with poverty and the illiteracy rates run over sixty percent. Although some changes are taking place, an extremely wide economic and cultural gap exists between the upper class, which comprises a small part of the population and the masses of rural and urban laborers who live in a separate, stagnant world of hopelessness and helplessness. The middle class is small and has little power in most countries.

The gulf between rural and urban society is also great, particularly in the countries with a large Indian and *mestizo* population, such as Bolivia, Peru, Ecuador, and parts of Mexico and Central America. Because of the miserable life in the isolated villages and countryside, uneducated and unskilled peasants are pouring into fast-growing, impressive cities. In six countries fifty percent or more of the population live in cities. The flight to the cities has created slums where illness, malnutrition, and poverty rob people of their initiative and form a volatile political pool of frustrated human beings.

The people in Latin America are poor in the midst of rich natural resources, for much of the continent is unexplored and undeveloped. Most of the people are engaged in agriculture, and in many countries a one-crop economy and the wildly fluctuating world market produce cyclical economic chaos. The system of big land holdings and peon-patron relationships limits competition and the need to be efficient and places the masses at the mercy of the good will of the elite. The primitive agricultural methods fail to produce a food supply that can keep pace with the annual increase in population.

Population experts are astounded by the patterns they chart for Latin America. Until recently, approximately half of the children died before reaching school age. Improvements in health services, sanitation, and diets during this century have brought about spectacular reductions not only in infant mortality but also in deaths from malaria, yellow fever, hookworm, and smallpox. As a result, the population in Latin America has doubled in the past thirty years; the annual growth rate of the population is now one of the highest in the world. Moreover, the education of this mushrooming school-age group must be provided for by a proportionally smaller economically-active age group.

Frequent military coups and chronic political instability, lack of capital and technical knowledge, and runaway inflation and flagrant tax dodging have had an adverse effect on the development of the Latin American nations. The industrialization of society and the growth of the physical education movement are impeded by the belief that physical labor and exercise are socially degrading and by the inadequacy of mass public education. Efforts to unify nations and to move forward are hampered by the cultural and geographical isolation of self-contained villages and by the meager means of communication and transportation between and within countries. Social change and national development are slowed down by nepotism and political favoritism. The tendency in Latin America is to place loyalty to extended family ties and regional leaders above that of the nation.

The problems to be solved in Latin America are formidable, but the passage from agrarian feudalism to industrial egalitarianism and the emergence of a new humanity through creative effort is getting underway. A fusion of many ethnic strains has been achieved with less racial discrimination than in many parts of the world. In general, however, the lighter the man's skin, the higher is his socioeconomic status. During the past fifty years considerable advanced social and labor legislation has been passed. In the future, less of the profit from industry and the exploitation of natural resources will go into foreign pockets. Many foreign concerns which, earlier in the century, were encouraged to come to Latin America have been placed under strict government control or their assets have been seized. Nationalism and resentment of foreign influence is strong in Latin America, some industrialization and economic independence are being realized, a small middle class is emerging, and the economic expectations of the illiterate masses and their aspirations for social justice are rising.

Militarism is still prevalent, as is often the case in underdeveloped nations. Since 1939, South America has experienced thirty-nine military coups which have affected nine of the ten principal countries. Not uncommonly, the army personnel administers elections, builds roads, develops physical education and sports programs, provides the doctors and teachers in desolate areas, and teaches illiterate recruits how to read and write. The military leaders have always been active in politics and have traditionally joined the social elite in resisting change. In recent years, however, some young officers, often in association with the civilian middle-class leaders, have rebelled against the powerful ruling elite, including some senior officers, and have fought for, and launched civil action and social reform programs.

The Church dignitaries who share power with the social elite have traditionally sought to preserve the status quo, have opposed secular education, and in many cases have been rather apathetic about the development of anything beyond a rudimentary education for girls and for the really poor. As a result of pressures from anticlerical revolutionaries, the Church, in most countries, has lost large landholdings and its absolute control over education. But Latin America is still predominately Catholic, and the Church continues to play a very active part in politics and education, and in family and community life. Some of the lower clergy played an important role in the independence movement, and in recent years, the Church has begun to awaken to the need for social justice, government reforms, and the modernization of its educational system and to voice the social doctrines expressed in the *Rerum Novarum* of Pope Leo XIII and in the *Mater et Magistra* of Pope John.

As a result of the influence of the Church, Latin American philosophy is dominated by Aristotelian-Thomism. Dialectical materialism has made some inroads in certain political circles, but empiricism and pragmatism have not had a strong influence. The consistent emphasis placed on the inferior nature of the physical being, the fatalistic acceptance of one's status in life, and the belief that the passive endurance of poverty and disease on earth is a means of attaining eternal salvation has tended to retard the development of physical education, health, science, and industry. Yet, in association with religious observances and holidays, the recreational life of the people is enriched by group activity, colorful parades, gay fiestas, and much dancing and singing in stunning costumes or native dress.

In most Latin American countries, educational administration and finance are the responsibility of the central government, but some decentralization exists in several countries. Because the Minister of Education is a political appointee, who changes with every change in government, educational development is impeded in politically unstable countries. The national directorates of the different types and levels of schools are isolated from each other to such an extent that little coordination exists. The national ministry of education determines what is to be taught and allows little or no flexibility for regional adaptations. In most countries, the national ministry also controls the certification, appointment, transfer, promotion, and inspection of teachers. Seniority and political affiliations are often given greater consideration than professional qualifications in the appointment of teachers and administrators.

The men in power in Latin America are beginning to bring about some improvements in education. But most nations still allot considerably more money to defense than to education and spend a large share of the educational funds for central administration. Centralized control of education also is, in part, responsible for the great discrepancy in the number and quality of the schools in the rural areas and capital cities. Because of the limited taxable resources and the reluctance of conservative elements to support anything more than a minimum education for the masses, insufficient funds for education are a chronic problem. Some moderate and some large increases in the percentage of the national budget for education are being made, but as yet the increase in Latin America as a whole has not been noteworthy.

In most Latin American countries, primary education is free and compulsory for six years, but the attendance laws are not enforced. No schools are available in many rural areas, and most of those that are, offer only a two- to four-year program. Many children do not attend school because of the lack of roads and transportation, the poor state of their health, the inadequacy of their diet, the apathy of their parents, the early age at which they must go to work, the unrelatedness of the curriculum to their needs and their culture, and the inability of teachers to communicate in the language that Indian children speak. Because of the low initial school attendance and the high drop-out rates, the average school attendance of the population is probably less than three years. Only half of the children between five and eighteen years of age are in school, and the absentee rate of the enrolled students is high. Out of every one thousand students who enter school, five hundred drop out the first year, sixty enter secondary school, six enroll in the university, and one earns a college diploma.

For the most part, only upper-class and some middle-class children can afford to go to secondary school. Between thirty and fifty percent of them attend private schools, usually church-related schools. Few comprehensive, coeducational, or rural secondary schools are found in Latin America. Most secondary schools offer a five- or six-year university-preparatory program, but some teacher-training secondary schools and more recently vocational and agricultural schools have been established that offer a two- to five-year program. The secondary school population since 1940 has outstripped population growth, but the training of high school teachers has not kept pace with the influx of students.

The colonial, Church-related universities, which were among the oldest universities in the world, trained an elite corps of men for the priesthood and traditional professions. The public universities that were established after the revolution continued to serve a small aristocracy. But the student reform movement which began in Argentina in 1918, the emergence of a middle class and their demands for a higher education, and the need for industrialization in Latin America have produced a sudden flood of students and pressures that promise to bring about drastic changes in the university system.

A few universities in Latin America offer students an excellent education, but most institutions are plagued with inefficient administration, instructional incompetence, and student strikes. A university usually consists of a loose union of independent nonresidential schools with duplicate courses, libraries, and activities, and they jealously guard their own identities. Most classes are taught by part-time professors. The curriculums are fixed and emphasize specialization in law, medicine, and civil engineering; little or no provision is made for research or graduate work. Rectors and deans have short terms; the professors on the university ruling councils are often outnumbered by the student and alumni representatives. Students take an active part in political life. Some of them remain in the university indefinitely and build a career on student leadership and subsidies from national political parties. The students have helped bring about reforms in society and education, but many youths neglect their academic studies to pursue campus and national political interests, some of them exercise their power in an irresponsible manner, and not uncommonly, their legitimate aspirations are exploited by other interests.

The training programs for teachers in many Latin American countries are inadequate. The preparation of elementary teachers, with a few exceptions, takes place in secondary-level normal schools. Rural teachers pursue a three- or four-year training program beyond their abbreviated primary education. Urban elementary teachers pursue a training program that is equal to or slightly longer than the secondary academic program. Many normal school graduates use their education as a stepping stone to other employment and do not remain in elementary school teaching. Approximately forty-five percent of the elementary school teachers have not had a normal school education.

Secondary school and normal school teachers attend either higher normal schools, pedagogical institutes, or universities, depending upon the country. Programs to prepare vocational teachers are just beginning to be developed. In Argentina, practically all teachers have been trained professionally, but in most countries many untrained, under-trained, and un-committed teachers are employed on all school levels. In a secondary school or university, two-thirds or more of the teachers may be part-time employees who may have university degrees but little or no professional preparation for teaching. These *por-hora* teachers are usually doctors, lawyers, government employees, or business men who look upon their teaching duties as secondary pursuits and do not always meet their classes. Physical educators are in short supply, particularly women physical educators. Many physical education administrators and teachers are political appointees who have had no training in the field.

The ratio of school children to taxpayers is excessively high—twice as high as in Western Europe. Close to half of the population in Latin America is under twenty-one years of age. The population explosion, plus the growing recognition of the desirability of education and the chronic lack of funds, has created an acute shortage of school facilities and equipment which were seriously deficient to begin with. Three shifts of classes are held in some schools; fifty to seventy pupils are crammed into bare classrooms where essential teaching equipment—chalk, paper, pencils, books—let alone games, sports, and gymnastic equipment are lacking or are inferior and in short supply. Many schools are located in crowded urban areas, many are rented, many were originally built as private residences or army barracks. Gymnasiums are not available in most schools. Little space is allotted for playgrounds; the patio, or a grassy or hard-surfaced area may serve the purpose, but dirt playgrounds are prevalent, particularly in rural areas. A school sports ground may be available, or the students may use the municipal athletic fields which may be some distance from the school. Some urban schools are impressive structures and well-equipped, but they are the rare exception, and because of insufficient maintenance funds, even well-constructed schools deteriorate rapidly.

The educational philosophy which prevailed in the United States was introduced in Argentina as a result of President Sarmiento's association with Horace Mann and the American school teachers Sarmiento brought to the new republic. More recently, Uruguay, Chile, Cuba, Brazil, Mexico and other countries have initiated educational reforms. Changes are underway, but for the most part, instruction still consists of formal lectures, rote memorization, and routine examinations. Little use is made of the scientific method, class discussions, laboratory experiments, or library experiences. Communication between teachers, teachers and students, and schools on the various levels is extremely limited. Dismally low salaries force many teachers to hold two or three jobs and to devote considerable time to politics and union activities, including strikes, which undermines their health and teaching efficiency.

On all school levels, the encyclopedic, fragmented, and uncoordinated curriculum is not sufficiently responsive to the needs of the community and fails to prepare youth adequately for a productive role in society. The many ministry-prescribed subjects are crammed into rigid time schedules; local modifications by perceptive teachers are not encouraged; the students often take twelve courses at the same time.

The programs, philosophy, and methods of education in Latin America are primarily geared to the social, economic, and intellectual objectives of the entrenched hierarchy of an earlier era. But the threat of Castro-type revolutions and concern about the economic vigor of their nations have convinced some members of the power elite that improving the lot of the underprivileged, providing them with the functional knowledges and skills that are the lifeblood of technological progress, imbuing them with a sense of nationalism, and helping them develop new attitudes and values are necessary for the development of their country as a whole.

The clamor for progress was translated into official language in the Act of Bogotá in 1960 and the Alliance for Progress in 1961 which stressed the need for land, tax, health, and educational reforms and launched an all-out attack to eradicate illiteracy, poverty, and narrow sectionalism. Long-term planning and cooperative action were tools to be used in fashioning a new society. During the 1960s, plans were made to accelerate the extension of education and the development of industry, to establish a common market that would unite Latin America in one free-trading zone, to build more roads, to improve harbors, and to construct telecommunications that would enable Latin Americans to trade goods and ideas more easily.

Some Latin American countries are now beginning to effect the long-term plans for education which they drafted according to the manpower needs for carrying out socioeconomic development. The large-scale reform of education is being carried out with the help of the Organization of American States (OAS), UNESCO, WHO, UNICEF, The International Labor Organization, the Pan-American Union, the United States Agency for International Development (AID), the Peace Corps, and many foreign companies, foundations, and universities.

The educational reform laws of some countries provide for a greater degree of decentralization and flexibility in their educational system. Many Latin American governments are striving to build more schools and play areas, to extend primary education to all children, to renovate the secondary school curriculum and teaching methods, to develop science, physical education, and sports programs, to provide guidance services and health services, to train intermediate-level agricultural, industrial, and commercial technicians, to expand and upgrade teacher-training programs, to develop university research programs and extension programs, and to train more natural scientists, social scientists, agricultural experts, nurses, and business administrators.

To integrate the indigenous population into the national life and to close the great social distance between educators and rural people, centers have been established in Mexico, Chile, Puerto Rico, and Venezuela to teach leaders how to establish rapport with rural people, how to communicate in their language, and how to help them improve their economy and modify their fate through community action. In Bolivia and some other countries, education has been made compulsory for illiterate adults under forty years of age. Many rural teachers are not only helping eradicate illiteracy and providing elementary instruction for children and adults, but also helping families improve their housekeeping, health, sanitation, child care, farming, and recreational practices. Rural education and literacy programs are carried out by "cultural missions" in Mexico; mobile educational units; roving self-help action leaders; bilingual school in the Peruvian jungles; *nucleo* schools in rural Bolivia, Guatemala, and Peru; "radio schools" in Colombia and Chile; the Vicos self-help experiment in the Peruvian Andes; and through television programs in Mexico, Cuba, and Colombia and other countries. Regional centers have also been established in Mexico, Central America, and Brazil to produce low-cost textbooks and reading materials, some of which are bilingual.

The Latin American countries are slowly becoming integrated into the worldwide physical education and sports movements. Geographical isolation and great distances make it difficult for athletes and professional leaders to meet, but contacts have been made more frequently during the past few decades. Among the professional meetings that have been held to exchange ideas are the Pan-American Congresses on Physical Education in Brazil (1943), Mexico (1946), Uruguay (1950) where a separate sports medicine group was organized, and Colombia (1965); Inter-American seminars in Chile (1956) and Peru (1958); a World Congress on Sports Medicine in Chile (1960); an inter-American symposium in Chile (1963); and the sixth annual meeting of the International Council on Health, Physical Education, and Recreation in Rio de Janeiro (1963).

For many years, the Latin American Ling societies, affiliates of the parent Ling organization at Stockholm, have been represented in international meetings. A South American athletic meet was held in Buenos Aires as early as 1910. The first Central American Games were held in Mexico in 1926. The Bolivarian Games, in which countries liberated by Simon Bolivar participate, were first held in Bogotá in 1938. The Pan-American Games, which are staged one year prior to the World Olympic Games, have been held in Buenos Aires (1951), Mexico City (1955), Chicago (1959), São Paulo (1963), and Winnipeg (1967), and Colombia has been selected as host for the 1971 Games. Since first showing interest in the Olympic Games by coming to Los Angeles in 1932, Latin American countries have responded enthusiastically to succeeding Games.

In the crucial years that lie ahead, physical education can play an important role in the regeneration of human potential in Latin America. Traditionally, the opinions of sportsmen, journalists, and military men have often carried more weight than the voice of physical educators. The wealthy class and military men have given support to the sports club movement and the preparation of athletes for national and international competitions, but national leaders have not exhibited the same interest in earmarking funds for the development of physical education programs in the schools. Some of the educational reform programs have made firm commitments to support health, physical education, and recreation, but physical educators have not usually been represented on the decision-making levels where the priority of educational projects are determined.

In 1967, UNESCO-ICHPER initiated a project to study the role of health, physical education and recreation in developing countries. Dr. Leona Holbrook, the project chairman, selected Chile for a case study. A few of her recommendations[1] are summarized as follows:

1. Place professional personnel in the field on national decision-making bodies concerned with planning for curriculums, instructional materials, teacher training programs, school construction, and budgets.

[1]Leona Holbrook, "Report UNESCO-ICHPER, Study in Educational Planning for Health, Physical Education, and Recreation for School Age Youth In and Out of School—Pilot Project in Chile," (working copy, mimeographed) 1968.

2. Provide for health and physical education programs and facilities in all types and levels of schools and place professional personnel in charge of the programs.
3. Make schools responsible for meeting the requirements for physical education programs if they are to share in the educational equalization allotments.
4. Build model schools at each level with physical education, health, and recreation programs, facilities, and staffs that can inform regional administrators, teachers, and citizens of the possibilities for development.
5. Strengthen the concept of physical education as a part of the total education of both girls and boys, rather than as a junior professional sports program. Develop local and interschool sports programs which include all students and do not make early eliminations and selections for championships.
6. Coordinate the efforts of the physical education institutes. Make the institutes an integral part of the universities with the same general basic requirements rather than academically and geographically disassociated units.
7. Amplify the plans for developing day camps, play areas, recreation centers, and summer camps, particularly in rural and substandard housing areas; prepare professional recreation leaders to staff the programs and provide short-term courses for youths who can serve as assistants.
8. Encourage the national government and the Regional Center for School Construction for Latin America in Mexico to include adequate gymnasiums and play space in school building plans and give the proper authorities technical advice about the construction of facilities.
9. Give technical advice to vocational education departments and small industries to encourage the construction of a more complete supply of quality sports and play equipment and installations.
10. Introduce concepts concerning play, games, recreation, physical education, and health in the reading material for all children and adults and in publications distributed by government, labor, social, and educational agencies.
11. Develop a UNESCO-Chilean Commission to carry out the above recommendations, to advise various branches of the government, and to get professionals in the field to work productively in solving new problems.

In Latin America some remarkable results have been realized in the development of education, physical education, recreation and health in recent years. But the lack of financial resources, the shortage of trained administrators and educational specialists, the frequent turnover of the politically appointed ministry personnel, and the many traditions that are resistant to change impede progress. Moreover, needs tend to outpace progress and noble statements of objectives are not always implemented. Advances are made rhetorically, but the actualization of the plans is often frustrated. The announcement of the obituaries and rebirth of programs are not uncommon. Some progress is being made, however, and the people are convinced that the continued pursuit of their objectives is vital to the welfare of their nations.

PHYSICAL EDUCATION IN ARGENTINA

Three-fourths of the people of Argentina live in a semicircle extending three hundred miles around Buenos Aires. Here are concentrated the large cities, the industrial plants, the golden grain fields, and the rich grazing lands. In the south are the windswept sheep pastures of Patagonia; in the west are the wine-producing areas. Lacking a good supply of iron, coal, and water power, Argentina has been handicapped in the development of industry, but programs have been launched to stimulate manufacturing. Unlike most Latin American countries, Argentina has a large middle class, the fourth highest per capita calorie consumption in the world, and a population that is ninety-seven percent Caucasian. The public schools reach more children and the literacy rate is higher than in most Latin American countries. The federal government is responsible for public secondary schools and some public elementary schools, and enters into certain agreements with the provinces that provide the remaining elementary schools.

The secondary school reform in 1898 and the inauguration of a teacher training course in 1901 gave impetus to the development of physical education. The movement gained momentum in 1905 when a Special Inspection of Physical Education was established and a daily period of exercises was introduced in the primary schools. Dr. Enrique Romero Brest was placed in charge of the program and continued to give vigorous leadership to the profession for many years. He helped develop the *National Teaching and Physical Education Plan* in 1905 and created a course for teachers in Buenos Aires in 1906 which led to the establishment of the school that later became known as the National Institute of Physical Education.

A significant advance was made in 1938 when the Ministry of Education created a General Department of Physical Education. However, during the existence of the National Council of Physical Education, which was created under the Ministry of National Defense in 1947 and dissolved in 1951, both official and private physical education and sport were directed into centralized, military channels. But the General Department of Physical Education made considerable progress, particularly after it was reorganized in 1958. Among its accomplishments were the development of programs and facilities in the secondary schools, teaching guides and training programs, a corps of inspectors, medical services, and intramural and inter-scholastic competitions, including the *Juegos Intercolegiales Sudamericanos* (1960), and physical education festivals.

In 1963, a more comprehensive administrative agency was organized, the National Board of Physical Education, Sports, and Recreation, under the Ministry of Education and Justice, which has continued to provide leadership for the secondary schools, has elaborated plans for developing physical education in the elementary school, has drafted cooperative agreements with provincial governments, and has developed plans for the promotion of recreation, camping, and sports, including the establishment of the new National Institute of Sports. In addition to the leadership supplied by the national government, nearly all provinces have Boards of Physical Education, and some cities have boards that promote a number of sports, recreational, and camping activities.

Over the years the physical education program in Argentina has been subject to many influences. In the isolated and short-lived gymnastic programs that sprang up about the turn of the century, the French method predominated. Sports and games were introduced later in a few schools, and, owing to political conditions, military exercises and scholastic battalions replaced gymnastics for about five years. Between 1905 and 1938, the physical education program consisted of equal amounts of gymnastics and games and sports. The Swedish gymnastics and the techniques developed by Tissié predominated. Starting in 1938, the sports program and skill tests were improved and the calisthenics practiced by the Christian Youth Association of Buenos Aires were introduced. The results of the calisthenics were considered to be unsatisfactory because of their limited formative value, and Professor Carlos Hardelin, a graduate of the Central Gymnastic Institute of Stockholm, soon gave a new impetus to the Swedish method. A visit of Niels Bukh's gymnastic team in 1938 led to the adoption of some of his ideas.

During the 1950s several visitors created interest in improving the program, particularly on the elementary level. In 1951 and 1953, Professor Curt Johansson from Stockholm conducted courses in modern gymnastics showing the most advanced techniques. About this time, the influence of Thulin was felt, and the translation into Spanish of *Infantile Gymnastics* (1954) by Maja Carlquist and Tora Amylong also had an impact. The visit in 1954 of Ernst Idla's team of women gave impetus to the "education of movement." Courses and conferences were held by Professor Gerhard Schmidt from Austria in 1959, Professors Carl and Liselott Diem in 1961, and Liselott Diem and Irma Nicolai in 1962.

The present program of physical education places emphasis on gymnastics, but also includes games, dances, skill and capacity tests, track and field events, basketball, softball, soccer, rugby, handball, field hockey and *pelota al cesta*. Intramural and interscholastic contests are held in most sports, and physical education festivals, gymnastic galas, and evening folk-dance parties are held periodically. Wherever possible, swimming, open-air living, rowing, and skiing are practiced.

Physical education has been obligatory in Argentina on the primary and secondary school levels for many years. The federal government has been responsible for the secondary school program, but each province has had its own legislation regarding the elementary schools, and some provinces have had more advanced programs than others. In recent years, the federal government has launched a program to improve the provisions for physical education in elementary schools. The Department of Physical Education, Recreation, and Sports has made agreements with provincial governments to provide them with assistance and has developed teacher-training programs and instructional materials for the elementary school level.

In the secondary schools, specialists teach physical education classes, but they rarely work full time in one school; most of them work in two or more schools or also work for sports clubs. Physical education is not obligatory on the university level, but most universities have a Department of Physical Education that provides facilities for sports and organizes competitions.

Considerable effort has been expended to increase the number of qualified physical educators in recent years at the National Institutes of Physical Education of General Belgrano and Dr. Enrique Romero Brest in Buenos Aires, the national institutes founded at Santa Fé (1959) and at Mendoza (1960), the School of Physical Education of Tucumán National University (1953), the Physical Education Institute of the Province of Córdoba, and the National University of La Plata (1953), which also has a program concerned exclusively with research that was created in 1919. In addition, many short-term regional, national, and international physical education courses are offered. Recreation leaders are trained at the Physical Education School of the Municipality of Buenos Aires. Sports technicians are trained at the Institute of Sports which was created in 1963.

The Association of Physical Education Teachers, which has done much to upgrade and promote physical education programs since it was founded in 1939, organized the first Argentine Congress of Physical Education in 1943, and helped found the South American Confederation of Physical Education Professors Association in 1950. The Argentine Confederation of Graduates of the National Institutes of Physical Education, founded in 1955, has branches throughout the country. The Faculty Club of Professors of the National Institute of General Belgrano has published the *Physical Education Review* since 1958. Research and technical articles are published in *Amka, Kinesiologia, Medicina del Deporte y del Trabajo,* and *Medicina Fisica y Rehabilitacion.*

The Argentineans are soccer-mad, but they also love horse racing and betting, rugby, tennis, and other sports. Crowds flock to beaches and parks, such as Mar del Plata on the Atlantic coast and Palermo Park in Buenos Aires which includes a race track, tennis courts, polo fields, riding trails, and numerous athletic clubs. Affluent Argentineans ski and fish at the fashionable resort at San Carlos de Bariloche in the Andes. The Argentine National Park Service, which gets some revenue from a national lottery, operates twelve parks. In the cities in recent years there has been a revival of interest in folk dancing and native music, but the young people of the nation that gave birth to the tango at the turn of the century have abandoned it for the latest modern dances.

The Argentine cowboys are expert in throwing the *bola* or *boleadero*, a y-shaped arrangement of strands of rawhide with weights at the end. The rough riding game of *el pato*, which is said to have been developed by the gaucho herders of the pampas and the Calchaqui Indians, was banned in 1840. Alberto del Castillo Posse revived the game in 1937, and in 1941 the Pato Federation of twenty-four clubs was formed. The four gaucho-dressed, well-protected players on each team meet on a field resembling a polo area with baskets attached to tall poles on either end. By means of skillful riding and passing, the offensive team advances an inflated ball (*pato*) with six leather handles and strives to score a goal by tossing the ball into the opposing basket. The defensive combination tries to intercept the passing or to catch up with the ball carrier. The advancing rider must offer the *pato* to the defensive player who overtakes him, and they they wrestle for possession of it.

Some provinces and municipalities provide sports, camping, and recreational facilities and programs, and innumerable clubs offer facilities for sports. Membership in some clubs is based on nationality or work; some clubs are inexpensive and others are exclusive showplaces. The Gymnastic and Fencing Club of Buenos Aires has a ten-floor building as well as suburban open-air sections. Many of the federations that direct sports are affiliated with the Argentine Confederation of Sports. Argentina was host for the first South American athletic meet held in 1910 and the first Pan-American Games. The contingent of Argentinean athletes at Pan-American and Olympic games is quite large and their performance is noteworthy.

PHYSICAL EDUCATION IN BOLIVIA

The landlocked, mineral-rich Republic of Bolivia is sparsely populated. The tropical plains and mountain slopes that cover the eastern two-thirds of the nation are largely unexploited. Eighty percent of the people live on the barren western plateau which averages 12,000 feet above sea level. In this cold, windswept highland, cradled among the snowcapped peaks of the Andes, tough, discontented Indians gouge tin out of the mountains, derby-hatted women sort the lumps, and farmers coax barley, wheat, oats, and potatoes to grow with primitive agricultural tools.

Since winning their independence in 1825, the Bolivians have had no less than 180 revolutions and have lost four wars and half of their territory, including their outlet to the sea. About sixty-five percent of the Bolivians are Indians, and most of them live in relative poverty. When the National Revolutionary Movement (MNR) came to power after the Revolution of 1952, an effort was made to improve the status of the Indians by enfranchising them, instituting agrarian reforms, nationalizing three big tin combines, and launching an Educational Reform Program. Because of inexperienced management, run-down equipment, widespread strikes, and hyperinflation, the President was overthrown in 1964 and replaced by the vice-president and a military junta. Although considerable political and social unrest exists, some progress has been made in recent years in resettling highlanders in the fertile lowlands, building farm-to-market roads, rehabilitating state-owned mines and railroads, and improving agriculture, health care, and education.

Less than half of the school-age children attend school in Bolivia, but those who do attend may participate in some physical education activities, for the subject has been obligatory since 1928. Early in the century, French and German military missions introduced some sports in the National Army and established gymnastics that were strongly influenced by the work of GutsMuths, Jahn, Amorós, and Hébert. Between 1914 and 1920, Henry De Genst and Julien Ficher, the leaders of a Belgian educational mission, trained teachers in the Ling gymnastics, wrote books, and created considerable interest in dances and sports. In addition, in 1914 De Genst helped found the La Paz Football Association. Political conditions interrupted the work initiated by the Belgian mission for a few years, but when the government changed, President Hernando Siles reinstituted the program and placed Saturnino Rodrigo in charge of it. In 1926–1927, a physical education course was offered at the University of La Paz, and the forty-two graduates of the program were assigned to positions throughout the Republic. The Normal Superior Institute of Physical Education was established in 1931 as a result of the urging of Professor Rodrigo and Captain Jorge Rodriguez H., who had previously been sent by the government to visit a number of European physical education institutions in Europe.

The physical education program in Bolivia is administered by the National Department of Physical Education in Schools which has two inspectors, one for boys and one for girls. The physical education program consists mostly of gymnastics, games, sports, track and field, hikes, and folk dances. Periodically, the National Department organizes gymnastic festivals, dances, or games which are held in stadiums throughout the country. The folk dancers in these events provide city dwellers with reminiscences of their rural childhood days.

Outside of school hours, the students may participate in Boy Scouts, Girl Guides, or mountain climbing, and skiing (Andinism). Some students compete in events that are sponsored by their sports clubs and associations. Sports equipment and awards for athletes are provided by the National Department which receives ten percent of the funds of the National Committee of Sports for the promotion of physical education in the schools.

Special departments promote sports activities in the universities which, through their clubs, organize national and international competitions. University students are also permitted to become members of nonuniversity leagues. The army and police corps have their own organizations for promoting physical education, which are administered by graduates of the Normal Superior Institute of Physical Education.

The Normal Superior Institute of Physical Education trains teachers for the schools, armed forces, and sports clubs. A secondary school teacher pursues a three-year course; a sports, athletics, or dance technician pursues a three-month course. The salaries that teachers receive are higher in city than in rural areas, but they are the same for both sexes and all teachers. Through the *Federación Nacional de Professores de Educatión Física* teachers disseminate information, protect their interests, and organize competitions and refresher courses. By ministerial decree, a special award is made to physical educators for meritorious service. All members of the profession receive free entrance to sports competitions.

The National Committee of Sports, founded in 1939, is composed of members of the sport federations, the army, the police force, the universities, the National Department of Physical Education, and the press. The Committee acts periodically as the Bolivian Olympic Committee, promotes sports among the nonschool population, engages technicians, and controls the sports fields and facilities that are financed through government subsidies and special taxes. Playgrounds and parks are built by municipal authorities. The most popular sports are football, basketball, boxing, volleyball, handball, Andinism, and fishing. Big trout are pulled from Lake Titicaca which has been a favorite fishing ground for balsa-boating Indians since the days of the ancient Incas. United States specialists stocked the lake in 1939 with trout to improve the protein content of the people's diet.

Most Indian children attend school briefly, if at all, and go to work at an early age. Many of them live in dirt-floored, one-room huts with no water or sanitary facilities, but pictures of football players and religious figures are usually tacked on the wall. Their mothers cook scanty meals over cow-dung fires. Because fuel is scarce, it is not used for heating the house or water for bathing. To help deaden pain, cold, and hunger, the Indians drink their native corn beer or raw cane alcohol or chew coca leaves. But the youths who survive on the high, forbidding plateau develop sufficient stamina to participate in sports and to dance madly in colorful costumes on religious feast days and national holidays.

Ball games among the Indians in Bolivia were first reported in the eighteenth century. The French anthropologist Métraux reports Indian tribes playing several ball games that have magical implications. In one game played by the Chiquitos, a rubber ball is headed back and forth between players "with a complex ceremonialism." Among the Chiriguano, the women throw stones or a hollow clay ball at rows of maize grains, an activity which may be connected with a fertility cult. The Araona play a game in which the ball is bounced by the stomach.

PHYSICAL EDUCATION IN BRAZIL

Beyond the picturesque tides that roll into the sprawling coastline of Brazil lies a nation that exceeds the United States in size and represents half of South America's land mass, wealth, and people. The economic center of the nation and half of the population is located near the coast in a few southeastern states. The vast, hot, Amazon jungle and the rich grazing lands in the southern interior lowlands are not easily accessible. In the barren, northeastern scrublands, the people are poverty-stricken and the average life span is thirty-five years.

Brazil has potentially more arable land than in all of Europe, a good supply of the important minerals, and the world's largest hydroelectric potential. Agriculture is the principal economic activity, but a significant amount of industrial expansion is underway, and a new capital, Brasilia, has been carved out of the wilderness to encourage the development of the interior. Yet this land of plenty has been more familiar with impoverishment than prosperity.

Politically, Brazil has been less rocked by revolutions than her neighbors. In 1822, the Brazilians declared their independence from Portugal and established a monarchy. A republic was established in 1889, and a new democratic constitution was adopted in 1891. Officially, the language in Brazil is Portuguese, but the more than one hundred and fifty Indian tribes speak scores of dialects. Veritable islands of unassimilated Italians, Poles, Germans, and Japanese are gradually being integrated into Brazilian national life. Brazil, like Cuba, Venezuela, and Panama is a land of great racial variety and Negroes and mulattoes have won national recognition in the arts, music, literature, and athletics.

The long neglect of education has caused some of the problems that Brazil faces today. During the first century of independence, some public authorities began to concern themselves with the development of education and exhibited some interest in physical education. In 1823, a deputy proposed offering an award to whomever should present a plan of physical, moral, and intellectual education, but no action was taken. In 1851, Law 630 included gymnastics in the primary school curriculum, and four years later, it was extended to the School of Pedro II, a model secondary school. But few children attended school, and considerable opposition to physical education was voiced, particularly when an attempt was made to extend the program to girls. After Rui Barbosa stressed the values of physical education in *Project of Reform of Primary Teaching in Various Complementary Institutions of Public Instruction* in 1882, physical education began to gain some acceptance.

When an educational reform movement was launched to establish schools for all Brazilian children after the Revolution of 1930, physical education was made compulsory in secondary schools and was given greater recognition and support. The Ministry of Education and Health, which was established in 1930 under the Vargas regime, organized a Division of Physical Education in 1937 and created a National Council of Sports as an advisory body. In 1953, the Ministry became the Ministry of Education and Culture and all health activities were transferred to a separate Ministry of Health. On the state level, an office under the Secretary of Education is usually responsible for physical education.

The police force and the army established the first schools to train physical educators. The Physical Education School of the Police Force was founded in 1909 in São Paulo, probably as a result of the arrival of a French military mission two years previously. A provisional course of physical education was offered in 1929 in which several officers and elementary teachers enrolled. The School of Physical Education of the Army, which was founded in 1933, served as a source of irradiation for the physical education movement in Brazil.

Two civilian schools were established in the 1930s, one in São Paulo and the other in Rio de Janeiro. The latter, the National School of Physical Education and Sports, which was incorporated in 1939 as one of the schools of the University of Brazil, developed a teacher-training course and a one-year course to qualify physicians as Doctors of Physical Education and Sports. Today, Brazil has ten schools that train physical educators and two of them fall under the federal universities. The programs for M.A. professors and for sports technicians are three years in length. The program for physical education instructors is one year in length for applicants who are already qualified to teach academic subjects in the primary schools. All teachers take a course in Physical Education, Recreation, and Games each year that they are enrolled in a normal school. In 1966, the 1140 students who were enrolled in the undergraduate physical education program in institutions of higher education constituted 0.6 percent of the total enrollment.

The 1961 Law of Directives and Bases of National Education which provided for some decentralization of education and many other reforms, also made physical education compulsory for primary and secondary students up to the age of eighteen years. Some school authorities comply with the law, but operate minimal programs because they are reluctant to expend money on physical education, and many youngsters do not benefit from the programs because they are not in school.

Until the last decade, gymnastics dominated the curriculum in Brazil. The German method of gymnastics exerted the greatest influence in the early days in the schools and until about 1920 in the army. The French method, de Joinville-le-Pont, which was introduced by a military mission, held sway between 1920 and 1950. The Swedish and Danish (Niels Bukh) gymnastics and North American (YMCA) calisthenics were also introduced. Today, the Brazilian students prefer sports to gymnastics; hence, sports have come to play an increasingly greater role in the curriculum. Some of the better schools have facilities for basketball, soccer, and tennis, and a few have swimming pools. Dance is a part of the girls' program.

Some sports contests are organized each year among the various secondary schools. Physical education and sports programs outside of school are generally managed by private clubs. The government sponsors some activities of a noncompulsory character. Student associations in the universities, which have achieved considerable power, sponsor social, cultural, sports, and physical education activities. The first Olympic Games of Brazilian Universities were held in 1935.

National sports-governing bodies are subject to governmental supervision through the National Council of Sports. Football, swimming, tennis, rowing, and track and field are affiliated with the Brazilian Sports Confederation. This body was in existence when the government decided to intervene officially in sports. Now, all new sports bodies must form a single confederation and must be approved by the government. Many sports organizations in the larger cities have built gymnasiums, pools, golf links, football and athletic fields, polo grounds, and camps.

Several accounts of the physical prowess of the original inhabitants of Brazil have been recorded. The Indians were skilled in the arts of hunting, fishing, canoeing, and swimming. Foot races were common, both in the hunt and war, and horsemanship was practiced by some tribes. Both the Indians and the Negroes, who performed the menial work under the Spanish, clung to ancestral collective forms of emotional expression. Through the years, the Negroes, who brought their African dances, music, and religious rites with them, have enriched the Brazilian dance movement, and some of their descendants, such as the soccer star, Pelé, have become national sport heroes.

The modern Brazilians are fond of sports; in São Paulo alone, five hundred sports clubs have been formed. Even the women have become more athletic as they have gained greater social freedom. Not surprisingly, Brazilian swimmers are recognized internationally, for in their country the magnificent bathing beaches attract everyone: the upper classes, the tourists, and the poorest favela-dweller. *Fútbol* (soccer) is the sport that intoxicates the nation. In the early days, Argentina and Uruguay dominated soccer in Latin America, but now Brazil is the dominant country. In Rio, 155,000 frenzied fans squeeze into the impressive Maracaña Stadium which has a seven-foot deep moat about the field. The moat protects the visiting players and referees from the famed "twelfth man" on the Brazilian team—the crowd. In addition to soccer, the wealthy Brazilians attend horse races, polo matches, and speedy *pelota* games. The gauchos of the cattle country love a good horse and ride well, and in the jungles, alligator-hunting with bows and arrows, spears and knives, or rifles is a common sport.

In the carefree carnival season, tambourines, gourds, and *cuicas* provide the tempo for folk dances and the latest modern dances. The rich attend exclusive balls in lavish couturier-designed *fantasias*, and the poor parade down gaily-decorated streets in their colorful costumes performing the intricate steps they have practiced for months in neighborhood *escolas da samba*. In the street dances the samba reveals its strong African influence; in the ballroom it is more restrained. Many community celebrations are held in Brazil that include parades, songs and dances stemming from the rituals of the indigenous Indians, the ceremonies of the Catholic church, and the rites of the Africans. Although the traditional *festas* have been diminished and tempered by time, several still remain popular.

Brazil has sixteen national parks, including the spectacular Iguaçu National Park. In Xingu National Park, created in 1961, the last of the Waurá Indians still observe many of the age-old ceremonies. At the close of the day, the men decorate their bodies with a sticky red dye to protect them from supernatural beings, wear bands about their arms and ankles which they believe will give them strength, and engage in wrestling bouts. In the war games at the climax of the dry season, each man's body is elaborately decorated in abstract designs, and the air is filled with the whir of blue-tipped spears, the chant of warriors, and the rhythm of rousing war dances. Several Brazilian tribes participate in ceremonial ball games, such as the tribal initiation ceremony in which Apinaye novices are coated with juice from a tree and are given paddle-like *battledores* with which they try to keep the ball continuously in the air. As a part of their harvest festival, the Eastern Timbira prepare twenty maize-husk balls and in the game keep batting each ball into the air with the palm of the hand until it hits the ground.

PHYSICAL EDUCATION IN CHILE

The boundaries of Chile follow the snow-covered Andes and curl some 2,600 miles along the Pacific Ocean, but in width the nation averages only about 110 miles. The northern area is extremely dry and barren, but rich in nitrate, copper, and other minerals. The "central valley of paradise," with its magnificent climate, is the home of eighty-five percent of the people, the industrial center of the nation, and one of the most fertile agricultural areas in the world. To the south, are found damp, dense forests, lumber camps, and sheep ranches as well as mountainous glaciers, sparkling streams, deep fiords, and island-dotted lakes that blend into a scenic splendor of breathtaking beauty.

Chile has less racial diversity, greater political stability, and a lower illiteracy rate than most Latin American countries. The nation was the first Latin American country to establish a system of public education, to pass a law admitting women to higher education, and to establish a social security system (1924) and other advanced social and labor legislation. The Chilean Armed Forces are divorced from national politics, and the separation of the church and state was achieved in 1925. As the middle class has grown, power has shifted from the conservative right to the democratic left. The democratic left is trying to effect an orderly change that will bring the lower class into fuller participation in the economic and social life and to provide a workable alternative to communism.

The first inhabitants of Chile, the rugged Araucanian Indians participated enthusiastically in sports and heroically defended themselves against their Spanish conquerors. From childhood the Indian boys were trained to swim swift streams, to run through brushwood while shooting arrows and throwing rocks, and to survive the greatest deprivation. At about fifteen years of age they practiced games that resemble certain present-day sports, such as *chueca* which is analogous to hockey, and *linao* which resembles handball.

The inhabitants of European origin in Chile first exhibited an interest in physical education toward the end of the past century. In 1885, the government admitted by contract a group of German teachers who cast the normal schools into the Herbartian mold and gave unprecedented emphasis to physical education, drawing, singing, and the manual arts. In 1889, the Pedagogical Congress discussed the promotion of gymnastics, military exercise, and hygiene and recommended the establishment of a special school to train physical educators. Joaquin Cabezas Garcia, a normal school professor, was sent by the government to Sweden to study physical education and manual arts. Upon his return, he struggled to implant the Ling system and to overcome the opposition of the people who preferred Jahn gymnastics. Joaquin Cabezas Garcia was appointed director of the Institute of Physical and Manual Education when it was opened in 1906, and he continued to provide leadership for physical education in Chile until he retired in 1942. Dr. Luis Bisquertt, a medical doctor and professor of physical education, succeeded him as Director of the Institute, which is now divided into three sections: physical education, home economics, and kinesitherapy. The School of Kinesitherapy was founded in 1944.

Since World War II, the Chileans have embarked on an important educational reform movement. In the 1960s, the plans for unifying the first eight years of general education and the alternative plans for the reorganizing the secondary schools were developed. During these years, the leaders in physical education revised their objectives and courses, developed new plans of study and guides for teachers, and reorganized the teacher training programs.

In general, the new programs allot two to three hours per week to physical education on all levels in all types of school programs. The curriculum includes the study of personal and community health and safety, educational gymnastics based primarily on the Ling system, games, the more popular sports, such as soccer, volleyball, track and field, and basketball, and the folk dances of Chile and other countries. The recommended complementary activities include tennis, weight lifting, swimming, underwater swimming, judo, rugby, water polo, skiing, rowing, mountaineering, orienteering, softball, badminton, and hockey on roller skates. The students are given physical examinations, and they receive grades in physical education which influence their promotion.

During the year, gymnastic exhibitions, field days, and sport competitions are held. School sports competitions are administered by the Primary Schools Sports Federation and the School Sports Associations (Secondary Schools). The leadership for these two bodies is supplied by teachers who sponsor sport clubs and conduct sport competitions from the local to the national levels without remuneration. Most schools have a playground or sports fields, but suitable gymnasiums are scarce. Some new schools and secondary schools have a room or hall that is outfitted for physical education classes.

For many years, classroom teachers and the normal school graduates who had had some specialized training in the field taught physical education classes in the elementary schools. Because of the shortage of teachers, some normal school specialists also taught on the lower secondary school level, particularly in the country. But most teachers in the secondary schools and normal schools were graduates of the Institute of Physical Education of the University of Chile and held university degrees and the title of Professor of State in Physical Education.

The Institute achieved the status of a university school in 1918, a status it later lost but regained in 1932. Until 1960, a physical educator at the Institute pursued a four-year program in contrast to the five-year program that other teachers pursued. In 1961, the Faculty of Philosophy and Education reorganized its administration into three central departments: mathematics and natural science, social studies, and philosophy and letters. The Institute of Physical Education became a professional school to which students were admitted after they had completed a preliminary course of study in one of the three central departments. In recent years, three other universities have begun to develop physical education teacher training programs. Under the new plan for educational reform, a student will obtain the title Professor of State in a Basic School with Specialization in Physical Education (Grades 1–8) by pursuing a three-year program. A student who wants to teach above the eighth grade will pursue the longer and more rigorous program of study and will attain the title of Professor of State in Physical Education. Because of the shortage of teachers, however, inservice training programs will continue to assume great importance.

Physical educators and academic teachers, both male and female, whether in a rural or urban area, are paid the same and have access to administrative positions. Many physical educators have become principals and superintendents. The Chilean Association of Teachers of Physical Education and *The Chilean Review of Physical Education* (formerly the *Bulletin of Physical Education* which was first published in 1934) provide teachers with some information and assistance.

Physical education programs are not well-developed on the university level. One technical university has an obligatory program, and one university offers a voluntary program. At the University of Chile and other universities, a Sports Department under the Student Welfare Section operates the Sports Clubs and the University Sports Association which controls sports competitions. Soccer is the most popular sport, and universities have teams formed of professional players.

The length of Chile presents transportation, time, and cost problems that hamper the development of national sports competitions, but every year sports are becoming more popular. Hundreds of informal sports clubs exist, and some clubs, such as the German Club and the Swiss Club have big athletic parks and send competitive teams all over the world. Many adults belong to the federations that are affiliated with the National Sports Council and international federations. The Council, which was formed in 1938 to control sports, is composed of government officials and representatives of the sports federations.

Soccer attracts fifty percent of the participants in sports and is the only professional sport with fourteen teams in the major league. Crew members of ships that came to Chile for saltpeter at the end of the last century competed in the first soccer games. The English introduced soccer, tennis, rugby, and track and field; the Germans popularized track and field and gymnastics on apparatus; and the YMCA introduced volleyball and the second most popular sport in Chile, basketball. The Scandinavians who surveyed the route of the Trans-Andean railroad in 1880 introduced skiing. The promotional work done in the 1930s by Wendell Hilty, a Swiss ski instructor, and the construction of ski resorts in recent years have made the sport popular. The Chileans, who are noted for their horsemanship and racing stock, love horse races. In many parts of the country, boating, sailing, deep-sea and freshwater fishing attracts both tourists and the local people. The Chilean Lake district, dotted with chalet-like resorts, many built by Swiss settlers, has become an international tourist center. Nineteen areas in Chile have officially been made national parks, many of which exist primarily on paper; but since the formation of the Latin American Committee on National Parks in 1964, the conservation movement has gained momentum.

PHYSICAL EDUCATION IN COLOMBIA

Colombia, occupying the northwest corner of South America, is the fourth most populous country in Latin America. Three mountain ranges, extending from Ecuador, divide the country into three distinct areas, long isolated from one another by poor communication facilities. The flat, grassy lowlands which cover the eastern two-thirds of the country are sparsely settled. The population is about seventy percent *mestizo*, twenty percent white, and the remaining ten percent is Negro, Indian, and mulatto. In this land of coffee, bananas, cattle, emeralds, oil, and gold, the growth of the economy has been relatively good during the last decade, and a high priority is now being given to the stimulation of industry and economic diversification.

The physical education program has developed slowly in Colombia. In 1904, Decree 491 declared physical education to be an indispensable part of education. A law was passed in 1925 which created a National Commission of Physical Education and a National Section of Physical Education. A number of reorganizations of the direction of physical education and sports have taken place since that time. Today, the National Section of Physical Education, under the National Ministry of Education, is responsible for the programs in the schools. The National Council of Physical Education authorizes participation in national and international sports events, recommends policies and means of promoting physical education and sports, and establishes appropriate regulations. The National Council consists of representatives from the Ministries of Education, National Defense, and Public Health; the Colombian Olympic Committee; the national sports associations; the Boy Scouts; the Colombian Association of Universities; the National Section of Physical Education; and the senior members of the faculty of physical education.

As in other South American countries, foreign leaders played a part in helping the Colombians develop their physical education and sports programs. In 1926, Hans Huber signed a contract in Berlin to serve for four years as a professor of physical culture in Colombia. In 1927, the first National Youth Olympics were organized under the direction of Captain

Plinio Pessina, a member of a Swiss Military mission, and Hans Huber played a major role in organizing this event the following year. In 1936, a mission from Chile under the leadership of Candelario Sepúlveda Lafuente, helped organize physical education in Colombia. In 1962, the American Association of Health, Physical Education, and Recreation entered into a contract with the Peace Corps to assist the Colombian people.

The early programs of physical education consisted primarily of gymnastics, marches, military drills, and mass exercises. Today, the official program includes gymnastics, rhythmics, games, Colombian and foreign folk dances, and sports. But in many schools, the European system of gymnastics and soccer predominate. The variety of activities that is offered depends on the availability of equipment, trained personnel, and facilities. The weekly time allotment for physical education classes is two to three hours, but many schools do not meet these standards. In the last two years of secondary school, boys may substitute military science for physical education. On the university level, an optional physical education program was organized at Universidad de Valle in Cali in the 1950s, which later became a required course. The classes were managed originally by students and no formal instruction and no grades were given.

Intramural programs are operated on the intermediate and secondary school levels, but to a lesser extent for girls and in rural areas. Interscholastic competitions for all sports and both sexes are usually concentrated into a few days each year rather than being conducted on a seasonal basis, in part because of transportation problems. On the university level, interfaculty games are held, and, since 1958, University Games (*Juegos Universitarios*) have been held annually in July. At the University Games, which are usually held at a different university each year, students compete in tennis, basketball, soccer, track and field, baseball, volleyball, swimming, ping pong, and chess. The Sports Councils which have been formed at universities are headed by a director who may merely plan for the University Games, or who may be employed as the supervisor of the university's physical education and sports program. The man may hold another position at the university, or, in some instances, he may be a student.

Finding ways of improving and expanding teacher training in health and physical education is of crucial importance in Colombia. A plan for organizing a National Institute of Physical Education was first presented in 1936. A plan for making the Institute an integral part of the National University of Colombia was presented in 1939, but this relationship was terminated in 1942. The school, which has had a rather precarious existence, and has graduated only about twenty students a year, became a section of the National Teachers' University in 1963. The general academic program has been improved, but the facilities for physical education are inadequate. To be admitted to the school, students must hold a secondary school certificate. They pursue a four-year program and earn a *licenciado* in physical education. The *Asociación Nacional de Profesores de Educación Física* keeps teachers informed of developments in their field through meetings and the publication of a bulletin. The National Section of Physical Education publishes teaching guides and organizes some in-service training programs.

The Peace Corps Volunteers who served in Colombia in the 1960s helped local leaders enlarge or establish compulsory service programs in some universities, helped develop intramural programs and strengthen athletic programs, created interest in sports other than soccer, organized summer school courses for teachers, worked with normal school teachers, and organized roving rural units to assist village teachers. Some Peace Corps workers assisted the National Section of Education in administering the American Association for Health, Physical Education, and Recreation Fitness Tests which were accepted in 1965 at the Fourth Pan-American Physical Education Congress in Bogotá. The Peace Corps also initiated discussions to encourage the establishment of teacher-training programs in institutions that had developed sound physical education programs, such as at the University of Valle in Cali.

On Sundays and feast days in Colombia, life revolves around the Church, but other agencies also serve as centers of social and recreational activity. Soccer games, bullfights, horse races, cockfights, and bicycle races attract crowds. The Colombians like to play baseball, and they enjoy swimming where climate and facilities permit. Men spend much time and money at bars where they play *tejo* on the adjacent courts and drink enormous quantities of beer or *aguardiente*, a type of rum. *Tejo*, which stems from a game played by the Chibcha Indians, is played with metal or stone disks that the players throw at a metal pipe which is imbedded in the earth and has a charge of gunpowder at the rim.

PHYSICAL EDUCATION IN ECUADOR

Ecuador straddles the equator, but because of its varying altitude enjoys a wide range of climates. About sixty percent of the population is concentrated in the valleys of the high Sierra country, but the new highways are encouraging migration to the rich agricultural belt along the coast. The vast eastern jungles are sparsely populated. Most Ecuadorians are Indians or *mestizos*, and they work at farming. Many Indian men and children are bilingual, but some women speak only Quechua.

In Ecuador, education received little support until a law passed in 1938 placed all public and private education under the control of the national government. Elementary education is now free, but secondary education is not free. In spite of the effort the government has made, most schools lack physical education facilities and equipment and an insufficient number of schools are available.

Early in this century, a series of foreign teachers introduced gymnastics, but political instability, lack of funds, and moral and religious prejudices impeded the development of the movement. In 1910, a Chilean military mission introduced German gymnastics and sports at the Military School, then army officers offered instruction in the secondary schools in Quito and Guayaquil, and Fernand Pons, a member of a Spanish educational mission, developed a program for primary teachers. In 1915, North American visitors assisted in the development of gymnastics for girls. In 1916, Franz Warzawa came to Ecuador with a German educational mission and did much to systematize and popularize physical education. One of his pupils. Luis Felipe Castro, later served as director of physical education in the leading secondary school, Mejia National School in Quito, and as Director General of Physical Education in Ecuador.

In 1922, F. W. Kooper arrived with another German mission and carried on Warzawa's work. As a result of Kooper's influence, legislation was passed that made physical education a compulsory subject in the primary and secondary schools. In 1925, Goesta Wellenius, a Swedish teacher, came to Ecuador and worked to advance Ling gymnastics. Because of the opposition of Ecuadorian teachers, his contract was eventually cancelled. The teaching of physical education was discontinued in 1930, and no Director of Physical Education was appointed until 1936. After Julio Torres, a pupil of Wellenius, became director, plans were developed for a national program of physical education based on a system approved by the International Congress of Physical Education held in Brussels in 1935.

The General Director of Physical Education in Ecuador serves in the Ministry of Education and is assisted by national inspectors of physical education. He is responsible for the planning and supervision of the school physical education and sports programs. In 1959, Julio Torres and Luis Castro, who did much to advance physical education when they held this position, were decorated by the government for the service they had rendered.

The time allotted to physical education each week is ninety minutes for elementary schools and one hundred and twenty minutes for secondary schools. Provincial and municipal inspectors supervise the elementary school program which is carried out for the most part by classroom teachers. Regulations require that all secondary school classes must be taught by qualified physical educators, but because of the lack of preparatory programs there is a shortage of teachers. In addition to the required program, annual mass demonstrations are held which have been subject to some criticism. Intramural and interschool competitions in gymnastics, games, and sports are also held. School sports competitions are controlled by provincial inspectors on the primary school level and by the Students Sports Federation on the secondary school level. In recent years, both the Student Sports Federation and University Sports League have come under the influence of commercial and professional interests.

Prior to 1936, Ecuador relied largely upon foreign teachers of physical education or native teachers who were trained in one- to three-month courses. Luis Felipe Castro organized a one-year course in 1936 and Julio Torres organized a second one in 1938. These courses were offered in Quito, and similar courses were offered at the University of Guayaquil. Julio Torres helped found the National School of Physical Education in 1943 which offered a three-year course for physical education teachers and a two-year course for athletic coaches and instructors of rhythmic gymnastics and dancing. The school was closed in 1950, however, and little activity took place for a decade. In 1958, Professor Genaro Fierro and his colleagues obtained the necessary authorization to establish a School of Physical Education at the Central University of Quito. This school and the Institute of Physical Education at the University of Guayaquil now offer a four-year training program. During vacation periods in recent years, refresher courses and meetings of the *Asociación Nacional de Profesores de Educación Física* have been held.

Among other government bodies that promote physical education and sports are the Ministry of National Defense and the Ministry of Government and Police, which provide physical education training for their personnel. The National Federation of Sports, which encourages and controls sports competitions from the local to the international level, also obtains considerable financial assistance from the government.

PHYSICAL EDUCATION IN MEXICO

Despite the stereotype of gaiety which we associate with the Mexican people, about two-thirds of whom are *mestizos*, a somberness of spirit and soberness of purpose has grown out of their long history of struggle against privation. The Mexican seacoast offers few natural harbors, most rivers are unnavigable, and jagged mountains or parched desert cover vast areas. To overcome these handicaps, the government has undertaken extensive education, irrigation, transportation, hydroelectric power, and communication projects. As a result, there is improved production in agriculture, cattle raising, and fishing. Rich oil and mineral deposits are also being developed and manufacturing is making impressive progress.

When the Spanish conquered the Aztecs, they established a feudal society which was dominated by Spaniards born in Spain. By the nineteenth century, the Mexican-born Spanish were sufficiently dissatisfied with the political and economic restrictions imposed upon them by Spain to crusade for political independence. Father Miguel Hidalgo touched off a revolt in 1810, and independence was finally achieved in 1821. Cycles of civil war prevailed however, until the Diaz regime (1877–1910) established greater stability and stimulated economic growth. But these gains were achieved at the expense of the masses who were pushed close to serfdom.

After the Mexican Revolution in 1910 and the adoption of the Constitution of 1917, the Mexican people began to mold a new social system. The Church, foreign capitalists, and hacienda owners lost much of their power. Great estates were distributed among the masses in communal or individual plots, and labor gained considerable influence. Education was made the function of the central government, and religious elementary schools were made illegal. Extensive public health and social security systems were established, and a concerted effort was made to extend education to the masses.

Mexico is a federal republic; powers not expressly vested in the federal government are reserved for the states, but the national government is the dominant political force. The Secretariat of Public Education (SEP) of the federal government provides schools for the Federal District and Territories, and, to alleviate deficiencies in state and local systems, it maintains "federalized" schools throughout the country. The SEP is responsible for curriculums, methods, and examinations in both state and federal schools. One of the special divisions of the SEP is that of the Director General of Physical Education. Education in each state, except for the federalized schools, is the responsibility of the Director General of Schools. Because of the dual system of education, some states have both a federal and state office in charge of physical education.

Extensive nonschool recreation programs have been developed by *Accion Deportiva del Districto Federal*, the National Institute of Mexican Youth (INAHUM), the government workers syndicate (ISSTE), municipal recreation departments, industrial concerns, and private clubs, such as Club Israelita and Club Deportiva de Chapultepec. The Social Security Institute, devoted to bringing about improvements in health and civic life, has also built centers that provide for sports, games, hikes, first aid instruction, military training, and social service activities.

In rural areas, cultural missions, which were first organized in 1923, help people construct recreational facilities, help them organize athletic activities and dance groups, and provide hygiene and agricultural demonstrations through the use of games and dances. The Mexican Pilot Project in Basic Education, which was begun in 1949, carries on more comprehensive programs.

The objectives of physical education in Mexico are to weld a homogeneous society and to provide for the "harmonious and balanced development of the human body; development of physical, intellectual, and moral abilities; training of the individual to make maximum efforts and to behave."[2] Through enriching the social and recreational life of the people, leaders are striving to break down rural isolation; to assimilate the Indians into the national mainstream; to combat gambling, drinking, cockfighting, and juvenile delinquency; and to help youths develop pride in themselves, their heritage, and their nation.

Students participate in physical education classes fifty minutes a week, but this requirement does not apply on the university level. Teachers are provided with a syllabus. The curriculum includes exercises, gymnastics, marching, games, track and field, soccer, volleyball, baseball, softball, swimming, and camping. In the girls' program, strong emphasis is placed on rhythmic activities with a folk background. In the Federal District, through instruction and competitions called *Juegos Escolares*, efforts are made to encourage the retention of traditional Mexican games. The class size may approach sixty students, two shifts a day is not uncommon, and in many schools, only a few of the activities that are listed in the curriculum are actually taught. Some schools have teams and engage in competitions. Some leagues exist, but they lack stability and central control. The Office of Physical Education sponsors carefully-controlled national student competitions.

The army adopted the Amoros system of gymnastics in the nineteenth century and was supplied with instructors in fencing and gymnastics by a school that existed from 1907 to 1914. As early as 1890, the schools were encouraged to introduce gymnastics according to Gayou.[3] In 1902, the government sent Professor Manuel Velasquez Andrade to several countries to observe gymnastics systems. The schools used the Swedish Ling system which Andrade brought back, cable exercises, and navy climbing ladders until the 1920s when the YMCA did much to promote physical education and to introduce new activities. Enrique P. Aguirre, who graduated from Springfield College in 1916, developed a modern type of program that had considerable influence on the school curriculum.

After the Mexican Revolution (1910–1917), leaders began to think of physical education as a means of bettering human life. The University of Mexico introduced a program in 1918. In the early 1920s, Dr. José Peralta, who had presented a plan for physical education to President Obregon, was appointed as the first director of the new office of physical education, and José U. Escobar was appointed as the first director of the Elemental School of Physical Education. In 1929 President Portes Gil approved a budget for national games which resulted in the construction of

[2]International Council on Health, Physical Education, and Recreation, *ICHPER Questionnaire Report, part I, Physical Education and Games in the Curriculum*. (Washington, D.C.: International Council on Health, Physical Education, and Recreation, c. 1963), p. 40.

[3]Lamberto Alvarez Gayou, "A National Sports Program," *Journal of Health and Physical Education* 14 (January 1943): 10.

several playing fields. In that same year, the first Congress of Physical Education met and organized cultural missions to give public demonstrations in the interior regions. In 1933 the government appointed a National Physical Education Committee to assist communities in surveying needs and promoting activities.

Most of the early teachers were not trained in the field; in 1936, under the initiative of General Tirso Hernandez, a teachers' college was established which later became the National School of Physical Education. Today, physical education is a required subject in each year of the normal school program. Specialists are trained at the National School of Physical Education in Mexico City or at the schools in Pueblo, Tobasco, or Chihuahua. Students begin their studies after the completion of the *secundaria* (grade nine), usually between the ages of fifteen and twenty-two years, and pursue a three-year course with the option of taking a fourth year to prepare for the examination. In the early days, the preparatory programs stressed skills, but the 1967 curriculum required more Spanish and English and introduced more theoretical content, including a course in tests and measurements. Students are also taught how to adapt games, to improvise where equipment and facilities are inadequate, and to work through *Padres de Familia*, the equivalent of the PTA in the United States.

Ninety percent of the teachers hold certificates which are based on minimal preparation; only ten percent of the teachers hold the title of "Professor" which is obtained after three years of study and the preparation of a thesis. In some schools, "monitores" assist the teachers. The beginning teacher is assigned twelve hours of work per week; he may advance to twenty-two hours or more of work if he becomes an inspector, state director, or regional inspector. Every two months, reports on teachers are sent to the national office; advancements are based on a point system. The teachers employed by the federal government receive free health and dental care, insurance, and other fringe benefits. Many of them, however, lack full government employment, and, hence, must seek additional work in private schools or clubs which tends to retard curricular and professional growth. The Association of Professors of Physical Education has operated spasmodically; its journal, *Educacion Fisica*, was published privately for only six issues.

Several extensive and imaginative sport complexes have been built in Mexico, such as the Magdalena Mixhuca Sports Center, the facilities on the spectacular campus of the University of Mexico, and the facilities built for the 1968 Olympics, which include the Aztec Stadium and flexible arena of the Sports Palace. Most schools, however, have inadequate facilities. In Mexico City, where space is limited, many students travel several miles to reach playing fields. In rural areas, many youngsters participate in games on hard, dusty, play fields and have little equipment available.

In 1923, the year that Count Henri de Baillet Latour, who was associated with the International Olympic Committees, toured several Latin American countries, the Mexican Olympic Committee was formed. Enrique Aguirre helped organize the Congress of Central American Games, and Mexico served as host in 1926 for the first of the games which later came to be known as the Central American and Caribbean Games. Mexico sent athletes to the Pan-American Athletic Games in Los Angeles in 1933 and served as host for the Games in 1934 and again in 1955, four years after they had been reorganized under the title of Pan-American Games. Mexico has participated in the Olympics since 1924 and served as host for the Games in 1968.

The *Confederacion Deportiva Mexicana* which was formed in 1933, coordinates and controls voluntary sports organizations through affiliated federations. The federal government helps sponsors and finance national championships and international trips. Mexico organized the Pan-American Junior Pentathlon in 1933, for boys under seventeen years. The National Sports Contest of the Revolution, patterned after the Olympics, was held in 1941 and then discontinued until 1949 because of the war. Just prior to the 1968 Olympics, the fourteenth Bureaucratic Games of the Union of Government Workers were held. In 1966, *XV Juegos Deportivos Infantiles Nacionales* and *XI Juegos Deportivos Juveniles Nacionales* were sponsored by sports bodies and government agencies.

The Mayas and Aztecs were fond of games, such as *patolli*, similar to parchesi, the *flying pole*, which is now considered a dance, and *tlachtli*, a ball game. From the accounts of Torquemada and the earlier work of Duran (1585) we know that the Spanish conquerors witnessed *tlachtli* and were particularly intrigued with the rubber ball. Columbus brought a ball back with him, no doubt examined with interest, for the Europeans used leather balls filled with hair or inflated bladders. Cortez staged a New World ball game at the court of Charles V in 1528. Christoph Weiditz, a German, who visited Spain in 1529, published illustrations of the game and some rules.

Many pre-Hispanic towns had one or more ceremonial ball courts which were usually an integral part of the temple. The nature of the game and courts varied in different eras and regions. One type of court was constructed in the form of a capital "I" and was recessed in the ground. The high side and end walls, which were decorated with religious symbols, were constructed of stone. Stone hoops were vertically fastened high on each of the side walls. In one form of the game, teams won points by propelling a solid rubber ball, about the size of a bowling ball, to the dead corner of the other team's end zone, or when their opponents missed a shot at the vertical hoop. All previous points were discarded, and the game was won if the ball was hurled through the stone hoops, which was no easy task.

Each variation of this fast and furious game had intricate rules. The ball could not be struck with the bare hands or feet. The buttocks, knees, and thighs could be used; elbows, hips, and head were used in some games; and a flat piece of rock held in the hand may have been used. For protection, the players wore kneepads, a wide, heavy belt, thick gauntlets or arm protectors, and a helmet. Despite their protective clothing, Duran reports, many players were injured severely or killed instantly. Sahagun (1529) reports that as a result of feverish betting some spectators lost their homes, jewels, children, and even their freedom. The winning players were lavished with gifts and treated as heroes. The captain of the losing team not infrequently was sacrificed to the gods to ensure the fertility of the land and the abundance of the harvest. A variation of this game is still played along the northwestern coast of Mexico.

A number of handball games are still played in Latin America. *Jai alai* in Mexico and *pelota* in other Latin American countries are essentially the same game. Some historians believe that *jai alai* is of Basque origin, but others think that it is a Mexican game taken to Spain by Cortez.

An effort is being made to preserve traditional games, sports, and dances in Mexico. Every region has a rich heritage of folk music, dances, and fiestas which usually have a ritualistic as well as a social function. The varicolored costumes, elaborate feathered headdresses, and expressive masks worn by the villagers blend into a dazzling pattern of rhythmic movement. The performances of the *Ballet Folklorica* of Mexico have won international recognition. Top-spinning games and a rudimentary form of hockey played with curved sticks and a ball have also been preserved.

Bullfighting is a national spectator sport. The two largest bull rings in the Americas are located in Mexico City and Lima, Peru. From October until March, the colorful Sunday spectacles are witnessed by enthusiastic crowds. At *jaripeo* or rodeo, the Mexican *charro*, or cowboy, performs feats in riding, rope spinning and lassoing. Other local, national, and international contests also attract many spectators. Soccer holds the spotlight, but gymnastics, and track and field events have been popular for some time. American football, *el beisbol* (Mexicanized baseball), and basketball are gaining in favor. Boxing, wrestling, swimming have also made advances in recent years. In equestrian sports and shooting, the Mexicans have taken many honors, and long-distance runners from the mountain regions have impressed the sports world.

PHYSICAL EDUCATION IN PARAGUAY

Because of the isolated and landlocked location of the country, the paucity of roads and obtainable natural resources, and the decimation of the male population by devastating wars, Paraguay is a poor and sparsely populated country. The population is concentrated in eastern Paraguay, for the vast Chaco region in western Paraguay is an inhospitable wilderness. Most Paraguayans are *mestizos*, many of whom speak both Spanish and Guaraní (Indian), and they engage in cattle raising, lumbering, and farming. The Paraguayans are less class-conscious than most South Americans because their nation does not produce sufficient wealth to create a great gap between the rich and the poor.

A strong military tradition prevails in Paraguay; the government allots fifty percent of the national budget to defense and twenty-five percent to education. Physical education received little support until after 1940 when a Commission for the Advancement of Physical Culture and a School for Gymnastics and Sports were founded. The Commission was reorganized in 1942, when the National Council of Physical Culture was created. The Council received technical assistance from a Brazilian officer, Silvio Amélio Santa Rosa, and was helped by the first Paraguayan teachers to graduate in Brazil. The Council effected the passage of legislation that was similar to that enacted in Brazil, created a National School of Physical Education, made physical education compulsory in teaching institutions, and adopted the French physical education method of Joinville. When the Council was reorganized in 1947, the following departments were established: (1) The Joint Assessory of Physical Education, a coordinating body, (2) The National Council of Sports, (3) The National School of Physical Education, and (4) The National Department of Physical Education.

The National Department of Physical Education directs and controls the program in the schools through councils in the Ministry of Education and Culture and the Regional Inspectorates of Physical Education. In the physical education classes, which are held once a week above the fourth grade in primary schools and twice a week in secondary schools, about sixty percent of the time is devoted to gymnastics. Each year, the Ministry of Education sponsors school competitions. On the university level, physical education is not organized, but some competitions are held between faculties, and students participate in the annual South American intercollege championships.

The National School of Physical Education is subordinate to the Ministry of Education and Culture, and, when convenient, is to become part of the National University. This school offered a one-year program between 1942 and 1946, extended it to two years in 1947, and is now considering a three-year program. A one-year course for sports technicians (five sports) was created in 1953, and an experimental course for specialists in one sport was created in 1962. The school was moved to a new campus in 1956 near the site where the National Sports Stadium was to be built. The School of Physical Education of the Army, which has functioned since 1950, also offers a one-year course, and the degrees it grants have been recognized by the Ministry of Education since 1962.

Although progress is being made in Paraguay, facilities are almost completely lacking and insufficient funds are available to employ physical educators in rural areas and small towns. Many physical educators are idle, and those who work in primary schools must teach in five schools to make the same salary as classroom teachers. In Paraguay, as in some other South American countries, more activity takes place in the sport sector than the school sector. Fourteen major institutions are a part of the National Council of Sports which promotes and controls sports and scouting. Basketball and volleyball are popular activities, but soccer is the national game. In this poor nation with a population smaller than Philadelphia, eleven soccer teams are in the top division alone.

PHYSICAL EDUCATION IN PERU

In Peru, which was the center of the highly developed Inca empire and later of the Spanish empire, the dry, healthful coastal area produces fifty percent of the gross national product. The vast, humid Amazon jungle to the east is sparsely populated and only partially explored. In the valleys of the Andean highlands, the descendants of the Incas eke out a living as subsistence farmers and cling to their ancestral languages, customs, dances, and fiestas. Forty-six percent of the people in Peru are full-blooded Indians who are largely illiterate, and most of the remainder have some Indian blood. Peru is underdeveloped, but the government is making a great effort to institute agrarian reforms, to spur economic growth, to build highways and schools, and to reorganize the educational system.

Dances, sports, and military exercises were a part of life in the days of the Inca. Youth engaged in ceremonial ball games that were associated with fertility rites or the cult of the dead. The aristocratic ceremony of *Huaca cu* was the culmination of a series of athletic and military contests. Youths who passed the tests of skill, bravery, and privation received the insignia of "Son of the Sun." According to some reports, the relay runners, *les chasquis*, who ran regular routes to maintain a communication system throughout the Empire, could cover the one thousand mile route from Cuzco to Quito in eight days.

As in other South American countries, the first modern physical education programs in Peru were the product of foreign leadership, were introduced through military channels, and were retained for some time after they had been abandoned abroad. Two members of a French military mission who arrived in 1903 stimulated interest in gymnastics. Captain Emile Gross worked for a decade to propagate Amoros gymnastics, and Fernand Charton, introduced the Ling gymnastics.

The national government did not actually assume responsibility for the administration of schools until 1905. Thereafter, with the establishment of the Teacher Normal School for men, a course in physical education based on the French gymnastic system was offered. Sports were added to the curriculum by two Americans, Joseph McKnight and Joseph Lockey, who were brought to Peru in 1910 and served as the Director of the Teacher Normal School and the Inspector of Primary Instruction, respectively. Unfortunately, all of the foreign leaders left Peru in 1914.

After World War I, physical education made some advances. The Peruvian Christian Association of Young People (YMCA) was founded in 1920, and Professor Carl H. Johnson, who served as director from 1921–1953, gave Peruvian leaders advice and assistance. Lieutenant Pucheu, who came with a French military mission in 1919, introduced Hébert's natural method of gymnastics, organized a three-month training course for soldiers in 1920, and with the Peruvian Captain, Carlos Nicholson, wrote a book titled, *Guide and General Rules of Physical Education*. As a result of Pucheu's efforts, the Hébert method became and remained the official system of gymnastics in the Peruvian schools for many years. An important step was taken in 1924, when Antonio Valdez Longaray succeeded in establishing the Inspectors of School Physical Education separate from the Premilitary Inspectors. During the eight years that Longaray served, a feminine section was created in 1925, sports championships were conducted, and gymnastics demonstrations were organized.

In 1930, the division of Physical Education and School Sanitation was established under Dr. Carlos Cacères Alvarez, who abolished the French gymnastic system and replaced it with the Ling system. He elaborated plans that made physical education compulsory in the schools on all levels, gave considerable attention to dosage of physical effort and the classification of contestants in interscholastic competitions, and succeeded in 1932 in establishing the National Institute of Physical Education. In 1940, Dr. Carlos Cacères Alvarez was replaced as director of the Institute by Antonio Valdez Longaray and as Director of Physical Education by Jorge de la Romana. Five years later, a pupil of Alvarez, Professor Evariste Gomez Sanchez, became Director of Physical Education and held the position until 1956.

At present, the inspectors of the men's and women's divisions in the Department of Physical Education and Recreation, which operates under the Ministry of Public Education, are responsible for the programs in both public and private schools. The Department is responsible for primary, secondary, and technical training school programs, but not for university or postscholastic programs.

Physical education, which is a required subject in the elementary and secondary schools, consists of educative gymnastics, sports, games, and folk dances. Some physically handicapped children receive training at the Institutes of Physical Reeducation in Lima or Callao. The practice of holding annual gymnastic exhibitions is still flourishing in Peru, the interest in national folklore is increasing, and the promotion of school championships is gaining momentum.

Physical education is a required subject in the normal schools, but not in the universities. The National University of San Marcos, which was founded in 1551 and is one of the oldest universities in the New World, established a department of physical education in the early 1920s, but most universities have not taken similar action. Some competition in sports takes place between universities, especially in Lima, but not on a regular basis. National Sports Games have been conducted a few times, and the International University Sports Games were held in Lima in 1958.

Physical education teachers are trained in the Carlos Cacères Alvarez National Institute of Physical Education. The Institute was founded in 1932 and was attached to the Faculty of Education of the University of San Marcos in 1946, but this relationship was terminated in 1949. The Institute is now equivalent to a normal school of higher education. The course offered by the Institute lasted for about a year in the beginning and was extended to two, three, and finally four years beyond secondary school preparation. Programs for sports technicians and a three-year, postgraduate course in kinesiology are also offered. Because of the shortage of teachers, athletes who have had no special training are employed in some schools, but they are expected to take courses during summer vacations.

The Peruvians have published two professional journals: *Revista de Educación Física Bimestral* and *Revista de Medicina Deportiva*. In recent years, the members of the *Asociación Nacional de Profesores de Educación Física* (ANPEF), *Consejo Consultivo Peruano de Aptitudes Físicas*, and the branch of FIEF have been active. The Council on Fitness has encouraged the adoption of physical fitness tests and has joined with the ANPEF in offering holiday courses. Some national physical education and physical fitness meetings have also been held.

Since the beginning of the century, the only physical education that many Peruvian youths have obtained has been in the army. The military school of physical education, which was started by Gross in 1903, functioned until 1932. Civilian teachers were employed by the army for a few years, but a new school of military physical education was founded in 1936. The military leaders also formed a Military Sports Federation which is affiliated with the South American Military Sports Federation and conducts championships independently from the civilian sport organizations.

The National Committee of Sports is responsible for the adult and after-school sport programs. The law which requires municipalities to provide playing facilities and fields is rarely observed. In Peru, soccer, basketball, and baseball are the most popular sports; bullfights attract throngs of spectators; and cycles of fiestas that include prayers, parades, games, and dances are the recreational as well as religious outlets of the people. The northern coast is one of the favorite areas in the world for big game fishing, and the Andean streams, which were stocked by the United States Bureau of Fisheries, teem with some of the world's largest trout.

PHYSICAL EDUCATION IN URUGUAY

Uruguay is a small nation with a temperate climate, vast ranches, and rich agricultural land. The government enforces the democratic constitution and administers an extensive social welfare program. The population is almost wholly of European descent. The size of the middle class is larger and the standard of living and literacy rates are higher than in most Latin American countries. Remarkably little racial, religious, or class prejudice exists. Included in the long list of social reforms is the provision of free education from elementary school through the university. Some unrest has developed in recent years because of the ruinous inflation and the unwieldiness of the bureaucracy that administers the welfare state.

The YMCA has done much to develop sports and physical education in Uruguay. The Christian Youth Organization was established in Montivedeo in 1909. When the National Commission for Physical Education (CNEF) was created in 1911, Jess T. Hopkins, a graduate of Springfield College, served as the technical director. Julio J. Rodríguez, who succeeded Hopkins in 1917, completed his studies at Springfield College as did other leaders in the CNEF. In 1922 the Technical Institute of the Christian Youth Associations was established in Montivedeo and flourished under the direction of James Stewart Summers. The Institute now offers a four-year course for future Association directors and physical education teachers from all South and Central American countries.

In Uruguay, the National Commission for Physical Education (CNEF) is responsible for physical education and sports in the schools, the training of teachers and coaches, and the promotion of sports and competitions from the local to the international level. Some leaders feel that the CNEF devotes more attention to voluntary and competitive sports programs than to the educational program, and they are concerned because members of the two major political parties serve as honorary members of the CNEF.

The CNEF makes agreements with school authorities on different levels concerning physical education and supplies them with teachers. The elementary schools and industrial schools lack adequate facilities, but a law requires that new secondary schools must include physical education facilities. Formative gymnastics constitute an important part of the curriculum. Elementary school children also engage in marches, games, rounds, and folk dances. Corrective gymnastics are offered in schools that have gymnasiums. In the secondary schools, where greater progress has been made, the program consists of gymnastics, dance, and sports, particularly soccer, basketball, and volleyball. In the industrial schools, a special effort is made to provide exercises that will counteract posture defects that arise from working conditions. Physical education classes are not organized on the university level.

The pioneer physical education teachers were athletes who were trained by the CNEF in short courses which had low admission requirements. From 1942 to 1950, the Ministry of Defense operated a Military School of Physical Education. The CNEF established The Superior Institute of Physical Education (ISEF) in 1939 to train "professors" of physical education and initiated a course for coaches in 1945. Considerable progress has been made in the training of teachers, but some professors object to operating within the political framework of the CNEF and want the ISEF to become dependent on the University. The academic entrance requirements to ISEF are a secondary school diploma for the professors' course and graduation from the sixth scholastic year for the coaches' course. CNEF publishes *Edufisica* and offers some summer school courses but no graduate work. Physical educators who wish to pursue further work usually obtain degrees in medicine, psychology, or physiotherapy.

An important part of the CNEF program is the distribution of state funds to institutions that promote sports, the organization of competitions through the intermediary of sports federations, and the provision of free gymnastics and sport classes in gymnasiums and free swimming classes at beaches and pools. All participants in CNEF programs must present a health certificate which they can obtain from the medical section without charge.

Soccer is the national sport in Uruguay. The annual soccer matches with Argentina are exciting spectacles that fill the huge stadium at Montevideo. A tide of pride sweeps over the nation when Uruguay wins the international football cup. Swimming, baseball, basketball, volleyball, and tennis are also popular. Uruguayans, Argentineans, and tourists from many other countries flock to the golden beaches of Punta del Este.

PHYSICAL EDUCATION IN VENEZUELA

The discovery of oil in Venezuela shortly before World War I brought sudden prosperity to this rather poor agricultural and cattle-raising country, but the new wealth created new problems and failed to correct some traditional ones. Besides the exploitation of oil and the more recent production of iron ore, modern Venezuela has had to cope with the lack of diversity of exports, the delayed development of industry and mass education, and the struggle between dictatorship and democracy.

The development of education fared badly from 1908 to 1935 under the dictatorship of Gomez, but after his death, the government began fundamental educational reforms. Physical education first received official recognition in 1936 when the Ministry of Education created a League of Physical Education which became the National Institute of Physical Education. The director of the Institute was Mr. Armando Alvarez de Lugo who had introduced gymnastics as early as 1912 in the Arts and Crafts School of Caracas.

After the Institute was established in 1936, six instructors began to organize physical education programs in the more important lyceums of Caracas. Two physical educators, one from Cornell University and the other from the University of California, Berkeley, joined the legion of foreign educators who were invited to Venezuela to work with the Ministry of Education. For over a decade some advances were made. In 1946, the National Institute of Physical Education became the National Department of Physical Education and the country was divided into administrative zones.

Under the dictatorship of Jiménez in the 1950s, physical education received a serious setback. Teacher training programs were terminated, the National Department of Physical Education was eliminated, and physical educators were relegated to an inferior position. But after the fall of the dictatorship in 1958, professional physical educators were once again designated as supervisors of programs in various types and levels of schools.

A national supervisor and zone coordinators now provide leadership for the physical education program which is required in the primary schools, in the secondary schools during the first three years, and in the normal schools. Some secondary schools exceed the one-hour-a-week requirement of the national program, but other schools have difficulty meeting this requirement. Most physical educators have had little or no professional training, but some of them have been successful athletes.

In the 1964 revision of the *Basic Program of Secondary Education*, the physical education program consists primarily of close order drills and gymnastics. Some elements of the dance are included in the girls' program, and each school, in accordance with its capabilities, is required to provide instruction in at least one sport each year. Most schools operate intramural programs, and some schools have interscholastic programs. In the 1960s, the United States Peace Corps volunteers assisted in organizing some leagues and encouraged substituting seasonal participation for the practice of concentrating competition in all sports at one time of the year.

The task of preparing a sufficient number of teachers to carry out physical education programs in Venezuela is a formidable one. Between 1936 and 1961 the national population more than doubled, but less than forty physical educators were graduated from the Pedagogical Institute during those years. The first plan to provide training was developed in 1936. The government sponsored the first course for one year in 1939 and a second course for eight months in 1946. A proposal was made in 1948 to establish a Superior School of Physical Education at the National Pedagogical Institute, and a Chilean, Humberto Díaz Vera, was invited to organize the program. This school was badly neglected and graduated few teachers before it was closed in 1954 by the National Department of Physical Education. Afterward, the Department established a training school which graduated three groups of teachers before it was closed in 1957.

After the change in government in 1958, the preparation of physical education teachers was reactivated at the Pedagogical Institute, and in 1963, the Department was transformed into a Division of Physical Education with the same status and privileges as other Divisions. The *Instituto Experimental de Formación Docente* was created in 1959 to train leaders for elementary and normal school and to prepare teachers in the area of physical education. In 1959, a second teachers college was organized, the *Instituto Pedagógico Experimental*. A four-year professional physical education program was developed by Peace Corps volunteers which was accepted by the *Pedagógico Experimental*.

In the 1960s, for the first time, some physical education graduates of the Pedagogical Institute were sent to other South American countries and to Europe to take courses and attend meetings. Some South American and Swedish teachers were invited to Venezuela to demonstrate the latest teaching techniques. The Ministry of Education also invited United States Peace Corps volunteers to assist teachers in the secondary schools. In addition, the Peace Corps volunteers conducted in-service training programs, taught in teacher-training schools, conducted sports clinics, helped coach teams and establish summer camps, worked in the *barrios bajos* (slums), and administered The American Association for Health, Physical Education, and Recreation Fitness tests.

The promotion and supervision of sports in Venezuela is carried out by the National Institute of Sports (IND) which was created in 1949 and operates from the national to the local level. The director is appointed from the ministerial level and a technical director is appointed by the Institute. The IND cooperates with the Ministry of Education in the area of physical education, particularly in respect to facilities. The national IND headquarters in Caracas consists of a large staff and a modern complex of sport facilities. The IND, which is closely related to the Venezuelan Olympic Committee, organizes the participation of athletes in international contests and sponsors *Los Juegos Deportivos Nacionales* which have been held since 1959. The national sport competitions are rotated among the different states which are provided with special funds to improve their facilities for the event and for future use. In 1960, the IND established the National Sports Training School which offers a two-year course for coaches. A diploma from this school has less prestige than one from the National Pedagogical Institute, but to ease the teacher shortage many IND graduates have been employed in the schools, particularly in the rural areas.

Venezuelans love games and gambling. Like all Latin Americans they play soccer, but baseball is the national sport. Some of their baseball players are internationally known and are recruited for the major leagues in the United States. Horse races, with the added attraction of betting known as "5 and 6," are extremely popular as are the bullfights which are held during fairs and festivals. Both the Venezuelans and the tourists enjoy swimming and other water sports and the excellent deep-sea fishing off the coast and in the inland lakes and rivers. Folkloric dance forms have been preserved, such as the *Diablos de yare* in the vicinity of Caracas and *Tamunangue* in the central area, and no fiesta or party is complete without the dancing of the fast, gay *joropo*.

27

Physical Education in Education in the African, Asian and the Pacific Nations

The Eastern and Far Eastern World was the cradle of civilization: here ancient cultures of a high order flourished and the great religions of the world arose. During a long and turbulent history, the peoples of these lands experienced the rise and fall of great empires and successive waves of invasion and conquest. But after World War II, a new era dawned. The sparks of nationalism that had sputtered early in this century suddenly burst into flames and swept throughout Africa and Asia. One by one the old colonial power structures were replaced by national governments. In Africa, thirty-six states became independent in eighteen years.

Today, a few nations in Africa, Asia, and the Pacific, are well-developed societies with a high standard of living, but many of them are underdeveloped with untapped human potential and unexplored natural resources. Some of the newly independent people are disappointed because rapid progress is not forthcoming even though they are now in control of their own destiny; all of them are aspiring to realize fuller human opportunity and are putting forth great effort to achieve this goal. Generalizations about the vast and varied African, Asian, and Pacific nations are dangerous, for data are meager, quickly outdated, and are not universally applicable. If these limitations are kept in mind, a separate discussion of physical education in Japan, China, Australia, New Zealand, India and Pakistan, and the Union of South Africa, and a brief survey of physical education in the other nations may provide some insight into developments that are taking place.

PHYSICAL EDUCATION IN SOME AFRICAN, ASIAN, AND PACIFIC NATIONS

Until relatively recently, little education was available beyond the home and village school in much of Africa and Asia and some Pacific Islands.

Some youngsters received a little fundamental education in colonial government or foreign missionary schools; some youngsters received a rote religious education or an indoctrination in traditional rites, games, dances, and self-defense activities from native teachers; few youths received a secondary school or university education. In Tanganyika, even recently, only forty-five of every one hundred eligible pupils entered school, only eight of whom remained after Standard V, and of these, only two secured places in secondary schools. Learning was impeded in countries that lacked a common language, for youngsters had to master a new language and literacy skills at the same time. Where tradition required that the government operate separate schools for boys and girls or for different racial, cultural, or linguistic groups, costs increased for facilities, teachers, and equipment, all of which deterred the advancement of education.

After World War I, some African and Asian countries made the radical decision to break with the ancient past. Within a few decades, they adopted many Western customs and methods and achieved a social revolution through education. After World War II, leaders of the newly independent nations also realized that the extension of education was essential for the preservation of their cultural heritage and the development of their countries. Many international agencies, foreign governments, and voluntary associations offered to assist them. Within a few years a number of promising programs and varied experiments were underway.

In Africa and Asia, considerable progress is being made in increasing support for education, and widening educational opportunity. An effort is being made to enroll more girls in school, provide literacy and fundamental education for unschooled adults, and develop vocational and technical training programs. In Iraq, for example, the education budget increased from 2.3 percent to 23.3 percent of the total state budget between 1920–21 and 1963–64. The number of primary schools increased from 89 to 4030, and the number of secondary schools from 3 to 409 between 1920–21 and 1961–62. Coeducational schools grew from a few in the early thirties to represent more than one-third of the total number of primary schools by 1961–62. An Iraq-UNESCO Agreement in 1950 marked the turning point in adult education. Since that time, many fundamental education centers have been established where unschooled youths and adults attend classes in literacy, home economics, child care, sewing, agriculture, nursing, or hygiene. As yet, compulsory, universal public education is not a reality throughout Africa and Asia, but a determination that it must be achieved clearly exists.

The leaders of thirty-six African states who attended the UNESCO-ECA Conference on the Development of Education in Africa, held in Addis Ababa in 1961, discussed the inadequacy of educational development. They established two long-range objectives: (1) by 1966, to raise primary school enrollment from forty percent of the school-age population to over fifty-one percent, and to increase the secondary enrollment from three to nine percent, and (2) by 1980, to establish universal primary education in Africa and to have twenty-three percent of the school-age population enrolled in secondary school and two percent in higher education.

Leaders in undeveloped countries of Africa and the Pacific Islands are making a tremendous effort to upgrade educational, health, and nutritional standards, but they are confronted with a combination of crucial problems. In many nations, anticolonial agitation and revolutionary activities, religious and tribal rivalries, or political strife have destroyed schools, disrupted student life, and interrupted normal economic and social development. Some governments must cope with the exodus of foreign capital and administrators, a serious shortage of native technicians and professional personnel, and the socioeconomic gap between rural and urban areas. The artificiality of some political boundaries, the assimilation of large groups of immigrants or religious refugees, and the religious tensions within and between countries also create problems.

The health and housing situation is desperate, and the population growth makes progressive reform programs inadequate as soon as they are established. Despite the efforts undertaken by the new governments, former colonizers, and international agencies, millions of people suffer from disease and malnutrition, and tens of thousands live and die in the streets. Almost half of the African children die before they reach five years of age. The high birth rate is as appalling as the death rate. Because of the high birth rate and the rapid expansion of educational opportunity, the school population is always increasing. Educating these children will be extremely difficult, especially in nations where planners are giving priority to the development of industry and the modernization of agriculture.

Combating illiteracy (the rate runs as high as eighty to ninety percent of the people in some countries) is going to require an enormous amount of effort. Many other obstacles to the development of education also exist: endemic unemployment; social and religious prejudices that impede reform movements; the lack of communication and transportation facilities. In a climate of adversity, educators in some newly independent nations must develop a sense of national purpose and individual civic responsibility for a mixed population, some of whose groups have their own customs, religious and dietary practices, and languages. Such diversity, which can be an asset, presents a challenge, but it also breeds bitter rivalries which interfere with unity and educational advancement. Intellectual emancipation is underway in Africa and Asia, but achievements will probably remain far behind aspirations for many years to come.

In most African and Asian countries, physical education, sports, and in some instances, scouting and other youth programs, are under the direction of a national supervisor or inspector of physical education with an office in the national ministry of education. But in some countries the responsibility for physical education, particularly sports, has been given to other ministries. In some countries, one authority supervises and develops both the school and community physical education and sports programs and facilities, grants financial assistance to sport federations and organizations, and supervises international sports relations.

All African and Asian countries have drafted similar objectives of physical education, but with differing emphases. Most political, academic, and military leaders recognize that the physical fitness of youth is a prerequisite for national development. In some countries physical educators want sports to be used to help youths acquire the cooperative skills and attitudes required for self-government. One leader points out, "As some of the basic requirements of a good citizen under the rule of democracy are a willingness and the ability to abide by law, and a spirit of compromise, tolerance, and fair play, athletic activities are one of the best and most effective means for training people in the cultivation of these qualities and capabilities. . . . As we Asians are marching on toward the achievement of true democracy, the cultivation of good sportsmanship of our people is certainly one of the most important missions ahead of us."[1]

Some countries in Africa and Asia are operating well-rounded physical education and recreational programs that cultivate cooperative skills and good sportsmanship, provide for personal development and satisfaction, and permit self-expression and responsible use of freedom. But self-interest causes other countries to emphasize physical fitness, discipline, military training, and nationalism, and to ignore the educational and recreational values of physical education. Some nations neglect the physical education of girls and unskilled students and concentrate their efforts on the development of competitive sports and the production of champion performers who can bolster national pride and prestige.

Physical education in Africa and Asia has been strongly influenced by the European colonials and by the Americans who were stationed in the Philippines after the Spanish-American War and in the Pacific area during and after World War II. The early African and Asian physical education programs which, for the most part, developed apart from sports and athletic competition, usually consisted of mass calisthenics, army-type drills, and some Swedish, Danish, or German gymnastics. This formal type of program was retained in many nations long after a more modern approach had been introduced in the mother country.

In the past two decades, several African and Asian nations have invited foreign physical educators to assist them in upgrading and expanding their programs. In some countries, such as South Korea, the Ministry of Education has provided grants to model schools for research in developing physical education programs. Many new syllabi have been developed that include more games, sports, and dances, and some physical fitness tests

[1]Gunsun Hoh, "Athletic Development in Asia and Its Influence Upon the Lives of Asian People," *Physical Education Today* 9 (March–June, 1962): 25.

and badges for youths and adults have been developed. But in many countries mass exercises and one or two popular sports still dominate the program, attention is focused on potential interscholastic athletes and the curriculum content is not suitable for girls.

In several countries, premilitary training is substituted for or provided in addition to physical education. In the Philippines, on the upper secondary school level, the physical education program for boys is integrated with preparatory military science. Israel has a required physical education and premilitary program on the secondary school level and a compulsory military and representative training program for all young men and women. In 1956, Egypt established compulsory military training in secondary schools and colleges and also encouraged students to participate in social service projects.

Some native leaders believe that "many African countries imitate with excess the patterns of former mother countries without sufficient financial backing to carry out the programs successfully. The tendency is to have the same conception, the same philosophy, the same organization as the mother country in spite of the big differences of climate, costume, and habits, as well as the lack of financial resources and a shortage of qualified personnel."[2] Throughout Africa and Asia, physical educators are reorienting their programs to meet the needs of their people and to give youths a better understanding of their own tradition and culture. To develop a sense of national identity, unity, and pride among disparate people, physical educators are encouraging youths to participate in cooperative team and game activities, hikes and camping trips, to points of local or national interest, and indigenous activities, such as yoga, judo, Thai boxing, *sipa* (a rattan ball kicking game), and tribal, regional, or national folk dances. Nationalism has created a desire to establish closer ties with neighboring countries and has aroused much greater interest in native games and dances.

Because of the rapid expansion of education and the many competing needs in underdeveloped nations, little money is available for physical education programs, and funds earmarked for physical education are often appropriated for other purposes. A few schools have excellent modern facilities, but these are the exception. Most classes are held in outdoor play areas which are often small and undeveloped. Fortunately, many countries have a favorable climate for conducting outdoor activities most of the year. During hot or rainy seasons or the hours of intense heat at midday, teachers suspend classes, hold them in classrooms, or conduct them in a school assembly hall, if available. In most schools the equipment and supplies are meager and substandard: cold sponge baths substitute for showers; first aid supplies, protective equipment, uniforms, sweat socks, and shoes are

[2]Kléber Viélot, "Egalité des Chances par L'Education," *International Council on Health, Physical Education, and Recreation, Eighth International Congress, 1965* (Washington, D.C.: ICHPER, 1966), p. 23.

unknown or in short supply. Swimming is not included in most programs because pools are not available; some parents fear the magical power of the sea; in Africa, crocodiles and the disease, bilharziasis, are prevalent.

Through initiative, industry, and improvisation, some African and Asian teachers develop programs with a minimum of financial assistance. With the help of students, they construct and maintain playing fields, courts, and play equipment. In Zambia a syllabus has been published which requires only apparatus that can be improvised. Students use seed pods for balls, bamboo sticks for marking off areas and for pulling and pushing contests, oil drums for balancing and for vaulting, old bicycle tires for hoops, and ropes and tires for swings. They fill sacks with grass for mats and unravel the thread in motor tires to make tenniquoit and volleyball nets.

Despite the progress that has been made in recent years, physical education has rather shallow roots in the curriculum. The subject usually appears in the timetables of elementary, secondary, and teacher-training schools, but teachers who lack space, equipment, and training and supervision in the field, do not always observe the timetable. Physical education is compulsory in most countries, but it is not always included among the entrance requirements for colleges or for civil service positions. Because education provides the key to preferred positions and social prestige, many headmasters, parents, and students believe that any time or money devoted to play rather than study is wasted. To promote their programs, physical educators must not only overcome this academic bias, but also fears about injuries, superstitions against certain types of participation, and the traditional reluctance to have girls participate in vigorous physical activity. Physical educators must also work closely with nutritionists, health agencies, and recreation leaders, for instruction in exercise and sport is no help to a child who is undernourished, or ill, or who has no playground or sports facilities available to him.

In addition to physical education classes, some African and Asian students participate in extramural, intramural, and interscholastic programs, sports clubs, regional and national competitions, hikes and camping trips, and scouting and community recreation programs. These programs are not universal, and they vary in quality; the isolation of many communities, the unavailability of transportation, and the lack of funds, equipment, and leadership often limit what can be accomplished.

Several African and Asian countries have established athletic associations to govern local, regional, and national school sports competitions. Early in this century the U.S. soldiers in the Philippines conducted leagues and tournaments among themselves and also provided competition for school teams. In 1905, W. C. Forbes, who later became the Governor General of the Philippines, stimulated interest in sports by providing athletic equipment to the schools showing the greatest progress. To bring students into competition in different sports, the Bureau of Education organized athletic associations. The annual national interscholastic meets, in the Philippines the first of which was held in 1910, have become important and colorful events that include many sports activities.

In Southeast Asia most countries conduct some sport competitions for youths. In Cambodia, interclass, regional, and national championship contests are held. In Malaya, students are grouped into "houses" for intramural competition and competition is based on "divisions." The State Schools Sports Council organizes programs of sports and games at the state level, and the Federation of Malaya School Sports Council controls competition on the national and international levels. In Burma, most after-school programs are sponsored by the National Fitness Council.

In Turkey, sport clubs occupy an important place in the schools and the recreational life of youths and adults, and some students participate in scouting activities and in weekend and vacation excursions. Turkish athletes excel in wrestling and participate in soccer, basketball, volleyball, and athletics. In Iran students are loyal to their separate sport clubs, and they have opportunities to participate in the national High School Olympic Games and in the University Olympic Games which are held annually. In Iraq, interclass and interschool competitions are held, bicycle and hiking trips are conducted, and the Department of Physical Education conducts summer swimming centers and camps for secondary school boys.

In the United Arab Republic, intramurals and sports days are a part of the elementary and intermediate school program. On the secondary level, interscholastic competitions are held, and some events are conducted on a national basis. On the university level, internal and external sports competitions are conducted. The University Students' Union, which includes committees for sports, for rovers, and for campers, operates in each university and on the national level.

Two years after the revolution of 1952, the United Arab Republic established the Supreme Council for Youth Welfare to promote the physical, social, and national education of youth. The Council was organized to realize its objectives through the ministries concerned with education, social affairs, labor, defense, and rural affairs and the national organizations and student unions concerned with youth welfare. Committees were appointed to spread physical training and sports in schools, sports clubs, rural areas, and factories; to obtain playing fields and equipment; to establish leadership training institutes, camps, and excursion programs; to encourage and to improve the organization of sport competitions; to raise the standards of games, referees, and instructors; to develop national social consciousness and social service work projects; and to provide for leisure time education. Regional Councils were established in the United Arab Republic to play the same role as the Supreme Council.

Many other African nations have also developed sports programs for youths. The Ethiopian Inter-School Athletic Association, which was founded in 1950, organizes interscholastic, provincial, and national competition and prepares athletes for international competitions. In the Congo (Leopoldville), soccer and other games are played after school, interschool competitions are organized, and a few students are members of the Football National Team. In Ghana, the Schools and Colleges Sports Federation is controlled by the Central Organization of Sports, which is responsible for the promotion and control of sports and competitions from the local to the international level. In Nigeria the National Sports Council and regional Sport Councils, which are either under the Ministries of Education or the Social Welfare Divisions of the Ministries of Labour, organize sport and recreation activities for youth. The Nigerian youth club organizers and social welfare workers, who assist youth in promoting dances, games, and competitions, have done much to develop sport activities and athletes for international competition.

For many years the physical educators and coaches in most African and Asian schools came from Great Britain, the Scandinavian countries, Germany, France, and the United States. Some natives who had studied abroad or who had been in military service also served in this capacity. Eventually some countries sent a few students overseas for training in the field and introduced short inservice programs that they later extended to one- to four-year programs. In Ethiopia, for example, native teachers who had been trained in Scotland and Sweden conducted two-month inservice courses from 1949 until 1961 and introduced a one-year teaching training physical education course in 1959. In 1964 The Haile Selassie I University opened a two-year physical education and health education diploma course.

In most African and Asian countries, full academic training is not available to physical educators. A few physical educators pursue degree programs in universities, but most of them are trained in teachers colleges in a certificate or diploma course. Some countries have established one or more special schools that train only physical education teachers or that also train coaches, national teams, and various sport specialists. In some countries medical doctors are the directors or serve on the staffs of the physical education training institutions.

There are various types of teacher training programs in African and Asian countries. Twelve four-year colleges in Korea provide training in physical education, and a four-year judo school provides training in that sport. ChulalongKorn University in Thailand offers a four-year degree program as does the University of Tehran in Iran and the Powell College of Physical Education in Nigeria, and in each country other schools offer two- or three-year nondegree courses. In the Philippines a teacher can obtain a certificate in four summers, a student can earn a Bachelor of Physical Education degree or a Master's degree with physical education as a major in four to six years. In Turkey, Swedish instructors conducted one-year courses from 1926 to 1933 when the Institute of Physical Education was established as a branch of the Gazi Teachers Training Institute. The Institute accepts high school and teacher-training school graduates and offers a three-year program for physical educators only. Recently, a bill was drafted to establish an Academy of Sports in Istanbul. At the University of Baghdad in Iraq, men are trained at the Higher Institute of Physical Education, which was established in 1952, and women are trained at the College for Women. A one-year program is provided by the National Institute for Physical Education and Sports in Cambodia and by the Specialist Teachers' Training Institute in Malaya. In Liberia, the Inservice Training School, Bureau of Physical Education, offers a three-year diploma program, and the Teachers' Training College, University of Liberia, offers a four-year, B.S. degree program. At the University of Algiers, which in preindependence days was the third largest university in France, is the *Institut d'Éducation Physique et Sportive*. In 1957 Afghanistan established a School of Physical Education and Sports where boys from grades seven to twelve are trained to become physical educators.

The United Arab Republic, which has considerable influence on the educational programs of other Arabic countries, has four higher institutes for physical educators only, two for men and two for women. In the four-year program, the general studies include Arabic, foreign language, sociology, and military training. The fundamental studies include anatomy, physiology, psychology, education, and health education. The professional studies include teaching methods, history of physical education, recreation education, popular games and sports, and practice teaching. Middle Institutes of Physical Education with lower admission requirements offer a simplified curriculum for primary teachers. The Olympic Institute trains coaches in a two-year evening school program. Former army personnel are no longer employed as physical educators in the schools in the UAR, and classroom teachers now teach the subject only during the first two years in primary school. In 1967, a recommendation was made to include physical education as a university course of study.

In the Jewish Community in Palestine during the 1920s most of the trained teachers came from abroad or were local students who went abroad to study, particularly to Denmark. In 1939 the Department of Physical Training was established which organized short-term courses to train instructors in premilitary training for sports and youth organizations. In 1944, a one-year physical education course was organized which in 1952 became incorporated in a permanent institution, the Physical Education Teachers' College. In 1948, the year in which Israel came into being, an Institute of Education for Movement was founded in Tel Aviv. Both the College and the Institute now offer a two-year program. In 1960, the year when the Physical Education and Sports Authority superseded the Department of Physical Training, the Physical Education Teachers' College was housed in the new Wingate Institute for Physical Education, which opened in 1957.

The Wingate Institute established a three-year program for high school teacher candidates in 1968. In the same year, the Institute sponsored the first International Seminar on the History of Physical Education and Sport. In addition to the physical education school, the Wingate Institute houses a three-year school for physiotherapists, a one-year school for coaches, a training center for national teams, an army physical instructor's school, a sport medicine research center, and a publication department.

Great strides have been made in the development of training programs, but a desperate need for more qualified teachers exists in all nations. Female teachers are in particularly short supply: in 1965 Ethiopia had only three women physical educators. To draw more women into the profession, the training programs must be made more attractive to them, and the tradition against women participating in vigorous physical activity must be overcome. The visits of women athletes and teachers from abroad are helping in this respect.

Since World War II, many multilateral and bilateral agreements have been made to help African and Asian countries develop physical education programs. UNESCO has been responsible for channeling assistance to many countries. The United States has sponsored goodwill tours of athletes and has provided scholarships, physical education teachers, coaches, health educators, textbooks, sports equipment, and other services through various educational and sports organizations, the United States Department of State, the Fulbright program, the Peace Corps, the American Point Four Program, and the Asia Foundation. Many other countries have supplied similar aid to developing countries.

Appeals are being made for scholarships that will enable more youths to study abroad, but some questions are being raised about the operation of these programs. When native students are all sent to the same foreign country to study, their nation does not benefit from the cross-fertilization of ideas. In some instances, the athletes and prospective teachers who are sent abroad are chosen on a basis other than ability and interest in sports and physical education. Perhaps more training should be locally conducted, for teachers who study abroad or in their own capital cities often become reluctant to return to rural areas. Critics complain that some overseas programs devote excessive time to political ideology or to studies of local interest. They also feel that the foreign programs do not prepare students for tropical and semitropical conditions where gymnasiums, indoor swimming pools, gymnastic apparatus, and modern equipment are lacking. They believe that at this stage of development their nations need more short-term, inservice programs and courses that will teach students how to improvise, to construct equipment, and to develop programs under pioneer conditions. In recent years there has been some interchange of ideas among the underdeveloped nations which should prove fruitful.

The Congo (Leopoldville) has sent students to Israel for refresher courses, the Winneaba Training College in Ghana has admitted students from other African nations, and Egypt has provided leadership for the Arab World.

The lack of textbooks and teaching aids has hindered the development of physical education in African and Asian countries. But in recent years educational missions and national governments have developed a number of syllabuses and sports training guides, and professional organizations and conferences have provided teachers with leadership training and guidance. Physical educators have formed professional organizations in the United Arab Republic, Turkey, Iran, Israel, the Philippines, Nigeria, Liberia, Congo (Leopoldville), Malaya, Thailand, Korea, and some other countries. The First All-African Conference on Health and Physical Education was held in Liberia in 1962, and the second one in Addis Ababa, Ethiopia in 1965. Some professional journals are being published to inform teachers of developments in the field. A quarterly journal is published by the Turkish Physical Education Teachers Association; the *Bulletin D'éducation Physique* is published by the Institut National Des Sports in Tunisia; *Chinuch-Gufani*, and a bimonthly journal is published by the Wingate Institute for Physical Education in Israel. In 1953, Dr. George G. Tan published the first issue of *Physical Education Today* in English and Chinese. This tradition was carried on in 1969 when the *ICHPER Asian Journal* was launched. Throughout Africa and Asia the status of physical educators is somewhat lower than that of other teachers, but their work is beginning to be recognized.

In the past century the African and Asian nations have adopted many Western sports. Wherever the Europeans established colonies, they made soccer, cricket, tennis, and track and field events a part of community life. Wherever American YMCA workers, educators, missionaries, members of the armed forces, or representatives of the government and business firms were sent, they introduced baseball and basketball. Athletes from Australia and New Zealand also assisted in cultivating sports interest, particularly in the older mainland countries. Since World War II, the sports movement in Africa and Asia has been stimulated by the presence of foreign soldiers and occupation forces, the international exchange of students and visitors, and the Olympic Games held in Melbourne, Rome, and Tokyo. Considerable sports assistance has been provided by foreign countries both as a goodwill gesture and as a part of the Communist-Capitalist and Sino-Soviet competition in underdeveloped countries. African and Asian countries have, in turn, enriched the Western sports and dance movement. Contacts with these cultures have cultivated a worldwide interest in judo, yoga, karate, badminton, and polo as well as in many native African and Asian dances.

In most African and Asian countries, the Europeans organized the first athletic and sports clubs and competitions, but native leaders eventually took over. Some schools and business firms sponsored clubs and competitions and provided playing grounds and sports equipment. Some governments developed sport programs for the defense and police forces and for railway and postal workers. In some countries, national associations were organized to promote and control specific sports which, in turn, became affiliated with national amateur sports federations. The pattern of development has usually been similar to that of the Philippines and Israel.

In the Philippines, soccer and fencing were popular sports under the Spanish. When the American forces and YMCA workers came, they introduced other sports. In 1911, Elwood S. Brown, a YMCA secretary, helped organize athletic clubs into a national governing body which later became the Philippine Amateur Athletic Federation. As an outgrowth of this organization, competitions with other Asian nations were organized and were held for two decades. The Philippines sent their first athletic representative to the Olympic Games held in Paris in 1924 and sent a larger delegation to succeeding Games. The sports leaders in the Philippines also took an active part in organizing the Asian Games, and they served as the host for these in 1954.

In Palestine, as in the Philippines, sports clubs were organized early in the century. By 1912, the clubs in the Jewish community united to form one association, the Maccabee, and an annual Sports Festival was held each Passover in Rehovoth. When the British took over Palestine from the Turks in 1918, the physical education and sports movement received further impetus, and soccer became the most popular game. The National Hapoel Association was founded for workers in 1926 and became a member of the International Labor Sports Federation (SASI) in 1927. This organization became the largest sports association in the country. The Hapoel Sports Festivals are now international events.

Since Israel came into being in 1948, an effort has been made to expand the sports movement and to improve performance. The Israel Sports Federation, which was formed by the Maccabee organization in 1931 and was joined by the Hapoel organization in 1951, now rules all sports in Israel except for football (soccer), tennis, and chess. The National Olympic Committee, founded in 1933, declined Nazi Germany's invitation to the Olympic Games held in Berlin in 1936. Athletes represented Israel in the Olympic Games for the first time in 1952. All sports in Israel are now affiliated with the Asian region except basketball which is affiliated with the European and Mediterranean region.

Early in this century a few African and Asian athletes began to compete with athletes from neighboring countries. The driving force behind the Far Eastern Championship Games, which did much to promote the development of athletics in Asia, was Elwood S. Brown and the Philippine Amateur Athletic Association. China, Japan, and the Philippines competed in these games from 1913 until 1934 when the games were dissolved over the political issue of whether Manchukuo should be affiliated or not. At that time, India organized the West Asiatic Games which were held once with Ceylon, Palestine, and Afghanistan participating. Plans for similar games to be held in 1938 were abandoned because of the war. After the war, G. D. Sondhi renewed the proposal to hold the games, and the first Asian Games were held in 1951 in New Delhi with fourteen countries attending. In 1962, seventeen countries participated in the fourth Asian Games in Indonesia. The multimillion-dollar stadium built in Djakarta for these games was financed by the USSR, and over thirty foreign coaches advised the participating countries. Because the local games committee, in excluding Israel and Nationalist China (Taiwan), violated the anti-discrimination principle, the International Olympic Committee withdrew its recognition of the 1962 games. Over the years, Japan, the host for the 1964 competitions, has captured most of the medals in the Asian Games.

A number of other regional games have been organized in African and Asian countries. The Maccabiah, which were held in Palestine for the first time in 1932 and are now held each year following the Olympic Games, have done much to raise the prestige of sports in Israel. In 1951 the International Olympic Committee granted Egypt permission to organize the Mediterranean Games, and invitations were sent to France, Greece, Italy, Lebanon, Malta, Monaco, Spain, Syria, Turkey, and Yugoslavia. At the request of Israel, whose athletes were barred from participation, the IOC refused to recognize the Mediterranean Games held in Naples in 1963. The Pan-Arab Games, which were organized in Egypt in 1953, were sponsored by the Arab Legion of Nations to further religious, cultural, and political relationships of youths in that part of the world. Competition in twelve sports was included in the first Southeast Asia Peninsula Games held at Bangkok, Thailand, in 1959. Suva, in the Fiji Islands, served as host for the first South Pacific Games in 1963. For the second Games three years later, New Caledonia built a $5,000,000 sport complex, and fourteen territories competed. In 1965, the first African Games were held in Brazzaville (the Congo) with about thirty countries represented; the United Arab Republic was the victor.

In recent years, developing countries preparing for international competitions have received considerable assistance from European, Russian, and American coaches and sport leaders. The American coaches who were sent overseas by the State Department to work with eleven foreign teams prior to the 1960 Olympics reported that the African and Asian athletes were determined to rank high in sports but were concerned about the effect that their climate, diet, and stature would have upon their performances. Foreign coaches who have worked in developing countries report that the native athletes need more technical sports training and practice, and more opportunities to compete, but that the youths display great enthusiasm and a strong desire to learn, to improve, and to excel for the sake of their countries.

Until quite recently, the sports and dance potential in African and Asian countries has been largely untapped. Many Far Eastern athletes participated in the Olympic Games for the first time in Los Angeles in 1932, but since that time, phenomenal progress has been made. Many stadiums are springing up in Africa. Today, recruiters from abroad come to watch Ghana's Black Star soccer team play Nigeria's Green Eagles. Tomorrow, many of the athletic superstars may come from Asian and African nations. The African and Asian nations are sending larger delegations to each international competition and when one of their athletes, such as Sergeant Abebe Bibila of Ethiopia, breaks a world record or wins an Olympic medal, wild enthusiasm breaks out in his homeland. A victory gives the people in developing countries a deep sense of national pride and self-respect and helps them overcome a lingering sense of inferiority. Some regional games have been marred by political manipulation, lack of crowd control, and inexperience with organization for competitive events, but at each international and regional competition observers have noted marked improvements in the performance of athletes in developing countries. Undoubtedly the gap that has existed between African and Asian sports records and those of the rest of the world will become narrower in the years that lie ahead.

PHYSICAL EDUCATION IN THE REPUBLIC OF SOUTH AFRICA

South Africa, which straddles the southern part of the African continent, is a multiracial, multicultural country about twice the size of Texas. The mountains that surround the great central plateau fall sharply to narrow plains that are fringed by the surf of the Atlantic and Indian oceans. In the past few decades, this land of gold and diamonds, wheat and maize, tobacco and sugar cane, and cattle and sheep ranches has experienced an industrial revolution that has made it the "workshop of the African Continent."

A few white men settled at the Cape of Good Hope in 1652 to raise green vegetables for the ships of the Dutch East India Company; French Huguenots followed in 1688; German immigrants came in 1757; and English settlers arrived in 1820, a few years after the colony had passed into the hands of the British. Because of grievances against British rule, the great trek into the interior was made in 1835–36 by the hardy Boer farmers, descendants of the Dutch and French immigrants who are now known as Afrikaners. Within a few decades, the discovery of diamonds (1865) and gold (1886) brought a flood of fortune seekers to South Africa and precipitated the Anglo-Boer War (1899–1902). The war cost the Boers their independence. Despite their strong resentment against the British, practical considerations and the postwar policy that was pursued encouraged the people of South Africa to merge their four provinces. In 1910 the Union of South Africa was officially proclaimed, and South Africa remained a self-governing dominion of the British Commonwealth until 1961 when the nation became a republic.

The black people in South Africa speak various Bantu languages, but the two official languages of the republic are English and Afrikaans (South African form of Dutch). Bilingualism among the whites is common. More Afrikaans-speaking white children attend public school than English-speaking white children. The white population of three and a half million people is in the minority. The nonwhite population is comprised of twelve million Bantu, a smaller group of coloured people (people of mixed blood), and some Asians, mainly Indians but a few Chinese.

The government has adopted a policy of separate development for the four racial groups (apartheid)—a policy which ideally aims at self-determination for each group. Hence, in education, separate bodies are responsible for each racial group. Education for the whites is controlled by the four provincial education departments and by the Department of Education, Arts, and Science in the central government. The departments in charge of education of the other races are: the Department of Bantu Education, Department of Coloured Affairs, and the Department of Indian Affairs. The higher positions in these three departments are now held by whites, but the trend is to replace them with persons of the various races.

The apartheid policy, which was drafted to keep Europeans and non-Europeans separate, has been subject to heated controversy. Critics throughout the world charge that the government denies nonwhites fundamental social, political, and economic rights and does little to improve their lot. White children enjoy better educational facilities and instruction, have a greater range of vocational opportunities, and remain in school longer than nonwhite children. But the South Africans believe they are making progress in providing better education for all children. Education is free for all races and is compulsory for white children until the tenth grade or sixteen years of age. Most coloured and Indian children attend at least primary schools, and the number of Bantu children in school is increasing. In 1946, seventy-two percent of the Bantu population ten years and older was illiterate. At present, eighty-three percent of the Bantu children attend school, and education may be made compulsory for them within the next few years. The South Africans believe that the transition to self-government of the Bantu people is progressing more peacefully than in other African states. They point out that the expenditures for Bantu education more than doubled between 1953–1963. Nonetheless, a great gap exists between the quality and quantity of education that white and nonwhite children receive.

The physical education movement got under way in South Africa toward the end of the nineteenth century. As early as 1874, a Transvaal Republic Education Law prescribed gymnastics for advanced education, but little action was taken. In 1892 Sir Thomas Muir, the third Superintendent-General of Education in Cape Province, organized short vacation courses and encouraged schools to introduce physical education. Thereafter, many short courses in Swedish exercises were organized, and gymnastic mistresses from abroad were appointed to teach in some girls' schools. A physical education teacher-training program was organized for women in 1921 by Miss M. C. Botha at the Cape Town Training College, for men in 1936 at the Paarl Training College, and for coloured students in 1938 at the Wesley Training School which was later transferred to the Hewett Training College in Cape Town. A program was organized in 1943 for Bantu students at the Healdtown Native Training Institution which has since been discontinued because too few students wished to specialize.

Between 1936 and 1939, provincial education departments established physical education teacher-training courses and appointed the first physical education supervisors. The University of Stellenbosch established the first degree course in physical education with Dr. Ernst Jokl as the department head. In 1938 the National Advisory Council for Physical Education (NACPE) was established to coordinate the efforts of the people working in the field in the municipal, provincial, and central governments and in the voluntary clubs. For a number of years, the NACPE, which was a subsection of the Union Education Department, provided subsidies and guidance for voluntary clubs and municipal recreation centers, assisted teaching institutions, produced teaching syllabi in English and Afrikaans, conducted and published research, and provided information and publicity services. After the Union Education Department became the Department of Education, Arts, and Science in 1950, the NACPE was dissolved. But since that time, an Adult Education Section under the Department of Education, Arts, and Science has supported some independent physical education projects on a national basis. These projects have usually been formulated by the South African Association for Physical Education and Recreation.

In South African schools, physical education is a compulsory subject through the secondary level, but not an examination subject. Both a physical education and a health education course are usually required for students who pursue a diploma course in education, but general university students are not required to take these courses. Playgrounds and sport fields are available at most schools, but gymnasiums are not; hence assembly halls are commonly used for physical education activities. Gymnasiums are being included in new schools, however, and a few are being added each year to old schools.

Many schools of thought have been incorporated into the physical education curriculum. The first immigrant teachers introduced Swedish gymnastics; in the early forties, the Austrian Gaulhofer-Streicher system was introduced; Bukh and German Turnen and the rhythmic gymnastic systems of Dalcroze, Bode, and Medau have also influenced the program. After World War II, greater emphasis was placed on total fitness and on social and recreational skills. A Fitness Council was formed in 1963, and a fitness scheme similar to the Canadian plan was put into operation.

Formality is disappearing from the physical education program which now usually consists of warm-up calisthenics, games skills, gymnastics, some track and field activities, and swimming if a pool is available. Game skills, folk dancing, rhythmic gymnastics, and modern educational dance form the main part of the girls' program. In regular classes, the techniques necessary to participate in the afternoon games program are taught, but the games are not usually played in their entirety. In 1967 legislation was passed to enforce uniformity of syllabi for all subjects in the various provinces, but physical education was excluded because it was not an examination subject. Indications are that such a step may be taken in the future.

In addition to teaching physical education and academic classes, physical educators supervise the school afternoon games programs and Saturday matches. Interschool competition is strongly stressed. The games program is voluntary, but well supported by parents and education authorities and the participation rate is high. Except on the provincial and national levels, games are played rather than watched. A school may field as many as fifteen teams on an afternoon. The main sports are netball and field hockey for girls and rugby and cricket for boys, but swimming, tennis, track and field, and gymnastic competitions are also popular. Softball and baseball were introduced some years ago but did not become established in the schools. Physical educators are usually in charge of the afternoon games program, but academic teachers assist them.

A shortage of trained teachers, particularly women, hampers the progress of physical education for all races. Teachers colleges offer a diploma course for primary school teachers which usually consists of three years of general training followed by a voluntary specialist course in a specific field, such as physical education. Generally, a university degree is required to teach in secondary schools. Students obtain a B.A. or B.S. degree with physical education as one of their majors after three years of study; after a fourth year of study, they obtain their secondary teaching diploma. The double major is required because most physical educators teach at least one other subject. A master's degree can be obtained two years after the first four years of study, and a doctorate at least three years after that. Grants for research can be obtained from the National Council for Social Research. Little research work is done by physical educators, however, because of the strong emphasis on teacher training and the lack of research facilities, trained personnel, and cooperation with related disciplines.

In 1966 a Department of Sport and Recreation was established by the central government with ministerial status and with trained physical educators as staff members. The new department is responsible for promoting participation and coaching for the masses with the hope of attaining greater achievements in the competitive field. The department has direct contacts with white organizations and donates to nonwhite sporting bodies through their departments. With the establishment of this new department, the South African Association for Physical Education and Recreation (SAAPER), which has done much to advance the physical education movement, was faced with the problem of deciding whether to remain attached to the Department of Education, Arts, and Science or whether to seek closer affiliation with the new Department of Sport and Recreation. A strong feeling exists that the SAAPER is basically an educational association. Another change took place when the new Department of Sport and Recreation was established. The publication of *Vigor,* the physical education quarterly which was first published in 1937, was discontinued; a substitute journal of a somewhat similar nature will probably replace it.

Sports play an important part in the life of all races in South Africa, perhaps because of the British influence, the favorable climate, the fairly favorable financial situation, and the absence of television. The sports clubs, which are common from the high school through the university and adult levels, hold interclub weekly matches. Coaching and umpiring are done voluntarily and without remuneration. The national sporting associations have provided some short training courses for coaches. Some industrial firms offer financial assistance for coaching courses and bringing out overseas teams. In the future, the Department of Sport and Recreation will probably provide some assistance.

South Africa has vied with New Zealand for the world champion rugby honors since the beginning of the century. Rugby and cricket, the national games, are amateur sports. Aside from golf, boxing, wrestling, soccer, and tennis, little professionalism exists. *Jukskei,* which is similar to horseshoes, is a distinctive South African game. The participants toss "skeys"—wooden pins that fit into the yoke of oxen—at a stick that is implanted in the ground.

Most voluntary sports organizations are virtually autonomous. A national body known as the Federation for Youth and Sport to which these associations belong offers them financial aid, which comes from private donations, particularly from business concerns, and from the Department of Sport and Recreation. In 1951, nineteen of the governing bodies of sports formed the South African Sport Federation. The central body for organized sport, which forms part of the Olympic Games, is the South African Olympic Games Association, but some sports, such as rugby, soccer, cricket, golf, and association football are not governed by this body. Non-European organizations have also been formed, such as Bantu football, lawn tennis, cricket, and rugby associations and similar Indian and coloured sport associations. The non-Europeans have also organized local and interprovincial sport contests. Since the republic is no longer a member of the British Commonwealth, South Africans do not participate in these games as before.

The South African Games, which were started in 1960, and take place every four years, are organized for all racial groups within their own groups and areas.

The apartheid policy has created some serious problems in respect to the promotion of sports. No racially mixed gatherings may be held except under special permit and special conditions in any place of entertainment. At the Olympic Games in 1964, South African sport leaders thought they could solve this problem by sending one black and one white team to international contests, but their appeals were not heeded by international authorities. In 1967, six months after Prime Minister Hendrik Verwoerd, a determined advocate of apartheid, was assassinated, the government amended the old ban on interracial sports to permit South Africa to send an integrated team to the 1968 Olympics. When several countries threatened to boycott the Olympics if South Africa participated, the International Olympic Committee reversed an earlier decision and voted not to invite South Africa to the Games. The apartheid policy again created tension when Arthur Ashe was accepted as a competitor by the South African Tennis Union in 1969, and his application for a visa was denied.

PHYSICAL EDUCATION IN INDIA AND PAKISTAN

In 1947, after two centuries of British rule and long-standing friction between the Hindus and Muslims, the subcontinent of India was partitioned into the two self-governing nations. Pakistan, which consists of two separate northern areas where Muslims are in the majority, faces many of the same problems as the Republic of India; hence, the following discussion will be focused primarily on the Republic of India.

Despite the progress that has been made in increasing agricultural production and improving education, India is still plagued with poverty, malnutrition, disease, and illiteracy. Providing schools, teachers, and textbooks for Indian children is a formidable task. There are a million babies born each month in India, fourteen languages and many dialects are spoken, and few roads connect the thousands of tiny villages where the majority of the people live. Although the constitution outlawed "untouchability," the caste system remains a powerful factor in society. Parochial interests are also thrust above national interests by the practice of nepotism and the prevalence of regional and religious animosities which produce political instability and hamper needed reforms.

Physical education is now accepted as an integral part of education in India, but previously it was viewed as a student welfare program. The program is impeded by the lingering ascetic philosophy, the strong emphasis on academic studies and examinations, the prejudices against female participation, and the lack of appeal that vigorous physical activity has for caste-conscious citizens and the poverty-stricken populace. The promotion of sports and games is hampered by marginal diets, the absence of a sports tradition, lack of trained coaches, inadequate facilities and equipment, and insufficient financial support. The princes who contributed generously to games and sports in the past are no longer able to extend their patronage to the same extent.

The administration of education in India is vested in the states, but a Central Advisory Board of Physical Education and Recreation advises the central government and assists the state director of education and physical education. Although many difficulties have been experienced, physical education and sports leaders have made encouraging progress.

In 1956, the Central Advisory Board published *A National Plan of Physical Education and Recreation* which included a more comprehensive curriculum than had been employed previously and also norms for physical efficiency tests. The objective of the program was to help youths acquire the physical fitness and neuromuscular skills, mental and emotional health, and recreational and social abilities that would enable them to assume the responsibilities of democratic citizenship.

The Indian leaders made an effort to revive or retain indigenous activities, such as *dands* (prone calisthenics), *baithaks* (squatting exercises), *asanas* (pose positions), *malkhamb* (pole exercises), *lezium* (a form of rhythmics), regional folk dances, and *kho-kho* (a vigorous team tag game), *kabaddi* (a native running and breath-holding game), *langadi* (a hopping game), *lathi* (a combative activity), and *jambia* (a self-defense activity).

Indian leaders soon found that the physical education programs in the schools were being adversely affected by competing programs that were financed by the central government. Many school authorities accepted the National Cadet Corps and the Auxiliary Cadet Corps programs which were operated by the Ministry of Defense. Some schools accepted the National Discipline Scheme, a physical education and patriotic program that was organized originally to combat the lack of discipline in refugee camps. In 1959 the Kunzru Committee was appointed to examine several overlapping youth programs. When the Chinese Communists invaded India, many leaders became concerned about strengthening discipline and instilling patriotism among youths.

As a result of the Kunzru investigation, the National Fitness Corps (NFC) was launched in 1965–1966. This integrated youth program replaced the existing physical education, Auxiliary Cadet Corps, and National Discipline Scheme programs, but the National Cadet Corps program was retained. The NFC handbook states that the new program aims to make youths physically strong for national defense and to develop patriotic fervor and appreciation for "the democratic values of life and love for their country."

The NFC handbook suggests the following core and optional activities for grades five through eleven and the number of classes to be devoted to each: Exercise Tables (Mass Physical Training Tables and Yoga Exercises are optional), 156; Military-type Drills and Marching, 138; *Lezium* (indigenous rhythmics), 66; Gymnastics (*Malkhamb* for boys) and Folk Dances, 114; Western and Indigenous Games and Relays, 222; Track and Field Events, National Efficiency Tests, and Hiking, 210; Combatives, such as simple and mass combat games and wrestling (girls may substitute folk dancing; judo is optional for boys; *jambia* is optional for girls), 58; and National Ideals and Good Citizenship, Practical Projects, and Community-Singing, 152. The last group includes the study of hygiene, sanitation, manners, the Indian Constitution and culture, optional training in first aid, organizing games and sports, firefighting, crowd control, camping, and social service. The National Fitness Corps Program stipulates that grades six through nine will have five periods of physical education per week and grades ten and eleven at least three to four periods a week.

In India few schools possess adequate gymnasiums, and the playgrounds, if available, may be some distance from the schools. Classes are often held in the school hall or in small open areas when the weather is not too hot or too rainy. Physical education classes are taught by classroom teachers on the primary level and by trained physical educators above that level. Recently, some specialist teachers have been appointed to supervise physical education in elementary schools, but they also teach a general subject. The NFC handbook recommends that wherever facilities exist, after-school intramural and interscholastic sports and games and a weekly period of mass physical training activities should be conducted. District and state competitions are organized, and the All-India School Games Federation conducts annual national competitions.

In the universities, all male students are required to participate in the National Cadet Corps. Some universities require other students in the first two classes to take physical education, but voluntary activity programs are more common. In India, the Inter-University Sports Board supervises a well-developed program of competition. In Pakistan physical education in the university is primarily an intramural-type program. In both Pakistan and India, the strong emphasis on academic studies deters participation in sports. India draws most of her athletes for international games from the armed forces, police, and railways, rather than from universities, as is the practice in Japan and the United States.

Under British rule, many retired military men taught physical education classes and they restricted the activities to mass drills and exercises; interested academic teachers organized sports and games for students after school. In the early part of this century, a new concept of physical education was introduced by two Americans, Henry Grey at the Calcutta YMCA in 1908 and H. C. Buck at the YMCA College of Physical Education in Madras, which he established in 1920 to train instructors. The broad Youth Welfare Scheme developed by J. Buchanan, an Englishman, while serving as Director of the College of Physical Education at Calcutta (c. 1930–1950), also influenced the development of physical education.

In Pakistan at the time of the partition, physical education leadership was partially depleted because many well-trained Hindu physical educators migrated to India, and the Ansars, a semimilitary organization, attracted many more. East Pakistan has continued the Buchanan Youth Welfare Scheme. The Director of the Program, who serves under the Director of Public Instruction, is responsible for the school physical education program and the sport clubs and organizations outside of educational institutions. West Pakistan has also placed physical education under the Education Department, but has made no provisions for a Director of Physical Education or the Youth Welfare Scheme.

There is a great need for more and better-trained physical education teachers both in Pakistan and India. A government college of Physical Education in West Pakistan and one in East Pakistan offer a one-year training program, and two National Coaching Centers have been established. In India, the syllabus of physical education in the elementary training schools has recently been revised. Over fifty institutions offer one-year teacher-training courses in physical education; the certificate course is for high school graduates and the diploma course is for university graduates. The National Lakshmibai College of Physical Education, which was established in 1957, inaugurated a three-year degree course, and in 1963, added a two-year postgraduate course. The Government College of Physical Education, Patiala, and the University of Punjab (Chandigarh) have made similar arrangements. These efforts to upgrade the teacher training programs, the government grants-in-aid to physical education colleges, and the founding of physical education professional organizations are improving the quality of leadership in the field.

To make people conscious of the need for physical fitness, the Ministry of Education has been conducting the National Physical Efficiency Drive since 1959–1960. Testing centers administer separate batteries of tests for men and women in various age groups. Badges are awarded for different levels of performance and a National Awards Competition is held annually for the most proficient performers.

Most communities have an *akhara*, an exercise center at which wrestling, gymnastics, and indigenous activities are practiced. Football (soccer), field hockey, and cricket are the most popular foreign games. The organization of sports on a national scale is fairly recent. The Indian Olympic Association was formed in 1927, and most of the national federations were formed after that date. To spur greater interest in sports, the Asian Games

Federation was founded by the Maharajadhiraj of Patiala, and the first Asian Games were celebrated in New Delhi in 1951.

The government is concerned about the quality and promotion of sports. The All-India Council of Sports, which was established in 1954, provides advice and assistance in this field, and most states have established similar sports councils. Each year the central government presents Arjuna Awards to outstanding sportsmen in different games and the Abul Kalam Azad Trophy to the university that has the largest number of participants in national and international tournaments.

The Ad Hoc Enquiry Committee on Games and Sports was appointed in 1958 to investigate the low standards of sports and the performance of Indian teams in international games. As a result of the Committee's recommendation, the National Institute of Sports was established at Patiala in 1961 to produce coaches of high caliber in as many sports as possible. In 1962 the first All-India Sports Congress convened at which members of government and voluntary agencies, the news media, and sports industries drafted recommendations for coordinating and improving the promotion of sports in India.

PHYSICAL EDUCATION IN CHINA

China, one of the oldest cultures and largest nations in the world, has had a turbulent history. After the Ching Dynasty was overthrown in 1911, a republic was established. Considerable internal dissension existed until 1928 when the Kuomintang (Nationalist Party) unified the nation. Within a few years, however, the Japanese aggression, World War II, and the Kuomintang-Communist conflict again plunged the country into turmoil. In 1949, the Kuomintang withdrew to Taiwan (Formosa), and the Communists began to build a new economic and social system on the mainland.

At the turn of this century, the Chinese adopted a modern system of education, for military defeats had convinced them that their traditional education was inadequate. As a part of the westernization movement, formalized calisthenics and athletic meets were introduced by missionary schoolteachers, YMCA leaders, Chinese students who had studied abroad, and well-trained specialists from Japan and America. Dr. Charles H. McCloy, who left the United States for China in 1913, promoted physical education through his work as a staff member of the Chinese National Council of YMCA, as director of a physical education school in Nanking (1921–1926), as editor of the *Chinese Journal of Physical Education and Hygiene* (1922–1924), and as an author of several books that were published in Chinese.

Between 1919 and 1927, a democratic movement developed in education that was influenced by Paul Monroe and John Dewey who were invited to visit China. Ball games and other modern activities were introduced during this period, and the title of the program was changed from Gymnastics to Physical Education. Even so, most sports were still considered to be extracurricular activities.

In 1929, a year after the Kuomintang unified the nation, a National Physical Education Law was passed and a National Physical Education Committee was established, both of which were reformulated in 1941. The law made physical education a required subject. The committee issued a standard physical education program and provided for teacher-training programs, facilities, and physical examinations for school children. Official regulations to establish playgrounds were formulated in 1939. In 1942 the Ministry of Education authorized the formation of provincial and municipal physical education committees.

Training for physical education teachers was instituted in 1916 at the Nanking Teachers College, in 1917 at the National Peking Normal University, and between 1920 and 1930 at several private teacher-training institutions. After the Nationalists unified the nation, all teacher-training institutions were gradually brought under the control of the central government. Later, owing to the teacher shortage, several provinces and municipalities founded their own training institutions.

When the democratic movement swept over the country, Chinese girls began to participate in physical education classes, morning drills, and athletics. Two women's teacher-training schools became well known: the Liang Chiang (Two Rivers) Girls' Physical Education Academy in Shanghai for its work in athletics and the Ginling Girls' College in Nanking for its work in dance and school physical education. After 1931, the physical education department of Peiping Girls' Normal University combined with the Peiping Normal University to inaugurate the first coeducational training program, an innovation that was eventually followed by other institutions.

During World War II, when many schools moved to the remote interior, the objectives of physical education were changed to meet the exigencies of the war. The Communist-Kuomintang conflict that followed the war further impeded the development of physical education. But since 1949, the leaders of the Republic of China on Taiwan and the Communist People's Republic of China on the mainland have recognized the important role that physical education can play in building a nation.

In Taiwan, physical education is a compulsory subject on all school levels and every school conducts physical examinations twice a year. Through these programs, students are encouraged to develop sound health, recreational, and living habits, and to acquire the motor skills and physical fitness necessary for personal development, national defense, and the redevelopment of China in the event of the hoped-for return to the mainland.

The time allotment for physical education on the elementary level is between 120 and 180 minutes a week and on the secondary level and above is 100 minutes a week. The elementary curriculum includes games, rhythmics, stunts, track and field, dodgeball, freehand exercise, walking, and swimming. In addition, the intermediate curriculum includes softball, basketball, soccer, and gymnastics. The secondary curriculum includes more team sports, water sports, archery, and self-defense activities, such as Chinese boxing, judo, boxing, and fencing. Students are encouraged to participate in the fifteen-minute morning exercises and in extracurricular outdoor activities, athletic meets, play days, physical education demonstrations, and sport contests. In colleges, physical education is a required subject, and intramural and intercollegiate programs are conducted. In 1957 an intercollegiate athletic federation of fifteen schools was organized.

Since 1957, physical education experts have been employed by the Ministry of Education, committees have been appointed to revise the physical education curriculum, syllabuses have been developed, and teaching demonstration tours have been conducted. The Ministry of Education now has a National Office of Sports, a Physical Education Committee with school, social, and research subcommittees, and a Commission of Provincial Education. The National Olympic Committee and Republic of China Amateur Athletic Federation come under the Ministry of Interior. The Ministry of Defense has a Physical Education Committee of Military. The China Youth Corps has an Improvement Committee of Youth Physical Education with subcommittees for some sports, research, and examinations of youth physical fitness.

Physical education teachers are trained at Taiwan Provincial Normal University in a five-year program and at Taiwan Provincial College of Physical Education or Taiwan Provincial Junior Teachers College in a three-year program. Physical educators for the armed forces are trained in the Political Cadre School which was established in 1952.

Beside teaching regular classes, teachers are responsible for morning exercises, intramural activities, and interscholastic programs. No educational organizations exclusively for physical educators exist, but several periodicals are published. The best physical education workers are honored during the Annual National Physical Education Festival. Because intensive competition for advanced study causes many students to neglect physical education, leaders in the field have urged that a physical education test should be included in the secondary school examinations for university entrance. Their suggestion is now being considered by the governmental authorities.

When the Nationalists lost power on the mainland, no professional sports were promoted in China, but amateur sports and athletic activities had gained enthusiastic support. Early in the century, Chinese students invited youths from other schools and from nonschool organizations to participate in their athletic meets. Interscholastic athletic associations were eventually formed. Local and provincial athletic meets were also organized for students and members of voluntary organizations. These meets later served as tryouts for the National Athletic Meet which was organized for men in 1911, and first added events for women in 1930. After the Nationalists became established on Taiwan, every city and district began to hold athletic meets and other contests at appropriate times. During the Ninth Athletic Meet held in 1960, about 2,300 athletes from 199 schools participated.

With the rising tide of interest in sports at the beginning of the century, many associations were formed to foster Western sports and to preserve traditional sports, such as *Kuo Shu* (Chinese boxing). Many of these associations became affiliated with the Chinese National Amateur Athletic Federation which was founded in 1910. The Federation promoted sports participation within the nation and in international games. Chinese athletes were sent to seven Olympic Games between 1932 and 1964, all but one of the Far Eastern Championship Games when they were held (1913–1934), and all but two of the Asian Games which have been held since 1951.

After the Communists seized power on the mainland in 1949, they established a crash educational program. Through literacy campaigns and technological training, they sought to catapult their predominately rural society with its difficult language and masses of uneducated peasants into a world industrial power. Molding youths into the Communist pattern of citizenship and morality was the objective of education. The school was to produce a student who was both "Red and expert," that is, who was politically conscientious and technologically skilled.

At the outset, almost all schools were supported by the national budget, but to meet the fiscal demands of the "Great Leap Forward" and to restore lagging farm production much of the responsibility for schools was later shifted to provinces, municipalities, communes, and industries. In principle, the administration of education was decentralized; in practice, the Communist Party made the important decisions.

Education was expanded rapidly on all levels and enrollments soared, but the quality of education suffered somewhat because of economic and political strains, the shortage of qualified teachers, and the amount of time that students had to devote to ideological education, mass campaigns and productive labor. The government established a two-track academic and vocational system of education and founded thousands of spare-time schools to eradicate illiteracy and to impress Communist ideology on the mass mind. To quickly realize economic goals, many school programs were made shorter and more intensive. Most colleges and universities became institutes that specialized in one field or closely related fields.

To relate learning directly to production, schools were encouraged to establish factories and farms, and factories and farms were encouraged to establish schools. The university and school factories were not merely laboratories, but actual productive units. Students and teachers on all levels were expected to respect the dignity of manual labor and were required to spend varying portions of their time working in factories and fields.

In addition to the regular educational network, many half-work, half-study schools and universities were established to make education available to more youths and to increase the supply of skilled labor. In these schools, which directed studies toward practical work in the fields and factories, the entrance requirements, curriculum, and standards of achievement were somewhat below that of the ordinary middle schools and universities.

Provisions in the Constitution of the People's Republic of China reveal that from the beginning the Communists attached great importance to physical education. Mao Tse-tung thought that the government should help youths cultivate themselves in those phases of moral, intellectual, and physical education that would enable them to realize their socialistic mission. Physical education was promoted to improve health and hygienic standards, to bolster productive labor and national defense, and to attain sports records and international recognition.

The Communists developed a physical education program for the schools that included gymnastics and sports, excursions that provided physical exercise, and military training for secondary school boys. In addition, they conducted a comprehensive youth program through The Young Pioneers and the Communist Youth League. Before the Sino-Soviet estrangement, Soviet coaches and educational leaders gave the Chinese assistance, and some Soviet textbooks and teaching guides were translated into Chinese. To expand the supply of Chinese leadership, the government established ten special schools to train physical education teachers and a number of junior and youth spare-time athletic schools to train promising athletes. In addition, *The New Physical Educator* and other periodicals and textbooks were published.

Physical fitness became an obsession in China after the government launched its massive physical education movement. Western activities were popular, and traditional sports and exercises were retained. *Wu Shu,* Chinese boxing, was preserved, and *T'ai-Chi Ch'uan,* an exercise that consists of shifting slowly from one stylized position to another, which was once performed only by older men, began to gain favor among young people.

Virtually everyone joined a physical education organization. In offices and shops, work was halted once or twice a day for sitting-up exercises. People were told to exercise for ten minutes a day so that they could serve the cause of socialism for ten additional years. Millions of people passed the "national sports prowess tests" which was initiated in 1955. The Peiping sports newspaper, *Ti Yu Pao* reported that the All-China Athletic Federation ratified 142 national records during 1958, and among the 142 were seven world marks.[3] Spectacular athletic displays were held on some occasions, such as the opening of Peking's Workers' Stadium in 1959, when eight thousand athletes performed for two weeks in a colorful sport show.

A visitor to China in the mid-1960s observed people participating enthusiastically in sports, dances, and exercises in streets, parks, schools, factories, gymnasiums, and Workers' Cultural Palaces. The Canton sports stadium, which seats fifty thousand people and has two Olympic-size pools, was one of the score of first-rate stadiums and pools seen in a brief visit. Young girls were observed doing folk dances for a half hour after working the night shift. The visitor reported, "There was nothing novel about this dancing session: all workers in China must do daily exercise of one kind or another—dancing, *tai chi chuan*, or more vigorous calisthenics."[4]

In two decades, the Communist Revolution had changed the lives of the great masses of Chinese people, but by 1970 their nation was caught in a vortex of natural calamities and political-economic problems. The economy had suffered because of poor harvests. Ideological conflicts with the USSR had precipitated the withdrawal of Soviet experts and supplies. Struggles between opposing political factions within the country had climaxed in another cultural convulsion. In the 1960s, the Communist Youth League was replaced by the Red Guards of Defense who were organized to defeat the enemies of Mao's teaching. In 1966 education was suspended for several months so that students could contemplate Mao's teaching and roam through the country spreading his gospel. A period of violent confusion and turmoil ensued during which the economy suffered. The outcome of this struggle cannot be predicted.

PHYSICAL EDUCATION IN JAPAN

Over the centuries Japanese culture has assimilated many ideas from other cultures. Chinese art, script, literature, sports, and Buddhism were introduced very early. Japan closed her doors to Western nations in the seventeenth century, but she reopened them involuntarily in 1854 and soon adopted Western ideas.

Some ancient sports are still popular in Japan, particularly the Japanese forms of self-defense (*judo*), fencing (*kendo*), archery (*kyudo*), and wrestling (*sumo*). Among the ancient sports that are now performed only on ceremonial occasions are the formalized kick-ball games (*kemari*), equestrian archery (*yabusame*), and equestrian ball-hitting (*dakyu*).

In ancient society, sports and dances were an integral part of such

[3]*New York Times*, Sunday, 22 February 1959, p. 4S.
[4]Lisa Hobbs, *I Saw Red China* (New York: McGraw-Hill Book Company, 1966), p. 128.

common activities as hunting for food, praying for good harvests, and training for war. In earlier times the Japanese hunted with bows and arrows and with falcons. When they settled down to agricultural life, they practiced archery as a sport, and dancing and sumo wrestling also became popular. Sumo matches were held every year from 734 to 1119. Two other ancient sports, *kemari* and *dakyu*, may have been brought to Japan from China during the seventh and eighth centuries.

When the samurai came into power at the end of the twelfth century, military training was stressed, sports and dances became an important part of shrine festivals, and the sports of noblemen became popular among the upper-class warriors. During the middle ages, equestrian archery, sumo, horse racing, *dakyu* were practiced mostly by warriors. *Kasagake*, an informal game of equestrian archery, was played at any time or place; *yabusame*, a highly ritualized form of the game, was played at religious festivals. *Kemari*, the noncompetitive game in which players keep kicking the ball in the air to keep it from touching the ground, was played by both court nobles and upper-class warriors, and eventually, by many other people, even women and children. When the sword and spear replaced equestrian archery in warfare during the sixteenth century, many schools devised secret systems for teaching these military arts. Judo gradually replaced sumo in the life of the warrior class in the middle ages. Like dancing and archery, sumo became a sport of the common people.

In 1603, Ieyasu Togugawa was appointed Shōgun and established the government in Edo (Tokyo). During the Edo Era, the clan schools offered a military and a cultural education. They formalized the teaching of judo and other military sports and awarded certificates for various levels of proficiency. Most feudal clan schools required training in swordsmanship, archery, judo, swimming, and cudgeling, and later added gunnery, regimental drill, and gymnastics. During the eighteenth century, equestrian ball-hitting was restored in a new form with only one goal. By the end of the feudal era, common people began to engage in many sports, sometimes furtively because of directives prohibiting participation.

The restoration of Emperor Meiji in 1868 marked the close of the feudal era and the beginning of a period of progress. A highly centralized national school system was established in 1872, and physical education was made a required subject. In 1878, a gymnastic training center was established and an American, George A. Leland, an Amherst graduate and a student of Edward Hitchcock, was invited to serve as a consultant. The post of school hygiene inspector was created in 1896. A School Hygiene Section was established in 1900 which was abolished in 1903, reestablished in 1921, and reorganized into the Physical Education Section in 1928.

The physical education program consisted primarily of light exercises until 1885 when a new law gave education a nationalistic orientation. But there were criticisms of the military-style gymnastics and appeals were made for the inclusion of the games, sports, and Swedish gymnastics that Westerners had introduced. A French engineer had organized a play day for workers as early as 1868. About a decade later, William Clark, an English teacher, introduced Japanese college students to rowing and track and field events. In the early 1900s Frank H. Brown, a YMCA director, introduced volleyball, basketball, and mass games. As a result of these influences, Japanese schools began to hold play days after the turn of the century. The university students began to organize sport clubs, and later, other students and workers followed their example. The Japanese became enthusiastic participants in Western sports, but they continued to practice their traditional sports and transformed some Western sports into Japanese forms, such as soft tennis and rubber-ball baseball.

A physical education syllabus that was largely based on Swedish gymnastics was published in 1913. In later revisions of this syllabus (1926, 1936, 1941), a liberalizing trend developed which was gradually enveloped by the emergence of a militaristic trend. The Showa Period (1926–1935) marked a shift toward informal teaching methods including more games and play. During this period, nonetheless, a military officer was stationed in each secondary school and a military training syllabus was prepared in 1926. After the Manchurian Incident in 1931, the militaristic trend became more pronounced. Judo and *kendo* were made compulsory, the time allotment for physical education was increased, and before the outbreak of the Pacific War, nationalistic physical fitness programs were developed. In 1941, the physical exercise course was renamed "physical training course," and a militaristic syllabus was compiled.

After the war "The Report of the Education Mission from the United States" encouraged the Japanese to develop more local initiative, freedom, and responsibility than had existed in their previous educational system. Physical education was made a required course in all schools, and the program was rid of all militaristic ideas. When the curriculum was revised in 1947 on a more democratic and scientific basis, the term "physical education" replaced the term "physical training," health education received considerable attention, a school lunch program was developed, and command-response forms of teaching gave way to more informal methods.

Today, emphasis is placed on the development of the individual student, rather than national power. Teachers strive to help students develop sound minds and bodies, approved health and safety practices, varied physical and social skills, and the ability to assume responsibility and to cooperate with others. The primary curriculum includes calisthenics, apparatus work, track and field, ball games, rhythmics, and other activities. The intermediate and secondary curriculums include the same activities plus combatives for boys, swimming, dancing, and ball games. More than one of the traditional sports of judo, *kendo*, or sumo must be taught. Above the fifth grade, classroom teaching of health and physical education theory is required. On the upper secondary school level, health and physical education are separate courses. Physical fitness and group methods of teaching have been emphasized recently.

School authorities also conduct intramural programs, motor ability measurement days, play days, excursions, skating competitions, and some seaside and open air schools. Interschool athletics are prohibited on the elementary school level, but a secondary school may have several sport clubs that participate in local and some regional contests. Lower secondary schools have participated in an annual All Japan Athletic Meet since 1953 and a National Swimming Meet since 1961. The results of the Athletic Meet, which is held simultaneously in all the prefectures, are assembled and ranked in Tokyo.

Some students participate in the National Sports Festival which has an Upper Secondary School Section. Practically all of the national contests on the secondary level, except for baseball, are supervised by the Physical Education Federation of Upper Secondary School, which has divisions for twenty-eight sports. Baseball, the most popular sport in Japan, is controlled by the All Japan High School Baseball Association which conducts a national baseball tournament that is broadcast on television and radio.

After the reorganization of education in 1947, a new type of university was established and physical education was made a required course. A Physical Education Department was established that was made responsible for the required activity courses and theoretical lectures, school athletics, and teacher preparation in the field. About a third of the university students belong to sport clubs, and some students participate in intercollegiate, national, and international contests. Before the war, no institution awarded a bachelor's degree in physical education. Today, fifty-eight universities and twelve junior colleges train health and physical education teachers, many of their students earn a bachelor's degree and some earn a master's or doctoral degree.

National physical fitness tests have been conducted in Japan since 1926 when the Athletic Test was formulated. A Physical Strength Badge Test was devised in 1939 to help build a stronger military power. In 1949 a Sport Badge Test was established to improve physical fitness and to popularize sports. In 1958 this test was superseded by the National Stadium Sport Test.

Research has not been neglected in Japan. The Research Institute of Physical Education under the Ministry of Education published a *Journal of Research on Physical Education* during the years it existed (1934–1941). Today several universities and some sport organizations are conducting research and some of them publish research journals. In addition, the Japanese Society of Physical Education, founded in 1950, publishes the *Research Journal of Physical Education*. The Japanese Physical Fitness Society, founded in 1949, publishes the *Japanese Journal of Physical Fitness*.

The Japan Physical Education Teacher Association informs secondary school teachers of developments in the field.

Sports have flourished in the community as well as in the schools. As early as 1897, the magazine, *The Sports World*, was published. With the introduction of Western sports in the nineteenth century, traditional Japanese sports began to decline. In an effort to counteract this trend, Jigoro Kano established *Kodokan* judo in 1882, and later established the Greater Japan Martial Arts Association in 1895. But the tide could not be turned for many organizations were formed to promote Western sports and public interest in these sports was heightened by the Olympic Games, Far Eastern Championship Games, Meiji Shrine Athletic Meets (1924–1938), and the sports events sponsored by the newspapers, the YMCA, and the scouting and youth organizations.

With the approach of the Pacific War, community recreation was directed toward militaristic goals, but the need for developing a new program was recognized soon after the war. The National Recreation Association was established in 1949. A Social Education Law was passed in 1949 to promote education, athletics, and recreation for out-of-school youths and adults. The National Stadium was built in 1958. The rebirth of the sport movement was culminated by the enactment of the Sport Promotion Law in 1961 which made provisions for establishing Community Sport Promotion Councils, holding an annual Sport Day and a National Sport Festival, and improving facilities and the training of sport leaders.

The Japan Amateur Sports Association (JASA), which was founded in 1911, now represents thirty-five sports associations. The JASA acts as a liaison body with sponsors of international games and a sponsor of the National Sports Festival in which as many as 100,000 athletes participate in thirty-five events. National associations for some sports, such as baseball, aviation, *Jukendo,* and football (American) function outside of the JASA.

Japanese athletes have participated in all but one of the Olympic Games since 1912, the Far East Championship Games (1913–1934), in the Asian Games which were organized in 1951, and the International Student Games which were first held in 1924 and were renamed *Universiade* in 1959. The progress that Japan has made in the development of sports was recognized when Tokyo was selected as the site of the eighteenth Olympiad in 1964, the first games in which judo was adopted as an official event.

PHYSICAL EDUCATION IN AUSTRALIA

Australia is a federation of six sovereign states that occupy an area about the size of the United States mainland. Approximately two-thirds of the eleven million Australians reside in coastal cities. Large-scale farming operations yield wheat, wool, lamb, beef, and dairy products, but a large part of the interior of Australia is arid and unfit for agriculture. In recent years, some shift from agriculture to industry has occurred.

The states control education in Australia with a highly centralized administrative system that is essentially the same in each state. The Commonwealth Office of Education, established in 1945, supplements the work of the state departments of education, but does not supervise their activities. The Commonwealth government levies major taxes and allocates amounts to the states, but does not control state spending. Except for special projects, the local community neither supports the schools nor has a voice in the operation of them. Because half of the people live in the six capital cities and sparsely settled areas cannot afford to support schools, state control ensures a more uniform standard of education in all districts.

The State Department of Education prescribes the educational program, sets the standards for the training of teachers, and acts as the final authority in all educational matters. Education is compulsory up to the age of fourteen to sixteen, depending on the state. Much has been done to broaden the curriculum since World War II, and more students are remaining in school beyond the school leaving age. Students in rural and outback (bush country) areas may receive instruction in area or consolidated schools, through correspondence courses and two-way radios, or in a school that travels to them by railroad.

Each state develops its own physical education program, but the Commonwealth National Fitness Officer provides some services that are available to both state and nonstate schools. The State Director of Physical Education is responsible for developing the course of study and teaching aids, training and hiring teachers, and providing leadership and supervision for the local program, and he may also organize recreation programs for the community.

The National Fitness Council, which was originally launched as a war measure, has given impetus to the training of physical educators and to the rise of school-community recreation in Australia. The National Fitness Council serves in an advisory capacity and coordinates the work of the State National Fitness Councils. The Commonwealth Government provides some grants to the states; the states appropriate additional funds and carry out the program. Where the State Director of Physical Education serves as the State Organizer for the National Fitness Council, considerable integration of school and council personnel and facilities is realized. The councils have established local committees and have affiliated the voluntary youth organizations and junior sports organizations as sub-committees. The councils have developed a number of play centers, recreation leadership training programs, year-round camps, swimming instruction programs, clinics to raise coaching standards, short-term training programs for youth leaders, and fitness booklets. Various aspects of the program have done much to assimilate migrant children—the "new" Australians.

Three men played a major role in molding the physical education movement in Australia. The pioneer work was done by a Dane, Bjelke Peterson, who was appointed as Federal Director of Physical Training in 1910. Fritz Duras, a German, established a diploma course at the University of Melbourne where he received an appointment in 1937 and trained a corps of future leaders. Gordon Young has been very active since he was appointed Director of Physical Education in New South Wales in 1938. These men had many problems to solve.

Because university courses that contain practical and applied work are heavily criticized in Australia, most secondary school physical educators are prepared at teachers' colleges in two- or three-year diploma courses. Elementary school teachers receive some training in physical education, and a combined professional and physical education specialist training program for elementary school teachers was introduced in 1966. Professional leaders have been pressing for the establishment of university degree programs in physical education, but only two programs are fully operative. A four-year degree program, which includes some research training, is offered at the University of Western Australia. Since 1961 the University of Sydney has also offered a degree program. The number of students completing the degree program is small, for the work is demanding and the degree is not needed for teaching. In recent years, many Australians have gone overseas to pursue graduate studies.

The State Education Departments set up scholarship quotas and pay most of the expenses of the students who are admitted to the teacher training program. In return, students enter into a contract to complete the course and to serve the Department for a stipulated number of years. After obtaining a diploma, teachers may receive inservice training through programs and publications provided by the State Education Department and the National Fitness Council. The Australian Physical Education Association, which was formed in 1954, publishes a journal and holds biennial conferences to keep teachers abreast of developments in the field; state branches of the Association conduct workshop sessions and special projects for their members.

Physical education is a required subject in elementary and secondary schools and also in teacher training colleges. Classroom teachers are responsible for physical education in most elementary schools, but recently a few full-time physical educators have been appointed to teach on this level. Full-time or at least part-time physical education specialists teach on the secondary school level; physical educators may also serve as the organizer of the sports afternoons or coaching sessions.

Because of the favorable climate, the physical education program is for the most part based on outdoor facilities. The distinctive character of each school is formed, in part, by local parents' and citizens' organizations that raise funds and sometimes obtain matching government grants for outdoor gymnasium construction, shelter sheds, and swimming pools. In Australia, school and community playing fields for football, rugby, soccer, field hockey, cricket, baseball, and track and field are usually available, courts for basketball, volleyball, and tennis are prevalent, and swimming pools are frequently found. But leaders are becoming concerned, because urbanization has whittled away at green spaces and open areas, and sport facilities have not kept pace with population growth.

The physical education program in Australia was strongly influenced by the English syllabi until 1942 when Western Australia produced the first non-European syllabus. A movement is now underway to introduce health education, and New South Wales has launched a pilot health-physical education-sports program which allots one period for health, two periods for physical education, and two periods for sports a week.

In the elementary schools the physical education program usually consists of conditioning and postural exercises, gymnastics, games and sports, rhythmics and dance activities. On the secondary level, conditioning or fitness exercises, gymnastics, track and field events, games and sports, swimming and lifesaving are an integral part of the program, and some emphasis is placed on dance for girls. Instruction and participation in sports and games are strongly stressed in class and out-of-class and in both the boys' and girls' programs. Girls participate in vigorous sports in Australia to a much greater extent than in the United States.

To supplement the physical education classes, a sports afternoon, morning coaching session, or sports day, which may be staggered for different grades, is set aside each week. The more competent teachers coach the interscholastic teams, but all pupils and all teachers are expected to participate in the sports afternoon. The absentee and truancy rates of non-skilled students are high, however, because many academic teachers are less enthusiastic about this responsibility than they were in the past. Schools organize their programs in somewhat the same manner. When a boy enters Melbourne High School, for example, he is allotted to one of four houses, and he remains in this house until he leaves school. On the first sports day of each season the boy selects his sport, but he is barred from other sports until he passes his twenty-five-yard swimming test. If a school team plays on the same day as a house team, then every boy on the school team can earn points for his house. Competitive sports, such as cricket, football, rowing, track and field, swimming, and baseball are controlled by public school amateur athletic associations. On sports afternoons, interschool meets are held for both boys' and girls' teams, and annual state championships are decided in separate sports. In the universities, sports clubs are run by students, and interfaculty and intervarsity sport contests are held, but no athletic department or ticket office exists.

Sports competition, beer, and mutton are a way of life with the Australians, who were hosts for the sixteenth Olympiad in 1956. People of all walks of life are keen spectator sportsmen and avid participants in sports. They join the clubs that have been formed for the various sports for both men and women many of which are affiliated with state athletic associations. Their sporting bodies engage professional coaches for competitive games and provide voluntary amateur coaches for boys and girls learning sports. To improve the quality of sport performance, the National Fitness Council and private enterprise have begun to promote coaching seminars.

Cricket matches and football games, the national pastimes, may draw 100,000 spectators. One of the first recorded cricket matches was played between two teams of the H.M.S. *Calcutta* in 1803, and organized football competition got underway after the middle of the nineteenth century. The big matches make use of the same facilities for cricket and football, the former in the summer and the latter in the winter. The England and Australian test match in cricket is of worldwide fame, and Australian rugby commands international attention. In the Australian football game, which is played without padding and without substitutes, eighteen men comprise a team, and the scores often total hundreds of points. With the influx of more immigrants, soccer has also gained a firm foothold in Australia.

Horse racing, which has had a long and colorful history, is more than a sport in Australia: it is a national frenzy. Boxing, which was popular at the time that Bob Fitzsimmons held three world's boxing championships, now attracts less public interest. The world-famous Australian tennis teams have won several Davis Cup matches, and Australia has sent many outstanding track performers to the Olympics. The public plays tennis and golf and uses bowling greens the year round. Cycling, camping, and hiking are also popular pastimes. Interest in outdoor life and adventure-type activities has been increased by the Outward Bound Movement and the Duke of Edinburgh Award Scheme. Although much of Australia has no snow, there are mountainous snow areas close to cities, and winter sports enthusiasts regularly spend weekends and holidays at these mountain resorts.

Because of the mild climate and the proximity of the cities to the beautiful ocean beaches, swimming is the most popular participant sport in Australia. Interest is growing in surfing, skin diving, and crew and sailboat racing. Volunteers who pay to belong to the Royal Lifesaving Society guard inland beaches, and volunteers who belong to the Australian Surf Lifesaving Society guard ocean beaches. In addition to many fine bathing beaches, the larger cities have modern swimming pools with excellent facilities for competitive swimming. Because of their love for water sports, the Australians have developed a strong sense of responsibility for learning lifesaving techniques and for teaching children to swim. The Australian crawl, introduced about the turn of the century, led to world-record-breaking results. The original two-beat, heavy muscular leg beat crawl quickly spread to Europe and America and later evolved into the more rhythmic six-beat American crawl.

In Australia, as in many British countries, not only how you play the game, but also whether you wear the proper form of dress counts. White is the color for tennis; cream is the color for cricket. House colors and school colors and club blazers, ties, and pocket crests are commonly displayed.

The English heritage, pioneer life, and mild climate have bred a strong sporting tradition in the Australians. Sports leaders take pride in the public's participation in sports, but they note that affluence and the automobile, travel, television, and glamorous commercial forms of entertainment are beginning to breed lazy leisure habits. This concern is somewhat alleviated, however, by the present trend toward greater participation in sports by the junor age group.

PHYSICAL EDUCATION IN NEW ZEALAND

The scenic beauty and temperate climate of the islands that constitute New Zealand rivals that of any country in the world. The nation is about the size of Colorado and has less than three million people. Most New Zealanders are of British descent, fewer than two percent are of foreign birth, and about seven percent are Maoris, descendants of the early Polynesian settlers. Sheep, cattle, and dairy products are basic in the economy of the nation which is highly dependent on foreign trade.

A national Department of Education controls education throughout New Zealand. It distributes the funds voted by Parliament, controls school inspections, and supervises staffing and curriculum. No local school taxes are levied, but the state elementary schools have locally-elected parents' committees, while state secondary schools, which conduct their own affairs, are controlled by boards of governors.

The first Director of Physical Training, who was employed by the Department of Education in 1913, recruited a field staff to offer a refresher course based on the 1909 English syllabus. From 1917–1920, a physician in the School of Hygiene was responsible for physical training. In 1920, a Chief Instructor was appointed who had served on the original field staff. The control of physical education is now vested in the National Adviser of Physical Education for New Zealand Primary and Secondary Schools and Universities. The office was filled by Philip A. Smithells when it was created in 1939; he was succeeded by Dudley R. Wills. The Physical Education Branch of the Department of Education produces books, pamphlets, films, and other teacher aids and employs itinerant specialists to assist secondary school physical educators. At present, no specialist inspectors of physical education are employed, but professional leaders hope that the policy of having ordinary inspectors do this work will eventually be changed.

When physical education was introduced in New Zealand, memories of the Maori war, the outbreak of the Boer War, and trends in other countries may have caused them to choose a military-type training. The New Zealand Education Act of 1877 stipulated, "In public schools provision shall be made for the instruction in military drill for all and in such of the schools as the Board shall from time to time direct, provision shall be made for physical training."[5] When a parliamentary report on the poor posture habits of children was made in 1912, the critics of the military-type program were able to bring about a change. In 1913, the 1909 English Physical Training Syllabus was officially adopted which provided a combination of Swedish exercises and military commands. The classes remained formal, however, and the cadet corps continued in secondary schools.

The syllabus that was officially adopted in 1928 was compiled by Dr. Renfrew White, an orthopedic surgeon, who introduced a full section on posture and added more athletics, games, and dances to the Swedish activities. Because the clinical posture exercises were unpopular and unsuited to class activities, the syllabus was replaced in 1939 by the English 1933 *Syllabus of Physical Training for Schools.* Since that time, New Zealand has added to this program. Today, a more informal atmosphere prevails in the classes, more individual expression is permitted, and the need for developing leisure-time activity skills is recognized. Considerable emphasis is placed on limbering and strengthening exercises, physical fitness, gymnastics, games, and track and field. In response to the interest in physical fitness, circuit training, target training, and weight training have been introduced. In the girls' program, rhythmical gymnastics, folk dancing, movement, mime, and "dance making," are gaining some momentum. Stick games, poi skills, spear drills, and other Maori games, as well as dances, and songs are kept alive. Educational gymnastics, in which children create movement patterns, is being introduced by more and more teachers. In this land of seacoast, lakes, and rivers, swimming instruction and life-saving techniques are stressed. About 1400 low-cost learner pools have been installed, which partly accounts for the fact that eighty percent of the elementary pupils learn to swim. The little health education that secondary school students receive is a "wet weather" activity.

In the primary schools, pupils have ninety minutes of physical education and thirty minutes of organized games a week. On the secondary level, where education is dominated by the school certificate and university en-

[5]D. R. Wills, *Physical Education in New Zealand* (Wellington, New Zealand: Department of Education, 1965).

trance examinations, physical education is not required above the fifth form (15 or 16 years of age), but an increasing number of schools offer it. On the lower secondary school level, students have ninety minutes of physical education and thirty minutes of organized games a week. The cadet corps is retained in many secondary schools, but not as a part of the physical education program.

Primary and intermediate students participate in interschool games and may have some camping experiences. At the secondary level provisions are made for games, and all students are encouraged to play. Interschool and interclub games and track meets are held, and on Saturdays, selected teams may compete with local clubs. Cricket and rugby are the most popular sports for boys. The girls participate in a well-organized sports program, but their games arouse less public interest. In recent years the awards made by the Gymnastics Association have contributed to the upsurge of interest in gymnastics and the formation of gymnastics clubs by school children.

Outdoor facilities for physical education are generally good. Until the mid-1960s indoor facilities were not available in many schools. In 1964 the government subsidy for building gymnasiums was doubled and one hundred were built within five years. Since 1968 all new secondary schools have had to include gymnasiums. In some instances school or community playing fields and pools are used that are not adjacent to the school. In inclement weather, teachers in the older schools may work with students in classrooms, assembly halls, or small gymnasiums that may lack adequate changing rooms and showers. Learner swimming pools are found in about forty percent of the schools, and a variety of playground apparatus has been created or adapted for free exercise. The school camping movement is getting underway: one or two camps have been operating for about ten years; five of the ten school districts now have permanent camp sites and the others hope to before long. To supplement their sports equipment budget, some schools use their "incidentals" funds or funds raised by students, Parent Teacher Associations, or sports clubs.

Until relatively recently, the teachers' colleges trained elementary teachers in two- or three-year courses, and all teachers took a minimum of eighty-one hours of physical education and health. During the "College Day," which was held each week, recreational clubs met and major games were held in the afternoon. In the mid-1960s plans were drafted for a three-year elementary school teachers program in which students would be given an introduction to physical education as a part of "curriculum studies;" thereafter, they would elect major fields to study in depth for three years. As a result, the students who now major in physical education are better trained in this area than elementary teachers before them were.

In universities physical education is not a part of the curriculum for all students. Sports, athletics, and recreational clubs are extracurricular activities, and physical educators are considered sport coaches rather than educators. Two colleges have begun to employ two or three recreation officers who conduct voluntary recreation and fitness classes and condition players for major games.

Universities do not offer degree programs in physical education, but one does offer an undergraduate diploma program. After years of effort by Sir C. E. Hercus, Dean of the Medical School, a School of Physical Education was established at the University of Otago in 1945 under Professor Philip Smithells. Students pursue four years of study to obtain a physical education diploma and a teacher's certificate. The graduates teach in secondary schools, teachers colleges, hospitals, and YMCAs, or serve on the itinerant staff. Because New Zealand offers no graduate study in physical education, many young people go abroad to study. The Physical Education Society of New Zealand holds professional meetings, conducts workshops, and publishes a professional journal. The Physical Education Branch of the Department of Education provides short courses and inservice training programs for itinerant and advisory teacher trainees.

In New Zealand, sports and outdoor recreational activities play a major part in national life. Everybody plays, every town has its clubs, and every sport has its district and national governing bodies. Rugby, cricket, tennis, and bowling on the green are popular. On the weekend, many young people play in an organized sport for their club on one day and participate in swimming, shooting, hiking, surfing, or rowing on another day. The entire population of this rather remote nation anticipates keenly the visits of teams from other countries.

28

Physical Education
in
Education for Internationalism

The preceding chapters have recounted the role of education and physical education in developing nationalism in the many countries around the world. Within the twentieth century, education for international understanding has become one of the most insistent requirements for modern civilization. Although the world has become materially closer by the technological developments in transportation and communication, it remains sharply divided by cultural and ideological convictions. There is a vital need for political, intellectual, and moral forces to strengthen the roots of international friendship and unity and to negate the horrible potential of the nuclear destruction of man himself.

Many people agree that education has a crucial role to play in reconstructing our world so as to achieve the goals of peace and brotherhood. Comenius visualized this educational concept in the seventeenth century, but subsequent progress has been characterized by some gains and many failures. The campaign to establish an office of education in the League of Nations was not successful, but in 1926 the League did create a Commission of Intellectual Cooperation. Unfortunately, nationalistic-minded members were unwilling to give much support to the Commission. After World War I, a number of private or semiprivate bodies were founded to improve international relations, such as the International Bureau of Education organized in Geneva in 1925. This Bureau promoted studies in comparative education, planned conferences, published educational yearbooks, and arranged exhibits. The Institute of International Education has done considerable work in furthering the exchange of students and teachers. The World Federation of Educational Associations was established in 1922 and eventually took its present name, World Confederation of Organizations of the Teaching Profession (WCOTP) in 1952.

During World War II, the desirability of forming a permanent international organization to build an enduring peace received additional popular support. This led to the creation in 1945 of the United Nations Educational, Scientific, and Cultural Organization (UNESCO). The preamble of the UNESCO constitution stated, "Since wars begin in the minds of men, it is in the minds of men that the defenses of peace must be constructed." UNESCO sought to provide the stimuli, facilities, and the personnel to accomplish such goals and to remove the physical and psychological barriers to the free exchange of ideas and knowledge.

Physical education and sports have played a part in this newer trend toward education for internationalism. However, nationalistic sentiments, ingrained over the years in older countries and burning hotly among the new nations of the world, have retarded maximum progress toward the goals of internationalism. Sports have sometimes become a political tool to serve narrow, nationalistic purposes. This has been true of both non-Communist and Communist countries.

The most prominent example of the use of sports for internationalism is, of course, the modern Olympic Games, founded by Pierre de Coubertin. At a meeting of the International Athletic Congress at the Sorbonne in Paris in 1894, Coubertin officially proposed a revival of the ancient Olympic Games as a means of stimulating universal interest in sports and physical fitness. The idea was not well received by some of the gymnastic societies who were critical of the trend towards sports and games. Furthermore, track and field events were not much emphasized outside the United States and Great Britain. Nevertheless, people rallied to his support, and the first modern Olympic Games were held in Athens in 1896. The complete record of subsequent Games is as follows:

IInd, Paris, 1900
IIIrd, St. Louis, 1904
IVth, London, 1908
Vth, Stockholm, 1912
VIth, Berlin, 1916 (not celebrated because of the war)
VIIth, Antwerp, 1920
VIIIth, Paris, 1924
IXth, Amsterdam, 1928
Xth, Los Angeles, 1932
XIth, Berlin, 1936
XIIth, Tokyo, 1940 (cancelled)
XIIIth, Rome, 1944 (not celebrated because of the war)
XIVth, London, 1948
XVth, Helsinki, 1952

XVIth, Melbourne, 1956
XVIIth, Rome, 1960
XVIIIth, Tokyo, 1964
XIXth, Mexico City, 1968
XXth, Munich, 1972

The initial Olympic program was composed of twelve track and field events, two weightlifting, one wrestling, four swimming, six cycling, two tennis, five target shooting, three fencing, and eight gymnastic events. In ensuing years many new events were added, notably team games and winter sports. The latter began with the 1924 Games. Women competed for the first time in 1912 in two events; their initial participation in track and field occurred at the 1928 Games. The Games also include exhibitions in the fine arts, as in ancient times, with entries in architecture, town planning, painting, drawings, graphic work, sculpture, literature, drama, and music.

The Olympic Games have had a far-reaching influence on sports and physical education throughout the world. Many countries have used the Olympic events as a basis for national programs of physical education. The Olympic rules for specific sports have been widely adopted. Less favored nations have sought coaches from other countries to train their athletes. The Olympic Games have encouraged the organization of regional and continental competition among many nations. The decision of the Soviet Union to enter the Olympic scene in 1952 was a profound stimulus to international sport because her satellite nations followed suit and it challenged the prestige of other big powers who took steps to improve their own athletic programs.

The modern Games have provided occasions for bitter disputes, lifelong friendships, and moments of deep emotion and high excitement. Some incidents of poor sportsmanship and dissension have been magnified by the popular press while the regular occurrences of goodwill and friendship receive little publicity.[1] Although wars and nationalism have at times dimmed Baron de Coubertin's dream, no one can fail to be stirred by his faith in the ultimate progress toward better world relationships. His words will continue to echo through the years as long as the Olympic Games are held:

> May joy and good fellowship reign and may the Olympic Torch pursue its way through the ages, increasing friendly understanding among nations for the good of humanity.

Since the revival of the Olympic Games in 1896, a number of other regional games have been organized despite many problems. These games include the Central American Games, the Bolivarian Games, and the Pan-

---

[1] Bill Henry, *An Approved History of the Olympic Games* (New York: G. P. Putnam's Sons, 1948), pp. 236–38.

American Games, which are discussed in Chapter 26. The Far Eastern Games, the Asian Games, the Mediterranean Games, the Pan-Arab Games, the Southeast Asia Peninsula Games, the South Pacific Games, the African Games, and the Maccabiah Games are discussed in Chapter 27.

Other kinds of competition have been organized between various countries. The British Empire and Commonwealth Games are an important event which began in 1930 and are held at four-year intervals. The International Federation for Sports at Universities (FISU), organized in 1947, sponsors the World University Games for college students every two years. International sports competition for workers is under the International Workers' Sports Committee. Since 1960, severely handicapped persons from many countries have held their own Paralympics following the end of the Olympic Games. Two interesting variations of international competition on a smaller scale are the Havalanta Games and the CANUSA Games. The former provided competition in a variety of sports for athletes from the cities of Havana, Cuba, and Atlanta, Georgia. Contestants met annually from 1949 through 1959 with the cities alternating as hosts. The story of the Havalanta Games was taken to Flint, Michigan by Thomas McDonough of Emory University and led to the inauguration of the CANUSA Games in 1958 between the people of Flint and Hamilton, Ontario. They have become an annual event climaxing the summer recreation program.

Thousands of individuals are brought together for international events under the auspices of the many international associations which deal with specific sports or activities. The oldest of these is the International Gymnastic Federation (FIG) which traces its origin back to a meeting called by Nicolas Jan Cupérus of Belgium in 1881 to form a European association of the national gymnastic societies. However, the most important organization today is the *Fédération Internationale de Football Association* (FIFA) which has 130 national members. It sponsors the famous World Cup competition which fans the passions of millions of soccer buffs every four years. This thrilling tournament for the Jules Rimet Cup was first held in 1930 and, after an interruption by the war, was resumed in 1950. The final game that year was played in Rio de Janeiro between Uruguay and Brazil. When the players jogged out onto the field, they were greeted by 200,000 *aficionados*. The championship match for the World Cup is the world's premier sporting event. A complete record of World Cup holders is as follows:

1930—Uruguay	1954—West Germany
1934—Italy	1958—Brazil
1938—Italy	1962—Brazil
1950—Uruguay	1966—England
	1970—Brazil

Other international federations exist for a variety of sports. Some of these are listed here with the number of national members indicated in parentheses:[2] athletics (track and field) (96); rowing (39); basketball (26); boxing (72); canoeing (29); cycling (70); equestrian (50); fencing (59); gymnastics (45); team handball (26); lawn hockey (43); ice hockey (25); wrestling (65); swimming (73); modern pentathlon (33); skating (28); skiing (39); shooting (70); volleyball (64); and yacht racing (40). The Davis Cup in tennis, which attracts international attention, was donated by Dwight F. Davis in 1900 for the winner of a match between England and the United States. The Walker Cup matches in amateur golf and the Thomas Cup competition in badminton are eagerly followed by other enthusiastic sports lovers from many nations.

Teachers of physical education were already exchanging information across national boundaries at the beginning of the nineteenth century as some came to observe the program at Schnepfenthal Institute and others read the books of GutsMuths in several languages. Later in the century the Turnfests and Sokol *Slets* acquired an international aspect, and the Royal Central Institute of Gymnastics drew many students outside Sweden. The first International Congress on Physical Education was held in 1889 in conjunction with the Universal Exposition in Paris—a meeting organized by Pierre de Coubertin. Another international physical education congress occurred in Paris in 1900 and was attended by Thomas Wood and R. Tait McKenzie, among others. The general secretary was George Demeny of France. Madame Österberg of England with thirteen of her students gave an exhibition in Swedish calisthenics, fancy steps, dancing, and basketball. Three propositions voted by the delegates are of some historical interest:

1. There should be one fundamental, international basis for physical education, with national application adapted to local conditions.
2. Scientific principles are necessary for application to practical education.
3. Gymnastics must conform to the laws of physiology, psychology, physics and chemistry.[3]

After this conference and before the outbreak of the war in 1914, several other international gatherings took place which mainly brought out the desire of the supporters of the Swedish system to have their own meetings. At a 1911 international conference in Denmark, delegates sympathetic to Swedish gymnastics established the International Institution of Physical Education. After a period of inactivity, it was revived in 1923 as the International Federation of Educational Gymnastics. This name was changed in 1930 to International Federation of Ling Gymnastics, and the Federation helped to organize the two great Lingiads held in 1939 and

[2]Council for Cultural Cooperation of the Council of Europe, *Physical Education and Sport* (Strasbourg: Council of Europe, 1964), pp. 193–207.
[3]Thomas D. Wood, "Letter to the Editor," *American Physical Education Review 5* (September 1900): 270.

1949 in Sweden. The organization assumed its present name, *Fédération Internationale d'Éducation Physique* (FIEP), in 1953. Its headquarters are in Lisbon, and it has published the *FIEP Bulletin* since 1931. Prominent leaders of the FIEP over the years have been Swedish: Sellen, Thulin, Kragh, and Homström.

The International Federation of Sports Medicine (FIMS) came into being at the first International Congress of Sports Medicine held at the time of the 1928 Olympic Games in Amsterdam. Twenty-one nations were represented, and several more meetings were held during the 1930s. The seventh Congress took place in Prague in 1948. Since then, meetings have occurred on a biennial basis.[4] The FIMS publishes the quarterly *Journal of Sports Medicine and Physical Fitness*. More than thirty nations had national federations of sports medicine by 1965.

1930 to 1940 was a disappointing decade for international developments in physical education. A major factor was undoubtedly the worldwide depression which severely restricted travel funds. An International Congress of Physical Education and Sports scheduled for Los Angeles in 1932 was cancelled because of economic conditions, and a series of lectures was substituted.

Since 1945, however, many significant happenings have reflected a universal desire to promote international good will and professional understanding. The devastation from the war and the onset of the nuclear age seemed to accelerate a desire to cross national lines in spite of political tensions.

The National Association of Physical Education for College Women in the United States took the initiative to underwrite the First International Congress for Girls and Women which was held in Copenhagen in 1949 and represented twenty-four nations. Dorothy Ainsworth and Agnete Bertram of Denmark worked together to make the necessary arrangements, and both women presented papers at the congress. A second conference met at Paris four years later, and the International Association of Physical Education and Sports for Girls and Women (IAPESGW) was officially organized. Ainsworth was elected as the first president and served eight years. Subsequent congresses have been held at London (1957), Washington (1961), Cologne (1965), and Tokyo (1969). Ainsworth also was the organizing chairman for the Connecticut Valley Congress on the Essentials of Physical Education for Youth in 1954 which was held in the United States and sponsored by the American Association for Health, Physical Education, and Recreation.[5]

[4]Giuseppe La Cava, "The International Federation for Sports Medicine," *Physical Education Today* 10 (March–June 1963): 7–8.

[5]Hazel C. Peterson, "Dorothy S. Ainsworth: Her Life, Professional Career and Contributions to Physical Education" (Doctoral dissertation, Ohio State University, 1968), pp. 304–423.

As these and other conferences were held, many physical educators began to think of an international organization for teachers of physical education. The result was the formation of two such organizations by 1960: the International Council on Sports and Physical Education (ICSPE) related to UNESCO and the International Council on Health, Physical Education, and Recreation (ICHPER) associated with the World Confederation of Organizations of the Teaching Profession.

The idea for ICSPE evolved during the International Congress for Physical Education held just prior to the 1956 Olympic Games in Melbourne. A committee worked on a constitution and eventually the ICSPE was officially recognized three years later at a conference on Sport, Work and Culture and International Relations in Helsinki, sponsored by UNESCO and the Finnish government. It began publication of the *Revue Analytique d'Éducation Physique et de Sport* and has organized working groups or committees. The scope of ICSPE includes both school physical education and out-of-school amateur sports clubs.

ICHPER originated in the appointment of a small committee on health, physical education, and recreation by the WCOTP in 1958. Ainsworth served as committee chairman, and its recommendations to create an ICHPER were approved by WCOTP delegates the next year. The first president was Dorothy Ainsworth who served two three-year terms. She was succeeded by Julien L. Falize of Belgium, and he was followed by Klaas Rijsdorp of The Netherlands. Carl A. Troester, Jr., has held office as secretary-general since its inception. ICHPER started an official periodical, *Gymnasion*, in 1963, and it has conducted half a dozen international studies and surveys concerning physical education and games. It holds annual congresses in conjunction with the meetings of the WCOTP.

Thus, the internationally minded physical educator of the 1960s could participate in three leading professional organizations—FIEP, ICSPE, and ICHPER. These organizations are beginning to cooperate for the benefit of the profession. A Congress for Sports Sciences met at the Tokyo Olympics in 1964 with the help of all three organizations and FIMS. The World Congress of Sports and Physical Education held in Madrid in 1966 was organized by FIEP in cooperation with ICHPER. Three associations, ICHPER, ICSPE, and FIEP, jointly sponsored both the First International Seminar on the History of Physical Education and Sport in Israel in 1968 and the World Conference on Sport and Education which met at the time of the 1968 Olympic Games in Mexico City. This joining of forces rather than the fragmentation of effort seems the most desirable and productive procedure for the years ahead.

There are other examples of international cooperation. The first All-African Conference took place in Liberia in 1961, and several Asian meetings have been held. The first Pan-American Congress dates back to 1943 with two more following in 1946 and 1950. Unfortunately, for various reasons, there was a fifteen-year gap until the Fourth Congress convened in Colombia in 1965. A Pan-American Institute for Research was formed at the 1946 meeting with Charles H. McCloy as president. On the European continent the Council for Cultural Cooperation of the Council of Europe seeks to coordinate efforts and promote cooperation. One project was the development of a 100-hour minimum short course for trainers in sports and physical education by a group of experts from sixteen countries who met together for a week.[6]

Another recent phenomenon which indicates the international trend in physical education is the growing interest in comparative physical education. The father of comparative physical education was Marc Antoine Jullien who published a remarkable book, *Esquisse*, in 1817. It was little noticed by his contemporaries, but in a section on "Physical Education and Gymnastics," he outlined the need for information on program, methods, and measurement. In 1928 Pierre de Coubertin established the *Bureau Internationale de Pédagogie Sportive* in Lausanne to serve as a world center for scientific and systematic information on sports and physical education. During the 1960s comparative physical education has become accepted in the curriculum of an increasing number of universities in the United States and Europe. Anthony has outlined the aims of comparative physical education as follows:

a. to establish reliable data on each country and system, separately and collectively.
b. to search for regularities by analyses of differences and similarities with particular attention paid to the relation of theory to practice.
c. to try to understand the past and to predict future trends: and to assist in the formulation of policy.
d. to examine the need for the reform of one's own methods and systems and to contribute to a universal improvement of standards and knowledge.
e. to relate knowledge in the specific field of sport and physical education to that in all other relevant disciplines.[7]

If physical educators are to accept the challenge and utilize their potential influence for world peace, the present time is a propitious one in which to study comparative cultures. It is an obligation for members of the profession to have a grasp of world problems. Knowledge stimulates sympathetic understanding and appreciation. Sympathy in associating with other people and a familiarity with their ways of life may not completely expunge all national differences, but it will make it possible to define prob-

[6]Council for Cultural Cooperation of the Council of Europe, *Training the Trainer* (Strasbourg: Council of Europe, 1964).

[7]D. W. J. Anthony, "Comparative Physical Education," *Physical Education* 58 (November 1966): 73.

lems and create a more wholesome emotional atmosphere in which to seek cooperative solutions to the difficulties that are faced.

Physical educators today live in a world which "is now too dangerous for anything but the truth, too small for anything but brotherhood."[8] We must join with all people in our own country and in other countries to work incessantly for international truth and brotherhood. We have no other choice.

[8]A. Powell Davies quoted in Adlai E. Stevenson, "The Political Relevance of Moral Principle" (mimeographed, 1959), p. 1.

Bibliography

GENERAL WORKS

Boykin, James C. "History of Physical Training," *Report of the Commissioner of Education for 1891–92*. Vol. 1. Washington, D.C.: U.S. Government Printing Office, 1894. Pp. 451–594.

Brubacher, J. S. *A History of the Problems of Education.* 2d ed. New York: McGraw-Hill Book Company, 1966.

Butts, R. Freeman. *A Cultural History of Western Education.* New York: McGraw-Hill Book Company, 1955.

Carr, Edward H. *What is History?* New York: Alfred A. Knopf, Inc., 1962.

Cohen, Alan and Norman Garner. *Readings in the History of Educational Thought.* London: University of London Press, 1967.

Commager, Henry Steele. *The Nature and the Study of History.* Columbus, Ohio: Charles E. Merrill Books, Inc., 1965.

Cubberley, Ellwood P. *The History of Education.* Boston: Houghton Mifflin Company, 1920.

Danto, Arthur C. *Analytical Philosophy of History.* Cambridge: Cambridge University Press, 1965.

Diem, Carl. *Weltgeschichte des Sports und der Leibeserziehung.* Stuttgart: Cotta, 1960.

Dixon, J. G.; P. C. McIntosh; A. D. Munrow; and R. F. Willetts. *Landmarks in the History of Physical Education.* 2d ed. London: Routledge and Kegan Paul, 1960.

Eby, Frederick. *The Development of Modern Education.* 2d ed. Englewood Cliffs, N.J.: Prentice-Hall, Inc., 1952.

————, and Charles F. Arrowood. *The History and Philosophy of Education, Ancient and Medieval.* Englewood Cliffs, N.J.: Prentice-Hall, Inc., 1940.

Gardiner, Patrick. *The Nature of Historical Explanation.* London: Oxford University Press, 1952.

649

Good, H. G. *A History of Western Education*. 2d ed. New York: The Macmillan Company, 1962.

Graves, Frank P. *A History of Education Before the Middle Ages*. New York: The Macmillan Company, 1909.

———— *A History of Education During the Middle Ages and the Transition to Modern Times*. New York: The Macmillan Company, 1910.

———— *Great Educators of Three Centuries*. New York: The Macmillan Company, 1912.

———— *A History of Education in Modern Times*. New York: The Macmillan Company, 1928.

Hackensmith, C. W. *History of Physical Education*. New York: Harper and Row, Publishers, 1966.

Higham, John et al. *History*. Englewood Cliffs, N.J.: Prentice-Hall, Inc., 1965.

Hockett, Homer C. *The Critical Method in Historical Research and Writing*. New York: The Macmillan Company, 1955.

Howe, George Frederick, ed. *The American Historical Association's Guide to Historical Literature*. New York: The Macmillan Company, 1961.

Kinney, T. and M. W. *The Dance*. New York: Tudor Publishing Co., 1935.

Leonard, Fred E. and George B. Affleck. *A Guide to the History of Physical Education*. Philadelphia: Lea and Febiger, 1947.

Mayer, Frederick, ed. *Great Ideas in Education*. 3 vols. New Haven, Conn.: College and University Press, 1966.

McIntosh, P. C. *Sport in Society*. London: C. A. Watts and Co., Ltd., 1963.

Meyer, Adolph. *Educational History of the Western World*. New York: McGraw-Hill Book Company, 1965.

Monroe, Paul. *A Textbook in the History of Education*. New York: The Macmillan Company, 1916.

Mulhern, James. *A History of Education*. 2d ed. New York: The Ronald Press Company, 1959.

Nakosteen, Mehdi. *The History and Philosophy of Education*. New York: The Ronald Press Company, 1965.

Nevins, Allan. *The Gateway to History*. rev. ed. Chicago: Quadrangle Books, Inc., 1963.

Quest 11 (December 1968). Entire issue.

Randall, John H. *The Making of the Modern Mind*. Boston: Houghton Mifflin Company, 1926.

Rice, Emmett, John Hutchinson, and Mabel Lee. *A Brief History of Physical Education*. New York: The Ronald Press Company, 1969.

Sachs, Curt. *World History of the Dance*. New York: W. W. Norton and Company, Inc., 1963.

Social Science Research Council. *Generalizations in the Writing of History: A Report of the Committee on Historiography*, edited by Louis Gottschalk. New York: Social Science Research Council, 1963.

Szukovathy, I. "Some Notes on the History of Sport Bibliography," *Research Quarterly* 8 (March 1937): 3–14.

Ulich, Robert. *History of Educational Thought.* 2d ed. New York: American Book Company, 1950.

———— *The Education of Nations.* Cambridge: Harvard University Press, 1967.

Vuillier, Gaston. *A History of Dancing.* New York: D. Appleton and Co., 1898.

Wilds, Elmer H. and Kenneth Lottich. *The Foundations of Modern Education.* New York: Holt, Rinehart, and Winston, Inc., 1961.

PART I

General Works

Bogeng, G. A. E. *Die Geschichte des Sports Aller Völker und Zeiten.* 2 vols. Leipzig: Seamann, 1926.

Gardiner, E. N. *Athletics of the Ancient World.* Oxford: The Clarendon Press, 1930.

Laurie, Simon S. *Historical Survey of Pre-Christian Education.* New York: Longmans, Green and Co., 1907.

Marrou, Henri I. *A History of Education in Antiquity,* Translated by George Lamb. London: Sheed and Ward, Ltd., 1956.

Piggott, Stuart, ed. *The Dawn of Civilization.* New York: McGraw-Hill Book Company, Inc., 1961.

Woody, Thomas. *Life and Education in Early Societies.* New York: The Macmillan Company, 1949.

Chapter 1: Primitive Survival

Birket-Smith, Kaj. *Primitive Man and His Ways,* Translated by Roy Duffell. London: Odhams Press, 1960.

Catlin, George. *Letters and Notes on the Manners, Customs, and Condition of the North American Indians.* Minneapolis: Ross and Haines, 1965.

Culin, Stewart. "Games of the North American Indians," *Twenty-fourth Annual Report of the U.S. Bureau of Ethnology.* Washington, D.C.: U.S. Bureau of Ethnology, 1907.

Hambly, W. D. *Origins of Education Among Primitive Peoples.* London: The Macmillan Company, 1926.

Kidd, Dudley. *Savage Childhood.* London: Charles and Adam Black, 1906.

Means, P. A. *Ancient Civilizations of the Andes.* New York: Charles Scribner's Sons, 1931.

Stumpf, Florence, and Frederick W. Cozens. "Some Aspects of the Role of Games, Sports, and Recreational Activities in the Culture of Modern Primitive Peoples," *Research Quarterly* 18 (October 1947): 198–218.

Todd, A. J. *The Primitive Family as an Educational Agency.* New York: G. P. Putnam's Sons, 1913.

Wilder, H. H. *Man's Prehistoric Past*. New York: The Macmillan Company, 1924.

Chapter 2:   *Perpetuity of Civilized Culture*

Breasted, J. H. *A History of Egypt*. New York: Charles Scribner's Sons, 1912.
Erman, A. *Life in Ancient Egypt*, Translated by H. M. Tirand. London: The Macmillan Company, 1894.
Farquhar, J. N. *The Crown of Hinduism*. London: Oxford University Press, 1915.
Giles, Herbert A. *The Civilization of China*. New York: Henry Holt and Co. 1911.
Herodotus, Book I, Articles 136–138. London: G. Bell and Sons, Ltd. 1889.
Kuo, Ping Wen. *Chinese System of Public Education*. New York: Teachers College, Columbia University, 1915.
La Tourette, Kenneth S. *The Chinese: Their History and Culture*. New York: The Macmillan Company, 1934.
Lexova, J. *Ancient Egyptian Dances*, Translated by K. Haltmar. Prague: Oriental Institute, 1935.
Mac Kay, E. J. H. *The Indus Civilization*. London: Lovat Dickson and Thompson, 1935.
Marshall, John. *Mohenjo-Daro and the Indus Civilization*. 3 vols. London: Probsthain, 1931.
Maspero, G. *The Dawn of Civilization: Egypt and Chaldea*, Translated by M. L. McClure. New York: D. Appleton and Co., 1894.
Mehl, Erwin. *Antike Schwimmkunst*. Munich: Ernest Heimeran, 1927.
Müller, F. M., ed. *The Sacred Books of the East*. 50 vols. Oxford: The Clarendon Press, 1879–1910.
Rajagopalan, Shri K. *A Brief History of Physical Education in India*. Delhi: Army Publishers, c. 1962.
Wilkinson, J. Gardner, *The Manners and Customs of the Ancient Egyptians*. Revised by Samuel Birch. London: John Murray (Publishers) Ltd., n.d.

Chapter 3:   *Hebrew Religious and Civic Ideals*

Day, Edward. *The Social Life of the Hebrews*. New York: Charles Scribner's Sons, 1916.
Drazin, Nathan. *History of Jewish Education*. Baltimore: John Hopkins Press, 1940.
Ellis, G. Harold. "The Origin and Development of Jewish Education," *Pedagogical Seminary* 9 (March 1902): 50–62.
Jewish Encyclopedia. New York: Funk and Wagnalls, 1905.
Margoliouth, G. "Games, Hebrew and Jewish," *Hastings Encyclopedia of Religion and Ethics*, Vol. VI, 171d–175b.
Swift, F. H. *Education in Ancient Israel*. Chicago: Open Court Publishing Co., 1919.

Chapter 4: Greek Individualism

Beck, F. A. *Greek Education 450–350 B.C.* New York: Barnes and Noble Inc., 1964.

Botsford, G. W. and Charles A. Robinson. *Hellenic History.* 4th ed. New York: The Macmillan Company, 1956.

Cahn, Joseph L. "Contributions of Plato to Thought on Physical Education, Health, and Recreation," Doctoral dissertation, New York University, 1942.

Chryssafis, Jean E. "Aristotle on Physical Education," *Journal of Health and Physical Education* 1 (January 1930): 3–8, 50; and (February 1930): 14–17, 46–47.

——— "Plato on Physical Education," *Pentathlon* 1 (April 1929): 3–9; and (May 1929): 6–10.

Davidson, Thomas. *Education of the Greek People.* New York: D. Appleton-Century Co., 1906.

Fairs, John R. "The Influence of Plato and Platonism on the Development of Physical Education in Western Culture," *Quest* 11 (December 1968): 14–23.

Forbes, Clarence A. *Greek Physical Education.* New York: The Century Co., 1929.

Freeman, K. J. *Schools of Hellas.* London: The Macmillan Co., 1922.

Gardiner, E. N. *Greek Athletic Sports and Festivals.* London: The Macmillan Co., 1910.

Gulich, Charles B. *The Life of the Ancient Greeks.* New York: D. Appleton-Century Co., 1912.

Harris, H. A. *Greek Athletes and Athletics.* London: Hutchinson and Co. (Publishers) Limited, 1964.

Plummer, Edward M. *Athletics and Games of the Ancient Greeks.* Cambridge: Lombard & Caustic, 1898.

——— "Toys and Games for Children Among Ancient Hellenes," *Mind and Body* 7 (August 1900): 124–32.

Robinson, Rachel S. *Sources for the History of Greek Athletics.* Cincinnati, Ohio: Published by the author, 1955.

Wilkins, A. S. *National Education in Greece.* New York: C. E. Stechert and Co., Anastatic Reprint, 1911.

Woody, Thomas. "Philostratos: Concerning Gymnastics," *Research Quarterly* 7 (May 1936): 3–26.

——— "Professionalism and the Decay of Greek Athletics," *School and Society* 23 April 1938, pp. 521–28.

Chapter 5: Roman Utilitarianism

Bury, J. B. *A History of the Roman Empire.* New York: American Book Co., 1927.

Fowler, W. W. *Roman Festivals of the Period of the Republic.* London: The Macmillan Co., 1899.

Friedländer, Ludwig. *Roman Life and Manners Under the Early Empire*, Translated by L. A. Magnus et al. 4 vols. London: G. Routledge and Sons, 1908–1913.

Gwynn, Aubrey. *Roman Education*. Oxford: The Clarendon Press, 1926.

Johnston, H. W. *Private Life of the Romans*. Chicago: Scott, Foresman and Company, 1932.

Mommsen, Theodor. *The History of Rome*, Translated by Dero A. Saunders and John H. Collins. New York: Meridian Books, Inc., c. 1958.

Preston, H. W. and L. Dodge. *The Private Life of the Romans*. Chicago: Benjamin H. Sanborn and Co., 1936.

Rostoutsev, Mikhall. *The Social and Economic History of the Roman Empire*. 2d ed. Revised by P. M. Fraser, Oxford: The Clarendon Press, 1957.

Wilkins, A. S. *Roman Antiquities*. New York: D. Appleton and Co., 1878.

PART II

General Works

Laurie, S. S. *Rise and Early Constitution of Universities*. New York: D. Appleton and Co., 1902.

———— *Studies in the History of Educational Opinion from the Renaissance*. Cambridge: University Press, 1905.

Chapter 6:   Medieval Disciplines

Ballou, Ralph. "Early Christian Society and its Relationship to Sport," *National College Physical Education Association for Men 71st Proceedings*, 1968. Pp. 159–165.

Block, M. L. B. *Feudal Society*, Translated by L. A. Manyon. Chicago: University of Chicago Press, 1961.

Boulton, W. B. *The Amusements of Old London*. London: J. C. Nimmo, 1901.

Cornish, F. Warre. *Chivalry*. New York: The Macmillan Company, 1911.

Coulton, G. G. *A Medieval Panorama*. New York: The Macmillan Company, 1938.

———— *Life in the Middle Ages*. Cambridge: Cambridge University Press, 1928.

———— *The Medieval Village*. Cambridge: Cambridge University Press, 1931.

Cripps-Day, Francis H. *The History of the Tournament in England and France*. London: B. Quadrich, 1918.

Davis, W. S. *Life on a Medieval Baroney*. New York: Harper and Brothers, 1923.

Evans, Joan, ed. *The Flowering of the Middle Ages*. New York: McGraw-Hill Book Company, 1966.

Haskins, C. H. *The Rise of Universities*. New York: Henry Holt and Co., 1923.

Heywood, William. *Palio and Ponte*. London: Methuen and Co., Ltd., 1904.

Jusserand, J. J. *Les Sports et Jeux d'Exercices dans l'Ancienne France.* Paris: Plon-Nourrit, 1901.

Leach, A. F. *The Schools of Medieval England.* New York: The Macmillan Company, 1918.

Marique, Pierre J. *History of Christian Education.* New York: Fordham University Press, 1924.

Moore, Ernest C. *The Story of Instruction; The Church, The Renaissance, and The Reformation.* New York: The Macmillan Company, 1938.

Painter, Sidney. *French Chivalry.* Baltimore: John Hopkins Press, 1940.

———— *A History of the Middle Ages (284–1500).* New York: Alfred A. Knopf, Inc., 1953.

Perry, A. W. *Education in England During the Middle Ages.* London: Oxford University Press, 1926.

Rait, Robert. *Life in a Medieval University.* Cambridge: Cambridge University Press, 1912.

Rashdall, Hastings. *The Universities of Europe in the Middle Ages.* Oxford: Clarendon Press, 1936.

Reisner, Edward H. *Historical Foundations of Modern Education.* New York: The Macmillan Company, 1927.

Salzman, L. F. *English Life in the Middle Ages.* London: Oxford University Press, 1926.

Southern, R. W. *The Making of the Middle Ages.* New Haven: Yale University Press, 1953.

Strutt, Joseph. *The Sports and Pastimes of the People of England.* London: Methuen and Co. Ltd., 1903.

Thomas, Ralph. *Swimming.* London: Sampson, Low, Marston and Co., 1904.

Chapter 7:   Humanistic Education

Castiglione, Conte Baldassare. *The Book of the Courtier.* Translated by L. E. Opdycke. New York: Charles Scribner's Sons, 1903.

Chappell, William. *Popular Music of Olden Times.* London: Chappell and Co., 1859.

Compayre, Gabriel. *The History of Pedagogy.* Boston: D. C. Heath and Co., 1890.

Elyot, Sir Thomas. *The Boke Named the Governour.* London: Kegan, Paul, Trench, and Co., 1883.

Giles, Rev. Dr., ed. *The Whole Works of Roger Ascham.* London: John Russell Smith, 1864.

Hay, Denys. *The Age of the Renaissance.* New York: McGraw-Hill Book Company, 1967.

Henderson, Robert. *Ball, Bat and Bishop.* New York: Rockport Press, 1947.

Hyma, Albert. *Erasmus and the Humanists.* New York: F. S. Crofts and Co., 1930.

Kristeller, P. O. *Renaissance Thought.* New York: Harper & Row, Publishers, 1961.

Martines, Lauro. *The Social World of the Florentine Humanists 1390–1460*. Princeton, New Jersey: Princeton University Press, 1963.

Monroe, Paul. *Cyclopedia of Education*. New York: The Macmillan Company, 1911.

Mosellanus, Petrus. *The Paedologia; Renaissance Student Life*. Translated by R. F. Seybolt. Champaign: University of Illinois Press, 1927.

Robinson, J. H. and H. W. Rolfe. *Petrarch: The First Modern Scholar and Man of Letters*. New York: G. P. Putnam's Sons, 1909.

Simon, Joan. *Education and Society in Tudor England*. Cambridge: Cambridge University Press, 1966.

Strutt, Joseph. *The Sports and Pastimes of the People of England*. London: Methuen & Co. Ltd., 1903.

Vegius, Mapheus. *De Educatione Liberorum et Eorum Claris Moribus*, Libri Sex; A Critical Text of Books I–III by Sister Maria Walburg Fanning. Washington, D.C.: Catholic University of America Press, 1933.

Woodward, W. H. *Vittorino Da Feltre and Other Humanist Educators*. Cambridge: Cambridge University Press, 1905.

Chapter 8:   Educational Moralism

Bruce, G. M. *Luther as an Educator*. Minneapolis: Augsburg Publishing House, 1928.

Carson, Jane. *Colonial Virginians at Play*. Charlottesville: The University of Virginia, 1965.

Collinson, Patrick. *The Elizabethan Puritan Movement*. Berkeley: University of California Press, 1967.

De La Fontainerie, F. *The Conduct of Schools of Jean Baptiste de la Salle*. New York: McGraw-Hill Book Company, 1935.

Dickens, A. G. *Reformation and Society in Sixteenth-Century Europe*. London: Thames and Hudson, 1966.

Dulles, F. R. *America Learns to Play*. New York: D. Appleton-Century Co., 1940.

Earle, A. M. *The Sabbath in Puritan New England*. New York: Charles Scribner's Sons, 1896.

———— *Customs and Fashions in Old New England*. New York: Charles Scribner's Sons, 1896.

———— *Child Life in the Colonial Days*. New York: The Macmillan Company, 1927.

Eby, Frederick. *Early Protestant Educators*. New York: McGraw-Hill Book Company, 1931.

Farrell, A. P. *The Jesuit Code of Liberal Education*. Milwaukee: The Bruce Publishing Co., 1938.

Fiske, John. *Old Virginia and Her Neighbors*. Boston: Houghton Mifflin Company, 1902.

Hulme, E. M. *The Renaissance: The Protestant Reformation and the Catholic Reformation*. New York: The Century Co., 1925.

Marique, Pierre J. *History of Christian Education.* Vol. 2. New York: Fordham University Press, 1926.

Smith, Preserved. *The Life and Letters of Martin Luther.* Boston: Houghton Mifflin Company, 1911.

Trevor-Roper, H. R. *Crisis of The Seventeenth Century: Religion, the Reformation and Social Change.* New York: Harper & Row, Publishers, 1968.

Chapter 9: Educational Realism

Ainsworth, D. M. *Milton on Education.* New Haven: Yale University Press, 1928.

Monroe, Will. *Comenius and the Beginning of Educational Reform.* New York: Charles Scribner's Sons, 1900.

Montaigne, Michel Eyquem de. *Essays.* Translated and edited by Jacob Zeitlin. New York: Alfred A. Knopf, 1934.

Mulcaster, Richard. *Positions.* London: T. Vautrollier for T. Chare, 1581.

Plattard, Jean. *The Life of François Rabelais.* New York: Alfred A. Knopf, Inc., 1931.

Quick, R. H. *Essay on Educational Reformers.* New York: D. Appleton and Co., 1904.

Sarafian, K. A. *French Educational Theorists.* Los Angeles: C. C. Crawford, 1933.

Watson, F. *Vives and the Renaissance Education of Women.* New York: Longmans, Green and Co., 1912.

Woodward, W. H. *Studies in Education During the Age of Renaissance.* Cambridge: University Press, 1924.

Chapter 10: Educational Disciplinarianism

Adamson, J. W. *The Educational Writings of John Locke.* New York: Longmans, Green and Co., 1912.

Gay, Peter, ed. *John Locke in Education.* New York: Teachers College, Columbia University, 1964.

Locke, John. *Essays.* London: Ward, Lock and Co., 1883.

St. John, J. A. *The Philosophical Works of John Locke.* London: G. Bell and Sons, 1913.

Chapter 11: Educational Naturalism

Archer, R. L. *Rousseau on Education.* New York: Longmans, Green and Co., 1912.

Cassirer, Ernest. *The Question of Jean-Jacques Rousseau,* Translated by Peter Gay. Bloomington: Indiana University Press, 1963.

Davidson, T. *Rousseau and Education According to Nature.* New York: Charles Scribner's Sons, 1903.

Green, Frederick. *Jean-Jacques Rousseau: A Critical Study of his Life and Writing.* Cambridge: University Press, 1955.

Guts Muths, J. C. F. *Gymnastics for Youth.* London: J. Johnson, 1800.

Lang, O. H. *Basedow: His Educational Work and Principles.* New York: E. L. Kellogg and Co., 1891.

Moolenijzer, Nicolaas J. "The Concept of 'Natural' in Physical Education: Johann Guts Muths-Margarete Streicher." Doctoral dissertation, University of Southern California, 1966.

Rousseau, J. J. *Émile, or Education,* Translated by B. Foxley. London: J. M. Dent and Sons, 1911.

———— *Émile, or, Treatise on Education,* Translated by W. Payne. New York: D. Appleton and Co., 1895.

PART III

General Works

Comparative Education Review. Teachers College, Columbia University, and Comparative Education Society, New York.

Council for Cultural Cooperation of the Council of Europe. *Physical Education and Sport.* Strasbourg: Council of Europe, 1964.

Cramer, John and George Browne. *Contemporary Education: A Comparative Study of National Systems,* 2d ed. New York: Harcourt, Brace & World, Inc., 1965.

Diem, Carl. *Weltgeschichte des Sports.* 2 vols. Stuttgart: Cotta Verlag, 1967.

Dixon, J. G., P. C. McIntosh, A. D. Munrow, and R. F. Willetts. *Landmarks in the History of Physical Education.* 2d ed. London: Routledge and Kegan Paul, 1960.

Easton, Stewart C. *World Since 1918.* New York: Barnes & Noble, Inc., 1966.

Hackensmith, C. W. *History of Physical Education.* New York: Harper & Row, Publishers, 1966.

Hartwell, Edward M. "On Physical Training," *Report of the Commissioner of Education for 1897–98.* Vol. I. Washington, D.C.: U.S. Government Printing Office, 1899.

Howell, Maxwell. *Sources for Comparative Physical Education and Sport.* Mimeographed. Edmonton, Canada: Faculty of Physical Education, University of Alberta, n.d.

Howell, M. L. and M. L. Van Vliet. *Physical Education and Recreation in Europe.* Ottawa, Canada: Fitness and Amateur Sport Directorate, 1965.

International Council on Health, Physical Education, and Recreation. *Physical Education and Games in the Curriculum. ICHPER Questionnaire Report, Part I.* Washington, D.C.: ICHPER, c. 1963.

———— *Physical Education in the School Curriculum. ICHPER International Questionnaire Report, Part I, 1967–68 Revision.* Washington, D.C.: ICHPER, 1969.

———— *Status of Teachers of Physical Education. ICHPER Questionnaire Report, Part III.* Washington, D.C.: ICHPER, c. 1963.

——— *Teacher Training for Physical Education. ICHPER Questionnaire Report, Part II.* Washington, D.C.: ICHPER, c. 1963.

——— *Teacher Training for Physical Education. ICHPER Questionnaire Report, Part II, 1967–68 Revision.* Washington, D.C.: ICHPER, n.d.

International Council of Sport and Physical Education. *Sport and Leisure. Report of the First International Seminar.* Stuttgart: Verlag Karl Hofmann, 1965.

International Yearbook of Education. Paris: UNESCO and the International Bureau of Education. 1948 to date.

Jackson, C. O. "Elsewhere in the World," *Physical Educator.* 1953 to date.

Johnson, William, ed. *Physical Education Around the World.* Indianapolis, Indiana: Phi Epsilon Kappa. Monograph No. 1 published in 1966; Monograph No. 2 published in 1968; and Monograph No. 3 in 1969.

Kandel, I. L. *Comparative Education.* Boston: Houghton Mifflin Company, 1933.

Leonard, Fred E. and George B. Affleck. *A Guide to the History of Physical Education.* Philadelphia: Lea & Febiger, 1947.

Molyneux, D. D. *Central Government Aid to Sport and Physical Recreation in Countries of Western Europe.* Birmingham, England: The Physical Education Department, University of Birmingham, 1962.

National College of Physical Education Association for Men Proceedings of Annual Meetings. See "Foreign Relations" in issues for 1958–1960; see "History of Sports" from 1961 to date.

Pollard, Hugh M. *Pioneers of Popular Education, 1760–1850.* Cambridge: Harvard University Press, 1957.

Report of the WCOTP Committee on Health, Physical Education, and Recreation, International Conference, 1959. Washington, D.C.: International Council on Health, Physical Education, and Recreation, 1960.

Seurin, Pierre. *L'Éducation physique dans le monde.* Bordeaux: Éditions Bière, 1961.

Thut, I. N. and Don Adams. *Educational Patterns in Contemporary Societies.* New York: McGraw-Hill Book Company, 1964.

United Nations Educational, Scientific, and Cultural Organization. *The Place of Sport in Education: A Comparative Study.* Paris: UNESCO, 1956.

Vendien, C. Lynn and John Nixon. *The World Today in Health, Physical Education, and Recreation.* Englewood Cliffs, N.J.: Prentice-Hall, Inc., 1968.

Weir, L. H. *Europe at Play.* New York: A. S. Barnes & Co. Inc., 1937.

Year Book of Education. New York: Teachers College, Columbia University and Institute of Education, University of London, 1932–1941, 1948 to date.

Zwarg, L. F. *A Study of the History, Uses, and Values of Apparatus in Physical Education.* Philadelphia: Temple University, 1929.

Chapter 13:   Germany

Arntz, Helmut. *Facts About Germany.* Bonn: Federal Government of Germany, 1968.

Bernett, Hajo. "Aspects of Contemporary History of Physical Education in Germany," *Proceedings of the First International Seminar on the History of Physical Education and Sport*. Netanya, Israel: Wingate Institute for Physical Education, 1969. Pp. 20–1–6.

Dambach, John. *Physical Education in Germany*. New York: Teachers College, Columbia University, 1937.

Diem, Carl. "Development and Aims of Physical Education in Germany," *Journal of Health and Physical Education* 19 (June 1948): 390–92, 430–31.

Diem, Liselott. "Federal Republic of Germany—Health, Physical Education, and Recreation." In *The World Today in Health, Physical Education, and Recreation*, edited by C. Lynn Vendien and John E. Nixon, Englewood Cliffs, N.J.: Prentice-Hall, Inc., 1968. Pp. 126–50.

Dixon, J. G. "Prussia, Politics and Physical Education." In *Landmarks in the History of Physical Education*, edited by J. G. Dixon et al. London: Routledge & Kegan Paul, 1957. Pp. 107–148.

Fletcher, Arthur W. *Education in Germany*. Cambridge: W. Heffer and Sons, Ltd., 1934.

Haag, Herbert. "Teacher Training for Physical Education in West Germany," *Physical Educator* 26 (December 1969): 182–83.

Karbe, Wolfgang. "Physical Education and Sports in East and West Germany," *Physical Educator*, 19 (October 1962): 108–13.

Kiefer, Paul. "The Support of Physical Education and Sport by the Ministry of Education," *International Council on Health, Physical Education, and Recreation, 10th International Congress, 1967*. Washington, D.C.: ICHPER, 1968. Pp. 83–85.

Kohn, Hans. *Prelude to Nation-States: The French and German Experience, 1789–1815*. Princeton, New Jersey: D. Van Nostrand Co., Inc., 1967.

Lindegren, Alina M. *Education in Germany*. U.S. Department of Interior, Office of Education, Bulletin #15. Washington, D.C.: U.S. Government Printing Office, 1938.

Oktavec, Frank. *The Professional Education of Special Men Teachers of Physical Education in Prussia*. New York: Teachers College, Columbia University, 1929.

Richter, Peter. "Physical Education in Germany." In *Physical Education Around the World*, edited by William Johnson. Monograph No. 1. Indianapolis, Indiana: Phi Epsilon Kappa, 1966. Pp. 23–26.

Rosenkranz, W. et al. *Polytechnical Education for All*. Dresden: Verlag Zeit im Bild, 1965.

Schultze, Walter and Christoph Führ. *Schools in the Federal Republic of Germany*. Weinheim: Verlag Julius Beltz, 1967.

Chapter 14: Sweden

Amylong, Tora. "Gymnastics in the Lower and Middle Departments of the

Swedish Comprehensive School (grades 1–6)." Mimeographed. Stockholm: National Swedish Board of Education, 1966.

———— "Physical Education in the Schools of Sweden." Mimeographed. Stockholm: National Swedish Board of Education, 1966.

Carlquist, Maja. *Rhythmical Gymnastics*. London: Methuen and Co. Ltd., 1955.

Högberg, Paul. *The Principles of Physical Education in Sweden*. Stockholm: The Swedish Institute for Cultural Relations with Foreign Countries, 1963.

International Council on Health, Physical Education, and Recreation of WCOTP, International Congress, 1962, Washington, D.C.: ICHPER, c. 1963.

National Swedish Board of Education. "Physical Education in the Swedish School System." Mimeographed. Stockholm: National Swedish Board of Education, 1960.

Posse, Nils. *Handbook of School Gymnastics of the Swedish System*. Boston: Lee and Shepard, 1891.

Sports and Recreation in Sweden. Stockholm: Swedish Tourist Traffic Association, c. 1967.

Thulin, J. G. *Gymnastics Hand-Book*. Lund: Berlingska Boktrycheriet, 1947.

Wiberg, Albert. *Gymnastikhistoriska Studier*. Vaxjo: Nya Vaxyobladet, 1949.

Chapter 15:   Denmark

Begtrup, H., H. Lund, and P. Manniche. *The Folk High School of Denmark and the Development of a Farming Community*. London: Oxford University Press, 1936.

Brickman, William W. *Denmark's Educational System and Problems*. Washington, D.C.: U.S. Government Printing Office, 1967.

Bukh, Niels. *Fundamental Gymnastics*. New York: E. P. Dutton & Co., Inc., 1928.

Danish Foreign Office Journal. Some articles almost every year.

The Danish Ministry of Education. *Physical Education in Denmark*. Mimeographed. Copenhagen: The Danish Ministry of Education, c. 1966.

Dixon, Willis. *Education in Denmark*. Copenhagen: Centraltrykkeriet, c. 1958.

Hansen, Emanuel. *Danmarks Hojskole for Legemsovelser*. Arsberetning, 1947–1948.

———— *Sports in Denmark*. Copenhagen: Det Danske Selskab, c. 1955.

Knudsen, K. A. *A Text Book of Gymnastics*. London: William Heinemann, 1920.

Lindhard, Johannes. *The Theory of Gymnastics*. London: Methuen and Co. Ltd., 1934.

National Association of Physical Education for College Women. *Report of International Congress of Physical Education of Girls and Women*. Washington, D.C.: American Association for Health, Physical Education, and Recreation, 1950.

Chapter 16:   France

du Cateau, Bellin. "The Development of Physical Education in France," *Journal of Health and Physical Education* 3 (November 1932): 52–53, 57.

Education in France, no. 27, *Special Issue on Sports*. Paris: Cultural Services of the French Embassy, 1964, pp. 1–34.

Fraser, W. R. *Education and Society in Modern France*. London: Routledge and Kegan Paul, 1963.

La Génération Montante en France. Paris: Ministère Des Affaires Étrangères, c. 1967.

Hewitt, Jack E. "International Scene, France," *Journal of Health, Physical Education, and Recreation* 35 (October 1964): 71–73.

Jokl, Ernst. "G. B. Duchenne's Physiology of Motion," *Journal of Health, Physical Education, and Recreation* 38 (February 1967): 67.

Lazard, Christian. "Organization of Physical Education in France," *Journal of Health and Physical Education* 5 (January 1934): 8–11, 55.

Ministère De l'Éducation Nationale. *Certificat d' aptitude au professorat d' èducation physique et sportive*. Paris: Institut Pédagogique Natural, 1965.

"National Sports Training in France," *The Australian Journal of Physical Education* 32 (November 1964): 30–35.

Physical and Sports Activities from Birth to Maturity, Brochure 106, Physical Education. Paris: National Pedagogical Institute, 1962.

Chapter 17:   England

Barnard, H. C. *A History of English Education*. London: University of London Press, Ltd., 1964.

Board of Education. *Syllabus of Physical Training for Schools*. London: His Majesty's Stationery Office, 1933.

———— *Recreation and Physical Fitness for Girls and Women*. London: His Majesty's Stationery Office, 1937.

———— *Recreation and Physical Fitness for Youths and Men*. London: His Majesty's Stationery Office, 1937.

Darwin, Bernard. *British Sports and Games*. London: Longmans, Green & Co. Ltd., 1940.

Department of Education and Science. *Moving and Growing*. London: Her Majesty's Stationery Office, 1952.

———— *Planning the Programme*. London: Her Majesty's Stationery Office, 1953.

Ellis, Michael. "Physical Education in Great Britain." In *Physical Education Around the World*, edited by William Johnson, Monograph no. 1. Indianapolis, Indiana: Phi Epsilon Kappa, 1966. Pp. 1–7.

Hackwood, Frederick W. *Old English Sports*. London: T. Fisher Unwin, 1907.

Hale, Christina. *English Sports and Pastimes*. London: B. T. Batsford, Ltd., 1949.

Hoyle, Eric. *The Role of the Teacher*. London: Routledge & Kegan Paul Ltd., 1969.

Laban, Rudolf and F. C. Lawrence. *Effort*. London: MacDonald & Evans, 1947.

Maclaren, Archibald. *A System of Physical Education—Theoretical and Practical.* Oxford: Clarendon Press, 1869.

McIntosh, Peter C. *Physical Education in England Since 1800.* London: G. Bell & Sons, Ltd., 1968.

Ministry of Education. *A Guide to the Educational System of England and Wales.* London: His Majesty's Stationery Office, 1945.

Morison, Ruth. *A Movement Approach to Educational Gymnastics.* London: J. M. Dent and Sons Ltd., 1969.

National Association of Organizers of Physical Education. *Physical Education: Its Aims, Scope, and Organizations.* Chelmsford, Essex: The Association, 1945.

Pollard, Hugh M. *Pioneers of Popular Education, 1760–1850.* Cambridge: Harvard University Press, 1957.

Savage, H. J. *Games and Sports in British Schools and Universities.* New York: Carnegie Foundation, 1927.

Smith, Horatio. *Festivals, Games, and Amusements, Ancient and Modern.* London: Henry Colburn and Richard Bentley, 1831.

Strutt, Joseph. *The Sports and Pastimes of the People of England.* Glasgow: R. Griffin and Co., 1838.

The Wolfenden Committee on Sport. *Sport and the Community.* London: The Central Council of Physical Recreation, 1960.

Chapter 18:   Russia

Dawson, Percy M. "Physiculture in the Soviet Union," *Research Quarterly* 8 (March 1937): 33–45.

Foster, Mildred Y. "A Comparison of the Programs in Physical Education in the United States of America and the Union of Soviet Socialistic Republics." Unpublished master's thesis, Springfield College, 1967.

Hans, N. and S. Hessen. *Educational Policy in Soviet Russia.* London: P. S. King and Son, Ltd., 1930.

Harsky, J. E. "Development of Physical Education in Schools of Soviet Russia from 1919 to 1931." Master's thesis, University of Pittsburgh, 1932.

Howell, M. L. and M. L. Van Vliet. *Physical Education and Recreation in Europe.* Ottawa, Ontario: Fitness and Amateur Sports Directorate, 1965.

Kryachko, I. A. *Physical Culture in the Schools.* Moscow and Leningrad: Government Publishing House, 1948.

McRae, D. *Education in the Soviet Union.* Melbourne: Ruskin Press, 1945.

Minnerly, Frank S. "Physical Education and Recreation in Soviet Russia," *Journal of Physical Education* 58 (November-December 1960): 27–30.

Morton, Henry W. *Soviet Sport.* New York: Collier Books, 1963.

Roberts, Glyn. "Physical Education in Russia." In *Physical Education Around the World,* edited by William Johnson. Monograph no. 1. Indianapolis, Indiana: Phi Epsilon Kappa, 1966. Pp. 51–57.

Simmons, E. J., ed. *U.S.S.R.: A Concise Handbook.* Ithaca: Cornell University Press, 1947.

Sinfield, G. *Soviet Sport*. London: Russia Today Society, 1945.

Singer, Gusta. "Health, Physical Education, and Recreation in Communist States." In *The World Today in Health, Physical Education, and Recreation*, edited by C. Lynn Vendien and John E. Nixon. Englewood Cliffs, N.J.: Prentice-Hall, Inc., 1968. Pp. 353–74.

Starbuck, E. A. *Soviet Sports*. New York: National Council of American-Soviet Friendship, 1945.

Techetikov, Georgi. "Exercise for Young and Old," *World Health* (October 1967): 32–33.

Washburn, John N. "Sport as a Soviet Tool," *Foreign Affairs* 34 (April 1956): 490–99.

Chapter 19:   Other European Countries

Anthony, Don. "Physical Education and Sport in England and Rumania: Observations and Remarks," *International Review of Education* 14 (1968): 81–84.

Broekhoff, Jan. "Physical Education in the Netherlands." In *Physical Education Around the World*, edited by William Johnson. Monograph no. 2. Indianapolis, Indiana: Phi Epsilon Kappa, 1968. Pp. 46–53.

Burgener, Louis. *Geschichte der Leibesübungen in der Schweiz*. Langenthal, Switzerland: Buchdruckerei Merkur Ag., 1950.

Epuran, Mihai. "General Training of Physical Education Teachers in Romania," *International Council on Health, Physical Education, and Recreation, 11th International Congress, 1968*. Washington, D.C.: ICHPER, 1969. Pp. 61–63.

Finnish Society for Research in Sports and Physical Education, ed. *Physical Education and Sports in Finland*. Helsinki: Werner Söderström Osakeyhtiö, 1969.

Georgeoff, Peter J. *The Social Education of Bulgarian Youth*. Minneapolis: University of Minnesota Press, 1968.

Hallberg, David D. "Physical Education in Norway," *Physical Educator* 20 (May 1963): 83–87.

Hewitt, Jack. "The Education of Physical Education Teachers in Belgium," *Physical Educator* 25 (October 1968): 137–38.

——— "Physical Education Teacher Training in Europe," *Journal of Health, Physical Education, and Recreation*, 35 (September 1964): 63–65; and (October 1964): 71–73.

Hirt, E. "Physical Education in Switzerland," *Physical Educator* 22 (December 1965): 179–81.

Hoff, Robert D. and Randi Norman. "Physical Education in Norway." In *Physical Education Around the World*, edited by William Johnson. Monograph no. 2. Indianapolis, Indiana: Phi Epsilon Kappa, 1968. Pp. 54–63.

"International Conference on Physical Education," *Journal of Health and Physical Education* 3 (November 1932): 15–64.

Jernigan, Sara Staff. "A Composite of Olympic Sports Development," *Physical Educator* 23 (October 1966): 136–39; and (December 1966): 178–81.

Klissouras, Vassilis. "Greece: Health, Physical Education, and Recreation." In *The World Today in Health, Physical Education, and Recreation*, edited by C. Lynn Vendien and John E. Nixon. Englewood Cliffs, N. J.: Prentice-Hall, Inc., 1968. Pp. 173–89.

Koski, W. Arthur. "Observations of the Physical Education and Sports Programs of Finland," *Gymnasion*, 1 (Spring 1964): 54–58.

Mihovilovic, Miro "L'Éducation Physique en Yougoslavie." In *L'Éducation physique dans le monde*, edited by Pierre Seurin. Bordeaux: Éditions Bière, 1961. Pp. 411–17.

———— "Physical Education in Yugoslavia," *Physical Educator* 15 (October 1958): 111–13.

Moehlman, Arthur H. and Joseph S. Roucek eds. *Comparative Education*. New York: The Dryden Press, 1952.

Molnár, Sándor. "Physical Education in Hungary." In *Physical Education Around the World*, edited by William Johnson. Monograph no. 2. Indianapolis, Indiana: Phi Epsilon Kappa, 1968. Pp. 18–25.

Moolenijzer, Nicolaas J. "Physical Education in Austria." In *Physical Education Around the World*, edited by William Johnson. Monograph no. 3. Indianapolis, Indiana: Phi Epsilon Kappa, 1969.

National Association of Physical Education for College Women. *Report of the International Congress on Physical Education of Girls and Women*. Washington, D.C.: American Association for Health, Physical Education, and Recreation, 1950.

The Organization of Physical Education and Tourism in Poland. Warsaw: State Committee for Physical Culture and Tourism, 1961.

Piasecki, E. "Physical Education in European Universities," *Journal of Health and Physical Education* 1 (May 1930): 3–5, 48–49.

Pihkala, L. "Physical Education in Finland," *Journal of Health and Physical Education* 3 (November 1932): 47–48, 57.

Polish Organization Committee. "Physical Education in Poland," *Journal of Health and Physical Education* 9 (June 1938): 348–49, 396–98.

Programme for Physical Education. Oslo: The Royal Norwegian Ministry of Church and Education, 1963.

Recla, Josef. "Physical Education in Austria," *Journal of Health and Physical Education* 20 (May 1949): 310, 346–48.

Reitmayer, L. "Physical Education in the Czechoslovak Schools," *Physical Educator* 23 (May 1966): 84–88.

Riess, L. W. "Physical Education in Czechoslovakia," *Journal of Health and Physical Education* 3 (October 1932): 6–13, 63.

Salazar Carreira, José. "L'Éducation Physique au Portugal." In *L'Éducation physique dans le monde*, edited by Pierre Seurin. Bordeaux: Éditions Bière, 1961. Pp. 316–25.

Schroeder, L. C. "Physical Education and Sports in Europe," *American Physical Education Review* 34 (November 1929): 516–21.

Sheridan, Leora J. *Secondary Education in Portugal: Its Origin and Development*. An Essential Portion of a Dissertation. Philadelphia: Published by the author, 1941.

Staley, Seward C. "The European Sports Scene," *American Academy of Physical Education, Professional Contributions No. 6.* Washington, D. C.: American Association for Health, Physical Education, and Recreation, 1958. Pp. 13–24.

———— "Sports in Europe," *Journal of Health and Physical Education* 2 (October 1931): 3–8, 52.

Van Der Stock, Maurice. "L'Éducation physique en Belgique." In *L'Éducation physique dans le monde*, edited by Pierre Seurin. Bordeaux: Éditions Bière, 1961. Pp. 41–54.

Vassev, A. "L'éducation physique en Republique populaire de Bulgarie." In *L'Éducation physique dans le monde*, edited by Pierre Seurin. Bordeaux: Éditions Bière, 1961. Pp. 67–79.

Vetö, József, ed. *Sports in Hungary.* Budapest: Corvina Press, 1965.

Villalba Rubio, Ricardo. "L'Éducation Physique en Espagne." In *L'Éducation physique dans le monde,* edited by Pierre Seurin. Bordeaux: Éditions Bière, 1961. Pp. 125–34.

Woody, Thomas. "Sokols: 1948," *Journal of Health and Physical Education* 19 (June 1948): 393, 442–43.

Xme. Conférence Internationale de l'Instruction Publique Convoquée par l'UNESCO et le BIE. *L'Éducation Physique dans l'Enseignement Secondaire.* Geneva: Bureau of International Education, 1947.

PART IV

General Works

Betts, John R. "Organized Sport in Industrial America." Doctoral dissertation, Columbia University, 1951.

Boyle, Robert H. *Sport—Mirror of American Life.* Boston: Little, Brown and Company, 1963.

Classen, Harold. *The History of Professional Football.* Englewood Cliffs, N.J.: Prentice-Hall, Inc., 1963.

Cozens, Frederick W. and Florence S. Stumpf. *Sports in American Life.* Chicago: University of Chicago Press, 1953.

Davis, John P. ed. *The American Negro Reference Book.* Englewood Cliffs, N.J.: Prentice-Hall, Inc., 1966.

Dean, Cyril F. "A Historical Study of Physical Fitness in the United States, 1790 Through 1961." Doctoral dissertation, George Peabody College for Teachers, 1964.

Dulles, Foster R. *A History of Recreation: America Learns to Play.* New York: Appleton-Century-Crofts, 1965.

Durant, John and Otto Bettmann. *Pictorial History of American Sports.* New York: A. S. Barnes & Company, Inc., 1952.

Flath, Arnold W. *A History of Relations Between the National Collegiate Ath-*

letic Association and the Amateur Athletic Union of the United States, (*1905–1963*). Champaign, Illinois: Stipes Publishing Company, 1964.

Hackensmith, C. W. *History of Physical Education.* New York: Harper & Row, Publishers, 1966.

Henderson, Edwin B. *The Negro in Sports.* Washington, D.C.: The Associated Publishers, Inc., 1939.

Lee, Mabel and Bruce L. Bennett. "This Is Our Heritage," *Journal of Health, Physical Education, and Recreation* 31 (April 1960): 25–33, 38–47, 52–58, 62–73, 76–85. A special issue for the 75th Anniversary of the AAHPER.

Lee, Robert. *Religion and Leisure in America.* Nashville, Tennessee: Abingdon Press, 1964.

Leonard, Fred E. and George B. Affleck. *A Guide to the History of Physical Education.* Philadelphia: Lea & Febiger, 1947.

McDonald, Forrest. *The Torch is Passed: The United States in the 20th Century.* Reading, Massachusetts: Addison–Wesley Publishing Co., Inc., 1968.

Menke, Frank E. *Encyclopedia of Sports.* New York: A. S. Barnes & Company, 1969.

Morison, Samuel E. *The Oxford History of the American People.* New York: Oxford University Press, Inc., 1965.

Postal, Bernard, Jesse Silver, and Roy Silver. *Encyclopedia of Jews in Sports.* New York: Block Publishing Company, 1965.

Rice, Emmett, John Hutchinson, and Mabel Lee. *A Brief History of Physical Education.* New York: The Ronald Press, 1969.

Rinsch, Emil. *The History of the Normal College of the American Gymnastic Union of Indiana University, 1866–1966.* Bloomington: Indiana University, 1966.

Rudolph, Frederick. *The American College and University.* New York: Alfred A. Knopf, 1965.

Schwendener, Norma. *History of Physical Education in the United States.* New York: A. S. Barnes & Company, 1942.

Treat, Roger. *The Official Encyclopedia of Football.* New York: A. S. Barnes & Co., Inc., 1967.

Voigt, David Q. *American Baseball: From Gentleman's Sport to the Commissioner System.* Norman: University of Oklahoma Press, 1966.

Wacker, Hazel M. "The History of the Private Single Purpose Institutions Which Prepared Teachers of Physical Education in the United States of America from 1861 to 1958." Doctoral dissertation, New York University, 1959.

Weston, Arthur. *The Making of American Physical Education.* New York: Appleton-Century-Crofts, 1962.

Young, A. S. *Negro Firsts in Sports.* Chicago: Johnson Publishing Company, Inc., 1963.

Zeigler, Earle F. "History of Professional Preparation for Physical Education in the United States, 1861–1948." Doctoral dissertation, Yale University, 1950.

Chapter 21: The United States, 1787–1865

Barrows, Isabel C., ed. *Physical Training: A Full Report of the Papers and Discussions of the Conference Held in Boston in November, 1889.* Boston: George H. Ellis, 1899.

Cheever, David W. "The Gymnasium," *Atlantic Monthly* 3 (May 1859): 529–43.

Cole, Arthur C. "Our Sporting Grandfathers," *Atlantic Monthly* 150 (July 1932): 88–96.

Eastman, Mary F. and Cecelia C. Lewis. *The Biography of Dio Lewis.* New York: Fowler and Wells Co., 1891.

Fink, Ruth White. "Recreational Pursuits in the Old South," *Research Quarterly* 23 (March 1952): 28–37.

Harveson, Mae E. *Catherine Esther Beecher, Pioneer Educator.* Lancaster, Pa.: Science Press Printing Co., 1932.

Henderson, Robert W. *Ball, Bat, and Bishop.* New York: Rockport Press, Inc., 1947.

Higginson, Thomas W. "The Murder of the Innocents," *Atlantic Monthly* 4 (September 1859): 345–56.

Holliman, Jennie. *American Sports (1785–1835).* Durham, North Carolina: The Seeman Press, 1931.

Lewis, Dio. *New Gymnastics.* Boston: Ticknor & Fields, 1862.

Manchester, Herbert. *Four Centuries of Sport in America, 1490–1890.* New York: The Derrydale Press, 1931.

Marr, Harriet W. *The Old New England Academies.* New York: Comet Press Books, 1959.

Monroe, Will S. "Joseph Neef and Pestalozzianism in America," *Education* 14 (April 1894): 449–61.

Smith, Horatio. *Festivals, Games, and Amusements.* New York: Harper & Brothers, 1836.

Stowe, Lyman B. *Saints, Sinners, and Beechers.* Indianapolis, Indiana: The Bobbs-Merrill Co., Inc., 1934.

Warren, John C. *Physical Education and the Preservation of Health.* Boston: William D. Ticknor and Co., 1846.

Weaver, Robert B. *Amusements and Sports in American Life.* Chicago: University of Chicago Press, 1939.

Zucker, Adolf E., ed. *The Forty-Eighters.* New York: Columbia University Press, 1950.

Chapter 22: The United States, 1865–1900

Ainsworth, Dorothy. *History of Physical Education in Colleges for Women.* New York: A. S. Barnes & Co., 1930.

Aller, Anne S. "The Rise of State Provisions for Physical Education in the Public Secondary Schools of the United States." Doctoral dissertation, University of California, 1935.

Bealle, Morris A. *The History of Football at Harvard, 1874–1948*. Washington, D.C.: Columbia Publishing Co., 1948.

DeGroot, Dudley S. "A History of Physical Education in California (1848–1939)." Doctoral dissertation, Stanford University, 1940.

Douglass, H. Paul and Edmund Brunner. *The Protestant Church as a Social Institution*. New York: Harper and Brothers, 1935.

Gibson, H. W. "The History of Organized Camping," *Camping Magazine* 8 (January–December 1936).

Hart, Albert Bushnell. "Status of Athletic Sports in American Colleges," *Atlantic Monthly* 66 (July 1890): 63–71.

Hartwell, Edward M. *Physical Training in American Colleges and Universities*. Bureau of Education Circular of Information No. 5, 1885. Washington, D.C.: U.S. Government Printing Office, 1886.

Hill, Lucille E. ed. *Athletics and Out-Door Sports for Women*. New York: The Macmillan Company, 1903.

Kindervater, A. G. "Early History of Physical Education in the Public Schools of America," *Mind and Body* 33 (June 1926): 97–103.

Leonard, Fred E. *Pioneers of Modern Physical Training*. New York: Association Press, 1919.

Naismith, James. "How Basketball Started and Why It Grew," *Journal of Physical Education* 30 (November 1932): 43–48.

Petroskey, Helen. "A History of Measurement in Health and Physical Education in the United States." Doctoral dissertation, University of Iowa, 1946.

Posse, Nils. *The Special Kinesiology of Educational Gymnastics*. Boston: Lee & Shepard Co., 1894.

Rainwater, Clarence E. *The Play Movement in the United States*. Chicago: University of Chicago Press, 1922.

Ray, Harold. "Chautauqua—Early Showcase for Physical Education," *Journal of Health, Physical Education, and Recreation* 33 (November 1962): 37–41, 69.

Richardson, Sophia F. "Tendencies in Athletics for Women in Colleges and Universities," *Popular Science Monthly* 50 (February 1897): 517–26.

Sargent, Dudley A. *Physical Education*. Boston: Ginn and Company, 1906.

Seymour, Harold. *Baseball. The Early Years*. New York: Oxford University Press, 1960.

Shaler, N. S. "The Athletic Problem in Education," *Atlantic Monthly* 63 (January 1889): 79–88.

Stecher, W. A. ed. *Gymnastics, A Textbook of the German-American System of Gymnastics*. Boston: Lee and Shepard, 1895.

Swanson, Richard A. "American Protestantism and Play: 1865–1915." Doctoral dissertation, Ohio State University, 1967.

Chapter 23:   The United States, 1900–1930

Athletic Research Society. "Report of the Committee on Intramural Sport," *American Physical Education Review* 23 (April 1918): 198–212; and (May 1918): 279–86.

Butler, George D. *Pioneers in Public Recreation*. Minneapolis: Burgess Publishing Co., 1965.

Coffey, Margaret A. "The Sportswoman," *Journal of Health, Physical Education, and Recreation* 36 (February 1965): 38–41, 50.

Dorgan, Ethel J. *Luther Halsey Gulick. 1865–1918*. New York: Teachers College, Columbia University, 1934.

Dudley, Gertrude and Frances A. Kellor. *Athletic Games in the Education of Women*. New York: Henry Holt and Company, 1909.

Fisher, George J. "Athletics Outside Educational Institutions," *American Physical Education Review*, 12 (June 1907): 109–20.

Hetherington, Clark. *School Program in Physical Education*. Yonkers, New York: World Book Co., 1922.

Hunter, Adelaide M. "R. Tait McKenzie—Pioneer in Physical Education." Doctoral dissertation, Columbia University, 1950.

Kallenberg, Henry F. "The Federation Form of Organization in Athletics," *American Physical Education Review* 17 (June 1912): 507–10.

Lawrence, Helen B. and Grace I. Fox. *Basketball for Girls and Women*. New York: McGraw-Hill Book Company, 1954.

Lewis, Guy M. "The American Intercollegiate Football Spectacle, 1869–1917." Doctoral dissertation, University of Maryland, 1964.

Martin, John. *The Dance*. New York: Tudor Publishing Co., 1946.

McCurdy, J. H. "A Study of the Characteristics of Physical Training in the Public Schools of the United States," *American Physical Education Review* 10 (September 1905): 202–13.

Mitchell, Elmer D. *Intramural Athletics*. New York: A. S. Barnes & Co., 1925.

Ray, Harold L. "The Life and Professional Contributions of William Gilbert Anderson, M.D." Doctoral dissertation, Ohio State University, 1959.

Ritter, Lawrence S. *The Glory of Their Times*. New York: The Macmillan Company, 1966.

Savage, Howard J. et al. *American College Athletics*. Bulletin No. 23. Carnegie Foundation. New York: The Carnegie Foundation for the Advancement of Teaching, 1929.

Sefton, Alice A. *The Women's Division, National Amateur Athletic Federation*. Stanford: Stanford University Press, 1941.

Somers, Florence A. *Principles of Women's Athletics*. New York: A. S. Barnes & Company, Inc., 1930.

Welch, J. Edmund. *Edward Hitchcock, M.D. Founder of Physical Education in the College Curriculum*. Greenville, North Carolina: Published by the author, 1966.

Whigham, H. J. "American Sport from an English Point of View," *Outlook* 93 (27 November 1909): 738–44.

Chapter 24:   The United States, 1930–50

Ashton, Dudley. "Contributions of Dance to Physical Education," *Journal of Health, Physical Education, and Recreation* 27 (December 1956): 21–22, 34.

Brace, David K. "Physical Fitness in Schools and Colleges," *Journal of Health and Physical Education* 15 (November 1944): 488–90, 528–29.

Brammell, P. Roy. *Intramural and Interscholastic Athletics*. U.S. Office of Education. Bulletin 1932, No. 17. National Survey of Secondary Education, No. 27. Washington, D.C.: U.S. Government Printing Office, 1933.

Caulkins, Edward D. ed. *School Athletics in Modern Education*. New York: Wingate Memorial Foundation, 1931.

Clarke, H. Harrison. "History of the Research Section of the American Association for Health and Physical Education," *Research Quarterly* 9 (October 1938): 25–36.

Diehl, Leonard and Floyd Eastwood. *Industrial Recreation, Its Development and Present Status*. Lafayette, Indiana: Purdue University Press, 1940.

"Fiftieth Anniversary of the Athletic and Recreation Federation of College Women," *Journal of Health, Physical Education, and Recreation* 38 (January 1967): 34–35, 66.

Gerber, Ellen W. "Three Interpretations of the Role of Physical Education, 1930–1960: Charles Harold McCloy, Jay Bryan Nash, and Jesse Feiring Williams." Doctoral dissertation, University of Southern California, 1966.

"International Conference on Physical Education," *Journal of Health and Physical Education* 3 (November 1932): 15–64.

Ley, Katherine and Sara Staff Jernigan. "The Roots and the Tree," *Journal of Health, Physical Education, and Recreation* 33 (September 1962): 34–36, 57.

Neilson, N. P. "The Report of the Committee on Teacher Training in Physical Education in the United States," *Research Quarterly* 4 (March 1933): 51–57.

Palmer, Gladys E. "Policies in Women's Athletics," *Journal of Health and Physical Education* 9 (November 1938): 565–67, 586–87.

Radir, Ruth. *Modern Dance for the Youth of America*. New York: A. S. Barnes & Co. Inc., 1944.

"Report of the Committee on Physical Education and Athletics," *The North Central Association Quarterly* 8 (June 1933): 26–69.

Schlundt, Christena L. "Individuals Who Determined the Dance Philosophy of Graduate Education," *Research Quarterly* 39 (December 1968): 1077–79.

Steiner, Jesse F. *Research Memorandum on Recreation in the Depression*. New York: Social Science Research Council, 1937.

Tunis, John R. "Sports Return to 1900," *Harper's Magazine* 186 (May 1943): 633–38.

U.S. Office of Education. *Physical Fitness Through Physical Education for the Victory Corps*. Washington, D.C.: U.S. Government Printing Office, 1943.

Valentine, P. F., ed. *Twentieth Century Education*. New York: Philosophical Library, Inc., 1946.

Von Borries, Eline. *The History and Functions of the National Section on Women's Athletics*. Washington, D.C.: National Section on Women's Athletics, 1941.

Washke, Paul R. "The Development of the American Association for Health,

Physical Education, and Recreation and Its Relationship to Physical Education in the United States." Doctoral dissertation, New York University, 1943.

Chapter 25:   The United States Since 1950

American Association for Health, Physical Education, and Recreation. *This Is Physical Education*. Washington, D.C.: AAHPER, 1965.

Duer, A. O. "Basic Issues of Intercollegiate Athletics," *Journal of Health, Physical Education, and Recreation* 31 (January 1960): 22–24.

Frost, Reuben B. "Recent Trends in Certification of Men Physical Education Teachers and Coaches," *National College Physical Education Association for Men 69th Proceedings*, 1965. Pp. 44–50.

Haag, Herbert. "An Analytical Survey of Selected State Guides and Examples of Physical Education Programs at the Secondary Level Offered in Selected School Districts in the United States, 1965." Unpublished master's thesis, University of Washington, 1966.

Holbrook, Leona. "Physical Education and Its Interpretation in Universities in the United States," *International Council on Health, Physical Education, and Recreation, 10th International Congress, 1967*. Washington, D.C.: ICHPER, 1968. Pp. 86–93.

Hoover, Francis L. "A History of the National Association of Intercollegiate Athletics." Doctoral dissertation, Indiana University, 1958.

Hunsicker, Paul A. and Guy G. Reiff. "A Survey and Comparison of Youth Fitness 1958–1965," *Journal of Health, Physical Education, and Recreation* 37 (January 1966): 23–25.

Kraus, Richard. *Public Recreation and the Negro*. New York: Center for Urban Education, 1968.

Lambert, Charlotte. "Pros and Cons of Intercollegiate Athletic Competition for Women: A Middle of the Road Position Paper," *Journal of Health, Physical Education, and Recreation* 40 (May 1969): 75–79.

Lawther, John D. " 'Movement Education' and Skill Learning," *Gymnasion* 6 (Spring 1969): 13–16.

Meredith-Jones, Betty. "Understanding Movement," *Journal of Health, Physical Education, and Recreation* 26 (May-June 1955): 14, 59.

Miller, Ben W. "Physical Education Programs in the United States," *International Council on Health, Physical Education, and Recreation 10th International Congress, 1967*. Washington, D.C.: ICHPER, 1968. Pp. 109–18.

Olsen, Jack. "The Black Athlete—A Shameful Story," *Sports Illustrated*, 29 (1 July 1968), pp. 12–27; (8 July 1968), pp. 18–31; (15 July 1968), pp. 28–43; (22 July 1968), pp. 28–41; and (29 July 1968), pp. 20–35.

Outdoor Recreation Resources Review Commission. *Outdoor Recreation Trends*. Washington, D. C.: U.S. Government Printing Office, 1967.

Porter, Lorena. *Movement Education for Children*. Washington, D.C.: National Education Association, 1969.

President's Council on Youth Fitness. *Youth Physical Fitness: Suggested Elements of a School-Centered Program.* Washington, D.C.: Government Printing Office, 1961.

"There Were No Greener Pastures," *Sports Illustrated* 31 (22 December 1969): pp. 38–79.

Van Dalen, D. B. "Dynamics of Change in Physical Education," *Journal of Health, Physical Education, and Recreation* 36 (November-December 1965): 39–45.

PART V

General Works

Comparative Education Review. Teachers College, Columbia University, and Comparative Education Society, New York.

Cramer, John and George Browne. *Contemporary Education: A Comparative Study of National Systems.* 2d ed. New York: Harcourt, Brace & World, Inc., 1965.

Department of State Publication. *Background Notes.* Washington, D.C.: U.S. Government Printing Office. This is a series of State Department publications about various nations of the world.

Diem, Carl. *Weltgeschichte des Sports.* 2 vols. Stuttgart: Cotta Verlag, 1967.

Hackensmith, C. W. *History of Physical Education.* New York: Harper & Row, Publishers, 1966.

International Council on Health, Physical Education, and Recreation International Congress Proceedings. Washington, D.C.: ICHPER. Published annually from 1960 to date.

International Council on Health, Physical Education, and Recreation. *Physical Education and Games in the Curriculum.* ICHPER Questionnaire Report, part I. Washington, D.C.: ICHPER, c. 1963.

————— *Physical Education in the School Curriculum.* ICHPER International Questionnaire Report, part I, 1967–68 Revision. Washington, D.C.: ICHPER, 1969.

————— *Status of Teachers of Physical Education.* ICHPER Questionnaire Report, part III. Washington, D.C.: ICHPER, c. 1963.

————— *Teacher Training for Physical Education.* ICHPER Questionnaire Report, part II. Washington, D.C.: ICHPER, c. 1963.

————— *Teacher Training for Physical Education.* ICHPER Questionnaire Report, part II, 1967–68 Revision. Washington, D.C.: ICHPER, n.d.

International Council of Sport and Physical Education. *Sport and Leisure. Report of the First International Seminar.* Stuttgart: Verlag Karl Hofmann, 1965.

International Yearbook of Education. Paris: UNESCO and the International Bureau of Education. 1948 to date.

Jackson, C. O. "Elsewhere in the World," *Physical Educator.* 1953 to date.

Johnson, William, ed. *Physical Education Around the World.* Indianapolis, Indiana: Phi Epsilon Kappa. Monograph no. 1 published in 1966; Monograph no. 2 published in 1968; and Monograph no. 3 in 1969.

National College of Physical Education Association for Men Proceedings of Annual Meetings. See "Foreign Relations" in issues for 1958–1960; see "History of Sports" from 1961 to date.

Physical Education Year Book. Ling House, London: Physical Education Association of Great Britain and Northern Ireland.

Report of the WCOTP Committee on Health, Physical Education, and Recreation, International Conference, 1959. Washington, D.C.: International Council on Health, Physical Education, and Recreation, 1960.

Seurin, Pierre. *L'Éducation physique dans le monde.* Bordeaux: Editions Bière, 1961.

Thut, I. N. and Don Adams. *Educational Patterns in Contemporary Societies.* New York: McGraw-Hill Book Company, 1964.

Vendien, C. Lynn and John E. Nixon. *The World Today in Health, Physical Education, and Recreation.* Englewood Cliffs, N.J.: Prentice-Hall, Inc., 1968.

Year Book of Education. New York: Teachers College, Columbia University and Institute of Education, University of London, 1932–1941; 1948 to date.

Chapter 26: Pan–American Nations

Augusto, Maurette. "Physical Education in Brazil." In *Physical Education Around the World*, edited by William Johnson. Monograph no. 3. Indianapolis, Indiana: Phi Epsilon Kappa, 1969. Pp. 18–30.

Belevan-Garcia, Cesar. "Physical Education in Peru," *Physical Educator* 10 (May 1953): 54–55.

Bisquertt, Luis. "Physical Education in Latin American Countries," *International Council on Health, Physical Education, and Recreation 6th International Congress, 1963.* Washington, D.C.: ICHPER, 1964. Pp. 42–48.

Chile Ministerio de Educación Pública. *La Reforma Educaciónal Chilena.* Vols. I and II. Santiago, Chile: Ministry of Education, 1967.

Clark, Gill. *Chile: Education and Social Change in Chile.* Washington, D.C.: U.S. Government Printing Office, 1966.

Clay, Maurice. "Physical Education in Mexico," In *Physical Education Around the World*, edited by William Johnson. Monograph no. 2. Indianapolis, Indiana: Phi Epsilon Kappa, 1968. Pp. 34–45.

———— "Physical Education in Colombia." In *Physical Education Around the World*, edited by William Johnson. Monograph no. 3. Indianapolis, Indiana: Phi Epsilon Kappa, 1969. Pp. 31–45.

Colombo, Alfredo. "Brazil," *International Council on Health, Physical Education, and Recreation 6th International Congress, 1963.* Washington, D.C.: ICHPER, 1964. Pp. 49–52.

de Borhegyi, Stephan F. "America's Ball Game," *Natural History* 69 (January 1960): 48–58.

Duque, Vincente Padilla. "Ecuador," *International Council on Health, Physical Education, and Recreation 6th International Congress, 1963*. Washington, D.C.: ICHPER, 1964. Pp. 61–68.

Elizeche, Ignacio. "Paraguay," *International Council on Health, Physical Education, and Recreation 6th International Congress, 1963*. Washington, D.C.: ICHPER, 1964. Pp. 69–74.

Ferrer, Pérez Vincente. *Salud y Educación*. Vols. I–VII. Santiago, Chile: Talleres Gráficos de Eng. Hispano Suiza Ltda., 1966.

Harrell, William. *Educational Reform in Brazil. The Law of 1961*. Washington, D.C.: U.S. Department of Health, Education, and Welfare, 1968.

Hauch, Charles. *The Current Situation in Latin American Education*. Washington, D.C.: U.S. Department of Health, Education, and Welfare, 1963.

Hernandez, Angel Humberto Vaca. *Compilacion De Disposiciónes Sobre Educación Física De Colombia*. Bogota: Imprenta Nacional, 1958.

Howell, Nancy and Maxwell Howell. *Sports and Games in Canadian Life: 1700 to the Present*. Toronto: Macmillan Company of Canada, 1969.

IND XVIII Aniversario. Caracas, Venezuela: IND Department of Public Relations, c. 1968.

La Belle, Tom. "The Peace Corps in Colombia," *Journal of Health, Physical Education, and Recreation* 37 (November-December 1966): 57–59.

Ministerio De Educación Nacional, Seccion de Educación Física. "Consejo Nacional De Educación Física." Mimeographed. Bogota: Ministerio de Educación Nacional, 1966.

Ministerio De Educación y Justica, Dirección General de Educación Física, *Programs de Educación Física*. Buenos Aires: Ministerio De Educación y Justica, Dirección General De Educación Física, 1961.

———— *Creación De La Dirección Nacional De Educación Física, Deportes y Recreación*. Buenos Aires: Ministerio De Educación y Justica, 1963.

Ministerio De Educación y Justica, Dirección Nacional De Educación Física Deportes y Recreación. *Instituto Nacional De Deportes (Su Creación)*. Buenos Aires: Ministerio De Educación y Justica, Direccion Nacional De Educación Física Deportes y Recreación, 1963.

Plan De Estudios y Programas De Educación Normal Urbana Aprobados Por El Consejo Nacional Technico De La Educación. 2d ed. Mexico, D.F.: Secretaria De Educación Publica, 1964.

Pond, Charles. "Educación Física in Colombia, S.A.," *Physical Educator* 19 (December 1962): 149.

"Problems and Promises of Education in Latin America," *Phi Delta Kappan* 45 (January 1964): 162–229.

Rodriguez, Julio J. "Reseña Historica De La Educación Física y La Recreación en El Uruguay." Mimeographed. Montevideo: Comisión Nacional De Educación Física, Dirección Téchnica, n.d.

Schurz, William. *Latin America*. New York: E. P. Dutton & Co., Inc., 1963.

Tannenbaum, Frank. *Ten Keys to Latin America*. New York: Vintage Books, 1966.

Torres, Evelino and Manuel Gallagos Carratu. "Venezuela," *International Council on Health, Physical Education, and Recreation 6th International Congress, 1963*. Washington, D.C.: ICHPER, 1964. Pp. 75–78.

Trigo, Carlos Pozo. "Bolivia," *International Council on Health, Physical Education, and Recreation 6th International Congress, 1963*. Washington, D.C.: ICHPER, 1964. Pp. 53–61.

Van Vliet, M. L., ed. *Physical Education in Canada*. Scarborough, Ontario: Prentice-Hall of Canada Ltd., 1965.

Chapter 27:   *African, Asian, and Pacific Nations*

The Central Advisory Board of Physical Education and Recreation. *A National Plan of Physical Education and Recreation*. Publication No. 692. New Delhi: Ministry of Education, Government of India, 1964.

Ching-Szu Chen, Paul. "Dr. C. H. McCloy, the Physical Education Scholar and His Works," *Physical Education Today* 6 (June 1959): 9–12.

Chopde, Sadanand D. "Physical Education in India," *International Council on Health, Physical Education, and Recreation 9th International Congress, 1966*. Washington, D.C.: ICHPER, 1967. Pp. 68–72.

Department of Education, New South Wales. *Curriculum for Primary Schools: Natural Science, Health, and Physical Education*. Sydney: U. C. N. Blight, Government Printer, 1965.

Department of Education, Queensland. *Teacher Training: Scholarships and Fellowships*. Brisbane: S. G. Reid, Government Printer, 1965–6.

Department of Physical Education, University of Stellenbosch. "Physical Education and Sport in the Republic of South Africa." Mimeographed. Stellenbosch, South Africa: Department of Physical Education, University of Stellenbosch, 1967.

du Toit, Stephanus. "Physical Education in South Africa." In *Physical Education Around the World*, edited by William Johnson. Monograph no. 1. Indianapolis, Indiana: Phi Epsilon Kappa, 1966. Pp. 58–62.

Habte, Aklilu. "Education—Africa's Unfinished Business," *Journal of Health, Physical Education, and Recreation* 36 (November–December, 1965): 28–31.

Ichimura, Souichi. "Physical Education in Japan." In *Physical Education Around the World*, edited by William Johnson. Monograph no. 1. Indianapolis, Indiana: Phi Epsilon Kappa, 1966. Pp. 32–36.

Ikai, Michio and Shinshiro Ebashi. "Physical Education in Japan," *International Council on Health, Physical Education, and Recreation 9th International Congress, 1966*. Washington, D.C.: ICHPER, 1967. Pp. 79–83.

Imamura, Yoshio. "Special Lecture: Traditional Sports in Japan," *Proceedings of International Congress of Sport Sciences, 1964*. Tokyo: Japanese Union of Sport Sciences, Kannami-cho, Shibuya, Tokyo University. Pp. 28–35.

Johnson, William. "Physical Education in Pakistan." In *Physical Education Around the World*, edited by William Johnson. Monograph no. 1. Indianapolis, Indiana: Phi Epsilon Kappa, 1966. Pp. 43–50.

Kunzru Committee Report. *Report of the Committee for Coordination and Integration of Schemes Operating in the Field of Physical Education, Recreation, and Youth Welfare*. New Delhi: Ministry of Education, Government of India, 1964.

McLendon, John B., Jr. "Asian Games—Olympics of the East," *Journal of Health, Physical Education, and Recreation* 34 (January 1963): 55–57.

Miller, Jeffrey. "Physical Education in Australia." In *Physical Education Around the World*, edited by William Johnson. Monograph No. 2. Indianapolis, Indiana: Phi Epsilon Kappa, 1968. Pp. 1–9.

Ministry of Education, Japan. *Physical Education and Sports in Japan 1964.* Tokyo: Tokyo Printing Co., 1964.

Miyahata, Torahika. "Physical Education in Japan," *Physical Education Today* 5 (October 1958): 15–24.

The National Fitness Corps: Handbook for Middle High and Higher Secondary Schools. New Delhi: Ministry of Education, Government of India, 1965.

Physical Education and Sports in Israel. Jerusalem: Israel Olympic Committee, c. 1964.

Scholer, E. A. "Teacher Training in Physical Education in New Zealand," *Physical Educator* 33 (March 1966): 36–39.

Tan, George G. and Wu Wen-Chung. "The Present Situation of Physical Education in the Republic of China," *Physical Education Today* 7 (December 1960): 1–16.

Tsai, Min-Chung. "Physical Education in the Republic of China," *International Council on Health, Physical Education, and Recreation 9th International Congress, 1966.* Washington, D.C.: ICHPER, 1967. Pp. 61–67.

Wills, D. R. *Physical Education in New Zealand.* Wellington: R. E. Owen, Government Printer, 1965.

Wright, Edward J. "Physical Education in New Zealand." In *Physical Education Around the World*, edited by William Johnson. Monograph No. 1. Indianapolis, Indiana: Phi Epsilon Kappa, 1966. Pp. 37–42.

Chapter 28: Internationalism

Ainsworth, Dorothy S. "Your Part in International Relations," *Journal of Health, Physical Education, and Recreation* 33 (September 1962): 73–74.

American Association for Health, Physical Education, and Recreation. *Proceedings of a National Conference, International Relations Through Health, Physical Education, and Recreation, 1967.* Washington, D.C.: AAHPER, 1967.

Anthony, D. W. J. "Comparative Physical Education," *Physical Education* 58 (November 1966): 70–73.

Bucher, Charles A. *Foundations of Physical Education.* St. Louis: The C. V. Mosby Company, 1968.

A Decade of Progress. Washington, D.C.: International Council on Health, Physical Education, and Recreation, 1967.

Emery, Curtis R. "The History of the Pan-American Games." Doctoral dissertation, Louisiana State University, 1964.

Falize, J. "International Structure of Physical Education and Sports," *Gymnasion* 4 (Spring 1967): 6–10.

Leonard, Fred E. and George B. Affleck. *A Guide to the History of Physical Education.* Philadelphia: Lea and Febiger, 1947.

Lucas, John A. "Baron Pierre de Coubertin and the Formative Years of the

Modern International Olympic Movement, 1883–1896." Doctoral dissertation, University of Maryland, 1962.

McDonough, Thomas E. and Donald L. Moore. "The Havalanta Games," *Journal of the American Association for Health, Physical Education, and Recreation* 22 (November 1951): 32–34.

Peterson, Hazel C. "Dorothy S. Ainsworth: Her Life, Professional Career and Contributions to Physical Education." Doctoral dissertation, Ohio State University, 1968.

Putnam, Betty J. "A Study of National and International Physical Education Associations." Unpublished master's thesis, Smith College, 1956.

Ryan, Allan J. "History and Scope of the Medical Aspects of Sports," in *Proceedings of the Sixth National Conference on the Medical Aspects of Sports*. Chicago: American Medical Association, 1965.

NAME INDEX

SUBJECT INDEX